SRILA PRABHUPADA
TRIUMPHANT
DEPARTURE

COMPLETE BOOK OF
POISONING EVIDENCE

~VOLUME ONE~
PERSONAL AMBITION SERIES

SRILA PRABHUPADA

TRIUMPHANT DEPARTURE

COMPLETE BOOK OF POISONING EVIDENCE

~VOLUME ONE~
PERSONAL AMBITION SERIES
Version 2.1 May 6, 2023

PRABHUPADA TRUTH COMMISSION

QUOTES FROM LATE 1977 CONVERSATIONS:

"Better To Be Killed By Rama" (Srila Prabhupada)
"Someone has poisoned me." (Srila Prabhupada)
"Some Rakshasa Has Given Poison" (Damodara Sastri)
"My Guru Maharaja Also (re: poisoning)" (Srila Prabhupada)
"So they may kill me also." (May 1976, Srila Prabhupada)
"So who is it that has poisoned?" (Tamal Krishna Goswami)
"He's saying that someone gave him poison." (Bhakticharu)
"At the last stage, don't torture me and put me to death." (SP)
"The poison is personal ambition…" (SPL, Nov. 1, 1970)
*"During times of universal deceit, telling the truth
is a revolutionary act." (George Orwell)*
Please Study The Facts And Truth, And Be Rightly Informed

*REAR COVER PHOTO: Sept. 6, 1977 Srila Prabhupada in UK
at the Bhaktivedanta Manor with very swollen hands, dark sunglasses
due to photophobia, 10 weeks before his physical departure.*

©2022 NEW JAIPUR PRESS
ISBN: 978-0-923519-12-4

PRABHUPADA TRUTH COMMISSION

Prabhupada Truth Commission consists of present and former ISKCON institutional leaders and senior devotees who have served as GBC members, Temple presidents, Directors of special projects, who resigned, withdrew, or are anonymous and do not support the deception, cover-ups, and corruption of ISKCON's leaders. They are loyal and dedicated to the unadulterated teachings of His Divine Grace Srila Prabhupada and restoring his divine mission. Contact: *(srigovinda@gmail.com)*

ABBREVIATIONS INDEX:

NAA: neutron activation analysis
SP: Srila Prabhupada
SHPM: *Someone Has Poisoned Me* (1999)
JFY: *Judge For Yourself* (2003)
N14C: November 14 Commission
SPL: Srila Prabhupada Letter
SPConv: Srila Prabhupada conversation
CC: *Chaitanya charitamrita*
NTIAP: *Not That I Am Poisoned* (2000)
ABHI: Abhirama's memoirs
Tamal: Tamal Krishna Goswami
ISK70: *ISKCON in the 1970's*
SPLila: *Srila Prabhupada Lilamrita*
BCS: Bhakticharu Swami
BTG: *Back to Godhead* magazine
ConvBk: *Conversation Books*
KGBG: *Kill Guru Become Guru* (2017)
GBC: ISKCON governing body
SPLecture: Lecture by Srila Prabhupada
SBhag: *Srimad Bhagwatam*
BGita: *Bhagavad Gita* (Srila Prabhupada)
TransD: *Transcendental Diary*
PTC: Prabhupada Truth Commission
BHAV: Bhavananda das
KAV: Damodar Prasad kaviraja
JPS: Jayapataka Swami
HSUnpub: Hari Sauri unpublished diary for Oct-Nov 1977 (printed 2022)

The "Personal Ambition" series:

Volume 1: Triumphant Departure: Complete Book of Poisoning Evidence
Volume 2: Anti-Prabhupada: Deviant Impact of Tamal Krishna Goswami
Volume 3: Pursuit of Srila Prabhupada's Poisoners
Volume 4: Srila Prabhupada's Mysterious Health Decline
Volume 5: ISKCON's Hidden History: Coup, Scandals, Schisms, Utopia Lost
Volume 6: The Poisoning of ISKCON: Corruption, Deviation, Cover-Ups
Volume 7: Kill Guru Become Guru: Crushing the Naysayer Rogues
Volume 8: Restoring Srila Prabhupada's Divine Mission
Volume 9: Srila Prabhupada: The Current Living Acharya
Volume 10: Vedic Villages: Experiments in Varnashrama Projects
Volume 11: Srila Prabhupada: Shaktavesh Avatar of Truth and Mercy
Volume 12: Let The Jackals Howl: The Caravan Will Pass

DEDICATION

INTRODUCTION TO SRI SIKSASTAKAM

"Lord Chaitanya Mahaprabhu instructed his disciples to write books on the science of Krishna, a task which His followers have continued to carry out down to the present day. The elaborations and exposition on the philosophy taught by Lord Chaitanya are, in fact, the most voluminous, exacting, and consistent, due to the unbreakable system of disciplic succession, of any religious culture in the world. Yet, Lord Chaitanya in His youth, widely renowned as a scholar Himself, left us only eight verses called Siksaktakam."

TABLE OF CONTENTS
SRILA PRABHUPADA - TRIUMPHANT DEPARTURE
COMPLETE BOOK OF POISONING EVIDENCE

FOREWORD 1

INTRODUCTION.. 10

PART ONE: IRREFUTABLE FORENSIC EVIDENCE 15
CHAPTER 1: THE FIRST HAIR TESTS.. 15
CHAPTER 2: GBC ABANDONS UNTESTED HAIR SAMPLES 21
CHAPTER 3: DISCOVERY OF CADMIUM 29
CHAPTER 4: FURTHER HAIR TESTS 33
CHAPTER 5: SUMMARY OF HAIR TEST RESULTS 38
CHAPTER 6: THE CADMIUM EXPERTS 41
CHAPTER 7: MALICIOUS, HOMICIDAL POISONING 55
CHAPTER 8: POISONING TIMELINE 67
CHAPTER 9: CADMIUM POISONING CASES.. 71

PART TWO: PRABHUPADA TALKS OF POISONING 79
CHAPTER 10: SOMEBODY HAS GIVEN ME POISON 80
CHAPTER 11: HE SAID LIKE THAT 87
CHAPTER 12: SOMEONE HAS POISONED ME 95
CHAPTER 13: WHO IS IT THAT HAS POISONED? 98
CHAPTER 14: USELESS CHATTER.. 102
CHAPTER 15: THE WORDS OF THE PURE DEVOTEE 104

PART THREE: WHISPERS OF POISONING 109
CHAPTER 16: ORIGINS OF POISON INVESTIGATION 109
CHAPTER 17: THE SCIENCE OF AUDIO FORENSICS 117
CHAPTER 18: MITCHELL'S AUDIO FORENSIC ANALYSIS 122
CHAPTER 19: TESTING FOR TAMPERED TAPES 125
CHAPTER 20: SECONDARY WHISPERS 129
CHAPTER 21: THE MITCHELL STUDY REVIEWED 132
CHAPTER 22: DR. McCAFFREY CONFIRMS WHISPERS................ 137
CHAPTER 23: J P FRENCH ANALYSES POOR QUALITY TAPE 138
CHAPTER 24: OWL INVESTIGATIONS: POSSIBLE HOMICIDE 140
CHAPTER 25: FBI ANALYST CONFIRMS WHISPERS 142
CHAPTER 26: SUMMARY OF ALL AUDIO FORENSICS.................. 144
CHAPTER 27: FORENSIC ANALYSES SINCE 2006 148

PART FOUR: MEDICAL EVIDENCE 150
CHAPTER 28: SRILA PRABHUPADA'S MEDICINES 150
CHAPTER 29: VERY GOOD HEALTH 161
CHAPTER 30: AN INEXPLICABLE ILLNESS 166
CHAPTER 31: THE MYSTERY SYMPTOMS 171
CHAPTER 32: TOO MANY MISDIAGNOSES 182
CHAPTER 33: LONDON HOSPITAL VISIT.. 191
CHAPTER 34: REJECTION OF PROPER MEDICAL CARE................ 197

PART FIVE: TESTIMONY AND SUSPECTS 209
CHAPTER 35: FRIGHTENED MEXICAN WITNESS............................ 209

CHAPTER 36: FOUR KAVIRAJAS AGREE ON POISONING 213
CHAPTER 37: LIME AND OTHER TESTIMONIALS 226
CHAPTER 38: THE PRIMARY SUSPECTS 235
CHAPTER 39: POISONING IN HISTORY 239

PART SIX: COVER-UPS BY LYING PROPAGANDA 252
CHAPTER 40: MERCY KILLING INTERVIEW 253
CHAPTER 41: MINISTRY OF COVER-UPS 257
CHAPTER 42: *SOMEONE HAS POISONED ME* VILIFIED 263
CHAPTER 43: BALAVANTA'S INVESTIGATION AXED 265
CHAPTER 44: GBC BOOK DENIES ALL EVIDENCE 271
CHAPTER 45: NOVEMBER 14 COMMISSION SNUFFED 273
CHAPTER 46: *JUDGE FOR YOURSELF* IGNORED............................282
CHAPTER 47: WAS IT THE WATER? 285
CHAPTER 48: SRILA PRABHUPADA'S ARSENIC...........................288
CHAPTER 49: HAIR ANALYSIS 301
CHAPTER 50: DEAF TO THE WHISPERS 310
CHAPTER 51: SMOKE AND MIRRORS 316
CHAPTER 52: BEARING FALSE WITNESS 326
CHAPTER 53: DESPERATE LIES OF *DECEPTION* 336

PART SEVEN: THE QUEST FOR TRUTH 342
CHAPTER 54: TRUTH AND COGNITIVE DISSONANCE........................342
CHAPTER 55: PRIVATE INVESTIGATION 349
CHAPTER 56: ENORMOUS RAMIFICATIONS 362
CHAPTER 57: EVIDENCE AUTHENTICITY 369
CHAPTER 58: FLAWED OBJECTIONS ANSWERED 373
CHAPTER 59: HORSES, FOLLY, COMPLICITY................................374

PART EIGHT: TRIUMPHANT DEPARTURE 380
CHAPTER 60: SRILA PRABHUPADA'S HOROSCOPE 380
CHAPTER 61: HIS AMAZING TOLERANCE AND MERCY 389
CHAPTER 62: CAN THE PURE DEVOTEE BE KILLED? 397
CHAPTER 63: EXHUMATION OR LEGAL CASES? 407
CHAPTER 64: IRREFUTABLE EVIDENCE SUMMARY.......................413

APPENDIX 1: CHIEF MEDICAL EXAMINER'S STATEMENT..................419
APPENDIX 2: TRANSLATIONS OF THE LAST TAPES 420
APPENDIX 3: McCAFFREY REPORT.....................................435
APPENDIX 4: ABOUT ARSENIC AND ANTIMONY..........................435
APPENDIX 5: DR. J. STEVEN MORRIS CREDENTIALS.....................439
APPENDIX 6: CREDENTIALS: DR. PAGE HUDSON 441
APPENDIX 7: CADMIUM POISONING CHARTS 442
APPENDIX 8: HEALTH HISTORY 1975-77 443
APPENDIX 9: ABHIRAM AND WIFE TESTIMONIES.........................471
APPENDIX 10: NONE SO BLIND AS THOSE WHO WILL NOT SEE 479
APPENDIX 11: SP'S TRAVEL ITINERARY 1976-77 480
APPENDIX 12: SHARP SWORD TRUTH FILMS...............................481
APPENDIX 13: SRILA PRABHUPADA'S TEETH AS EVIDENCE...............486

FOREWORD

By Dhira Govinda das

My purpose in life is to encourage people to establish and cultivate their personal, direct relationship with Srila Prabhupada. I endeavor to inspire them to serve and relate to Srila Prabhupada as their current link to the disciplic succession originating with Sri Krishna. I offer my immense gratitude to the "Prabhupada Truth Commission" for so courageously and determinedly serving this mission of making Srila Prabhupada available to the world, through its efforts in producing this volume related to the disappearance pastime of Srila Prabhupada. I came to Krishna consciousness, initially, through years of consuming massive amounts of prasadam, with little to no interest in any other aspects of the process, philosophy or culture of bhakti-yoga (thank you, Stambha das prabhu, for opening and running the bhakti-yoga center in State College, Pennsylvania). Gradually, though, I read Srila Prabhupada's books, and heard some classes from his representatives, and, by the purifying effects of prasadam, was able to realize, or admit, despite myself, "This makes sense." "Despite myself," in the sense that, as far as I was aware, I really wasn't searching for spirituality, or Truth, and certainly not God. I had a life and a future, and it was fine, even exciting, wonderful, and rich. But, this philosophy of Krishna consciousness, and the lifestyle that accompanied it, though quite distinct and radically foreign from what I had come to accept through my conditioning, seemed rational, in its assertions and in the process of purification provided for experiencing the veracity of those assertions.

Since I liked to think of myself as an honest person, I knew that, to be sincere, I needed to give myself to this process of Krishna consciousness, and experientially assess firsthand the statements regarding reality that Srila Prabhupada was giving. Srila Prabhupada's teachings confronted my assumptions regarding all the important questions I had ever considered, and many that had not occurred to me, ranging from the nature of the self, evolution, consciousness, life's purpose, death, etc. I needed to rearrange my entire internal structure to accommodate the principles given by Srila Prabhupada. "Needed to," meaning, again, though I didn't want it to, the philosophy of Krishna consciousness made sense, as contrary as it was to what I had come to believe most all educated, sophisticated, scientifically-minded, progressive people knew. To quote Mark Twain, *"It ain't what you don't know that gets you into trouble. It's what you know for sure that just ain't so."* To be truly independently thoughtful, a term I got later from Srila Prabhupada, it was necessary for me to acknowledge the logic and profundity of these teachings, and to give myself to the process of Krishna

1

consciousness, at least on a trial basis. Thus, I decided to give myself to the process for six months. That was in Israel, 33 years ago. In a sense, I'm still doing the experiment, with some very small measure of earnestness, and am highly satisfied with the result, feeling forever indebted to Srila Prabhupada and his representatives.

A servant of Srila Prabhupada is naturally interested to hear and understand about all of Srila Prabhupada's pastimes- his embarking on the Jaladuta, rising at 1 AM to speak his purports into the dictaphone, viewing Charlie Chaplin, dancing in kirtan, leading Jaya Radha Madhava, and his disappearance pastime. Of course, each pastime of Srila Prabhupada has its distinctive flavor, and invokes diverse emotions. Truth about events surrounding Srila Prabhupada's disappearance have been concealed, and thus we can appreciate the efforts to reveal them, if not exhaustively, at least thoroughly, comprehensively. While there are more details to emerge, this volume provides a clear picture of what happened, through the tremendous research and efforts that were made.

As we learn more and more about the events surrounding the disappearance of Srila Prabhupada, our admiration for his inconceivably transcendental character is enhanced- at least, that's the case for me, and I trust that it will be similarly so for those who carefully study the happenings surrounding Srila Prabhupada's disappearance. My preference, for sure, in relation to the disappearance pastime of Srila Prabhupada, would be to simply, directly glorify Srila Prabhupada for the awe-inspiring transcendental qualities he demonstrates. As I indicated above, though, truths related to his disappearance have been deliberately concealed. Thus, to maximize the possibility that the information in this volume will be examined and received by as many people as possible, it's necessary, or at least real helpful, to expose the deception that has been perpetrated, so that readers and potential readers are free from the influence of the knowledge filter created by ISKCON (Intern'l Society for Krishna Consciousness).

For many years I endeavored to serve Srila Prabhupada's movement as a participant in the ISKCON organization, in services such as sankirtana leader, temple president in Tel-Aviv, leading a book distribution party in Arab towns and villages, Board of Directors Chairman of ISKCON of Alachua, and Director of the ISKCON Central Office of Child Protection. As years went on I realized, through repeated experience, that the atmosphere of bold, innovative, groundbreaking thought that so vitally characterized my experience with Srila Prabhupada's spirit and teachings, was conspicuous by its absence in the organization that was supposedly representing him. For sure I found there were forums for discussion in relation to issues of moment. To quote Noam Chomsky, *"The smart way to keep people passive and obedient is to strictly limit the spectrum of acceptable opinion, but allow very lively debate within that spectrum."* So, yeah, on vital issues there was lively debate, in a range the size of a postage stamp. I came to the point where I could no longer, with clean conscience, identify with the organization, or encourage others to connect with the organization, and simultaneously I find myself increasingly enthusiastic to practice the process of Krishna consciousness given to us by Srila Prabhupada, and to serve Srila Prabhupada and his mission.

I understand and appreciate that, amongst those connected with the ISKCON organization in various capacities, there will naturally be diverse viewpoints in regards to what I've expressed above. There can be, though, no reasonable objection to the assertion that what I've written applies to how the ISKCON organization has handled the topic of the disappearance of Srila Prabhupada. The official resolution of the ISKCON Governing Body Commission (GBC) is *"There is no evidence at this time to support the allegations of poisoning of Srila Prabhupada."* Professionally conducted tests on samples of Srila Prabhupada's hair, from the weeks and months shortly before Srila Prabhupada's disappearance, reveal cadmium levels about 250 times above average. There is no rational accidental or environmental cause for this level of cadmium in the samples of Srila Prabhupada's hair. By far the most reasonable explanation, as far as I am able to determine, is that someone, or more than one person, deliberately, with homicidal intent, gave cadmium to Srila Prabhupada. Forensic toxicologists have confirmed that the level of cadmium found in Srila Prabhupada's hair constitutes clear indication of deliberate poisoning. One described it as *"...prima facie evidence of poisoning with malicious intent."* Yet, the GBC stands strong in its stance that *"There is no evidence at this time to support the allegations of poisoning of Srila Prabhupada."*

On May 14, 2004 I wrote to a GBC member regarding the issue of Srila Prabhupada's disappearance: *"I'll briefly go over some points regarding this topic of Srila Prabhupada's disappearance pastime. First, Srila Prabhupada clearly expressed concern that he seriously considered the possibility that he was poisoned. As far as the argument 'But maybe he was referring to unintentional poisoning effects from medicine'- I don't see how someone conversant with the relevant conversations, and who is sincere about excavating the truth of the matter, can pose such an argument. Sure, there was discussion about poisonous effects of medicine. And there was also distinct and manifest discussion by Srila Prabhupada and those around him about deliberate murder by poison. Why else, for example, would they be discussing a case in Calcutta of a husband deliberately murdering his wife by poison? Clearly they were discussing murder by poison. If accidental poison by medicine was also talked about, that's a separate point. The relevant point is that Srila Prabhupada was speaking about being deliberately poisoned by other human beings. This is clear.*

"I'm not saying that it's conclusive evidence. But let us, and the GBC, at least take Srila Prabhupada's words seriously. And if the GBC body won't actively pursue an investigation, then let's at least refer interested persons to Srila Prabhupada's direct words. Who can argue with hearing from Srila Prabhupada on this topic? I won't include herein the conversation transcripts where Srila Prabhupada clearly expresses he suspects he is being poisoned, and the conversations where those around him clearly believe that Srila Prabhupada thinks that it is very possible that he is being murdered by poison. I am assuming that you have carefully studied these conversations. If you have, and you don't agree with my assessment above, I humbly request that you share with me the basis for your views. If you haven't studied these conversations by this time, then I'm doubtful whether you should be in any sort of leadership position in Srila Prabhupada's movement, especially considering the statements you have implicitly and explicitly made about this subject. Again, what I'm presenting here is simply that Srila Prabhupada expressed serious concern that he was deliberately poisoned. People should know that Srila Prabhupada had this concern. It is not helpful, except maybe in the most short-sighted sense concerned solely with immediate institutional protection, to cover this up..."

But I didn't receive a response on this from that GBC member.

Srila Prabhupada several times expressed his concern that someone was giving him poison, and, as mentioned in my above letter, he was clearly referring to the possibility that someone, or more than one person, was attempting to murder him through poisoning. For those surrounding Srila Prabhupada it was obvious that Srila Prabhupada was concerned that he was being given poison with malicious intent. This is clear in the Conversation Books Vol. 36, pages 367-8 where Srila Prabhupada speaks with his caretakers: **BHAV:** *Prabhupada was complaining of mental distress this morning also.* **BCS:** *Srila Prabhupada?* **SP:** *Hmm?* **BCS:** *[Bengali] ...mental distress?* **SP:** *Hmm-hmm.* **KAV:** *[Hindi—bole bole]* **SP:** *Vahi bat jo koi hamko poison kya. (That same thing – that someone has poisoned me.)* **BCS:** *O aacha, uno soch na ki koi... (Oh, okay, he thinks that someone....)* **KAV:** *(speaking over Bhakticharu): Dekhiye bat yehi hai ki kisi rakshas ne diya ho...* **BCS:** *Someone gave him poison here.* **KAV:** *[Hindi, long explanation about Sankaracharya disciple being poisoned]* **Tamal:** *Prabhupada was thinking that someone had poisoned him?* **BCS:** *Yes.* **Tamal :** *That was the mental distress?* **BCS:** *Yes.* **KAV:** *[Hindi]* **Tamal:** *What did Kaviraja just say?* **BCS:** *He said that when Srila Prabhupada was saying that, there must be something truth behind it. [People all speaking at once; asking about the acharya that was poisoned by powdered glass]* **Tamal:** *Srila Prabhupada, Shastriji says that there must be some truth to it if you say that. So who is it that has poisoned? [13 seconds pause with no answer]*

Srila Prabhupada unmistakably expressed concern that he was being poisoned. Those in close proximity to him in Nov. 1977, unambiguously acknowledged Srila Prabhupada's concern about this. The ISKCON GBC remains firm in its assertion that *"There is no evidence at this time to support the allegations of poisoning of Srila Prabhupada."* Multiple top-level audio-forensic professionals, working independently, confirm that in the days prior to Srila Prabhupada's departure, those close to Srila Prabhupada are speaking in whispers in the background, and multiple audio-forensic analyses determine that the word "poison" is used in at least some of the whispers. This includes whispers with content such as *"The poison's going down"* and *"Is the poison in the milk?"* Srila Prabhupada's words, the prime evidence for Srila Prabhupada followers, leave no doubt he was thinking/knowing that one or more persons were giving him poison.

Hair samples of Srila Prabhupada reveal levels of cadmium that indicate deliberate, chronic poisoning with cadmium. In the days prior to Srila Prabhupada's departure there are recordings with whispers in the background, and multiple professional, audio forensic analyses reveal a few of Srila Prabhupada's disciples whispering about "poison." The ISKCON GBC insists *"There is no evidence..."* ...my stance is that if you want truth in regards to Srila Prabhupada's disappearance pastime, do not seek it from the ISKCON GBC, who are committed to cover-ups and concealment. Surfing the net, I find a talk related to the disappearance of Srila Prabhupada (www.youtube.com/watch?v=VdsG_v948XA), by someone in the leadership of the ISKCON organization. Below is a transcription of a lecture, May 27, 2014, first 5 min.). [This video and others are now removed by the GBC.]

Question: "Is it true that Srila Prabhupada was poisoned?" Maharaja laughs, and responds: *"It is not true that Prabhupada was poisoned. Actually, I was one of the people who did the investigation as to the allegations of whether Prabhupada was poisoned or not... and we did a thorough investigation, we did a hair analysis... so the hair analysis did not show any poison, interestingly enough, and therefore we can conclude that Prabhupada was not poisoned, simply on that basis... also we did an analysis of all the recordings, and everything else... there was a book that was put out, by a devotee in Australia, called* 'Not That I am Poisoned'... *Prabhupada said 'Not that I am poisoned...' it was very clear... There's no evidence that Prabhupada was poisoned. The only thing they came out with was playing Prabhupada's recordings backwards, and it maybe sounded like something... it's just like one of these Beatles songs, Lucy in the Sky With Diamonds, and you play it backwards, and it means something... and that was the only evidence.*

"There's no evidence that Prabhupada was poisoned... Why do people say that- because, basically, they're upset that they didn't get any position

5

in the Krishna consciousness movement, or they have some personal animosity, or problem with people who have some position in the Krishna consciousness movement. It's all based on an emotional thing. ...when someone says something, there's always an emotional background to it. There are emotions that are stimulating... when there are strong emotions, logic is thrown out. So, this is actually the case. Logically there's nothing; physically there's nothing. And also there's devotees who were taking care of Srila Prabhupada, such as Bhakticharu Maharaja, and Tamal Krishna Maharaja. And specifically Bhakticharu Maharaja, who had so much love for Srila Prabhupada, they would kill themselves rather than hurt Prabhupada. There was nobody with any motive that would have hurt Prabhupada who was around Prabhupada at that time... What's the next question; that was an easy one... and you can just go on the internet and read that book, Not That I Am Poisoned, *is the name of the book."*

The Maharaja giving the talk starts with a hearty laugh in response to the question regarding whether Srila Prabhupada was given poison with homicidal intent, indicating that the issue of Srila Prabhupada being murdered is a laughing matter, really not worth serious attention. Then he unequivocally asserts, *"It is not true that Prabhupada was poisoned."* And he affirms that he's not just stating opinions he has heard from others, but rather, he was a member of the team that conducted a "thorough investigation," and he declares, "There's actually no evidence." Not content to oppose Srila Prabhupada's words and an abundance of high-level forensic audio and toxicology evidence, the Maharaja goes on to share his apparently conclusive psychological analyses of those who contend that there is compelling evidence that Srila Prabhupada was given poison with murderous intent. The Maharaja explains to his audience that persons who make such claims are driven by personal ambition, envy, anger issues, and other such emotional disturbances, implying, pretty straightforwardly, that members of the ISKCON GBC, such as himself, are not motivated by such lower-self emotional drives as personal material ambition, when they continue to declare, *"There is no evidence to support the allegations of Srila Prabhupada's poisoning."*

I also find www.youtube.com/watch?v=TOUmm2UMmYo (first 2 minutes). This different Maharaja says: *"My question is that a few times I hear about killing Srila Prabhupada by Tamal Krishna Goswami. Can you make it clear for me what is going on? [...] There is an idea, from some people, that Srila Prabhupada was killed by some of his close disciples; well, short of doing a forensic study, it's not possible to prove anything. If you want to take my opinion, this is nonsense; extremely offensive to both Srila Prabhupada and his close disciples. And, furthermore, what difference does it make to you? You have to chant Hare Krishna and go to Krishna. So, even if, just for the sake of argument, Srila Prabhupada had been so horribly dealt with by his disciples, what difference does it make to you? You have to chant Hare Krishna. Now, interestingly, when we see, when Prahlad Maharaja, was fed poison, in the Bhagavatam, by his father Hiranyakasipu, it had no effect on him. So, Krishna protects his pure devotee. So, Prabhupada, we understand, he's not an ordinary person. He went to Krishna in that time, and in that way, because Krishna wanted him to. That's all. You probably got this from the internet. So, again, you won't get Krishna conscious by wandering around the backyards of the internet. There are all sorts of weird things out there."*

I get the impression it's "this or that." Care about Srila Prabhupada's disappearance pastime, or chant Hare Krishna. Can't do both. While I appreciate that it is important to utilize discretion with respect to time, circumstance and person, in sharing and discussing various pastimes of Srila Prabhupada, also it's true that this Maharaja's statement, perhaps with the intention to protect his listeners and himself, seems to deprecate the intelligence of those to whom he is speaking, as if he needs to protect them from the truth, or even, from their natural propensity to want to seek truth.

This volume states, *"Once one recognizes the truth that Srila Prabhupada was intentionally poisoned, how can he remain silent? Silence and complicity are close friends. Let us not take this subject as entertainment reading and then forget the matter, doing nothing about it. There is already too much history in Srila Prabhupada's movement of hiding truths from devotees with a privileged few manipulating those in the dark. This is not a matter of airing our dirty laundry in public. It is a question of defending Srila Prabhupada, the truth, and his mission – the prime benediction for humanity."*

Anton Chekhov- *"The illusion which exalts us is dearer to us than ten thousand truths."* As I mentioned above, followers of Srila Prabhupada, in their deep gratitude and affection for Srila Prabhupada, will want in most every instance to at least have the opportunity to hear the truth about his disappearance pastime, and for those serving in positions of leadership in the ISKCON organization to discourage intelligent and honest exploration of Srila Prabhupada's disappearance only adds to the already mountainous evidence that the organization is dedicated to cover-up, deception, and a culture of fear and repression. I trust that the Maharajas to which I've referred, as well as the vast majority of other devotees in positions of leadership in the ISCKON organization, are, in a sense, innocent, or, perhaps more precisely, simply ignorant. What I mean is, they've allowed themselves to be influenced, covered, by a knowledge filter that became prominent in the organization decades ago. Information that conflicts with the dominant paradigm strongly tends to be filtered out. We don't need to succumb to such a mushroom culture. This book provides ample opportunity for each to be independently thoughtful on this issue of the disappearance pastime of Srila Prabhupada. This book states:

"There has been an almost miraculous assemblage of pieces of evidence which cannot be denied or swept away except by dishonest persons whose interests are threatened by emergence of the truth. Some will be reluctant, even vehemently so, to accept that Srila Prabhupada was poisoned because this disrupts personal attachments, conceptions, views, psyche, and their major paradigms. But anyone can become free of these limiting constraints with an open and honest mind." As Upton Sinclair says, *"It is difficult to get a man to understand something, when his salary depends upon his not understanding it."* This book continues, *"Again, we maintain that even though most of ISKCON's leaders had no direct involvement in SP's poisoning by heavy metals, they are deeply implicated in this crime by: (1) Covering up the crime by denials, lies, and refusal to conduct or even allow an honest investigation, and (2) Demonizing all who have privately investigated and protested the poisoning."*

Through the organizational strategy of diversion and deception, many, or practically all, connected with the ISKCON organization have been fooled in relation to the disappearance pastime of Srila Prabhupada. I know that I was, till the early 2000s, when a few events, including attendance at an international GBC meeting in the year 2000 where the topic of Srila Prabhupada's disappearance was discussed- or, a thinly veiled appearance of discussion occurred. That discussion, or smokescreen of one, which seemed to convince most everyone that the issue had been handled, led me to consider that there was more to the issue than the institutional party line. Mark Twain again- *"It's easier to fool someone than to convince them that they've been fooled."* By humbly accepting we may have been deceived by lies perpetrated by ISKCON on Srila Prabhupada's disappearance, we open ourselves to be touched and moved by strikingly wonderful qualities evinced by Srila Prabhupada in the pastime of his disappearance.

Of course Srila Prabhupada's departure is pastime, and Sri Krishna and Srila Prabhupada co-created this pastime according to their desire, for our illumination and inspiration. That it was a pastime doesn't mean that those involved in the pastime were consciously acting as pure servants of the will of Sri Krishna and Srila Prabhupada, just as the Romans involved in the crucifixion pastime of Jesus are not generally regarded as pure-hearted devotees of God. Sometimes I've heard the argument that Krishna would not allow Srila Prabhupada to be poisoned. For me it's not clear how it makes sense that Srila Prabhupada and Krishna would be okay with a disappearance pastime that involved, say, germs, or a virus, or some other form of attack on the body, though not poisoning. Also of course those who gave poison to Srila Prabhupada did not succeed to murder him.

Srila Prabhupada lives through his vani, his sound vibration, his instructions, his books, through the many sincere followers who dedicate their lives to serve his mission. This volume is evidence of this; it reveals the pastimes of Srila Prabhupada's disappearance, and Srila Prabhupada is alive through this revelation. He is alive in the revelation, and he is instructing us, and opening our eyes with the torchlight of knowledge. For decades there have been flagrant, often gross, shameful and repulsive efforts to block and obscure Srila Prabhupada's direct relationship with his sincere followers. This has been the source of untold anguish, pain and suffering for countless people. The information revealed in this volume moves us great strides forward in understanding the consciousness and actions that are at the root of this offensive obstruction, and opens the floodgates of the ocean of the gifts given to us by Srila Prabhupada.

Perhaps the truths that are revealed in these pages will catalyze profoundly auspicious changes throughout Srila Prabhupada's movement, including in the ISKCON institution. I hope so, though, to whatever extent that occurs, or not, it is doubtlessly auspicious, though not necessarily comfortable or pleasant, in itself to hear the actual story of what happened in the disappearance pastime of Srila Prabhupada. The efforts made with this publication are heroic, standing courageously for truth on behalf of Srila Prabhupada. I regard this volume as a monumental achievement in the history of Srila Prabhupada's movement. When I first heard rumors about Srila Prabhupada's disciples giving him poison, I regarded them as ridiculous. Then, a few months later, late in 1997, I heard about this topic from Ambarish Prabhu, and he convinced me there might be validity to the allegations that Srila Prabhupada poisoned with murderous intent. Later Ambarish wrote a Foreword for *Srila Prabhupada: The Prominent Link*. There, he quotes Herbert Spencer, as follows- *"There is a principle which is a bar against all information, which is proof against all information, which is proof against all arguments, and which cannot fail to keep a man in everlasting ignorance. That is contempt prior to investigation."*

In that spirit of discovery, with willingness to accept and do what is right, and not merely convenient, let us give careful consideration to this volume. Hare Krishna. Jaya Srila Prabhupada!

David Wolf (Dhira Govinda dasa), Ph.D., Founder and Director- Satvatove Institute School of Transformative Coaching, Founder and Director (1998-2004)- Association for the Protection of Vaishnava Children, Author of several books including- Relationships That Work: The Power of Conscious Living; Krsna, Israel, and the Druze: An Interreligious Odyssey; Srila Prabhupada: The Prominent Link; Effects of the Hare Krsna Maha Mantra on Stress, Depression, and the Three Gunas (doctoral dissertation); Member-Board of Directors, ISKCON of Alachua, 1995-2001 (Chairperson for four of those years). Temple President- ISKCON Tel-Aviv, Israel, 1987-88.

INTRODUCTION

MYSTERY OF SRILA PRABHUPADA'S DEPARTURE

From mid-1976 Srila Prabhupada unexplainably became increasingly weak and ill. Despite treatment from various Ayurvedic doctors, he did not improve. Amazingly, in a bedridden state, Srila Prabhupada continued translating *Srimad Bhagavatam* until his departure. He left this mortal world on Nov. 14, 1977 to rejoin Lord Sri Krishna in the eternal abode of Goloka Vrindaban, from which perfect, liberated devotees descend to spiritually benefit the conditioned souls. Srila Prabhupada, a pure devotee of Lord Krishna, is not dead. He lives forever in his instructions, and his bona fide followers will always live with him. Krishna's eternally liberated associate is not an ordinary man. His appearance and disappearance in this world are arranged by Krishna. Bhaktivinode Thakura stated: *He reasons ill who tells that Vaishnavas die, While thou art living still in sound. The Vaishnavas die to live, and living try, To spread the Holy Name around.*

His Divine Grace A.C. Bhaktivedanta Swami singlehandedly began, organized, nourished, and built up the worldwide Hare Krishna movement from a 1965 beginning in New York's Lower East Side. Through his society, named ISKCON, in 12 short years, he initiated 5000 disciples, opened 108 temples, published eighty books of Vedic scriptures and philosophy, and distributed 60 million of pieces of literature in dozens of languages across the globe. His health was very good even though he had reached 80 years of age, and his vigor and strength was far beyond any of his much younger students. He slept a few hours a day and maintained a challenging schedule of exercise, study, writing, teaching, management, and counseling.

In July 1976, he suddenly became very ill and weak, with no appetite. In Feb. 1977 his health again sharply declined, marked by chronic mucus and bronchitis. No doctor (there were many Indian kavirajas and several allopathic doctors) could pinpoint the actual problem, as diagnosis suggestions ranged across the board, from diabetes to kidney ailment, from nothing was wrong to perhaps asthma. No doctor was ever engaged for long nor allowed to do proper medical tests or x-rays, and his belated death certificate incongruously listed heart attack as the cause of death. After 10 months of hardly eating, Srila Prabhupada's physical condition resembled starvation, yet his Krishna consciousness never wavered. It was a mystery illness until 20 years later, when the "poison issue" erupted in late 1997, just as the internet went mainstream.

A series of whisperings by Srila Prabhupada's caretakers about poison was discovered on tape recordings made in Srila Prabhupada's quarters during his last days. That was sobering enough, but when actual conversations a day earlier than these "poison" whispers were stumbled upon, which hardly anyone had seen before, where Srila Prabhupada said repeatedly he thought he had been poisoned, and his caretakers discussed homicidal poisoning at length, then the dots were being connected. Many suspected Tamal Krishna Goswami of foul play, especially after an interview was found with him claiming Srila Prabhupada asked for "medicine to die now." The GBC leadership of ISKCON was compelled to appoint an investigator and undertake an internal inquiry. Hopes were high that the truth of the matter would be revealed.

A year later, little had been done. Some of Srila Prabhupada's followers decided to investigate on their own. The GBC investigator was ill-funded and a busy attorney, and after 30 months he made an inconclusive report which simply recommended further investigation. Simultaneously, the primary suspects secretly organized and funded their own whitewash report with obvious lies, deceit, and fraud. ISKCON hastily endorsed the position that there was no evidence of poisoning. Move on folks, nothing to see here... But the private, external investigation by honest devotees continued. A forensic breakthrough occurred by chance in 2002 when Srila Prabhupada hair samples that the GBC themselves had wanted to test, but abandoned in Wisconsin, were found to have sky-high levels of the heavy metal cadmium. The GBC had declined to pay for the tests. Further audio forensics, research, interviews, and hair tests added to the pool of evidence. There was little room for doubt about Srila Prabhupada being homicidally, maliciously poisoned in 1977, apparently by some of his own caretakers and senior disciples. It was not until 2017, however, that a full updated report was made public on this new evidence, posted online as an e-book, and then printed in India as a two book hardcover set in 2022. This updated softcover edition features the complete poisoning evidence, and subsequent volumes in a "Srila Prabhupada" series will feature related topics such as Tamal, suspects, health decline, ISKCON history, etc.

A struggle to effect a full, honest, and unbiased investigation into this matter was undertaken by a broad spectrum of devotees. Many have contributed to the "private" investigation, only one of whom is the compiler-editor of the accumulated evidence in this volume. The "poison issue" is not promoted by a disenfranchised, splinter group nor is it manufactured by those who have old grudges to avenge nor by those who have psychological imbalances. It is not coming from troublemakers and faultfinders, emotional and "wounded souls" who are an unpleasant annoyance. ISKCON deceitfully shut out their own honest "independent" investigator (Balavanta das), and then, after cooking up a disgraceful cover-up, they prohibited and penalized any further investigation into Srila Prabhupada's poisoning. Outsiders then quietly completed the investigation that ISKCON should have done themselves. The resulting evidence stands on its own merits, although it is totally ignored and dismissed by ISKCON leadership.

The "poison issue" is extremely relevant to the health and future of the Hare Krishna Movement. The established fact of an actual poisoning cannot be honestly denied in the face of the overwhelming evidence. Many follow-through questions naturally arise, which is exactly what the misleaders of ISKCON are very fearful of facing, and why they have deviously avoided the issue. This alone more than disqualifies them from continued leadership in Srila Prabhupada's ISKCON. Aside from criticism of the GBC for failure to honestly investigate Srila Prabhupada's poisoning and their devious cover-up of obscuring the evidence, this volume focuses on the evidence itself and on unraveling the myths propagated by the institutional deniers. *Ultimately this investigation will be continued by a government agency pursuing mundane justice.* However, we should focus on spiritual purity instead.

This volume is also a response to the book *Not That I Am Poisoned (NTIAP)*, published by ISKCON (Feb. 2000) and endorsed by its GBC. *NTIAP* was a response to *Someone Has Poisoned Me* (*SHPM*, May 1999), which presented the evidence which at that time indicated Srila Prabhupada had endured arsenic poisoning. Later hair sample tests revealed shockingly high cadmium levels. The debate on the lethality of the arsenic levels found in an early hair test became largely irrelevant due to the cadmium discovery. The evidence and conclusions in *SHPM* remain valid, but with a significant addition to the body of evidence: *Cadmium was the primary poison, and arsenic was secondary.* Cadmium was found in similarly elevated levels in three separate forensic analyses of Srila Prabhupada's hair. These cadmium levels could not be due to accident, pollution, industry, shampoo, medicine, or bad water. It was due to malicious homicidal poisoning by ingestion of contaminated food or drink. Some remaining questions in Srila Prabhupada's poisoning:

(1) Who did it, who benefited, and what to do with them? **(2)** Of them, who is in ISKCON or its leadership? **(3)** Can we trust what the poisoners have done to ISKCON since 1977? Or their policies, position papers, doctrines, philosophical interpretations? What deviancies have they introduced into ISKCON? **(4)** Is it not problematic if those who poisoned Srila Prabhupada supported the endless changes to Srila Prabhupada's books, lied about being successor acharyas, made multiple revisions to ISKCON's initiating guru system, disenfranchised thousands of devotees, and remain financially unaccountable as supposed gurus? **(5)** Should Srila Prabhupada's poisoners and those who joined their new guru regime be trusted to guide ISKCON forward? **(6)** Did some ISKCON leaders have Srila Prabhupada removed for their own material gain and then corrupt the institution with defective doctrines to enable pursuit of their own personal, material ambitions? **(7)** Shouldn't everything that has happened in ISKCON since Srila Prabhupada's departure be re-evaluated? Shouldn't we start over from square one, like it was the day after Srila Prabhupada left?

WHO IS BEHIND THE PRIVATE INVESTIGATION?

"A global body of very serious and dedicated followers of Srila Prabhupada with massive resources have been working quietly for years to bring these issues to full understanding in all the different forums trying to follow Srila Prabhupada. No stone will be left unturned in establishing the truth in facts and philosophy on all these issues and doing what is necessary to drive out the deviations and give back to Srila Prabhupada his global mission the way he wants it. All we want is the truth. If it is being hidden from us, then we will go looking for it. And find it we did..." (Naveen Krishna das, 2020)

Working together, these individuals adopted an identity: **Prabhupada Truth Commission**, a fully independent investigative group, focused on the discovery of truth. Unfortunately the corrupted ISKCON does not want truth and maintains institutional control through an artificial harmony of repression which will not last. Open philosophical discussions and exchange of views and realizations are actually healthy because: **(1)** it helps an individual to attain self-fulfillment. **(2)** It assists in truth discovery. **(3)** It strengthen the capacity of an individual in decision-making. **(4)** It helps to form our sincerely-held beliefs and communicate them freely to others.

Prabhupada Truth Commission is an informal group of Srila Prabhupada followers tasked to uncover Srila Prabhupada's hidden glories in his disappearance pastimes. This is a collaborative effort by many devotees aiming to discover the truth and please Srila Prabhupada, wanting to share the plain facts and evidence. Those who had never met each other worked together with common ideals. The forensic tests and early private investigation was undertaken by Naveen Krishna das, Jitarati das, Mandapa das, and Nityananda das. Historical records, essays, and philosophical materials were collected from varied sources. Input on Srila Prabhupada siddhanta came from brahminical devotees. Nityananda das did compilation and editing with submissions and advice from a working team of about ten devotees, scattered worldwide. Our appreciations go to the authors of various materials, much of it used without due credit. We ask pardon for these and other shortcomings.

SHORT SUMMARY OF THE POISON ISSUE

A brief history of the key "poison issue" history:

(1) Up to July 1976 Srila Prabhupada had very good health.

(2) Then Srila Prabhupada's health declined relentlessly and no doctor could tell why. **(3)** Immediately upon his departure, 11 leading disciples hijacked ISKCON as zonal acharyas. **(4)** For 10 years these gurus and ISKCON's managing body (GBC) caused havoc and huge damage.

(5) In 1987 the GBC admitted there was no appointment of new gurus- it was a hoax. **(6)** In 1997 whisperings of poisoning were found on a bedside audio recording of Srila Prabhupada's last days.

(7) Attention focused on discussions between Srila Prabhupada and his caretakers about him being poisoned.

(8) They were about homicidal poisoning; Srila Prabhupada said he thought he had been poisoned.

(9) ISKCON's GBC appointed Balavanta as a special investigator; after 30 months his findings were inconclusive.

(10) Balavanta had done a NAA hair test, finding elevated, health threatening but non-lethal arsenic levels.

(11) The "poison whispers" were forensically tested by many top audio labs, confirmed to be about poisoning.

(12) GBC denied there had been a poisoning and the suspects organized a sham GBC book of denials.

(13) *Someone Has Poisoned Me (2000)* and *Judge For Yourself (2003)* honestly presented the poison evidence.

(14) These books were condemned by the GBC and they banned discussion of the topic in ISKCON. **(15)** In 2002-05 hair samples arranged by the GBC were tested and found to have lethal cadmium levels.

(16) In 2017 *Kill Guru, Become Guru* was posted online with updated evidence of Srila Prabhupada's poisoning.

(17) In 2020 a GBC loyalist published *Deception*- full of deceit meant to discredit the poison evidence.

(18) 2022: a hardcover two book set was released as a reference library on the poison issue, the gurujacking of the divine mission, etc, titled *Srila Prabhupada's Hidden Glories*. **(19)** 2022: this revised edition released.

PART ONE:
IRREFUTABLE FORENSIC EVIDENCE

Tamal, Dec. 20, 1997: *"What is most needed is textual and __forensic evidence.__ We need researchers who can delve into all the materials and establish the truth on the basis of irrefutable facts."*

Part 1 ***does*** establish the irrefutable forensic evidence in Srila Prabhupada's malicious homicidal poisoning. *"All truth passes through three stages: First it is ridiculed. Second it is violently opposed. Third it is **accepted as being self-evident.**"* (M. Gandhi)

CHAPTER 1:
THE FIRST HAIR TESTS

"Every month I had the opportunity to shave Srila Prabhupada's head with the electric clippers. Srila Prabhupada was not a passive recipient during this process. He moved around and that made me more frightened. 'Turn the shaver off in between each stroke so it doesn't get hot,' he instructed. This wasn't very difficult, but the tricky part was shaving around his ears. 'Be careful of my ears,' he said whenever I got close to them. I was very careful. By Krishna's grace there was never a mishap during this service. It also gave me the opportunity to put many devotees into ecstasy by distributing Srila Prabhupada's hair."

(*What Is The Difficulty?* Srutikirti das, p 66)

HAIR TEST FOR MERCURY

After the whispers about poison were discovered and then the discussions of poisoning between Srila Prabhupada and his caretakers were brought forward, with the whole devotee world wondering what it all meant, the idea of professional audio forensic analyses took hold. As that developed into a series of audio studies, Nityananda das read books on solving poisoning crimes, poisoning case histories, and how law enforcement often exhumed a body to test for poisons and an unnatural death. Srila Prabhupada's exhumation, however, was unthinkable. But hair tests often uncovered hard evidence of poisoning. Forensic analysis of Srila Prabhupada's hair cuttings might confirm the discussions and whispers. The blood deposits and infuses its contents into growing hair. Srila Prabhupada became very ill in early 1977, so the presumed poisoning could be found in "sacred relics" of hair samples that some devotees had kept, provided they were cut during 1977. At the ISKCON farm at New Talavan, Mississippi, Nityananda had received in 1978 a gift of a goodly quantity of Srila Prabhupada's hair from a visiting sannyasi, maybe Prabhavishnu Swami. It was unknown when the hair had been cut, but maybe it was 1977. Nityananda decided to test some of this hair sample. He learned of a chemical process to detect elements or minerals in hair called hair mineral analysis (HMA). In Dec. 1997 he took half of his hair sample, named Sample W, about 40 milligrams, to First Analytical Laboratories in Chapel Hill, NC, which could only test for lead, mercury, or cyanide, one at a time. The lab analyst, Dr. Wadlin, explained that all chemical tests *except for mercury* required more hair than Nityananda had. So mercury it was. The result was 4 parts per million (ppm) mercury, which is in the normal range of 2-15 ppm as noted in toxicological texts. Highly abnormal amounts creating a serious health threat would be 50-200 ppm. *So, this hair was cut at a time when Srila Prabhupada was not being poisoned by mercury.* This test was regretted-- it did not help to settle matters but consumed a lot of sacred hair. Chemical tests required handfuls of hair, and were not viable for testing the few tiny amounts of hair relics that might be available from select devotees. Srila Prabhupada's hair was cut every 3-4 weeks, always half an inch at most in length, and the few known samples were as little as just a few pieces. So, were there any alternative testing methods?

FIRST NEUTRON ACTIVATION ANALYSIS

Dr. Wadlin suggested "neutron activation" analyses (NAA) which required no minimum amount, wherein a simultaneous reading of **multiple elements** was possible. NAA involved irradiating a sample, its constituent elements emitting different types of gamma rays and measured over a time period. Amounts of component elements are precisely measured. Elements like copper, sulfur, aluminum could be measured, but not chemical compounds like sodium nitrate. NAA can measure a single hair's linear profile, including spots of higher elemental concentration along the hair shaft, showing different exposures at different times. A profile analysis, however, requires hairs longer than an inch, and Srila Prabhupada's hair cuttings were only 2 to 10 mm in length. NAA tests of Srila Prabhupada hair samples would thus give an average reading, whereas profile tests on hair that were several inches long showed a historical timeline of varying poison levels over many months. Nityananda kept Naveen Krishna updated on the development of hair tests, who informed Balavanta, the GBC's "independent" investigator into the poison issue. In Jan. 1998 Balavanta disclosed he had obtained two very small quantities of Srila Prabhupada's hair (cutting date unknown) but that the forensic lab he located could not perform a chemical analysis on such a small quantity.

Through the FBI, in March 1998 Nityananda located two NAA facilities. One was Dr. J Steven Morris at the Research Reactor Division of the University of Missouri in Columbia, Missouri. Nityananda called Dr. Morris, who explained that he worked with and tested archeological artifacts, such as Peruvian and Aztec mummies, and so he was very familiar with hair testing. He offered to consider a written request for a series of pro-bono (free) tests. He was interested in our investigative case from an academic standpoint. Other-wise, normally, the university facilities were restricted from private parties or law enforcement.

Nityananda also called a Dr. A. Chatt of the Dept. of

Dalhousie University

SLOWPOKE-2 Facility
Trace Analysis Research Centre
Department of Chemistry
Halifax, Nova Scotia
B0H 4J3 Canada

1999 March 05

Mr. Niko Kuyt, President
Carolinas Vedic Village Society
P.O. Box 28
1851 Radharani Drive
Efland, NC 27243
U.S.A.

Fax: 919-563-8856

DR CHATT REPORT ON SAMPLE ND-1 (1999)

Dear Mr. Kuyt,

We have analyzed the very small sample (3.7 mg) of hair of Bhaktinedanta Swami (deceased 1977) that you provided. We have used instrumental neutron activation analysis for multielement determination in this hair sample. The following concentrations were measured:

ele-ment	Se	Cl	Al	Mn	Ca	Au	Zn	Br	As	Na	K	Hg
ppm	<3	3060	180	11	640	1.4	340	6.7	1.1	890	440	<1

It should be emphasized that the results given are approximate concentrations because of the very small sample size.

According to literature the normal range of As in human hair is 0.13 - 3.71 ppm; thus As poisoning seems highly unlikely.

Thank you very much for using our services. Please do not hesitate to contact us if you need any other information.

Yours sincerely,

A. Chatt, Ph.D., F.C.I.C., F.A.N.S.
Professor of Chemistry
Director of SLOWPOKE-2 Facility

enclosure: invoice

page 1 of 2

Telephone: 1-902-494-2065
Telephone/Answering Machine/Fax: 1-902-494-2474
Alternate Fax: 1-902-494-1310

E Mail: A.CHATT@DAL.CA &
CHATT@CHEM1.CHEM.DAL.CA
Time Zone: GMT -4

Chemistry, Dalhousie Univ., Halifax, Nova Scotia, Canada. Dalhousie had a nuclear reactor research facility and Dr. Chatt was a leading world authority on NAA hair tests. He wrote a book called *"Hair Analysis"* and he described his procedures and expertise. Nityananda decided to use Dr. Chatt at $400 instead of Dr. Morris who was not sure how soon he could a test. On May 1, 1998 Nityananda sent to Dr. Chatt most of his remaining sacred hair relic for NAA, labeled as *Sample ND-1*, weighing 3.7 mg. In Jan. 1999 Dr. Chatt, testing only for arsenic, found slightly elevated levels at *1.1 ppm*. This was not a very serious health hazard level. Later it was learned that Dr. Chatt's facilities were not very accurate on small amounts. More 1977 hair samples would be needed to do more tests. Where to find them?

ARSENIC POISONING CONFIRMED

Nityananda told Balavanta about Dr. Morris' pro bono offer, who then made arrangements with Dr. Morris for tests on Srila Prabhupada hair samples, starting with those he already had. Dr. Morris' work would be *"as his time would allow."* Few other facilities in the world have neutron accelerators and equipment capable of accurately analyzing tiny hair samples less than 1 mg in weight. Dr. Morris was an expert at forensically determining **abnormal levels** of toxic elements in human hair. Finally, in Feb. 1999 Nityananda heard from Naveen Krishna that Balavanta's hair test with Dr. Morris had **found arsenic at abnormal levels.** Balavanta was trying to maintain secrecy and Naveen Krishna, also a GBC, was canvassing ISKCON leaders to support Balavanta's investigation. But neither would tell more about the arsenic results.

On Feb. 19 Nityananda phoned Dr. Morris directly, who spoke openly, saying, as verified by numerous scientific studies, normally one finds *less than 0.05 ppm up to 0.2 ppm of arsenic in hair,* depending on diet, environmental exposure. Missouri farmers using agricultural arsenic chemicals often had elevated levels of 1.0 ppm, but Balavanta's *Q-1* hair sample had **"almost 3 ppm" arsenic.** (A year later Nityananda learned Sample Q-1 had exactly 2.6 ppm arsenic). Dr. Morris had collected *Sample Q-1* from Srila Prabhupada's hair clippers which Balavanta sent him. Dr. Morris summarized: Srila Prabhupada, at the time represented by that hair sample, had about <u>**20 times normal levels of arsenic**</u>. In his opinion, this would not come from environmental factors, but required ingestion of unusual amounts of arsenic. He was very knowledgeable on normal and abnormal levels of arsenic in human hair. The presence of high levels of arsenic in Srila Prabhupada's hair confirmed that <u>Srila Prabhupada had been poisoned with arsenic; any accidental, occupational, or industrial exposure was extremely unlikely</u> (Ch.47-8).

The GBC was upset when Nityananda reported results of "about 3 ppm" in *Someone Has Poisoned Me (SHPM)* in May 1999. Finally Balavanta publicly released the NAA report received from Dr. Morris in March 2000. *"The arsenic concentration in Q-1 was 2.6 ± 0.1 micrograms (μg) arsenic per gram (g) of hair (or 2.6 parts per million, 2.6 ppm). This concentration is approx. 20 times higher than what would be considered a normal average for unexposed individuals in USA."*

NORTH CAROLINA STATE CHIEF MEDICAL EXAMINER

In early 1999 Nityananda consulted with Dr. Richard Page Hudson, retired Chief Medical Examiner for North Carolina, a forensic pathologist teaching at East Carolina University doing private consultations in many toxicological investigations. He had been involved with many exhumations and testing various body tissues, including hair, to determine poisons. He had also been involved in many murder cases involving arsenic, including Blanche Taylor Moore, Velma Barfield. (Ch. 39). Dr. Hudson agreed that the symptoms from Srila Prabhupada's health history, as described, were definitely synonymous with chronic arsenic poisoning. Dr. Hudson was very familiar with chronic and acute arsenic poisoning from his criminal cases; a different set of symptoms will manifest in each chronic arsenic poisoning case, due to dose variances, the type of arsenic compound, the victim's constitution, etc. He did not think a chronic level of 2.6 ppm of hair arsenic would result in the dramatic symptoms that are virtually guaranteed at 10 ppm. He thought it would be valuable to broaden our results with more hair tests.

Hearing how the hair had come from hair clippers used over many months, Dr. Hudson agreed *Sample Q-1* represented an average from multiple cuttings as hairs had gotten stuck in the clipper blades (a time later determined to be up to 10 months, from about Nov. 1976 to early Sept. 1977). This composite hair sample from multiple cuttings averaged 2.6 ppm arsenic during this time, and was *chronic arsenic poisoning* for many months. This level was elevated, about 20 times over the average.

THE NAPOLEON POISONING CONTROVERSY

Nityananda (and others) now saw the need for a full unbiased investigation into Srila Prabhupada's poisoning, other than the slow-moving, one-man, secret, and under-funded GBC investigation by Balavanta. He decided to work with others in a private investigation. Hansadutta das told him of a 1972 book on Napoleon's poisoning: *The Murder of Napoleon* by Weider and Hapgood. Research into Napoleon's death and his poisoning took place in the 1960's by NAA hair tests (Ch. 39). Authenticated hair kept by collectors for 150 years were found to have very high arsenic levels. *Assassination at St. Helena: the Poisoning of Napoleon Bonaparte,* updated in 1995, proved to be very useful. Many different samples of his hair were tested by NAA. Although his elevated hair arsenic levels varied up to 50 ppm, the debate goes on whether this was accidental or homicidal, and whether Napoleon's final cause of death was stomach cancer or poisoning. Arsenic was prolific in Napoleon's time, so his poisoning could have been homicidal, environmental, accidental, or even medical. Interestingly, Napoleon's and Srila Prabhupada's symptoms were very similar.

CONCLUSIONS AND SUMMARY

UNIVERSITY OF MISSOURI-COLUMBIA

January 6, 1999

William H. Ogle, Esquire
Ledford, Mayfield and Ogle
787 South Yonge (U.S. 1)
Post Office Box 4118
Ormond Beach, Florida 32175-4118

Dear Mr. Ogle:

I have completed the analysis of a hair specimen (hereafter Q-1) obtained from an electric hair clipper which you transferred to my possession by letter dated June 15, 1998.

The individual hairs in Q-1 were embedded on the movable cutter between the fingers constituting the fixed comb of the implement. These were removed in a stream of acetone directed at that part of the clipper described above. The individual hairs were collected on a Whatman filter using vacuum filtration. After desiccation to produce a dry sample, the collected hair specimen, Q-1, was massed using an electronic balance having a sensitivity of 0.00001 grams. The individual hairs ranged in length from less than 1 millimeter to approximately 2 millimeters and the mass of the combined specimen, Q-1, was 0.00130 grams.

The arsenic concentration was quantified via neutron activation analysis using the procedure, with minor modifications, described in:

Nichols, T.A., Morris, J.S., Mason, M.M., Spate, V.L., Baskett, C.K., Cheng, T.P., Tharp, C.J., Scott, J.A., Horsman, T.L., Rawson, A.E., Karagas, M.R. and Stannard, V., "The study of human nails as an intake monitor for arsenic using neutron activation analysis", J. Radioanal. and Nucl. Chem. Articles, Vol. 236, Nos 1-2 (1998) 51-56.

The arsenic concentration found in Q-1 was 2.6 ± 0.1 micrograms (µg) arsenic per gram (g) of hair (or 2.6 parts per million, i.e., 2.6 ppm). This concentration is approximately 20 times higher than what I would consider a normal average for unexposed individuals living in the United States. The uncertainty (± 0.1) was propagated from the counting statistical error associated with the acquisition of the gamma-ray spectrum for Q-1.

Sincerely yours,

J. Steven Morris, Ph.D.
Leader, Nuclear Analysis Program

an equal opportunity institution

2.6 ppm arsenic is very abnormal, consistent with chronic poisoning, and the only plausible explanation is that it was due to ingestion. Normal hair arsenic is ±0.13 ppm, 1/20th that in *Sample Q-1* (Ch. 48). The likelihood of environmental contamination causing 2.6 ppm in Srila Prabhupada's hair is very low, and as seen in many chronic arsenic poisoning case studies, it represents a serious health hazard, especially if maintained for a period of many months, and especially in the case of an elderly person (App. 5). *The total evidence was that Srila Prabhupada was indeed deliberately poisoned.* Ch.'s 47-49 debunk many flawed explanations for the high arsenic levels in Srila Prabhupada's hair other than deliberate poisoning, such as tainted water, etc.

CHAPTER 2:
GBC ABANDONS UNTESTED HAIR SAMPLES

THE PRIVATE INVESTIGATION CARRIES ON

GBC member and attorney Balavanta das was disgusted when the GBC axed his two year investigation (Ch. 43) that had given reason to further investigate Srila Prabhupada's poisoning. The same hour he gave his report, March 2, 2000, the GBC endorsed the prime suspects' secretly produced and financed, sham whitewash book *Not That I Am Poisoned* (Ch. 50-52), and they declared there was no poisoning, banning even discussion of it in ISKCON at the risk of expulsion. Naveen Krishna and Balavanta resigned as GBC members. Naveen naively tried, with other senior devotees, to create an impartial tribunal for a full and honest investigation in cooperation with the GBC (Ch. 45). But the GBC's heavy hand blocked all efforts for further investigation as they hammered the poison issue into political oblivion. March 2, 2000 was ISKCON's Tiananmen Square massacre of the truth. By 2001 even the private investigation was at a dead end, and the issue was stalemated.

It became clear that any further investigative program would need be fully independent of the GBC, since they would not cooperate, and without their knowledge as well, so not to invite sabotage or interference from them. The poison issue had received widespread publicity as everyone around ISKCON knew about the hair test with high arsenic, the poison whispers and discussions, and Srila Prabhupada's statements about being poisoned. However, many doubts had been sowed by ISKCON's GBC, who flatly denied it all as being "beyond absurd," deeming it poisonous for anyone's spiritual welfare. Very few had even a basic understanding of the actual facts, and the zaniest things were repeated, such as it was impossible, blasphemous, Kali's trick, and based on no real evidence. ISKCON's GBC had successfully confused its members and congregations, indoctrinating their blind followers.

SHPM (Ch. 42) had really rocked the ISKCON boat, but by a flood of denials and obfuscation, the GBC had managed to quiet the storm. While the evidence had convinced many that Srila Prabhupada had been poisoned, and this deeply disturbed them, many paid little attention to the whispers or even Srila Prabhupada's own words of being poisoned, wanting instead more "scientific" proofs. And the 2.6 ppm arsenic hair test seemed to them rather inconclusive. Their secularly conditioned minds demanded court-quality, convictable evidence before accepting

Srila Prabhupada was homicidally poisoned. They had more faith in science than in Srila Prabhupada's words (Ch. 15).

How could scientific, irrefutable proof settle this issue? There was nothing more important for the future health of the Hare Krishna movement than historically establishing the truth about Srila Prabhupada's departure, one way or the other. The problems in the movement could never be resolved without this issue being irrefutably resolved. A small team of ISKCON "outsiders" decided to undertake more fact-finding and research. Those in the private investigation would have to use their own resources. Nityananda examined loose ends, studied *NTIAP* and *SHPM*, organized files of the evidence, scoured the internet, and gradually another book project coalesced. A thorough response was to be compiled, addressing the GBC denials, and including further facts, evidence, and forensic tests on audio recordings and hair samples, all made into a master compilation of all the evidence that established Srila Prabhupada's poisoning beyond doubt. Nityananda and Naveen commissioned several more audio forensic studies on the poison whispers. He liaised with the contingent of Asian private investigative devotees and retired from his business life, spending long days writing and studying. Almost two decades passed living in the far-off islands of Hawaii, Panama, and Fiji as the new evidence book took shape, interspersed with episodes of experimental simple living projects. But in 2001 the need was to find and test more Srila Prabhupada hair samples.

SEARCH FOR SRILA PRABHUPADA 1977 HAIR SAMPLES

Testing *Sample Q-1* by Dr. Steve Morris in 1999 showed 2.6 ppm arsenic, and was a big step forward in the poisoning investigation. *If further hair tests produced multiple confirmations of abnormally high levels of arsenic (or other poisons), the proof of poisoning would be final.* We believed Srila Prabhupada when he said he was being poisoned; what we needed was more proof for doubters. Multiple confirmations would eliminate any possibility that the first test result was a fluke. There were perhaps 10 or 20 devotees who still had samples of Srila Prabhupada's hair, kept as sacred keepsakes. To do further forensic hair tests, we set out to locate hair samples cut in 1977. This was our investigative priority. The two samples Balavanta had sent to Dr. Morris were dated well before 1977. The first dramatic downturn in Srila Prabhupada's health on July 20, 1976 was seen as the likely starting date of poisoning, so we wanted hair cut after that date.

But no other 1977 samples could be found even after much effort. We did not know that GBC agents in late 1999 had obtained two certified 1977 Srila Prabhupada hair samples, but that they failed to complete any test on them.

GBC BUNGLE THEIR OWN HAIR TESTS *By Nityananda das*

For a year and a half all our inquiries around the devotee world for 1977 hair samples were unfruitful. I still had some of my own hair relic. The owners of several 1977 hair samples were not even willing to exchange for earlier-dated hair. Yamuna dasi, Satyanarayan das, Hari Sauri das- they wanted nothing to do with this matter. They took me as a troublemaker. In late 2001, I was reading the GBC's *NTIAP*, p. 318-9 and intrigued by: *"At this time (Oct. 1999) we contacted Dr. Morris while trying to locate a lab to analyze a hair sample from Vrindaban... The devotee in charge ...testified that this hair was originally ON the clippers but was removed with a brush and kept in this container... Dr. Morris agreed to do the analysis... he wanted US$6000 to do the work... It then had to be decided if it was justifiable to spend US$6000 of GBC funds... it was decided that, considering the circumstances, it was not justifiable... To allay any fears of a 'cover-up', the Ministry for the Protection of ISKCON extends an open invitation to anyone who would like to fund this analysis by Dr. Morris. We will fully cooperate by providing full details of the specimens, which are already at a lab in the US, and what were their origins."*

An inspiration appeared in my mind's eye. A few times in life, one has a profound epiphany, and this was one of them. What if somehow these GBC hair samples could be tested? What if they produced further forensic evidence and confirmation of poisoning? Should I volunteer to pay for the tests? I doubted anyone else had taken up this offer, and I wondered if this offer was just a bluff to convince the masses, but which the GBC would never allow? Intimidated in 1999 by *NTIAP's* author Mr. Hooper, a disciple of Jayapataka, Dr. Morris had to set a price of $6000 to do any more hair tests. In March 2000 I had already asked Dr. Morris for cost concessions on a series of new hair tests, hoping that I could later locate 1977 hair samples, and he agreed to "re-negotiate." He felt it necessary to charge a commercial rate because Mr. Hooper had demanded unlimited free tests. I assured him I would be his only client and that others would need to arrange their own work, which he was entitled to decline. He agreed, and I told him I would contact him later.

YUDHISTHIRA DAS BECOMES A DOUBLE AGENT

Although *NTIAP* offered to cooperate in the testing of their hair specimens, I doubted this very much- especially not with myself, the author of *SHPM*. Maybe they would take the money, control the tests themselves, not turn over the test results, or they might even disappear the hair samples once an actual testing was proposed. Would ISKCON or the suspects risk facilitating tests with unpredictable results beyond their control? I suspected the GBC or Tamal stopped their own tests at the last moment by refusing the $6000 needed for Dr. Morris. My first objective was to obtain "full details of the specimens" and "what were their origins," without causing the samples to disappear. *NTIAP* described more than one sample and that one sample came from Srila Prabhupada's hair clippers, which would be 1977 hair. Where were these samples now? How could I arrange tests on these samples without having the GBC just disappear them? Hari Sauri was a GBC loyalist, so I could not approach him myself. I was already persona non-grata in ISKCON, publishing *Vedic Village Reviews* (1987-93) on Srila Prabhupada's intended initiation system, and the 1999book *SHPM*.

So I initiated email correspondence with him using the pseudonym Yudhisthira das, and posed as having the "no-poison" position, asking questions about the hair clippers. Hari Sauri replied Oct. 20, 2001: *"...a small batch of Srila Prabhupada's hair was collected by Daivi Shakti after Prabhupada's disappearance. She had cleaned off the clippers [with a brush] and put the hair in a box and kept it carefully. When Balavanta requested hair samples in 1998, I sent him the clippers*

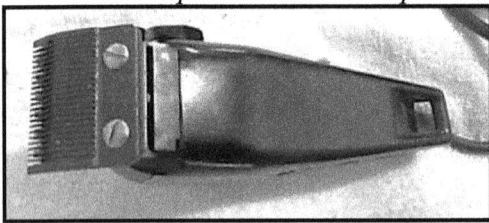

without knowing about the batch of hair that Daivi Shakti had... The hair samples I got later on from Daivi Shakti, which were sent to America for testing independently of Balavanta's investigation, were much bigger...There is no doubt that these samples were Srila Prabhupada's hair and it is highly likely that they were the last batch of hair clippings from His Divine Grace. It's also certain that they were clipped from his head in 1977..."

Hari Sauri said the last time he personally clipped Srila Prabhupada's hair was in early March 1977; March 13 he left Srila Prabhupada's personal service, not returning until October. Hari Sauri did not know about the clipper's use in his absence, but Tamal noted in his diary that Srila Prabhupada's hair was *last* cut by razor-shaving on Sept. 22, confirmed by Vrindaban das Parker. Tamal said in *NTIAP* that the last use of the clippers was early Sept. 1977. From Sept. to Nov. was apparently when Srila Prabhupada's hair growth had slowed, normal for those very ill, and so there were no clipper cuttings in those months, as per Tamal. This information was very useful. Hari Sauri further told me: *"I gave the sample of Daivi Shakti dd to Deva Gaura Hari* [Mr. Hooper] *in Brisbane... He did send it to a lab in the USA..."*

THE HAIR CLIPPER SAMPLES

The hair clippers Hari Sauri sent with Sesa das to be given to Balavanta in USA were taken from the Vrindaban ISKCON Prabhupada Museum display cases, labeled "Srila Prabhupada's Last Hair clippers," and were on display there since 1977. Balavanta sent these clippers to Dr. Morris in 1998. Srila Prabhupada used more than one hair clipper through the years, but this one was the last. In the same Oct. 20, 2001 email, Hari Sauri answered my questions about the hair clippers history: *"As far as the hair clippers go, they ...were sent as replacements for a clipper machine I had in late 1976 that burnt out in Vrindaban.* [As per SP's itinerary, he was in Vrindaban Oct. 20- Nov. 30, 1976.] *They were brand new and being Prabhupada's personal clippers they could not have been used by anyone else. I don't remember the exact date that we received these new ones but it would have been in either very late 1976, around mid-Nov. when Alex Kulik brought some things over from LA or they would have been sent over with devotees coming in early 1977. When Balavanta requested hair samples I sent him the clippers..."*

In *TransD Vol. 5 (*p. 431, 517), we see two times when the new clippers must have arrived: Nov. 14, 1976:*"Alex produced some other gifts for Srila Prabhupada- honey from his wife, a present from Visakha dasi in Los Angeles, and cow ghee... Alex also had something for me- two new power supplies for the Uher cassette recorder, sent by Krishna Kanti... I sent him with the latest batch of recordings for Krishna Kanti..."* Another likely arrival time for the new clippers was Nov. 22, 1976 when Alan Kallman brought BBT calendar samples from Los Angeles to Srila Prabhupada in Vrindaban.

Thus, based on the statements from Hari Sauri and Tamal, these clippers were used to cut Srila Prabhupada's hair from Nov. 14 or 22, 1976 until early Sept. 1977. During these 10 months, these clippers cut Srila Prabhupada's hair maybe 12 times, every 3-4 weeks, since during his 1977 illness, his hair grew slower due to the poisoning. It is concluded that the little container of hair collected from the clippers with Daivi Shakti's brush, which we wanted to find "at a lab in the US," was a MIXTURE from about 12 cuttings over 10 months. Each clipping would result in more hairs stuck around the clipper's blades due to the clipper's sticky lubricant oil. Daivi Shakti dasi brushed some hairs off these blades after Srila Prabhupada departed, and her sample represented an average over a span *10 months (Nov. 1976- Sept. 1977).* In 1998 Balavanta's *Q-1* hair sample had been washed off the same clippers by Dr. Morris because some pieces were still stuck there from 20 years earlier. So-- these clippers had provided *Sample Q-1* and the Daivi Shakti sample. But at which US lab was Daivi Shakti's hair sample?

FINDING THE GBC'S PRABHUPADA HAIR SAMPLES

NTIAP (p. 38) describes the GBC author, "...contacted various laboratories across the US regarding possible testing of a hair sample from Srila Prabhupada." NTIAP spoke of a Larry Kovar of General Activation Analysis (California): "After Larry found that his facility didn't have the required reactor time to perform the tests, he contacted Dr. Richard Cashwell at the Univ. of Wisconsin about performing the analysis." I surmised that just as Balavanta abandoned his 1974-75 hair samples with Dr. Morris, the GBC author sent hair samples to a US lab, not testing them, and abandoning them at that lab in 1999. These were Hari Sauri/ GBC authenticated 1977 Srila Prabhupada hair samples, exactly what we had been trying to locate. Maybe he failed to find an appropriate lab or their time ran out because they wanted the NTIAP book ready for the annual GBC meetings March 2, 2000. These samples might still be sitting at either Kovar's lab or at the Univ. of Wisconsin, if they had not been discarded. NTIAP: "...which are already at a lab in the US." There was no need to do hair tests once NTIAP was published. I emailed Larry Kovar, asking if he still had these hair samples, and he confirmed that he received the hair samples but that he could not test such small quantities at his facility. He then sent the samples to Dr. Richard Cashwell at the Univ. of Wisconsin, where he hoped the tests could be performed. Several of Srila Prabhupada's 1977 hair samples were sent to Wisconsin in late 1999. Were they still there?

GBC SAMPLES LOCATED IN WISCONSIN

I suspected that Dr. Cashwell also could not perform the testing due to the small hair quantities involved, otherwise why did the GBC author call Dr. Morris in late 1999 for tests? Mustering my nerve, Oct. 17, 2001 I phoned Dr. Cashwell, but he had retired a year earlier. Amazingly, his replacement, Dr. Robert Agasie, knew of the case, saying that their equipment was inadequate to test such a small mass of hair, just as suspected. He confirmed that *the samples were still there!* I boldly requested Dr. Agasie to send the hair samples to Dr. Steven Morris for testing at the Univ. of Missouri (MURR). Dr. Agasie promptly sent the GBC hair samples overnight to Dr. Morris. The Fedex invoice (ABOVE) shows the samples going directly to Dr. Morris. I could not have tampered with them, as I never saw or handled them. This chain of custody was important for the future. Nov. 1, 2001: Dr. Morris confirmed receipt of 4 hair samples from Wisconsin. The successful recovery of these hair samples could be of extreme import.

BELOW: Fedex invoice, Wisconsin to Dr. Morris directly

Nov 26 01 12:28P   River Village

FedEx.

Invoice Number: **4-003-11705**
Invoice Date: Nov 20, 2001
Account Number: 1909-8986-0
Page: 4 of 4

FedEx Express Payment Type Detail (Original)

Dropped off: Oct 30, 2001 | Payor: Third Party | Reference: OGLE 1008 | FedEx Internal Use: 4153847 10/01110/_/_

- Fuel Surcharge - FedEx has applied a fuel surcharge of 4.00% to this shipment.
- Distance Based Pricing, Zone 4

Tracking ID 790701173865	Sender	Recipient
Service Type FedEx 2Day	ROBERT AGASIE	DR STEVEN MORRIS
Package Type FedEx Envelope	UNIVERSITY OF WISCONSIN	RESEARCH REACTOR CENTE
Zone 4	750 UNIVERSITY AVE	UNIVERSITY OF MISSOURI
Pieces 1	MADISON WI 53709-1411 US	COLUMBIA MO 65211 US
Weight 1.0 lbs, 0.5 kgs		
Delivered Nov 01, 2001 09:25		
Service	Transportation Charge	8.00
Area Code AA	Declared Value Charge	0.00
Signed by D.WOLFE	Fuel Surcharge	0.32
Dec. Value USD 50.00	Total Transportation Charges	USD $ 8.32
Bundle ID 000		
	Payment Type Detail Subtotal .... USD $	8.32

LOST AND FOUND: NEW EVIDENCE

Dr. Morris quoted a minimum of $2500 for up to 5 NAA tests, and $500 for each additional test. I got contributions of $662 and sent Dr. Morris $3500 in advance for seven tests. Fortunately he never heard from any other GBC agents until 2017, when Mayeswara das called and harassed him after *Kill Guru, Become Guru* was posted free online in May 2017. (Ch. 53, App. 10) Dr. Morris described the 4 Wisconsin samples, labeled *Samples A, B, D, E. Samples B & E* obviously were not Srila Prabhupada's hair, being the wrong color and length, and were undoubtedly intended as comparison "controls." Only *Samples A* and *D* could be Srila Prabhupada's hair, and I got positive identification on Dec. 7, 2001 with a response from the GBC author by employing Hari Sauri as a go-between for "Yudhisthira das." Hooper wrote Hari Sauri, who then copied it to me: *"The only samples of Srila Prabhupada's hair I had were the one from Melbourne and the one from Daivi Shakti in Vrindaban... The other two samples should stick out because they were pulled from the heads of living people, and the ones from Prabhupada were obviously shaved hair which is very short."*

A few days earlier on Dec. 4, 2001, Hari Sauri wrote about the GBC author: *"I have spoken to him twice just recently... all he can say is that two of the samples are Srila Prabhupada's and the other two are controls. It should be very clear which are Srila Prabhupada's and which are the controls. As far as the controls go, one is Deva's own hair which should be brownish and about 2-3 inches long. The other control he doesn't remember."* So-- *B* and *E* were controls. Srila Prabhupada's hair was mixed clear-grey-black, not light brown or 3 inches long. In discussions with Dr. Morris, the best control samples would be from Srila Prabhupada himself and from an earlier, pre-poisoning time to compare with a post-poisoning time. We later did test some pre-1977

Srila Prabhupada hair samples to compare to his 1977 ones. I decided to test only *Samples A* and *D*- one of which was Daivi Shakti's- and the other was *"from Melbourne."* Later in 2002, Hari Sauri wrote Yudhisthira (me): *"For Srila Prabhupada's samples... the hair strands I got from Daivi Shakti were a little bit longer than the ones I left in Melbourne."* This confirmed that the shorter hairs in *Sample D* were from the Melbourne ISKCON temple, to which he had personally donated some hair, and that he cut from Srila Prabhupada's head in early

March 1977. It had been kept in Srila Prabhupada's Melbourne personal quarters since then as a sacred relic. In 1999 Hari Sauri retrieved some of this Melbourne sample and gave it to Hooper for testing, eventually reaching Wisconsin and then Dr. Morris.

Sample A (1-2 cm) had longer hairs than *Sample D,* and it was Daivi Shakti's Vrindaban museum exhibit. Hari Sauri also said *Sample A* was in an India-style tiny plastic container. *So A was for Daivi Shakti, D for Melbourne.* Miraculously, we had rescued 2 authentic 1977 samples of Srila Prabhupada's hair that had been abandoned by the GBC, and NAA testing on them by Dr. Morris was lined-up, all by countering the obstructive GBC with special tactics. There was no doubt in my mind (or Naveen Krishna) if the GBC or their agents found out what was going on, they would sabotage the tests or retake control of their samples. We had to use secretive methods to further the investigation. Yudhisthira had been useful. What would be the results? Hari Sauri, Tamal, and GBC were unaware of what was about to happen.

CHAPTER 3:
DISCOVERY OF CADMIUM

By Nityananda das
DEVISING THE TEST PARAMETERS

By 2002 we had only one poison-positive test result: Balavanta's *Q-1* with unusually high arsenic levels, but now **we would complete the GBC's own tests** on their abandoned Srila Prabhupada 1977 hair samples, without even taking possession of them. This could perhaps further forensically confirm the greatest crime of the millennium 25 years earlier. Dr. Morris was enthusiastic about the test program and he prepared for the neutron activation testing regime. Dr. Morris had impressive knowledge earned from thousands of previous hair tests for law enforcement agencies, court cases, and academic studies. On Jan. 7, 2002, we decided to start with GBC *Sample D* and test for arsenic. I asked if he would be able to test for more than one heavy metal in addition to arsenic with such small samples, asking about antimony and mercury, which I had read were also used as poisons. He said he would need to prepare the tests accordingly but that it was wise to broaden our search "while we were at it." Dr. Morris also suggested adding cadmium because it fit well with the parameters used to measure arsenic, antimony, and mercury. He geared the tests for these four elements. He explained how these four heavy metals had radioactive half-lives in the same range with common nuclear properties. They were measured "in coincidence" with other non-toxic elements which would serve as a benchmark to verify any disproportionately high values of heavy metals. The non-toxic markers to be measured simultaneously were: bromine, sodium, zinc, gold, silver, europium, and uranium.

Measurements of poisonous elements such as beryllium, thallium, lead, nickel, osmium and tin would require a separate and different nuclear activation parameter. With our small samples, only one set of elements could be measured, so we chose the heavy metals commonly associated with poisoning. Arsenic was the most "popular" poison in history. Mercury had been mentioned in the conversations re: makharadhvaja. High levels of antimony had been found in Napoleon's hair. Cadmium would be a bonus. Dr. Morris explained his methodology: after massive nuclear activation, the resultant radioactivity of the sample is measured over five days. Each element has a different optimum time for measurement. First the arsenic is calculated, then the cadmium, then the mercury, and finally the antimony. I am not a scientist, and this is from my defective memory but assumedly accurate.

Dr. Morris decided not to wash the samples before testing, which he said can very seriously compromise the results and was of limited value anyway. By powerful microscopic examination he had not found any external debris on the hair samples nor had he seen evidence of external contamination, such as from oils, dust, and chemicals. He referred to scientific studies on hair analysis that found that hair very close to the scalp, as these samples were, being the first half inch, was least likely to have been *externally contaminated*. Also another US study on the validity of hair mineral testing found that much of the variance in results was due to the washing steps used by some labs. (Ch. 49, *Exogenous or Endogenous?*) Since our samples were very small, Dr. Morris wanted to refine his testing techniques to maximize the accuracy. He would increase the neutron activation more than normal, and take the measurements over 5 days. Preparations were made for *Sample D* to "be put to the test" under 30 feet of water in the nuclear testing facility.

THE UNEXPECTED FORENSIC BREAKTHROUGH

In early March 2002 while I was gone to the Fiji Islands searching properties for a varnashrama project in the South Pacific, I got news that *Sample D* had been tested, and that the arsenic and antimony were rather normal. Ten days later I was back in Hawaii and called Dr. Morris. We reviewed the low arsenic and antimony in the test results and I told him *Sample A* should be next. Then Dr. Morris surprised me. *"I wanted to talk to you when you returned from your trip. Checking some of the other elemental contents in Sample D, and I checked the calculations several times to make very sure, <u>there is a most unusual and strikingly high amount of cadmium... It has 23.6 parts per million."</u>* "What does that mean?" I asked. Dr. Morris described cadmium as an extremely toxic heavy metal in the same family with arsenic, mercury, lead and thallium. From Dr. Morris' description, I recognized the symptoms of chronic cadmium poisoning in the history of Srila Prabhupada's final year.

CADMIUM LEVELS SKY HIGH ABOVE NORMAL AVERAGE

I was stunned at this dramatic development. How to explain these cadmium levels? We were focused on arsenic, but instead we had found abnormal cadmium levels. Research showed *<u>normal average societal levels of cadmium to be 0.064 ppm</u>*, half of normal average arsenic levels (Ch. 6). That is about 1/16th of one part per million. *Sample D*'s cadmium level was hundreds of times over normal. *<u>A breakthrough in forensic evidence was now in hand that would remove all doubts about Srila Prabhupada's poisoning,</u>* even in diehard non-believers. Scientifically-minded persons wanted indisputable forensic proof, and here it was. There would always be doubt of 2.6 ppm arsenic's significance, which was "only" 20 times normal, but these sky-high amounts of cadmium were undismissable. Arsenic was now a secondary poison, and *<u>cadmium had been discovered as the primary poison.</u>* Krishna had led us to stumble upon the evidence that would answer the question of Srila Prabhupada's poisoning with finality.

Srila Prabhupada **was** poisoned, primarily with cadmium and secondarily with arsenic. Dr. Morris had ascertained the cadmium values on Mar. 5 and I learned about them on Mar. 18. On the 15th, the Ides of March, the primary person of interest in Srila Prabhupada's poisoning was killed in a car crash in India. Why did Tamal depart just as the cadmium poisoning was uncovered? My college mate Satyanarayan das called me on March 16, and lamented that Tamal had perished. I was also dismayed, exclaiming, "Oh, that's very bad... now we'll never be able to interview him for the poison investigation..." He retorted in exasperation, "Is that all you can say!?"

CADMIUM: A RARE, EXOTIC, AND "FOREVER" POISON

On April 1, 2002 I conferred with Dr. Morris again. He was scheduled to irradiate the GBC's *Sample A* that week, including the little container that it came in. I asked where one would be able to find cadmium with which to poison someone. He replied: *"Many high school chemistry labs have cadmium salts such as cadmium sulfate, oxide or chloride. You won't find cadmium at the hardware or grocery store- one would need to know something about chemistry to know where to get it, such as a laboratory supplier. Cadmium is actually more poisonous than arsenic..."* Cadmium is not a restricted material, unlike plutonium, mercury, anthrax, or many chemicals. *But it is a "forever chemical" as its half-life is 17-30 years, how long it takes the body to expel just half*. Cadmium is not a well-known element, but available anywhere in the world. I asked Dr. Morris who would know of the unusual, rarely used poison cadmium, and who would have the expertise to use it in proper dosages in a chronic slow poisoning? Amateurs seemed out of the question. Dr. Morris replied, *"Someone with a very good knowledge of chemistry and poisons."* The recipe, doses, and application of chronic cadmium poisoning was beyond the ability or imagination of the average Joe and required some criminal sophistication, high level intelligence, or training in chemistry. The poisoners knew what they were doing.

RESULTS OF THE SECOND GBC HAIR *SAMPLE A*

On Apr.18, 2002, I received an email from Dr. Morris about the second test in the new series. *Sample A*, which had been brushed off Srila Prabhupada's 1977 hair clippers by Daivi Shakti, had these results:

GBC SAMPLE A:

CADMIUM = 12.4 ppm (194 X the norm of 0.064 ppm)
ARSENIC = 0.200 ppm (near normal)
ANTIMONY = 0.186 ppm (2 X normal)
MERCURY = 5.16 ppm (normal)

Dr. Morris cryptically noted: *"Again, the most striking finding in Sample A is the very high level of cadmium."* Now we had double confirmation of cadmium poisoning from two samples fully authenticated as Srila Prabhupada's hair, from different sources and times. *Sample A* (Daivi Shakti, from the clippers used Nov. '76 to-Sept. '77) and *Sample D* (Hari Sauri, early March '77) had fully vindicated our conclusions in *SHPM*. These two tests were solid evidence and irrefutable proof that Srila Prabhupada was indeed maliciously poisoned.

GBC SAMPLE D:

CADMIUM = 19.9 ppm (311 X the norm of 0.064 ppm)
ARSENIC = 0.640 ppm (5 X normal)
ANTIMONY = 0.661 ppm (10 X normal)
MERCURY = 3.72 ppm (normal)

Dr. Morris: *"...with such small samples the so-called analytical blank must be carefully determined so that one does not assign analytical signal to the sample that is actually from some other source. In this case there are two possibilities that could confound the hair analyses: external contamination and impurities in the small vials used to contain the hair specimens during the NAA. External contamination cannot be completely ruled out without a detailed history of the sample; but one can search for possible sources. In the instant case: I now have checked the containers the samples have been stored in and find no evidence of significant contamination sources for arsenic, cadmium, antimony, or mercury. I also carefully analyzed the high-purity vials (blanks) that I use in the NAA experiments and as expected there is a minute presence of the elements of interest in these vials. Insofar as trace elements are concerned, there is "everything in everything" if one has a technique sensitive enough to make the measurement. I have now made these sensitive measurements and have 'blank-corrected' the results."*

The difference between 23.6 and 19.9 ppm cadmium in *Sample A* was due to the test vial being very slightly cadmium positive but much higher in mass than the hair. Dr. Morris clarified the vial was not 3.7 ppm cadmium, but that a tiny amount multiplied by 1000s X in mass made the difference. He described *Sample D* was in a small cardboard pillbox; *Sample A* had a translucent plastic bottom and top. He tested the pillbox and found *"no evidence of significant contamination..."* *Sample A* had not been tainted with cadmium from the container in which it had been stored for many years. The Srila Prabhupada hair samples that the GBC planned to test for arsenic were abandoned in Wisconsin, and I was able to locate them, test them properly, and discover that the primary poison was **CADMIUM**. How remarkable it was to finish the GBC hair tests for the GBC, and find proof positive Srila Prabhupada had actually been poisoned primarily with cadmium. Anyone who doubted these results could do further hair tests on 1977 samples that are available.

CHAPTER 4:
FURTHER HAIR TESTS

By Nityananda das
SAMPLE M

In 2002 I underwent a complex swap arrangement with an ISKCON temple to obtain a few pieces of hair which was supposed to be Srila Prabhupada's 1977 hair. It was sent to Dr. Morris and denoted as *Sample M* for "maybe" from Srila Prabhupada. I spoke with him on Oct. 15, 2002. He had examined *Sample M* closely and remarked that the coloration did not match the other Srila Prabhupada hair samples in his possession. *Sample M* had two pieces of "coal black" hair and four pieces white hair. *It was Dr. Morris' opinion that M was NOT Srila Prabhupada's hair.* Dr. Morris was very suspicious, asking about the sample's origins. He asked if I trusted the source, even though I had given him no reason to doubt the sample's authenticity. The conclusion was we could not trust the source. Dr. Morris later tested *Sample M* and, as expected, it was found to have normal levels of all the four toxic elements: cadmium, arsenic, mercury, and antimony.

TEST RESULTS FROM JAGAT'S SAMPLE J

In late 1999 Mandapa das in Australia informed me that he had located a sample of Srila Prabhupada's hair owned by Jagat das, who did not know when it was cut, but he had received it directly from Hari Sauri. Mandapa arranged to send the sample directly to Naveen Krishna, who then sent it in Dec. 2001 to Dr. Morris. It was not possible to establish the dating of *Sample J*, as it was named. I asked Dr. Morris to test it anyway. On May 16, 2002 the test results were received. There were no unusual amounts of arsenic, cadmium, antimony, or mercury. Actually, the levels were much lower than found in the previous samples. The blank-corrected concentrations:

RESULTS OF SAMPLE J TEST:

CADMIUM= undetected, below 2.3 ppm   ARSENIC= 0.082 ppm
ANTIMONY= 0.080 ppm   MERCURY= undetectable, ≥ 1.62 ppm

Due to the mass of the sample and his measurement settings, Dr. Morris had detection limits of 2.3 ppm cadmium and 1.62 ppm mercury, both of which were undetected in *Sample J*. So although we could not obtain an exact reading on cadmium, it was presumed to be in a normal range, below 2.3 ppm. We concluded *Sample J* was cut before poisoning began and it was useful in comparison to Srila Prabhupada's samples that showed sky-high poisoning levels.

RE-TEST OF SAMPLE ND-2

I reflected on the 1999 test of *Sample ND-1* done by Dr. Chatt, reported in *SHPM*. ND-1 was my own personal Srila Prabhupada hair relic that I had received around 1978 in New Talavan. There were compelling reasons to do another test on that sample. First, there was cause to doubt the accuracy of Dr. Chatt's results. Dr. Chatt had found under 1 ppm mercury whereas Dr. Wadlin in Chapel Hill, NC had earlier found 4 ppm mercury in another part of the same sample. This wide disparity in mercury readings indicated inaccuracies produced by either Dr. Wadlin or Dr. Chatt. One of them was quite inaccurate.

RESULTS OF ND-2 TEST: (All near normal values)

Dr. Morris knew Dr. Chatt and his NAA facility very well, as there are very few NAA experts, and they all know each other. Dr. Morris emphatically stated Dr. Chatt's facility was far less accurate than his facility. This was later confirmed by Dr. Chatt himself- he even said he would be unable to measure cadmium in such small samples due to his equipment's limitations. All this justified a re-test of my own personal hair relic. I took some more of my dwindling hair relic. About 25 pieces were moved by tweezers into an empty film canister and labeled *Sample ND-2*. It was sent on Jan. 14, 2002 to Dr. Morris, specifically to test for cadmium. The *ND-2* test results came on June 28, 2002, and the values were nearly normal. I concluded my hair relic was dated before Srila Prabhupada's poisoning had begun.

CADMIUM = 0.206 ppm   **ARSENIC = 0.141 ppm**

ANTIMONY = 0.013 ppm   **MERCURY = 1.85 ppm**

This was the second sample showing Srila Prabhupada's normal, pre-poisoning values, and interestingly, both confirmed that

From:	"Steve Morris"
To:	"ABC" <govinda@starband.net>
Sent:	Monday, May 20, 2002 3:25 AM
Subject:	Re:

Nico:

Your speculation is largely correct. The analysis is optimized for arsenic and the sub-milligram sample size does limit the sensitivity. The only other thing that I can add is that every element has a sensitivity determined by its nuclear parameters --its propensity to capture neutrons, half life, gamma-ray energy and abundance-- and matrix effects. For cadmium and mercury, these parameters are not as favorable as they are for arsenic. Consequently, the detection limit is higher. You are also correct in your observation that with cadmium we cannot detect a normal level in these small samples. That is precisely why I was surprised, and almost completely missed, the appearance of Cd in Sample D to begin with. These sensitivity limitations on Cd do prevent us from concluding that Sample J is at normal levels for this element; but we certainly can conclude that it is significantly lower than the D or A samples.

Q-1's 2.6 ppm arsenic is 20 X more than Srila Prabhupada's own normal. All the debate about what was a normal hair arsenic level was settled because what was normal for Srila Prabhupada was now established by *Samples J* and *ND-2*. Importantly, we now saw the huge gap between Srila Prabhupada's pre-poison and post-poison cadmium and arsenic levels. Also of great interest was that average normal societal levels of cadmium (0.064 ppm) and arsenic (0.13 ppm) compared quite closely to Srila Prabhupada's pre-poisoning values of 0.206 ppm cadmium and 0.141 ppm arsenic. I asked Dr. Morris if *ND-2* had greater accuracy than J in the cadmium results because of the samples' weight difference. *Sample J* was only 0.00085 grams, whereas *ND-2* was 4 X more, 0.00310 grams. *"Yes, most of the difference in detection limit can be attributed to the considerably larger mass of Sample ND-2 compared to Sample J. I have also been fine-tuning the analysis procedures which have resulted in a better sensitivity for ND-2."*

RE-TEST OF SAMPLE Q-1 WAS NOT POSSIBLE

I discussed with Dr. Morris the feasibility of re-testing *Q-1* for cadmium since he had tested it ONLY for arsenic (2.6 ppm). In June 2002 he notified me that the first test on *Q-1* had prohibitively reduced its structural integrity, and it was not re-testable. It was "now dust." Balavanta had also sent Dr. Morris two pre-1976 hair samples in 1998. (*Sample 1-A*, 17 pieces, 1-2 cm long, from Sashikala dasi; *Sample 1-C,* from Sruta Kirti das, only 2 pieces, 1-2 cm long). I decided not to test *Samples 1-A* or *1-C*. For comparison we already had two

From:	Morris, Steve [MorrisJ@missouri.edu]
Sent:	Friday, July 22, 2005 5:23 AM
To:	govinda
Subject:	Hair Sample from Clipper

July 21, 2005

TO: Nico Kuyt
FROM: J. Steven Morris
RE: Analysis of Hair Specimen Recovered from Hair Clipper

I was able to recover a small hair sample from the clippers. This sample is a few small clippings of a few millimeters each having a cumulative mass of 0.00012 grams. I was able to analyze this sample for arsenic. I have now optimized the analysis parameters for cadmium, which will be reported next week.

I will state for the record that the sample discussed in this report was collected by me after removing the head from a set of hair clippers that were purported to have been used to cut the hair of Srila Prabhupada. Obviously, I cannot attest to the factual validity of that assertion.

normals with *Samples J* and *ND-2*, and there was no need to test more 1974-75 hair, a time when there appeared to be no poisoning.

3 YEARS LATER: A THIRD CADMIUM CONFIRMATION

Two ultra-high cadmium results in *Samples A* and *D* were positive proof and a double confirmation of cadmium poisoning. But a third confirmation in another test would add even more certainty of cadmium poisoning. A forensic toxicologist advised: "More is better." But three years passed without finding any more 1977 samples. I reread Dr. Morris' report to Balavanta: *"The individual hairs in Q-1 were embedded on the movable cutter between the fingers constituting the fixed comb of the implement. These were removed in a stream of acetone...*" So I phoned Dr. Morris and asked my big question. *"By removing the clipper's lower blade, could he find any more hair inside, any that might still be there?"* Was there some more hair hidden inside? Decades ago Daivi Shakti dasi had brushed off hairs stuck to the outside of these clipper blades which became *Sample A*. In 1999 Dr. Morris washed off with acetone a few more hairs stuck **BETWEEN** the cutter teeth, and was labelled *Sample Q-1*. But what about dismantling the hair clippers with a screwdriver and looking **UNDER** the blades? During the phone call, Dr. Morris pulled the clippers from somewhere in his office and removed the lower plate. Yes, he said casually, there were a few more pieces of hair trapped under the blades. He would test them that week! Dr. Morris, July 21, 2005: He recovered *three pieces of hair* from the clippers, 2 mm long; total weight 0.00012 grams. This was *Sample Q-2*. The NAA test showed arsenic at 0.85 ppm. Counting the cadmium radiation took a few more days; on July 25 those results were received. *Q-2 was the third sky-high cadmium confirmation. Same hair clipper hair, but new test.*

RESULTS OF Q-2 TEST:

CADMIUM   = 14.9 ppm (233 X normal)
ARSENIC   = 0.85 ppm (6.5 X normal)
ANTIMONY = not measured (not known why)
MERCURY = not measured (not known why)

3 CONFIRMATIONS

With renewed impetus, the investigative and evidence compilation work resumed again. There was now no more doubt: Srila Prabhupada's cadmium poisoning was **proven** by three confirming tests. Next, the task was to research a definitive, accurate, scientific interpretation of these sky-high cadmium levels found in Srila Prabhupada's 1977 hair samples. How abnormal were these amounts and what consequences would they have on one's health?

From: Morris, Steve [MorrisJ@missouri.edu]
Sent: Tuesday, July 26, 2005 5:20 AM
To: govinda
Subject: Hair Sample from Clipper

Q-2

July 25, 2005

TO: Nico Kuyt
FROM: J. Steven Morris
RE: Analysis of Hair Specimen Recovered from Hair Clipper (Cadmium)

The cadmium (Cd) concentration in the hair specimen previously described (see July 21, 2005 report copied below) was measured by neutron activation analysis. The mean concentration of three measurements is 14.9 PPM and the standard deviation is 1.9 PPM. The 95% confidence interval (CI) range is 11.1 to 18.7 PPM. As previously stated, the large uncertainty is the result of the small sample mass (0.00012 grams).

CHAPTER 5:
SUMMARY OF HAIR TEST RESULTS

ALL HAIR TEST RESULTS 1998-2016

HAIR TESTS WITH ELEVATED CADMIUM & ARSENIC LEVELS

ID	Date	Mass	Size	Tested	Source	ARS	ANT	MER	CAD
D	Mar77	.00072	½ cm	3.4.02	Melbrn	0.640	0.661	3.72	**19.9**
A	1977	.00064	1-2 cm	4.15.02	DaiviSh	0.200	0.186	5.16	**12.4**
Q-2	1977	.00012	2-3mm	7.26.05	Clipper	0.85	n/a	n/a	**14.9**
Q-1	1977	.00130	<2mm	1.6.99	Clipper	**2.6**	n/a	n/a	n/a

Samples D (Melbourne), A (clippers), Q-2 (clippers) average 15.73 ppm.

TESTS WITH NORMAL CADMIUM, ARSENIC, ANTIM, MERC

ID	Date	Mass	Size	Tested	Source	ARS	ANT	MER	CAD
J	Pre-77	.00085	1 cm	5.15.02	Jagat	0.082	0.080	1.62	<2.3*
ND2	Pre-77	.00310	¾ cm	6.11.02	Nityand	0.141	0.013	1.85	0.206
ND1	Pre-77	20 mg	1 cm	1998	Nityand	1.1			
W	Pre-77	40 mg	1 cm	1998	Nityand			4.0	

Sample J's cadmium under 2.3 ppm. Sample M not Prabhupada's hair.

OTHER SAMPLES AVAILABLE FOR TESTING

ID	Date	Mass/g	Size	Tested	Source	Details
Tooth	1975	?	2 root	Not Yet	Stolen	In acrylic, viable mt DNA
1-C	1974	2 pcs	1 cm	Not Yet	Sruti Kir	Vrindaban museum
1-A	1975	17 pcs	1 cm	Not Yet	Sashik	Vrindaban museum

KNOWN SAMPLES OF SRILA PRABHUPADA HAIR, TEETH

ID	Date	Tested	Source	Location etc.
Tooth	April 1977	No	Tamal K Goswami	TKG Mayapur Samadhi tomb
Tooth	Aug 1976?	No	Hari Sauri	GBC took from Hari Sauri
Tooth	??	No	Ramesvara	Los Angeles
Tooth	Late 1975	No	Kumar das	Pittsburgh, PA, USA
Hair	1977	No	Satyanarayan	He needs to find it
Hair	1977	No	Yamuna dd	Florida, with Dinatarine dasi
Hair	1977 ?	No	Prabhupada das	London, UK
Hair	1968	No	Samba das	Los Angeles/ from Hayagriva
Hair	Late 1977	No	Nrhari/ Hawaii	Packed away (2005)
Hair	1977	No	Abhiram das	In his personal belongings
Hair	??	No	Taruni/ Yadunad	Unknown-
Meds	Late 1977	No	Indradyumna Sw	Had a "tin" of last medicines

Research Reactor Center

University of Missouri-Columbia
Research Reactor Center
1513 Research Park Drive
Columbia, MO 65211

J. Steven Morris
PHONE: (573) 882-5265
FAX: (573) 882-6360
e-mail: morris@missouri.edu

November 23, 2015

Nico Kuyt
PO Box 903
Savusavu, FIJI

Dear Mr. Kuyt:

Pursuant to your August 19, 2015, request I have combined the results from three previous reports on the neutron activation analysis of human hair specimens for arsenic (As), cadmium (Cd), antimony (Sb) and mercury (Hg). The three previous reports from which the concentration data are combined here are:

November 11, 2002: J.S. Morris to Nico Kuyt
July 21, 2005: J.S. Morris to Nico Kuyt
July 25, 2005: J.S. Morris to Nico Kuyt

All element concentrations are reported as micrograms of the element per grams of hair (μg/g), which is equivalent to parts per million (PPM), the concentration unit used in the data table below. The error in the element concentration reported has been estimated from consideration of the sample mass measurement and the counting statistical error. These error estimates are expressed as 95% confidence intervals and are given in [ ].

Sample ID	Mass (g)	Analysis start date	As (PPM) [95% CI]	Cd (PPM) [95% CI]	Sb (PPM) [95% CI]	Hg (PPM) [95% CI]
"D"	0.00072	March 4, 2002	0.640 [0.064]	19.9 [2.0]	0.661 [0.066]	3.72 [0.56]
"A"	0.00064	April 15, 2002	0.200 [0.020]	12.4 [1.2]	0.186 [0.019]	5.16 [0.77]
"J" (77-3)	0.00085	May 15, 2002	0.082 [0.021]	<2.3	0.080 [0.020]	1.62 [0.41]
"ND-2"	0.00310	June 11, 2002	0.141 [0.021]	0.206 [0.052]	0.013 [0.007]	1.85 [0.46]
"M"	0.00077	November 6, 2002	0.357 [0.036]	<1.45 [0.22]	0.100 [0.010]	5.37 [0.81]
Q-2*	0.00012	July 19, 2005	0.85 [0.49]	14.9 [3.8]	not measured	

*Sample Q-2 was recovered from electric hair clippers and included a few clippings approximately 2 mm in length with a combined mass of 0.00012 grams.

Sincerely yours

J. Steven Morris, Ph.D.
Sr. Research Scientist

Dr. Morris had written to Nityananda das in 2002: *"Do you know the chronological relationship of these two samples (A & D) to each other and of each to the time of death of the subject?"* After the revelation of the astronomical cadmium values in these three Srila Prabhupada hair samples, Nityananda compiled answers to this question, plus many conclusions from the new evidence provided by *Samples A, D,* and *Q-2.* They are shown above.

CADMIUM: The *average normal* levels of about ***0.064 ppm*** hair cadmium in human society was researched thoroughly and is detailed below. Thus *A, D,* and *Q-2* were 194, 233, and 311 times over *average normal* cadmium societal levels. The average cadmium level in Srila

Prabhupada's hair throughout 1977 is 15.73 ppm, or ± 250 times above normal. *This is elaborated below.* Sample *D* (Melbourne) was cut in early March 1977, and represents about 3-4 weeks hair growth (the average time between Srila Prabhupada's hair cuttings), a time during which the average cadmium level was 19.9 ppm- a lethal level if maintained over this time, also documented below. *Samples A* and *Q-2* (hairclippers) were a mixture of hair from a number of cuttings from mid-Nov. 1976 to early Sept. 1977, and show an **average** of almost 14 ppm cadmium through those 10 months. Another severe, dramatic health decline began Feb. 26, 1977, and *Sample D* reflects cadmium levels from mid Feb. to early March 1977. Thus Feb. 26 is obviously a poisoning incident- this hair was cut just 2 weeks later by Hari Sauri das. There is no plausible explanation how Srila Prabhupada acquired these astronomical cadmium levels by environmental pollution, accidental exposure, occupational hazard, etc (as seen in next chapters.)

ARSENIC AND ANTIMONY

The *average normal* levels of hair arsenic in human society was researched and found to be about *0.13 ppm* (App. 4), corresponding to pre-poisoning levels in *Samples J & ND-2*. Yet, arsenic was notably elevated in *D* (5 X normal), *Q-2* (6 X normal), and *Q-1* (20 X normal)- **Why?** *Arsenic was secondarily present at elevated levels along with the cadmium.* While cadmium was the primary poison, arsenic was secondary. The varying levels of arsenic in three tests, namely 5, 6, and 20 X normal, are *too elevated to ignore* or attribute to normal variances. Srila Prabhupada's 1977 arsenic was unusually elevated, although not lethal like the cadmium levels were. The pre-poisoning average of arsenic shown in *J* and *ND-2* was 0.112 ppm (vs. 0.13 normal), and the four 1977 samples (*D, A, Q-1, Q-2*) averaged 1.07 ppm arsenic.

Thus there is almost 10 X more arsenic in 1977 than pre-1977, and is very hard to explain except by some deliberate cause. The average normal levels of hair antimony in human society was researched and found to be about *0.066 ppm*, which corresponds to pre-poisoning levels found in *J* and *ND-2*. Yet, antimony was quite elevated in *Sample D* (10 X normal) and in *Sample A* (3 X normal). **Why?** *Antimony was also secondarily present at elevated levels.*

CONCLUSIONS: Srila Prabhupada's poisoning was via a *heavy metals cocktail of primarily cadmium and including arsenic and antimony.* It is possible that other poisonous ingredients had also been used in Srila Prabhupada's poisoning, but we do not know of them because of limited testing. Also noted is how the 2.6 ppm arsenic in

Sample Q-1 was 32 X more than in *Sample J*, a very unusual jump from pre-poison to post-poison levels. This is not a standard variation. Values in *Samples J* and *ND-2* conform to average normal societal levels as noted in the scientific literatures. *All these cross referencings and comparisons of test results confirm the accuracy of Dr. Morris's calculations.* Cadmium was the primary poison with antimony and arsenic coincidental in lesser elevated amounts as secondary poisons. Why this is the case is unknown. Srila Prabhupada was poisoned with sky-high levels of cadmium deliberately and intentionally over 10 months, demonstrated by the dating of the hair samples that were tested, constituting proof of deliberate homicidal intent (see Ch. 6). Srila Prabhupada travelled widely during these months, which shows that the poisoning was in-house-- it came from someone on the inside, not from the air, water, etc of any one location. Whether 2.6 ppm arsenic is health threatening is now irrelevant in light of 250 X average normal cadmium. *And cadmium is* **TWICE AS POISONOUS** *as arsenic.*

CHAPTER 6:
THE CADMIUM EXPERTS

By Nityananda das

Naveen Krishna das, former GBC, advised that various forensic experts should be consulted to give authoritative weight to the conclusion of malicious chronic cadmium poisoning. We were able to locate several heavy metals experts and obtain their opinions. Also the scientific literature available online at PubMed provided expert opinions and studies on cadmium and hair analysis. The body of scientific literature on cadmium poisoning continues to grow. In 1977 cadmium was not a well-known poisoning method, so Srila Prabhupada's poisoners learned about it from a chemist, doctor, professional, or poison tantric such as Chandra Swami. (see Volume 3)

#1 EXPERT OPINION: DR. HUDSON, Forensic Pathologist

The former North Carolina Chief Medical Examiner, Dr. Page Hudson, Jr. was a forensic pathologist teaching at East Carolina University, and earlier he had reviewed my first book, *SHPM.* He specialized in solving heavy metal poison murders in North Carolina. His work had been detailed in several popular books about arsenic poisonings. (App. 2). I sent a letter to Dr. Hudson with a description of

Srila Prabhupada's 1977 illness and symptoms and included the test results on *Samples A* and *D*, asking for his insights and comments on the hair tests, Srila Prabhupada's medical history, and cadmium toxicity.

His reply: *"I suggest Medical Toxicology: Diagnosis and Treatment of Human Poisoning, 1988, by Ellerhorn/ Barceloux. [...] but they are remarkably few who possess expertise with this material."* Based on his professional and medical experience, he opined: *"One ppm is considered a rather hefty load of cadmium. About 20 ppm is distinctly abnormal. Wasting, kidney disease, and the spillage of sugar are certainly consistent with cadmium toxicity, but unfortunately are common with many other conditions and diseases... It appears to me that if the cadmium concentration is correct, the exposures to the material must have been small and over a period of months. To administer intentionally this poison in this fashion would call for amazing subtlety and patience. I reasoned in a vague sort of way that a person reaching the high concentration the subject did would more likely have received multiple doses or had chronic exposure to reach the hair level he did – without having some clinically acute, dramatic episode marking the exposure. Perhaps Dr. Morris might find very irregular peaks in the cadmium concentrations if there were a serial analysis of the hair, measuring from the root. But the cadmium may have done irrecoverable damage months before death and all subsequent hair growth may have been drawing from the body pool of cadmium – without new exposures."*

COMMENT: Serial analysis requires much longer hair than Srila Prabhupada's less than 1 cm hair that was cut every month. Napoleon's hair was several inches long and suitable for NAA serial analysis. Interestingly: *(1) He surmised a case of multiple doses and chronic exposure, administering cadmium with "amazing subtlety and patience." (2) Cadmium poisoning symptoms are similar to many other conditions and diseases. (3) 20 ppm: distinctly abnormal; 1 ppm: rather hefty load.*

#2 EXPERT OPINION: DR. ANIL AGGARWAL, FORENSIC TOXICOLOGIST, MAULANA AZAD MEDICAL COLLEGE

We came across a colorful character, Dr. Anil Aggarwal, a Forensic Toxicologist in New Delhi. A Professor of Forensic Medicine at Maulana Azad Medical College since 1985, he specializes in solving mysterious deaths and is an expert in poisons. His website chronicles many bizarre cases he solved, including one of acute cadmium poisoning. Dr. Aggarwal also maintains an *Internet Journal of Forensic Medicine and Toxicology* and an *Internet Journal of Book Reviews.* Contacting him about our investigation, he agreed to review our case. We sent him a medical symptoms summary and detailed the cadmium findings in hair tests, providing the initial report from Dr. Morris for *Samples A* and *D* in 2002. One of our team members, in India on a fact-finding mission, went to see Dr. Aggarwal in person and brought him a copy of *SHPM.* In May 2002 we had very pr oductive meetings with Dr. Aggarwal and his associates, all top university scientists in toxicology and medicine. The particulars of Srila Prabhupada's case were presented, discussed, and analyzed. Dr. Aggarwal rendered his professional opinion: *"Cadmium 20 ppm in hair is prima facie evidence of poisoning with malicious intent."*

In June 2002, Dr. Aggarwal wrote to me further: *"A perusal of your book, and other facts as discussed with your friend, point strongly in favor of cadmium (poisoning)... I am able to defend your contention in any forum."* Dr. Aggarwal then passed my book to a colleague, Dr. Satbir Singh, a consultant in toxicological radiology at G.B. Pant Hospital, saying: *"I had immediately handed over your book Someone Has Poisoned Me to one of our experts for his opinion. I was discussing your case with Dr. Singh..."* These medical and forensic experts remain ready to assist our investigation.

#3 EXPERT OPINION: DR. DIPANKAR CHAKRABORTI, Director Of Environmental Studies, Jadavpur University, India

In 2002 Dr. Dipankar Chakraborti was at the head of the arsenic crisis in Bengal, imminently qualified in heavy metals poisoning, hair analysis, and heavy metals intoxication. He was interviewed in India by a member of our Asian investigative team in April 2002. He elaborated that his field of expertise included poisoning by mercury, antimony, arsenic, and cadmium. Asked what is the significance of a hair level of 20 ppm cadmium, he replied *"He will be finished. He can't survive more than 3 or 4 days."* Yet Srila Prabhupada survived with such high cadmium levels for many months – only, we surmise, by the will of

43

the Lord and due to mystic yoga perfections, by being a topmost yogi. Otherwise one may wonder why these massive amounts of poison did not have the expected results.

Dr. Dipankar's recent activities in brief: **(1)** Visiting Faculty, Big Data Analytics Programme, S.P. Jain Institute of Global Management, Mumbai, 2015-2016 **(2)** Visiting Faculty, CSE Department, NIT Mizoram, 2014-2015 B93) Assistant Professor, CSE Dept, NIT Meghalaya, 2012-2014 **(4)** Visiting Research Scholar, Precision and Intelligence (P&I) Laboratory, Advanced Information Processing Division: Okumura Group, Tokyo Institute of Technology (TIT), Tokyo, 2011 **(5)** Research Fellow, India-Japan Cooperative Programme-Project (DST-JST), Multi-disciplinary research field on "Sentiment Analysis where AI meets Psychology" 2010-2012, CSE Department, Jadavpur University, Kolkata, India **(6)** Research Engineer, DIT, MCIT, Gov't of India sponsored project "Development of the Cross-Lingual Information Access (CLIA) System" 2009-2010, CSE Dept, Jadavpur University, Kolkata, India **(7)** Visiting Faculty, CSE Department, GCETTS, 2008-2009 **(8)** He wrote a searing report (www.ncbi.nlm.nih.gov) on the arsenic in water crisis in India in 2018 titled Groundwater Arsenic Contamination in the Ganga River Basin: A Future Health Danger: this affects 500 million people and 19% of India's population drinks water with lethal arsenic levels over time.

#4 EXPERT OPINION: DR. AMARES CHATT, DALHOUSIE UNIVERSITY, HALIFAX, NOVA SCOTIA

In 1998 Dr. A. Chatt in Halifax tested our first hair sample, *ND-1*. He uses neutron activation analysis, although his facility has lesser accuracy on very small mass samples than Dr. Morris at MURR. He authored a book, *Hair Analysis*. Dr. Chatt remarked on Srila Prabhupada's 20 ppm cadmium found by his friend and colleague Dr. Morris: *"The level of 20 ppm seems to be very high if external contamination is ruled out. I have done thousands of hair tests over many years and sometimes see at most 2 ppm cadmium."* His first reaction to a level of 20 ppm was to ask what kinds of shampoos, creams, etc might have externally contaminated the hair. My reply: *"None of these things were used."*

#5 EXPERT OPINION: ARL LABS ANALYTICAL RESEARCH LABS, PHOENIX, ARIZONA

Analytical Research Labs does commercial hair analyses for individuals, doctors, and medical clinics. The Standard Industrial Classification (SIC) of Analytical Research Labs is 807101 - Laboratories-Medical. A medical or clinical laboratory is where tests are done on clinical specimens to derive information about the health of a patient as pertains to the diagnosis, treatment, and prevention of disease. ARL is one of the largest such outfits in the US, and has a very professional and respected performance rating. As of 2003, they were doing 35,000 hair tests annually; as of 2017 they were in operation almost 4 decades. President Kenneth Paul C. Eck was interviewed by me in 2004. He disclosed these facts derived from their hair mineral analysis operation: *(1) They rarely see cadmium levels over 1 ppm (2) That the usual range was from 0.02-0.10 ppm (average 0.06 ppm) (3) That: "20 ppm was off the chart."* I also spoke to Russ Madarash, ARL's head chemist, who confirmed: *(1) Cadmium values are usually under 0.10 ppm (2) That their "red alert level" is 2 ppm, which would require a second test to verify such an elevated amount (3) The highest value that he remembered was 4 ppm.* (see www.arltma.com)

So after many years of operation, and out of perhaps a million tests, one ARL client had 4 ppm hair cadmium, while no one had the levels we found in Srila Prabhupada's hair. Srila Prabhupada's cadmium levels were **"OFF THE CHART."** I also used ARL several times to check my own hair for environmental contamination, due to lead paint dust after sanding antique window frames. Sure enough, my lead was quite elevated, confirming the accuracy of commercial hair testing. ARL's president and head chemist, interviewed separately, gave confirming same data and facts.

#6 EXPERT OPINION: AYURVEDIC PHYSICIAN

Dr. Metha, an Ayurvedic physician from Texas, was shown in 1998 several photographs of Srila Prabhupada during his last days, and he also watched the video documentary of Srila Prabhupada's last months titled: "The Final Lesson." Dr. Mehta had been a practicing Ayurvedic physician since 1948. From an interview in 1997: *"The expression and symptoms of the face, the eyes and the manner of speaking indicate to me that Srila Prabhupada was poisoned, most probably by arsenic or mercury. He himself said that he was poisoned, confirmed by dullness of the face, how the body's natural color is gone. This is very hard for the average person to understand; only the experienced eye can tell."*

#7 EXPERT OPINION: CD POISONING SCIENTIFIC STUDIES

WHAT ARE AVERAGE NORMAL CADMIUM LEVELS?

Published scientific studies are generally accepted as presentation of scientific facts, subject to due diligence and discretion in application to specific circumstances. So exactly what do scientific studies show to be the *average normal* level of cadmium in human hair? Below is a large cross section of studies separated into (A) unexposed subjects, (B) exposed subjects, (those working or living in environmentally or occupationally contaminated situations). We collected the findings from numerous authoritative sources, and note that even the levels of persons exposed occupationally, environmentally, or accidentally to abnormal cadmium amounts are still a fraction of ONE PPM, very far below the levels seen in Srila Prabhupada's hair.

CADMIUM UNEXPOSED SUBJECT STUDIES:

(1) Laurie Miller, Center for Disease Control (CDC), sent us a thick manual on cadmium poisoning, which put the average normal amount of hair cadmium at **0.07 ppm** (Sharma, et al, 1982) (2) Analytical Research Laboratories, Phoenix, AZ disclosed that in their hair analyses for their clients was an average **0.06 ppm** (0.02-0.10 ppm) (3) Dr. J. R. Montonte of Trace Minerals International in Cleveland uses a normal for hair cadmium at **0.10 ppm** (4) Dr. Max Sutton, Hill Laboratories, CA uses a reference range for cadmium in hair of **0.0-0.15** ppm (average **0.075 ppm**) (5) A 1994 study by Wolfsperger M, et al of 79 healthy adults in Vienna & Rome found an average of **0.038 ppm** cadmium in non-smoker's hair (6) A 1999 study by Liu XJ (Japan) compared hair cadmium of **0.109** ppm in residents of a cadmium polluted area in 1979 to **0.055 ppm** levels in 1999 after cleanup by soil replacement (7) A study in 1988 by Wilhelm M, et al in Germany of school children in different areas found hair cadmium levels ranging 0.0637-0.1161 ppm (average **0.0745 ppm**) (8) A 1990 study by Wilhelm M, et al at Germany's Institute of Toxicology measured normal cadmium hair levels at 0.060–0.085 ppm (average **0.072 ppm**) (9) A study in 1991 by Wilhelm M, et al in Germany found young children to have an average of **0.09 ppm** hair cadmium in their hair (10) A study in 2003 by Benes B, Sladka J, et al in Czech Republic measured cadmium levels in the hair of 3556 children. The medium amount of cadmium was **0.14 ppm** (11) A study in 2003 in Slovenia by Erzen I, et al measured the median cadmium content in the hair of 245 random young men to be only **0.004 ppm** (12) A study in 1994 by Wilhelm M, et al in Germany found **0.111 ppm** hair cadmium in a control group of children (13) A 1991 hair cadmium study by Bosque MA, et al in Spain of 226 children compared average results from an industrial area (**0.327** ppm) with a rural area of **0.002 ppm**. (14) A study of 5846 healthy Japanese showed average

cadmium in both men and women to be **0.028 ppm** (Yoshikazu, Yoshio, 2005) **(15)** The hair cadmium reference value for Italy is 0.03 mg/kg or **0.03 ppm** (2012, Abdulrahman) **(16)** The hair cadmium reference value for England is **0.11 ppm**. (2012, Abdulrahman) **(17)** The hair cadmium reference value for Japan is **0.05 ppm**. (2012, Abdulrahman) **(18)** Cadmium levels in the hair of elderly Koreans was found to be on average **0.052 ppm** (Kim M, Kim K, 2011) **(19)** A 2016 study in China showed a mean of **0.062 ppm** (Zhou T, et al)

CADMIUM: AVG. NORMAL FROM 19 STUDIES: 0.064 ppm

(1) The 19 above studies ascertain an "average normal" amount of hair cadmium found in "normal" unexposed persons. There are variations due to location, environment, nearby industries, etc. We calculated an **average of the studies of normal values** for both unexposed persons (above) and exposed (see below), and this disallows criticism that selective studies were used to push the figures up or down. We call this the **"Average Normal."** One could "cherry-pick" the lowest value studies like the GBC author did when he chose only two unusually high arsenic studies in Mexico City and Glasgow (Ch. 48), which would be dishonest, so our average of many studies is much more accurate.

(2) *That average of normal cadmium in human hair comes to 0.064 ppm*, about 1/16th of one ppm, or about half of the average normal *arsenic* hair levels. Srila Prabhupada's 1977 cadmium levels in hair *Samples D, A,* and *Q-2* (12.4, 14.6, and 19.9 ppm) is an average *15.73 ppm*. **(3)** *Srila Prabhupada thus had about 194 to 311 times more than the average normal of hair cadmium, sustained over a period of 10 months. His 1977 average is 250 times above average normal.* Note that cadmium levels in vegetarians are significantly lower (Gonzalez-Reimers, 2014). **(4)** Srila Prabhupada's cadmium poisoning was very serious. As per the expert opinions below, *this is a lethal amount over a short period of time.* My own two personal hair test results conformed to the "average normal" of 0.064 ppm. In 2005 I had my hair tested by Doctor's Data through my physician in a general physical check-up. The cadmium was normal: **0.067 ppm**. When my wife and I tested our hair a few years earlier, we both had cadmium levels of **0.10 ppm**.

CADMIUM STUDIES OF EXPOSED PERSONS

(1) A 1989 study by Bergomi M, Borella P, et al in Italy of 142 children in an industrial area found average hair cadmium of **0.17 ppm** **(2)** A 1994 study by Muller M, Anke M noted that a German factory had extensive cadmium emissions since 1960, resulting in the local residents having high hair cadmium levels averaging **0.389 ppm** **(3)** A 1995 study,

Chlopicka J, et al, Poland studied children in industrial areas, finding average hair cadmium levels of **0.43** ppm **(4)** A 1996 study by Kasnia-Kocot J, et al in Poland examined the hair cadmium levels of 69 children living in "the most polluted district" of Chorzow, finding average levels of **0.44** ppm in girls **(5)** and **0.91** ppm in boys. **(6)** A 1996 study by Zaborowska W, et al in Poland found **0.31** ppm of hair cadmium in 157 children, including those living in high exposure areas **(7)** A 1997 study by Zaborowska W, et al in Poland found **0.37** ppm hair cadmium in another group of exposed school children **(8)** A 1998 study by Chlopicka J, et al in Poland found **0.91** ppm hair cadmium in children from a highly industrialized and contaminated area **(9)** A 1991 hair cadmium study by Bosque MA, et al in Spain of 226 children from an industrial area had **0.327** ppm **(10)** A study in 1994 by Wilhelm M, et al found **0.265** ppm in a group of German children who had high cadmium exposure **(11)** A 1999 study by Liu XJ in Japan compared hair cadmium of **0.109** ppm in residents of a cadmium polluted area in 1979 to lower levels of **0.055 ppm** in 1999 after environmental cleanup by soil replacement. **(12)** A 1991 hair cadmium study by Bosque MA, et al in Spain of 226 children from an industrial area had **0.327 ppm**

NOTE: (www.webhart.net) reviews screenings tests for toxins, stating: "Cadmium in hair exceeding 1 ppm is cause for concern."

CADMIUM: AVERAGE OF 12 *EXPOSURE* STUDIES: 0.387 ppm

The above 12 studies of hair cadmium in persons environmentally or occupationally exposed shows how Srila Prabhupada, with average 15.73 ppm cadmium throughout 1977, had *40 X those exposed to serious or significant environmental or occupational contamination.* How can anyone suggest Srila Prabhupada's cadmium was due to "exposure" to factory or environmental contamination? In all the very many studies we came across, we never found an instance of hair cadmium levels even close to Srila Prabhupada's, whose levels were off the "exposure" chart. It is amazing he lived for so many months with such levels.

HOW THESE SCIENTIFIC STUDIES WERE SELECTED

There are some studies which include what are called "outliers" that result in misleading ranges and averages for cadmium and arsenic hair levels. Therefore we selected studies that did not have obvious outlier values, to arrive at a more accurate average normal in human hair (namely 0.064 ppm cadmium and 0.13 ppm arsenic). When one finds range highs many times higher than the average, that high end value is not average or normal. It means that among those selected in a study, a few are unexpectedly abnormal. In statistics, this phenomenon is called

48

"outliers." Scientific studies may include "outliers" that result in misleading ranges and averages for hair levels. When one sees range highs unusually or several times higher than the average, that high end value is *not average or normal*. In some studies, one or a few may be unexpectedly abnormal.

OUTLIER: a data point on a graph or in a set of results that is very much higher or lower than other data points. Wikipedia explains how outlier data points distort an average value: *"Naive interpretation of statistics derived from data sets that include outliers may be misleading... outliers may indicate data points that belong to a different population than the rest of the sample set. In most larger samplings, some data points will be further from the sample mean than what is deemed reasonable. This can be due to incidental systematic error or flaws in the theory that generated an assumed family of probability distributions, or it may be that some observations are far from the center of the data. If an individual data point can be considered anomalous with respect to the rest of the data, then the datum is termed as a point outlier. The two common approaches to exclude outliers are truncation ...or trimming... [which] discards the outliers..."*

Outliers and distribution irregularities are often problematic in scientific studies. Sometimes *legitimate corrections are made via truncations*. However, we did not employ any corrective process of adjustments. We simply chose relevant studies without obvious outliers to ascertain average normal hair values for cadmium, arsenic. However, the GBC chose two highest values they could find, which was cheating (Ch. 48). Our careful avoidance of a few studies with obvious outliers is legitimate because these studies that do not correspond to the majority of studies can be misleading. Actually, science has established that *normal* in heavy metals is close to zero. To select studies without abnormal high outliers is common sense and actually is a more accurate "normal."

#8 EXPERT OPINION:
CADMIUM POISONING SCIENTIFIC STUDIES

LETHALITY AND MORBIDITY

Cadmium poisonings (and deaths from it) are rare. Although many studies on cadmium have been done since the 1950's, the relationship between dose and health effects is still being refined. The paucity of clinical cases of serious cadmium poisoning (chronic or acute) has largely restricted the scientific record to animal studies and neutral to mild cases of exposure in human society. Nevertheless, the body of scientific literature does provide ample knowledge of cadmium's toxicity and does shed bright lights on the lethality and morbidity of Srila Prabhupada's high cadmium levels (our research has not been updated since 2005). There is no doubt the high cadmium concentrations found in Srila Prabhupada's hair was a primary factor in his sharp deterioration of health and his physical demise. A review of the scientific studies below helps to understand the effects of Srila Prabhupada's cadmium levels. Even though there was no study specifically with ± 16 ppm cadmium in hair, still, many studies were found to illustrate very clearly: *The sky-high cadmium levels that Srila Prabhupada endured over 10 months is an imminently life-threatening and lethal level.*

(1) Cadmium has reached *up to* 4 ppm in the soil at hazardous waste sites. *(Srila Prabhupada had 4 times the level in the worst waste dump.)* (2) OSHA characterizes: *"Cadmium is extremely poisonous and toxic at extremely low levels, and thus tests may miss its detection... even amounts of cadmium dust in occupational situations previously thought safe are now shown to cause kidney disease."* Cadmium is now known to be much more poisonous than previously believed, and OSHA has issued much more stringent restrictions on cadmium pollution. (3) Even in areas of heavy industrial and environmental cadmium pollution, as in southern Poland, residents still only had roughly $1/70^{th}$ what Srila Prabhupada had. (Note that Srila Prabhupada's high cadmium was NOT due to environmental or industrial pollution.) (4) A blood cadmium level above 7 millionths gram per liter indicates significant exposure. (5) Cadmium is about twice as toxic than arsenic, and normal hair values of both are a tiny fraction of one ppm. A hair level of 5 ppm arsenic can lead to a fatal chronic poisoning. *(Cadmium levels of 19.9 ppm are therefore extremely elevated.)* (6) The village of Ergates in Cyprus lies downwind from a cadmium foundry, resulting in 150-300% the national average of brain, kidney, pancreas, lung, and leukemia cancers amongst the residents. Blood cadmium levels were 5 X the norm. *(This would correspond to 5 X the norm in hair cadmium. If Srila Prabhupada's hair had ± 250 times the norm, then Srila Prabhupada would have been 50 times as ill as these unfortunate villagers.)*

(7) Kidney dysfunction is associated with 10-100 times normal cadmium concentrations accumulated in the liver and kidneys. Hair is an excellent indicator of internal cadmium concentrations. (Srila *Prabhupada's hair had up to 311 X normal amounts, and Srila Prabhupada's kidney failure was thus primarily due to cadmium poisoning.)* (8) Average cadmium in US food is 0.002-0.040 ppm; in most drinking water it's below 0.001 ppm. (9) The EPA has reduced allowable cadmium in drinking water to a maximum of 0.05 ppm and the

FDA restricts cadmium in food coloring. **(10)** A study in 2001 by T Osawa et al on the relation between cadmium in rice and kidney dysfunction found that the maximum allowable amount of cadmium in rice before adverse health effects became visible was 0.05-0.2 ppm. High cadmium in rice resulted in kidney dysfunction after a short time.

(11) Cadmium is seldom used as a deliberate poison; yet it is extremely toxic, more than mercury or arsenic. Compared to 19.9 ppm cadmium in hair, note the normal blood and urine cadmium values: Blood- 0.0000003 gram/ liter; urine creatinine- 0.29 ppm. **(12)** A study by Yao-Min Hung et al in 2004 of a self-poisoning case stated that ingestion of >100 mg of soluble cadmium salts can be lethal. **(13)** www.ilocis.org/documents/chpt63e.htm Kidney dysfunction and damage are the most prominent findings after long-term exposure to lower levels of cadmium via polluted food. As kidney dysfunction progresses, amino acids, glucose, minerals (calcium and phosphorus), are lost into the urine. Kidney stones are frequently reported by cadmium workers. Severe cases may develop uremia. Studies have shown irreversible glomerular dysfunction. Cadmium kidney damage is irreversible and worsens even after exposure has ceased.

SUMMARY: LETHALITY AND MORBIDITY

(1) Srila Prabhupada's hair was 4 X as cadmium polluted than the worst hazardous waste dump. **(2)** Even amounts of cadmium dust in occupational situations previously thought safe are now shown to cause kidney disease. **(3)** Srila Prabhupada had 40-70 X more cadmium than those exposed to serious pollution. **(4)** Srila Prabhupada's cadmium levels were far above what would cause serious kidney disease and kidney failure within a year's time. **(5)** Srila Prabhupada's hair had 16,000 X more cadmium than in most of the world's drinking water. **(6)** Srila Prabhupada's hair had 400 X more cadmium than the maximum limit allowable in drinking water by the EPA. **(7)** According to one website, the lethal dose of cadmium is 30-40 mg. But the "lethal" level of cadmium poisoning varies by body weight, age, health, gender, chronic vs. acute, and other factors, all of which determine how soon someone dies from the poisoning or from the conditions and diseases caused and aggravated by the poisoning. Due to Srila Prabhupada's age and health, a lethal cadmium dose would be less than 30-40 mg or 1/900 oz. **(8)** "…even less than a milligram of cadmium salt may be enough to produce fatal toxicity." Clinical Chemistry (2011) p. 1488. **(9)** Henry Lee Lucas, a Texas serial killer was subjected to medical tests in 1985 to

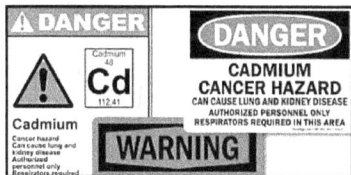

study his criminal nature. The chemist, Dr. Walsh, analyzed locks of his hair to determine the category of body chemistry. *"His cadmium concentration is more than 30 times the population median value, and is the highest level we have ever observed in a human being out of thousands tested,"* says Walsh. And Srila Prabhupada had 8 X as much as that...

#9 EXPERT OPINION: STUDIES IN THE SCIENTIFIC LITERATURE ON CADMIUM POISONING

PATHOLOGY & TOXICITY

Various studies provided a general overview of cadmium's extreme and widespread destructiveness to the body, giving *some idea of what it does, and how, to its unfortunate victims.*

(1) Unlike other toxic heavy metals, *ingested cadmium is primarily cumulative;* since body excretion is so slow, limited to at most 2 micrograms/day, regardless of the amount ingested, so ingested amounts greater than bodily excretion rates will accumulate in the body until a fatal threshold is reached. Poisoning with arsenic (since it is quickly excreted) requires regular doses, whereas poisoning by cadmium, being cumulative and with a half-life of 17-30 years, can become fatal very quickly. **(2)** Cadmium is so poisonous that even 10 mg ingested has caused severe toxic symptoms. (Rumack BH: Poisindex Information System) A lethal dose is about 0.5 grain or 30-40 mg cadmium, far less than the 300 mg arsenic required, and is the weight of a small postage stamp. This is about 0.035 grams or 0.001235 ounce. **(3)** Cadmium is a general metabolic poison and competes (replaces) with zinc, disrupting essential biological processes. Ingested cadmium is primarily deposited in the kidneys and liver, with a very limited amount being carried by the blood and excreted through the urine. Since the amount of cadmium deposited in hair depends on the blood level of cadmium, hair cadmium is like the tip of the iceberg as to the actual total body burden.

(4) A 2000 study in Belgium by MK Viaene et al stated that "animal studies have shown cadmium is a potent neurotoxicant." Its cumulative toxic effect depends on the amounts ingested. **(5)** The target organ for cadmium toxicity via oral exposure is the kidney. Cadmium causes irreversible renal tubular damage, which progresses into complete Fanconi syndrome with decreased tubular reabsorption of proteins, glucose, amino acids, calcium, phosphorus, with decreased ability to acidify or concentrate the urine. **(6)** Renal tubular dysfunction and proteinuria (in kidneys) results in overall physical deterioration. Rather than assimilate nutrients, minerals and protein, the kidneys allow them to pass out with urine, with whatever stores are in reserve. Leaching due to cadmium poisoning (protein, sugar spilled in the urine) denies the victim any sustenance with progressive malnutrition, starvation, indigestion, diarrhea, vomiting, stomach pain, etc. *(Exactly Srila Prabhupada's condition... Part 4)* **(7)** Cadmium poisoning is irreversible; there is only mediocre chelation therapy and no antidote.

(8) From ncbi.nlm.nih.gov /pmc/articles/PMC5596182: Cadmium has no known beneficial effect on the human physiology. **(9)** Daily excretion of cadmium is about 0.01% of the total body burden; cadmium takes 17 to 30+ years to excrete half of what is in the body. Cadmium's half-life in the blood is 3-4 months, which is deposited in the hair as it grows (compared to a few days for arsenic). **(10)** Normal cadmium concentrations in the adult kidney cortex are about 50 ppm and when it reaches 200 ppm a critical threshold is reached, and then serious kidney disease/ dysfunction /failure develops. *(Exactly Srila Prabhupada's condition)* **(11)** Cumulative effects of cadmium continue after exposure ends; disease then tends to be progressive. Once sufficient cadmium is chronically ingested, death follows from disease progression.

(12) Long-term chronic cadmium poisoning results in various bone and prostate diseases, and lung cancer. The liver and cardio-vascular system are also adversely affected by cadmium. **(13)** Cadmium intake is distributed widely in the body but accumulates mostly in the liver, kidneys. It binds to protein and non-protein sulfhydryl groups and macro-molecules e.g., metallothionen, effecting especially the liver, kidneys. **(14)** Because the toxic effects of cadmium are a function of a critical concentration being attained in the kidneys, similar effects will occur following long-term poisoning at low levels, and short-term poisoning at high levels. Kidney/liver toxicity can occur with cadmium levels accumulated even by sub-chronic exposure. *(which is why it was not recognized by so many "short-term" doctors)*

(15) Breathing difficulties, emphysema develop even 10 years later at chronic levels. *(Oct. 1977 Dr. K. Gopal was focused on SP's lungs, consistent with cadmium poisoning)* **(16)** The IARC regards cadmium as cancer-causing due to chromosomal aberrations in the blood lymphocytes and lesions in the central nervous system, liver/kidneys, causing blood disorder eosinophilia. **(17)** Cadmium is one of the most dangerous environmental nephrotoxic agents, causing hearing/eyesight loss, kidney stones, decreased bone density, alters calcium metabolism. Cadmium, arsenic, antimony interfere with the basic chemical processes that sustain life. **(18)** Cadmium is present only in tiny trace amounts in the environment.

#10 EXPERT OPINION: DR. J. STEVEN MORRIS

SEVEN HAIR SAMPLES TESTED BY NAA

DID DR. MORRIS MAKE AN ERROR?

It is extremely unlikely Dr. Morris made an error in his calculations on the cadmium in Srila Prabhupada's hair. He has done thousands of neutron activation analyses on tiny samples for several decades, and this is his unique expert qualification. Through thousands of earlier tests he perfected and refined his techniques, eliminating any meaningful errors. His reports admit a slight variance of accuracy up to 5%± higher or lower, so he achieved 95+% accuracy. This low variance factor makes his findings highly accurate. *We can justifiably have millions of times more confidence in Dr. Morris' results than in the dishonest, fraudulent denials of ISKCON's GBC,* who are politically motivated to bury the "poison conspiracy." Dr. Morris, on the other hand, has no motive to find elevated levels of anything. We should simply take it that the forensic scientific breakthrough discovered "accidentally" by Dr. Morris is the arrangement of Lord Krishna to reveal the truth of Srila Prabhupada's final pastimes. If Dr. Morris' results are doubted, more hair tests can be done. Why doesn't the GBC test other Srila Prabhupada hair samples that they have now hidden away somewhere? They are scared to do so.

Dr. Morris did 3 separate NAA tests finding similarly extreme cadmium in *Samples A, D,* and *Q-2.* Thus he would have had to make the *same miscalculations* 3 times over 3 years, while he was doing countless other NAA tests and when he would have corrected any anomalies in his testing regime that might have surfaced. Dr. Morris was not testing for cadmium for the first time. His Srila Prabhupada's hair tests were done amongst many other tests using the same NAA method. And he is only one in the MURR team of NAA experts who work together. On each of Dr. Morris' three cadmium tests, he uniquely refreshed his testing calibrations and calculations, consistently finding similarly elevated levels of cadmium and also similar levels of arsenic, antimony, and mercury. Seven tests, four elements, and a total of 22 values that fit together compatibly without contradictions. *This consistency and cross-correlations four tests of elevated 1977 hair and the three tests of normal pre-1977 hair strongly validates his findings as very accurate.*

Srila Prabhupada's last year hair cadmium levels were lethal, and even more so due to any existing heart, kidneys, and diabetes health problems. This is the clear verdict of the above ten expert opinions, confirming the lethality of Srila Prabhupada's hair cadmium levels.

CHAPTER 7:
MALICIOUS, HOMICIDAL POISONING

CADMIUM WAS THE PRIMARY POISON

SHPM (1999) stated that Srila Prabhupada was poisoned with arsenic, based on the evidence at that time. Arsenic was 2.6 ppm in one sample of Srila Prabhupada's hair, or about 20 X above the average normal. *There is no innocuous explanation as to how Srila Prabhupada would have acquired this amount of arsenic in his hair, even if it was not a lethal level.* The arguments that Srila Prabhupada drank arsenic tainted Bengali water, or that 2.6 ppm is normal, must all be discarded after honest scientific evaluation (Ch. 47-48). However, hair tests on *Sample D* (2002), *Sample A* (2002), and *Sample Q-2* (2005) found an average 15.73 ppm cadmium in Srila Prabhupada's hair *throughout* 1977, a level 250 X above average normal. This cadmium is sky-high; the arsenic was very high; the antimony elevated. We assessed, based on scientific literatures, that these cadmium levels would be lethal over the 10 months represented by the hair samples, while the arsenic would be health debilitative over this time. Srila Prabhupada was poisoned with cadmium as the primary poison, and arsenic secondarily. Also the antimony that was 8 X above normal.

POISONING CLASSIFICATIONS

"All things are poison and nothing is without poison; the dosage alone makes the poison." (Paracelsus, 1538) Gradual poisoning by heavy metals occurs in one of three ways: **Accident:** There is misuse of some dangerous manufactured product or substance. **Pollution:** There is environmental or occupational pollution or exposure. **Homicide:** Someone secretly and maliciously introduces one lethal dose in food or drink, or multiple doses over time, producing the appearance of a chronic illness and causing slow death. Since cadmium is begrudgingly expelled from the body, a hefty dose of cadmium would act adversely for years with unsure recovery. A persistent, gradual health deterioration would result from regular cumulative small doses of cadmium. Cadmium poisoning can be classified in four degrees of intensity, as follows: **ACUTE,** with sudden, dramatic symptoms, intense and often fatal; **SUB-ACUTE,** with serious effects but not immediately lethal; and **CHRONIC**, with regular extended lesser doses and longer survivability. Which was applicable to Srila Prabhupada?

Srila Prabhupada's hair cadmium levels were far above the low-level chronic poisoning typical to factory pollution, which can produce serious health problems such as kidney failure and prostate cancer after 10-40 years, with values of 0.5 up to ±2 ppm hair cadmium. Srila Prabhupada's case is far more substantial than low-level chronic poisoning. Acute poisoning would result in death within hours or days. The continuity of Srila Prabhupada's symptoms and a gradual, progressive health decline over a year or so does not indicate a one-time acute poisoning. (Unless Srila Prabhupada survived one or more acute doses by dint of his mystic powers.) This is a distinct possibility.

Srila Prabhupada's first dramatic health attack and decline was July 20, 1976, a second time Feb. 26, 1977, a third time May 16, 1977 in Hrishikesh, and again Sept. 8, 1977. Each of these sub-acute episodes was a sudden onset of a crisis pushing his health down again. **Mid-Level Chronic Cadmium Poisoning?** Yes, this was his condition *in between the sub-acute episodes described above*. As Dr. Hudson opined: *"the exposures to the material must have been small and over a period of months."* The gradual ingestion of small amounts of cadmium resulted in a delayed, cumulative, and irreversible effect on health from mid-1976 to Nov. 14, 1977. The hair tests and medical history of Srila Prabhupada indicate *mid-level chronic poisoning* mixed with a series of regular *sub-acute* episodes with higher doses, or the extended ingestion of small amounts of cadmium with insidious, hidden, deadly effects and punctuated with sub-acute doses (which Srila Prabhupada endured.)

A MALICIOUS, HOMICIDAL POISONING

Srila Prabhupada was in good, strong health until mid-1976 (Ch. 29). He had minor health problems but he was literally superhuman in endurance, outdoing his youthful students. In mid-1976 his health mysteriously began to decline, and many doctors could not put a finger on the real cause. There were many misdiagnoses as there were doctors! His health was afflicted by chronic cadmium poisoning punctuated by sub-acute episodes. Hair tests and medical history evidences an insidious, secret poisoning by difficult to detect heavy metals, primarily cadmium, the effects of which look like the symptoms of diabetes and kidney disease. Administration of many low doses over many months was punctuated with periodic more potent "surprise" doses, which discredited all doctors and Ayurvedic or allopathic medicines. Access to Srila Prabhupada was severely restricted by Tamal. The unexplained mysterious, progressive health decline was characterized as a divine pastime to deflect inquiry. Chronic cadmium or arsenic poisoning resembles old age, arousing little suspicion. *It is a state of chronic invalidism and starvation. Srila Prabhupada suffered a severe cadmium poisoning of virtually unprecedented, catastrophic proportions. There was a distinct methodology for the homicidal cadmium poisoning.*

METHODOLOGY

The cadmium poisoning was a prolonged ingestion of small amounts of cadmium with insidious, hidden, deadly effects, then sometimes punctuated with heavier or more acute doses. The hair tests show that *the poisoning was chronic over a period of 10 months;* Srila Prabhupada's medical history indicates up to 18 months (Ch. 8). *Hair tests confirm massive cadmium poisoning and medical symptoms indicate a start in May to July 1976.* Knowledge of poisoning methodologies has always been available (Ch. 39). The discovery of Napoleon's high arsenic levels in the 1960's highlighted the subject of poisoning. Srila Prabhupada's poisoners had to be "very close" to administer periodic doses. Caretakers were the only ones with access to carry out a secretive tainting of food or drink which Srila Prabhupada then ingested. Since it was not a one-time poisoning, with the hair tests and physical symptom history showing a start as early as May 1976 and up to Nov. 1977, namely in a chronic manner, the poisoners would need regular access to Srila Prabhupada, ruling out outsiders like Gaudiya Math, caste brahmanas, or visitors. This narrows the poisoners to those who were stationed around Srila Prabhupada, especially after the severe February 1977 health decline.

Cadmium would produce the slow health debilitation and starvation syndrome found in Srila Prabhupada's health history. A "cosmetic" poisoning of small doses would result in a feeling of malaise, increased weakness, and a reduction in the body's general strength. Between the first two major episodes of July 20, 1976 and Feb. 26, 1977, Srila Prabhupada partially recovered. Srila Prabhupada's health history fits all too well with cadmium poisoning (Ch. 31, App. 8).

CADMIUM SALTS

How could cadmium have been introduced into Srila Prabhupada's physical body? *Toxicology of the Eye* by WM Grant (1974) states: *"Ingestion of cadmium salts has caused severe and sometimes fatal poisoning."* Cadmium salts are very suitable for homicidal poisoning. Perhaps it was the common, readily obtainable compound cadmium chloride ($CdCl_2$), which is very soluble in water (1400 grams/ liter), has no taste, color or odor, and is a white crystalline powder, similar to salt or sugar. It could easily mix into Srila Prabhupada's salt, sugar, or food supplements. The same is true of arsenic trioxide. *"I clearly remember cadmium chloride as one of the bottled chemicals in our high school chemistry class, and it was included in Edmund Scientific chemistry kits that I remember looking at in a Genesee St., Rochester, NY hobby shop in 1965."* (Nityananda das) Cadmium is widely available in various inorganic salts. The most important is cadmium stearate, used as a PVC heat stabilizer. Cadmium sulphide is used as yellow and red plastic pigments. Cadmium chloride is a fungicide, ingredient in electroplating, colorant for pyrotechnics, tinning solution additive, and mordant in dyeing and printing textiles. It is used in production of photographic films and in mirror manufacture and in electronic vacuum tubes. Cadmium oxide is an electroplating agent and a component of silver alloys, phosphors, semiconductors and glass and ceramic glazes.

AVENUES FOR ADMINISTERING CADMIUM POISON

The form of cadmium most likely used would be a crystalline cadmium salt and not pure cadmium metal, which is not colorless, tasteless, or water soluble. Cadmium chloride, stearate, and sulfate salts are common, tasteless, odorless, transparent, and readily water soluble, looking like salt or sugar. Here are some avenues how cadmium could have been given to Srila Prabhupada for oral ingestion by tainting any of his

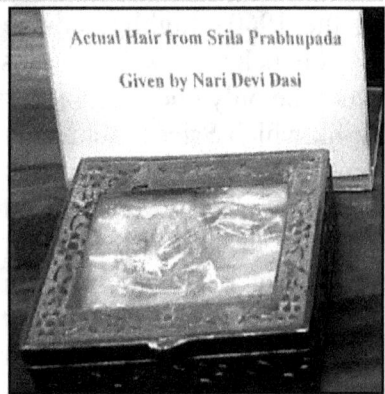

Actual Hair from Srila Prabhupada

Given by Nari Devi Dasi

exclusive, regularly used personal ingredients: *(1) Sprinkled on top of food, as claimed by Bhakta Vatsala das (Ch. 35) (2) Sprinkled in milk, water, or fruit juice (readily dissolvable) (3) Mixed in his kitchen's sugar or salt jar (4) Mixed in his tooth powder.* Other avenues: **(5)** The dry powder Horlicks or Complan food supplements **(6)** His special vegetable salt **(7)** His *Hedges* snuff powder **(8)** His cooking spices in his personal, unguarded Vrindaban kitchen **(9)** Medicinal compresses used in some 1977 treatments (absorbed through skin, but this was seldom) **(10)** Mixed in various medicines, but we note that no one medicine was taken regularly in the last 18 months.

A sprinkle or pinch of colorless, tasteless, and odorless cadmium salt crystals, such as what might fit on the very tip of a key, would be unnoticed and could produce another serious downturn in health. Cadmium is potently poisonous. No one else dared to use Srila Prabhupada's personal items, meant only for his use, so an insider could secretly taint any of those items, and the caretakers would unknowingly (or knowingly) be agents in a gradual homicidal poisoning. Then someone would administer a periodic more acute, higher dose, e.g., July

20, 1976, and Feb. 26, May 16, Sept. 8, 1977. Bhaktisiddhanta das, resident of ISKCON Vrindaban, said all of Srila Prabhupada's cooking and food preparation was done in a separate kitchen (which no longer exists), attached to his apartment, supervised by Tamal and BCS. Only sometimes were temple offerings sent to Srila Prabhupada.

In the health history (App. 8), April 10, 1977, Tamal, BCS, and Bhavananda are all involved in refilling Srila Prabhupada's tooth powder container: **Tamal**: *Yesterday you were questioning if we had an extra quantity of that, er, to fill up your container... of one of the things that you use... Oh, tooth powder.* **SP**: *Ah, yes, that.* **Tamal**: *Do you know where it is?* **BHAV**: *It hasn't been filled up yet?* White, tasteless cadmium salts could easily be mixed with Srila Prabhupada's tooth powder and absorbed just like nicotine from chewing tobacco. Cadmium could be mixed with food, salt, drinks, etc. Easy. Thus poison was taken in small doses regularly, maintaining a constant drain on Srila Prabhupada's health while the poisoners watched or went elsewhere, knowing that their work went on automatically.

Mustard seed oil was used to massage Srila Prabhupada daily, including his head (with hair), so was cadmium in the massage oil? No... Srila Prabhupada's masseurs were not poisoned through their hands. Massage oils can thus be ruled out.

POISONING, LITTLE BY LITTLE

The nature and progressive history of Srila Prabhupada's declining health in his last year, with its ups and downs, level plateau periods, and sudden onsets of a new crisis, suggests a scenario of a *steady "maintenance" poisoning punctuated by periodic, more intense doses.* This comprises a mixed regimen of mid-level chronic and sub-acute poisoning, and overall, an extended slow poisoning. Every so often, after some weeks or months, as the circumstances were "favorable," the poisoners would terminate the intervals of health stabilization and some feeble recovery with a more sub-acute dose to generate the onset of yet another attack of increased illness and accelerated health decay. This greater degeneration of health due to the mysterious and persistent "ailment" appeared to be nothing more than *"Srila Prabhupada's body being old and worn-out from constant travelling and preaching."* (TransD) Meanwhile, awkward situations with new doctors or treatments were avoided that might discover the "disease's" true nature.

Srila Prabhupada's decision to return to Vrindaban avoided any chance that Western medicine, hospitals tests, or competent doctors discovered poisoning. The accumulating cadmium would continue to wreak havoc and cause physical deterioration. The constant anemia, lack of appetite, no taste for food, and muscle weakness seen in Srila Prabhupada's health history (App. 8) was a result of background chronic poisoning, enough to produce a "starvation program." His body slowly lost weight, becoming progressively weaker, primarily from being unable to eat or digest food, with no taste or appetite, the kidneys "spilling" sugar and protein back into the urine. *Assassination at St. Helena*, p. 505: *"The dosages (chronic arsenic intoxication) may be small enough that none will produce immediate distress, though a general sense of discomfort and sickness will be apparent and may baffle diagnosis."* A summary of the method of covert poisoning: *"The doses are increased and reduced to create the impression that the 'patient' with a mysterious illness is getting better from some treatment, and worse from another. Then the dose is much increased and no one is surprised when there is a severe turn for the worse that defies medical diagnosis or doctors' medications."*

FINAL DOSE THE DAY AFTER THE POISON WHISPERS

Finally, after a program of chronic poisoning had reduced Srila Prabhupada's health to the brink of extinction by Nov. 1977, a final dose was administered, clearly indicated by the forensically confirmed, tape-recorded murmurs and whispers about poisoning Nov. 11, 1977. As protocol, a tape recorder was routinely left on in Srila Prabhupada's room to capture all his words of wisdom. These "poison" whispers were also captured and have been repeatedly confirmed by audio experts to contain the word *"poison."* The confirmed poison whispers are: **(1) JPS:** *"Poisoning for a (long) time..."* **(2) Tamal:** *"The poison's going down... (giggles) the poison's going down"* **(3) Tamal:** *"Is the poison in the milk?"* **Bhav:** *Uhhuh.* (Srila Prabhupada then is heard drinking milk.)

Significantly, after Srila Prabhupada said several times, **"Someone has poisoned me,"** (Nov. 9-10) and his caretakers extensively discussed homicidal poisoning (Nov. 10), the ***next day*** certified poisoning whispers occur (Nov. 11) on tape recordings. Is this coincidence? We think not, and surmise the poisoners became alarmed that Srila Prabhupada had discovered them and would soon expose them. The chances of several separate poison whispers, out of thousands of days, popping up on the very next day after the "poison discussions" is next to zero. It was not coincidental. It was the consequence of Srila Prabhupada's dropping the bombshell that he thought he was being poisoned. The poisoners were rushing to finish before being caught. Srila Prabhupada *(whom Tamal also whispered about: "He's as sly as they come")* was now wise to them and the situation had become extremely critical. Was it a coincidence that the caretakers, after discussing homicidal poisoning and acknowledging Srila Prabhupada was very distressed about how he had been poisoned, that they did nothing and just ignored and dropped the matter, and then whispered about poisoning him the very next day? The statistical probability of these three coincidences three days in a row is also next to zero. Think about that.

HOMICIDAL CADMIUM POISONING

Advanced testing by NAA of hair *Samples D, A,* and *Q-2* with 250 X more than the *average* normal levels of cadmium in human hair has established and confirmed Srila Prabhupada's **homicidal cadmium poisoning**. Scientific research confirms these amounts are lethal over the 10 to 18 months during which Srila Prabhupada was exposed. Cadmium was the primary ingredient in a *heavy metals cocktail* that included elevated levels of arsenic and antimony, which were cadmium enhancers. But the cadmium itself was sufficient to cause rapidly declining health and premature death. These levels accelerate, exacerbate any existing kidney disease and diabetes, entirely consistent with Srila Prabhupada's surprise health decline in 1976-1977 (Part 4). *The evidence overwhelmingly supports a homicidal cadmium poisoning.*

CHRONIC INVALIDISM, CHRONIC STARVATION

Chronic cadmium or arsenic poisoning causes a physical condition which appears typical to old age and therefore arouses no suspicion. It is a state of chronic invalidism and chronic starvation. Both Satsvarupa and Hari Sauri postulate in their writings that Srila Prabhupada's illness was just part of old age and the physical body wearing out. Of course, now we know that the cause of Srila Prabhupada's gradual health deterioration was **heavy metal poisoning.** The poisoners prolonged the poisoning, lest suspicions be aroused by a sudden death. It would need to look natural, entailing a frustrating, gradual, unexplainable decline of health over a year. If it appeared as anything other than a prolonged illness, then an autopsy, investigation, or serious questioning might discover the poisoning. It was also necessary to maintain Srila Prabhupada's state of chronic invalidism until he made his will and turned over management and bank accounts to his disciples. A sudden death by poison would have left ISKCON's assets in legal limbo.

After the kidneys become overloaded with cadmium poisoning, "leaching" occurs, causing protein and sugar to spill into the urine, denying the victim of any sustenance from what they eat. Cadmium ingested early in 1977 would still be wreaking havoc on the health at the end of 1977. Slow death follows with malnutrition, starvation, indigestion, diarrhea, vomiting, stomach pain, etc. These were Srila

Prabhupada's medical symptoms, and any analysis of Srila Prabhupada's medical condition must address the ± 16 ppm cadmium which was maintained for 10 or even 18 months.

"BASICS OF HOMICIDAL POISONING INVESTIGATIONS"

From: Office of Justice Programs (ojp.gov) Abstract: (scientific study with relevancies to be noted): *[Our comments bracketed] "Those at highest risk for being victims of poisoning are ...the elderly ...The offender is usually personally involved with the victim and is often a caregiver. Poisoners often assume the role of attempting to "nurse" the victim back to health... poisoners usually enjoy the thrill of having power over the life and suffering of the victim.* **["The poison's going down... giggle, giggle"]** *...Substances that can be lethal in small amounts appeal most to perpetrators. The ideal poison for a homicide is odorless, tasteless, difficult to detect, and a bearer of symptoms similar to naturally occurring diseases. It has become increasingly difficult to find a poison with all of these features,* [which is why cadmium was chosen] *since modern scientific methods and advances have made it easier to detect poisons. This article profiles the following poisons that have been used to perpetrate homicidal poisoning:* **arsenic**, [or other heavy metals] *cyanide, thallium, strychnine, aconitine, atropine, and* **antimony**. *Some "red flags" that indicate homicidal poisoning are sudden death; the association of a caregiver with other illnesses or deaths; whether the victim received medical treatment, appeared to recover, and then died later; caregiver access to restricted drugs or other chemicals; and caregiver isolation of the victim. The forensic toxicologist narrows the list of poisons that may have been used."* [Note the many parallels in Srila Prabhupada's case.]

INSIDIOUS AND VIRTUALLY UNDETECTABLE

Arsenic, strychnine, cyanide, curare, and other exotic poisons are routinely overlooked and go unrecognized, and heavy metals are even more rarely used in homicide (what to speak of cadmium, although there are a number of cases- see Ch. 9). The term for this is "insidious," namely, working or spreading harmfully in a subtle, treacherous, or stealthy manner. *Cadmium is a "masquerade" poison much like arsenic, and it is virtually undetectable.* In *Unnatural Death: Confessions of a Medical Examiner*, Dr. M. M. Baden explains that autopsies rarely can tell poison is present, and that separate tests for each possible specific poison are necessary but very expensive. Heavy metals are virtually invisible and usually missed by homicide investigators, physicians, coroners, and medical examiners. *For every murder by poisoning, 5-10 others go undetected, or a 10-15% detection rate.*

Asked why arsenic poisoning was not previously suspected in Napoleon's death, Ben Weider replied: *"...Henri Griffon, the poisons expert at the Paris police laboratory ...said that in no case of arsenic poisoning, and he has investigated many, did a doctor diagnose arsenic correctly and in time. The symptoms are characteristic of several diseases more familiar to doctors; one must see them in their totality to make the right diagnosis. Certainly a doctor is more comfortable with disease than with the idea of poison."* Homicide by chronic arsenic poisoning has been documented and prosecuted on many occasions, even though it is very difficult to diagnose. *Chronic cadmium poisoning is somewhat a rarity in the annals of criminal poisoning.* Srila Prabhupada's nefarious poisoning was planned and executed in a most sinister manner, carried out without arousing too much suspicion. But Lord Krishna arranged for it to be discovered and revealed. Even the best laid plans of mice and men are foiled by Providence.

CADMIUM POISONING RESEMBLES COMMON DISEASES

Srila Prabhupada seems to have had some degree of diabetes and kidney weakness for years prior to 1977, indicated by occasional swelling of bodily extremities (dropsy, or edema). Whoever master-minded Srila Prabhupada's cadmium poisoning probably knew that the resulting symptoms would closely resemble those of diabetes and kidney disease, or any number of other ailments. Thus it was next to impossible to discover. At www.toxnet.nlm.nih.gov it cautions *"persons with kidney disease may be hyper-susceptible to cadmium (compounds) and should be excluded from exposure."* Cadmium was a good choice of poison for Srila Prabhupada as it would be confused with his already existing health problems. Who would suspect? This hints at professional advice or involvement. Tamal was very intelligent and knew about arsenic poisoning (as recorded on tape in 1970.) Bhakticharu studied chemistry at university in Germany. Thorough investigation of the scene and circumstances, consideration of medical history, and comprehensive toxicology testing, progressing from one poison to another, are key to detection of poisoning. *Each poison must be specifically, individually tested for- or it will be missed.* This was never done during Srila Prabhupada's prolonged, mysterious, and persistent illness lasting 18 months. Only basic urine tests were done, e. g., for infections or diabetes.

CADMIUM: ACCIDENT, ENVIRONMENT, OCCUPATION?

Could Srila Prabhupada's poisoning be accidental where he

somehow ingested sufficient heavy metals to produce such high levels over 10 or more months? Scientific evaluations in previous chapters practically rules out any accident: **(1)** His sky-high levels in three hair tests are not seen in any other person in the scientific literatures involving accidents or environmental/ occupational exposure, as these levels are so lethal that no victim would have survived 10 months as did Srila Prabhupada. **(2)** The poisoning was slow and chronic, so how can there be an accidental exposure that remained constant up to 18 months while Srila Prabhupada's health unexplainably deteriorated and he moved to numerous different locations?

We must remember that the hair tests indicate high levels over 10 months or more– what consumer product, pollution, etc could have caused an average of ± 16 ppm hair cadmium? Others would also have been affected. So this idea is totally implausible. Environmental pollution or occupational hazards are also ruled out because no one else in Srila Prabhupada's entourage suffered his "disease." His cadmium levels were unique to he alone and the result of a deliberate, person-specific poisoning in food or drink. How could Srila Prabhupada alone be exposed to some environmental contamination when he was constantly surrounded by others, none of whom were exposed? *This was a pin-pointed, exclusive poisoning.* It is tiring to hear so many excuses of "ifs, thens, buts" from the GBC about how this astronomical cadmium level might have come from ceramic mugs, medicines, water, air, clothes, the Yamuna River, asteroids, or aliens. *If the GBC really wanted to find truth, why don't they test their own Srila Prabhupada hair samples and teeth that they have?* And settle the issue? With less time and money than all their books, videos, and cover-ups to fault the factual evidence that they deny with deceit and hypocrisy?

HOW MANY LETHAL DOSES WERE GIVEN?

We could not find any other examples in the scientific record of cadmium poisoning over a long time where someone had as high levels in their hair as did Srila Prabhupada. It was an unprecedented poisoning. And he "survived" these levels many months from <u>at least</u> Feb. to Nov. 1977. Was there a final lethal poisoning on Nov. 11? *("is the poison in the milk?")* Were earlier lethal poisonings given to Srila Prabhupada? Being a pure devotee with mystic powers, he had the power or means to overcome all physical obstacles and bodily attacks, including poisoning. On July 20, 1976, Feb. 26, 1977, May 16, 1977, and other dates he suffered sudden, intense health attacks (suspected lethal poisonings). Only after Srila Prabhupada revealed his poisoning on Nov. 9-10, 1977 did he decide to leave and go to his next service to Lord

Krishna. Toxicology and pathology experts will opine specifically on what 10 months of 15.75 ppm average cadmium would do to an 81 year old with perhaps some pre-existing diabetes and kidney problems. *These levels are unprecedented and lethal over that amount of time.* Srila Prabhupada was definitely maliciously, homicidally poisoned with sky-high levels of cadmium at levels of toxicity and morbidity that would kill an ordinary man much sooner than the months he was being poisoned.

Further expert opinions on these cadmium levels are forthcoming. It was not: **(1)** Due to any exogenous contaminant **(2)** Due to the water he drank (Ch. 47) **(3)** Due to the medicines he took (Ch. 28) **(4)** Due to the air, mustard oil, etc. / The question: ***Was Srila Prabhupada Poisoned?*** has now been conclusively answered, and it was clearly a lethal, homicidal, malicious poisoning that cannot be explained in any other way. *Cadmium levels this high only occur when one is given cadmium chemicals to ingest through food or drink as a homicidal poisoning.*

ADVANTAGES OF CADMIUM POISONING

(1) No gore **(2)** Weak can overcome the strong **(3)** No mess to clean up **(4)** Mental distancing from the act **(5)** Stealthy mechanism **(6)** Time to establish an alibi **(7)** Anybody is vulnerable **(8)** Don't have to confront the victim **(9)** Cadmium is virtually unsuspected, an ideal poison **(10)** Obtainable without rousing suspicions **(11)** Very toxic in small quantities **(12)** Is colorless, tasteless, and odorless **(13)** Can be hidden in food or drink **(14)** Has a delayed onset of action **(15)** Effects mimic many natural diseases **(16)** Is chemically stable **(17)** Suits those who are cowards.

CADMIUM HAIR TESTS: FACTS SUMMARY

Three new tests of Srila Prabhupada's hair in 2002-05 revealed sky-high levels of the heavy metal cadmium from Feb. to Nov. 1977, about 10 months, but medical symptoms unique to cadmium poisoning indicate poisoning began in mid-1976, for a total of up to 18 months. The arsenic was secondary. Chronic cadmium poisoning with sub-acute episodes was the poisoning methodology. Cadmium levels were 194-311 times above the average normal, which is clearly homicidal. These levels are "off the chart" and would be lethal within a short period of time. If not for Krishna's choosing when Srila Prabhupada would depart, we could say Srila Prabhupada was removed by those who wanted him gone. The secretive poisoners' false hopes that a quarter century had dissolved the molecular needle hidden in the chemical haystack has been miraculously shattered by these hair tests. Russia's most famous serial killer admitted at his execution that he never expected the advancement of forensic science by which he was caught and convicted. Similarly, Srila

Prabhupada's "cold case" cadmium poisoning was amazingly and unexpectedly unveiled by advancements in forensic science as Lord Krishna's special arrangement. The GBC resolution, *"There is no evidence at this time to support the allegations of poisoning of Srila Prabhupada,"* makes a mockery of ISKCON leadership.

(1) The GBC failed to complete tests on two samples of Srila Prabhupada's 1977 hair, abandoning them. These samples were located and forwarded to Dr. Morris, an expert in NAA. Hari Sauri das gave all background details on these two samples and confirmed their authenticity. **(2)** Dr. Morris executed two NAA tests in 2002, finding sky-high levels of cadmium. Prime suspect Tamal quit his body, hampering the investigation by his permanent unavailability for interviews or depositions. A third hair test in 2005 by Dr. Morris again confirmed sky-high levels of cadmium. **(3)** Average cadmium in the 3 tests was 15.75 ppm, about 250 X the 0.064 ppm normal average of "unexposed" persons, as ascertained from 19 studies. Srila Prabhupada had 41 X the cadmium found in the average industrially-exposed person (0.387 ppm), ascertained from another set of studies. Srila Prabhupada's hair had 4 X more cadmium than the worst hazardous waste dump, 15,000 X more cadmium than in most drinking water (and 400 X more than the EPA allowable limit). **(4)** There is no plausible explanation how Srila Prabhupada acquired these high cadmium levels by environmental pollution, accidental exposure, or occupational hazard. Scientific studies and many expert opinions point to homicidal poisoning and that these cadmium levels are *unprecedented and "off the chart."* **(5)** Two more Srila Prabhupada hair tests from an earlier time were normal, comparing pre- and post-poisoning levels. **(6)** Cadmium was the primary poison; arsenic and antimony were secondary. **(7)** Other Srila Prabhupada hair samples and teeth can be tested for further confirmations.

(8) The target organ for cadmium toxicity via oral exposure is the kidney, causing irreversible renal tubular damage or kidney failure with the appearance of malnutrition, starvation, indigestion, diarrhea, vomiting, and stomach pain, *exactly Srila Prabhupada's medical symptoms.* **(9)** Cadmium poisoning is very difficult to recognize, and looks like common diseases such as kidney disease and a normal "old-age" deterioration of physical health. **(10)** Many cadmium compounds are colorless, tasteless, odorless, a white crystalline powder that is very soluble in drink, food, or medicine. It is readily obtainable and virtually undetectable. **(11)** Srila Prabhupada's case was a mix of chronic and sub-acute poisoning, or small doses punctuated with heavier doses. Leaving New York, July 1976, there was a sharp, sudden illness with no appetite, weakness of the legs, mucus and coughing, indigestion, vomiting. **(12)** By mid-1977 he displayed photophobia, conjunctivitis, hoarse voice, rhinitis, and constant mucus, which are not diabetes or kidney disease symptoms but which are uniquely associated with cadmium poisoning (Ch. 31). **(13)** Hari Sauri cut *Sample D* (19.9 ppm) in early March 1977, was ±0.5 cm long or 3 weeks of growth, and represents blood deposits from about mid-Feb. to early March 1977. *Sample D* reflects the Feb. 26, 1977 massive cadmium poisoning.

(14) Cadmium was found again in *Sample A* (12.4 ppm) and *Q-2* (14.9 ppm). Both these samples were found in the hairclippers, accumulated as a mixture from numerous hair cuttings from Nov. 1976 to early Sept. 1977, reflecting average cadmium over 10 months, or a *"poisoning for a long time."* Because half the cadmium is eliminated from the body after 17-30 years, whatever cadmium Srila Prabhupada had in early Sept. 1977 would still be 99% there when he departed on Nov. 14, 1977. Even with no further poisoning after early Sept. 1977, his cadmium would be about the same Nov. 14, 1977. Thus Srila Prabhupada's *average* hair cadmium was 14.9 ppm for one year, Nov. 1976 to Nov. 1977, as seen from *Q-2*. **(15)** Cadmium levels varied during this year. Once a level was reached, however, it never significantly declined, as in poisonings with arsenic that has a shorter half-life. **(16)** But there was further cadmium poisoning in Srila Prabhupada's last 2-3 months because it is clearly indicated in his health history, seen in the continued health downturns and in the poison whispers. Thus Srila Prabhupada's cadmium levels would simply rise with each successive dose due to its accumulative nature and extremely long half-life. **(17)** 2.6 ppm arsenic and 16 ppm cadmium in the hair of a 70 lb, very ill, elderly Srila Prabhupada, is a much more serious poisonous intoxication than if in a healthy, 200 lb person.

CHAPTER 8:
POISONING TIMELINE

HAIR TESTS WITH ELEVATED CADMIUM LEVELS

Samples A, Q-1, Q-2 were taken from accumulated hairs stuck on/in Srila Prabhupada's hair clipper blades. *Sample D* was cut in Bombay, early March 1977, and we estimate there were perhaps a few more hair clippings after that. Dates of the hair tests, their results, and quantities are given above. This will help to understand the poisoning timeline.

Srila Prabhupada's health suddenly and mysteriously began an inexorable and accelerating decline from mid-1976 until late 1977.

ID	Date	Mass	Size	Tested	Source	ARS	ANT	MER	CAD
D	Mar77	.00072	½ cm	3.4.02	Melbrne	0.640	0.661	3.72	19.9
A	1977	.00064	1-2 cm	4.15.02	DaiviSh	0.200	0.186	5.16	12.4
Q-2	1977	.00012	2-3mm	7.26.05	Clippers	0.85	n/a	n/a	14.9
Q-1	1977	.00130	<2mm	1.6.99	Clippers	2.6	n/a	n/a	n/a

POISONING TIMELINE KEY EVENTS AND DATES

SP: Nov. 9, 1977: *"Hothat hoye galo. (It all happened suddenly.)"* The hair tests are proof of massive cadmium poisoning from at least Feb. 1977 until Nov. 14, 1977, and medical symptoms indicate poisoning may have started as early as May 1976, with the first drastic episode on July 20, 1976. We note below the key events in the poisoning timeline:

(1) Suspicions are that Srila Prabhupada's cadmium poisoning might have begun as low level poisoning on May 4, 1976 upon suspect Tamal's arrival in Hawaii. After May 1976 we see in Srila Prabhupada the classic cadmium poisoning symptoms, very similar to, albeit less severe, those in the severe health decline after Feb. 26, 1977, a date when the sky-high cadmium poisoning is confirmed by hair tests. These symptoms included persistent heavy mucus congestion, weakness, no appetite, and nausea.

(2) From May to July 1976, Srila Prabhupada had weakness, loss of appetite, heart palpitations, and persistent mucus with cough, cold/flu, bronchitis and rhinitis. **(3)** On July 20, 1976 in New York, as Tamal's guest, Srila Prabhupada became extremely ill as he left on a flight to London, lying prostate on three seats and remaining seriously ill and weak. For weeks he was quite bedridden and thereafter he walked little and with difficulty, partially, slowly recovering while away from Tamal over the next 7 months, travelling in Europe and Asia. Harikesa wrote Tamal on July 24, 1976: *"Srila Prabhupada has been very sick since he has come. On the way back from the airport he vomited every 5 minutes, we had to stop the car. He did not eat for 3 days and is very weak."* Tests of 1976 hair or teeth would confirm what is suspected: *Srila Prabhupada's cadmium poisoning began in May to July, 1976.* July 20 appears to have been a very serious episode of poisoning.

(4) Tamal joined Srila Prabhupada in Mayapur on Feb. 14, 1977, became his personal secretary Feb. 22, and Feb. 26 Srila Prabhupada became deathly ill, moaning for days in bed. The very serious July 1976 and Feb. 1977 health attacks were in Tamal's presence, and he was absent in between. **(5)** After Feb. 1977 Srila Prabhupada no longer went on morning walks, walking at all was difficult, he ate very little. **(6)** Srila

Prabhupada's hair was regularly cut with his personal hairclippers every 3-4 weeks and some of it was saved by devotees as sacred relics. Dr. Morris tested hair *Sample D,* finding 19.9 ppm cadmium. This hair grew from mid-Feb. to early March, 1977. **(7)** Afterwards, the health condition declined steadily, with no appetite, digestion, and significant weight loss. Mucus congestion was present almost constantly. In March-April 1977 Bhakticaru became Tamal's primary assistant and a nurse-caretaker to Srila Prabhupada. **(8)** May 7, 1977 Srila Prabhupada flew to Delhi. Feeling stronger, he walked down the plane stairs himself. Srila Prabhupada went to Hrishikesh. He began to feel better and eat again.

(9) May 16, 1977: His health suddenly, severely worsened and he rushed back to Vrindaban, thinking to die soon. This was another acute poisoning episode. **(10)** Srila Prabhupada's health languished all summer of 1977, punctuated by further minor downturns. **(11)** SP did not walk nor eat hardly at all. **(12)** At the end of Aug. 1977 SP flew to London, bedded down flat in the car and plane, then he was carried about in a palanquin. **(13)** *Samples A* and *Q-2* confirmed 12.4 to 14.9 ppm cadmium; both samples came from SP's personal hair clippers used Nov. 1976 to Sept. 1977. These values are an average for 10 months. The cadmium tests show ± 250 times average normal levels. **(14)** Sept. 8 there was a medical emergency of inability to pass urine; SP had a minor surgery. **(15)** SP returned to Bombay on Sept. 13, but Sept. 15 brought another health "crisis" and SP was now fully bedridden. He took food supplements. The excessive mucus worsens whenever he eats or drinks anything. **(16)** He went to Vrindaban Oct. 1 and asked all disciples to come see him a final time (this message was suppressed); his health is the worst. **(17)** Oct. 25-26 he took 3 makharadhwaja doses but then discontinued it. **(18)** Nov. 9-10 he disclosed his thoughts that he has been poisoned and his caretakers openly discussed homicidal poisoning. **(19)** Nov. 11 there are tape recorded murmurs and whispers by caretakers about poisoning, and Srila Prabhupada departs Nov. 14.

MISDATED TAPES?

The poison whispers (see Part 3) indicate a final poisoning on Nov. 11, 1977, and Srila Prabhupada departed 3 days later. Why would it take 3 days to work? We see on Nov. 12-14 there were many more conversations, something unusual if a final poisoning took place on Nov. 11 *("The poison's going down").* One plausible explanation is the last 3 tapes (T-44, 45, 46, Nov. 11-14) were dated out of order and that the whispers/ final poisoning were actually on Nov.13. This better explains how the last poison whisper "poisoning for a long time" and "get ready to go" fit in with a final poisoning. The poison whispers may have taken place Nov. 13, not Nov. 11. Also, Bhagwat Maharaja has documented that Narayan Maharaja had significant discussions with Srila Prabhupada in his last two days, but these discussions are unexplainably not on any tapes.

Our research shows that a conversation at 3:10 pm, supposedly Oct. 8, was on Oct. 6 instead. ConvBk Vol 35, p. 121-4 appear to belong after p. 105, and p. 125 should come after p. 138, being chronological errors. This is clearly ascertained by studying the sequence of events, speakers, and content of the conversations. The morning of Oct. 8, BCS was sent to consult with Narayan Maharaja; however, the ConvBk shows a discussion about the two allopathic Vrindaban doctors occurring at 3:10 PM on the 8th, wherein BCS had not yet arrived from Mayapur. This discussion really took place on the Oct. 6, as per *TKG's Diary*. Also Tamal notes Narayan Maharaja's visit on late Oct. 8 as before Jayatirtha's arrival, whereas the ConvBk (based on the tapes' dating) have them reversed. Also, Tamal records that right after Srila Prabhupada discussed Sri Lanka with Hansadutta, telling him to develop it like New Vrindaban, Srila Prabhupada called Brahmananda from the back of the room and told him to develop Africa and try to bring back Pusta Krishna. However, in the ConvBk, these two events are separated by 12 pages and a dozen "breaks," but the two incidents appear to be consecutive.

CHART CORRELATES HAIR TESTS WITH HEALTH HISTORY

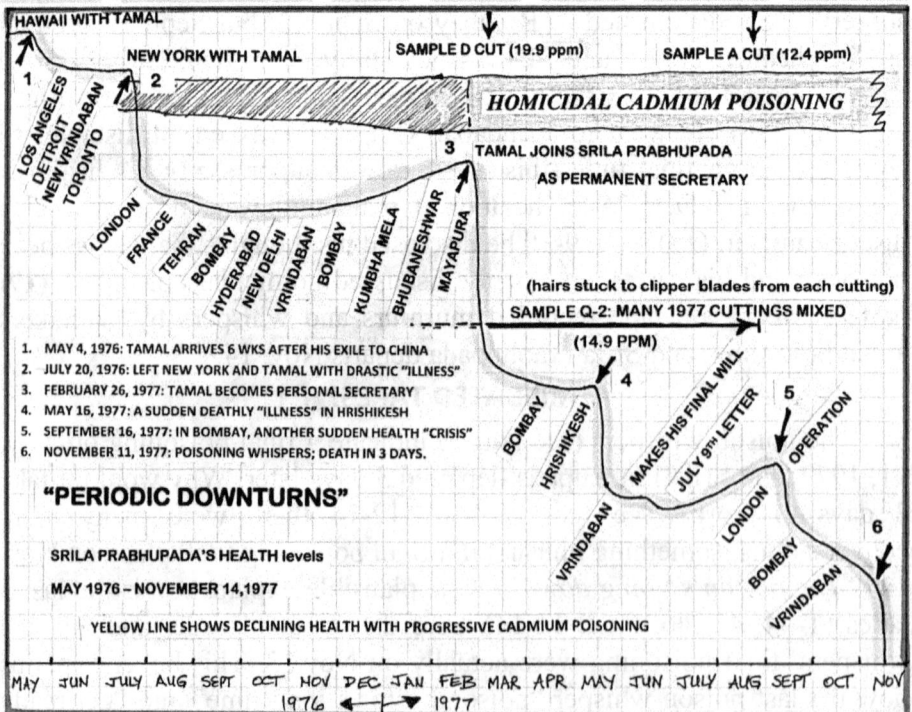

HAWAII WITH TAMAL

NEW YORK WITH TAMAL

SAMPLE D CUT (19.9 ppm)

SAMPLE A CUT (12.4 ppm)

1

2

HOMICIDAL CADMIUM POISONING

LOS ANGELES
DETROIT
NEW VRINDABAN
TORONTO

3

TAMAL JOINS SRILA PRABHUPADA

AS PERMANENT SECRETARY

LONDON
FRANCE
TEHRAN
HYDERABAD
NEW DELHI
VRINDABAN
BOMBAY
KUMBHA MELA
BHUBANESHWAR
MAYAPURA

(hairs stuck to clipper blades from each cutting)

SAMPLE Q-2: MANY 1977 CUTTINGS MIXED

(14.9 PPM)

1. MAY 4, 1976: TAMAL ARRIVES 6 WKS AFTER HIS EXILE TO CHINA
2. JULY 20, 1976: LEFT NEW YORK AND TAMAL WITH DRASTIC "ILLNESS"
3. FEBRUARY 26, 1977: TAMAL BECOMES PERSONAL SECRETARY
4. MAY 16, 1977: A SUDDEN DEATHLY "ILLNESS" IN HRISHIKESH
5. SEPTEMBER 16, 1977: IN BOMBAY, ANOTHER SUDDEN HEALTH "CRISIS"
6. NOVEMBER 11, 1977: POISONING WHISPERS; DEATH IN 3 DAYS.

BOMBAY
HRISHIKESH
MAKES HIS FINAL WILL
JULY 9TH LETTER

4

5

OPERATION

"PERIODIC DOWNTURNS"

SRILA PRABHUPADA'S HEALTH levels

MAY 1976 – NOVEMBER 14, 1977

VRINDABAN
LONDON
BOMBAY

6

VRINDABAN

YELLOW LINE SHOWS DECLINING HEALTH WITH PROGRESSIVE CADMIUM POISONING

MAY   JUN   JULY   AUG   SEPT   OCT   NOV   DEC   JAN   FEB   MAR   APR   MAY   JUN   JULY   AUG   SEPT   OCT   NOV
1976 ←   → 1977

Then the talks about the two different Dr. Ghosh's (Allahabad, Kodaikanal) is at the end of the tape marked Oct. 10, yet Tamal says it takes place around noon on Oct. 12. Perhaps the end of the Oct. 10 tape was recorded on Oct. 12 because someone noticed it had not been used up, fully recorded? Several caretakers put tapes were in and out of the recorder and there was bound to be confusion and errors. The ConvBk has parts of Oct. 12 conversations out of order. The correct sequence is p. 199-200, then 181-2, then 201-212. Tapes were often misdated or recorded out of chronological sequence. Talks were recorded on one tape, the next conversation on another tape, and then back to the first tape, etc. The tape recordings were often "time-line jumbled."

Multi-day tapes were sometimes labeled when recording was started, and sometimes when recording was finished. Tapes were accidentally re-recorded, so side A was actually *after* side B and the original side A was over-recorded and lost. Mistakes happened as Tamal engaged others to do things for him, and he was rarely the one recording tapes. Sometimes the wrong tape would be put in the recorder. Days later several tapes were labelled at the same time and the dates were wrong. Ranjit das in 1999, as the Bhaktivedanta Archives' senior editor, confirmed the many misdates in the ConvBks. E. g., a Feb. 18, 1977 tape was actually March 18, seen when a news article was read to Srila Prabhupada. Some tapes were off by 2 days, even 30 days. Research shows that dates on the last tapes were jumbled or incorrect. Thus the poison whispers may very well have been on Nov. 13, not Nov. 11.

CHAPTER 9:
CADMIUM POISONING CASES

WAS CADMIUM POISONING EVEN POSSIBLE IN 1977?

The GBC insists the idea of homicidal cadmium poisoning is ludicrous because: (1) it was unknown in 1977, (2) and there are no such cases on record. *Both are totally untrue.* Knowledge of poisoning methodologies were readily available in 1977 in literatures and medical publications. The 1960's discovery of Napoleon's high arsenic levels in hair brought much attention to the subject of poisoning. Those involved in the 1977 poisoning may well have read the 1972 book *Who Poisoned Napoleon?* From *Toxicology of the Eye* by WM Grant (1974): *"Ingestion of cadmium salts has caused severe and sometimes fatal poisoning."* Many sources confirm cadmium is entirely suitable for homicidal poisoning and was well known as such before 1977. Many cadmium poisonings were studied from the 1950's and the most well-known is Japan's "itai-itai" incident involving hundreds in the 1960's with cadmium poisoning of rice fields. That there have been no cadmium homicide cases is also not true at all. We found many of them (below).

FOURTEEN CADMIUM POISONING CASES

(1) Turgut Ozal, the President of Turkey (1989-1993) died suddenly Apr. 17, 1993. A suspicious heart attack indicated an assassination by deliberate poisoning. His remains were exhumed Oct. 2, 2012 and a leaked autopsy report revealed a high level of "strychnine creatine" (leads to respiratory arrest in 20 minutes and could cause a heart attack). The autopsy report was destroyed by the authorities, test results went missing, and an inquiry interrupted. The Kurdish separatists claimed Ozal was poisoned by the Turkish special services. An autopsy of his exhumed remains revealed four poisons. The banned insecticide DDT was 10 X the normal. *"Experts also detected the presence of cadmium in his body. In addition, experts also found the radioactive elements americium and polonium. Experts said his body was weakened with americium and polonium over a long period of time, and with the use of DDT [and cadmium], ingested in food or drink, his death was accelerated."* **(2)** Aug. 8, 1995 the funeral for a prominent Moscow businessman was attended by the Russian prime minister and noted dignitaries. Ivan Kivelidi and his secretary were *killed with cadmium* smeared on a phone and in their tea.

(3). John Harris Trestrail III, of the Center for the Study of Criminal Poisoning, in his database of 900 poisonings worldwide, documented one case of murder by cadmium. **(4).** July 23, 1981: Two youths (14 and 15) gave cadmium chloride mixed in a drink to 11 children who suffered as a result, but no one died. **(5)** John Creamer was arrested Dec. 19, 2002 in Florida and indicted for his wife's murder. *"Cadmium toxicity and the death resulting from that is extremely rare. This is my first case. We are dealing here with a combination. So it's not the pure cadmium, but I've given the cause of death as combination of cadmium, alcohol and Xanax. The combination would cause suppression of the respiratory center."* Searching his home, deputies found three containers of cadmium. Before her death, Jayne Creamer had told her sisters, hairdresser and others she feared her husband had been poisoning her. Detectives accused him of slipping cadmium into his wife's drink in a romantic getaway.

(6) In early 2019 a California chemical engineer, David Xu, was charged with lacing a colleague's water with cadmium, which was not fatal. He was caught on a video recording. **(7)** Cadmium (7 X normal) is one of the toxic substances that Italian prosecutors detected in the blood of Imane Fadil after her death from organ failure in hospital. The 33-year-old Moroccan-born model had been a key witness in the "bunga bunga" sex party trial of former Italian PM Silvio Berlusconi. She died in hospital on Mar. 1, 2019, and suspicions that she was poisoned are under investigation. She shared suspicions she had been poisoned after falling gravely ill in Jan. 2019. **(8)** Robert W Hall describes a postmortem laboratory analysis of the sub-occipital proximal hair of Patrick H. Sherrill, who, on Aug. 20, 1986 committed mass murder, and then committed suicide. Akathisia, alcohol, and prior psychiatric history were eliminated as possible explanations of his behavior. The analysis revealed very elevated levels of cadmium and lead. An underlying, immunotoxic biochemical pathology due to heavy metal poisoning may have affected inhibitory control mechanisms. (PsycINFO, 2012)

(9) Yukai Yang, a chemistry student at Lehigh University in Pennsylvania was charged for poisoning his roommate in Dec. 2018. He mixed thallium and cadmium in drinks, food, and mouthwash, and the victim still suffers ill effects. **(10)** In 2018 a 57-year-old man was arrested in the deaths of 21 co-workers at a valve manufacturing plant in Germany. The suspect "Klaus O." was convicted in 2019, sentenced to life in prison for poisoning his colleagues by spiking their sandwiches with *high levels of cadmium and mercury,* caught on a surveillance camera. In a search of his home police discovered a makeshift laboratory where they found a number of heavy metals, including lead acetate, cadmium, lead, and mercury. Two suffered serious kidney damage. A third has brain damage and is currently in a vegetative state, unlikely to recover. One eventually died. **(11)** Jan. 16, 2003: Three Pennsylvania family members were to be exhumed with suspicions of cadmium poisoning in 1995 and 1997. Ann Nagg's body had already been exhumed in connection with the homicidal cadmium poisoning of a fourth person, Russell Repine.

(12) July 8, 2019: The son of Nigeria's Muslim leader Sheikh Ibrahim al-Zakzaky warned about the deteriorating health of the 66-year-old cleric, who has been held in detention along with his wife for more than three years. He was shocked by his father's worsening medical condition after visiting him, stressing that he needed to be immediately hospitalized as "large and dangerous quantities of lead and cadmium have been found in his blood." Islamic Human Rights Commission (UK) received reports Zakzaky's health had further worsened. IHRC sent a medical team to Nigeria to examine Zakzaky and wife and said the treatment they require can only be accessed outside Nigeria. Islamic Movement in Nigeria also said he was poisoned in prison and required urgent medical care abroad. **(13)** Aslan Bzhania accused the leader of Abkhazia (on the Black Sea), Raul Khajimda, of poisoning him. He is the top challenger to incumbent Khajimda. Along with 2 security guards, he was hospitalized in Moscow. *"According to the results of the analysis conducted in a Munich laboratory, heightened levels of mercury and aluminum were found in Bzhania's blood, as well as a heightened level of benzodiazepines and cadmium."* (May 17, 2019)

(14) Suspected murder: ***Acute Cadmium Ingestion*** (Buckler Et Al 1986) *"A woman (age 17) was admitted to hospital with facial swelling and vomiting. She was too ill to provide any history. She had facial, pharyngeal and neck swelling and was hypotensive. Subsequent gastric washout (roughly 3 hours after ingestion) produced a white crystalline material confirmed to be cadmium chloride. She suffered a respiratory arrest, becoming hypothermic [...] Full supportive measures including chelation treatment... were unsuccessful, and she died 30 hours after admission... There was hemorrhagic necrosis of the stomach, duodenum and jejunum, focal hepatic necrosis and slight pancreatic hemorrhage. At autopsy the following cadmium concentrations were measured: blood 23 mg/l, urine 17 mg/l, liver 0.4 µg/kg wet tissue, lung, 0.2 µg/kg. The patient had ingested a massive dose of 150 gm of cadmium chloride, and although the initial diagnosis was delayed, it seems unlikely that any treatment would have prevented the membrane dysfunction and destruction of tissue. The case illustrates the catastrophic effects of ingested cadmium on organ function."*

Fourteen cases of cadmium poisonings. *Note:* 90% of poisonings go undetected, so we can assume hundreds of cadmium homicide poisonings have taken place worldwide in recent times. Political assassinations worldwide appear to be using cadmium as one ingredient in a mixture with others, just as was done with Srila Prabhupada's heavy metals cocktail which included arsenic and antimony.

ACCIDENTAL CADMIUM POISONINGS ARE COMMON

Still, aside from those who develop cancer or kidney failure after many years of environmental or occupational exposure, quick death from cadmium poisoning is not common. Most human cadmium studies and case histories involved typical environmental exposure and a few instances of occupational exposure wherein very long-term effects resulted from low-level chronic poisoning. The body of medical literature shows cadmium to be a rare poisoning agent. But using cadmium salts to poison someone is very feasible, it is very poisonous and can kill very effectively and secretly. We have listed 14 examples above, a list that is not complete. By the 1940's cadmium became prolific in modern industrialized society and accidental cadmium poisoning was frequent, and it was soon understood as very poisonous. Cadmium poisoning studies began with Friberg/1950, Bonnell/1955, and cadmium's causing critical, life-threatening kidney malfunction was well known in medical circles by 1977. Most cadmium poisoning studies focus on hazardous occupational or environmentally contaminated situations, such as Polish factory pollution.

Accidental cadmium poisoning examples: (**1**) Dr. Aggarwal, an Indian toxicologist, reported that in Japan a patient died when he was mistakenly given an injection of cadmium chloride instead of calcium bromide. (**2**) In 1960's Japan, a large-scale soil and water contamination resulted in "itai-itai" (ouch-ouch) disease with brittle bones, great pain, kidney failure. Residents on the Jinzu River also had osteomalacia due to disturbed phosphate reabsorption resulting from atrophy of the proximal tubules of the kidney. This came from the upstream Mitsui Mining's industrial cadmium pollution in the river, used for drinking and rice field irrigation. (**3**) Cadmium pollution-related disease was found in New Zealand due to unregulated aerial spraying with cadmium pesticides for decades, with large areas of agricultural land having many times the acceptable limits, resulting in contaminated produce. Especially root crops such as turnips and potatoes absorb cadmium from the soil. NZ potatoes should only be eaten sparingly. (**4**) In 2001 a de-forested area in Honduras had caused naturally cadmium-contaminated soil to run-off and spoil a local town's water supplies. Over 400 were admitted to hospitals and thus far 11 died with kidney failure symptoms.

(**5**) A hospital patient was accidentally injected with cadmium chloride instead of calcium chloride; and he died. (**6**) Consumption of cadmium contaminated oysters in Tasmania led to nausea and vomiting in victims. (**7**) Fatalities have resulted from using oxy-gas flame to cut cadmium-plated objects, or grilling with cadmium-coated refrigerator racks, or using high temperature flames with cadmium-bearing solder.

(8) In 2016 there were news stories about cadmium plated or cadmium alloy costume jewelry responsible for illnesses all over the world. Cheap jewelry was traced to remote Chinese factories where jewelry manufacturing costs were lowered by use of cadmium due to its low melting point. Soldering fumes and dust caused much disease. **(9)** Medical Case History: Adult, Acute Cadmium Inhalation (Lucas et al., 1980) *"A welder worked for 30 minutes with an oxyacetylene torch and silver solder. He was in a large airy building, high ceiling, large open doors... He became dyspnoeic with a persistent non-productive cough within hours. His symptoms worsened and he died 5 days later. Both lungs showed changes typical of acute pneumonitis. The rod of silver solder had 20% cadmium. The case illustrates that death from cadmium fume inhalation can occur in an apparently well-ventilated environment, particularly if the presence of cadmium is not suspected."*

(10) Another mass cadmium poisoning case (BBC, Sept. 18, 2012): *"Sri Lanka Kidney Disease Blamed on Farm Chemicals:"* a study of thousands of farmers who developed serious health problems pointed to chemical pesticides and fertilizers. 15% of the mostly rice farmers in one province suffered with various stages of kidney failure. Investigations by testing blood, urine, tissue, and hair samples suggested arsenic and cadmium had contaminated food, air, or water. Cadmium is found in some fertilizers and arsenic in some pesticides, most from China, notorious for dangerous chemicals. Central American farmers are also noticing a similar "epidemic" of kidney disease problems.

(11) Mikheil Shaakashvili, former president of Georgia, was found in Dec. 2022 by his medical team to have been poisoned in prison with high levels of a bevy of heavy metals: arsenic, bismuth, barium, and mercury. Exotic cocktails of heavy metals in poisonings is a creative affair, and cadmium would have been a logical choice for anyone with some chemistry background. To say, "it was not possible in 1976 because it was unknown," is another attempt at creating doubts and disinformation.

ABOUT CADMIUM POISONING AND SYMPTOMS

Cadmium is a naturally occurring metal used in various chemical forms in metallurgical and other industrial processes, in alloys, pigments, fluorescent lighting, batteries, motor bearings, plastics, chemical reagents, solders, galvanization, electroplating. Cadmium is in pesticides, phosphate fertilizers, and electronic components and nuclear reactor control rods. Cadmium (and arsenic) are by-products of lead, zinc or copper mining. Pure cadmium is rare; its common compounds cadmium acetate, chloride, sulfate are most soluble, odorless, tasteless, colorless, extremely toxic. defiled by civilization's touch. Cadmium was safely locked up in nature prior to modern industry, exposure negligible by diet, water or air. Cadmium is now regulated with fewer poisoning episodes. Since the early 1950's, when the hazards of cadmium exposure were recognized, the toxic effects of cadmium have been better understood. Toxicological properties of the several different salts and oxides of cadmium are similar, although differences in absorption and distribution lead to different effect levels. Cadmium salts, oxides, and the Cd+2 ion are all soluble to various degrees. Cadmium is a cumulative toxicant and can be absorbed by the body via air, water, food, dust, fumes, or soil through breathing, ingestion, and the skin. Once the accumulation rate in the body exceeds the rate of excretion, and the critical concentration is exceeded in the kidneys, detrimental health effects follow.

The sky-high cadmium findings hair demanded research of medical literature for chronic cadmium poisoning symptoms, especially those not typical in Diabetes Type 2 or kidney failure. Srila Prabhupada *clearly had all the signs of chronic cadmium poisoning in his medical symptoms.* (Ch. 31) **Toxicity:** Cadmium is extremely toxic, with acceptable levels *one tenth* that of most of the other toxic metals. Its effects are many, but it mainly affects the kidneys, the cardiovascular system, and causes cancer. Cadmium has no known beneficial biological function or effect. **Degenerative Diseases:** Cadmium is involved in all of the major diseases of our time, including cancer, diabetes, arthritic syndromes, heart disease, kidney disease, and others. Cadmium replaces zinc in the body, required for over 100 critical enzymes, including those needed for proper immune system activity, digestion, cardiovascular health, etc.

CADMIUM FOCUSES ON THE KIDNEYS

Cadmium poisoning most frequently affects the kidneys, and once cadmium-induced proteinuria is detected, it is usually irreversibly progressive. Dr. Friberg, who did many studies on heavy metals: *"When discussing the kidney damage from cadmium, it is important we make it clear we are talking about serious, but often insidious effects on the vital organs. The kidney has a reserve capacity but once this is consumed, symptoms may appear in swift succession and the condition of the patient then deteriorates rapidly."* The critical concentration level of 200 ppm cadmium in the renal cortex, when reached by accumulations over time, signifies a descent into kidney failure/disease. Severe cadmium-induced renal damage may develop into chronic renal failure and uremia at which point dialysis or kidney operation is needed (which was Srila Prabhupada's diagnosis by Dr. Khurana, Aug. 1977).

Cadmium-induced renal damage is compounded due to there being no medical treatment for cadmium accumulation in the kidney. Recently, chelating techniques were found for cadmium poisoning, the first sign of which is decreased reabsorption of filtered low-molecular-weight proteins, indicating damage to renal tubules. Even after exposure ends, damage continues. Cadmium affects kidney vitamin D metabolism with subsequent disturbances in calcium balance and bone density. Tamal wrote, June 7, 1977: *"Unfortunately His Divine Grace's health has taken a turn for the worst. Prabhupada's body is practically worn out and all of the internal organs are no longer functioning properly. This includes the kidneys, the liver and the heart."* Scientific studies confirm cadmium poisoning targets these organs, just as Tamal said.

OTHER EFFECTS OF CADMIUM POISONING

Toxicological Profile: Cadmium, US Dept Health/ Human Services (1999): **(1)** Animals had birth defects, many other negative physiological effects due to cadmium poisoning. **(2)** Cadmium is toxic to a wide range of organs and tissues, but primarily the kidneys/liver. **(3)** Cadmium alters zinc, iron, selenium, copper metabolism. **(4)** Cadmium reduces the blood's glycogen levels and increase blood glucose levels. **(5)** Lung damage follows air inhalation or gastrointestinal ingestion of cadmium, often related to liver/ kidney damage. **(6)** Gastrointestinal irritation with nausea, vomiting occur at higher cadmium doses. **(7)** Cadmium poisoning increases blood pressure. **(8)** Cadmium causes anemia due to reduction of iron uptake and absorption, resulting in weakness. **(9)** Cadmium may lead to painful and debilitating bone disease with loss of calcium, phosphate and causes gastrointestinal tract atrophy, reducing ability to absorb essential elements such as calcium, phosphates. **(10)** Cadmium accumulates in the liver (and kidneys), causing liver damage and death at higher levels. **(11)** Decreased body weight, rates of growth (incl. hair) are common findings. **(12)** Many cancers are related to cadmium. **(13)** Majority of studies focus on effects of occupational/ environmental cadmium exposure, so effects of deliberate, higher levels in homicidal poisonings are not as well understood. **(14)** Cadmium levels in blood, urine, liver, kidney, hair, other tissues are used as biological exposure indicators. Blood cadmium levels are more indicative of recent exposure than whole body burdens. Urine cadmium levels primarily reflect total body burden of cadmium. Hair reliably indicates cadmium body burden, esp. at higher levels. Exogenous hair contamination is primarily in those exposed at lower levels but not usually in hair cut close to the scalp. **(15)** Liver & kidney tissues accumulate cadmium, measured by NAA or X-ray fluorescence analysis.

PART TWO:
PRABHUPADA TALKS OF POISONING

In his Vrindaban, India private quarters on Nov. 9-10, 1977, Srila Prabhupada surprised everyone by stating he thought he was being poisoned, and he repeated this twice more. He and his caretakers engaged in lengthy, full-voice, bedside discussions about his being poisoned, not by medicine, but by someone with malicious, homicidal intentions. These talks are called the "poison discussions." Srila Prabhupada's statements carry great weight and for many are the strongest evidence that Srila Prabhupada was poisoned. (Ch. 15). Since the words of His Divine Grace are of the utmost importance to his followers, who accept his words as absolute, faultless, and truth, they are the evidential foundation of Srila Prabhupada's poisoning. Since the following transcripts of recorded conversations are the actual words of Srila Prabhupada and his caretakers, and because they are extensively discussing with Srila Prabhupada about him being *maliciously* poisoned, it is the epicenter of the poison issue. The Bhaktivedanta Archives Vedabase has recently completed their VedaBase translations of all 1977 Bengali or Hindi portions. These foreign language parts of the poison discussions were translated in *SHPM* (1999), but afterwards a more complete translation of tapes T-44, 45 and 46 from His Divine Grace's final days was made by a well-educated, 22 year Calcutta resident Bengali who knows Hindi and Bengali fluently. Hindi professional teachers and translators assisted him, and Naveen Krishna das, a former GBC and Indian national, supervised, reviewed and confirmed these new translations. *Key parts from these poison discussions are excerpted in ten sections in the following chapters with the English translations to the Hindi or Bengali portions which are included only in Appendix 2.*

Much of the Bengali and Hindi conversation regarding poisoning is between Srila Prabhupada and the Calcutta *kaviraja* Damodara Shastri, who generally spoke in Hindi with Srila Prabhupada and BCS, whereas BCS spoke in either Hindi or Bengali, and all of them also speak in English, so the three languages are intertwined. There has been little disagreement over the translations because they are quite obvious and clear. A native of India who was born and raised with the language can easily understand the subtle nuances of meaning in these conversations. Naveen Krishna das, a native of Delhi, stated from his own judgement that he has no doubt Srila Prabhupada was thinking that he was being poisoned. It is the *interpretation of the translations* that are debated, not the translations themselves. The phrase *"not that I am poisoned"* is reviewed in Ch. 11, where *the GBC deviously pulled this ONE phrase from the context of all the discussions, and twisted its meaning while ignoring the balance of the talks.* This is a deceitful cover-up, understood upon a closer look. We should give close attention to the words of the pure devotee and one whose consciousness cannot be adversely affected by the material energy or conditions. *"When a pure Vaishnava speaks, he speaks perfectly. How is this? His speech is managed by Krishna Himself from within the heart."* CC Mad 8.200 /See Appendix 6 for the <u>full</u> transcript and translations of the "poison discussions."

CHAPTER 10:
SOMEBODY HAS GIVEN ME POISON

On Nov. 9, 1977, Balarama Misra, a Vrindaban priest whom Srila Prabhupada had long known, came to visit. He offered to do a Tulasi leaf puja for Srila Prabhupada's recovery, and also asked for money to repair his Chaitanya Mahaprabhu temple. Suddenly, out of the blue, Srila Prabhupada chose this old acquaintance, a most unlikely person, to casually inform that *someone said that he has been poisoned*. Srila Prabhupada raises the issue himself, unprompted. We note that Shastri and Balarama Misra had also known each other for a long time.

SECTION ONE: MAHARAJA CALLED FOR ME (NOV. 9, 1977)

KAV (Shastri): (Time: 05:14) Here is Balarama Misra come to see you. Do you know him? (He) is from Chaitanya... **Balarama Misra (BM):** I am over here Maharaja. I am Balarama Misra, do you recognize me? **SP:** Yes. **BM:** I am known to kaviraja for long time. Well, yesterday I met him (kaviraja), he said, Maharaja (SP) has called for me. It is a great honor for me, that is, this way I get a chance to meet you. Because many days ago, when the deity had not been installed.

SP: Give him a chair. **BM:** Yes, yes Maharaja, it is here. I thought, if I could come and meet you. **SP:** Suddenly I fell sick. Everything was all right, I don't know what happened. Is work going on well? **BM:** Yes.

SRILA PRABHUPADA CALLED FOR BALARAMA MISRA

Srila Prabhupada had asked Shastri to request Balarama Misra to come see Srila Prabhupada about going to the Bombay ISKCON temple opening to officiate as a priest. Perhaps Srila Prabhupada also had planned to reveal his mind to Balarama Misra, whose son Dr. Sri Pran Gopal Acharya knew Srila Prabhupada very well in the 1960's when he was a college student in Vrindaban, and *who also came with his father and attended this meeting.* This is described by Gopal Acharya himself in the book *Our Srila Prabhupada: A Friend to All: "...Prabhupada became very ill. So a kaviraja who lived in Calcutta, named Damodar, attended to Prabhupada's treatment. Prabhupada sent a message to our residence to call Balarama Misra. Fortunately I also went. Prabhupada was in his room and told us in Bengali, 'Baba, we are...'"* (p. 225-8) Srila Prabhupada asked Balarama Misra to preside as the priest for the upcoming Bombay temple opening ceremonies. But Srila Prabhupada first confided *that he thought he was being poisoned.*

SECTION TWO: SOMEONE SAYS I HAVE BEEN POISONED

SP: (Whispers) **SP: Someone said that poison has been given. May be true. BM:** Hmm? **KAV:** What are you saying? **SP: Somebody says that someone has given poison. KAV:** To whom? **SP: To me.**

WHY TELL OUTSIDERS BEFORE DISCIPLES?

Why did Srila Prabhupada not raise this issue first with his own trusted and intimate disciples? Why choose Balarama Misra, whom Srila Prabhupada had not seen for a long time, and then the second person to know of it was the kaviraja, and both were outsiders? Why did Srila Prabhupada not simply tell Tamal, his personal secretary, or any one of his own disciples? The GBC argues against Srila Prabhupada telling outsiders first because he thought his disciples were the poisoners, as though the "poison theory" hinges on this detail, which of course it does not. Still, whoever he spoke to first or last (which is a side issue), Srila Prabhupada *is talking of actually being poisoned.* Being always perfectly guided by the Supersoul in every action and word, he made this shocking revelation to outsiders first, and then by default, to his caretakers. *The tapes were controlled by Tamal, so maybe Srila Prabhupada was trying to bypass the tapes that went missing under Tamal's care* (Volume 2.)

Srila Prabhupada's message seemingly was meant to reach beyond his caretakers. Did he circumvent his poisoners to ensure his disclosure got outside his rooms and past his caretakers?

Dr. Śrī Pran Gopal Acharya

Tamal had for many months already set up a very tight security cordon around Srila Prabhupada, who was practically quarantined. Only those screened by Tamal were allowed to see Srila Prabhupada, and most devotees, dignitaries, Godbrothers, and locals were refused entry. Many who came to Vrindaban to see Srila Prabhupada could not enter and were frustrated. Many of Srila Prabhupada's old friends later said they were turned away, e. g., Nrshimananda Goswami, OBL Kapoor, Vishwambhar Goswami, Dr. Khurana, Dr. Ghosh (VRI), etc. Is it any wonder that when an opportunity arose, Srila Prabhupada asked Shastri to bring Balaram Misra and tell him about his poisoning and get the word out to the Vrindaban locals, bypassing Tamal and his own caretakers? This is only a logical assumption. Tamal somehow failed to disappear this tape with so much on it. Still, Srila Prabhupada treated the matter casually.

He said in Bengali, "*somebody said that someone poisoned him.*" The *kaviraja* asked what he was saying, and Srila Prabhupada repeats himself in Hindi. Then, with "to me," he confirms he is speaking of himself. Srila Prabhupada **(1)** is talking of actual poisoning, **(2)** not just the symptoms of poisoning, and **(3)** he states it three times. We note that there are clearly two unknown persons to which Srila Prabhupada has made reference, namely the **informant** ("someone") and the **poisoner** ("somebody"), neither of whom are identified.

WHAT WAS SRILA PRABHUPADA'S PURPOSE?

Why would Srila Prabhupada initiate a discussion of his own poisoning if it were not true? Did Srila Prabhupada talk about being poisoned in several discussions (as we will see) over two days because: **(1)** He wanted to create confusion? *(no, he did everything for preaching, even his poisoning revelations.)* **(2)** He was speculating or just cranky? *(forgive the crazy suggestion.)* **(3)** He brought up the poisoning so he could later clearly state that he was NOT being poisoned? *(this is the GBC's ridiculous position, which makes no sense at all.)* He said these things because they were *true and he wanted us to know that he thought he was being poisoned.* That he did not aggressively pursue the matter is another discussion (Ch. 61), and does not minimize the importance of what he *did* say. Perhaps the purpose to his revelation a few days before his departure was to leave the service of follow-up and investigative work to us, at least to those who would take his words seriously.

SECTION THREE: "ALL THESE FRIENDS" SAID IT

KAV: (07:28) Who told that? **SP: All these friends. BCS** Who said that Srila Prabhupada? **SP: They all say. Tamal:** Krishna das? (whispers)...(blowing conch) **KAV: Who would give you poison? And**

why? Tamal: (07:35) **Who said that, Srila Prabhupada? SP: (07:48) I do not know, but it is said.** Devotee whispers: (07:53) (indistinct) **...it's Poison. SP:** You do know astrology? **KAV:** What is he saying?

WHO WERE "ALL THESE FRIENDS"?

Srila Prabhupada referred to an informant who said he was given poison, and the Kaviraja then asked __who__ was saying this. The answer: "All these friends" and "They all say." So who were these "*all these friends*"? Who were "they"? "They" refers to many persons, more than one. A logical and sensible understanding is that the "friends" were those persons who were right there, namely Srila Prabhupada's caretakers. Bedridden and incapacitated, Srila Prabhupada hardly had the strength to raise an arm, and so he **verbally** pointed out those in his immediate presence as the ones who had said that he had been poisoned. Who else could he have meant? Not visitors, who would have already left, and who could not be "these." *All these friends* means plural and present persons, namely the caretakers who were with Srila Prabhupada.

Another explanation is that Srila Prabhupada learned of his poisoning from one of the four kavirajas who diagnosed poisoning in early Nov.1977 (Ch. 36). *One of them (or someone they told about their diagnosis) could have discreetly told Srila Prabhupada about their poisoning diagnosis.* Tamal did not know who told this to Srila Prabhupada (or when), meaning someone told Srila Prabhupada while Tamal was out of the room, or perhaps in Hindi or Bengali. Shastri asks, "*Who is saying?*" -so it was not Shastri who had told Srila Prabhupada. When interviewed, Narottama Lal Gupta, one of the kavirajas, did not claim to have told Srila Prabhupada. Maybe Bonamali heard it from one of the three kavirajas that had determined poisoning.

If Srila Prabhupada *overheard* his caretakers speaking or whispering about poisoning, this is parallel to the discovery of poison whispers *"overheard"* by the tape recorder. Ultimately there are no secrets.

"...Just like you are fighting with your enemies, that is very clear. 'The other party is my enemy.' But if somebody's treating as your friend and within he's trying to kill you, enemy, oh, that is very dangerous enemy." (SPLecture Feb 20, 1967) Maybe Srila Prabhupada heard some talk or whispers about poisoning, but did not recognize who was speaking, or he did not want to name them. First he says "all these friends," but when pressed by Tamal, he says, "I do not know" But it is unlikely that Srila Prabhupada did not know. As seen later, Tamal also thought Srila Prabhupada knew who told him about his poisoning, and so he asked him again. Prahlad Nrsimha das, 2017: *"Even the way Tamal*

asked: 'Who told you, Prabhupada, that you were poisoned?' is very strange and sounds much more to be the question of someone who wants to know who had revealed the plot to poison Srila Prabhupada."

OBSERVATIONS

Adridharan das in 1999 gave a very technical opinion on Srila Prabhupada's poisoning statements, whether poisoning was confirmed beyond any iota of doubt, and *NTIAP* used it in their "no poison" position. But Srila Prabhupada's opinion is worth far more. Adridharan was a ferocious adversary of the GBC and ISKCON Mayapur at that time. Jayapataka Swami sent 250 Mayapur disciples to physically storm the Calcutta temple in Aug. 2001, chasing temple president Adridharan into the street, and later charging him with embezzlement due to poor record keeping. Why does the GBC quote Adridharan in one instance, but expel him from Calcutta temple, refusing to hear his other opinions on ISKCON's guru system? The GBC arguments were so weak in defense of their no poisoning position, they had to quote an avowed adversary and enemy, hoping no one would notice. Adridharan felt *Srila Prabhupada had not absolutely stated he was definitely being poisoned.* Still, Adridharan strongly advocated for further investigation and he did not say that Srila Prabhupada denied being poisoned (as the GBC does). The difference between these two positions is vast.

Srila Prabhupada *3 times* stated someone said that he was poisoned (twice, shown above, and again the next morning, Nov. 10). In total he affirms no less than *nine times* he was poisoned throughout the "poison discussions." Although Srila Prabhupada so far only refers to *someone else* having said that he was poisoned, the subject was raised by Srila Prabhupada because he believed it true, or why bring it up at all? Note: Srila Prabhupada was told that *he had actually been poisoned*, and he says it was possible. The discussion will then shift to poisoning symptoms, which may confuse some, as they look to equate symptoms to medicines, diabetes, etc. Later Srila Prabhupada and his caretakers will extensively discuss actual *homicidal* poisoning, referring to rakshasas, murder, court cases, ground glass in food, and so on.

SRILA PRABHUPADA CHANGES THE SUBJECT

As colossal as a revelation of poisoning is, Srila Prabhupada only casually mentioned it and then went on to discuss other things, like the Bombay temple opening. Even though it was a shocking topic to bring up, he casually moved on to ask Balarama Misra if he knew astrology. He could have continued discussing his poisoning, but did not. After dropping a bombshell, the three further episodes of poison discussions were initiated by caretakers who are curious or worried about the matter. This appears to be the case from the *available* recorded tapes, but it is suspected that 200 tapes went missing in 1977 (Volume 2). Srila Prabhupada seems satisfied to have brought it up once, and afterwards he declined to give much more information. Indeed, Srila Prabhupada appeared guarded, evasive and reluctant to discuss the matter further, what to speak of revealing his mind fully. Srila Prabhupada chose not to make much fuss about being poisoned, as though he just wanted to plant the seed for a future investigation (Part 7). And this is where ISKCON leaders rationalize that if Srila Prabhupada did not aggressively pursue the matter, that this means there was no poisoning. They say Srila Prabhupada would certainly have fought tooth and nail to "protect his movement," all his hard work, and his own body so he could do his service. This argument has unfortunately lured many into thinking that if there was a poisoning, Srila Prabhupada would have stopped it. *But there are other explanations.* His bringing it up casually can be seen as his resignation in his imminent departure and reluctance to make commotion about himself. This is a philosophical understanding *(Ch. 61).* But, although Srila Prabhupada may have been tolerant of being poisoned, followers and disciples must adhere to the duty of finding the truth and ensuring justice is done. How can we not take his words seriously?

"WHEN GIVEN POISON"

The *kaviraja* and BCS try to convince Srila Prabhupada he will live for another ten years. Then, later, while Balarama Misra is still there, the kaviraja, returns to the topic of poisoning.

SECTION FOUR: SOMEBODY GAVE YOU POISON?

KAV: (25.15) This thing Maharaja. How did you say today **that someone said somebody gave you poison?** Did anyone tell or you got some indication somewhere? **SP: No, someone said that these kind of symptoms manifest if someone is poisoned. Maybe there is such a mention in some book..** **KAV:** Yes I know that such things happen if raw mercury is administered. Or there are some other things also which can cause such illness. But who will do such a thing to a Godly person like you. According to me if someone has such thoughts for you then he is a rakshasa/ demon. **Indistinct (BREAK)**

ABHAAS: APPEARANCE-INDICATION-SYMPTOM-FEELING

The kaviraja asks about some "abhaas" to confirm a poisoning that Srila Prabhupada was told about by "someone." Srila Prabhupada says no, that he was told by someone that he had poisoning symptoms. The audio tapes are clear that no one disbelieved Srila Prabhupada's first poisoning statements, which were understood and acknowledged by everyone present. No one tried to refute them, but decades later the GBC does exactly that. The deniers will tell Srila Prabhupada not to say these "useless and ridiculous" things? Today they are unaffected about the discussions of homicidal poisoning. Why does Shastri say maybe a rakshasa-demon gave Srila Prabhupada poison? Those present made multiple affirmations and were shocked by Srila Prabhupada's words. Shastri later said, *"There must be some truth to it. There's no doubt."*

ACTUAL POISONING *PLUS* POISONING SYMPTOMS

Srila Prabhupada elaborates that someone said that when poisoned, a person will develop the symptoms of poisoning as seen in Srila Prabhupada's physical condition. Would he have said this if he thought there was no poisoning? Yet the GBC dismisses Srila Prabhupada's poisoning symptoms as being due to diabetes! So far, Srila Prabhupada: **(1)** earlier stated that *someone said that somebody had poisoned him,* **(2)** he now adds that *someone said that he had the symptoms of poisoning,* **(3)** and that these *poisoning symptoms may be described in some book.*

Srila Prabhupada spoke both about *being actually poisoned and having symptoms of poisoning.* Of course, the dishonest GBC ignores the part about actual poisoning, and tries to dismiss the symptoms as due to diabetes or medicines. In other words, no poisoning... Not only did Srila Prabhupada hear about his being poisoned from "all these friends," but he *also* heard that he had the symptoms of poisoning from someone he felt was qualified to recognize them. Or why say all this if there was no poisoning, as *NTIAP* asserts? Due to his medical expertise Srila Prabhupada was himself fully qualified to recognize poisoning symptoms. Due to Srila Prabhupada's pre-eminent qualifications as a life-long chemist, pharmacist, medicines compounder, and a supremely empowered, perfected mystic yogi, his own recognition that he had poisoning symptoms **cannot be ignored**. He knew the symptoms and effects of poisons and medicines. *"Srila Prabhupada knew very well the symptoms of all disease; after all he was a pharmacist for years. As far as I could tell, he knew everything." (What Is The Diff.* p. 55)

KAVIRAJA AGREES WITH POISONING AND SYMPTOMS

Shastri, an experienced, highly qualified kaviraja, grappled with the poisoning revelation. That only a demon would maliciously poisoning a saint shows he took Srila Prabhupada's talk of being poisoned most seriously. The GBC rationale that Srila Prabhupada is contradicting his own earlier statements by now qualifying that he was told only of having symptoms is ridiculous. Shastri accepts that there is talk of an actual poisoning, **and** talk of the symptoms. Why else talk of demons if he thought Srila Prabhupada was only talking about some bad medicine as the GBC claims? Shastri seriously wondered which poison could cause his symptoms, mentioning mercury (symptoms similar to cadmium.)

EITHER WAY IT IS VERY ALARMING

The misunderstanding that Srila Prabhupada was clarifying his previous statements about **being poisoned** to mean **only having poisoning symptoms,** should still lead to great alarm and support for a full, unbiased investigation. After all, the reason for having poisoning symptoms would be because of actual poisoning! Srila Prabhupada did not say he had diabetes symptoms, he said poisoning symptoms, and he knew the difference (unlike the GBC). He would not confuse diabetes symptoms with poisoning symptoms. *Neither should we.* Poisoning symptoms are due to poisoning, and since all 1977 doctors failed to give a correct diagnosis, that further points to a hidden poisoning. Srila Prabhupada's homicidal poisoning has been confirmed beyond a doubt (Part 1), so hollow denials from the GBC will not suffice. GBC: *"He [SP] replies that it was the talk from the day before about the possibility that someone poisoned him."* Sometimes the GBC talk of poisoning, and at other times of only symptoms. They should never be listened to.

CHAPTER 11:
HE SAID LIKE THAT

Later on Nov. 9, after Balarama Misra leaves, and after the lengthy visits of Svarupa Damodara and Giriraj Swami, and after Tamal reads a long letter from Jitarati das about preaching in China, during a pause, Tamal questions Srila Prabhupada again. *Carefully note Tamal's exact question, since it is to this exact question that Srila Prabhupada will answer. It was all about what someone else had said.* (Skip ahead)

SECTION FIVE: PRABHUPADA HAD POISONING SYMPTOMS

Tamal: Srila Prabhupada? You said before that you... **that _it is said_ that you were poisoned?** **SP:** No, these kind of symptoms are seen when a man is poisoned. *He said like that*, **not that I am poisoned.**

Tamal: Yeah. Did anyone tell you that, or you just know it from before? **SP:** I read something. **Tamal:** Ah, I see. That's why actually **we cannot allow anyone to cook for you. SP:** That's good.

Tamal: Jayapataka Maharaja was telling that one acharya, Sankaracharya, of the Sankaracharya line - this is a while ago - *he was poisoned to death.* Since that time, none of the acharyas or the gurus of the Sankaracharya line will ever take any food cooked except by their own men. **SP: My Guru Maharaja also. Tamal:** Oh. You, of course, have been so merciful that sometimes you would take prasada cooked by so many different people. **SP:** That should be stopped.

"NOT THAT I AM POISONED"

This phrase has been unjustly exploited by the GBC, by taking it out of context and even changing the wording, trying to establish that Srila Prabhupada said that he was **not** poisoned. But the GBC's assertion of no poisoning is totally untenable. It is laborious but necessary to confront *NTIAP's* 6 page chapter *denying* Srila Prabhupada spoke of being poisoned. Their twist of Srila Prabhupada's words is a colossal and desperate deception, and not just an innocent difference of opinion.

OUT OF CONTEXT PARAPHRASING, TWISTED MEANING

NTIAP repeatedly asserts Srila Prabhupada never stated he was poisoned, and that the poison discussions Nov. 9-10, do not support the "poisoning theory." *NTIAP:* "*...the clear and simple fact [is] that Prabhupada himself denied that he was poisoned.*" *NTIAP* (p. 51) then massacres the truth: "*In contrast, the phrase **Not that I am poisoned** is a direct reply to Tamal's question asking Prabhupada, 'Did you say you were poisoned?'*" But actually, Tamal's question was: "*You said that... it is said that you were poisoned?*" *NTIAP* changed the conversation to suit their needs. ***Nowhere*** does Tamal ask, "*Did you say you were poisoned?*" He asks about *who said, who did it, and what was said*, but never does Tamal ask ***did you say*** you were poisoned? *NTIAP* asserts Srila Prabhupada denied being poisoned, *but this would be an answer to a question that was never asked*. *NTIAP* has deceptively separated the "*not that I am poisoned*" phrase from the preceding "*No, these kind of symptoms are seen when a man is poisoned. He said like that...*" The two sentences should be read together to be properly understood.

As a test, let's use *NTIAP's butchered version*: **Tamal:** Did you say you were poisoned? **SP:** Not that I am poisoned. //This makes no sense: it is grammatically untenable. Or we can look at the GBC's longer version: **Tamal:** You said before that you... that it is said that you were poisoned? **SP:** Not that I am poisoned. //Srila Prabhupada did not say "No, I did not say that." He explains that *the informant told him he had poisoning symptoms and the informant did not say that Srila Prabhupada was poisoned.* Taken out of context, "*not that I am*

88

poisoned" makes no sense as an answer, and needs to be connected to the whole. *NTIAP's* manipulation game contradicts the flow of discussion. This is dishonesty. They do the same with the May 28, 1977 talks: take out some words and discard the rest. The GBC needs truth lessons, not just remedial English grammar. Thus *"not that I am poisoned"* is **not** Srila Prabhupada's declaratory statement of not being poisoned, but it qualifies what was **not said** by his informant. Srila Prabhupada is explaining what someone else told him.

Another look: *[correct meaning in brackets]* **Tamal:** SP? You said before that you… that it is said that you were poisoned? **SP:** No, *[he said that]* these kind of symptoms are seen when a man is poisoned. He said like that, *[and he did]* not *[say]* that I am poisoned.

SRILA PRABHUPADA SAID HE WAS NOT POISONED??

The truth is, Srila Prabhupada never said *"Not that I am poisoned"* as a statement in itself. The 21 word communication is in its entirety on *NTIAP* p. 47, but on p. 48, 16 words are missing, leaving us with: *"No... Not that I am poisoned."* By p. 51, it is reduced to: *"Not that I am poisoned."* This is word fraud. If Srila Prabhupada denied his poisoning, everyone would have believed it, but they didn't, and the proof is in their lengthy discussion about murder, poisons, demons, etc. (ConvBk 36. p. 359) Also note this: **Tamal:** *Ah, I see. That's why actually we cannot allow anyone to cook for you.* (Why would Tamal want to stop "anyone" from cooking for Srila Prabhupada? Because he said he was NOT poisoned?) Directly after Srila Prabhupada supposedly admitted (as per *NTIAP*) he was **not** being poisoned: **(1)** Shastri said: *"...maybe some rakshasa gave him poison. If he says* (that) *there must be some truth to it. There's no doubt."* (He doesn't think there was no poisoning.) **(2)** BCS said: *"He's saying that someone gave him poison.* (He doesn't think there was no poisoning.) **Tamal:** *Prabhupada was thinking that someone had poisoned him* (He doesn't think there was no poisoning.) **BCS:** *Yes.* (he agrees again.) **Tamal:** *That was the mental distress?* (Why distress when there's no poisoning?) **BCS:** *Yes.* (he agrees again.) So, if no one present in 1977 believed Srila Prabhupada said "Not that I am poisoned" as a statement in itself, how do they expect us to believe it now?

GBC CONTRADICTORY POSITIONS

NTIAP, p. 48: *"Srila Prabhupada gives an unequivocally straightforward answer to a straight-forward question, "No ...not that I am poisoned." No amount of word jugglery now or in the future can take away the clear and simple fact that Prabhupada himself denied that he was poisoned."* But what is supposedly clear to the *NTIAP* author in

2000 was "confusing" to Hari Sauri das in May 1998 when he wrote: *"These translations and transcripts do in any case reveal a <u>confusing</u> scenario. Srila Prabhupada indicates first to Tamal that he had the symptoms of someone poisoned, not that he was being poisoned. Later he states more positively that he thinks he is being poisoned. We may never know exactly what was in Srila Prabhupada's mind..."* So what is at one time clear to the GBC is at another time confusing to them. In 1998 one arm of the GBC says they are CONFUSED, then in 2000 another arm of the GBC says that CLEARLY Srila Prabhupada stated that he was **not** being poisoned. Why can't they get their story straight? Their slippery dishonesty leads to contradicting themselves (what to speak of SP.).

FURTHER EVALUATION

Earlier Srila Prabhupada spoke of a different person: *"**Someone says that I have been poisoned... it's possible."*** And *"**Someone says that, somebody has given me poison**."* Then later, Srila Prabhupada spoke of another person who told him he had poisoning symptoms.

Points in understanding the phrase, *"...not that I am poisoned"* are:

(1) "He" (the informant) spoke of symptoms only and was not speaking of poisoning. This is understood from *"He said like that..."* **(2)** Tamal did not ask IF there was a poisoning; he asked WHAT was said. **(3)** If Tamal thought that Srila Prabhupada had just said that he was not poisoned, surely Tamal would have repeated it or sought elaborations. Instead, he asked whether he knew about poisoning symptoms. **(4)** Srila Prabhupada, in response to Tamal's question, is clarifying what someone else (**"he"**) said, and not his own thoughts on the matter. His own thoughts were expressed earlier and will be again expressed the next morning, and these thoughts are that **he has been poisoned. (5)** This is not the last statement Srila Prabhupada makes on the poison issue. He states the next morning: *"That same thing – that someone has poisoned me."* So even if there is some confusion over the meaning of *"not that I am poisoned,"* it is cleared up the next morning, leaving no further doubt about Srila Prabhupada's thoughts or meaning. *He thought he had been poisoned.* **(6)** Srila Prabhupada did not say he was not poisoned, he said someone else had said he had the symptoms of poisoning. Srila Prabhupada replied that he was not told he had been poisoned.

WHY RESTRICT WHO WAS COOKING?

(1) Tamal: Ah, I see. That's why actually we cannot allow anyone to cook for you. *(Why stop "anyone" from cooking? Why take precautions or worry about cooks if there is no poisoning? Was Tamal going to blame Srila Prabhupada for unrestricted cooks if poisoning* *came to be known? The GBC interpretation is flawed.)* **SP:** That's good.

(2) Tamal: Jayapataka Maharaja was telling that one acharya, Sankaracharya, of the Sankaracharya line - this is a while ago - he was poisoned to death. Since that time, none of the acharyas or the gurus of the Sankaracharya line will ever take any food cooked except by their own men. *(Why bring up an* <u>actual homicidal poisoning story</u> *if there was no poisoning and only innocent symptoms?)* **SP:** My Guru Maharaja also. *(Bhaktisiddhanta took measures to prevent actual homicidal poisoning.)* **(3) Tamal:** Oh. You, of course, have been so merciful that sometimes you would take prasada cooked by so many different people. **SP:** That should be stopped. *(Stop accepting food from different sources because there is no concern about poisoning? Tamal has acknowledged real poisoning.)*

Srila Prabhupada practically stopped eating after the health attack in Hrishikesh on May 16. When his sister Pishima came and cooked in Oct. 1977, he ate a full meal for the first time in months. He instructed Srutirupa and Pishima to cook for him and let no one else cook. On Oct. 2, Srila Prabhupada instructed Kuladri not to allow anyone to cook for him without his permission. *These are three times that Srila Prabhupada ordered restrictions on who cooked for him by choosing cooks from* <u>outside the circle of caretakers</u>. It appears Srila Prabhupada was making efforts to avoid the poison being given to him in his food.

"MY GURU MAHARAJA ALSO"--POISONED

Srila Prabhupada states *"My Guru Maharaja also"* was cautious about what food he took. So then why be incredulous about Srila Prabhupada's poisoning? Bhaktisiddhanta was given an injection by a doctor the day before he departed. *TKG's Diary* (p. 43): *"He had a sentiment that the doctor was paid to kill him."* Srila Prabhupada said the regional head of police confessed someone tried to bribe him to kill Bhaktisiddhanta, but he could not do it since he was a great saint, and also told how his guru made a will on a scrap of paper just before a hernia operation, in case he be murdered by the doctor. He skipped the operation at the last moment. Srila Prabhupada told Brahmananda das that Tirtha Swami had poisoned Bhaktisiddhanta (confirmed by Lalita Prasad who said he saved his brother the first time, but could not do so the second time by Bhaktisiddhanta's own disciples). *"They conspired to kill him. Guru Maharaja told me personally. [...] He was so kind that he used to talk so many things with me. So he personally told me that 'These people, they wanted to kill me. They collected 25,000 rupee and went to the police officer in charge of that area, that "You take this 25,000 rupees. We shall do something against Bhaktisiddhanta Sarasvati. You don't take any step."'* (SPLecture Feb. 7, 1969)

TAMAL'S SHARP MEMORY

Tamal: *You said before that you... that it is said that you were poisoned?* Tamal corrected himself from *"that you (said?)"* to *"that it is said"*? Why? We find 196 lines back in the transcript: **Tamal:** *Who said that, Srila Prabhupada?* **SP:** *I do not know, but it is said...* Tamal's sharp memory is focused on exactly what is transpiring in these poison discussions. We would not normally expect someone to remember verbatim what had been spoken so far back in continuous multi-party conversations. It was all about what was said by some unknown informant and who he was. *"It is said..."*

Tamal pressed Srila Prabhupada **four times** for disclosure of the unknown informant's identity, while Srila Prabhupada stalwartly remained vague. What Tamal is really concerned about? Is he worried about a poisoning or who informed Srila Prabhupada? Who ratted? It is the latter, because he wanted to deal with whoever leaked the big secret. He did not seem to care if Srila Prabhupada was actually being poisoned. The 4 times he tries to discern the informant: **(1)** Krishna das? *[Babaji? Did KDB tell SP about the poisoning?]* **(2)** Who said that, Srila Prabhupada? **(3)** You said before that you… that it is said that you were poisoned? **(4)** Did anyone tell you that, or you just know it from before? Tamal wants to know **who** told Srila Prabhupada that he had been poisoned and had poisoning symptoms. *He is concerned with finding who the informant is, not about stopping the poisoning itself.* This indicates he wants to neutralize the informant. If it was a local resident, a devotee, or a kaviraja, Tamal could then act accordingly. The final absurdity is Tamal's doing nothing as a result of all these discussions, even after clearly acknowledging Srila Prabhupada was speaking of being homicidally poisoned. Tamal was acting very suspect.

POISONING SYMPTOMS ARE OF SERIOUS CONCERN

NTIAP implies Srila Prabhupada is now negating his former statements that someone said that he was being poisoned. We disagree. The "poison discussions" leave us with the clear impression Srila Prabhupada thinks he has been poisoned. The next morning (Nov. 10) Srila Prabhupada admits he was in distress due to the idea that someone has poisoned him. Even *IF* Srila Prabhupada was modifying his statements (and he does not) to refer to symptoms and not actual poisoning, still, poisoning symptoms in itself should be of great concern to all his followers and be more than adequate grounds for investigation.

To have poisoning symptoms, which Srila Prabhupada clearly believes he has, indicates being actually poisoned. Symptoms are indications of the real thing. Srila Prabhupada talks of poisoning again the next day. The GBC is skilled at duplicitous deception. These poison discussions are a mountain of actual poisoning evidence.

RATIONALE FOR EVASIVENESS

Srila Prabhupada has now spoken twice of an unknown informant ("he"), who told him he had poisoning symptoms. Srila Prabhupada had earlier swung the kaviraja away from talk of poisoning to talk of symptoms, as he does with Tamal too. It seems Srila Prabhupada is now reluctant to discuss his actual poisoning, for obvious reasons. Srila Prabhupada was more forthcoming with Sastri than Tamal, and throughout these poison discussions, he is very guarded and vague with Tamal. The vagueness, ambiguity, and refusal to name the informant was quite telling. We assume he had good reasons for this. Was it mercy towards his poisoners, or indifference, or self-defense, or surrender to the Lord's desire and destiny? (Ch. 61)

TAMAL DOWNPLAYS THE POISONING

Tamal was very intelligent, a master politician, and expert at manipulating people, language, and situations. Many times he would *downplay* the significance of Srila Prabhupada's poisoning revelation.

TAMAL'S FIRST DOWNPLAY: "JUST KNEW IT FROM BEFORE": Doubting whether Srila Prabhupada was *actually* told by anyone that he had poisoning symptoms, Tamal asked him if anyone told him, or he "**just knew** "about them "**from before**." This downgrades the poisoning to just a theory, just a hunch. It is a downplay of significance.

TAMAL'S SECOND DOWNPLAY: COOKING IN THE FUTURE: Tamal said *"that's why actually we cannot allow anyone to cook for you,"* as though Srila Prabhupada's statements about being poisoned only warranted concern over food being *maybe* poisoned *in the future.* "Oh, let's watch who brings you food *in the future*?" Tamal knew Srila Prabhupada spoke of being *already* poisoned, but he cleverly diverts to taking future precautions. Tamal has *still* not responded appropriately to the real poisoning that is being discussed. Srila Prabhupada is not making idle talk. Tamal makes it sound like a good preventive measure, just in case somebody might try to put poison in some food. Yet he did absolutely nothing about it? Tamal just makes diversionary small talk…

Srila Prabhupada's health was mysteriously declining for many months, he was on the verge of departure, he could hardly move or speak, he just stated very clearly that someone said that he had been poisoned, and then he also says that he had the symptoms of poisoning. And Tamal talks about precautions with future cooks? How crazy is that? It downgrades the poisoning revelations to something that *might* happen in the future-- but it has ***already*** happened! If someone on his deathbed speaks of having been poisoned, wouldn't more than future cooking precautions be in order? Call the police, call for medical tests? Full alert to all devotees? But Tamal's failure to deal with the true weight of Srila Prabhupada's words points a big finger at himself as an avoidance tactic, diverting to absurd talk of future cooking arrangements, which he did not do anyway. Tamal *pretended to miss the point*. Homicidal poisoning is finally fully acknowledged by all caretakers the next day (Ch. 14). Even then, Tamal does nothing! Amazingly, no action is taken and two days later the suspects are whispering in his room about "poison and the use of it." (Ch. 26)

THE NEXT MORNING, NOVEMBER 10

Early the next morning on Bhavananda's watch, Srila Prabhupada was very restless, kicked off all his covers, and great so-called "mental distress." Shastri came and gave some pain medicine *(TKG's Diary)*.

SECTION SIX: "MENTAL DISTRESS" NOV. 10, 1977

(Skip ahead:) **Devotee:** The distress is less now? **KAV:** The uneasiness is less isn't it? **BCS:** It's less now, this restlessness and the pain. *Skip:* **BHAV** So what was the cause of that distress? **BCS:** What happened this morning? [Shastri found SP's body now functioning properly; heart rate, pulse and blood pressure amazingly became normal. They talk about Srila Prabhupada's "mental distress."] *(Skip ahead)*

Tamal: (background) But what did Prabhupada just say? **KAV:** (speaking over BCS) How the position was this morning... the position was; there were problems, wasn't there ? Had I given ten doses his heart would not have been in the position it is. Now with one dose his heart is... What can I say tell me? What definition can (I) attach (to this)? **BCS:** He said, "How can you define it? How can you explain it?" **Tamal:** (background) But what did Prabhupada just say? **BCS:** Like the condition couldn't have improved by ten medicines also but one medicine it becomes perfect. **Tamal:** What did Prabhupada just say? **BCS:** Prabhupada just said that I mean, this morning his condition was bad, not now. **BHAV:** Prabhupada was complaining of **mental distress** this morning also.

Tamal asks three times what Srila Prabhupada said. He is trying to keep up - he did not want to miss anything about the poisoning.

TAMAL'S THIRD DOWNPLAY: "MENTAL DISTRESS"
Bhavananda again states Srila Prabhupada complained not just of pain, but *also* of mental distress earlier that morning ("mental disturbance" in *TKG's Diary*.) Apparently the mental distress was not from pain, but of being poisoned. This is the day after Srila Prabhupada said he has been poisoned. Was mental distress/ disturbance a characterization by Tamal and Bhavananda to downplay the talk of being poisoned? Mental distress characterizes Srila Prabhupada as old, dying, senile, and thus what he says should not be taken seriously, which later Tamal evinces. (Vol. 2)

CONCLUSION: Extracting a phrase to use it out of context with a contrary meaning- this is how the GBC claims Srila Prabhupada denied being poisoned. *"Not that I am poisoned"* refers to what someone else said about Srila Prabhupada, namely, that this person did not say Srila Prabhupada was poisoned, but instead said that he had poisoning symptoms. But Srila Prabhupada earlier already made it clear he thought he was poisoned, and he did so again the next day. The poison discussions show Srila Prabhupada spoke of actual poisoning *and* poisoning symptoms.

SP: No, *[he said that]* these kind of symptoms are seen when a man is poisoned. He said like that, *[and he did]* not *[say]* that I am poisoned.

CHAPTER 12:
SOMEONE HAS POISONED ME

BCS asks about the "mental distress" and the kaviraja encourages a reluctant Srila Prabhupada to disclose his thoughts. Not shown in the transcript below, Jayapataka can be heard in the background of the tape recording asking, *"What did the kaviraja say about Sankaracharya?"*

SECTION SEVEN: SOMEONE GAVE HIM POISON HERE
BCS: Srila Prabhupada? **SP:** Hmm? **BCS** What was that problem? Mental distress? **SP:** Hmmm. Hmmm. **KAV:** Say, say. **SP: That same thing– that someone has poisoned me.** **BCS:** Oh, okay, he thinks that someone.... **KAV** (speaking same time) **BCS: Someone gave him poison here.** **KAV:** Charu Swami... **BCS:** Yes. **KAV:** Listen, this is the understanding that **some demon** (may) have given **(poison)**. Charu Swami... **some demon has given [poison].** This can happen. It's not impossible. Sankaracharya was there, **someone gave him poison.** For six months he suffered. There is glass you know? Bottle glass? It was

95

ground and fed in food. What befell him; after twelve months leprosy spread inside his body. Everyone suffers their karma. But the medicine I have given, **the poison cannot stay.** I give a guarantee, that even if there are effects, they will not stay. Because right now **I cannot detect [poison]** has been given to him. If it is found that his kidneys go bad, then it could be by sickness or astrological reason **or by poison.**

Tamal: Prabhupada was thinking that someone had poisoned him? BCS Yes. **Tamal:** That was the mental distress? **BCS:** Yes. **KAV:** This is what [he] says, then **there must be some truth in it. In this there is no doubt. Tamal:** What did Kaviraja just say? **BCS:** He said that when Srila Prabhupada was saying that, there must be **something truth behind it. Tamal: Sheessh!** (Everyone speaking) **KAV: It's some rakshasa, the poisoner,** will put something in pan. What to say, something in milk. To eat, [he] will put a medicine in pan, by the morning [your] whole life can be forgotten.

DISTRESSING THOUGHTS OF BEING POISONED

Explaining the cause of his "mental distress" and restlessness, Srila Prabhupada said: *"that same thing– that someone has poisoned me."* It was the same thing, or *vahi bat*, as the day before. In other words, Srila Prabhupada was "mentally distressed" about thoughts that he has been poisoned. The GBC has offered that Srila Prabhupada was only distressed about a previous conversation and not about poisoning itself. This is really ridiculous. Obviously Srila Prabhupada was "distressed" about being poisoned. *NTIAP: "He replies that it was the talk from the day before about the possibility that someone poisoned him."* The implication is that yesterday's discussions are the cause of disturbance, and not those discussions' contents, namely being poisoned. The GBC is grasping at straws! Due to his illness, senility, grumpiness, etc. the GBC says we cannot take Srila Prabhupada's words very seriously (Ch. 51). *The "mental distress" was due to the thought of being poisoned.* But Srila Prabhupada was "distressed" over the previous day's discussions: **(1)** Someone had said that somebody had poisoned him, **(2)** that someone was "all these friends," indicating the caretakers around him **(3)** that someone also said that he had the symptoms of poisoning, **(4)** and that he recognized having these symptoms by his own medical knowledge. Further: **(5)** Srila Prabhupada was almost paralyzed, yet so restless, he kicked off his covers in the night, **(6)** The novel and inappropriate phrase "mental distress" is used to describe Srila Prabhupada's mood, **(7)** The kaviraja was called due to Srila Prabhupada's "mental distress" being so profound that pain medicine was given, **(8)** His attendants felt compelled to ask about the cause of the "mental distress."

POISONING IS AFFIRMED AND ACCEPTED

The previous day ended with Srila Prabhupada seemingly reluctant to talk about his poisoning, but now talk of actual poisoning is again in the forefront. No longer does Srila Prabhupada say, "It's possible." Poisoning now has become a factual reality and everyone is quite shocked, evident by the new flurry of conversation. *Everyone present proceeds to affirm and acknowledge that Srila Prabhupada was saying that he thought he had been maliciously poisoned in an attempt to kill him.* Eleven acknowledgements of malicious poisoning: **(1)** TKG's Diary: *"Prabhupada disclosed his thoughts that someone has poisoned him."* **(2)** BCS confirms: *"...he thinks that **someone gave him poison here.**"* **(3)** Shastri confirms: *"...some demon has given **(poison)**. This can happen. It's not impossible."* **(4)** Tamal: *"Prabhupada was thinking that someone poisoned him?"* **(5)** BCS: ***"Yes."*** **(6)** Shastri: *"This is what he says, then **there must be some truth in it.** In this there is no doubt."* **(7)** BCS: *"He said that when Srila Prabhupada was saying that, **there must be something truth behind it.**"* **(8)** Tamal's *"Sheesssh!"* is an affirmation. **(9)** Srila Prabhupada, listening to all these poisoning affirmations, never corrected them, *as he certainly would have if there was no poisoning*. He confirmed with not protesting. **(10)** Tamal poses his ***final "Who did it" question*** to Srila Prabhupada. **(11)** They then spoke of real poisonings- a wife poisoned, Sankaracharya's poisoning.

CONCLUSION: Srila Prabhupada never named who poisoned him or who told him about it. The discussions are about **who** said there was a poisoning, and it was **not** about **IF** there was a poisoning. *They all clearly acknowledged that Srila Prabhupada spoke of actual, malicious, homicidal poisoning by someone trying to kill him.* An honest reading of the poison discussions concludes Srila Prabhupada **believed he was poisoned**. He said that his being poisoned was possible, and then he solidifies his assertion, and many confirmations of his poisoning are pronounced by those around him.

CHAPTER 13:
WHO IS IT THAT HAS POISONED?

SECTION EIGHT: THERE MUST BE SOME TRUTH TO IT

Tamal: Srila Prabhupada, Shastriji says that there **must be some truth to it if you say that.** <u>So who is it that has poisoned?</u> *(then- 13 seconds dead silence- Srila Prabhupada never answers this question)*

TAMAL ACKNOWLEDGES THE POISONING

Tamal's question is *who did it*, not if it was done, or who told him. Tamal has now gone to *"Who did it"* from his earlier *"Who said it."*

Srila Prabhupada thought he was poisoned, and thus his "mental distress." Tamal and others acknowledged Srila Prabhupada thought he had been poisoned (on Nov. 10). Yet incredibly, the GBC and Tamal adamantly insisted Srila Prabhupada said he was **not** poisoned, so there is **no** reason for further investigation since they already investigated and found nothing! Although Tamal asserted after 1997 that there was no poisoning, the record shows he clearly acknowledged the poisoning in 1977. Tamal never asked, "Who is it that has *not* poisoned?" Even if we were to accept that Srila Prabhupada said he was not poisoned (which is untrue), still, Tamal was so convinced on Nov. 10 that he asks Srila Prabhupada who poisoned him. There was a poisoning. Who did it?

WHY DID SRILA PRABHUPADA NOT ANSWER?

Tamal's grave question resulted in an eerie 13 seconds of dead silence as everyone waited for Jagat Guru to reveal his poisoner. They all thought Srila Prabhupada knew who it was, or why ask him and wait so long for an answer? The day before he was evasive, but today Srila Prabhupada is silent and gives give *no* answer-- he does not want to answer Tamal. Tamal believes Srila Prabhupada knew the poisoner's identity, and he seems unconcerned about being named as the culprit. He was always confrontational. Being the primary suspect, and deemed guilty of the poisoning beyond a reasonable doubt in Volume 2, it is remarkable Tamal would so brazenly risk being named as the poisoner. He had no fear of being named? Was Tamal so confident that Srila Prabhupada would not name him? Was there some blackmail?

The long silence implies Srila Prabhupada knew but did not wish to say. Srila Prabhupada chose **not** to answer and his silence is another confirmation that he was poisoned, simply because he failed to deny it. Also: if someone asks you something and you do not reply, it is usually because **(1)** you know the person asking already knows the answer, or **(2)** you know he is the culprit. Srila Prabhupada's silence subtly hints that Tamal is the poisoner. Srila Prabhupada knew who did it. Perhaps he was silent because he considered it unnecessary, or too late, or he just did not want to disturb the all-redeeming service that his caretakers were still giving, considering their advancement more valuable than his own life. Did he magnanimously decline to disturb his poisoners? See *Ch. 61: His Amazing Tolerance.* But he obliquely answered Tamal the next day by *"Ravana will kill, better to be killed by Rama."*

Divine or Demoniac offers a rationale for no answer: *"Pariksit came across the personality of Kali cutting the legs of the bull Dharma. Inquiring from Dharma who had hurt him, Dharma refuses to identify Kali as the wrong-doer... 'Although the bull, or the personality of religion, and the cow, the personality of the earth, knew perfectly well that the personality of Kali was the direct cause of their sufferings, still, as devotees of the Lord, they knew well that without the sanction of the Lord no one could inflict trouble upon them.'"* (SBhag 1.17.18 Purport)

From SBhag 1.17.22: **TEXT:** *The King said: O you, who are in the form of a bull! You know the truth of religion, and you are speaking according to the principle that the destination intended for the perpetrator of irreligious acts is also intended for one who identifies the perpetrator. You are no other than the personality of religion.*

Purport: *A devotee's conclusion is that no one is directly responsible for being a benefactor or mischief-monger without the sanction of the Lord; therefore he does not consider anyone to be directly responsible for such action. ...in case of benefit, no one will deny that it is God-sent, but in case of loss or reverses one becomes doubtful about how the Lord could be so unkind to His devotee as to put him in great difficulty. Jesus Christ was seemingly put into such great difficulty, being crucified by the ignorant, but he was never angry at the mischief-mongers. That is the way of accepting a thing, either favorable or unfavorable. Thus for a devotee the identifier is equally a sinner, like the mischief-monger. By God's grace, the devotee tolerates all reverses. Pariksit could understand that the bull was no other than the personality of religion himself. ...a devotee has no suffering at all because so-called suffering is also God's grace for a devotee who sees God in everything. The cow and bull never placed any complaint before the King for being tortured ...although everyone lodges such complaints before the state authorities. The extraordinary behavior of the bull made the King conclude that the bull was certainly the personality of religion, for no one else could understand the finer intricacies of the codes of religion.*

This is why the pure devotee would not identify his poisoners.

PRABHUPADA BECOMES EVASIVE AS TO WHO SAID

We note how Srila Prabhupada became progressively evasive as he was repeatedly pressed by Tamal over two days to reveal who said that he was poisoned. Note the progressive evasion: **(1)** Shastri asked "Who is saying?" answered by, "All these friends." (unspecific) **(2)** BCS asks who said this; the answer, "They all say." (unspecific) **(3)** Tamal asks if it was Krishna das (Babaji). (no answer) **(4)** Shastri asks "Who will give you poison? For what, why?" (no answer) **(5)** Tamal asks who said this, and SP said obliquely, "I don't know, but it is said." **(6)** Finally, Tamal asks who poisoned him, and Srila Prabhupada gives no answer at all.

HE TOLD OUTSIDERS, THEN RELUCTANT TO SAY MORE

Srila Prabhupada, as he did the day before, told the kaviraja very frankly in Hindi, _"That same thing– that someone has poisoned me."_ Srila Prabhupada again spoke to the *kaviraja* about being poisoned and not to the devotees. He answers Shastri but not Tamal. He did not want to speak with his disciples and Tamal's "Who did it" is unanswered. Why does he speak with Balaram Misra and Shastri, but not his caretakers?

Srila Prabhupada would not say more, for whatever reason. Once he revealed he believed himself poisoned, he did not bring it up again. He chose not to name his informant or poisoner. After these poison discussions are 41 pages of talks in ConvBk's, including with Krishna das Babaji, Narayan Maharaja, and Bon Maharaja. Srila Prabhupada not speaking further of his being poisoned in no way minimizes or negates his earlier statements. *Rather, it contributes to the mystique of the pure devotee's wonderful pastimes.* He briefly revealed that he thought he was being poisoned, so now we all know about it, and then he left the matter alone. That's all he wanted to accomplish. The long silence is broken by Shastri and useless chattering ensues with various speculations, none which was of practical in dealing with a poisoning. It is like someone drowning while spectators debate how it happened rather than making a rescue! And decades later, this matter is suppressed by the GBC with every cheap trick. They must have a strong motive to keep this darkest incident a secret. All the caretakers acknowledged homicidal poisoning; and there is nothing about bad medicine as the GBC today claims.

SECTION NINE: WHICH POISON WAS USED? Conv. continues:

KAV: The biggest poison is mercury. BCS: That was Gaya, that which... **KAV:** No, no. That was Svarupa Guha. You read about it didn't you, Swamiji? In Calcutta? **SP:** Hmm. **KAV**: Svarupa Guha? **BCS:** He doesn't know **KAV:** Her husband had given it. For it there is no medicine or antidote. Such a heavy dose was given. It's what we call Rashkapoor. **BCS:** No. That mercury was in... the makharadhwaja. **KAV:** No, no. That's not mercury. It's called by another name. **BCS:** Ok. **BHAV:** What did he say? **BCS:** He said that it's quite possible that mercury, it's a kind of poison. **Tamal:** That makharadhwaja... **BCS:** Rashkapoor? **KAV:** Aamer Rash. That's one preparation. **It's very poisonous. BCS:** Is that like makharadhwaja? **KAV:** Makharadhwaja is nectar, although not suitable for him, that's a different story. But that [Raskapoor] **is poison** for everybody. **BHAV:** What medicine was he taking before that? **BCS:** What? **KAV:** Nothing. **BCS:** He was referring to a case, a big **murder** case in Calcutta, the husband **poisoned the wife. BHAV:** Guha. **KAV:** Svarupa Guha... the case is now... **BCS:** Shankara Bannerjee was... **BHAV:** Our lawyer is the... (giggles)

Why is Bhavananda giggling because ISKCON's lawyer Bannerjee also represented the murderer Svarupa Guha? He giggles in the poison whispers too. What is amusing? This is disturbing, suspicious. This time Krishnadas Babaji is not present to take the blame for his giggling.

MAKHARADHVAJA AND DIFFERENT POISONING CASES

Shastri talks of mercury, Raskapoor and Svarupa Guha. When BCS suggests mercury was in the *makharadhvaja*, which Tamal also suggests, Shastri says it is not poison, but too strong for Srila Prabhupada. The Calcutta murder case was known to Bhavananda, who giggled. Why? Jayapataka earlier told Tamal about the powdered-glass Sankaracharya poisoning, so it is clear that everyone recognized that Srila Prabhupada was talking about *actual, homicidal poisoning*. Why do they today say it was just bad medicine? *This points to guilt, or why be so dishonest?* Poison cases were a vogue topic for these four men. Not only do Tamal, Bhavananda, BCS, and Jayapataka discuss various poisoning cases, but the same four are also the ones whispering of poisoning the very next day, Nov. 11. One day talking of various poison murder cases, and the next day whispering about the use of poison. *Thus they are suspects.*

TAMAL'S FOURTH DOWNPLAY: Makharadhvaja? BCS, Tamal try to blame *MKD* but Shastri says it is nectar, although inappropriate for SP's condition; but *Raskapoor* is poisonous for everyone. SP was not taking *MKD*. The attempt *to blame the poisoning on MKD*, which SP had taken only 3 times, 2 weeks earlier, was rejected by Shastri. (Ch. 28) SP's health decline from Feb. 1977 came from a poison other than the *MKD* taken Oct. 25-26. *Tamal is trying to deflect talk of poisoning towards talk of MKD and bad medicines (as the GBC does today).*

CHAPTER 14:
USELESS CHATTER

After the reaffirmations of the poisoning, the talks turn chaotic.

SECTION TEN: NO POISON IS STRONG ENOUGH:

Tamal: Bhagatji doesn't think the... **KAV** In my mind, his body is such that it is like a thunderbolt. You can beat it a 1000 times, but nothing will happen. **BCS:** No need for bewilderment. The way God protects his own, similarly Prahlad Maharaja was also. **KAV:** Swamiji, one verse comes to my mind: "Without protection, one remains fixed if protected by fate, whereas one who protects himself but is condemned by fate is destroyed. Without a protector, one person can live carelessly alone in the forest, whereas another takes all precautions in his home, and still dies." You are a divine soul, that is why there is no need to be anxious. **Tamal: No poison is strong enough to stop the Hari Nam, Srila Prabhupada. KAV:** Right. Before the Holy Name, how much poison was given to Mira, a single drop was enough to kill a man. Mira drank it all. Poison when offered to the Lord becomes nectar. **Devotee:** Prahlad Maharaja. **BCS:** Prahlad Maharaja. **KAV:** Halal gave Mira a stronger dose of poison than Prahlad got. It was so strongly made... Like there is one poison in allopathy, even till today nobody can tell the... **Tamal:** Would you like some more kirtan Srila Prabhupada? Lokanatha can lead. Lokanatha, you lead. **SP:** (??) **Tamal:** Lokanatha.

Tamal thought kirtan would avoid further poison discussions.

TAMAL'S FIFTH DOWNPLAY: Poison cannot stop Harinam: Chaotic, useless conversation. Shastri speculates that an allopathic tasteless poison may be involved (a heavy metal?) Finally Tamal has the perfect solution: *"No poison is strong enough to stop the Hari Nam, Srila Prabhupada."* Although somewhat spiritually valid, this is not an appropriate response when one's guru says he is poisoned. We recall Tamal's statement, *"Now you have to choose which suicide."* (Ch. 51)

KIRTAN FOR TAMAL'S PROSTATE CANCER?

When Tamal developed prostate cancer in 1996, he used the best physicians and hospitals for surgery, spending $500k. Tamal's hypocrisy is that he rejected any proper medical care for Srila Prabhupada in 1977, arranging only Hari Nam, even after Srila Prabhupada spoke several times about being homicidally poisoned. This medical hypocrisy on the part of all the caretakers is telling. What does Lokanath Swami have to say about these discussions at which he was present?

TAMAL'S SIXTH DOWNPLAY: MORE KIRTAN: Tamal urgently puts an end to the poison talks by pressing Lokanatha to do kirtan. And after the kirtan, nothing was done, no police, investigation, tests, autopsy, not even any more discussion. Chant Hare Krishna and keep poisoning? This is simply demoniac. This downplay is the most outrageous. Srila Prabhupada saw the pretense of his poisoners' false devotion. They totally ignored his poisoning complaints. The next day the poisoning continues, confirmed by the poison whispers. (Part 3)

NOTHING DONE ABOUT THE POISONING COMPLAINTS

Throughout these talks Tamal is anxious to find out **who** told Srila Prabhupada that he had been poisoned, who was exposing the poisoning. Tamal was not at all concerned whether the poisoning was *true, much less doing anything about it.* Did Tamal, as the primary caretaker and personal secretary: **(1)** Call law enforcement? **(2)** Do any in-house investigation? **(3)** Call senior devotees together to discuss Srila Prabhupada's statements? **(4)** Arrange for expert medical care or do urine tests to test for poison? **(5)** Make any changes to Srila Prabhupada's cooking or care? **(6)** Arrange for an autopsy or medical exam after Nov. 14? No, he did none of these things, which is very incriminating for Tamal and the caretakers, now that poisoning has been positively confirmed (Part 1).

CONCLUSION: The deniers say there was no poisoning, only innocent symptoms. But poison symptoms indicate actual poisoning, so *talk of symptoms is a strength for the poisoning position, not a weakness.* One should search for the poison which is causing those symptoms, not to dismiss poisoning because there are only symptoms! This tells us much about the deniers. Tamal was fully responsible for Srila Prabhupada's care, in complete control of the day's events, assisted by BCS and Bhavananda. He knew the poisoning revelation could naturally lead to he being accountable as the primary suspect, especially in light of his history (Volume 2). So, if you were Srila Prabhupada's secretary Tamal, you'd call the police and get tests done, right? Or you could end up being blamed, right? Why didn't he do that, as would be logical?

This only increases suspicions that Tamal shoved the poison issue under the rug because he was a poisoner. Tamal's total dominance precluded anyone, without Tamal's approval, from even suggesting an appropriate response to the talk of poisoning. Everyone was intimidated by him, lest he flare up again. Tamal, BCS, Bhavananda, and Jayapataka participated in the Nov. 9-10 poison discussions, but they went silent on the subject until 1997 when the issue became public, and then they made denials blatantly contradicting their 1977 recorded statements. Even a moron can see the extremely suspicious circumstances here. Why does the GBC cover-up the poison evidence? Amazingly Srila Prabhupada's concerns about being poisoned were never addressed by his caretakers. Did they think Srila Prabhupada was talking gibberish to be politely entertained? Or, as poisoners, were they glad to bury the issue?

CHAPTER 15:
THE WORDS OF THE PURE DEVOTEE

1998 LETTER: BHAGWAT MAHARAJA (abbreviated)

I am amazed at everyone's inability to focus on the most important point of this investigation, which are the words of His Divine Grace- *"Someone is poisoning me."* They were the reason for launching the investigation and continue to be the most compelling reason for the investigation. After a closer examination of the tape, to see whether there was more information to shed more light on His Divine Grace's statements, the whispers were found. Unfortunately everyone has focused on the whispers instead of His Divine Grace's statements, which are the real evidence for his being poisoned. First, from a practical point of view, Srila Prabhupada was during his grihasta days the manager of a pharmaceutical house. He designed, manufactured, and marketed his own medical preparations. He was very conversant with how herbs, chemicals, and poisons acted on the human body. He owned a pharmacy in Allahabad and sold prescriptions where he would need knowledge of drug interactions with the body. He was educated in medical science to recognize poisoning just from the reactions he was feeling in his body.

Second, he is the Nitya Siddha pure devotee of Krishna, and he is by the grace of Supersoul fully conscious of the hearts and minds of his devotees. In 1974 there were several leaders in our society who claimed it was foolish to think that he knew what was going on in his temples and in the hearts of his disciples. When I was in Bombay Srila Prabhupada received a letter from Sarva Mangal dasi. She described these statements, and she wanted him to please clarify. Srila Prabhupada told his secretary, *"For a greatly advanced pure devotee of the Lord this was not difficult."* The secretary asked, *"So I should tell her that you know this?"* Srila Prabhupada replied, *"That's not what I said. I said a greatly advanced pure devotee of the Lord would know these things. I am not a greatly advanced pure devotee, I am not even a devotee. I am just trying to be a devotee."* Srila Prabhupada has elsewhere stated that Supersoul tells him whatever he needs to know. We can thus conclude Srila Prabhupada is a greatly advanced pure devotee and he most certainly knew he was being poisoned and by whom. Where is the proof Srila Prabhupada was not a greatly advanced pure devotee and did not know he was being poisoned?

Unfortunately there are some devotees who have been diminishing the words of the greatly advanced pure devotee Srila Prabhupada by portraying him as an ordinary man. Some of them are the same devotees who I argued against over 20 years ago about the same thing. I have heard statements like "he was old and sick and could not understand," "he was senile," "usually old Indian men who are dying think they are being poisoned," "he was confused," and other mundane assessments of His Divine Grace. If these assessments are accurate then how could he translate Srimad Bhagavatam until his last days? Are we to accept this last translation work as the ranting of a confused, senile old man?

Just because doctors were examining Srila Prabhupada doesn't mean they could ascertain that he was being poisoned, unless they tested for it specifically. Many poisons cause the rapid onset of certain diseases (like heart attacks, strokes, kidney failure, etc) and death. It was said in certain circles that when Indira Gandhi held Jayaprakash Narayan under house arrest she slowly administered poisons that caused kidney deterioration and his death. This kind of poisoning cannot be detected by routine medical tests. So the statements of some that doctors did not notice poisoning is not evidence that he was not poisoned. Srila Prabhupada, conversant with the effects of various substances, and as he was experiencing it first hand, makes him the most likely person to ascertain the truth of the situation. Also he is the greatly advanced pure devotee who knows what is going on.

This truth is being obfuscated by all this rhetoric about the whispers and whether they are real or not. The whispers don't even really matter! What matters most is that the greatly advanced pure devotee of the Lord said, *"Someone is poisoning me."* Doesn't the *Nectar of Instruction* warn us that to consider the spiritual master as an ordinary human being is greatly offensive? Are there not many other verses that say the same thing? How many verses are there, which state that faith in the words of the spiritual master is the real key to enlightenment?

It has been asked how Srila Prabhupada, the greatly advanced pure devotee, could be poisoned. But didn't Jesus Christ accept crucifixion, praying, *"Let this cup pass from me, but thy will be done"*? Didn't Jesus forbid Peter from fighting with the Roman soldiers when they came to take him? Srila Prabhupada died for the sins of his disciples: that is the initiation covenant. He could have stayed with us. *"Krishna said it is up to me -I can stay or I can go, but what do you want?"* Obviously there was a Judas element among us, and so he departed. That is not the same as being vanquished. *"He reasons ill who says that Vaishnavas die when living still in sound."* Srila Prabhupada left us his words, and his voice beckons us to bring him justice.

Which devotee is there who will argue that the words of the spiritual master, *"Someone is poisoning me,"* are wrong? The core of this issue is faith in the eternally transcendental position of the spiritual master and his words. The entire political diatribe and semantics only conceals the truth. We know somebody poisoned Srila Prabhupada, because he said so! The only question is who? If the whispers fail to prove who, it is not the end of the case! It is only insufficient evidence! Maybe Srila Prabhupada wants us to look at it from another angle. One thing we can be sure of he is in control! It is up to him when, where, and how we find the truth *[Note: hair tests did that]*.

There are many who were in Vrindaban during these last days who feel it would have been impossible for them to not notice this was going on. But how many times were we involved in difficult situations and only Srila Prabhupada understood everything? And we didn't even have a clue. No one knew about Judas except Jesus Christ. Didn't Srila Prabhupada tell us he was being poisoned? Still we did nothing about it. Some may try to distract from the truths written in this letter by discrediting me. But this letter is about Srila Prabhupada and his words. I am easily discredited, there is much I do not do, but one thing I have never done is considering my Spiritual Master to be an ordinary man or doubted his words. I can say with conviction, however, that anyone who follows all the rules but fails to accept that Srila Prabhupada is a greatly advanced pure devotee of the Lord whose words are never wrong, is a spiritual failure. The issue is do we believe our Spiritual Master when he says, *"Someone has poisoned me"*? Do we believe that his words are never wrong? Do we believe that he would make a mistake about something so serious as this when he is receiving his information from the infallible Supreme Personality of Godhead Sri Krishna? It is faith on trial here, faith in the Spiritual Master's words. The line is drawn: on one side are those who doubt the words of the greatly advanced pure devotee of the Lord. On the other side are those who believe that if the spiritual master says it's a rope then it's a rope and if he says it's a snake then it's a snake. I know which side I am on. Which side are you on? **(END)**

HIS CONCERNS ABOUT POISONING WERE IGNORED

As of 2022 ISKCON's GBC, those charged with paying close heed to Srila Prabhupada's every word, still adamantly deny any possibility that Srila Prabhupada was poisoned, ridiculing and laughing at the "theory." Srila Prabhupada's shocking revelation generated a short buzz of conversation amongst the caretakers. It is puzzling and disturbing how Srila Prabhupada's senior leaders and main caretaker Tamal did not pursue the matter. No qualified doctor was consulted to investigate Srila Prabhupada's poisoning complaint in the next five days before Srila Prabhupada's departure, nor was any test done, nor even a simple coroner's examination of any kind performed. No local authority, medical professional, or law enforcement was consulted or notified. Devotees were not told Srila Prabhupada had repeatedly made clear statements about being poisoned. No one did a thing, much less try to protect Srila Prabhupada from unknown malicious poisoners. Today many who hear these taped discussions and the lack of response by the caretakers are shocked. The GBC now suggests Srila Prabhupada's talk of poisoning was due to senility, dying hallucinations in one near death which caused him to say things we cannot take seriously. But we don't agree, and neither did the *kaviraja*. His opinion, as is ours, was if Srila Prabhupada said it, it must be true. Note the clarity of Srila Prabhupada's consciousness during this time. Pradyumna das assisted Srila Prabhupada with the translation of the Bhagavatam and tells how he was lucid and focused, still translating just days before his leaving.

Srila Prabhupada's statements were ignored and brushed aside, and then lost in the dust kicked up by the mad rush to divide up the world and take Srila Prabhupada's place as the new gurus. (Volume 5) The pure devotee's words are never false or meaningless. By Krishna's design this truth has re-emerged from obscurity, like He also respoke *Bhagavad-gita* after it had been lost. Srila Prabhupada saying *"Someone has poisoned me"* beckons each disciple to study the truth of this these divine disappearance pastimes. We should study the complete evidence and be inspired to protect Srila Prabhupada's legacy and movement. Srila Prabhupada revealed his poisoning but did not name his poisoners. He left it up to us what we will do about it. Faithful followers place great stock in Srila Prabhupada's words, and his statements about poisoning are as important to them than forensics, witnesses, whispers, or all the other evidence. On top of his infallible words, forensic science has irrefutably proven that Srila Prabhupada was maliciously poisoned.

SUMMARY OF THE POISON DISCUSSIONS

(1) SP raised the poison issue himself. **(2)** He was told he had been poisoned. **(3)** SP maybe overheard those whispering in his room about poisoning, just as the tape recorder also heard the poison whispers. **(4)** SP was also told by "someone" that he had poisoning symptoms, and SP believed this accurate because he previously had read of poisoning symptoms. **(5)** <u>SP never said he was not poisoned</u>. **(6)** SP said *"Someone has poisoned me"* three times. **(7)** SP was evasive and oblique when Tamal asked WHO poisoned him. SP did not reveal his informant. **(8)** SP stated Bhaktisiddhanta also faced poisoning dangers (sources say he was poisoned by disciples). **(9)** After SP explained his "mental distress" was due to ***"Someone has poisoned me,"*** there were many clear acknowledgements and long discussions by all the caretakers of actual homicidal poisoning. No one argued or expressed doubts if SP was being poisoned. At the time it was accepted that SP was being poisoned. **(10)** Why would SP be in distress about being poisoned if (as Tamal claims, Ch. 40) it was a "mercy killing"? **(11)** The GBC's claim that SP said he was ***not*** poisoned is false. **(12)** Srila Prabhupada did not deny knowing who poisoned him, but he did not name who it was.

Srila Prabhupada's own infallible statements and the discussions about being poisoned, in themselves, and without any other evidence, make Srila Prabhupada's poisoning certain. Yet this was ignored until it became news 20 years later. Linking the "poison discussions" with the other evidence of forensically certified whispers, advanced scientific hair tests, medical symptoms, witnesses, ISKCON history, institutional cover-ups, suspects' denials, etc, then a very solid, clear conclusion emerges. The official unanimous GBC resolution, *"There is no evidence at this time to support the allegations of poisoning of Srila Prabhupada,"* makes a mockery of ISKCON leadership. For this dishonesty they all must be removed permanently and censured for life (at the minimum).

(Whispers) **SP:** *Why "phish-phish"? Why not talk? (Oct. 1977)*

In late 1997 several Florida devotees discovered background whispers and murmurings on tape recordings made in Srila Prabhupada's quarters, just before his departure on Nov. 14, 1977. Two whispers were quite clear: *"The poison's going down... (giggle) ...the poison's going down,"* and *"Is the poison in the milk?"* Others also contained the word poison or were highly unusual. A series of professional forensic audio analyses were conducted thereafter and the whispers' contents were consistently verified, but the ISKCON GBC dismissed them as just imaginary. For those who actually listened to the whispers recorded on Nov. 11, 1977, with decent audio equipment, there was practically universal acceptance of a poisoning conspiracy by Srila Prabhupada's caretakers. The GBC members and ISKCON leaders, however, somehow were not able or willing to decipher the whispers.

CHAPTER 16:
ORIGINS OF POISON INVESTIGATION

Rumors about Srila Prabhupada's being poisoned had circulated in ISKCON and in Vrindaban, India, the location of Srila Prabhupada's samadhi tomb, ever since Srila Prabhupada spoke about it just days prior to his departure on Nov. 14, 1977. Rupanuga das remembers the subject arose again in 1980. The *Vedic Village Review* editors heard about it in 1990. Partrikananda das documented these rumors and in early 1996 he tried to interest *VVR* in them. Puranjana das, a no-holds barred critic of ISKCON policies, raised the issue in mid-1997, publishing Srila Prabhupada's 1977 statements. In the mid 1990's, Satyaraja das, an ISKCON author, asked his friend Tamal about the poisoning rumors, and was told these persistent rumors arose every so often, much to Tamal's dismay, admitting they were not new. Rumors about a poisoning was too radical to believe-- until Sept. 1997, 20 years after Srila Prabhupada's departure, when the "poison whispers" were uncovered.

POISON WHISPERS DISCOVERED

In mid-1997 Naveen Krishna, an ISKCON GBC member, was in

Houston when he heard a local radio station was playing a recording of Srila Prabhupada's last days which was disturbing the local Hindu temple congregation. The tape indicated that Srila Prabhupada was poisoned. Naveen ordered a copy of the tape and listened to it with headphones. It was the Nov. 9-10, 1977 "poison discussions" between Srila Prabhupada and his caretakers, and he was very shocked, stunned. Badrinarayan and Anuttama, both prominent ISKCON leaders, visited him, and all three listened to the tape, with Srila Prabhupada complaining of being poisoned and discussing it with his caretakers. Badrinarayan said: *"If this turns out to be true, then we are all finished."*

Anuttama agreed the matter must be looked into by the GBC at once. Naveen listened to the tape again and heard the poison whispers for the first time, which hit him hard. Scores of devotees came to listen to the two whispers. News spread like wildfire amongst devotees worldwide. Isha das: *"I examined the whispers carefully using sophisticated electronic equipment, and had enhancements done on the tapes by FBI approved laboratories. My conclusion after hundreds of hours of analysis is that it is possible that Srila Prabhupada was poisoned. I called Balavanta and asked him if we could form an investigation committee. He agreed that Mahabuddhi, Jagajivan and myself would be on it..."* Mahabuddhi das, former temple president: *"We listened to Srila Prabhupada's tape of Nov. 10-11. We thought we had heard something like: LETS POISON IN THE MILK, and the more we heard it, about 100 times that night, the more it sounded that way."* Nityananda das, former temple president: *"Nov. 20, 1997: Mahabuddhi called and described shocking whispers he had found on a tape recording which indicated Srila Prabhupada had been poisoned in 1977. Thereafter I became involved in the effort to uncover the full truth behind these whispers and Srila Prabhupada's implied poisoning."*

GBC APPOINTS BALAVANTA AS SPECIAL INVESTIGATOR

In Sept. 1997 GBC member Naveen Krishna das was so concerned by Srila Prabhupada's poisoning discussions and whispers that, after consultations with senior devotees and GBC members, the GBC Executive Committee was convinced to make an "emergency" appointment of Balavanta das (William Ogle, attorney, former ISKCON GBC) to do an investigation. Balavanta was to research the alleged poisoning of Srila Prabhupada with Naveen's assistance, including a proper study of the alarming whispers. Balavanta posted online a statement that he was the new "GBC special investigator." Tamal, Srila Prabhupada's 1977 personal secretary and a leading GBC/ISKCON guru, called Naveen Krishna, trying his utmost to have the investigation handled internally by the GBC. But it was already official, funded, and moving forward. Naveen assured Tamal, with whom he had worked many years in Dallas, that this was meant to exonerate him from the rumors of poisoning Srila Prabhupada. The GBC gave $8000 for Balavanta's investigative costs- all he got over the next 2 1/2 years until his investigation was axed and superseded by a GBC cover-up.

FIRST PROFESSIONAL STUDY BY A SOUND STUDIO

Balavanta's initial and only public report in late 1997 stated about the "poison tape:" *"...it contains a whisper which refers to poison. This tape was digitally processed for clarity by an independent laboratory in Gainesville, Florida. According to the laboratory technician the following is the probable contents of the whispered statement. ....:* **'Let's not (or now) poison him and go'** *...We are currently sending the tape to another laboratory with more advanced equipment for further investigation. We will report the results of that study as available."* Balavanta collaborated with others, but he made no more reports of his investigative findings. Balavanta got a hush order from the GBC, due to Tamal's insistence. Tamal became the prime suspect with his unique voice recognizable in the whispers. Copies of Srila Prabhupada's conversations from his last days were circulated, including the Bengali and Hindi portions translated. The same tape with the poisoning whispers also had the "poison discussions" where Srila Prabhupada said three times *"Someone has poisoned me,"* and Tamal asked: *"Who is it that has poisoned?"* The shocking "poison discussions" between Srila Prabhupada and his caretakers went online. The poison issue was the main topic in the devotee world. The uproar and commotion was unlike anything seen before in ISKCON. Emotions ran high.

MORE POISON WHISPERS FOUND

Isha and Mahabuddhi found 4 damning whispers on the "poison tape." They were: **(1)** *"Is the poison in the milk?"* **(2)** *"the poison's going down, (giggle, giggle) the poison's going down"* **(3)** *"poison ishvarya rasa... get ready to go"* **(4)** *"put poison in different containers."* There was some uncertainty about the exact whisper contents, but the word "poison" was very clear to most everyone. On Nov. 30, 1997 Isha das, very adept with sound recording equipment, reported his own study of the poison whispers: *"After many devotees heard them, four of them were consistently and almost unanimously understandable. Based on these whispers, it was clear to these devotees that the whispers revealed Srila Prabhupada was poisoned in a conspiracy by his own caretakers. (1). Conv:36.373: After Srila Prabhupada asks to lie down flat: 'The* *poison's going down.. (giggle) the poison's going down.' (2). Conv:36.373: 'Is the poison in the milk? Um hum.' (3). Conv:36.374: After Srila Prabhupada says, 'Daytime we expose...' -Srila Prabhupada drinks something. (4). Conv:36.391: After Jayapataka says, 'Should there be kirtana?' we hear a Bengali phrase, and then the whisper 'Poison ishvarya rasa.' Srila Prabhupada says weakly and very surprised, 'To me?', then we hear, 'Take it easy, get ready to go,' then... 'The poison's in you Srila Prabhupada.' Then, 'He's going under... He's going under.' Then Hansadutta's kirtan began."*

It was soon realized that to properly hear the whispers, one needed a good quality tape played in ideal conditions with rapt attention. Many were listening to poor third or fourth generation copies. The best audio was a direct copy of the original at the Bhaktivedanta Archives in North Carolina. In Alachua many devotees went to SkyLab, a local sound studio, to listen to the enhanced and "cleaned up" whispers, with excessive background noise removed. The almost unanimous consensus was that the whispers revealed *Srila Prabhupada was being poisoned in a conspiracy by his own closest disciples*. Naveen met with many GBC members and reviewed the tapes and conversations with them. Without exception, they left very concerned and disturbed.

NORMAN PERLE'S BUNGLED AUDIO ANALYSIS

Balavanta knew that another ISKCON attorney, Mrgendra das in Los Angeles, had a few months earlier employed Norman Perle (National Audio Video Forensic Laboratory, CA) to study the May 28, 1977 "appointment tape" for any post-recording editing. Balavanta sent a poor quality copy of the Nov. 11, 1977 whispers tape to Perle, whom Isha das then called to discuss the whispers' locations on the tape. Perle told Isha that he had been asked by Balavanta to study only one whisper on a shoestring budget of $500. Perle's "one whisper" analysis did not verify any poison words. Surprised, Isha das called Perle again. *"I had discussed with Perle about several whispers locations on the tape but when Balavanta received his report there was confusion what Perle had actually analyzed. I called Perle to discuss which sections of tape he was listening to. I could not get a clear answer from him."* Balavanta and Isha concluded Perle did not examine the poison whisper locations due to inadequate instructions. The tape was also seriously degraded and poor quality. This forensic study with Norman Perle was bungled and useless, not even examining the whispers.

GBC GOES SECRET; ANOTHER SOUND STUDIO STUDY

Mahabuddhi: *"Balavanta came to meet us. We were always working as a cooperative team but he said he's now the only investigator."* The GBC had silenced Balavanta, to report only to them, and they would decide what to disclose publicly. This was the start of the GBC poison cover-ups, solidified as the poisoning evidence increased. What began as a cooperative effort amongst a group of devotees had now split into two groups: Balavanta's one-man GBC investigation and Rochan's Independent Vaishnava Council (IVC), including Mahabuddhi and Isha. Isha was disappointed: *"Balavanta informed me that there was no longer an investigation committee and that he was going to act alone based on the GBC's instruction."* The ISKCON website Chakra.org refused to post Isha's audio files and research. The GBC did not like that devotees would be able to listen to the whispers online, even though they were found on tapes from their own Bhaktivedanta Archives..

Nityananda joined the team, which continued with audio research. The whispers were digitally enhanced and cleaned for clarity by a prominent sound studio, George Blackwell's Soundtrack, Inc of Miami, who did work for law enforcement. Blackwell reported, early Dec. 1997: *"...on this tape after cleanup was 'It's not poison in the milk' or... 'It's not poisoned milk.' ...one calls upon other skills besides engineering for this type of work. ...I relied heavily upon my 25 years of experience in musical training and in recording voices for commercials and narrations."* He adjusted the pitch, filters and equalizer to obtain a variety of listening conditions. His conclusions were based primarily upon listening with the human ear and did not include more sophisticated or software analytical methods. Still, it was a high quality analysis confirming one whisper as having the words "poison" and "milk."

HARIKESH IS SWAYED

In Nov. 1997 Naveen asked Harikesh Maharaja, the main ISKCON GBC/guru power-broker of the time, to listen to the whispers and poison discussions, who admitted he clearly heard the whispers about poisoning and that he was very concerned. On Naveen's request Harikesh sent the whispers and poison discussions to the entire COM list (thousands of worldwide devotees emails in Harikesh's control). Harikesh was about to send Balavanta an additional US$8000 for investigation costs, but Ravindra Svarupa caused him to change his mind, and Naveen arranged the funds from the GBC's account. Then Harikesh posted on the web that after listening with "better headphones" he **could not hear** "poison" in the whispers. He had been intimidated by Tamal and Ravindra. For the GBC, there must be no poisoning. Too much was at stake. The institutional cover-ups had begun. But it remained a mystery to Harikesh why Srila Prabhupada would say that he was being poisoned. Harikesh dreamt of being chastised by Lord Narasimha for not sending the $8000, but Naveen naively advised him to wait (and so these funds never came.)

GBC RESPONDS TO THE POISON CONTROVERSY

News of the poison issue was carried by VNN.org, an independent devotee website, and soon by two biased ISKCON GBC puppet media websites: CHAKRA and Dandavats. Thousands checked the "poison issue" news daily. Finally an official ISKCON statement was issued Dec. 7, 1997 by GBC vice-chairman Bir Krishna Maharaja, who said it was "stiffened-up" by Ravindra Svarupa and Mukunda Maharaja):

*"Certain **conspiracy theorists** have been propagating of late the allegation that [Srila Prabhupada] met his demise on Nov. 14, 1977 due to intentional poisoning at the hands of his own disciples. The GBC considers this charge both absurd and offensive. Based on considerable testimony from those present at the time, and on its own preliminary internal study, the GBC is convinced that no such evil deed or even intention existed at the time. The GBC is certain that Srila Prabhupada's passing away was due to entirely natural causes, as his doctors stated. Some persons have claimed that they heard the word 'poison' whispered on a tape said to have been made in Srila Prabhupada's room.*

*"Many others, however, find the whispers indecipherable. ...one can read into the whisper almost anything one chooses. ...some persons are bent on establishing **the false and malicious theory that some of SP's own disciples conspired to poison him.** To refute this charge beyond the slightest doubt, the GBC has given the original tape over to independent forensic experts for detailed analysis. The singular purpose is to lay to rest **malevolently motivated theories about SP's passing.** According to Balavanta das, head of independent investigation, 'Initial reports from two of the forensic laboratories, both of which used equipment more sophisticated than any previously applied, do not find the word poison on the tape and do not support allegations of any wrongdoing.' It is now clear that the report of taped whispering conspirators is a false alarm. GBC is confident the final forensic report will confirm."*

We note the GBC **never** produced any forensic analysis to invalidate the poison whispers. They now officially took a stance of total denial and cover-up. Balavanta gave the GBC the bungled Perle study and a non-forensic Gainesville sound studio perusal (not a laboratory), both of whom could not confirm whispers about poison, due to poor quality tapes. This GBC huff and bluff was soon contradicted by multiple forensic studies, yet they would then reject audio forensics that they had already referred to as having invalidated the whispers! Balavanta's initial mis-steps and learning curve was exploited by GBC deniers.

"MALICIOUS" THEORISTS ARE DEMONIZED

Bir Krishna Maharaja (GBC), Bhakticharu Swami (1977 caretaker, suspect), and Ravindra Svarupa (GBC) issued another statement Jan. 17, 1998 that they had individually listened to the "poison tape," and did not hear any poison word in any whispers. Also, in their opinion, the phrase *"poison in different containers"* was actually *"posing different opinions."* (Later forensic studies agreed with this.) They also translated the phrase "kayek din pare asha" to mean *"in a few days' time."* Thus they tried to invalidate the whisper *"poison ishvarya rasa"* which follows **separately** and **after** the Bengali phrase "kayek din pare asha." This was like Norman Perle listening to the wrong part of the tape, but for the GBC, it was a deliberate "mistake." They also had poor quality, fourth generation tape copies. Preservation of their status quo prevailed over the truth.

Tamal, architect of the GBC cover-ups, Nov. 23, 1999: *"You can see people got kicked out of ISKCON for taking different positions. ISKCON takes very strong stands; it's quite typical of religious institutions, that they are always trying to identify themselves correctly, to define their positions, by saying who's wrong, ...[they] are **demonized and driven out**, or (chuckling) burned at the stake..."* This attitude dismayed all who hoped ISKCON would be open to the truth. Now, one with justifiable and legitimate concerns over Srila Prabhupada's departure was an ISKCON enemy. This was a public relations smoke-screen cover-up. The dishonest GBC, who had kept a Pandora's box of scandals shut with a scandalous 20 year ISKCON history (Vol. 5). They denied everything even before any investigation (and which was never completed). It was a gross exaggeration that ISKCON findings of *"considerable testimony and preliminary internal study"* determined there had been no foul play of poisoning. Balavanta had hardly done anything yet. If ISKCON was to honestly refute the poison issue beyond doubt, Tamal, Srila Prabhupada's secretary and primary caretaker for most of 1977, should have undergone open questioning. In Dec. 1997, Dhanesvara das called Tamal, who refused to discuss the poison issue or answer any questions, deferring to Balavanta's investigation (which he never cooperated with). He said every question he would answer would bring up many more questions (which is why he should have been questioned). Balavanta and Naveen were dismayed by the GBC denials. They both resigned from the GBC in 2000, disgusted by the GBC deception and cover-ups.

BALAVANTA'S INITIAL EFFORTS

The GBC was already *"convinced and certain that Srila*

Prabhupada was not poisoned," while still stuck with Balavanta's continuing investigation which would hire "independent forensic experts." Balavanta had initially been engaged by honest GBCs, but the suspects and their allies moved the GBC elites to deny and cover-up the evidence. Balavanta told Nityananda in Jan. 1998 he was inadequately funded by the GBC for his investigative work and he was donating time as a very busy attorney for the investigation only when possible. He said that unless there was some new evidence, such as a witness or smoking gun, that his investigation would soon finish with an inconclusive report. But he never did interviews with any suspects, material witnesses, or even devotees with background information. Jayapataka, Bhavananda, Hansadutta, Satadhanya, Bhakticharu, Adridharan and others were not interviewed. Tamal refused him access to his original 1977 diary. He needed a suitable testing laboratory for a chemical analysis (for which chemical?) of a sample of Srila Prabhupada's 1977 hair. He retrieved 1977 containers from Srila Prabhupada's Vrindaban quarters. He wanted to test those containers for traces of poison, even though the whisper was "voicing different opinions." His investigation struggled to gain traction.

INDEPENDENT VAISHNAVA COUNCIL

In Nov. 1997, the Independent Vaishnava Council (IVC) was formed by Rochan das, former Seattle temple president: *"IVC was formed to investigate statements uttered during Srila Prabhupada's final days, indicating he was being poisoned... a website- harekrishna.com was launched to facilitate a virtual investigative council. The volume of e-mail and incoming calls was overwhelming. ...a number of individuals offered support for the investigation. There was a common sense of urgency to compile and distribute a comprehensive summary of all available facts. The Council began discussing investigative protocol, the philosophical implications, etc. ...members launched an audio CD project, a series of forensic tape analyses, and various inquiries. We were moving forward, and cooperating together to pursue the truth."*

And so a team came together to pursue a ***private investigation*** of Srila Prabhupada's poisoning: Mahabuddhi, Isha, Rochan, Dhanesvara, and Nityananda. They would not wait on Balavanta's work, which was GBC controlled. They would do their own investigation. First priority would be audio forensic studies of the "poison whispers." Although hard to imagine Godbrothers poisoning Srila Prabhupada, it was very possible, in light of the audio evidence and ISKCON's history (Volume 5). Transcending the GBC denials and Balavanta's secrecy, they would scientifically, forensically certify the "poison whispers," and settle what was in them. Courts accepted audio forensics as a valid evidence.

CHAPTER 17:
THE SCIENCE OF AUDIO FORENSICS

The GBC claimed that the poison whispers were differently heard by different people, according to their ears and mental predispositions, and they were not clear evidence. But professional audio forensic studies confirming the poison whispers would cancel the GBC denials that the whispers could be whatever one wanted them to be. The science of audio forensics was able to determine speech content *beyond the limitations of human subjectivity*. However, the limits of GBC dishonesty was underestimated. In spite of audio forensic analyses verifying the poison whispers, the GBC would continue their charade in March 2000, calling them, "Will-o-the Wisps." *NTIAP* p. 12: *"The Whispers Time Waster: Here the imagination finds no reins. Listen carefully and speculate. You, in your own home, can play FBI and catch the bumbling killers surrounding Prabhupada. Hear them blurt out their evil deed. Next you can jump on the internet and vilify the ISKCON leader of your choice."*

NTIAP would also extract words out of context so that Srila Prabhupada supposedly denied being poisoned (Ch. 11), so, if there was no poisoning, how can there be whispers about it? *NTIAP* ridicules the poison whispers and those who hear them. Just like crooked politicians. Why do 99% of devotees hear the poison words in the whispers but no GBC can? Many top-level audio forensic laboratories would certify the poison whispers after 1998, as seen in the coming chapters. Such is the hypocrisy that even "spiritual leaders" such as ISKCON GBCs and gurus will disregard clear evidence and the words of the Acharya. They concoct an apparent flaw in some detail, and then pretend that all the evidence is flawed. This fools maybe 50% and is the reason for this volume—to clearly present and interpret the full body of evidence.

Even normal speech is often contested, so creating doubts about the "poison whispers" was easy. Written words are clear, but spoken words sometimes must be verified by science and experts. Individuals making proclamations about what they hear is not the final verdict, even it be from the GBC. We needed the verdicts of accredited, reputable forensic audio analysts to determine with scientific equipment and advanced technology **what the whispers really were**. If we had several expert opinions agreeing on the gist of the whispers (at least the poison word itself), then this would be court-admissible evidence. The private investigation team would solicit a series of expert forensic audio analyses with multiple confirmations of the "poison whispers."

The GBC elite criticizes audio forensics science, saying it is "voodoo," quack science that is unreliable, and that sounds cannot be interpreted by technology, that this is only for the realm of human hearing and recognition, and that those who profess expertise in audio forensics are in the same league as fortune tellers, hypnotists, and chiropractors. However, the technology of audio forensic science has made more dramatic advancements even since 1998, and this GBC denial of audio forensics is ludicrous. In 2022 we now have audio language translators and voice recognition software (Google Voice, Google Translator). In *NTIAP*, the GBC employed a minor sound studio to review the whispers in 15 minutes and then lied about the results, and claimed they had discredited the science of audio forensics. (Ch. 50). As in any scientific profession, one must carefully vet and chose a reputable forensic specialist. Audio forensics science has great merit, credibility, and accuracy. There are many organizations of audio forensic specialists worldwide. Some work with law enforcement, or government, or cater to private clients. E.g.,: **(1)** Intern'l Assoc. for Identification **(2)** New York Institute for Forensic Audio **(3)** Audio Engineering Society **(4)** American Academy of Forensic Sciences **(5)** American Board of Recorded Evidence **(6)** American College of Forensic Examiners Institute.

GOVERNMENTS EMPLOY AUDIO FORENSICS

Governments routinely performs audio forensic authentication on messages from "terrorists" like Osama Bin Laden, Boko Haram's Abubakar Shekau, and Al Qaeda's Ayman al-Zawahiri. Audio forensics is regularly employed by law enforcement agencies worldwide in pursuit of criminal and civil investigations in court proceedings. The science of audio forensics is an established, credible scientific technology, widely used and accepted. Yet, the GBC has ignored these facts.

Audio Enhancement Techniques: For audio recordings, a variety of filters can be applied to enhance the material, bringing out specific aspects or events contained in the recording. *Spectral Noise Reduction:* Attenuation of unwanted background noise or ambiance in the recording to improve the Signal to Noise ratio (SNR). *Frequency Equalization:* Highly precise equalizers can be used to boost or cut specific bands of frequencies. This process makes speech more intelligible for identification purposes. *Amplitude Adjustments:* Overall amplitude may be increased/ decreased during these enhancement processes. *Compression & Normalization:* Quiet sounds in a recording such as whispering can be boosted by compressing the level of the signal so that the dynamic range of the material is reduced. This makes the wanted sounds in the audio recording more audible.

An audio forensic firm's resume and various services (Sound Testimony®) gives an idea of how sound is scientifically analyzed: **(1)** We specialize in audio forensic analysis and in improving recorded speech comprehension including intelligibility enhancement, audio recovery, and audio authentication. Our proprietary hardware/software system works to recover intelligible speech and other sounds from noise-intensive backgrounds & poorly recorded media. **(2)** We use advanced computer analysis to perform forensic audio recording authentication. **(3)** Our experience in criminal and civil cases includes murder, corporate fraud, employment discrimination, sexual harassment, labor, and family law. **(4)** We consult with counsel offering audio forensic evidence examination, analysis, restoration & recovery, litigation support, expert advice, expert testimony, and related expert witness services including preparation of cross-examinations and courtroom presentations. **(5)** We review other audio forensics investigators' work for any discrepancies, inaccuracies. **(6)** Our services also include voice recognition and/or elimination. **(7)** In most cases involving surveillance and evidentiary recordings, speech intelligibility is greatly improved. In some instances, the improvement is so significant that speech is revealed that was so hidden in noise that it was barely distinguishable from the background.

(8) Transcript creation, review and, if necessary, correction of existing transcripts is available after increasing intelligibility. **(9)** We also offer voice and sound extraction, tape verification, recording verification, signal, sound & event succession investigation, dialogue decoding, voice recognition and/or elimination, and surveillance recording preparation. **(10)** We use a proprietary system of hardware, digital signal processing (DSP), and computer analysis to recover speech from all devices. **(11)** Our unique audio forensic evidence examination, analysis, restoration, and recovery services are available to attorneys, law enforcement agencies, corporations, investigators, and private individuals. **(12)** Clients include Prosecutors, Defense Attorneys, Family Law & General Practice Attorneys, other Legal and Investigative Professionals, the National Security Agency (NSA), human resource departments, corporate directors, private detectives and individuals. **(13)** We work with high quality professional video editing suites to enhance audio from video surveillance tapes. **(14)** Although each case is different, our professional standards and pursuit of excellence never vary. Our decades of audio enhancement began before the computer age. Our experience combined with the latest computerized analysis and recovery tools provides professional solutions to your audio forensic analysis, recovery, recording authentication, and voice recognition needs.

SCIENTIFIC ADVANCEMENT IN AUDIO FORENSICS

The audio forensic science field relates to the acquisition, analysis, and evaluation of sound recordings that may ultimately be admissible evidence in a court of law or other venue. Audio forensic evidence may come from a criminal investigation by law enforcement or as part of an inquiry into an accident, fraud, slander case, etc. The primary aspects of audio forensics are establishing authenticity of audio evidence, enhancement of audio to improve speech intelligibility and the audibility of low-level sounds, and interpreting and documenting sonic evidence, such as identifying speakers, transcribing dialogue, and reconstructing crime or accident scenes and timelines. Modern audio forensics makes extensive use of digital signal processing, with the use of analog filters obsolete. Adaptive filtering and discreet Fourier transforms are used extensively. Recent advances in audio forensics techniques include voice biometrics and electrical network frequency analysis.

Until the early 1970's, tape recorders that captured Srila Prabhupada's spiritual voice were reel to reel, with a loose spool of magnetic tape threaded on the recorder and manually reversed for Side B. Then came cassette recorders with insertable closed tapes. Portable cassette recorders proliferated in the Hare Krishna movement from 1972 onwards, until the age of compact discs (CDs). All methods of preserving sound up to and including the CD involved a *medium,* whether wax, polyvinyl disc, magnetic tape, or plastic. The CD almost totally dominated the consumer audio market by 2000, but within another decade, rapid developments in computing technology saw it rendered virtually redundant by the most significant invention in audio recording— the *digital audio file* (.wav, .mp3, etc). Combined with new digital signal compression algorithms, greatly reducing file sizes, digital audio files rapidly dominated the market, such as with Apple's iTunes application and iPod portable media player. Downloadable digital audio has also enabled dramatic improvements in the restoration and remastering of recordings made on older media. Poor quality magnetic tape recordings of Srila Prabhupada's bhajans, conversations, and lectures have been "cleaned-up," greatly improved in sound clarity and quality, reducing unwanted background noise, and converted to digital audio files. This marked the beginning of a new era in recording. At the same time, dramatic advances in home computing and the internet meant that digital sound recordings are now captured, processed, reproduced, and stored- entirely electronically, on a range of magnetic and optical recording media, and these can be distributed easily, with no loss of fidelity, and crucially, without no need for any recording medium.

It is Lord Chaitanya's arrangement that science would develop ways to record, preserve, and playback sound spoken by the pure devotee. The Hare Krishna movement could be spread everywhere on this planet simply with Srila Prabhupada's books, but with his voice captured in digital audio files on personal computers and smart phones, it is the same as Srila Prabhupada being there. His coming to the West and modern sound technology are divine arrangements. Digital audio files have much improved quality and clarity. Software is also universally downloadable which can greatly improve the audibility of background whispers.

Audio forensics applies the tools/ techniques of audio engineering and digital signal processing to study audio data as part of an investigation, with authentication, enhancement, and interpretation. The enhancement, or clarification, of forensic audio is a common task related to the processing and analysis of audio evidence. Recordings which end up as forensic evidence are often made in non-ideal environments with non-ideal equipment leading to degraded quality and a poor ratio of signal to noise (SNR). Some recent advances include research into new algorithms for speech enhancement and recent developments in the evaluation of speech intelligibility. Since speech enhancement research is well established and contributions in this area are very frequent, the impact of innovative research is gradual but dramatic.

There are novel and relevant publications in the main areas related to forensic audio enhancement: deconvolution, speech intelligibility evaluation, and new areas of Compressive Sensing (CS) and Computational Auditory Scene Analysis (CASA). There are two recent reference publications related to this field. The *Encyclopedia of Forensic Sciences* (2nd Ed) featured a chapter on *Forensic Audio Enhancement and Authentication* by Grigoras & Smith, with a basic procedure for the handling and processing of forensic audio for both enhancement and authentication. Loizou's *Speech Enhancement: Theory and Practice* (711 p, 2013) continues to be a valuable reference in speech enhancement. It deals with the need to design algorithms to improve speech intelligibility without sacrificing quality evaluation measures, and enhancement algorithms aimed at improving speech intelligibility. It describes all the major enhancement algorithms and also covers noise estimation algorithms. It looks at measures to assess the performance, in terms of speech quality and intelligibility, of speech enhancement methods. Clear and concise, this book is an essential resource to implement the latest speech enhancement algorithms to improve the quality and intelligibility of speech degraded by noise (book comes with a CD). The Scientific Working Group on Digital Evidence (SWGDE) published guidelines and best practices related to forensic audio. The Audio Committee made up of law enforcement and academia released the updated "Core Competencies for Forensic Audio v1.0" in Sept. 2011, which is a valuable resource for the drafting of laboratory practices and Standard Operating Procedures (SOPs) respecting consensus driven best practices for forensic audio processing and enhancement.

CHAPTER 18:
MITCHELL'S AUDIO FORENSIC ANALYSIS

AUDIO FORENSICS, ADVANCED SCIENTIFIC METHODS

We wanted to go beyond the subjective human ear. Mahabuddhi learned that audio forensics was an extremely diverse and advanced science, as researchers improved equipment, analytical methods, computers, and software that accurately recognize the human voice. *Sounds of Speech Communication* by JM Pickett and *Acoustic Analysis of Speech* by Kent and Reed are two older definitive texts on the science of speech. One of the oldest tools used in speech recognition is still unexcelled in definitive identification of spoken words, namely the *Wide Band Voice Spectrograph*. It provides detailed information about the many frequencies and intensities of the various sounds in speech.

The spectrograph clearly presents the complex harmonic structure of the English language's 40 voiced phonemes, being the sound elements used to produce every word. The voice spectrograph (a printed sound "picture") displays one phoneme after another, providing an image of each word, with a similar pattern regardless of the accent, cadence, and the peculiarities of a particular voice. Unlike the human ear, the spectrograph is fully *objective* in identifying spoken words. Voice spectrograph analysis accurately determines even barely audible whispers with a confidence level of greater than 90% and has been used for decades by law enforcement and as court evidence. The whispers' true content could be determined by combining human interpretation with analysis by advanced technology and spectrographic image charts. Dr. Helen A. McCaffrey: *"Consequently, acoustic speech analysis does not yield absolute identification of speech sounds… acoustic analysis may confirm a message that has been perceived via listening to a signal and may also yield alternatives…"*

EXPERT AUDIO FORENSIC ANALYST ENGAGED

Mahabuddhi consulted with the American College of Forensic Examiners (ACFE) to locate a professional audio forensic laboratory, and he chose Jack Mitchell with Computer Audio Engineering (CAE) in New Mexico. Nityananda offered to bear the expenses (no one else would). Mitchell had $250K of equipment in his sound laboratory, and an impressive resume and credentials with 30 years working with sound, music, and recording arts. Mahabuddhi arranged the analysis, supplying a third generation copy (we had not yet understood the need to get original copies from Bhaktivedanta Archives) of the T-46 "Last Tape," carefully detailing the whispers' locations and that we wanted certainty on what was spoken. Mitchell was not told what the whispers were, with no information on the poisoning controversy; we wanted an objective analysis. CAE was told there were foreign language portions. After a week, Jack Mitchell called Mahabuddhi and advised: ***"You should be arranging for legal counsel,"*** as it appeared he had found a poison

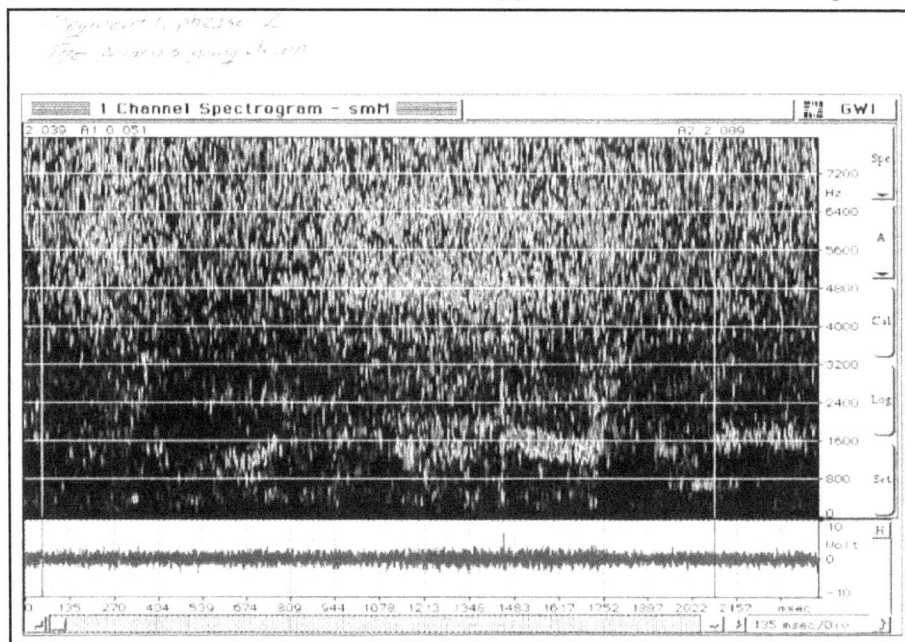

conspiracy. Mahabuddhi replied this was exactly what we had feared.

(Above: "THE POISON'S GOING DOWN" SPECTOGRAPH)

On Jan. 26, 1998, the report came with $4600 in costs, stating: *"Each segment was subjected to analysis using both Signalyze and Soundscope software. Methods employed were: F-T-A sonogram display, amplitude envelopes, 100ms segment FFT, LPC formant tracking– of particular interest was F2 trajectory tracking of the tongue movement, sound file amplification and normalization. The analysis activity involves data measurement, aural and visual alignment and segmentation of sonic events."* This first audio forensic report by CAE went into *Someone Has Poisoned Me (1999),* with 13 spectrographs (5 color) of the whispers.

MITCHELL ANALYSIS CONFIRMED BY SECOND EXPERT

The report included confirmation from a certified Texas audiologist *of all of his findings.* They meticulously discussed the technicalities of each phoneme. *"During signal analysis and dialog decoding, nine hours of consultation was done with Dr. Helen McCaffrey, Department of Communication Sciences and Disorders, Texas Christian University."* The report left the team members in shock. Two whispers had been verified containing the word POISON. Whisper #1 is from p. 373 ConvBk 36, Nov. 10, 1977. Srila Prabhupada: *"Hmmm. You make me flat,"* and then, in the background, Mitchell's analysis ascertained a person uttering softly a long, two part whisper to be: *"PUSH REAL HARD, ITS GOING DOWN HIM. THE POISON'S GOING DOWN"*

Most devotees and other forensic analysts found a similar version, namely: "The poison's going down, (giggle, giggle), the poison's going down." Uncontested was *"the poison's going down."* Mitchell had a low quality tape copy, and so Whisper #2 about poison in the milk was not confirmed, but it would be with many other experts. Mitchell did not return to this whisper after we later sent him an Archives original copy.

Whisper #3 is in ConvBk 36.391, Nov. 10, 1977. Someone fluent in Bengali speaks four Bengali words: "kayek din pare asha," meaning "in a few days' time." *After that* Jayapataka Maharaja (*definitely* it is his voice) says, not a whisper but a full voice in the distance: *"POISONING FOR A LONG (TIME?)"* Mahabuddhi and Isha had both heard this portion as: *"Poison Ishvarya Rasa."* Mitchell's and Mahabuddhi's versions are very similar phonetically (ish = ing, varya = for a) and both confirm the key <u>poison</u> word. *This whisper is about poisoning.* Interestingly, *rasa* means pastime, *Ishvar* refers the Supreme Controller. Was **JPS** speaking about "the poison pastime, taking one to God?" (or "Now you go meet your maker?") Some Ayurvedic medicines are called "rasayana." Immediately after this, was faint background speech:

SP: *To me?* Voice 2: *That's really original.* Voice: *Get ready to go.*

Srila Prabhupada's betrayers were informing him on the verge of death that they had been poisoning him all along, mocking him. Mahabuddhi and Isha, both with very high quality headphones and tape players, both respected, level-headed men, also found Srila Prabhupada replying to Jayapataka, "To me?' and then "Get ready to go." In 2022 an audio forensic lab studied and confirmed these findings (Ch. 27).

"WE KNOW HE'S TRYING TO TRAP US"

CAE also analyzed the "containers" whisper which takes place (ConvBk 36.380) Nov. 11, 1977. Balavanta and others thought Tamal was saying, *"Put poison in different containers."* The GBC said this was: *"we're voicing different opinions..."* This makes sense, as the word opinion was used just a little earlier in a discussion whether to go on parikrama or not. And Mitchell confirmed the GBC's version, proving the objectivity of audio science. And there were new discoveries. Just before this, Tamal was found by CAE saying: *"We know he's trying to trap us."* And: *"He's as sly as they come."* This fits in with a secretive plot, not caring lovingly for Srila Prabhupada. It seems Tamal knew Srila Prabhupada knew for quite some time they were poisoning him: he was tolerating and accepting this. With the Nov. 9-10 revelations, he told us about it, and then said no more about it for the next few days until departure. Was there a contest of wits with Srila Prabhupada?

CAE noted many other whispers as well (Ch. 20).

SUMMARY

There was a poison conspiracy; the certified whispers confirmed it. The unthinkable was reality. The CAE report pushed fence-sitters with weak hearts to take the "poison issue" seriously. Audio forensic analysis was key to verifying what the whispers were. CAE's analysis was, in quality and accuracy, far above any of subjective listening by human ears. Audio forensics is a legal method of evidentiary proof. When this matter comes to the courtroom, the Mitchell report will be hard evidence. Since then, technology has evolved even further. These poison whispers can be clearly heard online by a simple web search. Listen to them.

CHAPTER 19:
TESTING FOR TAMPERED TAPES

In Jan. 1998 Mahabuddhi left the team, encouraging Nityananda to continue, who contemplated further forensic analysis with Jack Mitchell and other experts. Ever since the "appointment tape" of May 28, 1977 was first circulated underground amongst devotees in the mid-eighties, first as various differing transcripts, then as actual tapes, there was suspicion it was edited or tampered. This tape had a conversation with Srila Prabhupada on who would initiate devotees after his physical departure. Devotees noticed clicks and strange noises on the tape, and many wondered if it had been spliced, if sections had been rearranged, or pieces were deleted to fabricate a different message from Srila Prabhupada's words. The tape seemed incoherent in places. As *VVR* editor, Nityananda wanted in 1990 to test of the appointment tape for tampering. He decided to have CAE analyze the May 28, 1977 and Nov. 11, 1977 tapes for "edits." Total costs came to $16k.

ANOTHER NORMAN PERLE BUNGLED "STUDY"

First, Nityananda had to uncover the details of another bungled "Perle study," other than Balavanta's early 1998 Perle audio test on the whispers tape. Mrigendra das (Harvey Mechanic), attorney and former ISKCON temple president, was asked by the GBC in mid-1997 (before the poison issue arose) to arrange a forensic analysis of the May 28, 1977 tape for alleged tampering or editing. The GBC wanted to address the widespread allegations that they had tampered with this tape many years earlier in order to support their zonal Acharya system (1978-1987). The Bhaktivedanta Archives sent a direct copy of the original tape to Norman Perle's audio forensics lab. Mrigendra's instructions were simple: *was the tape edited or tampered with?* Perle's report in Sept. 1997 caused great commotion: *"consistent with editing/tampering... this recording exhibits strong signs suggestive of falsification."* Perle identified six points, each documented with a waveform and spectrograph analysis, plus a brief commentary: *"...consistent with a recording made from an edited Master recording."* Perle thought the tape had six edits.

In Nov. 1997 Bir Krishna Maharaja explained to Nityananda that Perle had identified points where the tape recorder had been turned off and then on again. This was the method in which room conversations with Srila Prabhupada were taped, and recorded sections were separated by on-off "breaks." Mrigendra admitted to Nityananda he did *not* inform Perle as to this start-stop routine and neither did Perle ask about this. Perle's $500 budget was inadequate for a proper analysis. Mrigendra and the GBC realized the faux pas too late. So now there were two bungled, useless Perle tests. Perle's points of "falsification" were actually stop-start points and totally legit. Perle's "study" falsely increased suspicions of the May 28 tape being edited while not settling the question at all.

FORENSIC METHODOLOGY

Direct copies of the two tapes' originals were sent to CAE from the Archives. We finally understood the need for direct copies, called "DAT." Nityananda discussed with Mitchell the technical differences in spectrographic signatures of a start-stop compared to various types of illegitimate edits. Magnetic tape edits can be made by (1) over-recording,

(2) "punching in" electronically, or (3) the old-school razor blade butt-splice. Magnetic tape editing was not like today's "cut and paste" digital, on-screen computer editing. Magnetic tapes often snapped and were repaired with cellophane tape, often with a piece of damaged tape lost. Mitchell spoke of differing "ramp times" created by start/stops on different recorders. He could differentiate between stop/start points and editing points. Each recorder makes unique "signatures" on the magnetic tape, with its unique functions of pause, auto reverse, internal vs. external mike, fast forward, etc. To make a truly definitive analysis, we needed the actual tape recorders used May 28 and Nov. 11, 1977. Where were these recorders from 20 years earlier?

OBTAINING THE UHER

After many phone calls, we learned there was a UHER *reel to reel* recorder used to record Srila Prabhupada until early 1976. Then Hari Sauri das, Srila Prabhupada's servant, arranged to buy a UHER *cassette* recorder. Being easier to use, the quantity of recording increased dramatically in 1976. A second UHER cassette recorder was kept in Los Angeles for when Srila Prabhupada was often there and as a back-up. Parama-rupa das, Bhaktivedanta Tape Ministry founder (later Bhaktivedanta Archives), told Nityananda that he used the second cassette UHER in L.A. up to Feb. 1978, after which it was sent to India. Its location today is unknown. Hari Sauri also borrowed from Hansadutta in late Oct. to Nov. 22, 1976 a Uher 4400 Report reel to reel recorder. Nityananda had toured Puru das' Bhaktivedanta Memorial Museum at ISKCON Brooklyn in 1989 and remembered one of Srila Prabhupada's Uher tape recorders in a showcase. Puru took this museum with him after he left ISKCON. Tamal gave this UHER to Puru soon after Srila Prabhupada's departure and it was the most likely recorder to have made the two 1977 tapes we wanted to test for edits. Nityananda asked Puru to speak with Mitchell, and the UHER was sent. Mitchell repaired a short and the UHER was operational. Would this UHER's unique footprint signatures match those on either the whisper or appointment tapes? Were the anomalies on them due to edits and tampering? There was also a small silver SONY cassette recorder used in India when the UHER was unavailable or not working, now on display in Srila Prabhupada's Vrindaban quarters. Puru called Tamal about the history of this UHER and the silver SONY. However, Tamal politely declined. Why?

NO EDITS OR TAMPERING FOUND BY CAE

Mitchell had several technical consultations with Parama-rupa at the Archives, and they figured that any anomalies on Archives copies created by the *dubbing machine* would be eliminated if DAT (direct analog tape) copies were made. By Archives policy, original tapes *"do not leave the Archives without one of the Archives directors watching every second it is out of the vault."* A DAT copy was sent to CAE early March 1998. CAE also consulted with Norman Perle and Mrigendra on their appointment tape analysis. If Srila Prabhupada's sacred words on tape had been edited, it would be a significant discovery. Just as there is great consternation regarding the ongoing GBC-approved editing of Srila Prabhupada's books, if his sacred words on tape could also not be trusted, then what was left? It would be like the Bible, with current editions vastly changed from an unknown original.

CAE experimented with combinations of the UHER functions to replicate the "anomalies" identified on the two tapes, to determine if they were produced by tampering or normal operations. The anomalies were fully reconciled as normal. *No evidence of tampering or editing was found on both the appointment tape or poison tape.* On the May 28 tape, 2 of the 6 "anomalies" identified by Perle (1, 6) were lack of recognition of the tape "leader" at the start and end of the tape. This could only be ascertained on the original tape, which Jack Mitchell confirmed with the Archives. The other four anomalies were stop-start points.

The poison tape's "anomalies" were actually more challenging, and included: (1) a three seconds blank spot, (2) sudden amplitude changes, (3) spiked "ramps," etc. However, Mitchell reconciled the anomalies on *the poison tape: it was not edited.* However, there were conditions attached to these conclusions. **(1)** The Nov. 11 "poison" tape *was* made by this UHER. **(2)** CAE found the May 28 tape *was not* recorded on Puru's UHER cassette recorder (likely made by the Sony) **(3)** Even though the May 28 tape was not recorded on this UHER, there was no evidence of tampering detected and only had stop-start points with no irregular anomalies and no unexplained areas. *No anomalies were in the area of the critical "appointment" discussion.*

FULL CERTAINTY ONLY IF ARCHIVES ORIGINALS TESTED

Later Jack Mitchell noted that the certainty of no editing or tampering on the two tapes was about 80%. Final certainty could only be achieved if the ***original*** Archives tapes were tested by a "fluid magnetic development" process. He said such a test does not affect or damage the tape, but Parama-rupa thought it could potentially harm the original, and thus would not allow it. In this test, under 6X magnification, the magnetic signatures on the tape surface reveal "tank tracks" which would be broken by gaps every time the recorder was shut off for a "break." On copies the tank tracks are continuous. Testing the original tape could determine 100% the issue of tampering. An absence of gaps at stop-start points on the original tape would be proof that the "original" was actually a copy, and if editing had taken place, it would be revealed by the "tank tracks." There is still a 20% uncertainty. We hope in the future this question will be resolved by further analysis and tests, if possible.

POSSIBILITY OF NON-CHRONOLOGICAL TAPES

Early on, Mahabuddhi repeatedly mentioned his suspicion that the poison tape's sections seemed to be out of chronological order. He thought the *"Get ready to go"* episode was actually the very last of Srila Prabhupada's room conversations, with Srila Prabhupada given a final lethal dose and told *"poison ishvarya rasa"* or*" poisoning for a long time."* If so, why is this followed with more room conversations? Our research found several 1977 conversation tapes were not accurately dated. Perhaps "Get ready to go" was when Srila Prabhupada entered internal consciousness on Nov. 13, not Nov. 11 as the tape is marked. Misdating of tapes is examined in Ch. 8. Volume 2 looks at Tamal's missing tapes issue in depth. *The UHER is in the ISKCON Bangalore's Vrindaban Prabhupada Museum. The SONY recorder is in ISKCON Vrindaban Prabhupada Museum.*

CHAPTER 20:
SECONDARY WHISPERS

FURTHER WHISPERS FOUND

Jack Mitchell's first report came Jan. 25, 1998, and it verified the two primary poison-word whispers plus a number of secondary whispers. The last tape was full of whispers, unlike others. Due to the superior quality of the DAT tapes over what he had earlier studied, Mitchell decided to go back and review the whispers, going through the T-46 "last tape" carefully again. On March 26, 1998, Part One of an addendum report was received where CAE identified additional whispers. His original findings on the primary poison-word whispers remained the same. In late April 1998 Nityananda received Part Two of CAE's audio forensic analysis, with the report on no tampering on the May 28 "appointment" and Nov. 11 "poison whisper" tapes (Ch. 19). However, he found further secondary background whispers on T-46 (Nov. 11).

Whispering was common in Srila Prabhupada's room in 1977,

perhaps because Srila Prabhupada's hearing had become so poor there was no longer the same concern for secrecy. But the superior UHER German technology captured them and audio forensics ascertained more than the human ear could. These secondary whispers were isolated and studied by CAE, some of which also verified by Isha and Mahabuddhi's personal audio research. Most audio forensic labs were not given the mandate to search the entire T-46 tape for secondary whispers as was done with CAE. In Ch. 27 another elite audio forensics firm in 2022 also verified all three poison and secondary whispers. Some of these secondary whispers fit well with innocuous talks at that time, such as the health risks for Srila Prabhupada going on a very long, bumpy bullock-cart parikrama tour. But some are shocking and appear associated with the primary poison-word whispers.

CATEGORIZING SECONDARY WHISPERS

Below is the chronological sequence, with T-46's time markers, of the three main poison whispers *and* the secondary whispers, *including those confirmed by other audio analysts (before and after Mitchell's analysis)*, with comments. We categorized these whispers in three ways:

Multiple-verified poison whispers/ speech: BOLD CAPITALS
Multiple-Verified Secondary Whispers: PLAIN CAPITALS
Mitchell and 2023 forensic studies: secondary whispers: lower case
*All those that are **NOT** innocuous, are underlined.*

T-46 Side A:

Whisper: 00:57..."going down." (confirming next whisper)
WHISPER #1: 02.10   POISON'S GOING DOWN, (giggle, giggle) THE POISON'S GOING DOWN. (Tamal, answered by Bhavananda)
WHISPER #2: IS THE POISON IN THE MILK? UH-HUH
(spoken by Tamal and answered by Bhavananda)

Whisper #2 is the second "primary" poison whisper, not confirmed by Mitchell but later confirmed by many other experts, as we see below. It is significant that shortly after this whisper, Srila Prabhupada is offered milk to drink, wanting it a little warm, but then saying it was too sweet. He is clearly heard on the tape drinking the milk from the whisper. Someone answers affirmatively, with "uh-huh," meaning at least two persons are in the whispers.

Whisper: 03:25:"did it hurt?" WHISPER: 21:40:"HE'S GONNA DIE"
WHISPER: 21:58:"LISTEN, HE'S SAYING...GOING TO DIE."
Voice: 27.50: "it looks to me he's stupid... looks that way, yeah."
Soft voice: 33.36... "that's funny" Whisper: 33.41... "let's go out"
Tamal: 35.03... "Energies conserved and built up, and managed, and..." ()

Whisper: 35.19... "let's redeem ourselves"
Whisper: 35.32... "did you drink? How many?"
Whisper: 44.42... "god dammit JAY'S ...oh god"... "god damn..."
Whisper: 44.57: "fifty percent's your cut" 45.49: "well, no good reason" Whisper:
46.08: "you doin'?" Whisper: 46.51: "yes a heart attack time."

The whispers *"He's gonna die"* and *"heart attack time."* fit right in with the talks on how parikrama (walking tour) could cause a heart attack, since Srila Prabhupada was too frail for the bumpy roads. This is a remarkable validation of Mitchell's expertise by identifying these whispers when not familiar with the esoteric context of the talks.

T-46 Side B:

Whisper: 03.47... "do it again "Whisper: 05.19... "...maybe we...
Whisper: 17.05... "stay here" Whisper: 20.04... "somebody could
expect... experience..."Low voice: 21.18... "check these thing and..."
Tamal: *"WE KNOW HE'S TRYING TO TRAP US"*
Tamal: *21:25... "I told you what's going on. Ordered to...(?) HE'S AS SLY (SLAY) AS THEY COME."*

This "trap and sly" low voice speech (clearly Tamal's Bronx accent) has also been heard by many devotees. This increases suspicion of a conspiracy and some intrigue with Srila Prabhupada, where he accepts his being poisoned while cleverly dealing with his caretakers whom he loves and wants the best. Tamal is obviously *the prime suspect.*

Whisper: 23.21: "like this (his) last time out"
The "last time out" refers to Srila Prabhupada's final parikrama.
Soft voice #1: 28.44: "could have been ten percent of it"
Soft voice #2: 28.44... "can you buck the (?)..."
Jayapataka: 35.14: "You like kirtan?" (Bengali): "Kayek din pare asha" (In a few days' time...)
WHISPER #3: Jayapataka: *"POISONING FOR A (long) time"* (or *"Poison ishvarya rasa")* SP: *"TO ME?"* (high, squeaky voice) *Unknown: "(that's really) original."* **JPS: *Get Ready To Go.***
Voice: "My number's in the pass (port/book)." Voice: "Ok. Going now, (prabhu)." Voice: "(Yes, today or yesterday)." Voice: "Anything might of happened today." Voice: "(Look), I'm not afraid to die." Voice: "Very good." Voice: "You're taking it right now." Soft elder voice: "How's this?" Voice: "Let it go."

Following primary poison whisper #3 are disturbing secondary whispers; they come late on the last tape. Jayapataka Maharaja says to Srila Prabhupada in his distinct nasal voice "...poisoning for a long time." Srila Prabhupada's weak, high-pitch, wobbly response, "To me?" is heartbreaking. "Get ready to go" fits right in with a final poisoning, as does "You're taking it right now" and "Let it go." Most audible is the poison word and "To me?" Many devotees have heard all this quite clearly. You are taking poison right now? This does not sound like a voluntary assisted suicide like Tamal claims happened (Ch. 40).

These last whispers do not sound benign. The primary and secondary T-46 whispers are supportive of a poisoning conspiracy, and add significantly to the audio evidence. Srila Prabhupada's final poisoning is indicated with his poisoners heartlessly betraying him in his last hours. *Srila Prabhupada expired about 24 hours later, as best as can be determined.* There is too much here to be dismissed. **ALL** of the forensic studies in Part 3 agree upon the poison word in the primary 3 whispers, but **NONE** of the ISKCON leaders do. With the poison whispers, Srila Prabhupada saying he was poisoned, the caretakers talking about poisoning, the hair tests, and other evidence, how can the GBC say there is no evidence? The whispers themselves clearly indicate a poisoning conspiracy by Srila Prabhupada's leading disciples.

SUMMARY OF WHISPERS:

WHISPER: 00:57: "GOING DOWN."
WHISPER #1: 02.10 "POISON'S GOING DOWN, (giggle, giggle) THE POISON'S GOING DOWN."
WHISPER #2: "IS THE POISON IN THE MILK? UH-HUH"
Tamal: "WE KNOW HE'S TRYING TO TRAP US"
Tamal: 21:25... "HE'S AS SLY (SLAY) AS THEY COME."
WHISPER #3: JPS:"POISONING FOR A (long) time" SP: "TO ME?" (squeaky voice) JPS: "Get ready to go." Voice: "You're taking it right now." Soft elder voice: "How's this?" Voice: "Let it go."
WHISPER #4: "It's poison... "

CHAPTER 21:
THE MITCHELL STUDY REVIEWED

On Feb. 12, 2000, by phone Naveen Krishna interviewed Jack Mitchell of Computer Audio Engineering (CAE) in Albuquerque, New Mexico, who had done an extensive study on the poison whispers in early 1998. His audio forensic work had confirmed two whispers about poisoning, and was included in *SHPM* (1999). Due to the GBC's denials of the whispers evidence, Naveen wanted to clarify certain aspects of CAE's study and about the science of audio forensics, and to address GBC propaganda that audio forensics was a voodoo science. Abbreviated excerpts as follows:

JACK MITCHELL INTERVIEW:

Naveen: What kind of work you do as a professional in this field? **Jack Mitchell:** The broad category would be **audio engineering**. Specifically it is **forensic examination**. I specialize in that... 95% of my jobs are forensic examination. Past clients are various agencies of the US Dept. of Justice and that includes the DEA, US Attorney's Office, the Civil Rights Division. There have been municipal law enforcement agencies, public defender's office, attorneys countrywide, insurance companies, and individuals who just need answers. A lot of the work is enhancement of the recording so that it is intelligible so they can get official court transcripts. Sometimes they send a court reporter right into the studio environment to get a very accurate transcript. I can do things within the studio that I can't do on tape or CD... we make adjustments to the hearing ability of the court transcriber. We slow it down, use pitch correction and take a processed file and the unprocessed file and feed the two together. We document certain events on a recording where it may be claimed the recording is falsified. We do waveform and spectrographic signal analysis, and magnetic tape development. We look at the tape under high magnification.

Naveen: And the nature of the work where you actually try to establish what was being said in a whisper? **Jack Mitchell:** "We call that **speech decoding**. We use spectrographic, but a spectrogram does not tell us what is said. *The conclusions are based on the combining of an aural sense, a visual sense, and the technical data that is presented by the spectrogram.* **Naveen:** Just like a multiple side analysis then? **Jack Mitchell:** Yes, but it's all combined and happens simultaneously. We always use an unprocessed audio file so that we don't add or subtract important data. This is put into a spectrographic program that shows a lot of things. There is a **FTA display** which is frequency, time, amplitude. The frequency is on a vertical scale, the time is horizontal, and the amplitude is shown in both the vertical and horizontal, but it is shown as brightness of color. We also do **LPC form and tracking** where we track the movement of the tongue. We use **amplitude envelopes** to show how many syllables are involved. **FFT fast transform analysis** lets us look at very small segments of the signal to see the frequency content there. Is the signal a noisy signal such as a fricative or is it not as noisy such as a vowel? We put all of this together on screen. The waveform is lined up exactly with the displayed data. We segment the information into small components. We can make useful segments of 1-3 milliseconds. We align visually, aurally that waveform with the data into the FTA display, and we can confirm or disconfirm what we believe we are hearing. We can look at a FTA, an LPC, an amplitude envelope, FFT and waveform all at the same time. These things line up vertically, horizontally.

Naveen: Could you briefly describe the technology: hardware, software and the dollar value of the system that you have used in the work that you did for our particular case? **Jack Mitchell:** It's digital and computer-based, and there is a very high quality audio card inside the computer which is what we call the IO. It takes it in and puts it out. There's a high quality interface that will take an analog signal and convert it to digital, and vice-versa. My system costs $50k. The software is very high quality analysis software. For the spectrogram I use two analysis programs. One is **Soundscope,** a highly regarded program used in universities, hospitals, and research facilities. The other is **Signalize** which is favored by the academic community. I used both programs in this project. The primary program was Soundscope, then I would use Signalize; one would confirm the other. **Naveen:** Your equipment then ranks with the equipment that's used by top audio forensic labs in the world? **Jack Mitchell:** Absolutely. What you need to be concerned about is the input and output signal to noise ratio. A signal to noise ratio of 87 dv is quite good. My audio board has a signal to noise ratio of 104 to 105, the bigger the better. Then any noise within the system is down so low that it is not perceived. That's one of the primary considerations. *But what is really important is the knowledge and skill of the investigator.* This is important beyond a certain level of equipment. My system is way beyond what is needed for this kind of work.

Naveen: How did you receive these tapes and what instructions were you given? **Jack Mitchell:** Randy Stein called me in Dec. 1997. I asked what this was about, but he didn't want to tell me. I was given general instructions to enhance certain areas of the tape recording, but I had no idea what this was about. He sent me the first tape, which was very degraded, not a good tape to work from, and I told him it sounded to me like it was a fourth generation copy. He got another tape that was of higher quality, supposedly a first generation copy of the original, but was still somewhat degraded. They told me certain timings on the tape, try to enhance them, and let them know what I thought was being said. **Naveen:** Do you stand firmly behind your conclusions in that report? **Jack Mitchell:** Absolutely. There has been nothing presented to me that would change my mind even slightly. My conclusions are documented in the reports, which are extremely solid. I think it's going to be extremely difficult to discredit any area of the reports. **Naveen:** Is there anything in the reports that would go against your findings or conclusions or weaken your conclusions in any way?

Jack Mitchell: Absolutely not.

Naveen: Were you contacted by anybody else regarding your work besides Randy, Nico, myself and Bill Ogle? **Jack Mitchell:** I've had some calls in the last couple of weeks from a Mr. Hooper in Australia who had some questions and expressed some opinions. He had difficulty with the

COMPLETE BOOK OF POISONING EVIDENCE

segment **"the poison's going down."** He does not perceive the word "poison's". He agrees with the words "the" and "going down", but "poison's" he cannot agree with. *The first time he said what he hears is "boys are."* We focused on the "oi" diphthong. That is the same sound we get with the word "boy." But how do you account for the *double sylballents* there? POY-ZON. Mr. Hooper said, *"The boys are going down."* But that doesn't fit. It doesn't work in the spectrogram. Could it be, *"The boys is going down"?* But that's bad English. That would account for two sylballents, but in the section where we get "on" for poison there is an energy drop: if we have "boys is" we would have no energy drop in the lower frequencies. So that is not a credible alternative. **Then he called me again a week ago.** He said that he got a first generation copy from the Archives, and *now he is absolutely certain that it is "The swelling's going down."* That is not a credible alternative either because the "w" "e" in the spectrogram will not give us the type of formation that we see which is a movement in the frequencies from 800 to 1600 from a left-right direction. The "w" "e" in "well" doesn't work. If it were just the word "we", that could be credible as normally we would see a faster rise from 800 to 1600. But how does "we" fit in? It doesn't. If it could be "wheel," that doesn't fit. If it could be "weasels", that would take care of (the two sylballents), but did they say, "The weasel's going down?" That doesn't make any sense at all.

COMMENT: *So much for the GBC's Mr. Hooper's vain efforts at innocuous explanations. Weasel or swelling contradicts the distinctive "oy" in "poison." Hooper was desperate to find some plausible alternative to the poison word. He was so sure about boys, then changed his mind after hearing from Tamal that it was actually "the swelling's going down." Hey, maybe it could be "the swelling's in the milk" ?* ☺

Naveen: Did you do any kind of dictionary search to see if possibly the word "poison" was something else when you were considering all different possibilities? **Jack Mitchell:** We went through the process as to what could be alternatives. I had thought of "boy" and "ploy" and that doesn't fit the rest of the spectrogram. So I don't think so. I used a Random House unabridged and thought of every alternative, in every letter, leafing through to come up with reasonable alternatives. I could not do it. Every alternative goes full circle, coming back to the only word that fits with the spectrographic display and the oral sense: the word "poison's." **COMMENT:** *One interesting confirmation of Jack Mitchell's skills/ accuracy in his speech decoding of the tape is his picking up another faint whisper of the esoteric devotee-word PRABHU, as pahmbu or bahmbu.* **Naveen:** So you have not been able to come up with any other word except the word "poison"? **Jack Mitchell:** That's all I've been able to come up with. Our conclusion says, "Note, all features isolated and evaluated are consistent with "poison's." Analysis data combined with oral perception indicate it is "poison's." **I still stand behind this report 100%.** (*The GBC also claimed Tamal's Jewish Bronx accent could not be properly deciphered, as though this prevented Mitchell from ascertaining the whispered "poison" words. However, Mitchell said an accent does not change the science or the results.*)

Naveen: Would a session in your studio help with the aural hearing of these segments because of the quality of your equipment as compared to somebody's home stereo system? **Jack Mitchell:** This is why attorneys send certified court reporters into my studio because the quality is so much higher. The studio is acoustically designed by a professional. It has all kinds of absorbers and reflectors in the room. I have played this segment for people outside the studio. As a test I took it over to a friend's house and put it on their $500 system and my friend's wife who didn't know anything about any of this, picked out the poison word right away. She had to listen to it 2-3 times, then she picked out the wording. **COMMENT:** *This was invariably the experience with devotees: after hearing them a few times, almost all devotees clearly heard the POISON word in at least two of the three principal "poison whispers." Why can none of the GBC hear it?*

Naveen: You said earlier that any on-going controversy may be only based on audio and hearing, not the controversy of your report itself? **Jack Mitchell:** The report is extremely solid. I think it's going to be extremely difficult to discredit any area of the report. If there is an area they will try to discredit, they're going to try to say that what I hear is such and such, and that's different than what you've reported, so your report can't be correct. **Naveen:** That's why you were describing how the hearing perception changes from day to day. **Jack Mitchell:** Right. We call this auditory illusion. **Naveen:** All this work you've done is critical to coming up with the correct analysis. **Jack Mitchell:** That's right. It is my opinion the spectrogram locks this in. **COMMENT:** *To overcome the "auditory illusion" phenomenon, one needs forensic specialists to use scientific tools and methods for a vastly more accurate diagnosis. When many experts agree on the POISON word, then it is a very weighty piece of evidence, acceptable in most courts as well. Eight (8) sound studios and audio forensic labs have now confirmed the poison word.*

Naveen: You stand behind the other segment also? Segment 4? **Jack Mitchell:** Yes, absolutely. So far I have not even heard any controversy about that. *Segment 4 is really much clearer.* The voice production, although it was somewhat distant from the microphone, it was a normal speaking voice. It was not a whisper. It is really quite clear and I think anybody would have a very difficult time challenging that.

COMMENT: *Segment 4 was the third confirmed poison whisper where JPS says, "POISONING for a long time," and Srila Prabhupada* *weakly replies, "TO ME?" Jack Mitchell also had an accredited audiologist review his findings (see next chapter).*

In 2017, after Jack Mitchell passed away and CAE was defunct, the GBC found that ACFE, who had granted CAE's certification of forensic examiner in 1984, was selling some licenses fraudulently in 2014, 16 years AFTER Mitchell's study on the whispers. The GBC then celebrated and declared this proof that there were no poison whispers. Thus the GBC struggles to find ways to convince us mushrooms that there is no evidence!

CHAPTER 22:
DR. McCAFFREY CONFIRMS WHISPERS

When Jack Mitchell completed his study on the poison whispers, he collaborated with a colleague to verify his findings. He approached Dr. Helen McCaffrey, Ph.D., CCC/A from Fort Worth, Texas. On a 9 hour phone call they reviewed with the same software and techniques from their separate locations the background whispers on T-46. Jack guided her through his determinations, and she agreed with everything except the word "long" in the whisper, "poisoning for a long time." Dr. McCaffrey's statement was received April 13, 1998, and is another confirmation of the poison whispers that the GBC call "imaginary."

MITCHELL'S DESCRIPTION OF THE COLLABORATION

From Naveen's interview with Jack Mitchell on Feb. 12, 1998, on how he worked with Dr. Helen McCaffrey:

Naveen: Did anybody else review your work and agree with you or disagree or collaborate with you?

Mitchell: With the spectrographic analysis I felt it best to bring in a consultant with a strong background in speech science. I consulted Dr. Helen McCaffrey in the Dept. of Communication Sciences and Disorders at Texas Christian University [where Tamal attended in 1996]. I sent her the audio files of the various segments. She has the same Soundscope software, and after she set up the files, she reviewed them. Then we had a 9 hour telephone conversation where we analyzed each of the segments. We went back and forth segmenting them, looking at the various components, working with each segment until we were in agreement as to what we thought was said, what was the most likely that would fit into the particular formations, the data being presented by the spectrogram. Her conclusions are the same as mine. I then wrote the reports. I sent her the report for her review. She changed nothing. Her report is in Appendix 3.

CHAPTER 23:
J P FRENCH ANALYSES POOR QUALITY TAPE

On the basis of the above examinations, I offer the following opinion:

Whisper #1

In my view the likely content of this whisper is as follows:

"(It's going), it's going down. (It's going), it's going down.

Note: Parenthesis denote especially unclear sections.

Whisper #2

"It's not poison" [plus circa 2 further unintelligible syllables]

Whisper #3

[Circa 4-5 syllables - wholly unintelligible]

J P French PhD MAE FIOA   25th August 1998

Balavanta das had solicited a study in 1998 from a prominent audio forensic firm in the UK headed by Dr. J. P. French, who had been referred to him as being perhaps the world's foremost expert on audio forensics. Naveen Krishna sent a very poor quality copy of the poison whisper tape T-46 to Dr. French. As a result, in their Aug. 25, 1998 report, JP French was only able to verify whisper #2, as being **"it's not poison..."** The JP French report was made public Mar. 5, 2000. Balavanta was surprised that all three whispers could not be verified by such a prominent firm, as they seemed quite clear to most devotees. He asked Dr. French to check his findings again, but on the same poor quality tape recording that he had supplied earlier. Dr. JP French replied: *"I have re-considered the material against the interpretations you told me certain other people have put forward. However, my original view remains largely unchanged."* In Jan. 1999 Nityananda spoke with Balavanta about J.P. French's results, and he suspected that *Naveen Krishna had sent a fourth generation, degraded-quality copy of the "poison tape" original*, not realizing the difference that a superior-quality, first generation or direct DAT copy would make. Naveen wrote the GBC Feb. 23, 2000 just prior to their annual meetings, and before the submission of Balavanta's investigative report: *"...audio forensic engineers only had fourth generation copies of audio tapes from which* *they worked; thus they worked with very degraded quality. I know this because I was the one who sent these tapes to these engineers upon Balavanta's direction. So that makes it impossible for them to produce the same results as did Jack Mitchell."* Of course this letter was ignored.

Balavanta or Naveen never sent a DAT Archives tape to Dr. French to review his work, and therefore the study was greatly impaired. Still, Dr. JP French did confirm "(?) it's going down, (?) it's going down" in whisper #1, and the poison word in whisper #2. Dr. French partially confirmed the poison whispers, and, significantly, he did not contradict the results found by other studies.

FORENSIC REPORT FROM OWL INVESTIGATIONS (next chapter):

OWL INVESTIGATIONS, INC.

First Whisper

make

At approximately 2:00 Prabhupada speaks and says "Hum, you me flat"

After that statement, whispered in the back ground is the following

" Do This

Uh Huh

I swear all of it's going down

(someone laughing)

The poison's going down"

Second Whisper

Unintelligible

Third Whisper

"It's not poisoning"

Fourth Whisper

The word poison is clearly audible. Other words are audible but unintelligible.

Conclusion:

There is conversation about poison and the use of it. In my opinion there is certainly a basis for further investigation. Exhumation would settle the issue, although I am told that it is against religious beliefs.

A Forensic toxicologist and Homicide investigator should be consulted.

Opinion:

Based on my training and experience, the word poison is clearly audible and intelligible in several instances.

Respectfully Submitted,

Tom Owen
Owl Investigations, Inc

.2

P. O. BOX 189 • COLONIA, NJ 07067
VOICE (732) 574-9672 • 1-800-OWL-AUDIO • FAX (732) 381-4523

CHAPTER 24:
OWL INVESTIGATIONS: POSSIBLE HOMICIDE

In March 2001 Nityananda sought another top-notch audio forensic specialist to study the poison whispers; as more confirmations would leave less room for anyone to argue what they claimed to hear in the whispers. He located a highly reputable audio forensic investigator with substantial experience in law enforcement and courts: Tom Owens at Owl Investigations in Colonia, New Jersey. A DAT tape of T-46 was sent to Tom Owens directly from the Archives. Nityananda sent him a copy of *SHPM*, a tape transcript, the locations of the three different poison whispers. The $2500 fee for Tom Owen's work was pooled from Yasodanandana, Nityananda, Naveen, Mahatma, Jitarati, and Mandapa. The team was committed to the pursuit of truth and willing to sacrifice for it. Naveen Krishna communicated with Tom Owens to ensure a proper analysis. On Aug. 1, 2001 the brief but very concise and powerful results arrived. Tom Owens verified ALL three whispers as clearly having the poison word, another major confirmation.

WHISPER #1: "I Swear All Of It's Going Down (laughing) THE POISON'S GOING DOWN."
WHISPER #2: " IT'S NOT POISONING."
WHISPER #3: " POISON..." [Note: from "poisoning for a long time"]

EDUCATION

B.A. History 1969
Bellarmine College, Louisville, Kentucky

Certificate of Achievement, Electro-Acoustics,
Synergetic Audio Concepts, 1983

Completion of Voice
Identification Course, 1985

Certification as Voice Identification
Examiner, July 17, 1986 by the
International Association for Identification.
Certification Board Member 1987-1995
I.A.I. Life Member New Jersey Chapter
I.A.I. Life Member Kentucky Chapter

Audio Engineering Society N.Y. Chapter Board
of Directors 1989-1991, 1996-1998

Audio Engineering Society
WG-12 Working Group "Forensic Audio"
Chairman 1991-1999

Special Deputy,
Warren County Sheriff's Department
Bowling Green, Kentucky

Head Instructor, New York Institute
for Forensic Audio - 7 years

Experience in the Recording Arts 35 years

ORGANIZATIONS

Audio Engineering Society
American Academy of Forensic Sciences
American Board of Recorded Evidence
Law Enforcement Video Association
International Association for Identification

PUBLISHED ARTICLES

Mr. Owen has published more than twenty-five articles in the Audio Engineering Society Journal, the International Association for Identification Journal and other publications concerning Forensic Audio and the restoration of sound. He is also available on audio cassette from the Audio Engineering Society. Publications and references will be provided upon request.

We offer the latest in Voice Identification and Spectrographic Signal Analysis. Attributes such as Pitch, Amplitude, Time, and Frequency can be digitally captured and analyzed.

OWL
INVESTIGATIONS, INC.
AUDIO & VIDEO TAPE ANALYSIS

THOMAS J. OWEN - PRESIDENT

TAPE ENHANCEMENT
NOISE REMOVAL
TAPE AUTHENTICATION
VOICE IDENTIFICATION
VIDEO ENHANCEMENT

State-of-the-Art
Audio/Video Laboratory

Board Certified & Court Qualified

OWL INVESTIGATIONS, INC.
P.O. BOX 189 • COLONIA, NJ 07067
732-574-9672 • FAX 732-381-4523
1-800-OWL AUDIO • E-mail: owlmax@aol.com
Web: www.owlinvestigations.com

His conclusions and summary: *"There is conversation about poison and the use of it. In my opinion there is certainly basis for further investigation. Exhumation would settle the issue, although I am told that it is against religious beliefs. A forensic toxicologist and homicide investigator should be consulted. Based on my training and experience, the word poison is clearly audible and intelligible in several instances."*

CREDENTIALS: OWL INVESTIGATIONS, INC. Audio & Video Tape Analysis: Thomas J. Owens, President State of the Art Audio/Video Laboratory; Board Certified & Court Qualified, Forensic Audio Analysis, Forensic Video Analysis, Audio & Video Tape Enhancement, Voice Identification, Testimony in Courts of Law **SERVICES:** Forensic Consulting, including but not limited to: Audio Analysis, Video Analysis, Audio & Video Tape Enhancement, Audio & Video Authentications, Voice Identification, Voice Elimination, Training, Certification and Testimony. Owl Investigations, Inc. has a fully equipped audio-video processing laboratory with digital capacities for audio -video signal processing and voice identification. **CLIENTS:** Law Enforcement Agencies, State Police, the Federal Government, Prosecuting Attorneys, Defense Attorneys, Banks, Convenience Store Chains, Legal Aid Society, Public Defenders, Corporations and the business community in general. **EXPERIENCE:** Owl Investigations has one of the most sophisticated digital audio and video processing laboratories available. Mr. Owen, a nationally known forensic expert is

141

the Chairman of the ABRE. He also serves as the Chairman of the AES's Standards Group WG-12 on Forensic Audio. A graduate of Bellarmine College in Louisville, Kentucky, Mr. Owen worked 11 years at NYC's Lincoln Ctr Archives, appeared on network television, radio re: audio, video matters. He lectured extensively and has 25+ articles published in the AES Journal, IAI Journal, or the Forensic Examiner. Mr. Owen's qualifications as an expert witness have been demonstrated in 20+ states. Recording Arts Experience/35 yrs. **ORG'S:** AES, AAFS, ABRE, IAI.

"...the word poison is clearly audible and intelligible" Owl Inv's was the 4th top audio forensic laboratories to verify the whispers.

CHAPTER 25:
FBI ANALYST CONFIRMS WHISPERS

In 2003 Nityananda read a CNN story about several government specialists who were selected to test controversial content on one of the Richard Nixon tapes, and he chose one of these super-forensics labs to examine the three main whispers: JBR Technologies in Springfield, Virginia. After speaking for an hour with James Reames, he hoped JBR's research could lift the whispers study to a higher level than anything done so far. Nityananda was impressed with his abilities and techniques; he was a frequent contractor for FBI and CIA projects, and for 30 years had been an FBI audio forensics agent before going into private business. He was a true high-level audio expert.

ORIGINAL UHER TAPE RECORDER OBTAINED

Reames was very interested in our whisper certification project, and his study would bring the total of forensic studies to five, supplementing Mitchell, McCaffrey, French, and Owens. Nityananda sent a $3000 deposit. Mitchell had previously tested and repaired Puru's Uher cassette recorder in 1998 and believed it had recorded the poison tape. Therefore Reames wanted the Uher tape recorder and asked if he could get the original tape from the Archives. The "Final Days" video of Srila Prabhupada where he is dictating his Bhagwatam commentaries into a large UHER microphone, indicated it was the mother of the poison discussions and whispers tapes. Meanwhile Puru had sold the UHER to Jayanta das, a Prabhupada memorabilia collector. Jayanta sent the UHER to Reames for tests and inspections. Reames said he could verify 100% if there were any edits, while Mitchell was only 80% certain.

COMPLETE BOOK OF POISONING EVIDENCE

THE ORIGINAL TAPE T-46

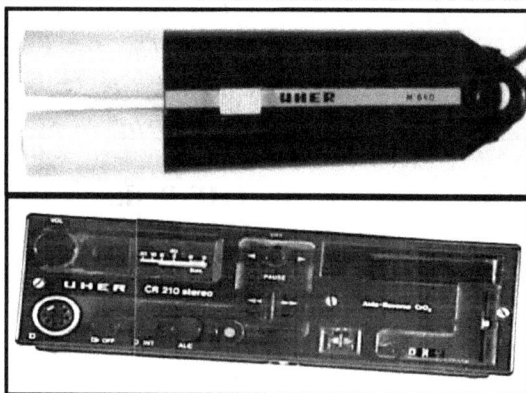

Meanwhile Nityananda spoke with Parama-rupa das at the Bhaktivedanta Archives in North Carolina, offering a donation if he would personally bring the original T-46 tape to Reames' lab for a day of tests while he watched to guarantee the safety and integrity of the tape. The Archives' trustees met and agreed to cooperate, saying it was in their interest to establish what was actually contained on the tape, as a matter of history and archival documentation. On July 23, 2003 (Nityananda resided in Hawaii), Parama-rupa brought the original tape to Reames' lab, a few hours' drive away. Reames performed various tests and inspections of the tape and was given a CD of the Archive's transcript of the tape. Reames made a copy of the tape utilizing all of his techniques for assuring the least loss of quality. Soon Nityananda received from Reames two binders with the transcript and a CD copy of the original tape, which had been formatted into 48 tracks for easy referencing and searching, and the transcript had times inserted for every sentence. Reames requested corrections to the transcript for accuracy according to our knowledge and information, and to pinpoint exactly which areas we wanted him to study. This was done, and we awaited his audio analysis.

RESULTS OF REAMES' WHISPERS STUDY

Nityananda finally received JBR's final report by email dated Feb. 1, 2006. It took 30 months to coax Reames to complete his report. To study the whispers, Reames made a better copy from the Archives original than the Archives could make, and he enjoyed using his tech skills and equipment. He described his physical examination of the original tape, how he repaired and did tests with the UHER, and he sent photographs. But he never looked for any edits. His hype about finding secret signatures and tracks and whether the Archives tape was edited or not proved to be all hot air. Although Reames stated that the original recorder and tape recording could help him discover information that was not possible to uncover otherwise, we got nothing in that connection. *Still, Reames did confirm two whispers,* the main thing we hoped for. Reames was asked to examine six spots. His essential report:

143

***Generation of the Direct and Enhanced CD Copies of the Cassette
Recording:*** *A direct and an enhanced copy of the audio information was
made on separate CD-R's. The track numbers are indexed to lapsed
minutes of playing time. Track 1 is 2 min. in length...*

Examination Of The Six Whispered Statements: **(Tape Side A):**

NUMBERLINE	TIME	SPOKEN WORDS
1: 037 – 042	02:10	**THE POISON IS GOING DOWN.**
		Laughter It's really going down.
2: 059 – 062	04:23	**THAT'S NOT POISON IN HIS MILK.**
		Uh-Huh.
3: 133–134	07:35	Do it now. Night time.
4: 617-618	27:43	Who is this Prabhupada's talking about?
5: 717–718	34:20	[unintelligible]

CONCLUSION: Later the UHER tape recorder that made the "Last
Tape" or poison whispers tape, the cassette recorder that immortalized
Srila Prabhupada's words in his last months and days of physical
presence with us, changed hands again. It is a UHER CR210 Stereo, type
1642, serial #33955. Tamal gave it to Puru, who loaned it to Jack
Mitchell in 1998 to confirm that it was Srila Prabhupada's last recorder.
Puru sold it to Jayanta. In 2003 Jayanta loaned it to Reames for his
poison whispers study. In 2012 Jayanta sold it to the Fiji Prabhupada
Museum, owned by Radha Govinda Vedic Charitable Foundation, who
donated it to ISKCON Bangalore's Vrindaban Prabhupada Museum in
2018, along with Srila Prabhupada's 1968 Mercedes and many other
items. JBR confirmed two principal poison whispers but never fulfilled
his work promise to analyze if the tape had been edited or tampered with.
The answer to this may be still on the CD copies Reames made in 2003.

CHAPTER 26:
SUMMARY OF ALL AUDIO FORENSICS

In 2022, as stated in Ch. 27, a new audio forensic study confirmed
all four poison whispers and all the dark secondary whispers as well.

**WHISPER #1: "THE POISON'S GOING DOWN, (giggle) THE
POISON'S GOING DOWN"** *(Speaker: Tamal, by his own admittance, but
he claimed he said "The swelling's going down")* The following sound
studio and forensic studies all agree on the above or a very similar
version, and *all agree on the poison word:* **(1)** Naveen, Balavanta,

Mahabuddhi, Isha, many others **(2)** JP French Assoc., 1998 (confirms "going down" **(3)** Jack Mitchell, CAE, 1999 **(4)** Dr. Helen McCaffrey, Ph.D., 1999 **(5)** Tom Owens, Owl Invest's, 2001 **(6)** JBR Technologies, VA, 2006 **(7)** Major Forensics Laboratory: 2022/ Tape location: ConvBk 36.373, just after "You make me flat." Side A Tape T-46, 1:55 minutes.

WHISPER #2: "IS THE POISON IN THE MILK?... UH HUH"

(Speaker: clearly Tamal's voice) The following all agree on the above or a similar version; such as but *all agreeing on the poison and milk words:* **(1)** George Blackwell's Sound Studio, Miami, 1997 **(2)** Skylab Studios, Gainesville, 1997 **(3)** Naveen, Balavanta, Mahabuddhi, Isha, and many others **(4)** JP French Assoc., UK, 1998 **(5)** Tom Owens, Owl Investigations, 2001 **(6)** JBR Technologies, Virginia, 2006 **(7)** Major Forensics Laboratory: 2022 / Tape location: ConvBk Vol. 36.373.22, just after Jayapataka says: "Like to follow the same treatment, only while traveling." Side A Tape T-46,

Gerry King
gk@skylabstudios.com
352.373.7288

CHIEF ENGINEER

2106 NW 67th Place · Suite 16
Gainesville, FL 32653
www.skylabstudios.com

3:20 minutes. A few minutes after this whisper, *"Is the poison in the milk?"* at 1:30 PM on Nov. 10, 1977, BCS gives Srila Prabhupada hot milk to drink. Srila Prabhupada said it was too sweet after BCS asked if it was too hot (only milk is hot; not juices or water). How can one not wonder if there was poison in BCS's milk?

WHISPER #3: "POISONING for a (long) time" (Srila Prabhupada replies weakly: "To me?") *(Speaker: Jayapataka's unique voice is clearly recognized)* The following all agree on the above or a similar version, and *all agree on the poisoning word.* **(1)** Naveen, Balavanta, Mahabuddhi, Isha, and many others **(2)** Jack Mitchell, CAE Studios, 1999 **(3)** Dr. Helen McCaffrey, Ph.D., 1999 (except for *"long"*) **(4)** Tom Owens, Owl Investigations, 2001 **(5)** Major Forensics Laboratory: 2022/ Tape location: ConvBk Vol. 36.391.4, after Srila Prabhupada says, "Yes" – and Hansadutta begins a kirtan, Side B Tape T-46, ± 21 min.

WHISPER #4: "IT'S POISON" Major Forensics Laboratory: 2022.

CONCLUSIONS: In 2005 we acquired Balavanta's investigation records, including the audio forensic study done by JP French in London. The results of the many audio forensic studies have provided extremely impressive, multiple confirmations of the poison whispers. How can anyone doubt that Tamal, Jayapataka, and Bhavananda were *"whispering about poison and the use of it,"* as stated by Tom Owens? Only ISKCON institutionalists with deeply embedded ulterior interests

145

deny that the whispers are certified evidence that establishes the conspiracy to poison Srila Prabhupada. (See also Volume 2, 3)

SONY TAPE RECORDER IN ISKCON VRINDABAN TEMPLE

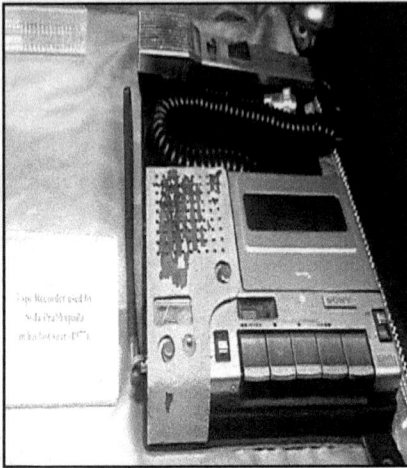

Isha's 9 year old son with headphones could hear "poison" in 3 of the above whispers. Yet the GBC claims that there are no poison whispers, and they cannot hear the word "poison." Yes, there are different versions with variations on the details of the whispers. But all the forensic studies *concur on the poison word* in the 4 principal whispers. This is why professional audio forensic laboratories with their specialized sound analyzing equipment need to be employed to ascertain the actual content of the "poison whispers." The fact is that the scientific methods of audio forensics rise far above human subjectivity. The many forensic audio experts confirm the majority of devotee's opinions on the whispers as well. Only the GBC stands out as not hearing them! The experts' exacting scientific studies speak for themselves and are accepted in courts. Major governments employ audio forensic specialists such as J P French to analyze audio recordings. The science is real, tested, authentic, and bona fide.

Someone wrote: *"...the whispers constitute weighty evidence. There are multiple whispers, confirmed by multiple audio-forensic professionals that include the word poison. The straightforward interpretation is the whisperers were involved in a plot to murder by poisoning."* Another wrote: *"I heard them in late 1997 here at home. And further confirmed at every step and every forensic report. "Poison going down" was confirmed several times, not just the word "poison"... they are totally incriminating whispers... nothing less. Giggles? Milk is being given? C'mon. Put on some headphones, and listen again please."*

Almost everyone hears them. The dishonest deniers, namely the GBC, ISKCON gurus, and suspects are contradicted by the devotees and audio forensic specialists. The whispers evidence strongly supports Srila Prabhupada being poisoned, and when joined with the other evidence, it is overwhelmingly irrefutable. The hair tests in Part 1 were the final nail in the coffin of denials. *The poison whispers now constitute solid and legal proof that caretakers in Srila Prabhupada's room were discussing his poisoning.* It can be taken that these whispers were arranged by Lord Krishna, as the testimony of the Supreme Truth.

NTIAP's assertion that the whispers are imaginary no longer cuts the mustard: by 2022 we had accumulated two professional sound studio opinions and six expert audio forensic specialist studies- all agreeing that the whispers are about poison. Any rational person would pay attention to the prominent scientific experts who have regularly solved crimes for various government authorities during their distinguished careers. To hear good quality recordings of these whispers, simply search online.

REVERSE SPEECH REVISITED

SHPM (1999) included two chapters on "reverse speech," a method of playing voice recordings in reverse to hear hidden messages as to the truth of the speaker's true intentions. There is some evidence that reverse speech can reveal a speaker's state of mind. Dhanesvara das was involved in some of the private investigative work in 1998-99 and he introduced reverse speech to others on the team. He had studied with David Oates, pioneer of the reverse speech method, and had experience with the technique, and had done evaluations of recorded conversations in 1977 of senior devotees with Srila Prabhupada. He convinced Nityananda to include his findings in *SHPM.* In retrospect, this was a mistake. Reverse speech is a controversial and unverified method of discerning the truth in recorded speech. The GBC ridiculed the "reversals," using them as a platform to portray all the poisoning evidence as humbug. The GBC contacted David Oates, who had a poor relationship with Dhanesvara. Oates then re-analyzed these "reversals" and found some to be "inconsistent" or "bogus." *However, he confirmed seven of Dhanesvara's reversals and half agreed with others, all of which clearly referred to poisoning and malicious intent by Srila Prabhupada's assistants.* Regardless, confirmed reversals or not, this technique is an insufficiently accredited method for use in determining facts. *It was a mistake to confuse and distract from the real evidence.*

In *NTIAP* (p. 306), David Oates confirms the accuracy of 7 speech reversals: *"The worst was just you kill," "Aye Govinda," "I kill the prophet," "Fail upon arsenic," "Heavy metal, that milk," "He create a sick pa ," "They've made your dying problem."* The GBC use of Oates to discredit the idea of Srila Prabhupada's poisoning was actually counter-productive as he actually confirmed a heavy metals poisoning by speech reversals. But somehow the GBC did not notice this. *"The CIA has published the theory of Reverse Speech, quoting my book, Hidden Messages in Human Communication. It has recently been declassified.*

147

This vindicates 34 years of my life's work! [...] It appears they have been using it all this time... Yours, David J. Oates

--www.reversespeech.com/ReverseSpeech-VoiceofUnconscious Mind

REVERSE SPEECH NOT CREDIBLE EVIDENCE

Reverse speech is an intriguing but unproven science. Methods to ascertain truth (CVSA) based on proven technology are widely used by law enforcement. (Vol. 2, 3) *"My apologies for bringing reverse speech into the conversation. This naïve act gave the deniers a foothold to ridicule the evidence. Bir Krishna Maharaja then stated 'poison conspiracists' only evidence was some speech reversals where we imagined something not there. What a liar and cheat, to characterize Srila Prabhupada's own statements, the hair tests, the certified whispers about poisoning, etc, as being nothing."* (Nityananda das, 2017)

CHAPTER 27:
FORENSIC ANALYSES SINCE 2006

Since JBR's study in 2006 (Ch. 25) there have been many studies of the "poison whispers" by various groups of devotees worldwide as well as by audio forensic analysts. A group of ex-ISKCON devotees in Europe concluded with advanced software and audio equipment that the three poison whispers were about poison and malicious poisoning. Around 2015 Naveen Krishna arranged for a legal affidavit including enhanced audio files from Isha das on the results of his new study of the whispers using more advanced software technologies and equipment. Isha, very experienced and proficient in audio technology, having also processed hundreds of Narayan Maharaja lectures, again confirmed his findings from 1997-8 (Ch. 16). Srila Prabhupada's caretakers were definitely softly speaking about a homicidal poisoning.

Hundreds of devotees worldwide had carefully listened to the poison whispers, being now easily available online, and invariably agreed on their contents. Of course, ISKCON GBCs still could not hear them! As such the GBC became known as the Governing Body of Cheaters, Crooks, and Criminals, due to their obvious dishonesty and corruption.

NEW AUDIO FORENSIC STUDY DONE IN 2020-22

In 2020 concerned senior devotees engaged one of the most reputed and globally acclaimed private investigation and forensic laboratories, who spent 500+ hours in the most comprehensive audio analysis to date of the Nov. 1977 tape recordings of Srila Prabhupada, his caretakers, and visitors. With new audio forensic technology, by updating, confirming, and revising prior results from 1998-2006, new and expanded findings and discoveries were made, strengthening the evidence of criminal poisoning. This study unambiguously confirms Srila Prabhupada's premature passing away by linking the lethal heavy metals and cadmium poisoning detected by NAA analysis of hair samples with incriminating audio evidence. Tamal, Jayapataka, and Bhavananda were identified as speakers of the homicidal poisoning whispers, bolstered by secondary whispers. The latest scientific technology, tools, and methods establishes the secret poisoning.

The conclusion that senior disciples criminally poisoned Srila Prabhupada was made as a group opinion by a broad panel of forensic experts, including medico-legal experts, toxicologists, pharmacologists, NAA experts, digital audio experts, homicide investigators, and psychologists. The investigative forensic team has handled 15,000 cases over five decades, received from governments, upper courts, senior attorneys, law enforcement, international agencies, multi-national corporations, and victims of crime and injustice. This new, sweeping, all-inclusive, encyclopedic, court-ready, revelatory study-report reveals AC Bhaktivedanta Swami's mysterious health decline was masterminded as a heinous crime of malicious cadmium poisoning. Several NAA experts are confirming Dr. Morris' cadmium hair test regime and protocols.

As per this study-report, a lengthy professionally produced film is being prepared to eviscerate all doubts that Srila Prabhupada was indeed poisoned with a lethal course of heavy metals in 1977. Thirty USA NAA labs are prepared to corroborate MURR's expertise. A consultants panel is designing the manner and style in which to employ this study-report. A summary of only the audio forensic determinations in this new study, which confirm/ expand on previous audio analyses, is as follows:

*Tamal WHISPERS: *So, The Poison's Going Down. (Bhavananda: Giggle). The Poison's Going Down.*
*Tamal: *Is The/That Poison In The Milk?* Bhavananda: *Uh-Huh.*
*Tamal: *We know he's trying to trap us.*
*Tamal WHISPERS: *Prabhupada keeps asking. He's not going to stop until he finds out.*
*WHISPER: [TIME: 07:53-57] *It's Poison.*
*(Bengali Speaker): Kayek din pare asha (In a few days' time)
Jayapataka: *Poisoning For A (Long) Time...*
[Srila Prabhupada]: (high, squeaky, weak voice) *To me?*
Jayapataka: *Get Ready To Go.* UNKNOWN: You're taking it right now.
SOFT ELDER VOICE: "How's this? UNKNOWN: Let it go.

PART FOUR:
MEDICAL EVIDENCE

Srila Prabhupada's medical symptoms do not prove his poisoning. This is not the purpose of this section, Part 4. But close examination of those symptoms does confirm the cadmium poisoning that has been proven by forensic hair tests (Part 1). Further, Srila Prabhupada's 1977 physical symptoms do not correlate to diabetes or kidney disease, although both are caused and aggravated by cadmium poisoning.

CHAPTER 28:
SRILA PRABHUPADA'S MEDICINES

According to **Prakruti: Your Ayurvedic Constitution**, by Dr. R.E. Svoboda, *"Anyone who wants to use mercury for rejuvenation <u>must be exceptionally careful about its source</u>, and must be sure that it has been properly prepared... The quantity of mercury in any one pill is very small thanks to the processing procedure known as Bhavana... Makharadhvaja (MKD) benefits all sorts of acute disease states, including especially respiratory ailments like cold, influenza, and pneumonia, and all sorts of chronic conditions, such as low blood pressure, general exhaustion, and nervous or mental debility... It is best to take MKD during coldest season of year so that their powerful innate fire does not increase pitta."* Dr. G. Ghosh, who was 82 in 1977 and a respected Allahabad allopathic doctor, said that any medicine which contains mercury and arsenic would be inappropriate for Srila Prabhupada. Damodara Shastri said the same. As far as is known, none of his medicines had arsenic, and Srila Prabhupada's hair mercury levels tested normal (Ch. 1).

MAKHARADHVAJA TAKEN 3 TIMES, NO SERIOUS REACTIONS

Srila Prabhupada took one dose of *MKD* Oct. 25, 1977 and 2 doses the next day (medical notebook), then discontinued it (only 3 doses out of 48 obtained). Tamal and BCS took charge of all his medicines. On Oct. 26 Srila Prabhupada said it was *"not acting."* On Oct. 27 Srila Prabhupada had diarrhea with no other ill effects. Some may think *MKD* contributed to his debilitated health, but with only 3 doses taken, that is hardly possible. The medicine obtained by Abhirama after Gaura

Purnima (March 1977) was not MKD but an Ayurvedic preparation called *somara rasayana* with gold, musk, pearls (no mercury).

CARETAKERS SEED "POISON" WORD INTO DISCUSSIONS

In Srila Prabhupada's conversations we hardly find any mention of the word "poison" previous to Oct. 1977, but then it was suddenly often used by caretakers, and Srila Prabhupada also. Why? It was used in reference to medicine or infection, not actual poison. Discussions were peppered with "like poison" or "poisonous." This seems a deliberate *seeding* of the poison word into conversations… to blur the difference between "like poison" and the real poisoning? Was it meant so that all future talk of poison could then be blamed on "bad medicine?" The inter-substitution of the words poison and medicine was peculiar. Was this intentional, to render everyone numb to a real poisoning, to create confusion if this leaked out? It appears a deliberate act to obscure the actual poisoning, describing medicines as poison, as a clever distraction from the secret poisoning that might be suspected or detected.

This confounding use of opposites is strange: **(1)** …"poisoning," referring to the blood and pus in his urine. **(2)** *"If the devotees are staying away, it is not because you are poisonous. It is because we are poisonous."* **(3)** *"That medicine turned out to be poison."* **(4)** *"...it had turned to poison."* **(5)** *"Satadhanya had also arranged earlier for the MKD, which had proved poisonous."* **(6)** *"drinking poison."* **(7)** *"poison to him."* **(8)** Srila Prabhupada called the MKD *"poisonous."* **(9)** "you said that it was poison. **SP:** Yes. […] …taking poison." **(10) SP:** So dead body, you take poison or ambrosia, it is the same..." **(11)** Ameyatma das recalled the confusion (in 1977): *"When Baradraja returned from India, he told us also that SP said the MKD was poisoning him…"*

ISKCON poisoning deniers have used *"the medicine was the poison"* argument repeatedly: **(1)** *NTIAP* p. 52: *"...when he is talking about the effects of the MKD."* **(2)** p. 13: *"When referring to poison, Prabhupada was merely hypothesizing about the possible effects of improper medicine. The symptoms could resemble poisoning, he noted."* **(3)** Tamal, p. 146: *"Some have suggested that even if one intentionally poisoned Prabhupada, the medicine he was given acted as 'poison.'"* **(4)** BCS, p. 198: *"Soon after the arrival of the MKD Srila Prabhupada started to speak about poison. Therefore it seemed to me that he was speaking about the adverse effect of MKD."* **(5)** BCS's book *Ocean of Mercy* also says the talk of poisoning was due to the bad effects of the MKD. **(6)** Tamal curiously interchanged the words poison and medicine in his two final pastimes books. **(7)** Shastri switched the poison and medicine words in the company of Tamal and Bhavananda, who introduced this clever idiosyncrasy a few weeks earlier.

THE DEEPLY FLAWED "MEDICINE IS THE POISON" IDEA

Now, decades later, the GBC deceitfully claims that when Srila Prabhupada spoke of being poisoned on Nov. 9-10, 1977, he was only referring to the MKD medicine from Oct. 25-26, 1977. They insist Srila Prabhupada could not have been poisoned maliciously by *any* of his own loving disciples, and *therefore* any talk of poison in 1977 *must* be about previous medicines with adverse effects that were *"like poison."* Ill-informing parties have posited that when Srila Prabhupada said *"Someone has poisoned me,"* this was in reference to the ill effects of the 3 MKD doses he took *a full two weeks earlier.* But this ruse does not fit with Srila Prabhupada's words about being poisoned. Yes, the MKD had some minor ill effect, some diarrhea. But *"the medicine was the poison"* false theory does not match the facts. Hair *Sample D* was cut in early March 1977 with 19.9 ppm cadmium, so how can Oct. 25-26 medicine affect hair levels many months prior? So that medicine was NOT the poison.

(LEFT: GBC's MKD test- no poison)

There is more: **(1)** How does talk of adverse medicinal effects Oct. 25-26 relate to the Nov. 10 talks of murder, rakshasas, homicide, lawyers, ground glass in food, and restricting who cooked for Srila Prabhupada, *two weeks later?* The two things have **NOTHING TO DO WITH EACH OTHER.** It had been 14 days since the *MKD* was taken, the diarrhea had ended 13 days earlier,

APPENDIX 4 - TEST RESULTS FROM PRABHUPADA'S MEDICINE

SCIENTIFIC SERVICES

Enquiries : Dr Henry A OLSZOWY
Phone : 32749071
Fax : 07-32749074
Our Ref : -1MX263/263:HAO

DATE: 06/01/2000

ANALYTICAL REPORT

CLIENT   INTERNATIONAL SOCIETY FOR KRISHNA CONS
              P.O.BOX 83
              INDOOROOPILLY QLD 4068

CONTACT   : DAVID HOOPER

CLIENT ORDER NO   : .

DATE RECEIVED   : 06/01/2000

DATE COMPLETED   : 06/01/2000

NUMBER OF SAMPLES : 1

SAMPLE ID   : MVAJ1

SAMPLE TYPE   : AQUEOUS SOLUTION

ANALYSIS REQUESTED   METHOD OF ANALYSIS
Identification (XRF Scan)   MXM-006; XRF

XRF = X-Ray Fluorescence Spectrometry

and Shastri's new program of different medicines, including *vrikkasan jivani*, had been underway for 10 days. The taking of *MKD* and Srila Prabhupada speaking of being poisoned are weeks apart and too disconnected to have any relation. By Nov. 10 the MKD was old history. The GBC artificially connects the two things just to confuse us. Also diarrhea and murder are quite different. **(2)** That Srila Prabhupada was secretly, maliciously poisoned since at least Feb. 1977, _and_ there is talk of poison in reference to non-poisonous things- *is suspicious and not coincidental*. The real poisoning is being obscured by loose talk of medicines being poison.

(3) In Tamal's Nov. 1977 taped interview he claims Srila Prabhupada asked for "medicine to die." (Ch. 40) But it is poison that kills and medicine that cures, unless we listen to Tamal et. al. using these words interchangeably. Tamal's mercy-killing interview involved extreme deception as to what was poison or medicine, and the current GBC also deceives that the medicine was the poison.

99MX263:HAQ Continued.

RESULTS

The following components were identified in the sample by XRF scanning. Major indicates >1%, minor 0.1 to 1% and trace <0.1%. These limits are only approximate and are intended to serve as a guide only.

Sample "MVAJ" (99MX263):
Major Components: Iron
Minor Components: Aluminium, Silicon, Phosphorus, Sulphur, Chloride
                  Potassium.
Trace Components: Zinc, Copper, Manganese, Calcium, Titanium.

COMMENTS:
The results relate to the samples as received. The responsibility for sampling rests with the client.

Dr Henry A OLSZOWY   06/01/2000

Note: This report shall not be reproduced except in full without the written permission of the Laboratory.

Queensland Health Scientific Services   PO Box 594   Phone (07) 32741111   Fax (07) 32741199
39 Kessels Road   Archerfield   International Code 61
Coopers Plains Qld 4108   Qld 4108

(4) Srila Prabhupada, being a medicine compounder, pharmacist, and realized pure devotee, would know if medicine from two weeks earlier was poisoning him. Instead, on Nov. 9-10, Srila Prabhupada spoke of someone telling him he had been poisoned, and that he also thought he had been poisoned, _but he did not speak of being poisoned by medicine._ If it was the medicine, why did Srila Prabhupada not just say so? **(5)** Why speak about being poisoned on Nov. 9-10 if it referred to a day of loose bowels two weeks earlier? This makes no sense. **(6)** Srila Prabhupada did not refer to *MKD* when he said *"Someone has poisoned me."* Someone is not something. **(7)** Oct. 25-26, Srila Prabhupada did not experience pain, fever, or vomiting from the MKD that comes with serious "poisonous" effects. Actually the *MKD* was NOT poisonous, as it only some caused some diarrhea, just as other medicines did previously.

(8) Why did Tamal ask "Who is it that has poisoned?" "Who" is not a medicine. **(9)** Why was Srila Prabhupada evasive about *who* had poisoned him, not answering Tamal's question, if it was just the medicine everyone knew about? Why did Srila Prabhupada not say he was poisoned by medicine? He did not say in the "poison discussions" that bad medicine was the poison, yet ISKCON tries to confuse by associating two unrelated events.

Reading the "poison discussions" (Part 2), it is clear Srila Prabhupada was not speaking on Nov. 9-10 of medicine as being poison. The caretakers acknowledged Srila Prabhupada was speaking about a malicious, homicidal poisoning, responding with discussion about murders, criminal cases, poison in food, rakshasas, etc. Unfortunately, many devotees have still not read these conversations and yet they make statements that are woefully contrary to the facts. To explain the "poison discussions" they make *MKD* a scapegoat. The theory that *"Someone has poisoned me"* (Nov. 9-10) refers to the negative effects of medicine on Oct. 25-26 makes no sense, meant only to deceive. Connecting the two incidents is dishonest, a scam trying to cover-up the poisoning and deny that Srila Prabhupada spoke of being actually poisoned. The 1977 conversations show that the talk of poisoning was not about bad medicine (or bodily toxins that had built up over the years). These are deliberate perversions of facts and truth. Srila Prabhupada spoke about homicidal poisoning, as was clearly acknowledged by his caretakers.

An ISKCON scholar (2020): *"I came to determine that the Kaviraja Ayurvedic doctor blew it. Unless those formulas are exact and precise, they can end up acting as poison, which is what happened in Prabhupada's case."* Which of the 40 kavirajas would that be? How does that explain the 10 months of sky-high cadmium in the hair samples since Ayurvedic medicines never have any cadmium? With the constant changes to new treatments, medicines, and kavirajas/ doctors, which medicine can explain 10-18 months of health decline? And why did the caretakers discuss homicidal poisoning and rakshasa poisoners, if it was bad medicine? These motivated denials contradict the facts.

THEY ALL SPOKE OF POISON, NOT MEDICINE

No medicine Srila Prabhupada took had truly poisonous effects. Srila Prabhupada was not speaking of MKD when he said, "Someone has poisoned me." Srila Prabhupada said he heard others speaking of how he was being poisoned, *which makes no sense if he was talking about medicines.* Still, the GBC uses "the medicine was the poison" as their "not-poisoned" defense to bewilder the naïve and ignorant. The conversation on Nov. 10 was about *rakshasas*, and who (not what) could possibly do such a thing, the Svarupa Guha and Sankaracharya poison murders, and "who is it that has poisoned you?" The kaviraja said there must be truth to it. The discussions were clearly about intentional poisoning and not about adverse medicinal effects. Srila Prabhupada did not say, "*Something* has poisoned me," or "The medicine has poisoned me." The poison deniers use talk of medicine from weeks earlier to re-define the Nov. 9-10 talks as innocuous. *But this subterfuge strongly implies complicity in the very same poisoning they are covering up.*

NO POISON IN MAKHARADHVAJA TEST BY GBC

Was the *MKD* donated by the notorious Chandra Swami (Volume 3) tainted with poison? Could this explain why the poisoning? Actually, the GBC tested the *MKD* by X-ray Fluorescence Spectrometry (XRF) at Queensland Health's Scientific Services in Australia on Jan. 6, 2000 (*NTIAP*, p.221-2). *No poison was found.* Strangely, there was no commentary on their *MKD* test in *NTIAP*, maybe because their test disproves "the medicine is the poison" theory! The MKD had no poison, so *NTIAP* said nothing about it. Perhaps these test results were included just to "pad" the book, to look good with (unexplained) scientific findings? Sample "MVAJ1" had no detectable mercury, arsenic, or cadmium, and primarily had iron, with traces of aluminum, sulfur, zinc, copper etc. So, without the essential ingredient of mercury, was it fake MKD? Maybe. Real *MKD* has mercury "sublimed" by an Ayurvedic "bhasma" process and would be in very tiny amounts. Their XRF test method was calculated in %, or parts per hundred rather than parts per million, which is very inaccurate. MKD's medicinal mercury would be far less than 1%. This XRF test could not detect the mercury levels in real *MKD. The MKD was tested by an inaccurate method and should be retested accurately with better equipment to see its mercury contents. But Srila Prabhupada was lethally poisoned with cadmium, which MKD never has as an ingredient anyway. His mercury levels were normal.*

TIMEWISE, MKD CANNOT EXPLAIN POISONING

Timewise, the *MKD,* taken Oct. 25-26, cannot explain the steady drastic health decline that Srila Prabhupada underwent from Feb. 26, 1977 (or earlier). *Sample D* was hair cut in early March 1977 and reveals *lethal cadmium poisoning had already been underway in Feb. 1977, eight months* before the October MKD was taken. Poisoning is not *retroactive.* Srila Prabhupada's health was fully deteriorated by cadmium poisoning by late Oct. How can the *MKD*, with no cadmium content, result in lethal cadmium poisoning 8 months before it was taken?

Also, we note that Satadhanya and Adi Keshava witnessed a highly reputable compounder of medicines take 48 doses of individually paper-wrapped packages from a stock in a large jar, in the front of a clinic full of clients. Chandra Swami had arranged to pay for the medicine, but he was away in south India at the time. (Volume 3) Further, this already prepared *MKD* was intended for another client, but some was given for Srila Prabhupada in deference of his spiritual status. *Thus it was very unlikely to be poisoned medicine.* The 45 doses of leftover *MKD* are still in ISKCON Vrindaban's Prabhupada Museum and could be accurately tested to determine its composition. Still, after 3 doses, the only ill effect was a day of diarrhea, which was common in those last months.

The *"medicine is like poison"* explanation may sound good to one who never read the 1977 conversations (Part 2), but it is actually rubbish. Indeed, **anything** Srila Prabhupada ate or drank as food or medicine could have been tainted with poison, so why zero in on the *MKD*? Tainting something more innocuous and regularly consumed, e.g., water, fruit juice, or milk (seen in the whispers) would be far less awkward.

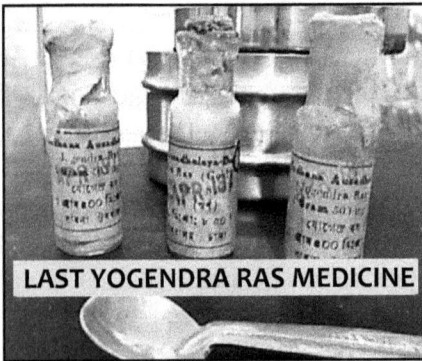
LAST YOGENDRA RAS MEDICINE

This was not like the CIA trying to smuggle poisoned chocolates into Fidel Castro's room. The caretakers had full access to all that Srila Prabhupada ate or drank, so why bother tainting the medicine that came from outside rather than the milk? Actually, the source of the MKD, Chandra Swami, is more to be suspected for supplying cadmium to the poisoners, who then tainted one of Srila Prabhupada's personal items. Ten months of cadmium poisoning is not from Oct.'s MKD.

MKD IS NOT THE POISON PRABHUPADA SPOKE ABOUT

In Feb. 2002 Bhailal Patel, president of National Fed. of Indian American Associations: *"It is clear to me, by hearing the available tapes of the room conversations of the time, that His Divine Grace referred to the said poisoning as a deliberate act of somebody poisoning him, not in the sense of some toxic side effects of medicines. When we met in Alachua ...nobody present had any different understanding after hearing the tapes and seeing the translations, than that Srila Prabhupada was raising the topic of somebody intentionally poisoning him."*

Saying Srila Prabhupada spoke of bad medicine is a cover-up tactic by the GBC and perhaps those who put the cadmium in what Srila Prabhupada consumed. The GBC has resorted to many dishonest tactics to discredit the evidence that Srila Prabhupada was poisoned. Talk of medicine as poison was a deliberate smokescreen to confuse us back in 1977, and the same is true again today. If the GBC really were honest, why don't they just test a Srila Prabhupada tooth or hair sample that they have in their possession?

BALAVANTA'S TEST RESULTS ON YOGENDRA RAS

In 1997 Balavanta obtained from Hari Sauri das three small glass vials of medicine pellets from Srila Prabhupada's Vrindaban quarters, and had them tested for cyanide and strychnine (a stab in the dark out of many things to test for). The results were negative, and no other tests were done. When Nityananda received Srila Prabhupada's hairclippers from Dr. Morris in 2005, these vials were included. The Yogendra Ras came to Dr. Morris after being tested by the National Medical Services in Pennsylvania. Balavanta's report in March 2000 included the test results. Yogendra Ras is pinkish-reddish pellets (unlike *MKD* which is a deep red powder) and an Ayurvedic medicine made from gold, iron, tin, and purified mercury, sulphur, silica, and pearl. Srila Prabhupada had taken it for many years but had stopped in late 1976 according to Hari Sauri. In April 1977 (date on the vials is April 16) he resumed again until June 1977, according to Tamal. On Oct. 7, 1977 Srila Prabhupada said he was again taking it, but we do not know for how long. It treats diabetes, frequent urination, urinary tract ailments, and many other health conditions. It balances vata and pitta. These 3 vials are now in a Vrindaban temple museum. In March 2004 Dhananjaya told Nityananda that Srila Prabhupada sent him in 1975 to a Delhi chain of Indian Ayurvedic shops for high quality Yogendra Ras (purified mercuric oxide). The pellets were crushed and taken with honey to control high blood pressure. No cadmium is in MKD or in Yogendra Ras.

SRILA PRABHUPADA'S HEDGES SNUFF

Srila Prabhupada sometimes used Hedges menthol snuff for congestion or "to defeat brain fag." Srutakirti das, 2016: *"Snuff! ... It was usually gotten in England. Srila Prabhupada took it at 1 or 2 o'clock in the very early morning when he was translating to relieve pressure in the head and for circulation, as far as I know..."* Since Srila Prabhupada rarely took snuff in 1977 when there was little translation work, we doubt snuff was a good medium for poisoning. Doubtful it was tainted with cadmium, but a test would tell; some of Srila Prabhupada's snuff is now secure at a museum in Vrindaban.

CADMIUM-TAINTED MEDICINE?

MKD is made with gold, sulfur, and mercury, and sometimes with other beneficent ingredients such as musk, pearls, and mica. *However, cadmium is never an ingredient in MKD or in any other Ayurvedic medicine.* Cadmium has no biological benefit, as it has no medicinal properties in small amounts like arsenic and mercury do. Srila Prabhupada's catastrophic cadmium levels cannot be explained as coming from medicines and can only be due to malicious, homicidal poisoning. The forensic hair tests show poisoning by cadmium, and not by mercury, as is found beneficially in MKD in tiny quantities. Dr. Morris' five hair tests showed normal mercury, even in those with high cadmium. Any cadmium sometimes found in Ayurvedic medicine will be very tiny traces due to component impurities. Anyone may ingest tiny amounts of cadmium from impurities in medicine, food, air, etc., which could conceivably result in cadmium levels a few times

more than normal, but **never** the 250 X normal Srila Prabhupada had. No one in the scientific literature has ever had these <u>unprecedented</u> cadmium levels. App. 3 shows Srila Prabhupada's cadmium is "off the chart." Expert opinions (Ch. 6) say these levels cannot come from food, medicines, environment, industrial contamination, water, air, soaps- they could only come by a deliberate malicious poisoning intended to kill.

Was there cadmium in the any other medicines that Srila Prabhupada took? This theory arose after some Ayurvedic medicines in recent years were tested and found to have heavy metals impurities slightly above acceptably safe levels, although usually with lead and mercury rather than cadmium. The amounts of impurities thus found were tiny and does not mean Ayurvedic medicines use cadmium as an ingredient. It means modern, industrial impurities at very low-levels had

---

National Medical Services, Inc.
Toxicology Specialists Worldwide Since 1970

3701 Welsh Road
Willow Grove, PA 19090
Phone: (215) 657-4900
1-800-522-6671
Fax: (215) 657-2972

EMAIL- NMS@PDND.COM

DATE OF REPORT: February 11, 1998

TO: Ledford, Mayfield & Ogle
787 S. Yonge
Post Office Box 4118
Ormond Beach, Florida 32175-4118
Attn: William H. Ogle

Ref: c/o William H. Ogle
NMS Control No. 980888
NMS Accession No. 97-198546

EXAMINATION: Heavy Metals Screen
Strychnine and Cyanide Screen

SPECIMENS: The following item was received via Federal Express No. 1963540051 on 11/28/97.

Item 1. One (1) metal canister contained three (3) glass vials, sealed with corks, which contained a dark red powder

Item 2. Hair clippers (no analysis)

ANALYSES and FINDINGS:

1. Inductively coupled Plasma Atomic Emission Spectrophotometry (ICP-AES) of all three (3) samples in item1 detected the following:

Elements (ug/g)	Item 1a	Item 1b	Item 1c
Boron	90	82	110
Aluminum	4900	4000	5000
Manganese	290	270	300
Mercury	1700	1160	1340
Lead	90	None detected	None detected

Note: Values are approximate

2. Microdiffusion and microchemical color tests did not reveal the presence of any potentially toxic concentrations of strychnine and cyanide on one (1) item chosen at random.
(Detection limit range: 50 to 100 ppm)

Comments:

The above findings for the metal screen may have been a result of environmental contamination.

Sincerely,

George F. Jackson, Ph.D.
Division Head of Criminalistics

---

found their way into the medicine, but these accidental trace impurities could not produce the ±16 ppm cadmium found in Srila Prabhupada's hair, even if he had taken hundreds of bottles of such tainted medicine. Cadmium impurities in medicines could not even explain a tiny fraction of the cadmium found in Dr. Morris' tests. Also, if there were cadmium, arsenic, and mercury impurities in Srila Prabhupada's medicines, why were his cadmium and arsenic highly elevated but his mercury normal? There is no credence to the idea that his cadmium came from tainted medicines. *The sky-high cadmium values speak of a deliberate, massive poisoning that simply cannot evolve from slightly impure medicines.* Do the math. In 1977 Srila Prabhupada did not stick with any medicine long enough anyway, even *if* they were slightly tainted. Note: cadmium levels in medicines do not translate to the same levels in hair, but instead will result in a tiny fraction thereof due to the great difference in mass between the body and a medicinal dose. *Slightly tainted medicines would explain nothing.* But the GBC tries their best to come up with baseless, deceitful theories just to confuse us. That is their expertise.

SUBLIMATION IN AYURVEDIC MEDICINES

Cadmium has no biological benefit. *It is never used as an ingredient in any Ayurvedic medicine.* There are some medicines which use tiny amounts of lead, gold, silver, mercury, arsenic, and antimony (but never cadmium), which have some beneficial biological function, but only as a *"bhasma"* compound such as in combination with sulfur and after being sublimely "purified" by an Ayurvedic process called *"bhavana."* Thus the mercury or arsenic acts medicinally upon the body; *it does not accumulate in the body due to its unique and innocuous chemical composition, but is expelled*. Again, cadmium is never used in Ayurvedic medicine. *This cadmium poisoning was possible only by deliberate, homicidal poisoning*. And yes, cadmium is everywhere in tiny amounts, and Ayurvedic medicines may sometimes be contaminated with very tiny amounts of cadmium, even sometimes slightly above acceptable "safe" levels. But this cannot result in levels 250 X above the average normal. *The GBC tested two of Srila Prabhupada's Ayurvedic medicines and found everything normal*. To reach Srila Prabhupada's sky-high cadmium levels could not come from snuff, Ayurvedic medicine, inks, cosmetics, shampoo, air, water, or food. His levels were far too high, and all these suggestions might result in only *slightly* elevated levels. Deniers like to pontificate with pseudo-science just to create doubts.

TOXIC BUILDUP DUE TO SO MANY MEDICINES?

Another dumb GBC theory about how Srila Prabhupada was

poisoned (but then why do they also say he was not poisoned?) is that he took so many medicines in his last years that he developed a toxic "build-up" of "chemicals" which then acted like poison. But that generality does not explain the specific sky-high cadmium or elevated arsenic. Trace amounts of a toxic element in a medicine cannot accumulate to Srila Prabhupada's sky-high cadmium levels. If so, thousands of people would have died from cadmium poisoning, not just the one case in question. *When it gets too difficult to completely deny the poisoning, the GBC then attempts to explain it as accidental.* Actually Srila Prabhupada took few medicines, and impurities in them would be inconsequential. He disliked them and typically he took them only for a few days, if at all. This is seen in his health history (Vol. 4). The GBC speaks of toxic build, instead of the actual cadmium hair test data.

Yet another crazy theory: some suggest Srila Prabhupada's cadmium levels came from medicines containing zinc with cadmium impurities (since cadmium is refined from zinc deposits). However, when looking at the 0.2-0.4% ratio of cadmium to zinc in natural deposits, this theory does not hold up, because, in order to accumulate 250 X the normal amounts of cadmium, one would die from zinc toxicity long before accumulating the levels of cadmium seen in Srila Prabhupada's hair. Srila Prabhupada's sky-high cadmium did not come from a medicine, food or drink containing zinc. Nobody has died from zinc medicines. *We need to identify a poisoning route unique to Srila Prabhupada.* There is not enough cadmium in zinc supplements to amount to even a tiny fraction of Srila Prabhupada's cadmium levels, *and Srila Prabhupada took no zinc supplements anyway.*

BAD MEDICINE OR HOMICIDAL?

Nowhere in the Nov. 1977 poison discussions does anyone accept that Srila Prabhupada was complaining about bad medicine (Part 2). Which medicine could that have possibly been? The MKD? No, not possible, since it was taken only 3 times. The medicines that Shastri was giving were all natural herbal tinctures. Srila Prabhupada's silence, after Tamal asked who poisoned him, affirms a homicidal poisoning, not from any medicine. Think about this bad medicine idea. Srila Prabhupada's health began a dramatic decline on Feb. 26, 1977, 9 months earlier. So what medicine was taken consistently through those many months that could kill? *There was so such medicine.* There is no validity to the flawed "bad medicine" theory. How can a variety of medicines that heal and strengthen the body, taken sparsely and mostly herbal or Ayurvedic, kill someone? The GBC deniers cannot support their flawed theories.

CHAPTER 29:
VERY GOOD HEALTH

ONLY MINOR INCONVENIENCES UP TO MAY 1976

Srila Prabhupada was in very good, strong health up until mid-1976. He was energetic, went daily on super-brisk morning walks lasting a good hour or more where even his youthful disciples had difficulty keeping up, he ate his meals heartily, slept only 2 to 4 hours a day, worked constantly to expand his mission, and so on. For his age at 80, he was literally superhuman in endurance, outdoing and amazing his students. He had a rigorous schedule of travel, engagements, meetings, writing, and managing a worldwide movement. Srila Prabhupada had some minor health problems, as anyone would at 80, such as occasional swelling of hands and feet, occasional high blood pressure, common colds, or occasional indigestion after eating a difficult food. He managed these minor inconveniences deftly with diet and a few basic Ayurvedic medicines and they did not slow him down. This good health was described by Melbourne temple president Balarama das (Aug. 2017): *"Srila Prabhupada visited Melbourne April 19-25, 1976, before going to New Zealand and Hawaii. Apart from being tired from the long plane ride from India, Singapore, Sydney to Melbourne, he was **in very good health** and we would accompany him on his **usual brisk morning walks**. As the Temple President, I had the opportunity to have some close association with His Divine Grace while serving him for a week. During that visit, he gave classes every day, was very vibrant, talkative and was visited by many important people. I mention this, as the visit was only a little over a year prior to his departure, and there was absolutely no reason at the time to suspect any problems with his health."*

Swami In A Strange Land (Yogeswara das, p. 217): *"...Prabhupada had trained himself to minimize physical needs and sleep. It was well known among followers that he rested at most 4 hours at night, then rose to write and chant. They had never met anyone like him. He was 75 years old and gave people less than half his age a run for their money."*

SP'S PERSONAL SERVANT SRUTIKIRTI DAS

(1) *"In April 2002 I contacted Sruta Kirti das about Srila Prabhupada's health. He was Srila Prabhupada's personal servant from Sept. 1972 until end of 1973, and then from Sept.1974 until mid-1975. Over this span of almost three years, Sruta Kirti had Srila Prabhupada's constant close association and knew about his health conditions from*

1972-75. If there was indeed a long-term condition of advanced diabetes, or something else significant, Sruta Kirti would have learned of it. However, he knew nothing of any diabetes. My first question was: 'While you were Srila Prabhupada's servant, what did you learn about his diabetes, his kidneys, or his difficulty in passing urine?" (Nityananda das) **(2)** Sruta Kirti: *"I was not even aware of Prabhupada's diabetes. I do remember he would pass urine often and remember him walking by me at one or two in the morning on many occasions. When he became very ill, like in Vrindaban (Aug. 1974), his body would shut down. He had no appetite and would try to eat a little fruit. Twice, while I was with him, he was very ill. Once in Vrindaban in 1974. That's when he said his illness was due to 80% of the leaders not following the principles. He was very close to leaving us at that time."* **(3)** Nityananda then asked: *"Were you aware of Srila Prabhupada's having any kind of kidney problems, such as difficulty passing urine, kidney stones-pain-infection, or swelling of the hands or feet? About diabetes, you were never aware of it, it was never mentioned, and that SP never said anything to you about it?"* **(4)** Sruta Kirti: *"Srila Prabhupada never spoke to me about any chronic problems, such as kidney ailments or diabetes. I massaged him daily and never saw any swelling of his hands or feet. He always had drinking water by his sitting place but I never noticed how much he drank. I did tell you I noticed he passed frequently."*

SP'S PERSONAL SERVANT HARI SAURI

In 1998 ISKCON responded to the "poison issue": *"We asked Hari Sauri, who, apart from being with Srila Prabhupada from Nov. 1975 until March 13, 1977, was also with His Divine Grace for almost three weeks in late May to early June 1977, and all of Oct. in Vrindaban, about Prabhupada's attitude towards his disease and curing it."*

Hari Sauri Reply: *"During the whole period I was with Srila Prabhupada I never once heard him mention that he had diabetes, nor did I notice that he ever made any specific changes in his diet in response to that condition. Nor did I ever hear the cooks that traveled with us at various times (Harikesh, Nandarani, Sruti Rupa, Jamuna, Palika, Arundhati) mention that they were preparing any kind of specific diet for him to counter that condition. As far as medicines go, he also never took anything for the treatment of diabetes. When I was with him he took some Ayurvedic medicines, none for diabetes - Yogendra Rasa, which I understood was a kind of brain tonic, every morning until the fall of 1976, when he stopped it completely; Triphala Churna on occasion for constipation; and Lavan Bhaskar (black salt), which he took occasionally for digestion."*

CONCLUSIONS FROM BOTH SERVANT TESTIMONIES

These two testimonies solidly establish that diabetes and kidney problems were not apparent, mentioned, discussed, nor of any concern while Sruta Kirti was serving Srila Prabhupada 1972 up to mid-1975, nor when Hari Sauri was serving Srila Prabhupada from Nov. 1975 until Nov. 1977. There were a few gaps in 1977 while Hari Sauri was away in Australia from March 13-late May (2 months) and June-Oct. (4 months). But if diabetes had developed by Oct. 1977, Hari Sauri would know about it, and he does not. *We can safely say that diabetes and kidney disease were not known health problems from 1972 to late 1977.* Srila Prabhupada's personal servants were unaware of any diabetes or kidney problems and never saw any edema (swelling of extremities) from late 1972 to mid-1975. However, today the GBC contradicts the above testimonies and deceitfully claims these ailments were well known in the 1970's and were the causes of Srila Prabhupada natural death. But at worst, diabetes and weak kidneys were a minor inconvenience, and not were NOT the cause of death. Instead, he was lethally poisoned.

Srila Prabhupada said once only, in Feb. 1977, that he had "a little diabetes," but he had a very strict, controlled diet and **was not insulin dependent** as is typical in advanced diabetes. He never experienced any diabetic emergencies or "incidents" like insulin shocks, diabetic coma, even in his last days. If his diabetes was serious or advanced in 1977, which all accounts and evidence do not support as being the case, it would be due to cadmium poisoning, which causes diabetes and kidney failure. No doctor ever produced any known quantitative assessment of Srila Prabhupada's diabetes or kidney ailments that were derived from blood or urine tests. If there ever were any such records, none are known or available today. Our conclusion is that the GBC's statements about Srila Prabhupada having advanced diabetes and kidney disease are simply a cover-up of the massive evidence of a malicious, sky-high, and lethal cadmium poisoning. If not for being poisoned, Srila Prabhupada may well have lived with his "little diabetes" and weak kidneys for another 20 years. He could have stayed as long as he liked, and he did.

DR. BABUR DOES URINE LITMUS PAPER TEST IN 1976

In March 2004 Nityananda das visited Vrindaban and visited an old friend, Dhananjaya das, manager of the MVT buildings. They last met in 1974 on a slow third class train ride from Calcutta to Navadwip. Dhananjaya told how in April 1976 Srila Prabhupada sent him from Vrindaban to Mathura to fetch a Dr. Babur, who came to see Srila Prabhupada. Later Dhananjaya took a urine sample to Dr. Babur's home, and watched as a litmus test showed high blood sugar. Dr. Babur declared Srila Prabhupada had "serious diabetes" and was concerned. Dr. Babur prescribed a very strict diet which Srila Prabhupada refused to follow, saying he *"would rather die than just eat boiled vegetables; the very thought of which was disgusting."* This was while Hari Sauri was his personal servant, so would he not know of this? And how definitive is a paper litmus test? Still, Srila Prabhupada's health was very good at this time and no one was concerned about any diabetes.

VRINDABAN MEDICAL DIARY

Oct. 17, 1997: internal GBC email from Hari Sauri das, describing a medical diary that would be valuable to the investigation into the circumstances surrounding Srila Prabhupada's disappearance. *"There is a diary book in the case in Srila Prabhupada's room in Vrindaban. It shows a lot of details about what he ate, how much urine he passed, etc. In the display you can only see one page. I don't know how far back it goes, but there must be a lot of info there."*

Balavanta's investigation files had only 12 faded copies of this medical diary pages, with many missing. Each day Srila Prabhupada was given unspecific "medicine" by BCS. Srila Prabhupada took milk, Horlicks, water, pomegranate juice, grape juice, whey, barley milk, and sometimes solid food like sweet rice, avocado, rasagula, papaya, or a tiny bit of lunch. Above is a page showing the last dose of MKD taken. *Tamal was in total control of Srila Prabhupada's medicines, with BCS's assistance.*

DIABETES AND POISONING CAN BE SIMULTANEOUS

In *SHPM*, a daily account of Srila Prabhupada's health and medical history from May 1976 to Nov. 14, 1977 was included as a resource. It shows Srila Prabhupada's and his caretaker's responses to a worsening, unexplained health crisis. App. 8 summarizes the mysterious circumstances of Srila Prabhupada's departure after a progressive illness, with essential medical information. It is useful for medical evidence, misdiagnoses, and physical symptoms analysis. Srila Prabhupada's full health history is found in Volume 4. A brief summary here:

1976:

5.4: *Health Decline:* Tamal visits, SP ill; weak, heart palpitations

6.23: New Vrindaban; weak, heart palpitations, indigestion, cold, mucus

7.9: SP arrives in New York as Tamal's guest for Rathayatra

7.20: *Health Crisis:* Very ill; vomit, edema, weak, cannot eat or walk

8.2: SP recovered enough to eat and walk a little at France farm

8.27: SP in Bombay, still weak with poor digestion for many months

1977:

1.13: *Health Decline:* Very ill, Kumbha Mela; weak, edema, mucus

1.19: SP arrives in Bhubaneshwar; weak, indigestion

1.26: SP collapses in Puri due to leg weakness

2.10: SP collapses in Navadwip due to leg weakness

2.14: SP in Mayapur; Tamal arrives with other GBCs

2.26: *Health Crisis:* Deathly ill; fever, pain, vomit, cannot eat/walk, weak, moaning, stays in quarters, hardly recovers in coming months

3.10: SP in Mayapur, his illness worsens, not eating, becomes weaker

3.13: Hari Sauri leaves; Bhavananda and Upendra replace him

3.22: SP arrives Bombay for pandal program; cannot walk without help

3.31: SP moves into his new rooms at Juhu temple

5.8: SP goes to Hrishikesh for health recovery in cool climate

5.16: *Health Crisis:* Hrishikesh: Suddenly very ill, returns Vrindaban to die, now he carried in a palanquin, needs help to go to toilet

5.17: SP prepares his will, starts final arrangements

5.28: SP instructs GBC about ritviks to initiate on his behalf

6.5: *Health Decline:* After GBCs leave, another health downturn

7.9: SP chooses 11 ritviks, signs & sends "Final Order" letter

7.12: SP calls for Bonamali *kaviraja* to tend to his health treatment

7.25: Abhiram starts as SP 's nurse, assistant (until Oct. 16, 83 days)

7.27: *Health Decline:* SP 's health takes another turn for the worse

8.25: *Health Decline:* SP becomes very ill, just before travelling

8.27: SP departs for London and the West, bedridden, very weak

9.8: *Minor Surgery:* Crisis: urine blocked; hospital, minor operation

9.13: *Health Crisis:* SP's health worsens, he returns to Bombay

10.2: *Health Decline:* SP returns to Vrindaban thinking his end is near

10.16: Dr. Ghosh and Dr. Gopal treat SP for kidney infection, etc

10.22: Dr. Gopal rejected; SP has dream of Ramanuja kaviraja's *MKD*

10.26: SP takes Chandra Swami's kaviraja's *MKD* 2-3 times, then stops

10.28: DP Shastri arrives, begins SP 's final treatment program

11.9: SP says he heard someone saying someone has poisoned him

11.10: SP says again someone has poisoned him, but nothing is done

11.11: *Final Dose:* Whispers: "Is poison in the milk?" "Poison's going down" "Poisoning for a long time…" "Get ready to go."

11.13: SP enters internal consciousness around midnight

11.14: SP departs from this mortal realm at 7:25 pm.

CHAPTER 30:
AN INEXPLICABLE ILLNESS

Re: Srila Prabhupada's reluctance to eat, drink for months, how he said he was being poisoned, Goldfrank's medical advice is interesting: *"...if homicidal intent is suspected, patients should be advised against accepting food or drink from anyone. Visitors should be closely monitored and outside nutritional products should be forbidden."*

MANY MISDIAGNOSES

No one in 1977 (and until 1997) could say exactly what was the cause of Srila Prabhupada's illness in his last year. Universally, this was a mysterious illness, without a description or name, amongst ISKCON devotees for decades. *"In the first twenty years after Srila Prabhupada's departure, no one I ever spoke with in the Hare Krishna movement, many hundreds of devotees, including leaders, equals, or rank and filers, ever articulated anything about the cause of Srila Prabhupada's final illness. It was just a big blank." (Thomas Getterly, 2020)* Yet, with the appearance of the poisoning issue in 1997, the GBC suddenly were knowledgeable experts on how Srila Prabhupada departed, claiming it was due to the natural causes of diabetes and kidney disease, but without any medical documentation and only newly revived memories.

However, in 1977 it confounded them and all devotees, all of Srila Prabhupada's doctors and kavirajas, and, seemingly Srila Prabhupada as well (until Nov. 9-10, 1977 when he stated he thought he had been poisoned). As Srila Prabhupada's mysterious illness worsened in 1977, there was *a bewildering parade of doctors and treatments.* There never was any conclusive diagnosis from a qualified doctor, based on proper medical tests (and no one knows if there were any or what the results were). There were many misdiagnoses: heart palpitations, liver/ kidney problems, diabetes, dropsy, just exhaustion, asthma, old age, indigestion, etc. Symptoms were cited as diagnoses. It was a mystery illness that grew progressively worse with anemia, indigestion, no appetite, weakness, and *constant "colds," mucus, cough, raspy voice, chronic bronchitis (classic heavy metal poisoning symptoms).*

Srila Prabhupada began to lose his vision and light pained his eyes. Reading the health history, clearly this search for a cure was urgent, constant, frustratingly evasive. No one could figure out why Srila Prabhupada was "ill" or what to do about it. Forty doctors and kavirajas were brought and consulted. So many treatments were undertaken (chart below). The central theme in 1977 was searching for a cure for Srila Prabhupada's illness (*whatever it was*). Everyone kept looking, and this was not because any diagnosis for Srila Prabhupada's illness was in hand, as the lying GBC claims today. *If they knew what the illness was, why did everyone in 1977 keep trying to find a cure* for Srila Prabhupada's health crisis? Why were so many treatments tried and rejected? No one knew what the illness was!

CONFUSION OVER THE MYSTERIOUS ILLNESS

Note the confusion in *ISKCON In The 1970's*: **(1)** *...because his disease was fatal- he couldn't eat, so his body was finished.* (May '77) **(2)** *...his sickness, which prevents him from eating, will cause his departure.* (May '77) **(3)** *...he is very ill; his body has "run out," he is going to die.* (May '77) **(4)** *News that SP is feeling better.* (June 17, '77) **(5)** *SP is "worse than ever" in ill health- dropsy.* (Aug. 4, '77) **(6)** *New word is that he is "even worse."* (Aug. 11, '77) **(7)** *Tamal said that his illness is psychological and subtle. A few days ago he was very bad.* (Aug. 17, '77) **(8)** *Tamal said, "This is one cure you haven't tried- going to the West." [and they tried a lot of cures.]* **(9)** *SP said, "I'm disgusted. These kavirajas come, say they will get me well in four days, and then later they say it will take a long time."* (Aug. 19, '77) **(10)** *SP's illness and his relation to it as his disciple was confusing, but he knew he should "stop all sinful acts."* (Aug. 20, '77) *[The idea was that disciples' sins were the illness's cause.]* **(11)** *Now we hear again that SP's health is in crisis, "the worst."* (Sept. 26, '77) **(12)** *The doctor says he has no particular disease now. He is exhausted. His inner organs aren't working. The body is coming to an end.* (Oct. 6, '77) *[Another super-vague diagnosis]* **(13)** *Early today there was some blood in his urine, which was sent to a lab.* (Oct. 12, '77) *[There are no records of Mathura lab results.]*

Satsvarupa's 1983 Srila Prabhupada biography in 6 volumes does **not** describe an illness of diabetes or kidney disease, as is the official ISKCON narrative today, and he describes only old age, travel stress, "overworked system." One would assume if the diagnosis for Srila Prabhupada's illness was so clear, as claimed by the GBC, that it would have been stated in his official biography? But it was not. *The truth is that their diagnosis only became "clear" when ISKCON leaders began their denials and cover-ups of the poisoning evidence.* In *TKG's Diary* (1998), no opinion about Srila Prabhupada's 1977 health and medical condition is given except for a myriad of vague, contradictory, misdiagnoses by 40 doctors and kavirajas, such as "internal fever," "gonorrhea," or "no disease, just weakness," none of which make sense. Tamal told Satsvarupa in 1977 it was "psychological and subtle."

Diabetes is not psychological and subtle. Hari Sauri's unpublished diary for Oct-Nov. 1977 (printed in 2022) contains a similar train of vague ideas as to what the mysterious illness was. *He never mentioned diabetes in all his 100 diary pages.* His five volumes of *Transcendental Diary* which goes to Oct. 2, 1976 also gives no clear diagnosis, only a list of *symptoms* like swelling of extremities, indigestion, old age, and *he never mentions diabetes*. Even on hundreds of tape recordings in 1976-77, we find the same vague descriptions, and nothing on diabetes.

The fact is there never was a clear diagnosis for Srila Prabhupada's health failure. That is, until the discovery of lethal levels of cadmium in three hair samples tested from 2002-05. ISKCON's diabetes defense that arose in 1998-2000, after the poison issue appeared, is not a medical diagnosis, it is **at best a theory** based on tenuous, conflicting testimonies and memories, and at worst a **dishonest cover-up** arising from corrupt motivations to maintain a status quo. What if ISKCON members thought some ISKCON gurus poisoned Srila Prabhupada? This could quickly end ISKCON's guru regime, as they all received their guruhood from the poisoners who concocted ISKCON's guru system. Today we palpably sense the GBC's desperation with vigorous denials of the evidence.

What was Srila Prabhupada's specific ailment in 1977 which led to his rapid health decline and passing away? Diabetes, kidney disease, heart disease, plain old age? Or were all of these accelerated, exacerbated by the now proven, massive cadmium poisoning? None of the biographical accounts of Srila Prabhupada's pastimes, including Tamal, Satsvarupa, Hari Sauri, Sruta Kirti, Vegavan, Giriraj, Abhiram, Srutirupa, and others say that the illness was diabetes. Nobody knew! Only **AFTER** the poison issue arose did this become the GBC's explanation! The GBC has little to substantiate their *"diabetes was the cause of demise"* idea, except for vague assertions from the memory of Dr. McIrvine (Ch. 33). The chart of the parade of doctors, their misdiagnoses, treatments, and results below shows a great confusion, **that there was no diagnosis at all**. Physicians, scientists, devotees, forensic toxicologists, law enforcement, investigators and medical examiners may find the health history in Volume 4 helpful.

PARADE OF DOCTORS, MEDICINES, TREATMENTS

Soon after Srila Prabhupada's serious health crisis on Feb. 26, 1977, a parade of doctors, *kavirajas* and different treatments ensued until his departure 9 months later. One is easily confused and lost by the constant treatment and medicine changes. Naturally one wonders about the unusual nature of Srila Prabhupada's "illness" and his medical care.

There was no logic or sense as to why treatments and doctors were switched/ abandoned one after another. We made an *partial* list of the doctors, treatments, and medicines. As Tamal said: *"so many doctors and medicines, nothing worked."* The poisoners knew the nature of the "illness" but everyone including doctors were mystified why Srila Prabhupada withered away in spite of all treatments.

Yes, in 1977 they all knew Srila Prabhupada's kidneys were failing... *but why?* If they knew in 1977 what the problem was, then why the continuous search with so many doctors? Symptoms were clear: dropsy, indigestion, anemia, no appetite, constant mucus and bronchitis, weakness, etc. But a symptom does not identify the illness nor the proper medical remedy. A symptom is not a diagnosis. Dr. Morris did NAA hair tests which uncovered the cause of Srila Prabhupada's health failure. *It was a massive, homicidal cadmium poisoning.* Perhaps diabetes and kidney problems were concurrent, we do not know for sure, but lethal poisoning was the real cause of health decline and of any diabetes as well. The facts ascertain a malicious poisoning of the greatest spiritual teacher in this age. The truth of history should be established, justice be served, the culprits identified and punished, and a complete cleansing be made of all the exploits, policies, and deviations that those poisoners injected into Srila Prabhupada's spiritual movement. His faithful followers must maintain, preserve, protect his divine gift to humanity.

THE PARADE OF DOCTORS IN 1977

1. Jan. 12   Dr. G. Ghosh of Allahabad   Kumbha Mela
2. End Feb.   Dr. G. Ghosh of Allahabad   Mayapur
        Diuretic caused blood in urine
3. Mar. 7   Bimal Tarka Tirtha, kaviraja   Mayapur
        Ayurvedic medicines, stopped in days, no results
4. Mar. 26   Dr. Oja   Bombay
        High blood pressure, rest and no strain prescribed
5. Apr. 5   New doctor   Bombay
        Unknown prescriptions but the treatment was rejected
6. Apr. 18   Dr. Sharma   Bombay
        Tried to give injection with pills, SP refused to take
7. June 4-5   Dr Ghosh Kodaikanal   Vrindaban
        Collapsed organs; recommended dialysis etc; treatments refused
8. June 24   Bhagatji's old baba   Vrindaban
        Medicine of 45 tree barks, SP took, felt better
9. June 12   Bonamali kaviraja   Vrindaban
        Milk, cow dung ashes, medicines, 3 weeks: no results
10. Date ??   Triguna kaviraja/Delhi   Vrindaban
        He told Yashoda dasi later he treated SP, details unknown
11. Aug. 15   Chief Dr of Delhi Ayurvedic Hospital, Vrindaban
        Came and left, Tamal rejected him
12. Aug. 15   Dr. Khurana   Vrindaban

Kidney failure; dialysis at temple; but Tamal declined
13. Aug. 15   Bhagatji's local Vaidya   Vrindaban
Dropsy, fast pulse; no salt, less strain; no results.
14. Aug. 25   Bonamali kaviraja   Vrindaban
Some Ayur. Meds; but SP left for London in 2 days
15. Aug. 27   Tamal, his own diagnosis   Vrindaban
SP illness was psychological/subtle, cure was to preach
16. Sept. 8   Dr. Andrew McIrvine   London
Kidneys, diabetes, malnutrition; performed circumcision
17. Sept.8   Dr. Kanodia   London
Courtesy follow-up check-up after circumcision
18. Sept. 9   Dr. McIrvine   London
More liquids, food, protein, antibiotics prescribed
19. Sept. 24   Ram Gopal Vaidya   Bombay
Liver/kidney problems; meds, special diet; SP rejected
20. Oct. 3-4   Bonamali kaviraja   Vrindaban
Only weakness; diet, Ayur. Meds caused cough, rejected
21. Oct. ?   Dr. Kapoor's Vaidya   Vrindaban
Ordered urine test, Vit. B, breathing exercises, massage,
supplements, no results after 10 days, treatment stopped
22. Oct. 12   Dr. Ghosh, Kodaikanal   Vrindaban
Tamal obstructed his treatment, he left after a few days
23. Oct. 13   Bhagatji intervened   Vrindaban
Arranged urine test; kidney infection; pills, SP refused
24. Oct. 15   Bonamali kaviraja   Vrindaban
Gonorrhea type disorder? -treatment rejected
25. Oct. 16   Dr. G. Ghosh, Allahabad   Vrindaban
Fresh air, protein, posture, urine test, treatment accepted
26. Oct. 17   Dr. G. Ghosh & Dr. K. Gopal   Vrindaban
Kidney infection/damage; Lassix, meds, liquids, nutrition
27. Oct. 20   Dr. G. Ghosh   Vrindaban
After his prescriptions, he left, Dr. Gopal took over
28. Oct. 20   Dr. K. Gopal   Vrindaban
Eat, drink more; treatment was continued for a week
29. Oct. 22   Dr. K. Gopal   Vrindaban
Suspected a lung problem, wanted at home X-rays, Tamal rejected
30. Oct. 22   Ramanuja kaviraja local   Vrindaban
Kidney, digestion; his ideas & his makharadhvaja rejected
31. Oct. 25   Delhi kaviraja gave makharadhvaja   Vrindaban
Self-treatment, makharadhvaja rejected after 3 doses, diarrhea
32. Oct. 28   Dr. Damodar Prasad Shastri   Vrindaban
Fresh Ayurvedic Meds to cure kidneys, treatment continued
33. Nov. 1   Dr. NL Gupta consulted   Vrindaban
Liver problem; prescribed a poison antidote, but not made, given
34. Nov. 7   Dr. D. P. Shastri returns again   Vrindaban
Kidney problem; new Ayurvedic herbal medicine to make blood
35. Nov. 10   Sri Ramduttji kaviraja came   Vrindaban
Milk, cough meds, Shastri stays to make fresh medicines
36. Feb. 1978   Death certificate obtained in Mathura
Heart attack listed; an arbitrary misdiagnosis 3 months later
37. At least several other unnamed doctors came, gave misdiagnoses and
ineffective treatments: ***The total for 1977 was at least forty doctors.***

CHAPTER 31:
THE MYSTERY SYMPTOMS

NON-DIABETIC SYMPTOMS UNIQUE TO CD POISONING

A careful review of Srila Prabhupada's 1977 physical health symptoms shows that a group of them are not readily reconcilable with Diabetes Type II (DM2), kidney disease, liver disease, heart disease, or anything else suggested by any doctor or ISKCON leader as being Srila Prabhupada's 1977 illness. We list 12 of these "mystery symptoms" below. Of course, the sequelae (complications) of diabetes and renal (kidney) disease could conceivably stretch to include some atypical ailments, *but not the entire group of these unique symptoms at once.* Although diabetes is a big door through which many consequent illnesses enter, it is highly exceptional that Srila Prabhupada prominently exhibited so many unique symptoms *not* typical to DM2. These symptoms are, however, ***unique to cadmium poisoning.*** These "mystery" symptoms are unique to cadmium poisoning but not to diabetes or kidney disease. They constitute a dynamic corroboration of the highly elevated cadmium hair tests. *Medical symptom analysis is standard evidence in all deaths under suspicious circumstances,* and our analysis demonstrates that even if Srila Prabhupada had advanced diabetes in 1977 (dubious) and if he therefore showed diabetes symptoms, he also simultaneously displayed a set of 12 non-diabetes symptoms, which are unique to cadmium poisoning. They are:

EYES: (1) EXTREME PHOTOPHOBIA/ light sensitive eyes
EYES: (2) CHRONIC CONJUNCTIVITIS & tearing eyes
LUNGS: (3) EXCESSIVE MUCUS, CHRONIC BHRONCHITIS
LUNGS: (4) COUGH and upper respiratory irritation
LUNGS: (5) LUNG IRREGULARITIES (short breath, pleurisy)
MUCUS:(6) COLDS, CHRONIC RHINITIS: wet nose congestion
LIVER: (7) ABNORMAL: weakness, enlarged, diseased
VOICE: (8) SCRATCHY, HOARSE, husky, gravelly, weak
DROOLING: (9) EXCESSIVE SALIVATION, DROOLING
URINARY: (10) Urinary/kidney infections/inflammation/phimosis
FACE: (11) EXPRESSIONLESS, colorless, pale, yellowish
MIND: (12) TEARFUL, SENSITIVE, melancholic, emotional

SYMPTOMS NOT FOUND IN DIABETES, KIDNEY DISEASE

DM2 is insidious and generally lies hidden. By the time it is diagnosed, often significant irreversible health damage has occurred, typically vascular, heart, neurologic, kidney, or eyesight degeneration.

Diabetes can lead to or be associated with a variety of physical ailments: obesity, weakness, dropsy, kidney malfunction, skin infections, just to name a few. It is no wonder some assume Srila Prabhupada had advanced DM2, although no history or records exist to support this. *These "mystery" symptoms exhibited by Srila Prabhupada cannot as a group be attributable to diabetes or kidney disease, but are typical of cadmium poisoning.* Also, all his other symptoms are compatible with cadmium poisoning, i.e., none of his symptoms conflicted with cadmium poisoning. Each "mystery" symptom is examined below.

PHOTOPHOBIA

Eye Sensitivity To Light: Photophobia (not skin photosensitivity) is when light hurts the eyes and one avoids light. The GBC claimed a search of the Medline database was unable to find photophobia as a symptom of heavy metals poisoning. To "enlighten" those in the dark on photophobia, a few references in "the scientific/medical world" are:

Photophobia: Arsenic/Mercury: (1) (www.praxair.com) Praxair Technology's safety sheet on arsenic trioxide where photophobia is listed among the "effects of repeated overexposure." Eye irritation and tearing are also listed here. **(2)** Rocky Mountain Arsenal Medical Monitoring Program (www.cdphe.state.w.us) lists the symptoms of arsenic poisoning, and photophobia is included. **(3)** Healthcentral.com, General Encyclopedia, shows light-sensitive vision, or photophobia, to be caused by, among other things, drugs such as amphetamines, atropine, cocaine, etc. **(4)** An article by Dr. KK Padlewska at www.emedicine.com about acrodynia, now a rare disease due to increased awareness of poisons, lists one of the symptoms as photophobia in 50% of cases. While acrodynia is caused by chronic mercury poisoning, the effects of arsenic are very similar. **(5)** PubMed (www. ncbi.nlm.nih.gov) cites an article, March 1989 (Ann Emerg Med) by DiNapoli, Hall, Drake and Rumack from the Dept. of Emergency Medicine, Parview Episcopal Medical Center, Pueblo, CO that documents photophobia as a result of arsenic poisoning. **(6)** PubMed also cited an article (Schweiz Rundsch Med Prax 1997) by French physicians in Switzerland who documented photophobia as a result of mercury poisoning.

Cadmium, Photophobia: 612 websites were found in 2005 when a search was made for "cadmium photophobia," and a perusal of them showed no doubt of photophobia being a prominent symptom of cadmium poisoning, as well as several other types of poisoning like mercury, etc. Two sites: (1). http://npic.orst.edu/RMPP/rmpp_inss.pdf and (2) www.espimetals.com/msds's/cadmiumsulfide.pdf

There is plentiful evidence from scientific sources to confirm photophobia is a symptom of cadmium and arsenic poisoning. *Further, photophobia is not associated with diabetes or kidney disease.* There are many references to allergic drug reactions, e.g., mustard gas and mercury, resulting in photophobia. Glaucoma sometimes causes photophobia, but Srila Prabhupada did not have the other symptoms of glaucoma. Diabetic retinopathy sometimes results in photophobia in early diabetes, but Srila Prabhupada had no other signs of retinopathy.

Health History References For Photophobia: From Srila Prabhupada's 1977 health history (many archival photos show him with sunglasses indoors), showing extreme photophobia due to cadmium poisoning: **(1)** "...put on sunglasses so your eyes won't be hurt by the sun." **(2)** ...someone asked, "Light?" [...] SP: "Oh. Just make it dark. (sound of curtains closing)" Tamal said, "We'll put your sunglasses on so you won't be disturbed by the light." (Oct. 29, 1977) **(3)** SP was brought onto the balcony veranda and put on his sunglasses. "...he again put on sunglasses, though we were sitting inside a dark room." (TkgD p. 137) **(4)** No translation work and darkened quarters. Going to the temple in the mornings, he wore his "dark sunglasses." (Sat:6.361-2) **(5)** Aug. 11, 1977: Guru Kripa gave SP a new pair of Polaroid sunglasses, which he used increasingly, even inside when there is a light on... (TkgD 50-1) **(6)** Aug. 11, 1977: Coming into the darkened room, SP had the light turned on. Abhiram read the report to SP. (ConvBk 35, p. 50-2)

(7) "He was reclining on a pillow and wearing sunglasses, which he always does now because his eyes are giving him some trouble." (Archive letters) **(8)** SP was wearing his sunglasses while lying on his back on a cot on the roof. (Iskcon70, 306-7) **(9)** Aug. 28, 1977: SP: ...again wearing his "dark sunglasses"... (TkgD.171; Sat:6.374) **(10)** SP came before the altar, slowly removed his sunglasses... (Sat:6.379) **(11)** At night, in a darkened room, Tamal (said), "...even though he put on his sunglasses, he kept his eyes shut because the light hurt his eyes." (TkgD.190) **(12)** "...eyes would hurt in bright light and he would always wear sunglasses." (Abhiram das, Sept. 2, 1977) **(13)** "Prabhupada's room was very dark except for a nightlight..." (Sat:6.390) **(14)** The room was very dark due to the windows being covered by curtains to accommodate Srila Prabhupada's sensitive eyes. (SPConv, Oct. 10, 1977)

(15) Oct. 2, 1977: SP's first order of business was that his servants "closed the curtains and dimmed the lights." (Sat:6.389) **(16)** "...Tamal brought out a flashlight for Pradyumna." (Oct. 14, 1977) **(17)** "Yadubara wanted to film you translating. We can have a little light here while he films for about half a minute?" (SPConv, Oct. 21, 1977) **(18)** Jayadwaita:

"Flashlight?" (ConvBk:36.14) **(19)** BCS: "Can I see it in the light, please?" SP could not tell that the sun had risen an hour earlier, because the room was so darkened. **(20)** "When Tamal tried to read to SP, he said, 'Is there a flashlight?'" (SPConv, Oct. 28, 1977) **(21)** Nov. 4, 1977: SP: "Get one small light." (ConvBk:36.280) **(22)** Nov. 8, 1977: The curtains were closed again... (ConvBk:36.344) **(23)** Bhaktisiddhanta das saw SP leave Vrindaban for London with dark sunglasses on at midnight. **(24)** SP asked for the light to be turned on. (ConvBk:36.67) **(25)** When Nityananda studied the Archives photos of SP taken in early 1977 (noted in SHPM): *"...it was shocking. Most of the scenes showed only a silhouette of Srila Prabhupada in his darkened rooms. He was averse to light."* **(26)** He wore *"dark sunglasses regularly, even late in the day or in a darkened room. He appeared to have troubles with his eyes, seeing properly, and with sensitivity to light."* (Sat:6.358-360)

Napoleon's Photophobia: No one knows if Napoleon's poisoning was deliberate or accidental. But what is relevant is a comparison of the poisoning symptoms in the two cases. Ben Weider, author of *Assassination at St. Helena,* spent 40 years studying Napoleon's arsenic poisoning, which is now widely accepted since new hair tests were done in 2001, showing unusually high arsenic content. Napoleon's arsenical photophobia is well known: *(1) "...he displayed symptoms of typical arsenical intoxication of an acute nature: ...sensitivity of the eyes to light" (2) "I accompanied him and was shown into a completely darkened room where General Bonaparte lay in bed. The room was so dark that I could not see..." (3) "Sensitivity of the eyes to sunlight or bright artificial light. The victim may prefer a nearly darkened room."*

Napoleon had extreme photosensitivity in his last six months. When the doctor visited Napoleon's darkened bedroom during daytime, it was kept so dark that he could not see Napoleon. Very high arsenic levels were found in many of Napoleon's hair samples (saved by collectors), which explains Napoleon's photophobia. **CONCLUSION:** *Photophobia is a symptom of cadmium and arsenic poisoning, but it is not typical in diabetes or kidney disease. Srila Prabhupada had increasing and obvious photophobia in 1977.*

CHRONIC CONJUNCTIVITIS, BRONCHITIS, RHINITIS

Chronic Cough, Mucus In Eyes, Chest Mucus, Tearing: *"Srila Prabhupada still chose not to drink anything although we are making mung jal with the hope that he will take later on. Just before, Tamal Krishna mentioned [to] Kirtanananda he was trying to persuade Srila Prabhupada to drink something. Srila Prabhupada would not do it and complained of mucus."* (HSUnpub, p 20) *"Any medicine, food, or drink,* *anything,* *would quickly cause lots of coughing up of thick mucus."* (TkgD) Constant mucus and cough are trademark symptoms of cadmium poisoning, but are not seen in diabetes or kidney disease. Chronic bronchitis and conjunctivitis are also not typically associated with DM2. An extensive search of scientific studies on Medline/PubMed showed no relationship between diabetes or kidney disease with chronic bronchitis, mucus, or conjunctivitis. In App. 8 (1977 health history) we see *an unending chronic, heavy bronchitis or cold, month after month, with heavy cough and chest mucus, conjunctivitis (watery irritated eyes with mucus), runny nose, tearing, and general irritation of the upper respiratory system and mucous membranes.* Sources attributing these symptoms to chronic cadmium/arsenic poisoning are:

(1) *"With respect to non-cancer diseases, we found.... Diabetes mellitus, and bronchitis..."* (Mortality for certain diseases with high levels of arsenic, Tsai SM, 1999) In other words, those poisoned with arsenic typically developed diabetes and bronchitis. **(2)** *"Chronic arsenic poisoning means... symptoms of... chronic bronchitis"* (Endemic chronic arsenic poisoning study, Zaldivar R, et al 1980) **(3)** *"...arsenic toxicity. The common symptoms are conjunctivitis..."* (Arsenic in ground water of West Bengal; Das D, Chatterjee A, 1995) **(4)** Emedicine.com: mercury or cadmium poisoning is associated with conjunctivitis and photophobia.

(5) www.magneticclay.com/productlist.shtml Symptoms/Diseases related to cadmium: **Bronchitis**, Cancers (bladder, esophagus, larynx, lung, mouth, pharynx, prostate, and stomach); headaches, heart problems, anemia, hypertension, and **kidney diseases**. **(6)** Cadmium in drinking water causes **Bronchitis**… www.triangularwave.com/f6.htm **(7)** Armstrong BG (1985): Prostatic cancer and **chronic respiratory and renal disease** in British cadmium workers. Br J Ind Med 42:540 **(8)** www.canoshweb.org/odp/html/cadmium Morbidity studies identified shortness of breath, obstructive patterns of lung function, **bronchitis**, emphysema in cadmium exposed workers. **(9)** Symptoms of cadmium poisoning include rhinitis, conjunctivitis, bronchitis, cough, dyspnea (shallow breath). www.inchem.org/documents/pims/chemical/cadm **(10)** www.environmentallamp.com/effects_of_cadmium Adverse health effects include **bronchitis (11)** There are endless references showing chronic bronchitis, upper respiratory tract irritation, conjunctivitis, rhinitis, cough, mucus, etc to be classic symptoms of cadmium poisoning, especially in sub-acute levels.

Health History References: Bronchitis, Conjunctivitis, Rhinitis, Cough: The following are *a few* references in Srila Prabhupada's health history with coughing, chest mucus, mucus in the eyes, with unremitting cold, cough and mucus through 1977. Srila Prabhupada's cough on late 1977 tape recordings is heartrending, especially knowing his chronic bronchitis and conjunctivitis were due to his cadmium/arsenic poisoning.

(1) 02.26.77: He could not sleep because he would be coughing so much. **(2)** 03.20.77: Srila Prabhupada (heavy coughing)... **(3)** 03.27.77: SP had a cough... **(4)** 06.30.77: SP needed a new bottle of eye wash (conjunctivitis) **(5)** 06.30.76: He is still weak and congested with mucus. **(6)** 07.04.76: His respiratory system is quite blocked with mucus. **(7)** 07.05.77: (SP) had a cough... "Until you're over your cold..." **(8)** 07.08.77: ...the Expectrin cough medicine that he's been taking... **(9)** 07.13.77: In the night the cough syrup prevented any translation work. **(10)** 07.21.76: Racked by a heavy cold, SP coughed up large amounts of mucus every few minutes. **(11)** 07.27.76: SP was still coughing and full of mucus. **(12)** 07.28.77: SP's eyes were being washed with rosewater 2 or 3 times daily. **(13)** 07.30.76: He is still full of mucus... **(14)** 08.07.76: ...still coughing but not dislodging the heavy mucus... **(15)** 08.21.76: ...(SP is) coughing up a lot of mucus. **(16)** 08.25.77: ...it is due to mucus... **(17)** 09.15.77: There was mucus buildup, much spitting and coughing... **(18)** 09.20.77: (SP) became very congested with a bad cough. **(19)** 09.23.77: (SP's) massage was skipped due to the cough. **(20)** 09.25.77: SP was constipated and coughing. **(21)** 09.27.77: (SP was) still coughing, which even the cough syrup did not help. Mucus was filling his whole system; even his eyes had too much mucus. **(22)** 10.03.77: ...causing SP to cough at night. **(23)** 10.04.77: ...coughing and spitting mucus all night. **(24)** 10.05.77: But today SP drank milk, and had NO mucus from it. **(25)** 10.06.77: SP's cough was back. Although drinking nothing, cough is coming. **(26)** 10.09.77: SP spat out some heavy mucus. **(27)** 10.12.77: (SP) coughed more again. (SP coughs heavily) **(28)** 10.15.77: SP answered, "I cannot" and coughed up mucus. **(29)** 10.21.77: There's a medicine for preventing any cough in the lung. **(30)** 10.22.77: Dr. Gopal suspected SP might have tuberculosis due to lung and breathing irregularities and wanted to take chest X-rays. He was confused as to why the cough would not go away. **(31)** 10.30.77: SP had a cough that gradually increased during the day. **(32)** Nov. 1977: We hear SP's bad cough on the tapes.

Does no one else find it unusual for someone to have mucus, cough, colds, bronchitis, rhinitis, etc NON-STOP ALL YEAR?? The accounts of various heavy metal poisoning victims invariably includes descriptions of cough, mucus, bronchitis, rhinitis, conjunctivitis, etc.

Mystery Of The Stop And Start Bronchitis: An unusual feature of Srila Prabhupada's last year was an almost constant cough and mucus.

These symptoms receded and resumed even day to day. While the milk was often blamed, mucus and cough came even during times of abstinence from milk. Or a new supplement or treatment was blamed for the mucus, *until everything caused mucus*. Eating, fasting, milk, or no milk. Finally Dr. K. Gopal became perplexed in Oct. 1977 and suspected something other than normal bronchitis. He wanted X-rays but Tamal demonized Dr. Gopal and no X-rays were taken, though the machine would be brought to Srila Prabhupada's rooms. No further investigation into these mysterious symptoms were made. X-rays would detect the radiopaque cadmium and be seen as white spots in the lungs. The constant bronchitis/ mucus is due to ongoing heavy metal poisoning. May/June 1976 was the onset of Srila Prabhupada's constant and heavy mucus congestion, leading to great suspicion the poisoning began at this time. Similar symptoms are noted in chronic arsenic poisoning case studies, such as in Blanche Taylor Moore's victims and Napoleon.

Persistent Conjunctivitis Mystery: Conjunctivitis is bacterial, viral, or allergic. Viral, bacterial clear up in days; allergic can last as long as the irritant is present. (Merck's Manual) *Srila Prabhupada's persistent, long-lasting conjunctivitis was allergic, from poisoning.*

DROOLING (EXCESSIVE SALIVATION)

Not typically associated with diabetes or kidney disease, excessive salivation and drooling is a prominent symptom of heavy metals poisoning.

(1) Cadmium causes excessive salivation: www.indiaagronet.com/ indiaagronet/Foods%20Technology/Food%20Adulteration.htm

(2) Increased salivation in arsenic poisoning: www. homeopathicdoctor.ca/GSDL/Sample_Reports/Nutrition/r_TotEC24.pdf **(3)** Cadmium ingestion is associated with salivation. www.canoshweb.org/odp/html/cadmium.htm#p2b

SCRATCHY THROAT, HOARSE, HUSKY VOICE

Not associated w/ diabetes/ kidney disease, a persistent scratchy, hoarse, husky voice is unique to chemical poisonings like Cd and As.

(1) www.cdc.gov/niosh/topics/pesticides/pdfs/pest-cd2app2v2.pdf **(2)** ww.chestnet.org/education/online/pccu/vol15/lessons1_2/lesson02.php **(3)** npic.orst.edu/RMPP/rmpp_inss.pdf

LUNG IRREGULARITIES- DYPSNEA, PLEURISY

On Oct. 22, 1977, Dr. K. Gopal of Mathura, after a week of various allopathic medicines, examined Srila Prabhupada again. He was perplexed: the appetite had not improved. The left lung was taking in less air, and he suspected asthma, pleurisy, dyspnea, or a type of lung infection. He prescribed a drug called *Isotoxin* and wanted to bring an X-ray machine to Srila Prabhupada's rooms to do a lung X-ray. Cadmium, being radiopaque, would have showed up.

Bhavananda and Tamal both vigorously nixed the X-rays, then criticized and dismissed Dr. Gopal. Nothing was done regarding Srila Prabhupada's unusual and mysterious lung irregularities, which are characteristic of cadmium poisoning and not associated with diabetes or kidney ailments. In 2002 Dr. Gopal clarified he suspected asthma (not tuberculosis as Tamal had written).

URINARY TRACT INFLAMMATION, Phimosis, Circumcision

From the description of the arsenic poisonings of Blanche Taylor Moore's victims, we find that Raymond Reid's symptoms *perfectly matched those of Srila Prabhupada in 1977.* The symptoms of cadmium and arsenic poisoning are similar. *"Raymond had nausea, vomiting, diarrhea, extreme weakness, swelling, anemia and blood irregularities, heart irregularities, failing kidneys. Then his kidneys stopped producing urine and he began coughing up large quantities of mucus. His intestinal tract was not working and he had a* **weak and raspy voice**. *He required a painful* **circumcision** *due to persistent inflammation and infection of the genital. ...his urine was blocked by inflammation in the urethra."*

Srila Prabhupada went to a London hospital in Sept. 1977 to relieve urinary retention with a circumcision. The attending ER surgical resident Dr. McIrvine said in 2000: *"His most obvious problem... was urinary retention... caused by a most unusual degree of phimosis... a long-standing scarring and thickening of the foreskin such that he was... virtually unable to pass urine."*

The unusual scarring and phimosis observed by Dr. McIrvine in Sept. 1977 is highly unusual, not typical to diabetes or kidney disease, but found in heavy metals poisonings. After many months of serious poisoning, this was likely a scarring from chronic urinary tract infections and inflammation, which would block the urine, and thus circumcision or urethral tubing is required. In Ch. 39 we see this in other heavy metal poisoning cases as well.

EXPRESSIONLESS, COLORLESS FACE

Srila Prabhupada, increasingly after his Feb. 26, 1977 severe health attack, exhibited a pale, expressionless, motionless, pallor-less, blank face that was unmistakable and can be noted in photographs of the time. This was also noted by Ayurvedic physician Dr. Mehta in 1997.

SENSITIVE, MELANCHOLIC, VERY EMOTIONAL

Srila Prabhupada, increasingly in his last months, was prone to sudden tears, crying, being very sensitive, melancholic, and prominently emotional, which was very much different than his prior demeanor. Though this should be seen as a transcendental symptom, its external correlative cause is heavy metals poisoning.

LATE DIABETES SYMPTOMS CONSPICUOUSLY ABSENT

At the bottom of this chart above are listed ten symptoms or complications very typical to diabetes that were *__not seen__* in Srila Prabhupada prior to his departure, and this creates great doubt whether he had advanced diabetes. No obesity, excessive hunger or thirst, insulin dependency, diabetic coma, infections, tingling, etc. These ten signs are not all guaranteed in advanced diabetes, but when a large number are absent, it creates grave doubts about an advanced diabetes diagnosis. So what was the primary cause of Srila Prabhupada's health deterioration? Answer: a heavy metals poisoning.

COMPARISON OF MEDICAL SYMPTOMS

Next is an analysis of Srila Prabhupada's medical symptoms.

SET #1: "MYSTERY SYMPTOMS": SEEN IN HEAVY METAL POISONINGS, NOT DIABETES/ KIDNEY DISEASE; ABSENT IN SRILA PRABHUPADA BEFORE MID-1976, INCREASINGLY SEVERE AFTER; VERY SUPPORTIVE OF CADMIUM POISONING

1.	*EXTREME PHOTOPHOBIA*	**SEVERE** last 6 months
2.	*CONJUNCTIVITIS, TEARING EYES*	**SEVERE** last 6 months
3.	*CHRONIC BRONCHITIS lung mucus*	**SEVERE** all 18 months
4.	*CHRONIC COUGH chest irritation*	**SEVERE** all 18 months
5.	*LUNG Irregularities short breath*	**SEVERE** last few months
6.	*CHRONIC RHINITIS runny stuffy nose*	**SEVERE** all 18 months
7.	*LIVER: weakness, enlarged, diseased*	**SEVERE** last 6 months
8.	*SCRATCHY, HOARSE VOICE*	**SEVERE** last 9 months
9.	*LOTS OF SALIVATION, DROOLING*	**Moderate** in 1977
10.	*PHIMOSIS, Urethra Inflammation*	**Severe** by Sept 1977
11.	*FACE No Color, Expression, Pallor*	**SEVERE** last 6 months
12.	*MIND Emotional, sensitive, tearful*	**SEVERE** last 6 months

SET #2: SEEN BOTH IN HEAVY METAL POISONING AND DIABETES/ KIDNEY DISEASE; AS SEEN IN SRILA PRABHUPADA BEFORE & AFTER HIS PROVEN POISONING:

		BEFORE	AFTER
1.	*HEART PALPITATIONS*	MINOR	**Severe increasingly**
2.	*HEADACHE*	MINOR	**Medium increasing**
3.	*BAD TASTE IN MOUTH*	NONE	**Severe increasingly**
4.	*PARESTHESIA/ ITCHING*	NONE	**Moderate late 1977**
5.	*ABDOMINAL UPSETS*	MINOR	**Moderate to Severe**
6.	*SEIZURES, FAINTING*	NONE	**Yes, late 1977**
7.	*HIGH BLOOD PRESSURE*	SOME	**High; On and Off**
8.	*WEIGHT LOSS, no appetite*	NONE	**SEVERE in 1977**
9.	*DIFFICULT URINATION*	SOME	**Severe increasingly**
10.	*DISCOLORED, CASTS IN URINE*	NONE	**Prominent late '77**
11.	*WEAKNESS ANEMIA FATIGUE*	MINOR	**SEVERE all 1977**

12.	/SWELLING/ Fluid Retention	ON-OFF	Severe increasingly
13.	KIDNEY DYSFUNCTION, UREMIA	MINOR	Severe increasingly
14.	KIDNEY STONES	NONE	Suspected
15.	LOW URINE CONCENTRATION	NONE	Medium increasing
16.	EYESIGHT LOSS	NONE	Severe last months
17.	LOSS OF HEARING	NONE	Severe increasingly
18.	MUSCULAR WEAKNESS, PAIN	NONE	Severe increasing
19.	OSTEOpenia/Malaci/ Bone Pain	NONE	Moderate late stage
20.	ATROPHY Gastrointestinal Tract	NONE	Severe increasing

SET #3: SEEN IN DIABETES/ KIDNEY DISEASE, NOT CADMIUM POISONING.
NOT SEEN IN SRILA PRABHUPADA BEFORE OR AFTER HIS POISONING,
STRONGLY INDICATING HIS DIABETES WAS NOT VERY ADVANCED

1.	OBESITY, WEIGHT GAIN	NO
2.	EXCESSIVE HUNGER: Polyphagia	NO
3.	INSULIN DEPENDENCY, Injections	NO
4.	INSULIN SHOCK, COMA, FAINTING	NO
5.	SKIN, FOOT INFECTIONS	NO
6.	EXCESSIVE THIRST: POLYDIPSIA	NO
7.	GANGRENE, Amputate Extremities	NO
8.	TINGLING IN EXTREMITIES	NO
9.	BOILS, ULCERS	NO
10.	SWALLOWING DIFFICULTIES	NO

SYMPTOMS ANALYSIS CONCLUSIONS

Nine of the 12 cadmium poisoning symptoms shown at the top of the chart are marked in the Health History (App. 8, Volume 4) so the reader can see their innumerable manifestations. **(1)** A group of symptoms is unexplainable by diabetes (DM2) or kidney disease and were produced by another "mystery" cause. **(2)** All the unexplained "mystery" symptoms are consistent with chronic cadmium poisoning. **(3)** Chronic cadmium poisoning is not only confirmed by symptoms but is proven by hair tests. **(4)** All of Srila Prabhupada's symptoms (including "mystery" symptoms) were consistent with cadmium/ arsenic poisoning. **(5)** Although Srila Prabhupada had some diabetes and kidney problems, his declining health after mid-1976 coincided with his cadmium poisoning, established by testing 1977 hair samples. **(6)** Srila Prabhupada's diabetes/ kidney problems were concurrent to the cadmium poisoning. **(7)** Srila Prabhupada's diabetes and kidney disease were aggravated and worsened by his cadmium and arsenic poisoning. **(8)** There are at least ten symptoms typical to diabetes that were **not** seen in Srila Prabhupada. *ALL Srila Prabhupada's symptoms match those of chronic cadmium and arsenic poisoning, whereas many usual advanced diabetes symptoms were conspicuously absent.*

METAL POISONING CASE STUDIES RE: SYMPTOMS

Assassination At St. Helena, p. 433: *"... German pathologist, Dr. A.*

Heffter, a specialist researching in the intricacies of diagnosis in cases of arsenic intoxication, writes that it is unforgivable not to suspect arsenic intoxication when gastric trouble is coupled with conjunctivitis, eczema or weakness in the legs." Also, Jim Schutze, in his book about Moore's arsenic poisonings, notes the difficulty in recognizing arsenic poisoning: *"Those same symptoms could just as easily steer a doctor toward acute alcohol poisoning, Guillain-Barre syndrome, diabetes mellitus, vitamin deficiency, lupus, blood disease, diphtheria, multiple sclerosis, or a host of other common diseases, including tick bite. In fact, it is the ability of arsenic to duplicate the symptoms of other diseases that makes it so difficult to detect... it remains one of the least accurately diagnosed of all afflictions. ...the possibility of arsenic poisoning simply is not a thought that leaps easily to the minds of physicians."*

Schutze explains that symptoms of arsenic poisoning resemble those of many other diseases, but *"all of these things together can mean almost nothing but... arsenic poisoning."* In hospitals, each separate symptom is analyzed by the respective specialist, and arsenic cases are rarely diagnosed quickly. The difficulty is that arsenic *"attacks life in so many ways and at such a fundamental biochemical level that each of its effects on the body perfectly mimics the effect of some other disease or problem."* And arsenic and cadmium have very similar effects, although cadmium is significantly more lethal.

COMMON SENSE ON COINCIDENCES

Obviously someone with diabetes and kidney disease could also have any of a number of other health problems, such as meningitis, leukemia, or poisoning. That a significant group of the "mystery" (non-diabetes/kidney) symptoms, co-existing all at once, were simultaneously manifest in Srila Prabhupada is highly unusual- such a complete set of respiratory tract and mucous membrane symptoms, on such a prolonged basis, day to day, up and down, more, then less, reveals a hidden and correspondingly applied cause. The probabilities of their coincidence evaporates and the likelihood of a distinct and separate physiological cause approaches certainty. *That cause is cadmium poisoning.* Critics of a diagnosis of cadmium poisoning by symptom analysis cannot account for these unexplained mystery symptoms. So many symptoms together were *atypical* to diabetes/kidney disease. We must account for **ALL** of Srila Prabhupada's physical symptoms, not just some. What are the probabilities of having prolonged, pronounced cough, mucus, salivation, conjunctivitis, and rhinitis due to natural causes? Answer: Zero To None. *The medical symptoms clearly validate the proven cadmium poisoning.*

FORENSICS COMBINED WITH SYMPTOM ANALYSIS

The hair tests show time periods with normal or very abnormal heavy metal levels. We have precise readings of Srila Prabhupada's normal cadmium, arsenic, mercury, and antimony. Since 1977 was a time of 250 X as much cadmium, 20 X as much arsenic, and 8 X as much antimony as he normally had pre-1977, this is a strong proof of poisoning. These levels are not from an accidental/ environmental exposure; it was a malicious homicidal poisoning. There was no way to reach these levels except by ingesting cadmium chemicals in food and drink. In 1977 Srila Prabhupada experienced a mysterious, persistent, undiagnosed, and debilitating "illness." His symptoms are fully consistent with heavy metal poisoning. The combination of forensics and medical symptoms analysis confirms the poisoning; this is basic, standard medical diagnostic practice. Sometimes symptom analysis is sufficient; but we make a poisoning diagnosis based on much forensic evidence as well. There was *a group of physical symptoms exhibited by Srila Prabhupada which are not attributable to diabetes or kidney disease, but which are typical of chronic cadmium poisoning.*

Chest congestion, heavy mucus/cough, apparent colds/ bronchitis/ rhinitis, heart palpitations/hypertension, weakness in legs, no strength or appetite, indigestion, swelling of extremities, and later, aversion to light, no taste, kidney infection, phimosis. This is a picture of a serious heavy metals poisoning, not diabetes. Note: In Srila Prabhupada's last days, he had great pain in one thigh and leg, and this is another symptom of cadmium poisoning, as was seen in the 1960's Japan "itai-itai" or "ouch-ouch" disease where victims had extreme bone pain. *"Cadmium intoxication also may lead to painful and debilitating bone disease compounded by loss of calcium and phosphate."*

CHAPTER 32:
TOO MANY MISDIAGNOSES

Nowhere can we find any conclusive diagnosis of Srila Prabhupada's 1976-77 illness based on proper medical tests. In 2002-05 Dr. Morris did NAA hair tests which discovered the cause of Srila Prabhupada's health failure to be a massive, homicidal cadmium poisoning. All else is speculation. The fact is that in 1977 no one understood what was the cause of Srila Prabhupada's failing health, even though there were many clear symptoms for which no cause was ascertained. Only by forensic hair tests 25 years later was a correct diagnosis finally reached, namely lethal cadmium poisoning. In 1977 there was a plethora of misdiagnoses of Srila Prabhupada's "illness."

Tamal told Naveen Krishna that Srila Prabhupada's fatal illness was dropsy. Dropsy or bodily swelling of extremities is not a disease, it is a **symptom**, due to fluid retention from diabetes, kidney disease, or heavy metal poisoning. In *Impaired Health: Its Cause and Cure* (JH Tilden): *"In chronic arsenic poisoning, patients lose their hair, dropsy develops, and many die of heart disease and dropsical accumulation."*

WHAT WAS SRILA PRABHUPADA'S "CAUSE OF DEATH"?

The actual cause of death is often a difficult thing to ascertain in cases where multiple factors are involved. Take the case of Dr. Josephine Brown of Glens Falls, NY, who died at home after being punched by an intruder, who assumed he had killed her, and then burned the house to destroy the evidence. Forensic examinations revealed that the thief had frightened the woman into having a massive heart attack, which was determined to be the "actual cause of death," though the fire would have killed her anyway. Murder charges were dropped, as it was found that death occurred prior to the fire and was not due to assault or injury from a fall. So determining the actual cause of death is often a predicament. Similarly there were many factors present at the time of Srila Prabhupada's departure, any of which, from the technical, medical point of view, or as in the proverbial straw that broke the camel's back, could be the "actual cause of death" at the last moment. There was old age, malnutrition, heavy metals poisoning and perhaps kidney or liver disease. One might prevaricate that all of these factors contributed to death and thus minimize the significance of poisoning. *However, the only* <u>abnormal and unnatural</u> *factor was the malicious heavy metal poisoning, a criminal act meant to interfere with divine arrangements and to effect Srila Prabhupada's premature demise by perhaps 15 years.* We note the fact that heavy metal poisoning causes and exacerbates malnutrition, diabetes, starvation, kidney-liver-heart disease. (see cadmium, diabetes: <u>www.ncbi.nlm.nih.gov/pubmed/19327375</u>: myocardial infarction <u>www.ncbi.nlm.nih.gov/pubmed/18053980</u>)

The very discovery of such high levels of cadmium and arsenic overrides the significance of all other diagnoses of Srila Prabhupada's condition, forcing them into the background of any analysis. Since a massive homicidal, lethal poisoning has been proven, then of what relevance or consequence is any debate about other health conditions? Srila Prabhupada's primary health problem was heavy metals poisoning.

An intentional, malicious, and lethal poisoning took place and that makes for a premature, unnatural death. That he expired on Nov. 14, 1977 with adverse health conditions is accepted, but the fact he was poisoned _establishes homicidal intent._ The undeniably established heavy metals poisoning was _intended_ to shorten Srila Prabhupada's life. The poisoners should be found and punished by the dictates of secular laws. When the GBC claims that there was a natural death and no poisoning, they are wasting our time and insulting our intelligence. As in any poisoning murder, what the health of a victim was prior to being poisoned matters little. Someone shot in the heart with a 9 mm pistol 6 times… does it matter if they were diabetic or had a weak heart? Homicide is homicide.

Srila Prabhupada's Death Certificate, Mathura, 2004

There was no autopsy or medical examination done by any government health officer, coroner, or doctor upon Srila Prabhupada's departure. This in violation of Indian law; all deaths must be reported and a cause of death determined by the government coroner. This was done with Kutichak's daughter in Vrindaban, mid-1977; she had eaten medicines from the trash. Kutichak took the body to the Mathura coroner's office for a death certificate before burial. But the law was broken in the instance of Srila Prabhupada's death. Obviously, complying with this legal formality may have exposed the poisoning. Over 100 days after Nov. 14, 1977, someone went to Mathura and filed for Srila Prabhupada's death certificate, listing the cause of death as "heart attack." There was no signature of the petitioner. If Srila Prabhupada had expired in the West, and especially under suspicion of foul play, certainly tests would have been done by the local coroner and an official autopsy report prepared. Conveniently for the poisoners, Srila Prabhupada chose to die in Vrindaban, where rules and procedures are loose. "Heart attack" is yet another misdiagnosis; his heart was strong until the last. Why was the death certificate filed so late, by whom, and why was "heart attack" listed as cause of death? This does not even relate to the various misdiagnoses at that time.

SHPM CRITICIZED OVER DIABETES ISSUE

NTIAP found a few minor errors in *SHPM's* description of diabetes as though they were catastrophic faults when they were only details of minor consequence. By clever emphasis on small things and ignoring the main points, *NTIAP* avoided the purpose of *SHPM's* symptoms analysis. *SHPM* was compiled in good faith. *NTIAP* then disparaged the "poison theory." But the bottom line remains the same: there are a group of physical symptoms exhibited by Srila Prabhupada which are not attributable to diabetes or kidney disease, but which are typical of chronic cadmium/arsenic poisoning. The GBC says the cause of Srila Prabhupada's ill health and death was advanced diabetes and kidney disease, and GBC insists everyone knew this in 1977. But this is contradicted by Srila Prabhupada's two personal servants who stated they knew NOTHING about diabetes from 1972-77 (Ch. 30). The GBC diverted the focus to a debate on whether there was diabetes and flimsy hearsay was trotted out, without hard proof, medical test records, or anything Srila Prabhupada himself said on tape. *And it is irrelevant anyway.* Diabetes, a little or a lot, the irrefutably proven cadmium poisoning was lethal, homicidal. Why is the GBC protecting poisoners?

The ISKCON GBC adopted a pretense of indignation, further confusing the issue by their character assassination and fear-mongering, saying the poison theory is a grave offence, thus obstructing the truth of the matter. Debate over diabetes became moot after forensic proof of lethal cadmium poisoning was discovered. Srila Prabhupada was poisoned with very high levels of heavy metals, regardless of any diabetes he may have had. *A diabetes diagnosis thus does not negate the proof of poisoning.* The cadmium exacerbated the diabetes, while being hidden by the diabetes. The debate over whether 2.6 ppm arsenic is a significant health debilitator is now overshadowed by the lethal levels of ±16 ppm cadmium. The GBC pretends to refute the poison evidence by pointing out irrelevant details (like taking sugar is anathema to diabetes).

THROUGHOUT 1977 NO ONE SPOKE OF DIABETES

In 1977 there were no insulin injections, diabetes medications, etc. Yet, in *NTIAP* 's *Introduction: "Advanced diabetes, plain and simple."* The GBC claims it was well-known by everyone that Srila Prabhupada had advanced diabetes. But this doesn't add up. If Srila Prabhupada was known to have advanced diabetes, why were there no discussions about it in any of the tape recordings, letters, biographies, and memories? Why are there no medical records about it? Why did Srila Prabhupada, his caretakers, and all his doctors/kavirajas go on looking for what was the mysterious cause of his illness, if they already knew that it was diabetes? Why did they not implement measures to manage it, and then keep looking for the cause of the illness?

Why did Srila Prabhupada and his servants vigorously undertake so many cure programs for a mysterious illness based on a myriad of diagnoses other than diabetes? Why was there no managing of diabetes with diet, medications like insulin, or a diabetes doctor? It was not until two months before Srila Prabhupada's death that a London doctor suspected diabetes and kidney disease, but this "news" never entered into the conversations or treatment programs afterwards. Why? Because all the kavirajas and doctors had other ideas as to the cause of ill health; diabetes was not one of them. Because there were different diagnoses, it is safe to say they were all incorrect. Nobody in 1977 thought diabetes was causing the dramatic health decline.

HARI SAURI CONTRADICTS HIMSELF: 1997 AND 2016

In 2016 Hari Sauri contradicted his own 1997 statement that diabetes and kidney disease were unknown in 1977. So much for his honesty. He reiterated *NTIAP's* position: *"The doctor who diagnosed Srila Prabhupada in London and who did the minor operation to clear the urinary tract blockage did give an interview several years ago ...he clearly states that Srila Prabhupada was suffering from irreversible kidney damage. NTIAP is quite thorough in its examination of the evidences and the conclusion is very clear and correct. Combined with my own personal experience in traveling with His Divine Grace for 18 months and ...Oct. 77, I have not, and there should not be for anyone, a shadow of doubt that Srila Prabhupada's body expired due to renal failure, a culmination of years of diabetes and exacerbated by a blockage of his urinary tract which caused a backup of uric acid and put pressure on his kidneys."* Hari Sauri stated two opposite things! Nityananda wrote him again in May 2017 with news of the cadmium in the hair samples that he had arranged for the GBC to test, but rather than acknowledging the forensic breakthrough results, he was irate that he had been tricked into providing information.

MORE MISDIAGNOSES

Amongst the misdiagnoses offered in 1977 were: **(1) Indigestion:** The body's disability to properly assimilate food. Srila Prabhupada's onset of poor digestion resulted from his poisoning. Kidney disease causes indigestion, but cadmium/arsenic poisoning causes indigestion *and* kidney disease. **(2) Tuberculosis:** Tamal said this was suspected by Dr. K. Gopal in Srila Prabhupada's last weeks because he was perplexed by the respiratory symptoms such as persistent cough. The private investigation team sent Sakshi Gopal and Abhinanada on April 21, 2002 to meet Dr. K. Gopal, Srila Prabhupada's last allopathic doctor at his clinic. Dr. Gopal said he had no idea in Oct. 1977 about diabetes, and was emphatic that his diagnosis had been for *asthma* or a chronic respiratory disorder caused by allergies (heavy metal poisoning will do this). **(3) No Disease:** This kaviraja did not know what was going on. **(4) Just Weakness:** Same as #3. **(5) Liver Disease:** Cadmium is filtered out of the body primarily by the liver, and causes liver problems. Previously there were no liver problems. **(6) Gonorrhea:** (??) **(7) Malnutrition:** Heavy metal poisoning causes indigestion, anemia, loss of appetite and taste, thus no eating leads to malnutrition. *(Horiguchi H, et. al. Cadmium induces anemia, Toxicological Sciences 2011;122 (1):198–210)*

(8) Diabetes Mellitus Type 2 (Dm2): The diabetes debate is irrelevant after discovery of sky-high cadmium plus elevated arsenic levels. DM2 is a metabolic disorder with the inability to properly maintain the blood sugar level, resulting in multiple organ deterioration and eventual failure. DM2 has an almost invisible late stage development over a 10-20 year period, and then complications develop during several years of poorly controlled hyperglycemia (high blood sugar). The symptoms are many and varied, including fatigue, skin infections, excessive thirst, frequent urination, ***increased* *appetite***, nausea. Complications include blindness, kidney failure, heart and blood vessel disease, boils/ulcers, gum disease, foot/ leg amputation. DM2 victims may or may not be insulin dependent, depending on the management and advancement of the condition. Diabetes is commonly caused by medications, poisons, drugs including cocaine, prednisone, oral contraceptives. Cadmium/ arsenic poisoning causes or worsens DM2. Sudden weight loss is typical to diabetes mellitus type 1, which Srila Prabhupada definitely did not have. DM2 generally is found in those who are overweight. *"Most people with DM2 do not lose weight."* (Merck Manual 1997) Srila Prabhupada's weight loss was due to poisoning, not diabetes. In DM2, the high blood sugar causes weakness because the body is unable to assimilate sugar into the cells. In 1977 Srila Prabhupada often fasted, eating little to nothing for days.

Arsenic and cadmium cause and worsen diabetes: www.diabetesnet.com: *"Researchers are now publicizing the health risks associated with the low, but dangerous levels of arsenic that is common in tap water. According to the EPA, exposures to low concentrations of arsenic over many years can lead to diabetes, anemia... recent research into the correlation between arsenic intake* *and the development of diabetes in populations in Bangladesh, India, Mexico, Thailand and Taiwan. ...a variety of journals have all indicated that there is a direct correlation between exposure to arsenic and the risk of developing diabetes."*

(a) *Arsenic in Drinking Water: 2001*: *"Arsenic has been implicated in a variety of adverse health effects, including... diabetes."* **(b)** Chin-Hsiao Tseng, *Chronic Arsenic Intoxication in Asia: "More recent studies also established the association between arsenic exposure and.... diabetes mellitus."* **(c)** *"In Bangladesh, a dose-response trend was also observed between the prevalence of diabetes mellitus and arsenic level in water."* **(d)** Tseng also published: *Long-term arsenic exposure and incidence of non-insulin dependent diabetes mellitus in Taiwan,* 1999. **(e)** *"Ingested inorganic arsenic and prevalence of diabetes mellitus,"* Am J Epidem (1994) by Lai MS, et al. **(f)** *Diabetes mellitus associated with arsenic exposure in Bangladesh,* Rahman M, 1998. **(g)** Merck Manual lists as a cause of diabetes as *"poisons that interfere with the production or effects of insulin, resulting in high blood sugar levels."*

For cadmium: **(a)** *"Cadmium toxicity exacerbated the destructive effect of diabetes on the peripheral nervous system." Effect on Cadmium in Diabetic Rats,* Demir N, et al 2002 July **(b)** *"These findings suggest that cadmium may cause prediabetes and diabetes in humans." Urinary Cadmium,* Schwartz 2003 **(c)** *"Cadmium is known to cause hyper-glycemia with diabetes-related complications in experimental animals." Cadmium & Impaired Glucose Tolerance,* Han 2003. **(4)** *"Cadmium increases the oxidative stress induced by diabetes":* Optic Nerve in *Cadmium Exposed Diabetic Rats,* Demir 2003.

(9) Kidney Disease: There are various kidney malfunctions which decrease the ability to filter toxins and excess fluids from the blood. Amongst the various types of kidney disease, Srila Prabhupada did not have symptoms of urethritis, cystitis, kidney injury, cysts, tumors, kidney stones, bladder stones, or acute kidney failure. The types of kidney disease which Srila Prabhupada *may have had,* judging by his physical symptoms, (although no known medical tests determined his type of kidney ailment) are: (i). Uremia (ii). Pyelonephritis (iii). Glomerulo-nephritis (iv). Chronic kidney failure (v). End-stage kidney failure. Various types of kidney ailments display symptoms quite different from each other. E.g., chronic kidney failure does not produce the swelling/ edema characteristic to nephritis. Still, kidney ailments are often "complex" and more than one disorder is present. No one knows which kidney ailments Srila Prabhupada may have had, due to the lack of specific medical tests and the complication of cadmium/ arsenic intoxication that has been established by hair tests.

Causes of kidney disease: Kidney disease can be caused by diabetes, drug abuse, high blood pressure, and among other things, poisoning by heavy metals. Srila Prabhupada's existing kidney weakness seen in the swelling of extremities on and off long prior to 1977, was surely aggravated by the poisoning. The swelling greatly increased in 1977, obviously in reaction to the proven, massive cadmium poisoning.

Symptoms of kidney disease: Gradual kidney failure may show few or no symptoms at first. Mild or moderate kidney failure may show only mild symptoms, and much damage usually has occurred before the symptoms become apparent. The metabolic waste product called urea increases in the blood due to the inability of the kidneys to eliminate it from the body. Nephritis (infection of or damage to the kidneys) causes swelling of the body, called edema or dropsy. Symptoms of kidney disease were seen in 1977: *swelling* due to edema, or fluid retention, *weakness/ anemia, urination in small installments, lack of appetite/ weight loss/ anorexia, nausea/ diarrhea/ gastric pain, high blood pressure, heart problems:* palpitations, irregular or fast pulse, ***anuria*** (difficulty in urination), *discoloration in urine, unpleasant taste or no taste, insomnia, stomatitis.*

Whatever kidney weakness Srila Prabhupada had before poisoning began then was drastically worsened due to cadmium poisoning throughout 1977. The two fit together like hand and glove. But, he had another group of symptoms not attributable to either diabetes or kidney disease. These *extra "mystery" symptoms* are unique to cadmium poisoning. The GBC completely and purposely evades this fact.

KIDNEY DISEASE/ DIABETES: ILLOGICAL DIAGNOSIS

Many DM2 and kidney disease symptoms are similar to those of chronic cadmium poisoning, but three hair analyses finding sky-high cadmium has confirmed a diagnosis of cadmium poisoning. No one can argue there was no cadmium poisoning. Although we know the extent of poisoning, we do not know the extent of DM2 or kidney disease, either before or after poisoning, because no records or test results (if any were done) exist. A misdiagnosis of diabetes or kidney disease would not account for the sky-high cadmium. With cadmium being the primary health deterrent, which *aggravated and accelerated* the diabetes and kidney disease, we must conclude a *premature and unnatural expiration. It was not a natural death.* From Ellerhorn's Medical Toxicology (1997): *"The most direct way to determine cadmium poisoning is to compare indicators of cadmium exposure, symptoms, and kidney damage to resultant adverse health effects."* I.e., Srila Prabhupada's cadmium readings combined with his having cadmium poisoning symptoms means he was homicidally poisoned. The GBC's debate about any coincidental diabetes or kidney disease is just a distraction from the poisoning crime.

Hair tests confirm heavy cadmium poisoning began at least by Feb. '77 and continued until Srila Prabhupada departed Nov. 14, 1977.

METALS POISONING ALMOST ALWAYS MISDIAGNOSED

Heavy metals poisoning is very difficult to recognize, and there is an extensive list of possible misdiagnoses from *Goldfrank's Text on Toxicology* that have been documented from case histories. Cadmium poisoning is far more rare than arsenic poisoning, its symptoms are also extremely generic and non-specific, and are at least as difficult to correctly diagnose than arsenic poisoning. Cadmium was certainly a superior choice among hard-to-detect methods of homicide; it went undiscovered for 25 years (1977-2002).

Regarding the confusion and difficulty in detecting heavy metals poisoning, Ben Weider said: *"Many medical writers ...have attempted to identify Napoleon's disease by analyzing his signs and symptoms. This has produced surprisingly disparate results. Thus, Napoleon is alleged to have had the following diseases: peptic ulcer, intestinal ulceration, liver inflammation, undulant fever, malaria, dysentery, rheumatoid arthritis, heart failure, congenital extremely slow blood circulation, epilepsy, tuberculosis, pleurisy, severe hormonal imbalance leading to obesity and impotence (dystrophia adiposogenitalis), intoxication from defective teeth, syphilis, gonorrhea, gout, piles, and severe constipation which, it is said, was fatal owing to auto-intoxication and poisoning by laxatives. ...it is a simple matter to make out a convincing case for every one of these diagnoses. But if what, after all, was a fairly unchanging disease pattern is taken as an entity, and allowance is made for all the signs and symptoms and their interrelations, then one cannot escape the impression that all the pieces form an orderly picture of two characteristic syndromes: the chronic and acute types of arsenic poisoning."* As they would to anyone, these cadmium levels destroyed his health over 10 months, a period of time shown by the hair tests.

Another misdiagnosis for Srila Prabhupada's health decline is in Brahmananda's book, *Swamiji*. *"Still, after beginning his mission in both New York and San Francisco ...he again suffered from severe heart palpitations and a stroke, which temporarily paralyzed his left side. Devotees later learned he had chronic diabetes, causing heart disease and eventually kidney failure as well." (p. 72)* Here, amazingly, Srila Prabhupada's 1967 stroke is associated with his 1977 mysterious illness. This is a total speculation, not supported by anything.

CHAPTER 33:
LONDON HOSPITAL VISIT

THE LONDON "SURGERY" AND DR McIRVINE

On Sept. 8, 1977, at Bhaktivedanta Manor near London, Srila Prabhupada, having severe pain the previous days, suddenly experienced a medical emergency, not being able to pass urine and fainting. Abhiram das, his personal nurse, convinced Srila Prabhupada to go to a hospital as an outpatient, and promised to restrict unwanted medical procedures. At Peace Memorial Hospital's emergency room they were attended by "surgical resident" Andrew McIrvine, who did a circumcision, after which urinary retention was relieved. Srila Prabhupada returned to the temple the same day, but the urine remained partially blocked, likely due to urinary tract inflammation or infection. In 2000 the GBC obtained statements from Dr. McIrvine, who remembered Srila Prabhupada from 1977. Dr. McIrvine's memories of diabetes and kidney failure supposedly refuted the poisoning (how does that work?) The GBC boasted that their interview with Srila Prabhupada's "surgeon" disproved poisoning, since it was only diabetes and as though the "poison theory" is predicated on misinterpreting symptoms. Such is the slippery deceit of the GBC. They create a false premise and then "defeat" it.

DR. McIRVINE CONFIRMS DIABETES

NTIAP (Ch. 2) features Dr. Andrew J. McIrvine, FRCS, who gave an *apparent* confirmation that Srila Prabhupada had diabetes (but which proves what?). Jan. 7, 2000 he gave his memories: *"Srila Prabhupada was presented to me in the emergency room of Watford General Hospital... obviously in poor health and showed signs of renal failure and was found to be diabetic. These diagnoses were made on clinical suspicion confirmed by blood and urine analysis. His most obvious problem was urinary retention. This was caused by a most unusual degree of phimosis. That a long-standing scarring and thickening of the foreskin such that he was at the time of his admission virtually unable to pass urine. This process would have taken many years to develop and during that time could well have produced back pressure enough to result in renal problems- as more often happens with prostatic obstruction. ...I am sure he would not have withstood a general anaesthetic. Somehow we persuaded him to have a circumcision to relieve the problem, which I carried out in the ER under local anaesthetic. He made a good recovery and was able to pass urine normally... Unfortunately his renal failure was by that time well advanced and irreversible, caused by a combination of diabetes and phimosis."* [This phimosis was likely due to chronic urethral infections and inflammation from heavy metal poisoning in the last year.]

DR. McIRVINE MAKES INTERESTING CLARIFICATIONS

Did Dr. McIrvine do blood and urine tests to confirm diabetes, kidney failure, and no poisoning? *NTIAP* blared: *"Prabhupada's Surgeon Confirms: Diabetes To Blame."* So, in late 2001 Nityananda exchanged emails with Dr. McIrvine to clarify in finer detail Srila Prabhupada's 1977 medical condition (this was before the cadmium discovery): **Nityananda das (ND):** *"I wrote a book detailing the evidence ...that strongly indicated Srila Prabhupada had been poisoned, a factor which likely caused/ contributed to death. I have read ...that you were contacted about your memories of Srila Prabhupada's condition and treatment. ...about diagnosing diabetes, phimosis, renal failure and the minor operation. Aside from having symptoms peculiar to chronic arsenic poisoning which are not found in diabetics, Srila Prabhupada also had 20 times the normal amount of arsenic in his hair. I and many others who are involved in trying to get to the bottom of this matter would very much appreciate if you would help us with a little further understanding of the case. Below I have some additional questions."*

McIrvine (MC): *"I will answer your questions best I can- but this was a long time ago- I was then a surgical resident in Watford- I very much doubt any written records remain. ...unfortunately there was never any suspicion of poisoning at the time and <u>no test would have been done to substantiate the argument in either direction</u>."* **ND:** What type of blood and urine analysis was done? Would those tested samples still be available for further testing? **MC:** *He came only to the emergency room ...so we would not have had full hospital notes opened. ...we usually only keep records for 7 years max. I would **probably** have done just simple tests, Hb, BUN, electrolytes, I do not think we would have kept tissue samples.* **ND:** Could not poisoning have exacerbated his diabetes and renal failure? **MC:** *Yes.* **ND:** Would a diagnosis of diabetes preclude the possibility of concurrent poisoning? **MC:** *No.* **ND:** Unless arsenic is confirmed by specific tests, would it not be missed entirely? **MC:** *Yes.* **ND:** What was it that indicated diabetes and renal failure?

MC: *The blood tests- specifically urea (BUN) and creatinine.* **ND:** One of the symptoms of chronic arsenic poisoning is the thickening of skin in certain places of the body: could this possibly explain his most unusual degree of phimosis? **MC:** *Very unlikely- this looked like a gradual problem probably developing over many years. I am afraid this is all from memory rather than actual records...* [A year of poisoning could result in this phimosis, as seen in Raymond Reid's poisoning. Ch. 39]

NO HOSPITAL RECORDS WERE FOUND

Investigation by Balavanta and Nityananda found that Peace Memorial Hospital was moved to another site in 1986 and became Watford General Hospital. The old hospital became a nursing home. All medical records were moved to the new hospital, but *"a major trawl was conducted for any records old enough to be destroyed as part of a housekeeping exercise."* Hospital records were routinely destroyed after 7 years. Balavanta hired Alexander Harris solicitors to search for Srila Prabhupada's medical records, but none were found, if any ever existed.

NO BLOOD TESTS WERE DONE

Srila Prabhupada was very much against needles and the drawing of blood. Tamal and Abhiram did not allow any blood tests. This was Srila Prabhupada's rigid policy- no blood tests had been done in years, even when doctors asked for them. Abhiram says he convinced Srila Prabhupada to go to the hospital only with assurances they were only going *"for some minor plumbing work."* The urgent reason for the Emergency Room visit was to relieve urinary retention, accomplished by a circumcision. Abhiram said he had to convince the doctor to accept Srila Prabhupada as an ER patient only for the urinary retention/blockage problem, and nothing else, and on the condition that intravenous feeding and general anaethestics were unacceptable. When various routine tests were about to proceed as per hospital policy, Tamal and Abhiram strenuously declined. Drawing blood for tests was refused. In Bombay on Sept. 14, Srila Prabhupada said: *"I could understand when he wanted blood that he would begin his allopathic treatments."* Tamal, Oct. 18, 1977 said he would not allow blood tests: *"...I mean we're not going to let them do anything bad [or] let anybody take you to the hospital. I wouldn't have done it in London, except that you yourself said we should do it. Otherwise your instructions told to everybody, 'Don't let them take me to a hospital.' So we're not thinking like that. Neither I'm going to let anybody put any, take any blood specimen or any of those things. It's not required."* In London no blood tests were done.

Maybe a urine test was done, as indicated by Dr. McIrvine. But since the urine was totally blocked, and upon circumcision the urine was dramatically released, it probably was difficult to collect any for testing. Regardless, no tests for poisoning were done and neither would poisoning be discovered with any of the usual urine tests the hospital may have done. Since Srila Prabhupada only spent a few hours in the emergency room and was not admitted as a patient to the hospital, and Dr. McIrvine said, *"...would not have had full hospital notes opened,"* and the caretakers' extreme prejudice against tests, *it is sure no tests were done.* Dr. McIrvine said "probably" *only simple tests* were done. He does not remember, nor are there any existing records, and the caretakers also do not remember if there were any tests done. Blood tests, surely not. After all, any test results would have come back after Srila Prabhupada had already left the hospital, so why bother?

METAL POISONING DETECTED ONLY BY SPECIFIC TESTS

Many assume that any poisoning would have been discovered simply by going to a hospital. But discovery of poisoning requires numerous, specific, and costly tests to check for each poison such as mercury, cyanide, thallium, arsenic, or cadmium. *Specific laboratory tests are required to detect each poison, and they could take days to be completed.* No one suspected poisoning much less order a test for cadmium. Heavy metal poisoning will require *many hospital visits and tests* before being discovered, if the victim does not die first. Attending physicians will not order specific tests for poisoning **unless suspected**. Cadmium/ arsenic poisoning is very difficult to discover, as it presents symptoms common to many other causes and ailments. Although Srila Prabhupada was suffering from a sky-high cadmium poisoning, the doctor, devotees, and hospital never suspected poisoning, and kept on trying various treatments, doctors, and medicines. Simply going to the ER would not result in a discovery of poisoning.

GBC'S HULLABALOO OVER DR. McIRVINE

(1) Dr. McIrvine was not "Prabhupada's Surgeon." In Sept. 1977 he was an ER surgical resident, not a doctor and in graduate medical training under the supervision of an attending physician. He performed a circumcision on a patient he had never seen before, and only saw once more the next day on a personal visit to the Manor. The GBC gave an impression that major testing and diagnosis work had been done by a professional surgeon, thus dispelling the poison theory. Let us not conclude too much from Srila Prabhupada's 2 or 3 hour ER visit. Dr. McIrvine's "testimony" of imperfect memories without any medical records is not a tell-all, iron-clad "testimony" of much at all. Any doctor would *assume* diabetes/ renal problems based on those appearances, even without tests. The GBC hyped the "surgeon testimony" as though this disproved a poisoning. It does not. **(2)** Going to a hospital for an ER day-patient circumcision procedure does not mean poisoning would have been discovered by blood tests, of which there were none. Were there any tests for poisoning? McIrvine: "*…no test would have been done…*"

(3) There are no medical records of any tests or doctor's notes, just vague memories. Diabetes or kidney disease was never documented, quantified, or recorded on paper, audio tape, or in any spoken memory. ISKCON leadership insists Srila Prabhupada's illness was diabetes, but this means nothing. So what if there was diabetes? It does not change the fact of poisoning. The question: *Was Srila Prabhupada poisoned?* is already settled. Yes, he was. The GBCs claim that *"Diabetes to Blame"* implies Srila Prabhupada's death was due to diabetes and not poisoning. Dr. McIrvine: *"Unfortunately there was never any suspicion of poisoning at the time and no test would have been done to substantiate the argument in either direction."* Dr. McIrvine confirmed poisoning would exacerbate diabetes and the two can exist together.

(4) Dr. McIrvine did not dispute the evidence of sky-high cadmium poisoning. **(5)** Later the *NTIAP* author wrote an open letter giving a new theory, namely that Srila Prabhupada's poisoning was simply a buildup of toxins due to kidney failure: *"That Prabhupada was being poisoned- by his own toxins due to kidney failure brought about by advanced diabetes- was diagnosed by Dr. Andrew McIrvine…"* But this speculation is not derived from Dr.McIrvine's "testimony" and ignores the fact that Srila Prabhupada was poisoned with cadmium and arsenic, which cause and worsen kidney disease and diabetes. The deceptive inference is there was no homicidal poisoning, just a natural death. **(6) Appraisal Of Dr. McIrvine:** We do not see any fault with Dr. McIrvine and his answers were honest. We appreciate his cooperation. However, in 2002, Nityananda wrote him again to advise of the sky-high cadmium NAA findings in Srila Prabhupada's hair samples. Unfortunately, he said he stood by the diabetes diagnosis because he had seen the *"cadmium orange dyed paint"* (actually it is beige clay) Hare Krishnas use which *"externally contaminated"* the hair samples, referring to the religious "tilak" marks on our foreheads. But tilak has no cadmium based orange paint. This ignorant speculation actually takes the cake.

(7) Diabetes Is Not Confirmed As Cause Of Death: Medically speaking, it is not plausible that Srila Prabhupada's illness from May-July 1976 to Nov. 1977 (before which he was in very good health, Ch. 29) can be attributed to diabetes or kidney failure, as these conditions rarely progress from invisible or mild condition to death in the span of 12 or 18 months. *Unless, of course, they are accelerated by sky-high cadmium.* The health decline was due to poisoning, and not a natural cause such as diabetes. Rather, the result of poisoning was diabetes and kidney failure. The GBC claims of *"longstanding serious diabetes and kidney disease for many years which led to a natural death in 1977"* is not supported by anything or anyone other than their own cover-up propaganda initiated after the poison issue arose in 1997. But even if true that there was longstanding serious diabetes, still, a lethal cadmium poisoning took place in 1977 as proven by three NAA hair tests.

(8) Diabetes Type 1, Type 2, Insulin: *NTIAP* stated that insulin was only for those with type one diabetes (incorrect). However, DM2 also requires insulin as it progresses. Endocrinology Diabetes and Metabolism (Gerald Bernstein, MD): *"Type 1 diabetes is an autoimmune disease that results in destruction of the insulin producing cells. People with this type of diabetes must take insulin. Type 2 diabetes is a multi-molecular disorder that causes, first, inadequate insulin secretion. It may be the amount or the way it is secreted. Second, most with type 2 also have a resistance to the insulin they make. Double whammy. Exercise, a proper diet to control weight may minimize the amount of medication you need for years but this is a progressive disorder so as you get older so does your ability to produce insulin. Sooner or later, diabetics will need insulin. It also may be advantageous to start insulin before that time to keep your blood glucose normal which leads to a better quality of life and reduce risk for complications."* On average a DM2 patient will start taking insulin 14 years post-diagnosis. That Srila Prabhupada was non-insulin dependent means his diabetes was not yet at a late stage, even in his last month. The GBC hullabaloo that Srila Prabhupada expired from diabetes, and not poisoning is deceit.

CONCLUSION

In light of the proven lethal, sky-high cadmium levels, any diabetes was ***irrelevant***. Before mid-1976 Srila Prabhupada's health was very good. The cadmium caused Srila Prabhupada's catastrophic health decline, and any degree of diabetes he may have had does not negate the cadmium poisoning. Both Sruti Kirti and Hari Sauri stated that diabetes was never mentioned by any doctor nor by Srila Prabhupada while they were with him from 1972 to 1977. The correct diagnosis for 1977's "illness" is cadmium poisoning. If a man with a weak heart is shot by a Magnum 38, what is blamed for his death? If an elderly man is poisoned at lethal levels, did he die from old age? If a diabetic is lethally poisoned and then expires, should malicious homicide be ruled out because he had diabetes? Since lethal poisoning is confirmed, any illness becomes secondary to the unnatural cause of death by poison. *There is no use debating if Srila Prabhupada's health decline was due to pre-existing diabetes or kidney disease, because the cadmium levels were lethal.*

Cadmium poisoning causes, aggravates, and accelerates diabetes, liver malfunction, and kidney disease, and it was the unnatural assailant on Srila Prabhupada's health, superseding any underlying natural illnesses. His hair tests have proven lethal cadmium poisoning, confirmed by a list of "mystery" health symptoms unique to heavy metals poisoning and atypical to diabetes or kidney disease. From 1966 to 1997, no devotees heard of Srila Prabhupada being diabetic, even those who were closely associated with him. Either Srila Prabhupada's diabetes was a very well-kept secret (where even his close servants did not know) or he did not have any significant diabetes. *But the diabetes debate does not negate lethal cadmium and elevated arsenic poisoning.*

CHAPTER 34:
REJECTION OF PROPER MEDICAL CARE

Tamal in late 1977: **(1)** *"They will introduce so many things-injections, operations- therefore I don't want it."* **(2)** *"No, these allopathic doctors have been totally a failure for you. There's no question of going back to them in any case... and strong medicine he prescribed... He would have created havoc with his testing... if you don't have the disease, then they'll make sure you get it, simply to be right."* **(3)** *"In terms of Prabhupada's medicines he would always have his secretary give his final conclusive opinion over what steps he should take and what treatments he should take..."*

Srila Prabhupada had a general policy of avoiding medicines but still, he took some and not others by choosing those he thought would be useful. Much of Srila Prabhupada's reluctance to take medicines was because no one knew what the actual ailment was, and Srila Prabhupada, being a pharmacist and chemist, could understand they were useless treatments. Unless one is convinced the doctor has made the correct diagnosis, why take his medicines? He would avoid useless medications. Otherwise, Srila Prabhupada was practical and very determined to cure his ailment, calling for doctors and kavirajas one after another (Dr. G. Ghosh, Bonamali, NL Gupta, Ramanuji in his dream, etc), and even self-prescribed his treatments. He was rightfully suspicious of allopaths with their injections, drawing of blood, and "experimental" treatments.

SRILA PRABHUPADA TRIED HARD TO CURE HIS ILLNESS

Feb. 17, 1971: **SP:** *...my Guru Maharaja was in his last days, these rascal doctors injected... Tirtha Maharaja brought so many doctors. And he protested, "Why are you giving me injection?" [...] And if you bring a doctor, the rascals will not stop. "Oh, that is our treatment. We must try our best." They will plead like that. "To give more trouble to the patient, that is our business." Inventing new medicines means inventing new means of giving trouble. [...] they will say, "No. There is no guarantee. Let us try, make experiment." [...] Whatever nonsense knowledge they have got, they make experiment, at the risk of other's life. [...] That is my opinion. [...] go to a medical man, especially in your country, first of all, you have to give blood, immediately. (laughter) One ounce of blood immediately. ...And then other injection. Because I underwent so many medical examination, I have got experience. For my immigration. I think, 3 or 4 times I was under health examination, and blood-taking, and injection. [...] "First of all give your blood; then talk of other things." Better to die without a doctor. (laughter) That's the best principle. Don't call any doctor. Simply chant Hare Krishna and die peacefully."*

Notwithstanding his attitude towards doctors, the historical record clearly shows Srila Prabhupada **_did_** want to cure his mysterious illness by qualified doctors and effective medicines. He disliked medicines (and guessing doctors), but if he thought they would work, he took them. He was practical and saw the defects in the modern medical system. He sent devotees to find the makharadhvaja from his dream. He seemed perplexed by his illness and he chose which medicines he took. Why did he and his servants undertake so many cure programs? Why did he repeatedly call for kavirajas and doctors? Why did he agree to go to Kodaikanal, Kashmir, etc under the care of a doctor? He wanted a cure with medical treatments. He always advised disciples to take care of their health with doctors, medicines, and hospitals when necessary. Abhiram das, Srila Prabhupada's nurse July 25-Oct. 16, 1977, notes Srila Prabhupada was actively involved in his own health care. To the chagrin of some caretakers, Srila Prabhupada's approach was to accept the help of anyone who came forward with sincere goodwill, accepting they were sent by Krishna. *He was very serious about restoring his health*. He repeatedly called for doctors he knew and he remembered or invented medicinal treatments. He was more inclined to natural, Ayurvedic medicines.

REJECTION OF MEDICAL PROPER CARE

A study of the historical record of Srila Prabhupada's last year shows *Srila Prabhupada's caretakers increasingly rejecting proper medical care for Srila Prabhupada.* This was aggressively vocalized and practiced by Tamal and supported by Bhavananda. Why? Srila Prabhupada was adverse to allopathic drugs, but the primary caretakers **(1)** opposed even visits by unintrusive kavirajas, whose treatment could be accepted or rejected, and **(2)** never made any effort to obtain a ***correct diagnosis*** for Srila Prabhupada's mysterious illness. /Throughout 1977 Tamal begrudgingly allowed doctors to do their initial inspections and make prescriptions, but then he would discredit them, one by one, as being unqualified, cheaters, imposters, unclean, etc. He would aggressively discourage simple medical procedures even if performed "at home" and when Srila Prabhupada did not object. There was a *perplexing parade of doctors*, coming and going, changing, accepting, discrediting, then rejecting, both Ayurvedic and allopathic doctors, even obviously competent ones willing to accommodate Srila Prabhupada's wishes. *It was a program of rejecting medical care.*

This stood out like a nose pimple. Why was there no proper medical care or even a proper diagnosis? Why were qualified doctors repeatedly engaged, criticized, and then discharged? Why was so much suspicion and distrust verbalized about all doctors, both allopathic and Ayurvedic? Why were only village kavirajas, babas, vaidyas, and quacks consulted, and then rejected? The list of a *parade of doctors* that resulted in confusion, with too many diagnosis speculations and treatments, is very long (Ch. 32).

COMPLETE CONTROL BY TAMAL

As 1977 progressed, Tamal, ever the controller, tightened his grip over Srila Prabhupada's life. Bhaktisiddhanta das was posted as a security guard by Srila Prabhupada's garden door, and remembers that nothing happened without Tamal's sanction. *"A security cordon was set up by Tamal around Srila Prabhupada. As security men we were instructed not to let anyone in without Tamal's OK first."* Tamal determined who visited or spoke to Srila Prabhupada. Tamal decided which medicines and doctors would be accepted or rejected. Tamal directed the health care, with Srila Prabhupada's input decreasing over the months. Tamal filtered the news, guests, and letters read to Srila Prabhupada. Tamal was firmly situated as Srila Prabhupada's guardian, advisor, primary caretaker, executor, and personal secretary. Tamal was in control, from an external perspective, and Srila Prabhupada appeared to acquiesce. Tamal had great latitude in charting the course of Srila Prabhupada's health care, travel plans and interaction with visitors.

TKG's Diary (p. 110): "Because I was treating him, Srila Prabhupada acted as though I was his doctor. He told Bhakticharu to consult with me regarding which foods he should be served and asked Upendra to consult me about the kind of massage and bath to give." Srila Prabhupada entrusted his health to his caretakers, depending on their decisions and arrangements. He would sometimes initiate some action regarding his health, but generally he deferred to Tamal, sometimes his other servants or the GBC members. This became more so as 1977 progressed. Everyone was extremely intimidated by Tamal and they were compliant with his avoidance of proper medical attention and doctors, as though this was spiritually intelligent. On Nov. 15, Tamal bypassed the local coroner and the required death certificate before Srila Prabhupada was placed in samadhi.

Tamal's India visa expired Aug. 14, 1977. He was overstaying and had to exit India, which would disrupt his being personal secretary and master controller. Then on Aug. 17: **SP:** *...Tamal Krishna wants me to go back to...* **Tamal:** *I was encouraging Prabhupada to... I said that if he goes to the Western temples, that the welcome from his disciples would be so much that he would live for hundreds of years. (ConvBk:35:65-71)* Thus Tamal made the plan to go to America. Needing to exit India, he promoted a foreign tour. He would take Srila Prabhupada with him to renew his visa.

POISONING SABOTAGES TRUST IN DOCTORS, MEDS

Effecting an insidious, creeping health debilitation, the poisoning would discredit all doctors and kavirajas by invalidating all diagnoses, medicines, and treatments. Faith and trust in each new medical practitioner and prescription was quickly sabotaged by the poisoning, as everyone thought the poison's ill effects and failure to recover were due to the new medicine or treatment. A pinch of cadmium would negate whatever beneficial effect a medicine would have. The kaviraja Shastri believed his herbs would rejuvenate Srila Prabhupada's strength, but all his efforts were frustrated by a continuing decline in health. Due to the adverse effects of the hidden poison, each new doctor was perplexed and his medicine was rejected for causing bad results (that actually came from the poison). The parade of doctors continued. The caretakers who had custody of medicines could tamper with them to discredit each treatment program, increasing the skepticism in all doctors and medical programs. It is suspicious that each time a competent doctor was treating Srila Prabhupada with medicines and careful attention, inevitably there appeared some ill side effects that resulted in the rejection of that doctor and treatment. The ongoing poisoning caused an adverse reaction, like sleeplessness, nausea, diarrhea, mucus, cough, etc, which was then attributed to the treatment and medicines. *"Oh, this doctor doesn't know what he's doing either! They are all idiots, cheaters, Srila Prabhupada! Reject them, and just depend on Krishna and kirtan!"*

No medicine or treatment could be effective in curing Srila Prabhupada's while the cadmium poisoning tore down his health. The Mathura District's best doctor, Dr. K. Gopal, in Oct. 1977 became perplexed that his medicines and treatment after a week were effecting no improvement. He began to re-think his diagnosis, wanting further testing. Immediately Dr. Gopal was severely criticized by Tamal, and his treatment and participation was rejected. Dr. Gopal did not bring the X-ray machine for examination of the internal organs, nor did he get a blood sample for analysis. Either of these two things could have discovered the heavy metals poisoning. Tamal smelled trouble and rejected Dr. Gopal. Bonamali kaviraja was rejected because Tamal claimed he raised his fees by 20 rupees, arguing that therefore he was dishonest and untrustworthy. Bonamali, even though an old friend of Srila Prabhupada, was then immediately dismissed. An atmosphere of intense distrust and suspicion of doctors and medicines, especially allopathic, served the interests of the poisoners well. When Satsvarupa visited in Oct. 1977, Tamal indoctrinated him with the understanding that all possible attempts had already been made with doctors and medicines, leaving no choice except to chant and pray to Krishna for a miracle. Without questions, Satsvarupa passively accepted, and Srila Prabhupada lay bedridden, slowly succumbing to the cadmium.

WHY WAS THERE NO QUALIFIED MEDICAL CARE?

Many times in 1977 Tamal rejected hospitals, doctors, medical tests. *"I'm not going to let anybody take you to the hospital. ...Neither I'm going to let anybody put any, take any blood specimen or any of those things. It's not required. (Oct. 18, 1977) "So we are not going to take you to the hospital under any condition. Neither... not only is it your order, but we also see absolutely no benefit from these hospitals." (Nov. 3, 1977)* Srila Prabhupada's 1977 health history (App. 8, Volume 4) shows an amateur's approach to health care coupled with a resolute avoidance of any qualified medical attention or evaluation. <u>There was no coherent or intelligent program for dealing with Srila Prabhupada's health problems</u>. Kirtanananda raised this issue in early Oct. Understandably, Srila Prabhupada would be cautious in dealing with hospitals and doctors, as Western medicine as often ruins one's health as helps it. Nevertheless, sufficient funds and contacts were available to select from a wide choice of qualified and cooperative doctors without being subjected to experiments, injections, and operations. At least four opportunities arose on their own that would have provided proper medical diagnostics and treatments on Srila Prabhupada's own terms, without hospitals, injections, or allopathic drugs: Dr. Khurana, Dr. Ghosh from Kodaikanal, the Madras Governor's estate, and Dr. K. Gopal, but all were dismissed, discredited, and demonized by Tamal. *The avoidance of modern medicine was deliberate* to prevent detection of the real cause of Srila Prabhupada's declining health, the poisoning. The poisoners' anxiety grew when a new doctor came, and they made sure he did not stay long enough to discover or suspect poisoning.

The nature of Srila Prabhupada's illness was a mystery, being elusive to all. This in itself is extremely telling. There was constant frustration in dealing with the mystery illness, as Srila Prabhupada did not respond to any treatment and he grew worse day by day. The secret poisoning brought about an atmosphere of hopelessness. On July 31, 1977 the very favorable Governor of Madras visited Srila Prabhupada, offering a wonderful opportunity for proper medical care:

Governor: I invite you warmly to come to Madras. Stay at Raj Bhavan (governor's mansion). And we have the best medical team of Madras government at your disposal. We have got the best doctors in whole of South Asia. ...very good physicians. SP: ...I am not very inclined for medical treatment, their injection, operation. (laughs) Gov: No, they won't give you injections. There, doctors give yogic treatment also, and nature cure treatment... So I would request you to come to Madras... SP: (to Tamal) If possible, take me there. Madras is not far away. ...Think over. His Excellency is inviting. It is a good opportunity. Gov: ...our Raj Bhavan in very comfortable place to stay. It's like ashram... SP: So accept this invitation and fix up. Gov: ...200 mango trees in our compound. Various fruit trees. Everything beautiful. Nearly 200 acres of land ... very fine, very cool... There is our small bungalow on the sea also. SP: So when you think it will be suitable? Gov: ...I'll be in Madras on the 8th back. Then I am there. (ConvBk:35.24-9)

"*Srila Prabhupada appeared enthused by the Madras invitation, where there were 'many good Ayurvedic kavirajas. I am 50 percent decided. If you agree, then we will go.' Tamal notes, 'I said I would have to contemplate the trip first.'" (TkgD.139) "Srila Prabhupada and his servants discussed the merits of travel to Madras and other places around the world." (Sats:6.359)*"

COMMENT: Why was this proper medical attention in Madras rejected by Tamal? Why was this great opportunity to restore Srila

Prabhupada's health rejected? There are no more tape recordings until 8 days later. Here was a chance, for free, the best allopathic or Ayurvedic treatment in a Governor's Mansion without injections, operations. In Bombay, Sept. 24, prominent life member Sri KJ Somaiya brought a well-known Ayurvedic *vaidya* named Ram Gopal to see Srila Prabhupada, whom Tamal immediately rejected, saying he *"wanted nothing to do with him."* After taking these new medicines, sure enough, Srila Prabhupada developed heavy mucus and discomforts that same night. The next day the vaidya was dismissed. This was a pattern repeated again and again; each new doctor was rejected by Tamal as the new treatment mysteriously caused immediate ill-effects.

TAMAL'S SCAREMONGERING

The horrors of modern medicine were repeatedly described to Srila Prabhupada in what appears to be a *determined attempt to steer Srila Prabhupada AWAY from any proper medical attention. Why?* Was there something only modern Western medical techniques could discover? Tamal was especially emphatic about this, a fact seen clearly in the taped conversations, but not in his own *TKG's Diary*. In HSUnpub, p. 17: *"Srila Prabhupada called Sachidananda in later and requested him to call another doctor. He asked Tamal for his opinion (who) was negative about the whole thing having become disgusted after so many doctors."*

Some 1977 fearmongering examples: **(1)** Oct. 22: Tamal heads up a discussion about the horrors of modern surgery, where scissors are forgotten and sewed up into a patient, requiring further surgery. **(2)** Oct. 6: Tamal strongly opposes Srila Prabhupada wanting to bring his old friend Dr. Narottama Lal Gupta. **(3)** Oct. 4: Tamal insists on rejecting Bonamali kaviraja's services, complaining over a fee increase of a few rupees, as though this was a criminal act. **(4)** Oct. 3: Tamal calls the former doctor in Bombay "hopeless." **(5)** Sept. 29: Discussion headed by Tamal against doctors and hospitals. **(6)** Sept. 25: Due to cough and mucus, the doctor of the day is rejected by Tamal. **(7)** Sept. 24: Tamal does not like the new doctor. **(8)** Sept. 17: Tamal discourages taking on any new doctor. /Do we see the pattern here? This went on all through 1977. Tamal (especially) had great prejudice against doctors and treatments. Was it feared doctors would discover the poisoning?

WHY DID ALL THE TREATMENTS FAIL?

Each remedy undertaken to restore Srila Prabhupada's health gave no lasting results. There had already been *a parade of various practitioners,* some good, some bad, all who came and went, and their treatments and medicines also came and went. Adridharan recalled feeling at the time a mood of frustration with these various and ineffective health care attempts. He and others like Kirtanananda hoped for a qualified doctor who would be able to treat Srila Prabhupada consistently until cured. Adridharan located and brought the last *kaviraja* (Damodar Prasad Shastri) at the end of Oct. 1977 to treat Srila Prabhupada. Despite his stellar qualifications, his treatments were also ineffective, as he had also misdiagnosed the ailment. No doctor was around long enough to suspect poisoning. Why was each new treatment discontinued? Why were there *adverse reactions **every** time* there was a new treatment? Thus the repeated rejection of doctors, medicines and treatments. Bhavananda and Tamal were *"relieved"* Srila Prabhupada decided to die peacefully, without further botheration with *"the struggle to live."* The real problem was that no one could detect the poisoning.

Treatments were often only for symptoms. _All the doctor treatments and medicines failed because they were treating either symptoms or a misdiagnosis._ The poison was not discovered until 2002. Heavy metals poisoning is only detected by modern medical facilities after a series of tests, eliminating various possibilities, one by one, so these doctors should not be criticized. To ensure the poisoning was NOT detected, the poisoners would change and discredit and reject any proficient doctor that came, just to perpetuate frustration and a resignation to fate.

MEDICAL CARE COMPARISONS

It is ironic and disturbing that 22 years after Srila Prabhupada was repeatedly denied proper medical attention, Tamal himself, using the modern medical system, was diagnosed with advanced prostate cancer that had spread to one kidney, and which was removed by surgery on Jan. 26, 1999. He employed the best physicians at the best ultra-modern hospitals, spending $500,000 on treatments, tests, surgery, medicines, and recuperation. With cancer, he no longer had the same aversion to modern medicine that he fervently professed in 1977, supposedly for Srila Prabhupada's protection. Tamal was cured, to the credit of modern medicine. *Why did Tamal not take the advice he gave to Srila Prabhupada,* and go to Vrindaban to chant and die without Western medicine and doctors? Why the double standard? This is hypocrisy.

No doctor was appropriate for Srila Prabhupada and each was rejected, one after another. But Tamal was very expert in finding proper medical attention, in proper diagnosis and treatment, at enormous expense, when it came to himself. But for Srila Prabhupada there was not even a diagnosis. Even Dr. McIrvine in London was only used for a minor surgical procedure and the specific crisis event of the moment, ***not*** for a thorough and scientific evaluation of Srila Prabhupada's health. Now that Srila Prabhupada's lethal poisoning with cadmium has been proven, we can guess why Tamal did not want doctors around: was he afraid they would stumble upon the poisoning? (Volume 2, 3)

Also in 2009, when the 400 lb. Jayapataka Swami, another of the primary poisoning suspects, almost died from a massive stroke resulting in serious paralysis and health issues, employed the very best that modern science had to offer. Rather than stay in the holy dhama of Mayapur to chant, or even a hospital in nearby Calcutta, he was often "airlifted" to Delhi or Bombay to the best "specialized" hospitals. Why was Srila Prabhupada so neglected and left in the care of a baba who prescribed a medicine made of bark from 45 trees? A report in 2014: *"...(Jayapataka) began from Kolkata hospital to be airlifted by an air ambulance for admission into a specialized hospital in Delhi. ...pray to the Lord to protect Guru Maharaja and that he successfully navigate any challenges during the flight. This moving of Guru Maharaja is being undertaken with thorough medical advice and approval from a panel of specialist doctors."* Specialized recovery trainers, therapy pool exercise equipment, best doctors and medical hospitals, "whatever it takes, whatever the cost"- all for Jayapataka Swami ever since 2009, and he continues in a semi-paralyzed condition. Tamal and Jayapataka did not reject proper medical care for themselves. This is hypocrisy.

NO RESPONSIBILITY, SUSPICIOUS EVENTS SEQUENCE

There was undeniably another factor why Srila Prabhupada never received proper medical attention. There was a lack of seriousness and irresponsibility on the part of the caretakers. A few examples: **(1)** The questionable source of Chandra Swami's *makharadhvaja* was not properly understood or investigated (Volume 3) **(2)** The Delhi *kaviraja's* cautionary disclaimer letter for the makharadhvaja was never shown to Srila Prabhupada **(3)** Srila Prabhupada chastised Tamal for not authenticating some eyewash brought to him.

Everyone was irresponsibly trusting in Tamal, totally intimidated by him. No one was thinking independently, or even thinking at all. Note the suspicious sequence of events: **(1)** No hospitalization. **(2)** No competent attending doctor. **(3)** No attending certified nurse. **(4)** Patient complains about being poisoned. **(5)** Patient overhears discussions about poisoning. **(6)** No report about possible poisoning to police. **(7)** No pathological investigation. **(8)** Ten months pass by as patient gradually withers away. **(9)** No autopsy or coroner's examination. **(10)** Death certificate issued after 103 days. **(11)** Body interred within 14 hours of death. **(12)** The registered cause of death as "heart attack" is nonsense. **(13)** When concerns of foul play led to a GBC investigation and arsenic was discovered in a hair sample, this investigation was terminated by the suspects and GBC with a whitewash, deceptive cover-up. **(14)** Funds for the investigation were redirected to the GBC denial book, compiled under direction of the suspects, produced by their disciples, with literary support from cronies. **(15)** The cadmium tests prove an malicious intent to murder Srila Prabhupada by poison.

TAMAL'S REJECTIONS OF DR. GHOSH OF KODAIKANAL

Iksvaku das (Heinz Dullinger) gave a statement (abbreviated below) on Oct. 4, 2001. Iksvaku received permission from Srila Prabhupada to bring well-renowned life member Dr. Ghosh from Kodaikanal to Vrindaban to treat him and restore his health.

"Dr. Ghosh's private clinic/retreat was highly rated, specialized in paralyses. SP's room was guarded, hard to get in. SP sat behind his desk looking weak, pale, yellowish, with a dim voice, sagging eyes, sensitive to light with blue rings underneath. I explained how I met Dr. Ghosh, a doctor who loved him and that I could ask him to come treat him. SP was skeptical and asked questions. Then, trusting me, he definitely agreed for the doctor to come. It would take a week for him to arrive. I went to Tamal's office and reported that I was to get the doctor. He said we don't need another doctor, everything was under control; I should not concern myself. He was very skeptical, wanted to know who I was, where I came from, and half the conversation was about my legitimacy of concern for SP's health. He was upset, and not accepting SP had agreed for Dr. Ghosh to come. I said I would get the doctor if he liked it or not.

"On May 27 I arrived in Kodaikanal, planning to drive Dr. Ghosh, his wife and his son Prahlad to the Madras airport. Unfortunately my radiator gave out and so they left on their own. On June 2 Dr. Ghosh arrived in Vrindaban, shifted room to room and asked to pay. June 12 I arrived and solved his accommodation problems. He told me of the troubles he had with Tamal. (1) He was not allowed to conduct a complete diagnosis, including tests, X-rays or a urine lab analysis. (2) He could not administer a time plan therapy treatment, without upsetting the massage routine. (3) His medicine was rejected by Tamal. (4) His failure to distance SP from management and allow him to relax.

*"We met with Bhagatji (Vishvambar Dayal) where we discussed how SP was fully in Tamal's hands and there was not much Dr. Ghosh was allowed to do. **Bhagatji was of the opinion that a conspiracy** was going on but nobody could confirm this. When Hansadutta and I stayed*

with Bhagatji in May for a week, he was already talking about a conspiracy against SP, but I did not understand what he meant. Dr. Ghosh asked me to promise that SP would stay in Vrindaban; any climate change would be bad for his health. He said his treatment proposal was at first rejected by Tamal but later accommodated into the existing massage treatment. He tried to take full charge of SP's treatment and recovery with massage, food management, etc, practically moving in with SP, whose health improved; he again gave classes. But Dr. Ghosh said he was bumping into corners every which way he turned. Then I had a hard time seeing SP. I only could see him mornings in the temple, weak but confident.

"Tamal implemented a new rule: 'SP cannot be disturbed.' Once I saw SP receiving an oil massage. His body was thin and fragile; massages activated the blood flow and was a stimulant. One day SP was walking a few steps with two devotees. I thought the long awaited improvements had come; he was getting better. But we had no access to SP; we all speculated from the outside. Dr. Ghosh thought there was not much more he could do in this situation, but he believed if SP would remain under stable conditions in Vrindaban, he had a chance to recover by year's end. Tamal would not even talk to him. Srila Prabhupada appeared trapped under Tamal's intense control over him.

*"Finally, Dr. Ghosh left on June 15, **frustrated and rejected**. On June 25 I left for Madras, thinking SPs health was improving. On Nov. 11 a sadhu baba came to me saying, 'Your gurudeva is very ill, you must go see him.' I arrived in Vrindaban Nov. 14, 6 pm in SP's room. I saw the Kaviraja testing SP's breath with the cotton swab. The day after SP's disappearance the GBC met. I was staying in Hansadutta's room, and he told me that during the meeting he became disgusted, walked out and paced the halls. 'They are already fighting over his inheritance.'"*

DR. GHOSH FROM KODAIKANAL COMES BACK OCT. 12

Dr. Ghosh from Kodaikanal came back to Vrindaban again on Oct. 12. Tamal was not happy and called Iksvaku crazy for bring Dr. Ghosh to impose on the existing program. Tamal blocked everything Dr. Ghosh wanted to do, who soon left again, further insulted. But first Dr. Ghosh fetched Dr. Krishna Gopal from Mathura's Rama Krishna Hospital, who tried to diagnose and treat Srila Prabhupada. After a week he was rejected. *Srila Prabhupada acquiesced to Tamal's negativity of doctors.* Tamal said by inviting hospital doctors, that tubes, operations, and drugs was unavoidable, so better to use kavirajas (with no poison-detecting X-rays). On Oct. 12, the talks about Dr. Ghosh from Kodaikanal:

Tamal: *...I would never communicate (with him). We already had our business with him 4 or 5 months ago. We already rejected him.* **Kirtanananda**: *It seems that someone has to be in charge of your care. One day it's this allopath, one day this quack, that quack. That's not good. I'd like to see you ask one of us... I'll be glad to do it. Anyone... Take charge of your care, and we can do the best we can...* **SP**: *But we have already asked Dr. Ghosh of Allahabad, but he has not yet come.* **Tamal**: *No, he hasn't. We received a letter from him. I think he may have missed our letter... But he hasn't come yet.* **SP**: *You can see that letter. He is qualified man.* **Tamal**: *Dr. Ghosh's letter... he suggests that we immediately take you to that Bombay hospital.* **Hari Sauri**: *He wanted to do that last March when he saw you there at Mayapur.* (ConvBk)

COMMENT: Kirtanananda saw the problem clearly, but Tamal could not? Tamal knew what he was doing in rejecting all doctors. Even Dr. Ghosh of Allahabad, an old friend that Srila Prabhupada said was qualified, was criticized before he even arrived!

NAVEEN KRISHNA'S FATHER DR. D. R. KHURANA COMES

Dr. D. R. Khurana, Naveen Krishna's father, came Aug. 15, 1977 and urged kidney dialysis treatment at a Delhi hospital. Tamal and Srila Prabhupada declined. Dr. Khurana then offered for a group of Delhi doctors to come with the kidney dialysis machine, do tests and treatments to treat Srila Prabhupada in his own quarters, with no need to go to the hospital. On Aug. 24, Tamal replied: *"SP very much appreciates your offer to treat him and care for him. Because he is just now under the treatment of an Ayurvedic Kaviraja he prefers to continue this treatment for some time. Besides ...he is travelling to the West to visit his temples there, with the thought that the devotional love of his disciples will be the best medicine of all."* Thus Dr. Khurana was rejected. He was one of the four professional, competent medical doctors who tried to offer their services to Srila Prabhupada, but who were all rejected by Tamal.

PART FIVE:
TESTIMONY AND SUSPECTS

Srila Prabhupada was poisoned with lethal amounts of heavy metals unexplainable except by deliberate homicidal intent (Ch. 7). Accidental or environmental contamination is ruled out (Part 6). Volume 2 and 3 look in depth at Tamal and other persons of interest and suspects in this crime, the evidence regarding some suspects being substantial. To date there are no direct witnesses or confessions. But this is typical for the hidden, cowardly act of homicidal poisoning. It is natural that witnesses will be scarce, especially 45 years later, but there are some substantial witnesses and testimonials that significantly contribute to the body of evidence. We note that the *cadmium poisoning is already proven*, even without direct witnesses or confessions, first by Srila Prabhupada's own words (for those who have faith in them), and second, by the forensic cadmium hair tests and certified whispers.

Witnesses, credible hearsay, and testimonies are valuable evidence that impressively adds to the hard forensic proof of poisoning, and include areas which should be further investigated. This evidence is documented herein, and what is fact or unverified is made clear. In time, these items may be confirmed or not. The total evidence already establishes that Srila Prabhupada was homicidally poisoned. Who did it is a question addressed in Volume 2, 3. There is sufficient evidence that Tamal was a poisoner (Volume 2) and that others were or may have been involved (Volume 3). The GBC resolution, *"There is no evidence at this time to support the allegations of poisoning of Srila Prabhupada,"* makes a mockery of ISKCON leadership. ISKCON's Orwellian double-speak (obscuring actual reality) is keeping the naïve membership in the dark, but those days are coming to an end as the light of truth prevails.

CHAPTER 35:
FRIGHTENED MEXICAN WITNESS

RUMORS OF MEXICAN BRAHMACHARI'S STORY

According to Partrikananda das, rumors circulated in Los Angeles' devotee community in 1982 that Srila Prabhupada's poisoning was witnessed by a Vrindaban gurukula schoolboy from Mexico. Bhakta

Vatsala das (BV), 13 years old in 1977, had regular cleaning duties in Srila Prabhupada's quarters. From a hallway *he reportedly overheard eight or so senior disciples discussing Srila Prabhupada's poisoning.* BV returned to Mexico in 1978; many devotees there remember him talking openly about what he had heard, including Ramanya, Durlab, Nandaprana, Mantri, Adhoksaja.

DURLAB CONFIRMS RUMORS AS FACTS

Durlab das remembered BV's testimony, and was childhood friends with BV's older brother Mantri das. He lived in Mexico City and ran his own business selling *Shiva* brand incense. *"I phoned Durlab das (Domingo) in Dec. 1997 and he openly verified how he, his older brother Adhoksaja das, Nandaprana das, and others repeatedly heard in 1978 BV's account about how he overheard eight senior devotees in a hushed discussion about poisoning Srila Prabhupada. The conversation took place in the Vrindaban temple near Srila Prabhupada's room as BV listened out of sight through the hallway doorway. Durlab also remembered that two ISKCON gurus, namely Kirtanananda Swami and Bhagavan das, had come to Mexico around 1982-84 looking for BV, who had by then left the movement with his family. Durlab stated that BV was afraid of ISKCON leaders, especially Tamal, and had deliberately adopted a very low profile, disappearing from view. Bhakta Vatsala resides near Mexico City. His mother still attends ISKCON programs."* (Nityananda das, 1999)

THE MEXICAN SECRET POLICE

Just after the "poison issue" had arisen, in Dec. 1997, Tamal traveled to Mexico for a week (it was not his GBC zone), going with Guruprasad Swami for a festival in Guadalajara, and then he went <u>alone</u> for "rest and recuperation," as described by Bir Krishna Maharaja, to Acapulco on the Mexican Riviera. Tamal stayed with his friend Hrdayananda in a 4 star Mexican hotel. Did this have anything to do with Bhakta Vatsala? We were told Tamal sent money to BV in Mexico in 1978 but this stopped after some time. Nityananda das: *"Shortly after our phone call and Tamal's visit to Mexico in Dec. 1997, Durlab's home was inexplicably stormed at night by police and he was severely beaten. Durlab excitedly related the incident to me on my second phone call to him in early 1998. Very afraid for his family, he said he would then regularly change his address and phone number. Durlab believed the attack must have been connected somehow to those in ISKCON who want his knowledge of BV's testimony about the poison conspiracy to remain silenced. The men were clearly "secret police" by virtue of their uniforms. After this, Durlab was very reluctant to talk anymore, and we lost contact with him. In 2015 we learned that he had passed away."*

MEXICAN WITNESS FOUND; "HOLY WATER," GBC TAPES

In April 1998, our team tried to find the 34 year old BV. Yasodanandan das, former Vrindaban gurukula headmaster, remembered him as his student. Rupa Vilas das, living in UK and a former Vrindaban gurukula teacher, also remembered this student. The boy was not so inclined to academics, but he worked hard. He remained in school for about five years until age 13, and returned to Mexico shortly after Srila Prabhupada's departure. Rupa Vilas and Yasodanandana knew nothing of him being a witness to poisoning discussions. On the tapes, Nov. 6, 1977: **SP**: *What is that sound?* **Tamal**: *That's one of the brahmacharis shaking out the dust in the rugs. In my office we have some rugs, so he takes them outside and shakes them. He's a nice brahmachari, young boy from the gurukula, from Mexico.* BV was engaged in cleaning by Srila Prabhupada's caretakers. He overheard discussions in those otherwise restricted areas. A few older gurukula boys were always assisting the resident or visiting sannyasis at ISKCON Vrindaban temple. BV was an assistant to Tamal, Srila Prabhupada's personal secretary. Tamal wanted him to come with him to Dallas after visiting his Mexican relatives in 1978, but he refused.

In July 1999, after reading *SHPM*, Ramanya das from Alachua called a truth team member, wanting to help with the investigation. He and Durlab das had both been childhood friends with Mantri das, who was the first of the three to join ISKCON (LA, 1970) and who was BV's older brother. Ramanya: *"I grew up at the same place with his family. I know his whole family. Our families are very close."* He was like an older brother to BV, and agreed to go to Mexico to interview him. He found BV through family and friends. But out of fear, BV then vanished for two weeks. Ramanya found him again and with Nandaprana das (ACBSP) convinced him to share what he was comfortable speaking about, and they tape recorded an interview at Durlab's home.

BV had been fearful for 20 years of certain ISKCON sannyasis. He asked, **"Where is Tamal?"** He was nervous and concerned for his family's safety. When he returned to Mexico in 1978, Tamal expected

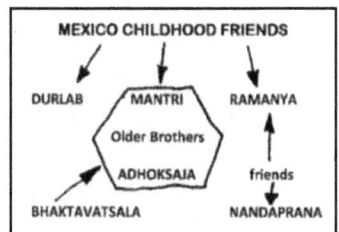

MEXICO CHILDHOOD FRIENDS

DURLAB   MANTRI   RAMANYA

Older Brothers

ADHOKSAJA   friends

BHAKTAVATSALA   NANDAPRANA

him to then come to Dallas, but he did not want Tamal in his life anymore, and when devotees came looking for him sometimes, he always hid out of fear. Once, he heard that Tamal and two disciples searched for him in Cuernavaca. BV related memories from his days in Vrindaban to Ramanya. He spoke as a simple, scared man, in Spanish and imperfect English. Srila Prabhupada had initiated him, and although away from ISKCON for decades, he still spoke like a devotee. He had 3 dreams of Srila Prabhupada telling him "to speak the truth" and remembered all the leader's names, explaining he was always serving sannyasis, cleaning Srila Prabhupada's rooms. Naveen translated the tape from Spanish in Oct. 1999. Adhoksaya was an older brother.

MAIN POINTS FROM BV's TAPED TESTIMONY

(1) He asked why did Bhavananda sprinkle the food with deity "holy water" for "purification," before it was brought to Srila Prabhupada? **(2)** When BV reported this to the headmaster, Jagadisha das, he was heavily reprimanded. **(3)** Twice he saw a group of GBCs having loud arguments, whether there should be one person in charge of ISKCON or to divide it up. Once Bhavananda punched Ramesvara, making his lip bleed. **(4)** He had found two cassette tapes hidden under Srila Prabhupada's bed mattress in early 1978 which he believed were recorded by the leading gurus. **(5)** He took and hid them in a hole behind a picture on the wall in his room. **(6)** Bhavananda, Jayapataka, Tamal and others searched everywhere for the missing tapes. **(7)** The day he left for Mexico, Bhakticharu sent him out to buy a tape player as a gift, then searched his luggage, finding and confiscating the two tapes. **(8)** BV never listened to these tapes, but he believed they were very important to the gurus since they had looked so hard to recover them. <u>What was on them?</u>

NOW THAT TAMAL AND OTHERS ARE FINISHED...

Interview: *What else you used to do in the gurukula in Vrindaban?*
A: *I cleaned the ashrams, I studied, and go and do the cleaning in the ashrams and Prabhupada's quarters, and take care of sannyasis... I used serve to Lord Krishna and all the gurus and sannyasis. I used to help cleaning especially Prabhupada's sleeping quarters, and also go in his kitchen. I used to help to prepare his meals, to clean the kitchen, I used to observe who used to cook and prepare his meals of Srila Prabhupada.*

BV declined to speak further and he wanted more time before saying more, and <u>it was clear to Ramanya and Nandaprana that there was much more he had to say but he was afraid to say it.</u> Ramanya told Nityananda he was convinced BV did not reveal all he had to say, out of fear of Tamal and others, and that we should try to interview him again. After

Tamal's demise in 2002, Nityananda called Ramanya and Naveen about pursuing another interview, but it did not happen. As of 2015, Kirtanananda, Bhagavan, and many others were also gone or now harmless. Durlab passed away in 2015, and Ramanya does not know where Mantri can be found: he left the movement in the 1970's. Ramanya sees BV's family every year, close to his own family home in Mexico. There must be other devotees in Mexico that could verify BV's speaking of overhearing the caretakers discussing poisoning, such as Astika das, leader of Mexico City's Sridhara Maharaja group, and Radha Krishna das, formerly Swami from the Spanish BBT. BV spoke about the poisoning in the late 70's in Mexico, long before the issue became public. A legal deposition with BV is needed. Where are Mantri, Adhoksaya (his older brothers) or other Mexican devotees who knew him, including Nandaprana, who can confirm BV and Durlab's testimonies. Please contact us if you have any information.

CHAPTER 36:
FOUR KAVIRAJAS AGREE ON POISONING

Three kavirajas (Ayurvedic physicians) in Oct. and Nov. 1977 each independently and collectively arrived at a diagnosis of poisoning for Srila Prabhupada. Reliable and independent sources with multiple confirmations provided different pieces by which this conclusion was reached. This is based on published materials and interviews with Balavanta, Nalinikanta, and other, as well as the tape recordings, the kavirajas themselves, and their descendants. A few dots in the picture were connected using common-sense, marked below in bold underlines. We are confident of the following accounts and conclusions below.

Bonamali kaviraja had an Ayurvedic practice and dispensary in Gopinath Bazaar, Vrindaban. Srila Prabhupada was his old friend before going to America in 1965, and he used to visit his dispensary to talk about philosophy and medicines. On July 12, 1977, after Srila Prabhupada had come back to Vrindaban to prepare for his physical departure, he called for Bonamali to diagnose and treat his persistent, unexplained illness. Bhakticharu was sent to ask for Bonamali, who came and diagnosed an inability to pass urine or stool. His prescribed a week-long, milk only diet, cow dung ashes over the body, and various medicines. After three weeks Srila Prabhupada discontinued this program, though it seemed to have been beneficial. Although Bonamali was not officially dismissed, other kavirajas and doctors continued to visit and make prescriptions during and after Bonamali's program.

Naveen Krishna das and his father Dr. Khurana of Delhi came to see Srila Prabhupada on Aug. 15, 1977. Dr. Khurana's offers of assistance and advice were not taken. Tamal sent a letter to Dr. Khurana explaining that Srila Prabhupada was already under the care of a kaviraja. The chief doctor from a prominent Ayurvedic hospital in Delhi also came, but after a few days, he was rejected due to Tamal's critical attitude towards him. On Aug. 27 Srila Prabhupada left for London, ending all treatments. On Sept. 8 Srila Prabhupada went to a London hospital for a minor operation to improve the ability to pass urine. On Sept. 13 Srila Prabhupada flew to Bombay, and on Oct. 2 he traveled by train back to Vrindaban.

MORE PHYSICIANS AND DR. K. GOPAL

On Oct. 3 Bonamali once again examined Srila Prabhupada, thinking there was no illness and only weakness, recommending a special diet and medicines to gain strength. One medicine produced more coughing and Srila Prabhupada decided not to use Bonamali again, asking Tamal to invite his old friend Dr. G. Ghosh from Allahabad to come treat him instead. Tamal declared Bonamali to be a "dishonest man," supposedly for raising his fees by a few rupees. But both Gopal Chandra Ghosh of Vrindaban Institute (another old friend of Srila Prabhupada) and Bonamali's son Braj Dulal Goswami deny this is true. Was Tamal creating deliberate misgivings about Bonamali? Gopal Chandra Ghosh quoted Bonamali as saying, *"I do not even want to sell them [medicines for Srila Prabhupada]."* On Oct. 6 Srila Prabhupada asked Tamal to call another local kaviraja, Narottama Lal Gupta, who was also an old acquaintance. But Tamal resisted this.

On Oct. 10 the retired principal of the Jaipur Ayurvedic College, Raj Vaidya Pandit Lakshmi Narayan, was brought and an examination resulted in recommendations involving diet, supplements, and medicines. On Oct. 12 Dr. Ghosh from Kodaikanal arrived unexpectedly, and he was shunned by Tamal and he soon left very disappointed (after bringing Dr. K. Gopal). On Oct. 15 Bonamali came again and proclaimed there was no illness, simply weakness. The next day Dr. G. Ghosh of Allahabad finally arrived. *"He personally took a urine sample to Agra for testing and then advised that Prabhupada should not take only liquid but also some solid food, like chena (fresh cheese) mixed with sugar, and he prescribed an enema with glucose and salt. He showed us how to massage Prabhupada's body from the feet upwards to improve circulation and help the blood move toward the heart, and how to massage his stomach in a clockwise direction.*" (Ocean of Mercy, p. 220) These urine test results are lost. Dr. G. Ghosh brought Dr. K. Gopal on Oct. 17, a young specialist from the local Ramakrishna Hospital, who thought the makharadhvaja prepared by Bonamali (not yet taken) was *moti-dristi* (similar but weaker). A serious chronic kidney infection was the diagnosis and medicines were prescribed. By Oct. 22, Srila Prabhupada had still not improved in strength. Dr. K. Gopal was perplexed why there was no improvement in Srila Prabhupada's condition. Tamal and Bhavananda heavily criticized Dr. Gopal's ideas for X-rays and he was rejected. Dr. K. Gopal was still at the Ramakrishna Vrindaban hospital in July 2020.

The private investigation team sent Sakshi Gopal and Abhinanada April 21, 2002 to meet Dr. K. Gopal at his Vrindaban clinic, who said he had no indications Srila Prabhupada suffered from diabetes, emphatic his diagnosis was not tuberculosis, but ASTHMA or a chronic allergic respiratory disorder [perhaps due to heavy metal poisoning?] Tamal's tuberculosis account was misleading. Dr. Gopal saw his medicine prescription in the display case at the Vrindaban ISKCON Prabhupada Museum, and advised it be checked to corroborate his 1977 diagnosis of asthma. His diagnosis of asthma fits with the effects of cadmium poisoning, namely chronic cough, bronchitis, and lung anomalies.

DREAMING OF THE MAKHARADHVAJA

On Oct. 22 Srila Prabhupada had a dream of a Ramanuja kaviraja who would supply genuine makharadhvaja, and Tamal sent devotees out in different directions to search for him. A local Ramanuji kaviraja was brought to see Srila Prabhupada and also said Bonamali's medicine was not makharadhvaja. Ultimately makharadhvaja was obtained in Delhi from a Shaivite kaviraja through the arrangement of the notorious Chandra Swami. Srila Prabhupada took 3 doses and then stopped due to some diarrhea. By Oct. 27 no doctor/kaviraja had been attending Srila Prabhupada for days. Late at night Adridharan in Calcutta was called to confirm approval for his bringing to Vrindaban a Ramanuji kaviraja that had been found in Calcutta, a Damodara Prasad Sharma "Shastri." It was thought he was the kaviraja from Srila Prabhupada's dream.

BONAMALI'S URINE TEST

Oct. 27, 1977: While discussing the two different batches of makharadhvaja (Chandra Swami and Bonamali) with Srila Prabhupada: ***TKG:*** *It may be we should take on Bonamali again?* ***Prabhupada:*** *And stick with him?* ***BHAV:*** *Kaviraja must be there all the time. (TKG's Diary, p. 304)* Bonamali had been absent from Srila Prabhupada's care since Oct. 15, and despite Tamal's earlier accusations about his "dishonesty," it was decided to call him again. Two devotees were then sent on Oct 27 or 28 to request Bonamali's return to Srila Prabhupada's care. This was confirmed by Bonamali's son, Braj Dulal Goswami (BDG), who has continued the family Ayurvedic practice and dispensary after his father's death. A 2001 interview of BDG by Jitarati, Mandapa, and others at his Vrindaban medical shop was recorded on a 25 min. audio CD, paraphrased, summarized as follows:

"My father was treating Srila Prabhupada, but he stopped... some other kaviraja was treating. When they came back again later [late Oct.] to my father for treatment, he was cautious, knowing other kavirajas were also treating Srila Prabhupada. He did not want to become involved without first doing urine sample and basic examination as a standard practice. He said to the two devotees who had come, 'I will not treat until I have urine sample.' I was 17 at the time and was my father's compounder. I was standing right there [points to a place nearby]. The next day the two devotees came back by rickshaw and brought the Swamiji's urine sample in a 50 gram Dabur honey jar. Bonamali lifted this bottle up to the sunlight. The urine sample contained three layers, three rings, and the colors were separate. My father turned and said to me, 'This is poisoning. The first layer is blood, the second is bone, and the third is marrow. This is slow poison. After giving this poison; the man will die slowly, slowly... no one can judge what is happening.' This thing my father explained me then and there, and he told them also, the two devotees, 'I think it is poison.'"

Bonamali then declined to resume Srila Prabhupada's treatment, for two reasons: **(1)** that other kavirajas were involved, and **(2)** the confirmation of poisoning from the urine test. *Braj Dulal Goswami explained that his father must have been afraid now that poisoning was understood.* Bonamali's diagnosis of poisoning was the first known instance of someone becoming aware of the real cause for Srila Prabhupada's health decline. BDG did not know if his father had determined the type of poison involved. He was also asked about how blood, bone and bone-marrow enters urine, and he said slow poisoning saps the energy and rots the body internally. This is amazingly verified:

SP: *Bichar hi... jo idhar me to... sarte sarte bilkul sab energy nasht ho gaya. Usliye parikama jayega.* (My thoughts are... that here... I am rotting and rotting. All my energy is wasted. That is why I want to go on parikrama.) Tape T-46A; ConvBk Vol. 36. *"Prabhupada was becoming increasingly weaker, despite the medicine. The kaviraja (Shastri) said all organs except for the kidneys, were all right. There was no <u>blood,</u>*

marrow, flesh, or muscles." *(TKG's Diary*, p. 332) Abhinandana in 2004 confirmed: *"...in 1997 I visited Bonamali's son. He is ready to testify, he is my friend. He said he saw the test tube of urine with the dhatus (bone, blood, flesh, marrow etc) separated in layers and different colors. Bonamali said, 'You see, this means poisoning, his body is dissolving, and my medicine is useless, therefore I will stop treating Him.'"*

DR. GOPAL GHOSH WITNESSES BONAMALI'S URINE TEST

Dr. Gopal Chandra Ghosh, Srila Prabhupada's old friend and Head Librarian at Vrindaban Research Institute, was at Bonamali Kaviraja's dispensary, on Oct. 27/28, 1977. As seen in *Our Srila Prabhupada* by Mulaprakriti dasi, Dr. Ghosh was Bonamali's good friend. He personally witnessed Bonamali's Ayurvedic analysis of Srila Prabhupada's urine, and in 2002 described the incident to Sakshi Gopal das when interviewed at the Institute (which preserves old historical documents and artifacts):

"Bonamali put down a plantain leaf. I was standing behind him looking over his shoulder. He had Swamiji's urine sample in a Dabur honey bottle. Carefully he put down a drop on the leaf and then added some Vedic powder. First the liquid went green and then slowly it turned a dirty brown. He did this thrice. Then he turned to us and said, 'This is poison. Swami Prabhupada has been poisoned.'" The double confirmation of Bonamali's urine analysis by Dr. Ghosh and Braj Dulal Goswami brings this evidence far above the uncertainties of hearsay and rumors. The Dabur honey bottle is a detail which two separate witnesses confirmed when interviewed separately, and confirms the credibility of both accounts.

Nityananda: *"In March 2004 I visited Vrindaban. I found Dr. Ghosh at the Vrindaban Research Institute. Eighteen months earlier he had suffered a stroke and heart attack, and was now very deaf, irritable, and almost unable to walk. My communication attempts* turned to writing my questions on paper. *'Did you witness Bonamali perform a urine test for Srila Prabhupada, and what was the result?'* He became quite agitated and began loudly stuttering. I pointed to the question again and again. Finally he said coherently: 'I heard about this* *urine test from Bonamali- I used to visit his shop very often- but because of my illness, my stroke, heart attack, I cannot now remember the results. But you should go and ask Bonamali's son Braj Dulal Goswami, he will tell you everything.'*

Dr. Ghosh then meticulously wrote down from his sharp memory Braj Dulal Goswami's name, clinic name, and exact Vrindaban address. Obviously he did not want to tell me the urine test results that he very well remembered. Again I asked, and he said in a guarded tone: 'Yes, the urine test showed something very untoward, something very unusual. Maybe the medicines caused the very negative results of the urine test. Ask Braj Dulal.' Was it poison, I asked? Dr. Ghosh became agitated and animated, and said I should go and study the artifacts, waving his arms at the exhibits. The exhibits were interesting, but his testimony more so. He would not confide in a white Westerner. Sakshi Gopal was Bengali and Dr. Ghosh had confided in him in 2002. He knew Braj Dulal would explain his father's urine test, so referred me there to get the real story which he himself was reluctant to go on record with. Also he was wary of the ISKCON complex which was almost next door."

CONFIRMATION FROM BRAJ DULAL GOSWAMI

*"During my 2004 Vrindaban pilgrimage I could not catch up with Braj Dulal Goswami. He was filmed in a 2005 documentary shown on Star TV in India wherein he again confirmed his father's determination of poisoning. URL: **www.youtube.com/watch?v=0h4YmilaL-c** In March 2010 my mother-in-law visited BDG in Vrindaban and put me on the phone with him. I spoke to him from Fiji, and asked whether he had seen his father test Srila Prabhupada's urine and heard his father declare that Srila Prabhupada was poisoned. He was at first rather cautious, but gradually relaxed and opened up. He was concerned for his life, stating that ISKCON was very powerful, that he was now 50 and had to think of his family and their future safety and livelihood. Since he had spoken to Sakshi Gopal in 2002, he no longer had patients or customers from ISKCON. After he spoke on the 2005 Indian television documentary arranged by Sakshi Gopal, he had indirectly received warnings from ISKCON that what was done was done, but he should not be involved with the poison controversy again. But he said he was devoted to the truth, and he stood by his statements in JFY and on the Star TV show. However, if he was to make these statements in print with an attorney or to a court, he asked how we could protect his family. Braj Dulal had been intimidated and*

was now cautious about further exposing his family to danger. I thanked him and promised to visit him on my next trip to Vrindaban." (Nityananda das, 2012) The photo above is from Mulaprakriti dasi's book *Srila Prabhupada: A Friend To All*. Braj Dulal Goswami is a brave man dedicated to the truth, even at personal risk. He is a significant witness and we pray for his health and safety. The interview notes of Dr. Ghosh of the VRI are included above as well.

DAMODAR SHASTRI TAKES UP THE TREATMENT

Just before midnight on Oct. 28, Damodar Prasad Sharma "Shastri," the Ramanuji Calcutta kaviraja, arrived with Adridharan in Vrindaban. He enthusiastically took up Srila Prabhupada's treatment, confident in success in a full recovery. He finding fresh herbs from local forests and preparing medicines. Shastri needed an ***assistant kaviraja***, herbal ingredients, and glass distillation equipment to prepare his medicines. Srila Prabhupada sent Shastri to Narottama Lal Gupta at his Ayurvedic clinic near Loi Bazaar, to borrow distillation equipment. Dr. NL Gupta told Nityananda in 2004 he went into the forests with Shastri to find herbs for medicines, advising Shastri about Srila Prabhupada's medical history and previous treatments, and that Shastri also consulted with Bon Maharaja and Vishwambhar Goswami of Radha Raman Mandir, both now deceased. Shastri met an unnamed young kaviraja at the Vrindaban Rangaji temple, and employed him as his assistant. On Oct. 29 Bhakticharu and Shastri went to see him. Shastri also went to Delhi for advice from an elderly expert at the Ayurvedic College, and he also went to Bonamali's dispensary. Shastri diligently, enterprisingly *networked* in Vrindaban and Delhi, and he built an informal Ayurvedic team to collaborate in treating Srila Prabhupada. However, Dr. NL Gupta did not favor Bonamali, saying he was not a certified, college-trained physician, and it was clear there were very poor relations between the two families.

PRABHUPADA'S OLD FRIEND NAROTTAMA LAL GUPTA

Narottama Lal Gupta kaviraja first met Srila Prabhupada at Kesi Ghat (in the 1950/60's) when he treated him for malaria. After a long time, Dr. NL Gupta again met Srila Prabhupada around Oct. 6, 1977 after some devotees came to his dispensary saying that Srila Prabhupada had asked to see him. ConvBk Vol35.122, records Srila Prabhupada's desire for Sacidananda das to bring a father and son doctor team near the post office and Loi Bazaar to see him. *Tamal strongly opposed the idea.* This doctor team, who practiced both Ayurvedic and allopathic medicine, *was Narottama Lal Gupta and son Liladhar Gupta.* Srila Prabhupada said this doctor was famous, expert, and had spoken at a temple function. Dr. NL Gupta came and was both happy and surprised to see Srila Prabhupada; he saw his condition was very serious. But Dr. NL Gupta's efforts at treatment were confused and mixed up with those of other kavirajas and doctors, and no one's treatment was effective. New physicians and treatments had become increasing frequent. Dr. NL Gupta was just one in the parade of 1977 doctors. Dr. NL Gupta and son still had their offices near the Loi Bazaar Post Office as of 2004.

THREE KAVIRAJAS DECIDE ON POISONING

After a week or so, when the combined, tireless efforts of Damodara Shastri, Dr. NL Gupta, Bonamali and others met with no results, they shared their frustrations in improving Srila Prabhupada's condition. Shastri learned about Bonamali's poison test and told NL Gupta about it, somewhere outside the ISKCON temple in early Nov. 1977. Dr. NL Gupta told Sakshi Gopal das in 2002 (summarized): *"When it was discovered that the medicines were having no effect, the three kavirajas working on Swamiji met to discuss the problem. After much deliberation all three of us expressed the same opinion that Srila Prabhupada's body had been poisoned. In all possibility the poisoning was chronic and had been administered over a period of many months. Srila Prabhupada was also saying that he had been poisoned. When we coupled his complaint to the unresponsive nature of his illness, we concluded that no matter how many purias (medicines/doses) we prescribed, Swamiji would not respond to the treatments. Unless we prepared a formula to first treat the poison in Swamiji's body, nothing was going to work. So we began searching for the necessary ingredients to combat the poison. But in that time Srila Prabhupada left his body. I still have the formula somewhere, it will take some looking to find it."* The poison antidote prescription was written down on a paper, but Dr. NL Gupta could not find it in his dispensary and its whereabouts are now unknown.

Dr. NL Gupta gave one possibility of the antidote's location: Srila Prabhupada's disciple Gaurimata dasi came to him to ask for some of His Divine Grace's "relics." He obliged her with some old prescriptions and letters, perhaps including the antidote document. Gaurimata passed away in recent years and when Vidya dasi (formerly married to Bhaktisiddhanta das) was contacted, she replied: *"I am sorry but I do not know of these prescriptions and medical papers you are referring to? I was Gauri's main care giver and did take care of all her material possessions after she left but have no memory of these precious artifacts of Srila Prabhupada's. If she had those from before, perhaps she gave them to someone else before she passed."* Some prescriptions are in Vrindaban ISKCON Srila Prabhupada museum's safe or displays.

Copies were obtained from Daivi Shakti dasi by Sadhusangananda in the mid 90's. In 2004 Nityananda saw 3 medical prescriptions written by Shastri in the display showcase of the Vrindaban ISKCON museum.

After his 2002 interview with Dr. NL Gupta, our Australian team member wrote Nityananda: *"Yes, I interviewed Narottama das kaviraja in Vrindaban. His revelations were amazing. He openly disclosed to me many things that confirmed Srila Prabhupada was poisoned. There is no doubt in my mind he would have said the same to Balavanta... hasn't Balavanta [told] what Narottama told him? When I went back later, his son Lila practically threw me out."* The following year in 2003 Sakshi Gopal went again with Jitarati das to speak further with Dr. NL Gupta, but his son Liladhar would not allow it. Liladhar had more or less taken over the clinic although his father still saw a few of his own longtime patients. The son had decided to be "neutral" and would not be pulled into the poisoning controversy. When Nityananda went to see NL Gupta in 2004, his son again prevented his father from saying much.

BALAVANTA AND NALINIKANTA CONFIRMATIONS

In Balavanta's March 2000 report to the GBC: *"I informally interviewed Dr. Narottama Lal (Gupta) who attended Srila Prabhupada in Vrindaban. He informed me that there should be no arsenic (99.9% for certain) in Makharadhwaja. He also stated that in his opinion, Srila Prabhupada had symptoms of liver damage. This, he thought, could lead to kidney damage and could also be responsible for swelling."* (ncbi.nlm.nih.gov/pmc/articles/PMC5596182: Cadmium poisoning causes liver damage.)

Balavanta and Nalinikanta went together to interview Dr. NL Gupta in Vrindaban on Apr. 9, 1999, and their separate testimonies and their written notes to our investigation team (PTC) were obtained for this chapter. All this amounted to much more than what was reported by Balavanta in his brief report to the GBC. Following is a composite report with the complete information: (compiled by Nalinikanta, Nityananda)

"There were three Indian doctors involved in the last treatments of Srila Prabhupada: Dr. NL Gupta, Damodara Shastri, and Bonamali. Srila Prabhupada told each of these kavirajas that he wanted nothing but what they gave him and that Srila Prabhupada would make note of it by writing it down. All three kavirajas became worried because they noted what appeared to be poisoning symptoms. All three were certain Srila Prabhupada was not suffering from advanced diabetes, and they decided the problem was an external cause, which appeared to be poisoning. Tamal was warned that no strong medicines, especially those

that might have arsenic [or mercury] in it, should be given to Srila Prabhupada. This shows they did not believe the poisoning was intentional. NL Gupta thought Srila Prabhupada had a liver disease.

"At first the three kavirajas did not suspect malicious poisoning, but may have later come to think it was intentional, and not the result of inappropriate or too many medicines. Nalinikanta saw an impression of distrust and suspicion from NL Gupta regarding an intentional poisoning, writing on Feb. 7, 2016: "I was there in person (1999). The younger Dr. Liladhar Gupta first received us and Balavanta explained that he was doing an investigation of the poisoning of Srila Prabhupada and wanted Dr. Narottama Lal Gupta's opinion. Dr. Liladhar Gupta first asked 'Are you from the GBC?' Balavanta said no, that this was an independent investigation. So after getting this assurance, then Dr. NL Gupta came downstairs to the room and he told us that yes, he had seen all the symptoms of arsenic poisoning. What I remember is that he was brief, and said yes, he saw all the symptoms of arsenic poisoning and he had said this to the people in Srila Prabhupada's room. That was it. The son did not contradict what his father said, did not say anything much. Then we left and they said if we come again he would meet us again."

We note that at this time Balavanta had already received the hair test results from Dr. Morris showing elevated arsenic.

DR. N L GUPTA INTERVIEW IN 2004 *by Nityananda das*

Dhanvantari Dham
Ayurvedic, Yoga, Naturopath, Dietetic,
Herbal & Spiritual Healing Centre

Dr. LILADHAR GUPTA
Director
B. Sc., PRE AYU., B.A.M.S., N.I.A. (JPR)
Ayurvedic Therapist New Zealand

House of Vaidya Narottam Lal Gupta
502-Purana Bazaza, **Vrindaban** 281121
Distt - Mathura (U.P.) India
Phone : 91.565.442665   Fax : 91.565.442914

In March 2004 I interviewed the elderly Dr. NL Gupta who still attended to walk-in patients most mornings of the week. I took my Hindi friend Yogesh with me to translate. After discussing his relationship with Srila Prabhupada, I asked if he thought Srila Prabhupada had been poisoned, and he suddenly became very nervous and agitated. He said (paraphrased): *"There was no poisoning. In the last month some of Prabhupada's urine was brought, and I tested it. But it showed no poisoning. This is the proof."* I reminded him of what he had told Balavanta and Nalinikanta in 1999, before his son Liladhar had started giving ISKCON Ayurvedic seminars abroad. Then he said: *"Damodara Prasad Shastri and I determined that Srila Prabhupada was poisoned due to too much Western medicine that was not properly prescribed. The overload of toxins became poison."*

Before I could ask if the urine test showed poisoning after all, Dr. NL Gupta walked out. Soon his agitated son Dr. Liladhar Gupta rushed in and took over the interview quite aggressively. I calmed him down with a paid medical consultation on my own health. Then I told Liladhar that Bonamali, as confirmed by Braj Dulal Goswami, had done a urine test in late Oct. 1977 and confirmed an intentional, malicious poisoning which was not from medicines, and he emphasized with great animosity that Bonamali was not a college-trained Ayurvedic physician. He did not know if Shastri had consulted with Bonamali. I mentioned that his father was brought some of Srila Prabhupada's urine to test for poison. Liladhar replied (paraphrased): *"Yes, but that urine test was not capable of checking for poisons; it was to gauge the bodily strength, how much age is left, like a pulse reading. No longevity was left. He had no life remaining. Even if Prabhupada was poisoned, what good will it do to bring it up now? The kidneys and liver were malfunctioning due to an over-exposure to toxins from medicines. He had a long-term, pre-existing kidney ailment that caused swelling of the hands and feet."*

This really sounded like he was coached what to say by ISKCON's foreign seminars sponsors. Why would a urine test show no poison if it was not for testing poison? Father and son had contradicted each other about this urine test. Why had their testimony changed from what they told Balavanta (1999) and Sakshi Gopal (2002)? Were they pressured to deny poisoning? My clear impression was that father and son were not being honest, intimidated by ISKCON (or why the agitation?) The economic stakes in their future ISKCON business tours would be a powerful motive. Liladhar proudly gushed about going to America to teach Ayurveda and that he was going again soon. Surely, to speak truth to me would end his career and commercial prospects in ISKCON, just as had happened to Braj Dulal Goswami. Telling me about New York (where I grew up), it was like he had gone to heaven. Amusing, sad. Still, I got some confirmation of the earlier interviews. **(END)**

SRILA PRABHUPADA TOLD ABOUT THE POISONING

From all of the above, we conclude that, at some point in early Nov., Shastri, Bonamali, Braj Dulal Goswami, Dr. NL Gupta, Liladhar Gupta, and Dr. Gopal Chandra Ghosh, at least six persons, had come to know of Srila Prabhupada's poisoning, either *intentional or accidental*. Surely these six relayed this very newsworthy conclusion to others, and this news circulated amongst the Vrindaban locals outside ISKCON. On Nov. 9 Srila Prabhupada repeats this news himself: *"Someone says that I have been poisoned."* This someone who told him was an unknown outsider. The next day he said *"Someone has poisoned me"* also that someone had told him that he had the symptoms of poisoning. We surmise that *one of these 6 persons, or someone they had told, confidentially informed Srila Prabhupada* that he had been poisoned and he had poisoning symptoms. This news came either directly from one of his kavirajas, or through others they had told. Tamal did not know Srila Prabhupada had been told, evident because Tamal repeatedly asks Srila Prabhupada *who* told him.

POISONED INTENTIONALLY OR ACCIDENTLY?

The question arises whether these six believed Srila Prabhupada was poisoning was intentional or accidental. Some thoughts: **(1)** How could they know either way? **(2)** They did not know which poison or medicines were responsible for this condition. **(3)** It would have been natural to assume poisoning was from too many medicines (although this is not a plausible theory, see Ch. 28). **(4)** If anyone suggested Srila Prabhupada was maliciously poisoned, this could invite trouble from the poisoners and be an uncomfortable position, maybe even dangerous. **(5)** Thus their suspicions about malicious poisoning would be kept discretely --Bhagatji also thought there was some conspiracy taking place. **(6)** Dr. NL Gupta said Tamal was warned not to give any strong medicines, but was Tamal told about their poisoning conclusion? **(7)** They assumed accidental poisoning because they had no proof otherwise. **(8)** When Srila Prabhupada said he was being poisoned (intentionally), Shastri accepted it as true, confirming their suspicions of poisoning.

DP SHARMA "SHASTRI" ACCEPTED POISONING

Kamsahanta das' son Namacharya had long attended the Mayapur gurukula. Dr. Ramesh K. Sharma, the son of Damodara Prasad Sharma ("Shastri," Srila Prabhupada's last kaviraja), used to visit Mayapur and the two became very good friends. In 1994 Dr. R K Sharma confided to Namacharya that his father Damodara Shastri spoke often to him about how Srila Prabhupada had been maliciously poisoned. We note that the poisoning of spiritual teachers in India is quite common, so the stigma of speaking about this privately on the fringes of ISKCON would have been negligible. In May 2002 our Asian team found Damodara Prasad Sharma's son, Dr. Ramesh Kumar Sharma, at their family home, Kalakar St, Calcutta. *When Dr. Ramesh K. Sharma was asked if his father Damodara Prasad Sharma had told him that* Srila Prabhupada was poisoned, he nodded, yes, to the affirmative.

It was confirmed by the son that his father Shastri had passed away in 1996. Unfortunately, Srila Prabhupada's last kaviraja expired prior to the rise of the poison issue. One less eyewitness; we should interview the remaining relevant persons and witnesses before they also pass away. May the full truth of Srila Prabhupada's disappearance also not be lost. As additional information, Damodara Shastri's wife was allegedly not allowed, by strict orders from Jayapataka Swami, to sell children's coloring books at the Mayapur ISKCON gate. Kamsahanta das stated that Damodara Prasad Shastri himself never went back to an ISKCON temple after Srila Prabhupada passed away. He was a good-hearted and faithfully religious man, and the poisoning must have affected him deeply. It is no surprise that he never spoke out in the face of such a powerful organization as ISKCON. What good could it accomplish?

ADRIDHARAN'S PERSONAL OPINION

The GBC's *NTIAP* (p. 48) reprinted Adridharan das' statements in 1999 about his association with the last kaviraja, whom he had brought from Calcutta to treat Srila Prabhupada and with whom he stayed in the same room in Vrindaban for two weeks in 1977. Just after the poison discussions on Nov. 9, 1977, Adridharan says he privately asked Shastri what he thought Srila Prabhupada meant by his statements on poisoning. Shastri supposedly told Adridharan that although he at first thought Srila Prabhupada was talking about a malicious poisoning, later he concluded he *"was actually referring to the effects of poison having been administered via bad medicine."* But this could simply reflect Shastri's fear of repercussions from unknown poisoners.

In the poison discussions, Shastri dismisses Tamal's suggestion of makharadhvaja and there were a total of 10 confirmations from those present that Srila Prabhupada was being homicidally poisoned. No one spoke of bad medicine, but about malicious poisoning and various homicidal criminal poisoning cases in India. Shastri's son clarified his father had often told him Srila Prabhupada was poisoned. This directly contradicts Adridharan's opinion. *"I visited their Kalakar Street clinic in Bagh Bazar, Calcutta in Jan. 1995. His son was not very informative. He stated that upon returning from Vrindaban in 1977 his father said Srila Prabhupada may have been poisoned, but did not go into any detail. At that time Damodara Prasad was at his Village in Rajasthan, on the opposite side of the country, but I failed to visit him."* (Abhinanda das) (Shastri's son may well have been reluctant to speak openly.)

CONCLUSIONS

On Nov. 9-10 Srila Prabhupada and his caretakers engaged in the "poison discussions." It was very clear to everyone Srila Prabhupada was thinking he had been maliciously poisoned. The poisoners worried they would be discovered. The very next day, Nov. 11, the poison whispers occur on the tape recordings: *"the poison's going down," "Is the poison in the milk?" "poisoning for a long time."* Did the poisoners decide to finish their work with a final dose? The answer is obvious.

The poison antidote prescribed by Dr. NL Gupta, probably to cleanse the liver, was never prepared or given, as Srila Prabhupada departed within days. Shastri believed Srila Prabhupada had been poisoned, seen in the poison discussions and in his son's testimony. Another valuable witness is the young kaviraja from the Rangaji temple, who needs to be interviewed. This information was assembled 20+ years after Srila Prabhupada's departure. Dr. Gopal Ghosh, Dr. NL Gupta, and Braj Dulal Goswami, when interviewed separately, provided complementary and compatible accounts. This is a powerful confirmation through witnesses and medical evidence that Srila Prabhupada was poisoned and confirms the forensic hair tests evidence, which is the final conclusive proof.

Four kavirajas: *Shastri, NL Gupta, Braj Dulal Goswami, Bonamali.*

CHAPTER 37:
LIME AND OTHER TESTIMONIALS

WAS LIME ADDED TO SRILA PRABHUPADA'S SAMADHI?

HSUnpub, Nov. 15, 1977: *"Marble which Mahaksha had purchased measuring 5 feet square was placed on the floor of the Samadhi pit. Srila Prabhupada was sitting in the asana position, then his transcendental body was covered with salt... and the pit was filled up with earth."* In 2002 Sakshi Gopal das received information that Tamal had lime mixed with the salt in Srila Prabhupada's samadhi pit. Bhaktisiddhanta das recalled that Tamal had ordered devotees to stamp the salt down on top of Srila Prabhupada's body and head by dancing in the funeral kirtan. Nara Narayan das also posted about Tamal adding lime to the salt during Srila Prabhupada's burial ceremony.

May 2020 we got another confirmation, Bhagwat Maharaja (Joseph Sylvester): *"Tamal arranged the lime **for obvious reasons**; Narayan Maharaja kept insisting it was not needed and was opposed to the lime. I was present and <u>saw the bag of lime with my own eyes</u>. I heard Srila Narayan Maharaja question why lime was needed; you are only to use salt. <u>I saw Tamal in the pit sprinkling lime on Prabhupada</u>. I witnessed this with my own eyes. I don't know how much of the bag he used. ...ask*

Sarvabhavana. He is forthcoming on details like this. I don't remember all who were there because there were 100s at the samadhi pit so I cannot see a clear picture of one person. But I saw who was in the pit. Ananda brahmachari who was Prabhupada's God Brother. Narayan Maharaja, Tamal, Bhakticharu and another brahmachari. Here is the picture. It was after this point that Tamal sprinkled the lime on Srila Prabhupada. I think the bag is behind Tamal in the dark of the picture. Tamal may have sprinkled lime on earlier as well; I cannot fully remember. I only remember seeing one bag with the word LIME written on it. I can see the picture in my mind's eye, it was leaning against the wall near the Samadhi pit. There were 100's of bags of salt that were being lowered into the pit. There was a smaller square hole that was made in the bottom of the pit in which some salt was poured and then Prabhupada was seated on a cushion, the edge of which is the line from Narayan Maharaja's foot in the photo."

"For obvious reasons" would refer to common folklore as found in murder mystery novels and mob-detective stories where lime chemically dissolves a body for a quick and anonymous disposal. In movies and TV shows, the quicklime destroys the body to prevent identification and destroy the evidence.

L to R: Unknown, Bhakticharu, Narayan Maharaja, Ananda, Tamal

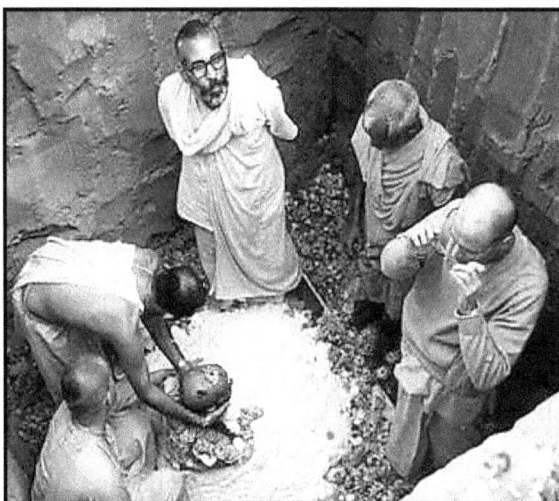

Lime is a mixture of calcium hydroxide and calcium oxide produced from calcining limestone. Typically lime is used to prevent odor from latrines or mass burials at shallow depths. Lime will harden over time as it did in "Roman cement." However, studies done many years after Srila Prabhupada's departure demonstrated that lime actually has the effect of ***preserving a body*** buried in the earth, by preventing putrefaction. It is very alkaline and prevents aerobic decomposition, which is slowed down. At greater depths there is less air and the decomposition delay can be long lasting, especially when, as is the case at Srila Prabhupada's Vrindaban samadhi site, there is very little moisture due to dry climate or overhead construction. Also, due to the marble slab at the bottom of the samadhi pit, leaching would have been limited to whatever water seepage came from above (about none). Just days before Nov. 14, 1977: **SP:** You must put salt around the body. **Narayan M:** I have explained to them everything. (A saint's body is placed in the ground with 12-18 inches of salt packed on all sides; and will be preserved for centuries.)

Sakshi Gopal in 2002 interviewed Dr. Gopal Ghosh, Vrindaban Research Institute, who also verified he saw lime mixed with the salt when Srila Prabhupada was put in samadhi. *Why did Tamal sprinkle lime over Srila Prabhupada? What was his idea, done despite Narayan Maharaja's protests, who explained how to do the ceremony?*

WAS ISKCON'S LAWYER ARORA POISONED?

"Acting on a suggestion from Bhaktisiddhanta das, a Vrindaban resident since 1975, my friend Yogesh went to Mathura in March 2004 to find Mr. Arora, the attorney who handled many of Srila Prabhupada's and ISKCON's early legal matters. Arora is seen several times in the 1976-77 audio recordings in his meetings with Srila Prabhupada, who trusted Mr. Arora and asked him to arrange trust documents for ISKCON properties in India. Yogesh found Arora in a typical lawyer's booth on the street and explained to him that Bhaktisiddhanta das had suggested he come to speak about Srila Prabhupada being poisoned. Very aged and with speech difficult to understand, Arora replied he knew only of his own poisoning which he suspected was done by some ISKCON leaders. As a result he had become speech impaired with paralysis on one side of his face. Whether Arora was actually poisoned or simply had animosity toward some ISKCON leaders, his story is recorded for historical purposes." (Nityananda das)

TRUSTS IMPROPERLY ALTERED?

Mr. V.K. Arora was also interviewed previously in mid-2002 by Sakshi Gopal. Arora described how some time after Srila Prabhupada's departure, he had been threatened with a gun by Gopal Krishna and Jayapataka in an ISKCON office. They wanted modifications to some ISKCON property trust documents, which he was forced to do. This fantastic allegation is not corroborated; obviously Arora has no love for these two ISKCON leaders. Mr. Arora's letter did not mention this since he was a cautious lawyer and wary of ISKCON. He was very proud of his service to Srila Prabhupada and received a letter from him in 1974.Taped conversations show a Mr. Sharma (lawyer) who also assisted with the trust documents for four ISKCON projects: Bombay, Bhubaneshwar, Vrindaban, Mayapur. The idea was to prevent the sale or encumbrance of properties, each secured by three trustees.

TKG's Diary, May 27, 1977: *"Atul Krishna Goswami of the Radha-ramana temple came. He praised Prabhupada. But he asked one question, 'After you, who will take charge of this property?' After he had left, Prabhupada called for Gopala Krishna. Bhavananda and I were also there. Prabhupada said, 'Now I can understand there is a very big undercurrent to take our property. Our position, property, everything is enviable. It requires very strong management to protect. But you are all children. Therefore I have to poke my nose in everything. There is no strong man amongst you. Of you all, Ramesvara is a little intelligent. Now make everything so it is safe.' Thus the G.B.C. held meetings and established a committee with Ramesvara, Jayapataka, Giriraja, Gopala Krishna, Jayatirtha and myself to form trust properties of all India holdings. A trust deed was drafted, based on the BBT document, and read to His Divine Grace. Prabhupada was very satisfied and said, 'Jaya future directors of ISKCON."*

Were the India property trusts altered as said by Srila Prabhupada's lawyer? Mr. Arora also came June 7, 1977 to have an affidavit signed and to register Srila Prabhupada's last will. (TkgD:63-4)

WHAT IS HEARSAY EVIDENCE?

Hearsay evidence is defined as: **(1).** Information received from others that one has not adequately substantiated (yet). **(2).** Evidence based on the reports of others, rather than on personal knowledge.

This volume is a compilation of evidence, some direct and substantiated, some circumstantial, and some hearsay. We may not meet court standards about types of evidence, rather we have compiled all the evidence, potential, credible, verified, including hearsay, aiming to facilitate *further honest investigation* into who poisoned Srila Prabhupada. Some hearsay may be found invalid, and some will prove accurate or lead to further revelations. Anything with potential credibility is included. In deciding what evidence to include, we have sifted through a voluminous amount of material, and selected only that which is credible or useful. We have made clear what is unverified, weaker evidence and what is the main evidence, such as forensics, whispers, poison discussions, interviews, etc. Any investigation will pursue all potential evidence. This volume has collected all the evidence and leads.

NARAYAN MAHARAJA SPEAKS ON SP'S POISONING

According to Bhagwat Maharaja and others who were present at a meeting with Narayan Maharaja (NM) in Alachua, Florida in 2003, NM was asked whether Srila Prabhupada was poisoned, and he answered:

"Your Prabhupada told me, 'I think I am being poisoned.'" However, NM's secretary Madhava Maharaja did not believe that NM would make an official statement to this effect, due to political pressure. Around that same time, Isha das played the "poison tape" for NM, who listened to the Hindi and English statements by Srila Prabhupada. NM then acknowledged that Srila Prabhupada was saying that he was being poisoned. At another time, while visiting Los Angeles, the ISKCON temple sent over a large plate of maha-prasadam to NM as a goodwill gesture, in spite of substantial tensions over his holding major programs close to ISKCON communities. NM declined to take anything from the plate, commenting that they had poisoned Srila Prabhupada and may poison him as well. Some claim that NM was a clever opportunist, and we do not consider these reports of NM to be of major import, but it is part of the record nevertheless. NM passed away in 2012. Another witness is now gone, never formally interviewed. Also, a NM disciple named Tarun Krishna (Tanmoy Chakravarty) was translating the Hindi on Srila Prabhupada's room conversation for Oct. 8, 1977 (or thereabouts) and found Srila Prabhupada speaking about poisoning in Hindi. This still needs to be verified and the exact location pointed out.

DIGPAL REMEMBERS & SOMETHING FISHY'S GOING ON

Digpal das sat in Srila Prabhupada's room in Oct. 1977 when Panchadravida Swami, GBC for Mexico, offered to give his youth to Srila Prabhupada, who graciously declined, encouraging him to use his youth for preaching, but then said, *"Unlike my other disciples, who are trying to poison me."* This is not found on the tapes, and has not been corroborated. Could Panchadravida verify this account? He should be interviewed anyway for whatever all information he may have.

Hasti Gopal das (2000):*" Ayodhyapati returned from India in late Oct. 1977; I saw him speaking to Viswakarma. He had a dark look in his eyes and when I approached, he looked at me and said something like, "We think something fishy's going on with Prabhupada's being sick."*

GOVINDA DASI AND BONAMALI KAVIRAJA

That Bonamali kaviraja was convinced of Srila Prabhupada being maliciously poisoned was confirmed by a note written to Nityananda das after *SHPM* was published (1999). Kusa dasi, ex-wife of Srutakirti (Srila Prabhupada's servant 1972-5) and Honolulu ISKCON temple president in 2002, wrote that her close friend Govinda dasi had visited Bonamali sometime after Srila Prabhupada's departure and was told *"What have they done to Swamiji? It appears Srila Prabhupada has been poisoned."*

It was not until 2015 that Nityananda das was able to clarify this with Govinda dasi and Kusa dasi. Govinda dasi wrote (abbreviated): *"I saw a Bengali doctor in Vrindaban named Banamali Kaviraj. I saw him a number of times in past, and I knew him fairly well, had been to his home and he also did some puja for me once. He was very brahminical, a simple, saintly person... I had left India soon after the big Kumbha Mela [Jan. 1977]. Kusha and I had traveled to the Kumbha Mela with Srila Prabhupada... From there we went to Mayapur, Calcutta, and then I returned to the US. ...when I next went to Vrindaban, perhaps a year or two after his disappearance I went to see Banamali Kaviraja. As I sat in his office, these were his exact words: 'What happened to your Swami Prabhupada? What did they do to him?! He was well when he left here? What did they do to him!?' I don't know why, I just started crying. Then he just shook his head, exasperated, and said, 'Never mind, never mind.' ...I didn't know what he was talking about... But he was upset, and definitely seemed to think that someone had done something to Srila Prabhupada. His mood was one more of outrage. So this is the factual history... Sadly, I was not there, as we were told he was fine and was going to live another ten years."*

Kusa dasi, however, insisted on one detail: *"Govinda dasi, I do remember you saying the doctor said, 'It appears that your Srila Prabhupada has been poisoned.'* Govinda dasi then replied: *'If Kusha remembers my saying this, then it is true. She has the memory of a she-elephant, so if she says I told her this, it is true, even though I can't remember that part. She has a better memory than me.'* Partrikananda also reported in 1998 that a kaviraja asked: *"What happened to your guru? He was in good health."* This confirms Govinda's recollection.

On May 30, 2022 Govinda dasi again confirmed her testimony: *"A [year or so] later, when I was in Vrindaban, I went to the Bengali Ayurvedic Vanamali Kaviraj. He began to say loudly to me, 'What did they do to him?! What did they do? He was well when he left here for the West. What did they do to him?!' [...] I began to cry. He then said, 'Never mind.' He saw I did not know what happened. Now I know."*

GBC PRIVATELY KNOWS WHAT THEY PUBLICLY DENY

Tamoharadasa@yahoo.ca (not the GBC) wrote: *"A Goswami told me that he heard it from a high ranking ISKCON GBC that the GBC is well aware and knows of the poisoning as a FACT. (Sept. 2015)* Interestingly, GBC videos and interviews referencing the poison issue have been deleted from the internet- the GBC is taking precautions because they know they are criminally liable. Another source confirms:

"In 2001, I spoke to an ISKCON guru/ GBC/sannyasi. He confided in me that he thought that it was very likely that there was truth to the assertion that Srila Prabhupada was given poison, by Tamal, and perhaps others. And then he was quick to follow up that statement by stating that he felt certain that they (ISKCON) had gotten it right about the guru issue and initiations system. This combination of statements was shocking for me to hear." (Dhira Govinda das, 2016)

Most ISKCON leaders privately worry the "poison issue" has more merit than they admit in public. The institutional stonewalling, denials, refusal to discuss the evidence shows a leadership afraid of the truth, trying to keep it hidden. Revelation of Srila Prabhupada's poisoning would naturally threaten the entire ISKCON status quo and their positions as gurus, thus their fierce opposition to the "poison theory."

SRILA PRABHUPADA ARRANGED FOR SPECIAL COOKS?

Abhiram's wife Srutirupa dasi explains in a *Prabhupada Memories* video that Srila Prabhupada asked her to cook for him and NO ONE else, with her husband assisting if necessary. She and Abhirama were part of Srila Prabhupada's caretaker team from July 25 to Oct. 16, 1977. Srila Prabhupada also asked his sister Pishima to cook for him, and when she did in Oct. 1977, it was the first full meal Srila Prabhupada ate in months, and he did with great relish. Srila Prabhupada also instructed Kuladri das on Oct. 3, 1977 that no one should cook for him without Srila Prabhupada's permission. From these and other instances, we see Srila Prabhupada's aversion to the prevailing cooking arrangements, meaning he knew he was being poisoned with tainted food at least 5 weeks before he outright said so on Nov. 9. It looks like he did not want to eat or drink from his caretakers. This was not suicidal, but survivalist. Sandamini dasi recalls helping Palika cook for Srila Prabhupada in 1977, and when the remnants came back: *"I said, 'Oh I'll help you transfer the plates.' But she understood my mind and she said, 'Yes, you can do that, but Prabhupada just said that when he's sick like this, that no one should take his remnants.'"* Was Srila Prabhupada concerned that those taking his remnants would also be poisoned? The deniers protest that if Srila Prabhupada was being poisoned in his food, those who took his leftovers would also be poisoned. But, no one was allowed to take his leftovers.

MORE ITEMS OF POSSIBLE RELEVANCE

A 1997 submission to the VADA website, Allegations of Poisoning, reads: *"I spoke with Prabhupada's sister Pishima just after Prabhupada's passing, in which she mentioned that Prabhupada had called her to Mayapur to cook for him some time before because he was concerned that he was being given poison. Prabhupada wanted her personally to supervise all aspects of his food preparation including purchasing bhoga."* This is credible. Of course, once Srila Prabhupada complained about Pishima's cooking as being too rich and it was "killing" him.

Yasodanandana was asked: *"Did Brahmananda tell you in early 70's that Srila Prabhupada said Tirtha Maharaja gave poison to Bhaktisiddhanta?"* His reply Dec. 1, 2020: *"Correct. This occurred in the Calcutta Iskcon temple (Albert Rd) about 7-10 days before 1972 Gaura Purnima. Brahmananda arrived from Bombay about 3 am and said Srila Prabhupada was concerned some of his Godbrothers might try to poison him, just like some of them tried to poison Bhaktisiddhanta. He told all the devotees to go to Mayapur early in the morning and protect Srila Prabhupada. Many of us left for Mayapur early in the morning."*

JAYADWAITA SWAMI ACCEPTS EVIDENCE, THEN DENIES

When the "poison issue" arose in late 1997, Jayadwaita Swami came to Naveen Krishna's home in Alachua to listen to the newly discovered whispers about poisoning on Srila Prabhupada's last tape recording. His office at the *BTG* building was behind Naveen's home. The two were friends. After he listened with headphones, Jayadwaita admitted: *"Yes, I can hear clearly, 'The poison's going down' and 'The poison's in the milk.'"* They reviewed the conversations where Srila Prabhupada spoke about being poisoned and how all his attendants acknowledged this without question. Yet, two years later, Jayadwaita Swami wrote: *"I've... listened to the enhanced audio-tapes... I've had the Hindi explained to me... by a native Hindi speaker. I've listened patiently to the arguments mapped out for me by close friends who believe it's all true... I dislike feeling obliged to respond to garbage... the scuttlebutt that Srila Prabhupada... was poisoned... nothing they've shown or told me has even begun to persuade me..."* Naveen met Jayadwaita later, asking how he could acknowledge the 1977 whispers and "poison discussions" at his home and then later say there was no persuasive evidence.

The reply: *"Oh, that was just one thing, not the whole picture."* Naveen thought, *"Who would stoop so low as to lie about such a thing as evidence in Srila Prabhupada's poisoning?"* Jayadwaita did not explain how the aural evidence was discredited to his mind. This was a major dishonesty, but (as many say) normal for him. Many complaints have been lodged against Jayadwaita for two-faced dishonesty, otherwise known as lying. This is also true about his replies to challenges over his book-changing. Gupta das, an attorney who has defended both sides in ISKCON-related cases, which included involvements by Jayadwaita Swami, said, *"Jayadwaita Swami is, in my opinion, among the top three most untrustworthy ISKCON leaders. "*

RELEVANT TO POISONING INVESTIGATION

WITNESSES AND INVESTIGATORS: **(1) Naveen Khurana** (Naveen Krishna das): US citizen, resigned from GBC, most knowledgeable about poison evidence and suspects. **(2) William Ogle** (Balavanta das): US Attorney, former GBC Chairman. Will voluntarily depose. Appointed by GBC in 1997 to investigate the poisoning allegations but his work was subverted by lack of funding, then sidelined and axed. **(3) Dr. J. Steven Morris**, Ph.D.: MURR of Univ of Missouri; did the NAA hair tests, finding the sky-high levels of cadmium poisoning. **(4) Nico Kuyt** (Nityananda das): In exile, private investigator in Srila Prabhupada's poisoning, compiled and researched the evidence, arranged Dr. Morris tests and audio lab tests. **(5) John Hanton** (Jitarati das): Very involved in investigative efforts, knows the suspects well.

WITNESSES IN VRINDABAN, INDIA: **(1) Dr. Sri Pran Gopal Acharya:** Vrindaban, prominent *purohita* priest. Interviewed by Mulaprakriti in her book, 1999. Father: Balaram Misra, to whom Srila Prabhupada first revealed the poisoning Nov. 9, '77. He came with his father at that time, knows what his father or others said about the poisoning. As a young man he knew Srila Prabhupada. **(2) Dr Gopal Chandra Ghosh (Gose):** Interviewed by Sakshi Gopal 2002, and Nityananda 2004. He confirmed the urine test by Bonamali who declared it was poison. Maybe he has sons who know more. **(3) Dr Braj Dulal Goswami**, Ayurvedic physician, son of Bonamali (Srila Prabhupada's kaviraja during much of 1977). Privately interviewed in 2002, again by phone in 2010, testified on Star TV 2005 that he witnessed his father's test of Srila Prabhupada's urine which determined poisoning. He is wary of ISKCON leaders, and has been threatened. He confirms his father believed Srila Prabhupada was maliciously poisoned. Did his father discuss Srila Prabhupada's condition in 1977 with Damodara Shastri? What Ayurvedic compound did his father add to the urine in the test?

(4) Narottama Lal Gupta, one of Srila Prabhupada's 1977 Vrindaban kavirajas, likely deceased. His son Liladhar continues the family practice, was financially entangled with ISKCON- the father told Balavanta das in 1999 that Srila Prabhupada was maliciously poisoned. Sakshi Gopal interviewed NL Gupta in 2002; four kavirajas concluded Srila Prabhupada had been poisoned. **(5) Bhaktisiddhanta Das:** lives near ISKCON Vrindaban Mandir since 1975, so he knows much. **(6) Shyama Ma:** This sadhu lady had ill-will towards Srila Prabhupada in 1977; should investigate, maybe deceased, check at her Vrindaban ashram (Volume 3). **(7) Bhagatji:** (Sri Vishwambhar Dayal) Surely he has passed away but what of children/family? He thought there was a conspiracy in 1977. His home was just around the corner from ISKCON. **(8) Sarvabhavana Das:** He said Bhakticharu Swami (his college friend) told him in 1977 that Srila Prabhupada said he had been poisoned. **(9) Dr. K. Gopal:** Mathura Ramakrishna Hospital; Srila Prabhupada's last allopathic doctor, he treated SP for a week and remembered the case very well in 2004. **(10) Dr. Rakesh Kumar Sharma:** (Calcutta) Son of Damodara Shastri, who was the last kaviraja; he confirmed his deceased father believed Srila Prabhupada was poisoned.

CONCLUSION

These testimonies, hearsay, memories, etc that indicate that Srila Prabhupada was poisoned might be dismissed as rumors if not for the cadmium hair tests that scientifically PROVE Srila Prabhupada was homicidally poisoned. They are part of the evidential record. There is much more evidence "out there." For those implicated in Srila Prabhupada's poisoning: your days in hiding are numbered, the truth will come out, and you will receive your dues either in this life or the next. Confession now would greatly relieve your karma and bring consideration of leniency. Otherwise be punished anyway, without leniency. You will be found out soon, definitely at the time of death.

From Mahabharata, Kashyapa Muni said: *"If one knows the truth but does not disclose it upon being questioned, or, if out of anger, fear, or some other motive, one gives a false reply, then he is bound up by 1,000 nooses of Varuna... If someone commits a sinful act in an assembly, then it is the duty of all those who are present to chastise the wrong doer. If they fail to do so, then the perpetrator of the sin receives one-fourth of the reaction, the leader of the assembly has to accept one-half, and all others present suffer one-fourth. A witness is one who has seen, heard of, or otherwise understood a thing, and he should always tell the truth, for in that way his pious merit will never suffer diminution."*

CHAPTER 38:
THE PRIMARY SUSPECTS

Srila Prabhupada's poisoning has been proven by the hair tests. The official GBC resolution, *"There is no evidence at this time to support the allegations of poisoning of Srila Prabhupada,"* makes a mockery of

ISKCON leadership. Srila Prabhupada's statements on being poisoned, the certified whispers by caretakers poisoning Srila Prabhupada, and astronomical levels of cadmium in three hair samples are irrefutable proof positive Srila Prabhupada was maliciously, homicidally poisoned. **Now we ask who did it?** There are some obvious suspects based on the abundant circumstantial evidence. The arrogant denial by all of the suspects while they defend each other in whitewash cover-ups and in the face of so much evidence, saying there is "no evidence," *is in itself a flashing red neon light which says, "We did it!"*

THE CARETAKERS ARE THE PRIMARY SUSPECTS

It is common sense to look closely at Srila Prabhupada's caretaker disciples who had direct access to him during his relentlessly debilitating "illness" of 1977. It is also common sense to look closely at those who would have gained materially from Srila Prabhupada's untimely or premature departure. As history shows, poisoners are usually a trusted confidant or close associate with direct access to the victim. They would be clever, good actors, intelligent and manipulative, patient, know the inner workings of Srila Prabhupada's life, habits, health, and medical situation. They had an overwhelming motive to remove Srila Prabhupada from the scene, and what they stood to gain was to them worth the risks and karma of such an abominable deed. And the caretakers and their allies did actually rise to the posts of all-powerful zonal acharyas and good-as-God gurus with thousands of surrendered, loving disciples.

The caretakers (Tamal, Bhakticharu, Bhavananda) all clearly acknowledged Srila Prabhupada spoke about a homicidal, malicious poisoning, yet they told no one, did nothing, and never mentioned it again. Then 20 years later when the whispers and poison discussions became public, they denied it had any meaning, saying Srila Prabhupada's words cannot be taken seriously. The GBC, led by Tamal, Bhakticharu, Jayapataka, and their cohorts amongst the elite GBC orchestrated a series of denials and obstructive cover-ups from 1997 onwards. An impartial ISKCON investigation has never been completed, but was done by Prabhupada Truth Commission (PTC). To question the involvement by these primary suspects in Srila Prabhupada's poisoning is not blasphemous nor improper, provided one carefully sticks to the facts, investigative protocols, and avoids baseless accusations or speculations. This volume has thus stuck to the facts and evidence.

Being the speakers of the forensically verified poison whispers, making conflicting statements between 1977 and since 1997, not acting on Srila Prabhupada's complaints of being poisoned, having immensely benefited from Srila Prabhupada's early departure and unnatural health decline, with overwhelming motive, easy opportunity, and the means, having questionable associations, character, and personal histories… all this makes certain persons highly suspected of Srila Prabhupada's poisoning. (See Volume 2, 3 for full study of this subject.)

TAMAL: THE PRIME SUSPECT

Tamal was involved in Srila Prabhupada's poisoning beyond a reasonable doubt, by virtue of the facts and evidence, fully explored in *Volume 2: Srila Prabhupada: The Life and Deeds of His Personal Secretary Tamal*. Tamal passed away in 2002 after a very checkered and controversial 34 years in ISKCON. Briefly, why he is the prime suspect:

(1) Tamal was in control of Srila Prabhupada's medicines and health care, assisted by Bhakticharu Swami and Bhavananda. **(2)** Days after Srila Prabhupada's departure, Tamal was interviewed (Ch. 40) for *BTG* magazine. He made bizarre statements that Srila Prabhupada had repeatedly asked his closest disciples to give him "medicine to die now," clearly implying an assisted suicide. He said *"We could have done that"* –as it was Srila Prabhupada's dying request. **(3)** Under his watch and surely by his design, about 200 tapes went missing with critical instructions by Srila Prabhupada on the future of the movement. **(4)** He was extremely ambitious to be the next sole Acharya, had a love-hate relationship with Srila Prabhupada, and suppressed Srila Prabhupada's instructions. **(5)** His 1980 confession that Srila Prabhupada never appointed gurus, and then his pretense of never confessing, and many other contradictory acts and statements 1977 to 2002, show he was not honest, truthful, or of a character by which he could be trusted. **(6)** He caused endless, untold destruction, chaos, and pain for the movement.

OTHER PERSONS OF INTEREST

There are a number of other high interest persons regarding Srila Prabhupada's poisoning that are fully explored in terms of facts and evidence in *Volume 3: Pursuit of Srila Prabhupada's Poisoners.*

(1) Bhakticharu Swami (died 2020) is highly suspected in the poisoning. He: **(a)** Made many contradictory statements, not being truthful, obviously hiding the truth. **(b)** Was instrumental in ISKCON cover-ups of the poison issue. **(c)** Was Tamal's 1977 close assistant and protégé. **(d)** Was clearly materially ambitious, after money and fame.

(2) Jayapataka Swami, the most powerful ISKCON guru with over 50k disciples, is suspected in Srila Prabhupada's poisoning: **(1)** He is the speaker of one poison whisper. **(2)** He has supported deceptive ISKCON cover-ups of the poisoning evidence. **(3)** See Volume 3.

(3) Bhavananda is highly suspected in Srila Prabhupada's poisoning because he: **(a)** Has a history of uncontrolled self-aggrandizement and low character. **(b)** Is heard in two of the poison whispers. **(c)** Was Tamal's closest friend. **(d)** See Volume 3. Bhavananda remains as a powerful manager in the huge Mayapur project even after all his history.

Others should be interviewed as well, to cross check various testimonies and dig deeper into the truth of the events, as to who is hiding something, who has supported the cover-ups and why, etc. Unfortunately, none of them are cooperative. Astonishingly they claim it has already been investigated via their own denials of deception and lies (Part 6). Satsvarupa is a person of interest, as he was close to Tamal, hid Srila Prabhupada's instructions, did Tamal's mercy-killing interview, and knows much more than he has divulged, which is nothing.

"NOW YOU HAVE TO CHOOSE WHICH SUICIDE"

On the day of the poison whispers, Nov. 10, 1977: **Jagadish:** Srila Prabhupada, can you tell us why you want to go on the parikrama? *(Parikrama is a walking tour of the sacred places)* **Tamal:** This seems like suicide, Srila Prabhupada, this program. It seems to some of us like it's suicide. **SP: And this is also suicidal. Tamal:** *(turning to others)* Hmm. Prabhupada said "And this is also suicide." *(turning back to Prabhupada)* **Now you have to choose which suicide. SP: The Ravana will kill** and Rama will kill. Better to be killed by Rama, eh? That Marica- if he does not go to mislead Sita, he'll be killed by Ravana. And if he goes to be killed by Rama, then it is better. **Tamal:** Who is this Prabhupada's talking about? **Devotees:** Marica.

What an astonishing statement from Tamal, spoken very cooly, calmly, and if one listens to the tape, a clear undertone of sarcasm! Many believe Srila Prabhupada marked Tamal as ISKCON's Ravana.

SERIES OF AUDIO EVENTS IN LAST WEEKS BY SUSPECTS

(1) Oct. 22, 1977: **SP:** ...Don't move me to the hospital. *Better kill me here.* [...] But if you are disgusted, that is another thing. **(2)** Nov. 3, 1977: **SP:** That is my only request, that *at the last stage don't torture me and put to death*. **(3)** Nov. 9: Srila Prabhupada said someone told him he was being poisoned. The caretakers discuss Srila Prabhupada's being poisoned and acknowledge a homicidal, malicious poisoning. (Part 2) Tamal asks who did it, but no answer. Also Tamal says: *"He's trying to trap us...He's as sly as they come."* **(4)** Nov. 10: SP again states that someone has poisoned him. **(5)** Nov. 11: Four forensically certified whispers. *"The poison's going down..."* *"Is the poison in the milk?"* *"Poisoning for a long time... get ready to go."* *"It's poison."* The speakers of three whispers have been ascertained to be Tamal, Bhavananda, and Jayapataka. And discussing parikrama: *"Now you have to choose which suicide"* And *"The Ravana will kill and Rama will kill."*

VOLUMES 2 AND 3 DEVOTED TO THE SUSPECTS

Because the ISKCON leaders so vociferously pretend that Srila Prabhupada's poisoning evidence is based on a blasphemous theory that it was done by his loving caretakers, this volume has largely avoided focus on WHO POISONED Srila Prabhupada. That subject is fully developed in Volumes 2 (Tamal) and 3 (other suspects). We have included herein the suspects' whispers and other aural evidence. But certified voice stress analysis tests of Tamal, Bhakticharu, Bhavananda, Jayapataka, as well as their histories, lies, contradictory statements, etc.

CHAPTER 39:
POISONING IN HISTORY

(1) *"Visat: 'from poison.' [...] Dhritarastra and his sons, they conspired to give them poison."* (SPLect Oct. 4, 1974) **(2)** *"Politicians, popes and parents were all victims at different times. Indeed white arsenic became known as 'inheritance powder.'"* (Hendrik Ball)

Poisoning has a long history with widespread prevalence, and by reviewing it, we can better appreciate that even within a spiritual movement poisoning often occurs. Whenever significant material assets are at stake, we can expect poisoning, murder, politics, or nasty affairs. This is the material world- competition, ambition, desire, and conspiracy. The intrigue of poisonings goes back to the earliest of recorded history. In the case of Napoleon, for example, historians have researched whether he was killed by arsenic and cyanide, and whether Empress Josephine and Napoleon's son, the Duke of Reichstadt, were also killed by arsenic poisoning. In the modern geopolitical sphere, we see many poisonings to remove rivals and eliminate enemies, more common than most know.

Toxicology dates to earliest man, who used animal venoms and plant extracts for hunting, waging war, and assassinations. The Ebers papyrus (c. 1500 BC) details many recognized poisons: hemlock aconit); opium; and metals like lead, copper, and antimony. Plants with substances akin to digitalis and belladonna were known. Hippocrates documented (400 BC) many poisons and clinical toxicology principles. Ancient Greek literature refers to use of poisons. Alexander the Great may have been poisoned. Cleopatra (69-30 BC) committed suicide by a poisonous snake. The Romans used poisons in politics. King Mithridates VI did many acute toxicity experiments on criminals and discovered *"an antidote for every venomous reptile and every poisonous substance."* He regularly ingested a mixture of 36 ingredients as an antidote. Poisonings in Rome took on epidemic proportions in the 4th century BC when a conspiracy of women killed men for inheritances. Widespread poisoning resulted in *Lex Cornelia* (82 BC), the first law against poisoning. The early Renaissance Italians, with characteristic pragmatism, took the poisoning art to its peak in the political scene. Victims were named, prices set, contracts recorded, payment made when the deed was done. A club of young, wealthy, married women became a club of eligible wealthy widows. Of the prominent families engaged in poisoning, the Borgias were most notorious. The deft applications of poisons to men of stature in the Church swelled the holdings of the Papacy.

Catherine de Medici took her skills from Italy to France, targeting husbands. She tested toxins on sick and poor. This was commercialized by Catherine Deshayes (*La Voisine*). Hired to poison Louis XIV, she failed and her business ended by her execution. She was convicted of many poisonings, including over two thousand infants. She was severely tortured and burned at the stake. The poisoning tradition spread through Europe, playing a major role in the distribution of political power in the Middle Ages. The study of the toxicity and the dose-response relationship for therapeutic agents was started by Paracelsus (1493-1541). Orfila, a French court physician, was the first toxicologist to use autopsy material and chemical analysis systematically as legal proof of poisonings, becoming the underpinning of forensic toxicology.

Arsenic was the preferred homicidal agent during the Middle Ages. A clinical description of acute arsenic poisoning in the novel *Madame Bovary* impressed readers with prolonged death throes. Arsenic featured in Kesselring's **Arsenic and Old Lace**, where strychnine and cyanide was also used to dispatch victims. Arsenic had widespread use in 18th/19th centuries' medicine as a tonic or "alterative." The prevailing professional opinion was: *"Arsenic is **a safe medicine**; none of the respondents having found it permanently detrimental..."* The heyday of arsenical chemotherapeutics occurred in the early 20th century, when Ehrlich discovered arsphenamine for treating venereal disease; replaced after WW2 by antibiotics. *For those who doubt that heavy metals and exotic poisons are much used in poisoning in modern day times, it may be useful to note the following case histories. This will dispense the idea poisoning is an antiquity. Unfortunately, poisoning is still very popular.*

ARSENIC AS POISON

The success of a criminal poisoning depends on imitating the effects of a natural disease. In 19th century Britain, arsenic was the poisoner's substance of choice. From 1750-1914 it featured in 237 cases before the English courts, but most got away with their crime. Arsenic was particularly popular with impatient heirs, keen to get their fortunes. Arsenic trioxide, known as white arsenic, was a harmless looking powder, resembling flour or sugar, and virtually undetectable in hot food and drink, fatal in small doses. From a 1855 London newspaper: *"If you feel a deadly sensation within and grow gradually weaker, how do you know you are not poisoned? If your hands tingle, is it arsenic? Your friends and relations all smile kindly upon you; how can you tell there is not arsenic in the curry?"* Of course you couldn't. Diagnosing arsenic poisoning was difficult. Doctors had only the patient's symptoms to go on, and clinical signs of arsenic (vomiting and diarrhea) were mistaken for food poisoning, dysentery and cholera. In 1862 toxicologist Alfred Taylor, giving evidence in a London murder trial, said he knew 8 deaths first recorded as due to cholera. When suspicions were raised later, and the body exhumed, the true cause was found to be arsenic.

If the poison was administered in small doses over time, the chances of being caught were very slim. Cyanide and strychnine work according to a strict timetable, dispatching victims predictably. Arsenic, by contrast, is mysterious, behaving like an infectious disease, so that the nature and length of the victim's suffering depends on their genetics and health. Miserable death from acute arsenic poisoning can take 2 hours to four days, even a fortnight. In 1851 Britain passed *The Sale of Arsenic Regulation Act* after many complaints from doctors, the press, and public. Buyers had to sign a "poison book." Gradually arsenic was harder to obtain, but its nasty and deadly career continued anyway.

When Srila Prabhupada said he had been poisoned in Nov. 1977, one of the discussion topics was the poisoning of a Sankaracharya guru with powdered glass, who suffered horribly for six months. Thereafter none of these gurus would eat unless cooked by their own men. Historically, poisoning in India was very common. Kings trained beautiful women as assassins by feeding them small doses of poison from childhood in ever increasing amounts, sending them to seduce their enemies with the "kiss of death." Srila Prabhupada told of his Godbrother Ananta Vasudeva who committed suicide with poison after his wife was found with a lover by his young son, whom the mother poisoned. Srila Prabhupada's guru was wary of doctors, injections, concerned of being poisoned. Bhaktisiddhanta was also poisoned in late

1936, confirmed by Srila Bhaktisiddhanta's brother Lalita Prasad *(from Yasodanandana das)*.

MURDEROUS DISCIPLES ARE A COMMON PHENOMENON

An Apr. 30, 2001 article "Gunmen of the Gods" quoted Divyanandji Maharaja: *"There have been many incidents in the past when a disciple has killed a head priest for ownership of the property attached to the religious places. There are miscreants who want to grab the land either by dethroning the head priest or implicating him in false cases or even eliminating him physically."* Maharaja never moved about without his armed "commandos." *"Most of us have firearms for our own personal security and to fight unscrupulous operators who are disguised as sadhus."* Mahant Anoop Das of Khaki Akhara always has 2 disciples and firearms with him, as the 13 acres attached to the temple makes him a target. In 1977 ISKCON had assets 1000s of times more valuable. The temptation for material gain in ISKCON was very attractive to disciples with selfish dispositions. No one should be naïve; to achieve a status "as good as God" is certainly motive enough to murder one's guru to sit in his seat. Kill guru, become guru. *"Poison claimed the lives of many acharyas and temple priests in India. By my count, the same year Srila Prabhupada passed away, no less than five other "acharyas" in the Mathura-Vrindaban district also passed away, and poison was suspect in every case. Guru poisoning is the same old story."*

The assassination of Swami Dayananda Saraswati in 1883 was the work of a dancing girl named Nanhi Jaan in the palace of Maharaja of Jodhpur Jaswant Singh II. Dayananda was a guest and asked the Maharaja to forsake the dancing girl, who became offended and bribed the cook to add ground glass in his milk. It took a month of agonizing pain and bleeding. The religious leader and founder of Arya Samaj passed away only after forgiving the cook who confessed, giving him money to escape the wrath of the hosting Maharaja.

NAPOLEON: POISONING SUSPECTED

In *Assassination at St. Helena* by Forshufvud and Weider, a theory of how Napoleon was slowly weakened by arsenic and then finished off with mercury cyanide is laid out in detail. We do not know if Napoleon was **intentionally** poisoned, which is irrelevant to Srila Prabhupada's case. New evidence after *SHPM* was published indicate: **(1)** Napoleon's serious poisoning may have been accidental or environmental, as arsenic was pervasive at that time without people being aware of its dangers (something not applicable in Srila Prabhupada's instance). **(2)** Napoleon sustained very high levels of arsenic intoxication for many years, revealed in many hair tests, while the final cause of death is uncertain.

Below we compare Napoleon's and Srila Prabhupada's physical symptoms, finding a striking similarity. Srila Prabhupada's symptoms are fully compatible with heavy metal poisoning; arsenic and cadmium poisoning symptoms are very similar. Srila Prabhupada had sky-high 250 times normal cadmium levels in three hair tests, so he *did* have heavy metal poisoning, just as did Napoleon. The parallels between the two poisonings are many. Both involved **(1)** suspicious symptoms, **(2)** a mysterious illness that baffled the doctors, **(3)** exhumation was not an option, **(4)** advanced hair tests, **(5)** a struggle to convince historians and vested interests as to the facts, and **(6)** study of historical records to identify poisoning suspects. Study of Napoleon's poisoning, suggested by Hansadutta das in 1998, gave insights how to do the investigation.

Weider and Forshufvud investigated the cause of Napoleon's death and in 1961-2 they tested samples of hair by NAA, finding high arsenic levels. In the decades to follow, many relics of Napoleon's hair were tested; all had very abnormally high arsenic levels, up to 51 ppm, a lethal amount depending on how long it lasted. In 1972 Forshufvud published *Who Poisoned Napoleon*, and *Assassination at St. Helena* in 1978 (updated, 1995). In 1999, Weider released *The Poisoning of Napoleon*. Historians, forensic scientists, politicians and the public have debated the evidence Napoleon was intentionally chronically poisoned with arsenic and finished off with mercury. Although everyone agreed with hair tests showing extremely high arsenic, some doubted the poisoning was intentional. In 1995 the FBI tested some of Napoleon's hair and said, *"the arsenic levels are consistent with poisoning."* The Praxis Post and the Nando Times in June of 2001 reported that five samples of Napoleon's hair were tested by Forensic Institute of Strasbourg. The director, Bertrand Ludes, said the tests showed from 7-38 ppm, confirming *"chronic long-term poisoning by arsenic."*

The experts say *"one nanogram per milligram (1 ppm) is at the high end of an acceptable level of arsenic."* Also, Ludes *"and Dr. Pascal Kintz, an institute toxicologist, said they analyzed, and dismissed, the possibility that the arsenic contamination came from other sources - as detractors of the murder theory claim – such as seafood. Both men have served as expert witnesses at trials."* The French Senate met to listen to Ben Weider's revelations: *"Both the FBI and Scotland Yard, confronted with the results of these tests, have said that if they came across similar results in the case of a recent victim, they would have no hesitation at all in **opening a murder inquiry.**"* A conference in France was held with a dozen eminent toxicologists, coroners, cancer specialists, and police forensic scientists on hand. Over 500 newspapers and magazines worldwide covered the story that Napoleon had been poisoned with arsenic and mercury. History books were amended.

Yet the GBC denies **both** Napoleon's and Srila Prabhupada's poisoning. Regardless of Napoleon's case, the GBC should recognize that the very substantial proof of Srila Prabhupada's malicious cadmium poisoning demands their support of an investigation rather than the denials and obstruction they have given instead. The significance of Napoleon's poisoning in relation to Srila Prabhupada's case is found in the similarities of chronic heavy metal poisoning symptoms as well as confirmation of the validity of hair testing science. That Napoleon was chronically poisoned with arsenic has now become widely accepted by scientists and historians alike. The GBC's mockery of the Napoleon poisoning "theory" simply embarrasses them. They missed the point. *Whether Napoleon was intentionally poisoned or not, does not change the fact that he had poison in his body at levels that are usually lethal.* These facts are indisputable. Napoleon's and Srila Prabhupada's symptoms were strikingly similar, due to heavy metal poisoning. Hair tests for both showed very elevated levels of arsenic or cadmium. However, Part 1 establishes Srila Prabhupada's poisoning as intentional.

SIMILAR SYMPTOMS IN NAPOLEON, SRILA PRABHUPADA

Napoleon's hair had arsenic spikes from 40+ doses over 6 months. Weider lists Napoleon's chronic arsenic poisoning symptoms as follows, many of which were *especially prominent* in Srila Prabhupada: (1) Restlessness. (2) General severe fatigue and exhaustion. (3) Noticeable change in disposition changing from depression to extreme optimism. (4) Disturbance in sleep rhythm (somnolence alternating with insomnia). (5) Pain mostly in lower legs & the region of the liver. (6) Feet, lower legs become swollen. (7) Calf muscles become very weak, walking difficult. (8) Swollen liver. (9) Skin turns bronze (jaundiced, yellow complexion). (10) Entire body may itch anywhere, everywhere. (11) Head hair grows very thin. (12) Lack of appetite, indigestion, stomach pains. (13) Impairment of hearing, deafness. (14) Impaired vision, dark rings under eyes. (15) Sensitivity of eyes to light, prefers a darkened room. (16) Tendency to periods of emotionalism, tearfulness. (17) Difficulty in urination, slow or painful, scanty. (18) Persistent dry cough. (19) Icy cold legs. (20) Severe hoarseness of voice. (21) Tachycardia or quickened pulse. (22) Irregular or very slow pulse. (23) Constipation alternated with diarrhea. (24) Conjunctivitis: cold in the eyes.

All these are very prominently seen in the health history (App. 8) and is a complete description of heavy metal poisoning symptoms.

COMPARISONS: NAPOLEON (N), PRABHUPADA (SP) CASES

(1) N's hair arsenic was 1-51 ppm; SP's 2.6 ppm arsenic is in that range. **(2)** N's walks became fewer, shorter, then ceased, as did his carriage rides, similar to SP's walks and car rides. **(3)** N's extremities swelling came and went in time with individual poisonings. SP's swelling also came and went, tied to poisonings *(see photo on back cover)*. **(4)** N's doctor noted lung damage, suspecting tuberculosis; SP's doctor suspected asthma. **(6)** In both, subacute symptoms lasted up to a week. **(5)** Dec. 3, 1816, N's skin had become yellow, suggesting an affected liver. Bhavananda suggested the same with SP on May 25, 1977, days after the severe Hrishikesh health attack. **(6)** On Dec. 14, 1816, N's severe illness caused muscular spasms and a brief fainting. The same with SP, Sept. 8, 1977. **(7)** N's poisoning description is remarkably similar to SP's. **(8)** No one tried to attribute N's symptoms to diabetes, whereas ISKCON does so with SP who had many "mystery" symptoms NOT typical to diabetes but compatible with heavy metals poisoning.

These comparisons clearly illustrate the striking similarities between Napoleon and Srila Prabhupada's health symptoms.

BLANCHE TAYLOR MOORE

Blanche Taylor Moore was sentenced to death in 1990 for the capital murder of her boyfriend by acute arsenic poisoning. She was also charged with, but never tried for, the murder of her first husband in 1973, and for the attempted murder of her second husband in 1989. She is also suspected in the deaths of her father, mother-in-law, and several others, all of whom are thought to have been fed food laced with arsenic ant poison. She denied everything and she was still in prison in 2022. Her life story is in *Preacher's Girl: The Life and Crimes of Blanche Taylor Moore* by Jim Schutze. He detailed the symptoms of arsenic poisoning.

Actually, 45 *known* murders have been attributed to arsenic poisoning in the last 50 years in North Carolina alone. Schutze highlighted how difficult it is to detect arsenic poisoning and how easy it is to get away with it. Blanche was well-liked, charming, church-going, and a grandmother with no criminal record. She raised two daughters diligently and successfully. She apparently loved all three men in her life. She worked hard and no one believed these evil deeds were her actions. She was convicted by *overwhelming circumstantial evidence* and her adamant lies which contradicted numerous witness testimonies. No one saw her poison anyone, although the 2% arsenic ant killer, a sweet syrup readily mixable in food, was found in her home. After 21 years of marriage, Blanche is believed to have poisoned her husband over several months until she gave him a massive and final, lethal dose.

"...the arsenic boiled off the inner lining of his stomach and bowels. He sat up straight in bed, and a jet of vomit shot out of his mouth and splattered against the far wall. His bowels exploded in a volley of thin rice-water stools. He fell back flat on the bed, fully awake, eyes wide open, convulsing and totally unable to control himself. But even as the toxin destroyed his muscles and nervous system, it already was sprinting even deeper into the physical and chemical structure that was his life. Moments later his abdomen bulged and then drooped, horribly distending as the external tissues of the walled organs and the blood vessels turned to mush and all of his fluids leached into his body cavity. He was conscious for at least the first hour of his death process. He cried out, moaned, and screamed in agony. There were waves and explosions of pain as the basic synaptic chemistry of his nervous system fell apart. His body was flung about both by the pain and the chaotic electrical storms in his nerves and muscles. Then finally, as the oxygen-bearing cells in the blood collapsed, he suffocated from within. His face turned purple. His body went flaccid as cells stopped converting sugar into energy. In brain suffocation, he escaped into a universe of hallucinations. The ferocious grimace on his dead face told that his body experienced wild pain to the very last. 'It must have been a heart attack,' Dot whispered. But rather, he'd been eaten alive, minutely and gradually, cell by cell, by arsenic. Its secret is that it loves life, races to life, embraces it, combines with it quickly and consumes it hungrily, converting it chemically from life into death. He had been extremely sick with flu-like symptoms of sore throat, diarrhea for two weeks..."

The descriptions of the acute poisoning symptoms below have many similarities to Srila Prabhupada's severe health attacks (App. 8).

Blanche Taylor Moore already had an intimate friendship with Raymond Reid for a dozen years or more before she killed James Taylor. She filed a multi-million dollar sexual harassment suit against her long-time employer Kroger Food Stores, and Raymond, an assistant manager, was caught in the middle. Apparently Blanche then decided to eliminate Raymond and began to feed him arsenic in her good home cooking. Raymond went to the local hospital several times but he was sent home each time, thinking it was stomach flu. The hospital did more tests and specialists came and went. He had nausea, vomiting, diarrhea, extreme weakness, swelling, anemia, heart irregularities, and failing kidneys.

His kidneys stopped producing urine and he began coughing up large quantities of mucus. His intestinal tract was not working and *he* had a _weak, raspy voice_. He required a _painful circumcision_ due to persistent inflammation and infection of the genital. Similarly Srila Prabhupada's surgery in London was a case of phimosis/ scarred tissue complicated by urethral inflammation and circumcision. All Raymond's symptoms perfectly match those exhibited by Srila Prabhupada. _His urine was blocked by inflammation in the urethra._ He grew worse, thick-tongued and restless. Blanche visited him in the hospital, bringing food whenever he could eat. Raymond received one last fatal dose of arsenic in his favorite foods Blanche made so well: banana pudding and peanut butter milk shakes. Arsenic in milk delays the effects a few hours, so suspicion of the food was never aroused. He changed his will to give one third of his assets to his beloved Blanche who came to care for him every day. He died horribly, with gargantuan swelling and open skin lesions everywhere. He leaked like a sieve, his body bursting from swelling and retained fluids.

Raymond's urine test detected 6.5 times normal arsenic, levels that can only come about by oral ingestion, but the report was unnoticed for years. Environmental contamination through the lungs or skin do not produce these levels, _established by expert witness testimony at the trial._

Blanche had already become involved with divorced preacher Dwight Moore, who "fell in love" with her. After some time he pressed her for marriage and she began to poison him as well with tainted food. He went to doctors and the hospital repeatedly; no one could figure it out. He had nausea, diarrhea, vomiting, and severe nasal congestion. They married and the poisoning continued. Finally he was transferred to the UNC Hospital Chapel Hill. It took six days, a battery of tests and several experts to determine arsenic was at the root of symptoms that included paralysis and a potentially lethal staph infection. It was discovered at the last moment, with Dwight on the verge of death, that someone was giving him arsenic _at the hospital;_ tests showed 20 X the _lethal_ amounts of arsenic, sufficient to kill many men but somehow withstood. He was put under guard and intensive care. Semi-crippled, he barely survived, but with serious neuropathy. _[Srila Prabhupada also survived a severely lethal level of cadmium poisoning.]_

Blanche failed a lie detector test, and a lengthy investigation ensued while she remained in jail for a year. There was great difficulty in preparing the case because of the long time between the deaths of Blanche's first husband and her boyfriend, and the attempted murder of her second husband. Many exhumations were ordered, including of Blanche's father and mother-in-law. Everyone had clearly died from arsenic poisoning or had highly abnormal amounts of arsenic in their bodies. NAA was done on Dwight Moore's hair and the exhumed bodies. The jury found her guilty. Thus we understand acute and sub-acute arsenic poisoning from a real case, the grotesque results of arsenic poisoning, and how difficult it is to detect and prosecute as a crime. Also interesting: Blanche's mother-in-law: *"...was found to have had elevated arsenic levels at the time of her death. She was old and weakened enough by other ailments that it was uncertain it could be proved arsenic had killed her. A large dose was found undigested in her stomach, suggesting she had been given arsenic moments before she died."*

James Taylor's hair had 42 X normal arsenic at death. Raymond Reid had 70 ppm hair arsenic at his death (500 X normal). Dwight Moore, who rewrote the texts on lethal arsenic poisoning, had 50 ppm (hair) in his first poisoning episode, and 100 ppm in his second, near fatal episode (750 X normal). *A lethal dose may be indicated by as little as 5 ppm of arsenic in the hair* (2.6 ppm in Srila Prabhupada's hair). While Blanche's victims were acutely and sub-acutely poisoned and their symptoms were dramatic, they shed light on Srila Prabhupada's chronic poisoning symptoms and the amounts of heavy metals required to cause deteriorating illness compared with amounts required to cause quick death. The similarities of symptoms in Moore's victims and Srila Prabhupada are remarkable (arsenic, cadmium symptoms are similar).

MORE NORTH CAROLINA ARSENIC MURDER CASES

Other North Carolina arsenic poisoning cases: **(1)** "Arsenic Annie" Doss, a grandmother who died in 1965 doing life in prison, who had fatally poisoned 5 husbands, 2 children, her mother, 2 sisters, a nephew. She found her husbands to be "dull." **(2)** Rebecca Case Detter was sentenced to life for killing her husband with household Terro arsenic ant killer. **(3)** Sally Holloman was sentenced to life for the arsenic murder of her husband, slowly poisoning him even in his hospital bed. Eleven years later she was convicted. **(4)** Susan Broadaway was sentenced to life for attempted murder of her husband. She mixed arsenic in his coffee. **(5)** Velma Barfield, or "Death Row Granny," died by lethal injection in 1984, the first USA woman executed in 22 years. She seemed pleasant, kindly, friendly and admitted using ant poison while under the influence of prescription drugs in the deaths of her husband, mother, and three others. She fed her husband oyster stew laced with arsenic, and he died a horrible tormented death of excruciating pain within hours. She sympathetically stood by and watched. **(6)** Robert F. Coulthard married into a prominent High Point furniture family, began an affair, took out a $351,000 life insurance policy on his wife. He spiced a hamburger with arsenic and his wife, mother of two children, soon died. Physicians were unable to correctly diagnose her condition until it was too late. Coulthard fed his wife a final dose at the hospital, but he was caught.

DR. MICHAEL SWANGO, "DOCTOR DEATH"

Dr. Michael Swango practiced in hospitals and medical companies in the USA until 1994, when he went to Africa for 2 years. He spent 2 years in a US prison for poisoning 6 co-workers. In 1996 he was arrested on his way to work at another hospital in Saudi Arabia, for felony fraud in lying on an employment application years earlier. He was convicted again and served time until 2000, when he was arrested upon his release for many other murders. A 1999 book on Dr. Swango called *Blind Eye* painted a narcissistic, psychopathic serial-killer suspected in ±50 deaths and dozens more attempted murders. Swango's method was poison, commonly arsenic, but he also used injections of nicotine, valium, adrenaline, ephedrine, xylocaine, nupercainal, botulism, cyanides, fluoroacetic acid, aclemine, and two very untraceable poisons, potassium chloride and ricin (a castor seed derivative).

Swango's first poisoning conviction was difficult to prove but the judge was convinced. One victim's hair had "a high concentration of arsenic." Arsenic ant poison was found in his apartment, plus a home laboratory to manufacture many poisons. The trial judge noted, *"..there are many tracks, and every track leads to the defendant's door, and I'm convinced beyond a reasonable doubt... that he is in fact guilty..."* One of Swango's Zimbabwe poisoning victims had arsenic *"...more than 12 times the norm"* and symptoms included nausea, headaches, weakness, and a nagging cough, which a doctor thought was chronic bronchitis. Recurrent bronchitis is a side effect of arsenic poisoning. (One of Srila Prabhupada's persistent symptoms was cough and bronchitis, and he had 20 X more arsenic than normal.) Although Dr. Swango was suspected since 1985 of poisoning his patients by many officials, his co-workers, and acquaintances, he moved from one job to another, killing as he went. Poisoning is detected only by specific tests, and is *"the perfect crime,"* as one Swango case investigator noted.

ALLEGATIONS OF ARSENIC POISONING IN MALAYSIA

In 1998 Anwar Ibrahim, Malaysia deputy PM, the cultivated successor to Premier Mahathir, was arrested on dubious charges. He had accused his mentor of corruption and wanted to replace him. Anwar arrested on charges widely seen as politically motivated. A year later he was still in prison, had lost 20 pounds and had loss of hair, numbness in the fingers, dizziness; high and fluctuating blood pressure, troubled lungs, dry skin, serious heart irregularities. (Srila Prabhupada had similar symptoms.) His wife and attorney suspected poisoning and tested his smuggled urine in Australia. Arsenic was 77 X normal (10 ppm). Due to publicity he was transferred to a hospital for 3 weeks, further tests found no arsenic poisoning, although levels were above normal.

Experts found above normal arsenic in Anwar's hair and fingernails. A senior Malaysian doctor said: *"...while the level of arsenic was not immediately lethal, more serious symptoms such as abdominal pains could develop and prolonged exposure at these levels would have eventually led to death."* We note similarities to Srila Prabhupada in 1977: a gradual poisoning. Anwar was proclaimed "not poisoned" (the GBC said the same), put back in jail, and he was convicted, serving an extended sentence. His poisoning is still unexplained. Anwar's story is a modern day example of an alleged arsenic poisoning that was not properly investigated and explained (like Srila Prabhupada's), in spite of widespread world publicity. Chronic arsenic poisoning is a very effective means of eliminating someone even in full view of the world. Anwar's hair was falling out, a symptom of antimony poisoning. He was pardoned in 2018 and slated to become the next PM in the near future.

POISONING IN POLITICS AND WAR

Victor Yushchenko underwent near-fatal dioxin poisoning months after dinner with head of Ukraine security services during his bid for the presidency. His face was disfigured by the poison, but he survived and won the election on a second round. Dioxin is unusual, almost undetectable, used in recent times. Cadmium is also unusual and nearly undetectable. In June 2022 Iran accused Israel's Mossad of poisoning its nuclear scientists. The West accuses Russia of poisoning its dissidents.

OTHER POISONING CASES (For Cadmium Cases: See Ch. 9)

A large number of suicidal, homicidal, or accidental arsenical poisonings by ingestion have been described in various medical texts.

(1) In Sept. 1998 there was a mass arsenic poisoning in Sonobe, Japan. Four deaths resulted when arsenic was laced into the curry at a town festival. **(2)** Georgi Markov defected from communist Bulgaria, working with Radio Free Europe in the 1970's. A large home audience listened to his criticisms of Bulgaria's regime. In 1978 he was shot with a tiny ricin-poisoned, metal pellet fired from an umbrella gun. He died in 4 days. **(4)** In 1776 Thomas Hickey was hanged for trying to poison George Washington. **(5)** Nero employed the assistance of a woman named Locusta and poisoned his brother, mother, and several wives.

(6) Claudius was killed by his wife Agrippina, who injected poison into figs he ate. Poisoning in ancient aristocratic Rome became widespread and eventually 170 women were convicted for their poisonings. **(7)** Between 1892-1905, Johann Otto Hoch used arsenic to poison a series of wives for his financial gain. From town to town he located new widows from obituaries in the papers, endearing himself, and after marriage, disposed of them. He was hung for murder by poison.

(8) Jonestown, Guyana was the scene of 913 deaths in 1978, most due to poisoning from a fruit drink laced with cyanide, which many drank or were forcibly injected by order of their leader Rev. Jim Jones. It was suicide, murder, and madness. **(9)** Donald Harvey, as a nurse's aide 1983-87, killed 24 persons with arsenic or cyanide. He had a compulsion to kill, and sentenced for life. **(10)** Since the 1960's Palestinian hero Yasser Arafat led the struggle for independence from Israel. Oct. 24, 2004 Arafat became ill and died in 2 weeks; many investigators searched for the cause of death for 9 years. The Swiss found high levels of polonium in Arafat's body and traces in his Ramallah compound and clothing. *"The Swiss forensic team found polonium levels in Arafat's body 18-36 times the average, and were 83% confident in polonium poisoning." (Nov. 6, 2013, Al Jazeera)*

(11) A similar case occurred in 2006 when a dissident Russian activist, Alexander Litvinenko, fell ill in London, dying 3 weeks later from highly radioactive polonium. **(12)** In 1981 Ali Agca shot Pope John Paul; the serious stomach wound was non-fatal. The bullet was thought tainted with poison. KGB, Bulgarians, Iranians were suspected. Religious leaders are often targeted by assassins executing secret designs of powerful concerns (may have happened with Srila Prabhupada?)

(13) SBhag 6.14: King Chitraketu's co-wives of his chief wife administered poison to his only child. **(14)** GBC Naveen Krishna participated in Balavanta's investigation. He went in 1998 to ISKCON Delhi temple and was given a plate "already prepared for you." In hours he was extremely ill, and on the plane laid down with nausea and chills. Arriving in Sweden, Harikesh hurriedly came and administered an Ayurvedic antidote which he kept in case of poisoning. **(15)** Many sources indicate Joseph Stalin was poisoned. In the 1990's KGB files were declassified and a doctor's report described clear symptoms of cyanide poisoning in 1953 from a fish dinner. (www.youtube.com/watch?v=mRIpQgk5V_o)

CONCLUSIONS

Homicidal poisoning is common, preferred since it is difficult to detect. Many are capable of this reprehensible crime. Many poisonings are only detected by investigation or accident. The poisoner strikes in secret, posing as neutral, a loved one, even a disciple.

PART SIX:
COVER-UPS BY LYING PROPAGANDA

(1) *"Make the lie big, make it simple, keep saying it, and eventually they will believe it." (Adolf Hitler)* **(2)** *"No lie can live forever." (Martin Luther King)* **(3)** *"...by too much lying propaganda, truthfulness is spoiled." (SBhag 1.17.25)* **(4)** *"The truth is not for all men, but only for those who seek it."* (Ayn Rand) **(5)** *"We use the same techniques as Aristotle and Hitler. We appeal to people on an emotional level and get them to agree on a functional level."* (N. Oakes)

Soon after the appearance of the "poison issue" in late 1997, ISKCON adopted a suppressive cover-up policy on the evidence in Srila Prabhupada's poisoning. Their first cover-up was in early 1998. Hari Sauri was spokesman for the new Ministry For The Protection of ISKCON (like George Orwell's Ministry of Truth). After *SHPM* was published in 1999 with the poisoning evidence, the GBC elite and suspects themselves orchestrated and financed a second fraudulent, deceitful cover-up of the poisoning evidence in 2000 with a book *Not That I Am Poisoned (NTIAP)*. ISKCON issued knowingly defective denials of the evidence in increasing desperation. They even said there was **no evidence at all** that Srila Prabhupada had been poisoned.

Another book in 2003, *Judge For Yourself,* included a CD with the poison discussions, whispers, and Tamal's mercy killing interview. ISKCON just ignored it. In May 2017 *Kill Guru, Become Guru* was released online, followed by 6 YouTube videos on the evidence that ISKCON wanted to fault and obscure. A secret GBC committee in late 2017 masterminded their third major poison cover-up, a project headed by notoriously dishonest Bir Krishna Maharaja and including Brahmatirtha, Gunagrahi, Malati, and prime suspect Bhakticharu Swami. Gunagrahi, dying from cancer, was a mole leaking key GBC emails. The GBC announced their rebuttal would soon be released. They misled their own "poison expert" Dr. VV Pillay. They anointed Mayeswara das, a feisty "independent" devotee eager for recognition, to do a thorough-looking pseudo-scientific rebuttal. In early 2020 came a 400 page, confusing, unreadable book titled *Deception: Poison Conspiracy Fraud* with Mayeswara's hour video as the sarcastic, fiery "defender of truth."

The GBC book *Deception* is filled with lies, distortions and deception ad nauseum. Since 1998 ISKCON has obstructed the truth with cover-ups of Srila Prabhupada's poisoning with misinformation, false narratives, fake facts, suppressing and censoring the actual truth, and, we believe, also by destroying key evidence. For this the entire GBC should be tried in criminal court as aiders and abettors after the factual crime. *Why don't they just allow one or two honest scientific tests instead of so much denying?* And let the evidence speak for itself? But they fear the truth too much. The scandal of the original poisoning is magnified by ISKCON's determined suppression of the hard evidence. Now the GBC and ISKCON too is an accomplice to Srila Prabhupada's poisoning and their time of reckoning shall surely come soon.

CHAPTER 40:
MERCY KILLING INTERVIEW

LATE 1977 TAMAL INTERVIEW FOR *BTG* MAGAZINE

On March 31, 1999, VNN.org published an article with audio clips from a 1977 tape recording that Isha das had found in his personal archives. The tape was an interview of Tamal by Satsvarupa for *Back to Godhead* magazine, recorded just days after Srila Prabhupada's disappearance. Isha was Satsvarupa's personal assistant at the time, and somehow this tape survived for 20 years through even a house fire. Tamal's interview contains shocking claims unsupported anywhere else. Any remaining doubts one may have that perhaps Tamal was simply a loving and faithful disciple will be put to rest permanently after listening to this tape. Anyone who understands even a little about Srila Prabhupada and then listens to this interview will be profoundly disturbed by Tamal's statements. His chilling voice evolves to a nervous, squeaky high pitch as he claimed that Srila Prabhupada stated: *"Can you give me a medicine, please give me a medicine that will allow me to disappear now."* To hear this audio recording is the clincher for many, the one thing that dispenses with any remaining sympathy toward Tamal, or doubt that Srila Prabhupada was poisoned.

This audio, in his own voice, shows Tamal was a mastermind calculator of dark intentions, consumed by personal ambition. His claims are incriminating, outrageous, evil, and frightening. He spoke of a rationale for Srila Prabhupada's mercy killing. The creepy, insidious undertones in his vile and stuttering statements are his laying a defense groundwork for an "untimely departure" with he having been only compliant with Srila Prabhupada's suicidal last wishes. Tamal justifies a poisoning as the dying request of one in great pain and misery, of one most anxious to "now die." Tamal's portrayal of Srila Prabhupada in this interview, as well as in his bizarre book *The Final Pastimes*, is an atrocious, nauseatingly offensive characterization of the pure devotee.

ESSENTIAL EXCERPTS FROM TAMAL'S INTERVIEW

Tamal: *"I was going to wait for the proper time to say this, but to me the incidents which stick most on my mind are how in the last few months, Srila Prabhupada would constantly ask to be allowed to, um, die peacefully.* **COMMENT:** Allow? Or help him die? *"And, um, how he would constantly succumb to the requests of his disciples not to leave us. Our relationship with Srila Prabhupada has always been one of total submissiveness, and complete, um... So, our position with Srila Prabhupada was one of complete submissiveness to his orders and instructions, his desires, just like a menial servant. It's hardly the position of the servant to, in any way, um, strongly request the master for anything. He should simply receive the instruction or order and carry it out. Yet we found in the later months, in the most recent months, that Srila Prabhupada seemed to be demanding from us a different type of attitude and emotion, at least especially from his most personal, you know, servants.* **COMMENT:** SP asked from his most confidential servants (like Tamal) something different, something unusual?

"Um. A number of times he would say 'Can you give me a medicine, please give me a medicine that will allow me to disappear now.' Another time he said 'I want most now to disappear. I want to die peacefully. Let me die peacefully.' Now on one hand we could take it and give him that medicine or let him stop eating and fast until death. We could have done that. And yet it seemed that, of course we could not do that out of our love for him." **COMMENT:** Asked for medicine to die? Medicine that kills is poison. Assisting Srila Prabhupada to "disappear now," "seemed" difficult due to their love for him, but "we could have done that." So did "they" give "medicine" to die? Tamal hints but then chickens out…

"I think we all had the feeling, at least a few of us who were in his personal attendance, that there wasn't really a question that he would live for a long time. But even though it was only a short time we wanted him to stay with us. And he would bring us to the point of complete despair, he would stop all doctors, all medicines, and bring us to the point where there was no return, where he would say 'Now there's nothing left but for me to die' I feel that these last months with Prabhupada were the most important months I ever spent with him. And, ah, somehow I feel that by seeing the way he acted and the way he dealt with me personally, that ah, that I'll be, ah... You can take this part off,

this last sentence. Somehow, I feel ???... I mean I want to say something, but I'd prefer not to say it. **COMMENT**: What was Tamal going to say? Why does he hesitate? Is he afraid we won't understand how the penultimate act of Tamal's loyalty to Srila Prabhupada was to assist him to "disappear"? That Srila Prabhupada trusted Tamal in this final test of submission and love? That Tamal was asked to give medicine to die?

Satsvarupa: *...a different kind of question. Right in the beginning without too much explanation you were talking about Prabhupada asking for something to let him disappear, that he wanted to die.*

COMMENT: Satsvarupa understood and accepted the mercy killing scenario, and wanted to explore it further. Just months later he also became one of the 11 new initiating ISKCON gurus, assuming command of a slice of ISKCON. Was he among "at least a few of us" whom Srila Prabhupada called upon to help him "die now," or was he just a silent consenter, an accessory after the medicine to die? Why would Srila Prabhupada be in distress about being poisoned (Ch. 8) if, as Tamal claims, he wanted his own "mercy killing"? This is totally contradictory and shows Tamal's mercy killing to be a cover-up.

Tamal: *Therefore after some time, the pure devotee wants to again go back to Krishna. And Krishna wants His devotee back. Prabhupada recently said, 'It is becoming unbearable.' We can understand that it wasn't simply the material pain that was becoming unbearable, but that Prabhupada also wanted to be with Krishna, and not be burdened with this physically incapacitated body. [...]* **Tamal:** *Oh yeah, painful. That why should he be burdened or incap... with this physically, you know, burdensome form.* **COMMENT:** This is absolute nonsense. If Srila Prabhupada repeatedly asked for medicine to die, there was no crime in poisoning him because that's what he wanted? Poisoner Tamal is clean because Srila Prabhupada wanted to die and Tamal was faithfully serving his final wishes... He was just following orders?

SRILA PRABHUPADA ASKED FOR MEDICINE TO DIE?

Tamal's statements are very frightening and are an assault on our understanding of Srila Prabhupada's stature as a fully self-realized soul. Below are eight direct, word-for-word quotes from Tamal's "euthanasia" interview: **(1)** ...in the last few months Srila Prabhupada would constantly ask to be allowed to die peacefully. **(2)** A number of times he would say "Can you give me a medicine, please give me a medicine that will allow me to disappear now." **(3)** Another time he said "I want most now to disappear." **(4)** I want to die peacefully. **(5).** Let me die peacefully. **(6)** ...we could take it and give him that medicine or let him stop eating and fast until death. <u>We could have done that</u>. **(7)** Prabhupada also wanted to be with Krishna, and not be burdened with this physically incapacitated body. **(8)** That why should he be burdened or incap... with this physically, you know, burdensome form. // At least six times Tamal clearly claims that Srila Prabhupada wanted assistance with "disappearing" now, meaning an unnatural, immediate, assisted death. Tamal was rationalizing Srila Prabhupada's poisoning, now proven by the cadmium hair tests. Euthanasia, assisted suicide, mercy killing? Justifiable and compassionate homicide? Or poisoning the pure devotee?

TAMAL PREPARED A EUTHANASIA DEFENSE

Tamal was concerned the poisoning was about to be discovered and he was rehearsing his explanation of the "mercy killing." The poison discussions just prior to Srila Prabhupada's departure must have gotten a number of people asking questions, and Tamal worried the truth would become public. Rumors or leaks from those who knew or suspected the poisoning, or from the "poison discussions" when Srila Prabhupada spoke of being poisoned- pushed Tamal to talk about "medicine to die." Many had discussed and heard about Srila Prabhupada's poisoning on Nov. 9-10 and the news was spreading. Even the kavirajas had concluded poisoning (Ch. 36). Tamal felt pressured to hone his defense that Srila Prabhupada asked to be assisted in dying. This sinister, clever defense was just in case the leaks got out of hand. Tamal was planting a radical rationale for a poisoning, doing the groundwork for a "mercy-killing" defense if it became public that Srila Prabhupada was poisoned. Tamal claimed Srila Prabhupada wanted to die peacefully by being given "medicine," which now we know was the poison cadmium.

But Tamal never mentioned assisted suicide again, after this one private interview, presumably because the poisoning lay well-enough concealed for 20 years until it looked him back in the face. Even after the poison issue became very public due to discovery of the poison whispers in 1997, Tamal never revisited his mercy-killing claims. Why? He changed his strategy, that's why. It was typical of Tamal to come up with radical positions and then drop them, as with his Topanga Canyon confessions in 1980 and his support for Narayan Maharaja in 1995. This phenomenon is the hallmark of deviation and untruthfulness.

EUTHANASIA CONTRADICTS POISON DISCUSSIONS

Tamal's euthanasia claim doesn't fit with the "poison discussions" where Srila Prabhupada raised the topic of being poisoned and was "mentally distressed" over it. If he wanted to die or asked for suicide-assistance, or made it clear he wanted his caretakers to help him die immediately, then why would he bring up his being poisoned or be "distressed" about it? If one wants to die, discovering he was being poisoned should be welcome, no? Why would Tamal later say this was the paranoia of an old, dying man not to be taken seriously, if this was what Srila Prabhupada had asked Tamal to do? Too many contradictions, and it makes no sense. If Srila Prabhupada was waiting for Tamal to facilitate his quick death, why talk on Nov. 9-10 about being poisoned? And why would Tamal ask Srila Prabhupada as to who had poisoned him if Srila Prabhupada had asked him to do that? Tamal's claims of Srila Prabhupada asking for medicine to die do not make any sense in the context of everything we understand about Srila Prabhupada's last year, the taped conversations, and the philosophy of Krishna consciousness. Therefore we reject Tamal's mercy killing claims as simply an awkward attempt to reframe the homicidal poisoning of Srila Prabhupada as the fulfillment of Srila Prabhupada's last wishes for an assisted suicide.

The full mercy killing interview chapter (above is an excerpt only) and the full examination of Tamal Krishna Goswami as the certain poisoner-in-chief is found in Volume 2. The full evidence and details of all the poisoning suspects, examining *who poisoned Srila Prabhupada,* is found in Volume 3. Of note is that the GBC, nor any ISKCON leader, has ever explained how Tamal's euthanasia claims are not evidence of a poisoning. This silence is another cover-up of the evidence.

CHAPTER 41:
MINISTRY OF COVER-UPS

GBC CREATES A NEW MINISTRY

In late 1997 the GBC Executive Committee (without approval of the full GBC) deputed Balavanta to conduct an "independent" investigation into the poison controversy, and expecting he would disprove and put it to rest completely. In March 1998 at the Mayapur annual GBC meetings, senior GBCs (and suspects) such as Tamal, Bhakticharu and Jayapataka thought the Executive Committee's action had been unwise and rash. After Balavanta leaked evidence supportive of a poisoning, the GBC quickly silenced him. Though Balavanta was employed and funded (albeit inadequately) by the GBC, he was a man of integrity and not a corrupted insider who would "protect" ISKCON's political interests. The poison issue was problematic for some GBCs who were widely perceived as primary suspects. There was a natural tension between

Balavanta and these suspects. Early in 1998 the GBC created The Ministry for the Protection of ISKCON (MPI) which engaged Hari Sauri das, a diehard GBC supporter through all the twists and turns of ISKCON's history, and Jahnu das, the right-hand man for Harikesh Swami's regime in Europe. Balavanta hardly had his investigation going when the GBC elite controllers, Tamal, Jayapataka, Bhakticharu, Bir Krishna Swami, and Ravindra Svarupa, arranged a cover-up and any honest investigation was thrown out the window. Denial, deceit, obfuscation, subterfuge, and stonewalling was the secret policy, with one cover-up after another. The GBCs fell in line behind the suspects to confront the common threat of the "poison theory." One for all, all for one. The "Cover-ups Ministry" was tasked with countering the poison theory, and specifically a CD project which was deemed a great menace.

THE POISON CD PROJECT

There was a widespread sentiment that the GBC was dishonest, blocking impartial investigation and sharing of the facts and evidence. A trio of Dhanesvara, Rochan, and Nityananda decided to make and distribute an audio CD with the "enhanced" poison whispers and a narrative commentary. Rochan enlisted the help of an odd character in Lockport, NY named Geoffrey Giuliano or "Jagannath das Puripada." Dhanesvara went to Lockport in Jan. 1998 to compose the storyline and create the CD in Jagannath's sound studio, offered at no charge. But Jagannath began to demand money and control in the project, and Dhanesvara had great difficulty maintaining the direction the team had decided on. It was made it clear to "Puripada," who pioneered the Ronald McDonald clown act, that he would be given $500 one time, and that Dhanesvara be allowed to finalize the CD without further interference. Still, Giuliano insisted on being the narrator. The storyline was edited to fit the available evidence at that time and the CD's purpose, mood, and content was developed conscientiously.

With the final "cut" on the day of the CD's completion, a dangerously angry Giuliano instigated a horrible confrontation and argument with Dhanesvara, who fled for Denver by bus, without the CD he had worked on for six weeks. Giuliano left the same day for India, stopping in Europe on the way. Weeks later Nityananda recovered a copy of the finished CD from the manager of the sound studio in Lockport where the CD was mastered. Giuliano claimed the CD was stolen and turned over to ISKCON by immigrant Bengali devotees in his ashram who also supposedly stole goods and US$19,420 cash. He even filed a robbery report with the local police. One of the Bengalis, Gaura Daya das, called from Washington, DC, saying that Giuliano stole the

CD and sold it to Harikesh Swami. He expressed sympathy, saying that he and his friends had also endured great abuse and exploitation by Giuliano, calling him a psychopath and con-man. He told many stories about shady business practices, misuse of tax exempt status, defrauding the electric company, and more.

HARIKESH ACQUIRES OUR STOLEN POISON CD

Apparently Giuliano stole the finished CD and sold it for $10,000 to Harikesh in Europe. Harikesh's operations had abundant cash. Thus the GBC had the audio Poison CD long before its makers did. Harikesh copied the CD for top GBCs. An urgent call to action was sounded in the GBC inner circle. They were worried about an impending release of a damning "poison audio CD" worldwide. MPI decided on a rebuttal of the CD, which was expected to flood the devotee world very soon. However, after recovering a copy, listening to the finished CD, and after consultations, the team decided to abandon the project. Nityananda would have gladly sold it himself to ISKCON at a fraction what they paid for it. It was a decent attempt, but everyone cringed at Giuliano's bombastic and irritating voice as the narrator. The team would continue investigations and a broader report would be made later. Also, an audio CD was only 72 Mb. A book was a better option; the "Poison CD" was never released. Yet, May 21, 1998, MPI released their *"Reply To The Poison Cd."*

The GBC thus responded to a Poison CD that was never printed nor distributed, thus actually increasing awareness of the poison issue, raising more questions, and arousing new interest in the investigation. The MPI's flawed response (reviewed below) was later included as 38 pages in *NTIAP,* the GBC book of denials. Giuliano later also gave an interview to the GBC claiming Dhanesvara and Nityananda wanted to tamper with the poison whispers in his sound studio, that they tried to contrive false evidence. *Giuliano gave no specifics* in his lies against an honest investigative team (Ch. 52). The GBC used a con artist who scammed both sides. Giuliano bragged to Nityananda how in ISKCON Toronto he had "taken" the original tape of Srila Prabhupada and Yamuna's Jan. 1977 studio kirtans, which he released under his own label in 1998 as *"The Lost Kirtans."* The GBC engaged in many cover-ups: the child abuse, zonal acharya hoax, guru fall-downs, its leaders deviations, etc. They also covered-up the poison issue with lies, misinformation, deceitful denials, and blocking any honest investigation. Is it any surprise so many have totally lost faith in the corrupted ISKCON leadership?

ISKCON'S REPLY TO POISON CD THAT NEVER WAS

May 21, 1998: MPI: Over the last few months a rumor has surfaced that Prabhupada supposedly was poisoned by some of his closest and most trusted disciples. Just recently a Poison CD came out, which, although hiding behind the banner of neutrality and claiming no other intention than getting to the truth of the matter, strongly suggests that Srila Prabhupada was poisoned by his Western disciples and that there is a conspiracy by the GBC to cover this up. The so-called evidence on the Poison CD is rather insidious at its core. First, logical arguments Srila Prabhupada was not poisoned by his disciples. **COMMENT:** *Let us focus on IF there was a poisoning, and not start with who did not do it.)*

MPI: A further point to consider is who exactly would want to kill Srila Prabhupada and what was their motive? Proponents of the "Ritvik" idea postulated that some GBC members [...] wanted him removed from the scene as quickly as possible so that they could become full gurus [...] According to their logic [...] they poisoned him to death. **COMMENT:** *Everyone knows some senior men were extremely ambitious to take Srila Prabhupada's place, and they did so. This was the poisoners' motive.* **MPI:** Obviously such a task would have to have been a conspiracy. How is it possible to keep such a conspiracy without any leaks for 20 years in ISKCON? How was it possible to keep Bhakticharu Swami out of it? [...] But what would be his motive? He [...] did he become guru until 1987. **COMMENT:** *The poison whispers and discussions ARE the leaks. Tamal's mercy killing interview shows there were leaks. Let's focus on the evidence not speculation. Bhakticharu joined in 1977 so he had to wait. Ten years was not long to wait at all.*

LONG STANDING AILMENTS DISPROVES POISONING?

[Next MPI gave Abhiram's report on Srila Prabhupada's medical symptom of dropsy (not a disease). But in 1977 40 kavirajas and doctors could not agree on a disease diagnosis.] **MPI:** ...The PCD authors would have it that Srila Prabhupada showed strong symptoms of someone being poisoned... **COMMENT:** *Yes, that is what Srila Prabhupada himself said several times. (Part 2)* **MPI:** ...but while they suggestively attribute this to sinister origins, we now present some more medical facts to show that such symptoms were indeed to be expected in someone of Prabhupada's physical condition... **COMMENT:** *MPI discusses Srila Prabhupada's medical condition trying to discredit a poisoning, saying that if there was diabetes, that rules out poisoning. But diabetics can be poisoned too, and Srila Prabhupada had medical symptoms not seen in diabetes or kidney disease, but are unique to heavy metals poisoning (Ch. 31).* **MPI:** From the Nov. 9-10 conversations, Shastri [kaviraja] did not detect any symptoms of arsenic in Srila

Prabhupada's body [...] even though Srila Prabhupada himself discussed directly with him the possibility of his being poisoned. Nor did Prabhupada's nurses, Abhiram and Bhakticharu Swami, nor any of the other doctors. **COMMENT:** *All the caretakers clearly acknowledged Srila Prabhupada spoke of being homicidally poisoned, including. Shastri. Read the conversations! MPI quotes BCS (a primary suspect) to show there was no foul play. In Nov. 1977 BCS said: "Someone gave him poison here!" Then in 1998 he denied it? Who will believe him?*

GBC'S "CONFUSING SCENARIO" PHRASE EDITED OUT

MPI: _These translations and transcripts do in any case reveal a confusing scenario._ Srila Prabhupada indicates first to Tamal that he had the symptoms of someone poisoned, not that he was being poisoned. Later he states more positively that he is being poisoned. _While we may never know Srila Prabhupada's mind exactly, or how seriously he took the suggestion that someone may be poisoning him_, what we do learn from these transcriptions is that the possibility of his being poisoned is discussed with his disciples present, both from a medical standpoint with the talk of mercury, and from the idea that an outside person could be deliberately doing it. We also learn Srila Prabhupada was not the first one to take up the matter of his being poisoned, rather he referred to "someone" telling him that he was being poisoned. No conclusion was reached. **COMMENT:** *Here Hari Sauri is more honest, admitting to a confusing scenario. But then this "honest" portion (underlined above) was **edited out** in NTIAP, p. 213. NTIAP changed their position to "**There definitely was no poisoning conspiracy.**" This is a dishonest, corrupt leadership which hides truth. Just as Hari Sauri's partial honesty was axed (1998 to 2000), Balavanta's investigation also was axed in 2000. The GBC was no longer "confused" by 2000.*

MPI: Thus Srila Prabhupada did not seem to think that his intimate servants were responsible. **COMMENT:** *First things first, it is not **who**, but **was** Srila Prabhupada poisoned? Later we can see who did it. MPI uses the incredulity of caretakers poisoning Srila Prabhupada to establish there was no poisoning. Cart before the horse?*

PRELIMINARY GBC WHISPER FINDINGS WERE WRONG?

MPI: It has been alleged that "whispers" have been found with the word "poison." ...have sent the tapes to forensic labs... spectrographic sound analysis as well as standard enhancement of the "whispers" by sophisticated audio playback equipment have been employed... it is inconceivable that a person or persons serving Srila Prabhupada... in the last days in Vrindaban could whisper *"the poison is going down [giggle],* *the poison is going down,"* watching Srila Prabhupada gulp down poison. *...there exists no evidence to support such a notion.* The GBC appointed an independent investigator to oversee a professional forensic analysis of the tapes to ascertain if there is any truth to these claims. ...after preliminary tests and lab feedback, Balavanta expressed doubt that any definite evidence will be found... several GBCs conducted tests with sophisticated equipment... the word "poison" simply does not appear. **COMMENT:** *The audio "tests" by various amateur, biased GBCs denied the poison word in any whispers. But many forensic audio studies (Part 3)* **confirm** *the poison whispers. GBC investigator Balavanta did two studies confirming the poison whispers (Blackwell & JP French).*

MPI: When one has an opinion as to what is being said, the ears and mind oblige us to hear that very thing. One can completely reprogram his hearing by just wanting to hear something else. It is extremely hard to understand what is being said if one has a preconception. **COMMENT:** *GBC cannot admit to what they do not want to hear... Audio forensic laboratories have no such prejudices and they all clearly hear "poison."*

MPI: The person giggling is Krishnadas Babaji, continuously giggling due his incessant chanting [...] **COMMENT:** *Bhavananda's unique voice is giggling. Krishnadas Babaji was not there at that time.*

MPI CONCLUDES THERE IS NO SOLID EVIDENCE

MPI: To build a whole theory of a poison conspiracy on such vague statements is certainly far-fetched [...] such a weak case would immediately be dismissed [...] very serious offense to accuse someone of murder, especially without any conclusive proof. On the flimsiest excuse for evidence they have accused devotees who love Prabhupada of committing an unspeakably monstrous crime against him, and they have systematically spread these charges. They have put the lives of devotees in danger. **COMMENT:** *They worry of danger to themselves, not caring that Srila Prabhupada complained of being poisoned. Their emotional plea that no one could do such a thing is just a cover-up. Let's start with an honest investigation, one not run by the suspects. Yes, the whispers alone are not an airtight case for poisoning. But with Srila Prabhupada saying he was being poisoned, certified poison whispers, and forensic hair test results, the conclusion is homicidal poisoning. How about lie detector tests, voice stress analysis, in-depth interviews and comparative depositions, rather than denials? Why did the GBC ask Balavanta to investigate if it was all nothing? Why were there poison whispers?*

MPI: ...no solid evidence exists either medically or on tapes to establish that Srila Prabhupada was deliberately poisoned, and certainly not by his disciples. Rather, we feel that the love of those surrounding Srila Prabhupada was genuine and self-evident. ...This theory should be dismissed and laid to rest. [...] not be disturbed by elements who do not have the best interest of his society and devotees at heart. The poison is the theory itself. **COMMENT:** *Those wanting an investigation are poisonous? The GBC's dishonest denials, orchestrated by the suspects themselves (Tamal, Bhakticharu paid for the expenses and printing of NTIAP), is the poison. They cut off Balavanta's funding and decided NOT to test their own hair samples which later proved the poisoning. They pay for their own luxuries but not an impartial investigation, otherwise their guru business is over. Srila Prabhupada himself started the poison issue. Should we ignore Srila Prabhupada's words and certified poison whispers to shield the GBC who have been exposed lying and cheating so many times before? MPI admits Srila Prabhupada's statements are "confusing" but then flips to saying "clearly there was no poisoning." Orwellian double talk. The clincher was the 250 X normal cadmium discovery in hair samples they arranged for. MPI drips with lies, deceit, and untruth just so the prime suspects can avoid scrutiny, while saying Srila Prabhupada cannot be taken seriously. See Vol. 2, 3.*

CHAPTER 42:
SOMEONE HAS POISONED ME VILIFIED

After Balavanta went silent, Mahabuddhi left the team, and the audio CD project was aborted. Nityananda continued, engaging forensic experts and doing hair tests. After more than a year, while Balavanta was not making much progress in his investigation, and there was nowhere one could obtain the actual complete facts and evidence, he decided to compile the evidence into a book. In 1998 Tamal published his 1977 *TKG's Diary* he kept as Srila Prabhupada's personal secretary. He portrayed Srila Prabhupada's departure as natural. It was a suspect's whitewash, full of tweaked fabrications to undermine the poisoning evidence (see Vol. 2). In May 1999 Nityananda published 2000 copies of *Someone Has Poisoned Me* with the categories of evidence on Srila Prabhupada's poisoning: whispers, poison discussions, witnesses, medical symptoms, hair tests, etc. The total evidence, especially Srila Prabhupada's statements *("Someone has poisoned me"),* was presented, concluding Srila Prabhupada had been maliciously poisoned. 408 pages, 45 chapters, 22 appendices, technical graphs, etc. A composite 150 page biographical record of Srila Prabhupada's health, from late 1975 until his departure was included. (See App. 8 and Vol. 4).

SHPM was widely distributed worldwide to devotees everywhere, largely free. It included the major CAE whispers audio forensic study and Balavanta's NAA forensic test finding about 3 ppm arsenic in Srila Prabhupada's hair. *SHPM* "rocked the ISKCON boat" and the poison issue was widely discussed, receiving good attention in the Indian media. The GBC urgently responded within 9 months with their own book of denials, *Not That I Am Poisoned* (March 2000).

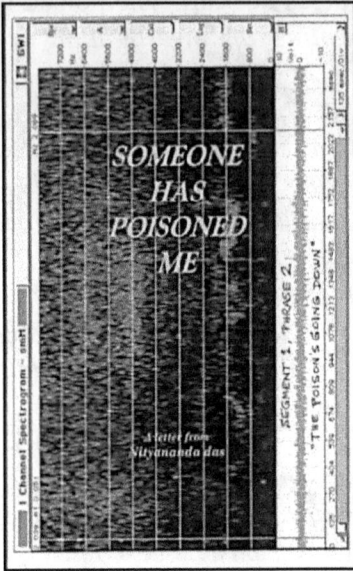

NTIAP tried to create doubts in all the poisoning evidence. As a result, many were confused. Parts per million, diabetes vs. poison symptoms, and audio forensics- everything was contested by ISKCON's GBC, and many were uncertain what was what. Some blocked their minds due to emotions. Some refused to even hear about it, but others wanted truth. *NTIAP* harped on a few tiny errors in *SHPM* as though this nullified all the evidence. But *SHPM,* a best and sincere effort, created a crisis of confidence in ISKCON, so the GBC simply denied that **any** of the evidence was valid, labeling it "the poison conspiracy." The evidence and conclusions in *SHPM* remain valid, and since 1999 the evidence has grown immensely. Forensic testing of the GBC's Srila Prabhupada hair samples found **cadmium was the primary poison, with arsenic secondary** (see Part 1). The poisoning has now been irrefutably proven.

Download *SHPM* online for free: http://killgurubecomeguru.org

SOMEONE HAS POISONED ME: TABLE OF CONTENTS

Chapter 1:	Poison Becomes an Issue	6
Chapter 2:	Poison Whispers Discovered	7
Chapter 3:	Whispers Alarm Devotees	8
Chapter 4:	Poison Investigations Begin	10
Chapter 5:	ISKCON Statement	12
Chapter 6:	Investigation Continues	14
Chapter 7:	Audio Forensics Commence	16
Chapter 8:	More Audio Forensics	20
Chapter 9:	Obtaining the UHER	22
Chapter 10:	Virtual Originals from Archives	24
Chapter 11:	More Whispers, No Editing	25
Chapter 12:	Witnesses	28
Chapter 13:	Are There Missing Tapes?	30
Chapter 14:	Researching the Tape Library	33

Chapter 15:   Chandra Swami Connection 34
Chapter 16:   "Someone Has Poisoned Me" 41
Chapter 17:   Introduction to 1977 Health Biography................................53
Chapter 18:   Kidney Disease Symptoms..58
Chapter 19:   Arsenic Poisoning Symptoms 60
Ch's 20-31:   Health Chronicle: Dec. 1975-Nov. 14, 1977 71-226
Chapter 32:   Health Biography Analysis..226
Chapter 33:   Hair Analysis...233
Chapter 34:   Napoleon: A Case History...245
Chapter 35:   Blanche Taylor Moore 256
Chapter 36:   Other Arsenic Case Studies 261
Chapter 37:   Reverse Speech Theory 264
Chapter 38:   Reverse Speech Analysis 267
Chapter 39:   Balavanta's Investigation 270
Chapter 40:   Poisoning Methodology 271
Chapter 41:   Possible Motives of the Assassins 276
Chapter 42:   Parade of Doctors, Treatments, and Mis-Diagnoses 278
Chapter 43:   Who Are The Suspects?...281
Chapter 44:   Dateline of Poisoning Highlights 282
Chapter 45:   Conclusions & Summary...283
Appendix 1:   Perle Appointment Tape Analysis 293
Appendix 2:   Audio Forensic Analysis: The Whispers 295
Appendix 3:   Audio Forensic Analysis: No Editing 314
Appendix 4:   Statement by Abhiram Prabhu...343
Appendix 5:   Appointment Tape Misquoted 345
Appendix 6:   Book Review: TKG's Diary..347
Appendix 7:   Diabetes Symptoms...350
Appendix 8:   Asutosh Oja Astrological Reports 352
Appendix 9:   Unverified Information..355
Appendix 10:   Are There Missing Tapes? 358
Appendix 11:   Hair Mineral Analysis...361
Appendix 12:   Sources of Arsenic 366
Appendix 13:   Possible Mis-Diagnoses 367
Appendix 14:   Poisoning Throughout History..368
Appendix 15:   History of Tamal Krishna Goswami 371
Appendix 16:   Was The Medicine Like Poison?...379
Appendix 17:   Astrology and Poisoning..382
Appendix 18:   Letter from Bhagavat Das...386
Appendix 19:   Tamal Talks at Pyramid House 389
Appendix 20:   Black Magic and Tantrics...392
Appendix 21:   ISKCON Answers CD That Never Was................................393
Appendix 22:   Arsenical Photophobia 406

CHAPTER 43:
BALAVANTA'S INVESTIGATION AXED

DISAPPOINTING AND INCOMPLETE

Soon after Balavanta was assigned by the GBC in Dec. 1997 to conduct an "independent" investigation, he went silent on his activities or progress. Twice, when Nityananda spoke with him, he confided frustration with arranging audio and hair tests. Nityananda also spoke with his assistant Naveen Krishna regularly, who shared as much as he could. Balavanta's progress was slow. At the 2000 annual India GBC meetings he finally presented his *initial* investigative report. It was brief, ambiguous, inconclusive, and he advised further investigation, noting that his GBC funding never came as promised. Many hoped Balavanta had accomplished a more comprehensive investigation after 2+ years. His report had several valuable discoveries and solid research, but it lacked follow-through. There were no interviews with suspects Tamal, Bhakticharu, Bhavananda, or Jayapataka. In regards to Srila Prabhupada saying he had been poisoned, Balavanta wrote inaccurately: *"On Nov. 8, 1977, Srila Prabhupada commented that "Someone has said that I have been given poison." Who said? "They say; they all say." He was pressed later and responded, "Not said, but that I have the symptoms of one who has been poisoned."* These few lines summarized the extensive discussions between Srila Prabhupada and his caretakers about poisoning, and he *incorrectly quoted* Srila Prabhupada, thus implying he had made conflicting statements. See Part 2.

TEST ON MEDICINES & HAIR FROM THE CLIPPERS

At Balavanta's request, Hari Sauri (Srila Prabhupada's personal servant) took some items from Srila Prabhupada's Vrindaban ISKCON quarters and gave them to Sesa das to bring to Balavanta in Florida. Balavanta tested 3 glass vials sealed with corks containing pink pellets (Yogendra Ras, Ch. 28). Balavanta: *"I also received a hair clipper from the (Vrindaban) museum which I sent to Dr. Morris of the Univ. of Missouri. Dr. Morris operates one of the world's most advanced technologies for microscopic analysis and is himself an authority on the subject. Having obtained a hair embedded on the movable cutter of the clipper, he subjected it to analysis. He found arsenic in the hair in the amount of 2.6 ppm which he considered to be 20 times greater than would be expected in an average person living in the United States."* [**Corrections:** Dr. Morris does neutron activation analysis, not microscopic analysis. Dr. Morris flushed a significant number of hairs from the clipper blades, (not pone hair) which was more than sufficient for an accurate analysis of arsenic.]

DELAWARE MEDICAL EXAMINER STATEMENT (*Appendix 5*)

Balavanta obtained an expert opinion on the arsenic levels of 20 X normal in Srila Prabhupada's hair. *"Richard Callery, M.D., the medical examiner of Delaware, stated that the amount of arsenic found in Srila Prabhupada's hair would not have been lethal in itself. ...over a duration of time or to a person already in frail health, this dosage could have been significant. He commented that a single exposure producing the indicated levels may not have produced specific symptoms although intermittent instances of exposure would likely have caused some level of gastric disturbance."* **COMMENT:** The hair found around the blades of Srila Prabhupada's hairclippers accumulated over about a year's time from multiple cuttings. A mix from many cuttings had average 2.6 ppm arsenic during the time the hairclippers were used (Nov. 76 to Sept. 77).

Dr. Callery concluded with a very powerful statement: *"It is my opinion, to a reasonable degree of medical certainty, that this individual, with the history of multiple myocardial infarcts (heart palpitations) and non-insulin dependent diabetes mellitus, and considering his age, would be an individual in frail health in which a chronic administration or exposure of arsenic leading to toxic levels would be expected to be a significant contributing condition to his death."* Gastric disturbances and other chronic arsenic poisoning symptoms would be expected. Srila Prabhupada's health history shows these symptoms (App. 8). Dr. Callery's valuable opinion established the serious effects of chronic arsenic poisoning- *"a significant contributing condition to his death."*

HAIRCLIPPER OIL CONTAINS NO ARSENIC

After Dr. Morris found 20 X normal arsenic in Srila Prabhupada's hair, Balavanta thought to see if the hair clipper lubricating oil contained arsenic. He called Exxon (USA), receiving a Material Safety Data Sheet on petroleum lubricating oils with its ingredients, absent any arsenic. Later in 1999 the GBC separately received a confirming report from Scientific Services, a health services of the Queensland, Australia government who had tested a sample of the Wahl brand hairclipper oil and it was found NOT to have any significant arsenic.

SP'S DRINKING WATER HAD NORMAL ARSENIC

Balavanta tested Srila Prabhupada's 1977 drinking water sources in Vrindaban and Mayapur (India) and they were *uncontaminated.* This proved that Srila Prabhupada's elevated arsenic was not due to water he drank in India. The water well at the Mayapur front gate, not used for drinking water *nor by Srila Prabhupada,* had arsenic at the very edge of government mandated safety limits. *Yet, unnecessarily, Balavanta still wondered if the drinking water could be the source of the arsenic, contradicting his own definitive evidence to the contrary.* Balavanta found Srila Prabhupada's 1977 water sources in India to be free of abnormal arsenic levels. Actually the arsenic crisis in India's drinking water *started* in the early 1980's and did not exist in 1977. (Ch. 47).

FRUSTRATION WITH POISON WHISPERS

Re: the poison whispers, Balavanta expressed frustration with the weak confirmation he received from Dr. J.P. French, *"an internationally recognized recording analyst."* But JP French was given a poor quality tape for analysis, a copy of a copy of a copy. Balavanta's view of the whispers was as skeptical as the GBC's. *"In general, the content of the whispers on the tapes is not clearly identifiable. Much is left to the ear of the listener. Although the above authorities have offered opinions as to what the voices likely say, doubt remains as to what they actually say. In other words we have not yet reached and may never reach a level of certainty as to content of the whispers. To a large degree this is inherent in the nature of a whisper; the very act of whispering involves a concealing of the substance if not the existence of the communication. Perhaps future technology will be of some benefit in this regard."* This was Balavanta's shortcoming- he used a bad tape and then speculated if the whispers could ever be certified. If JP French had been given a DAT copy from the Bhaktivedanta Archives, surely the whispers would have been confirmed, just as many later audio analyses on DAT tapes did verify the whispers as being about poisoning. Balavanta assumed the whisper were "not clearly identifiable," but *he was very mistaken.* The future technology he hoped for was already available. His investigation was limited to one busy man and $8000, so how much could be achieved? The constraints undermined the results which could have been dramatically improved had the GBC wanted a proper investigation. And the GBC loved Balavanta's errors and lack of results.

DR. NAROTTAMA LAL GUPTA AND ALFRED FORD

Balavanta also interviewed Dr. Narottama Lal Gupta, an Ayurvedic kaviraja who attended Srila Prabhupada in 1977 (Ch. 36). Dr. NL Gupta said there should not be any arsenic in makharadhvaja and that in his medical opinion, Srila Prabhupada had symptoms of liver damage *[this occurs in many kinds of poisoning]*. This, he thought, could lead to kidney damage and could also be responsible for the swelling that was visibly prominent. *[Now we know the liver damage was due to heavy metals poisoning.]* Balavanta also received from Dr. Gupta critical

information that *he did not include in his report* which was revealed later (Ch. 36 Four Kavirajas Agree on Poisoning).

Abhinanda das (Public Relations, Vrindaban ISKCON) wrote Naveen Krishna Dec. 18, 1999 that Ambarish das (Alfred Ford) offered to finance a full, legitimate investigation. He suggested attorney O.P. Sharma for the case (Rs. 100,000). Vineet Narayan introduced Abhinanda das to O.P. Sharma, whom Naveen had met a year earlier. Why was this opportunity missed? An heir to the Ford fortune could have adequately financed Balavanta's investigation to achieve far better results. This was a major mis-step.

SUSPECTS SABOTAGE BALAVANTA'S INVESTIGATION

Balavanta reported on interference to his investigation. *"I obtained additional samples of Srila Prabhupada's hair to submit to Dr. Morris for analysis. He was prepared to perform these tests (pro bono or cost-free) when he was contacted by a Mr. Hooper [Deva Gaura Hari] from Australia who said he was also working on the investigation. Mr. Hooper was not working with me and I do not know him or his role in your investigation. Following this contact, Dr. Morris decided to assess a substantial charge ($6000) for his tests. I contacted you (GBC) to ask for the funds to complete the study, but they have not been forthcoming."*

COMMENT: After the GBC gave Balavanta $8000 to investigate the poison issue, they declined to pay the $6000 asked by Dr. Morris to do tests on their own Srila Prabhupada hair samples (Part 1).

Mr. Hooper was secretly commissioned by the GBC poisoning suspects Tamal, Jayapataka, and Bhakticharu to do a pseudo-investigation to counter the evidence Balavanta and Nityananda had assembled. Balavanta was the official GBC investigator, but meanwhile, simultaneously, the suspects organized their own stealth report presented as *Not That I Am Poisoned (NTIAP)*. There was an official and a rogue investigation with different agendas. By intimidating Dr. Morris, Mr. Hooper sabotaged Balavanta's further hair tests. Later Dr. Morris told Nityananda how Hooper *harassed* him with demands for free tests: *"...a great number of samples need to be tested, and that fairness dictated if one was **pro bono**, all must be **pro bono**."* Dr. Morris had to charge fees for his work, whereas before he would help Balavanta and Nityananda simply out of academic interest. Although ISKCON temples would pay $9,500,000 in the child abuse lawsuit, the GBC would not pay $6000 to investigate the alleged assassination of their own Founder-Acharya. Why? The GBC was afraid of what Dr. Morris' results might be.

WAS BALAVANTA COMPROMISED?

Some devotees suspected Balavanta's investigation was partial to the GBC, not truly independent. One opinion: *"Three years have crawled by; many stalwarts for the cause have mellowed with waiting, or gone quiet. A typical ploy, using time to phase out the opposition and then conclude with being inconclusive. Where are the hard-hitting interviews with the suspects? Why did he not include the detailed Mitchell audio forensic report? Balavanta's report was commissioned by the GBC, paid for by the GBC, and conducted by a former GBC Chairman (Balavanta)."* But the truth is Balavanta was in a difficult situation, employed by the GBC, and constricted by the attorney-client privilege (legal rules of ethics). The GBC was his client, and as an attorney, he was bound to represent his employer's interests and instructions. So when the GBC ordered him not to release information publicly, he was bound by that, and thus his silence for years. Balavanta naively thought that there was still honesty and integrity in the GBC. But after giving his report in March 2000, and being crudely sidelined, Balavanta resigned from the GBC, disgusted by the GBC's cover-up of the poison issue. He told Nityananda he believed Srila Prabhupada was in fact poisoned but that it was difficult in establishing truth while obstructed by a corrupt ISKCON leadership. Years later, his investigation files and original documents ended up with the PTC.

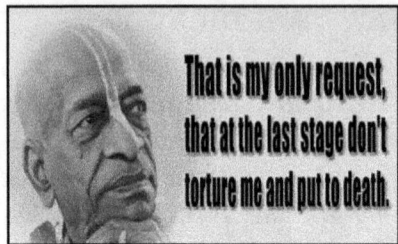

Balavanta was not compromised in his honesty on the poison issue. He felt his further investigation was futile, and he received a GBC e-mail advising he should be concerned for his family's welfare by further participation in the poison investigation. He took it as a "veiled threat." To lend it some credibility, Balavanta's investigation was called "independent," but Balavanta was ***dependent*** on the GBC, who silenced him, restricted his funding, and superseded him with their own secret cover-up. After the GBC's surprise book *NTIAP*, what could he do? His report concluded: *"The investigation is not complete. For example, Dr. Morris has additional hair samples to analyze. The diagnosis by history has not been accomplished. Additional areas of study can be considered. ...because the issue has arisen relative to his earthly pastimes and may be significant to the management of his mission, I recommend that the GBC now work toward the resolution of this matter with a view toward reaching a just and objective conclusion."* Balavanta's report included new, compelling evidence justifying further investigation into Srila Prabhupada's departure: **(1)** The hair analysis finding 20 X average arsenic **(2)** Medical Examiner Dr. Callery stating these amounts of arsenic would be a significant contributing factor to death in Srila Prabhupada's condition **(3)** Confirmation of one poison whisper by audio forensic expert Dr. JP French **(4)** Srila Prabhupada's hair arsenic was not due to Srila Prabhupada's drinking water in Vrindaban or Mayapur.

Balavanta, once GBC Chairman, was unprepared for the level of corruption in ISKCON's leadership. The GBC Exec. Committee

(Naveen, Madhusevita, Bir Krishna M) had appointed him, giving hope for a credible investigation into Srila Prabhupada's alleged poisoning, but the GBC suspects secretly arranged a devious cover-up to preserve their status quo. *"The investigation is not complete."*

CHAPTER 44:
GBC BOOK DENIES ALL EVIDENCE

"...to cut out its eyes and ears, to castrate its analytic capacity, to shut itself off from the truth because of blind prejudice." (P. Kattenburg)

SUSPECT'S SECRET BOOK NOT THAT I AM POISONED

Unknown to Balavanta, a second "investigation," more secret than his own, was launched in mid-1999 just after the release of *SHPM*, orchestrated by 3 primary poisoning suspects (Tamal, Bhakticharu, Jayapataka) with help from their disciples. This was a covert project to prepare a hard-hitting book to bury the poison issue and discredit the evidence in *SHPM*. When Tamal saw that Balavanta was doing honest research and forensics, he teamed up with Bhakticharu and Jayapataka to produce *Not That I Am Poisoned*. This was a rogue project, only known to some GBCs, to do whatever necessary to defend them from the truth. *NTIAP* was only approved by a full GBC vote *after the fact*. **Tamal engaged his disciple Tirtharaj das**, Brisbane temple president, as the coordinator of the book. **Jayapataka engaged his disciple Deva Gaura Hari das**, an Australian university science graduate, as the author and compiler. **Bhakticharu and Tamal funded the project and book costs** ($3000 each). Devamrita, Danavir and other ISKCON "loyalists" gave their autocratic, hypocritical, and deceitful essays of support.

Tirtharaj was an ambitious person with a checkered history (Vol. 6) and by defending the suspects/GBC regime he earned many brownie points (and pardons for his misdeeds). Deva Gaura Hari afterwards was sponsored on an 8 month European tour with his new wife. Disciples collaborated with their gurus (the suspects) to disseminate mis-information on the poisoning evidence. It was the classic modus operandi of the government minister orchestrating his defense by use of his office, subordinates, position, influence, while remaining out of sight. Tamal published his diary in 1998 to counter the poison controversy, using his doctored accounts of 1977 events to "reveal" supposed history that ruled out any poisoning. Tamal then orchestrated the GBC whitewash book, *NTIAP*. But at least the GBC and the suspects now were compelled to break their silence and start lying again.

Deva Gaura Hari and Tirtharaj, privately guided by Tamal, put together an insiders' sham investigation cover-up book. Minutes after Balavanta's report at the GBC meetings, concluding the "investigation is not complete," a surprise presentation was made by Deva Gaura Hari. Each GBC was given a fresh copy of *NTIAP*, deemed to be the full GBC "investigation" on the poison issue. CHAKRA website, Feb. 24, 2000: *"The GBC body today heard convincing evidence that Srila Prabhupada was not poisoned. After Balavanta's inconclusive report, they watched a presentation which convincingly concludes that Srila Prabhupada's passing away was due to entirely natural causes. Resolved: 1) There is no evidence at this time to support the allegations of poisoning of Srila*

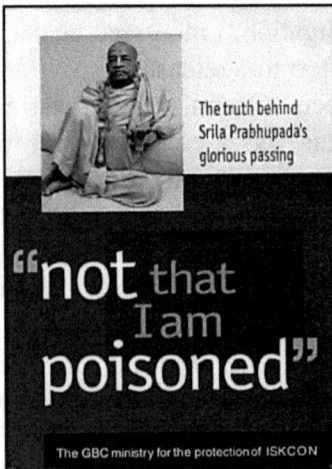

The truth behind
Srila Prabhupada's
glorious passing

"not that
I am
poisoned"

The GBC ministry for the protection of ISKCON

Prabhupada. This conclusion is based on two independent reports commissioned by the GBC Body. 2) The GBC body endorses the book, "Not That I Am Poisoned," as the most detailed and comprehensive exposition of these allegations to date, and it recommends the book strongly to devotees who may have been affected by or who are interested in this issue."

Mahabuddhi commented: *"The official GBC poison investigation was supposed to be Balavanta's report. What happened? So the 'committee to save ISKCON' needed to step in just in case Balavanta's investigation proved that more research needed to be done and the suspects were not fully vindicated? This political #### will not satisfy any intelligent devotee. Why did the GBC not give Nityananda and others the opportunity to present their case? Answer: because it was already decided what the outcome would be! So instead of finalizing the poisoning of Srila Prabhupada issue, the GBC has doubled the issue's credibility with the mishandling by the comic GBC leadership. Instead of giving proper funds to Balavanta or Nityananda's research, they shot in the back their own 'confidential investigator's' report and produced the old 'bait and switch' con game on everyone by announcing the 'PowerPoint Purana' as authoritative. What else to expect from the 'Good Old Boys Club'? CHAKRA is even more amusing with the 'Poison CD rebuttal' on their website, but this CD was stolen and sold to Harikesh. The CD never came out, and is hidden in the GBC X-files."*

GBC: MASTERS OF DECEIT

SHPM pressured the GBC inner circle of poison suspects to urgently disparage the mountain of poison evidence. They titled their response *Not That I Am Poisoned*, a true misnomer (Part 2), revealing the GBC's deceit. *NTIAP* is a continuation the GBC history of institutional cover-ups. All GBCs are tainted by this sinful book, which they know is rubbish meant to obscure the poisoning evidence. The statements and allegations in *NTIAP* are recognized by intelligent readers as a futile and desperate exercise in deception and dishonesty. It was said: *"Denial is standard GBC policy, not a river in Egypt."* May the light of the truth clear up the web of tangled shadows cast by the darkness in *NTIAP*.

SUMMARY CONTENTS OF GBC BOOK *NTIAP*

NTIAP has 320 pages, 20 chapters, 14 appendices, and **(1)** claimed 10 ppm arsenic was normal **(2)** diagnosed diabetes to refute a poisoning (?) **(3)** gave a twisted misinterpretation that Srila Prabhupada said he was NOT poisoned **(4)** scoffed at the poison whispers **(5)** analyzed Srila Prabhupada's symptoms as due to diabetes, not poisoning **(6)** ridiculed the idea of Chandra Swami being suspicious (Volume 3) **(7)** provided worthless fanatical, unsubstantive rhetoric from the suspects and GBCs **(8)** criticized Nityananda's character.

Even ISKCON GBCs unaware of the suspects' secretive cover-up book project seamlessly and compliantly endorsed *NTIAP* as soon as they saw it, relieved by this "solution" to the poisoning "theory." They did not read it and did not care if it came from the suspects. In their 2000 meeting, GBCs laughed and joked about the "poison theory." Those following the poison issue were shocked and appalled, this being the worst outcome. Institutional denials had again prevailed over pursuit of truth. *ISKCON would never do a full, unbiased investigation.* The ISKCON "old boy's club" scored another "victory" as members were intimidated to toe the party line and accept the GBC fraud cover-up.

CHAPTER 45:
NOVEMBER 14 COMMISSION SNUFFED

Naveen Krishna was deeply affected by Srila Prabhupada's poisoning revelation. Studying the evidence, especially Srila Prabhupada's own 1977 words on being poisoned, in 1998 he took a "leave of absence" from the GBC as a matter of conscience. He was well-respected as the Minister of Finance & Management, also heading fund-raising ISKCON Foundation. He coordinated establishment of GBC Ministries and various seminars globally, conducted as "ISKCON Conventions." Being an Indian national, he successfully developed Indian congregations and life-member programs. If the GBC properly addressed the poison issue, he was prepared to resume his service. He was deeply disturbed by ISKCON leaders' denials, obfuscation, and dishonesty, particularly by the prime suspect Tamal, with whom he had worked closely from 1984-98. Previously Naveen noted serious anomalies in ISKCON but hoped societal purity would improve. The idea of Srila Prabhupada poisoned by men still in ISKCON was the last straw. He assisted Balavanta in his investigation and worked to apprise many devotees of Srila Prabhupada's words about being poisoned and he extensively distributed the poison whispers. Finally in Feb. 2000, Naveen gave his full resignation from the GBC, knowing that Balavanta was about to submit his investigative results to a GBC not interested in the truth of the matter. He could no longer participate in ISKCON if it refused to do an honest investigation into Srila Prabhupada's poisoning, in which he saw the entire ISKCON leadership complicit.

Kavichandra Swami (Feb. 17, 2000), re: Naveen's resignation, in the typical ISKCON leaders' way of covering things up: *"I don't think we should send this out to everyone, as he (Naveen) has requested. The simple info that he will not be giving any seminars should suffice."*

NAVEEN STARTS THE NOVEMBER 14 COMMISSION

Balavanta's investigation was axed and the GBC had done their *NTIAP* whitewash. Naveen Krishna invited respected leaders from various sectors to cooperate in an impartial investigation. Since the GBC felt that there was no need for further investigation, but many were unconvinced that the issue was settled, Naveen organized a non-confrontational group to privately investigate Srila Prabhupada's poisoning, in friendly cooperation with the GBC. (This proved naïve.) Ever the diplomat and tactful coordinator, Naveen attracted a broad spectrum of devotees under the banner of the **November 14th Commission (N14C)**. On Sept. 27, 2001, Naveen Krishna sent an announcement to all GBCs:

"On March 2, 2000, the GBC resolved: 'The GBC Body accepts the resignation of Naveen Krishna Das. The GBC Body requests Naveen Krishna Das to give careful and dispassionate consideration to the case presented in the book NTIAP, and then enter into discussion with the Executive Committee for a resolution of this issue.' My resignation as a

GBC was due to troubling questions over Srila Prabhupada's disappearance. By early 2000, I had come to see that, at the very least, these issues deserved further investigation and study. In taking the March 2nd resolution to heart, I could not just close my eyes to disturbing evidence and accept the conclusions contained in the book NTIAP, which had many shortcomings and discrepancies. [...] many of my Godbrothers thought and felt as I did. [...] a comprehensive, professional and dispassionate methodology was sorely needed if this issue was to be properly dealt with. ...as a result of this GBC directive, N14C was formed. Through this organization, all of us who share similar concerns can now 'give careful and dispassionate consideration to the case presented in the book NTIAP' - after which I will then beg to 'enter into discussion with the Executive Committee for a resolution' of this issue, as was requested. The announcement of N14C is attached..."

Naveen announced the formation of the N14C: "... *It is with heavy heart and sober mind that the undersigned announce the N14C, whose mission is to research, investigate, study, document, preserve, honor and glorify the life and times of Srila Prabhupada, including circumstances surrounding his disappearance... as many feel spiritually impelled to (unravel) the circumstances surrounding his disappearance... to those of us who have heard Srila Prabhupada's own voice in those final days. Unanswered questions linger. ...for the sake of his Mission, the issues surrounding his disappearance need resolution... the unequivocal intention of N14C is to pursue a fair and comprehensive investigation in a thoroughly professional manner. We will seek honest answers to straightforward questions. All evidence obtained will be professionally documented and evaluated. N14C has no agenda other than to fully investigate and preserve the facts. We beg the cooperation of all. ...Together we must do the needful... a Special Liaison and Mediation Panel [will] facilitate communication and mediate disputes... between the GBC and N14C. ...In addition, Balavanta prabhu has offered to advise N14C... Anyone, anywhere, who has any information, experience or knowledge to share on this topic is asked to contact us. Naveen Krishna das, Chairperson"* **Commissioners:** *Dhira Govinda das, Guru Prasad Swami, Jahnavi dasi, Naveen Krishna das, Bhailal Patel, Rochan das, Veda Guhya das, Vrindaban das, Yasodanandan das.* **Liaison Panel Members:** *Ambarish das, Gunagrahi Goswami, Rasaraja das, Sesa das.* **Advisors:** *Balavanta, Gupta das*

COMMENT: Secret sympathizers included Prahladananda Swami and others; obvious vocal opponents were Tamal and the whole GBC.

INTRODUCTION LETTERS, N14C PARTICIPANTS (*abbrev.*)

Ambarish Das (Alfred Ford): *"...I would like to state the nature of my participation in the N14C... As a disciple of Srila Prabhupada, I have to take with gravity... Srila Prabhupada has stated three times in one day that he has been poisoned by someone, I have to hear these words with the utmost seriousness. To dismiss these statements as trivial or lacking authenticity is extremely offensive and cruel. As such, I am not satisfied with the results of any of the investigations or reports issued so far. I do not believe that Balavanta was given adequate facility to complete his investigation. He has stated as much himself. Although there are some members of our society who believe this subject is better forgotten, I do not believe it can or should be until a full and proper investigation has been carried out. We may never know the entire truth behind Srila Prabhupada's final pastimes... the events surrounding these pastimes effect... Srila Prabhupada's legacy and enduring society, I support... the newly formed N14C... to set the record straight. My participation is purely for honesty, fairness and justice. My role is to try... to keep an investigation from becoming a trial. The process needs to be a professional and systematic gathering of facts... we need to put to rest, as much as possible, the lingering questions... in the minds of many. We need to create an accurate historical record..."*

Sesa, Balavanta, Gunagrahi. Dhira Govinda: *"The GBC [...] book "NTIAP"- will, upon examination, simply cast further doubts, and will not clear anyone's name... one example to illustrate this is the title of the book itself which is that SP did not speak about being murdered by poison. However, if one simply listens to the taped conversation it is clear (he) did speak about (that), and that devotees around SP were also discussing this topic. So, the central premise of the GBC book on this matter is quickly torpedoed by even a cursory examination. I don't see what good it will do to pretend that the GBC book deals professionally with the issue.... In my participation in N14C I will work to ensure that a fair and professional investigation is conducted (and) because of a conviction that it is vital to the well-being of SP's movement that we resolve the issue of his disappearance pastime. Lacking such resolution, doubts about the matter will fester and impede the healthy progress of the sankirtana movement. Based on the documentation I've seen till now, I do not believe that the issue has been satisfactorily concluded."*

Gupta Das: (letter to Vipramukhya Swami): *"I am in receipt of an email note generated under your header, reproduced below, which was forwarded to me. As regards your comments... the point is that a Commission is necessary in order to professionally explore all of the as-yet-unexplained circumstances and events surrounding the* *disappearance of Srila Prabhupada, a small portion of which was reviewed in NTIAP. From that neutral perspective, it is not "sad" that Naveen Krishna does not feel that the 'evidence in NTIAP was convincing.' What is sad is you are obviously far from neutral on this issue -- you have already made up your mind that nothing will be uncovered by a professional and thorough investigation which has **not** already been done in the rather weak lay analysis which is the basis for NTIAP. ...much of the problematic evidence was barely dealt with in that report, and additional problematic evidence has developed since. Balavanta's conclusion was "the investigation is not complete." It's as if you think potential criminal exposure can be repressed by way of a top-down public relations effort. ...politics -- as opposed to a desire for the full truth -- is the motivating force at the core of your uninformed opinion... if we are all very fortunate, a true investigation into all of the as-yet-unexplained circumstances and events surrounding Srila Prabhupada's disappearance will show no untoward... We should all pray for such a result... In the meanwhile, if you don't have the knowledge base to lend your support for this critically important work, at least don't embarrass yourself by getting in the way of it."*

INDIAN COMMUNITY INVOLVEMENT

After the N14C was launched, many of Naveen Krishna's former comrades in the GBC pressed him to give up this program and instead privately deal with the GBC Executive Committee. However, Naveen politely declined their requests, convinced of that option's futility. Bhailal Patel, Naveen old friend, was president of National Federation of Indian American Associations. In early 2002 he sent a letter to Naveen which was widely distributed, indicative of many Hindu's sentiments.

"I wanted to write to you about my opinion on the investigation being done by the N14C regarding SP's statements about being poisoned. I have been kept informed about this for over a year now. In the middle of 2001 you informed me of an initiative you are undertaking along with many other devotees to more fully understand the circumstances under which SP left this world. During the days immediately preceding his divine disappearance, he raised several times the topic of his being poisoned. It is clear to me, by hearing the available tapes, that SP referred to the said poisoning as a deliberate act of somebody poisoning him, not in the sense of some toxic side effects of medicines. When we met, nobody had any other understanding after hearing the tapes and seeing the translations, than that SP was raising the topic of somebody intentionally poisoning him. The reports you

presented from 3 different forensic experts with very high credentials clearly pointed to evidence from the tapes about incriminating whispers.

"I have all the documents and tapes with me and the whispers seem to confirm an act of deliberate poisoning. All three experts found and confirmed-'It's going down, the poison's going down'- just at the time when SP was being given milk to drink, which he then is drinking. These experts recommended an investigation for homicide. The medical reports indicated symptoms that were consistent with chronic poisoning. Further, all present with SP in Nov. 1977, namely Tamal, Bhakticharu, Bhavananda, and the Kaviraja, all understood and confirmed SP was thinking he had been poisoned. Nevertheless, the GBC presently do not accept even this much, and further, their book NTIAP intentionally contradicts the recorded statements and available evidence. Thus it is highly misleading to the vast majority of innocent devotees and life-members who have not taken the time to study all the direct raw evidence themselves. Since we rely on the honesty and truthfulness of the GBC, this action by the GBC leaves the great majority of devotees and life-members either uninformed or misinformed about this very grave matter.

"Thus, as President of the National Federation of Indian American Associations, NFIA, representing more than 1M Indian Americans, I am compelled to lend support to any effort that thoughtfully arrives at the truthful conclusion about this matter of the poisoning of SP. I am for helping that the truth on this matter is clearly understood and resolving this matter internally and peacefully. I am also co-leading the efforts to organize cooperative action on many issues of the more than 20 million international Indian NRI's this coming Dec. in New Delhi. You also know that in the past I was involved with a major effort to discover the truth about a former Prime Minister of India and we spent more than a million dollars and worked with the highest ranking officials. SP is no less important to us. He is India's greatest Spiritual."

Clearly, the commitment to fully investigate Srila Prabhupada's disappearance was strong, and it was due to the force of truth and the insatiable thirst in honest persons for that truth.

ISKCON ATTORNEY GUPTA DAS WRITES TO THE GBC

In late 2001, Gupta das, an attorney who was involved in many ISKCON legal cases, stated: *"Clearly, the standard to determine if an investigation is conducted into the unexplained circumstances surrounding Srila Prabhupada's disappearance should be about uncovering the full truth at the risk of perceived inconveniences. Yet, after reviewing the work already done, including SHPM, Balavanta's*

GBC Report and NTIAP, my opinion is that a complete investigation into this matter has not yet been done. In fact, not only have the preliminary research and reports generated more questions than provided answers, in addition, troubling questions regarding the forensic work remain unresolved. Accordingly, I fully support the effort... to undertake a professional, objective and comprehensive investigation into the circumstances surrounding Srila Prabhupada's disappearance. Moreover, I encourage all, esp. those with direct knowledge of Srila Prabhupada's final pastimes, to cooperate... All effort should be made to bring this matter to closure during the lifetime of those contemporary to Srila Prabhupada. His legacy deserves nothing less. Gupta das"

GBC INTIMIDATES N14C PARTICIPANTS TO RESIGN

In response, the GBC mobilized its intimidation program and convinced 4 of the N14C participants, all ISKCON "office bearers," to resign from N14C, or be removed from their office and service. Gunagrahi Swami privately apologized for his N14C resignation and was ready to help later. Sesa, Dhira Govinda, Guruprasad Swami decided to retain their positions and service within ISKCON while confirming their continued but unofficial support for a full investigation. Dhira Govinda found it preferable to resign from the ill-fated N14C to continue as director of the Child Protection Office, where he felt he would be able to accomplish more good. A 9.30.01 email from Vipramukhya Swami, organizer of ISKCON's Chakra website, to the GBC Chairman was leaked: *"It is sad that Naveen Krishna doesn't feel the evidence in the "NTIAP" book was convincing. I don't think this commission [N14C] will be able to come up with anything not covered in that book."*

GBC PASSES URGENT, REPRESSIVE RESOLUTION

Within weeks, the GBC had strongly reacted to N14C, passing an urgent resolution, not wanting to wait til the March Mayapur meetings.

PROPOSED CORRESPONDENCE RESOLUTION FOR VOTE:
(by Ramai Swami, GBC Chairman): Below is a proposed resolution in response to the creation of a Commission set up to re-investigate allegations of Srila Prabhupada being poisoned. GBC members have discussed the implications of revisiting this issue at length [...] We are concerned for several reasons: Firstly, we feel we looked into this matter at great length. We commissioned Balavanta to investigate this matter. After some expenditure and much time, the study was inconclusive. Then a thorough investigation was done by Deva Gaura Hari. He presented his findings in NTIAP to the GBC [...] We were satisfied by his work and we accepted the book's conclusions as solid, logical, and well

researched. Secondly, to this date, we have not found any evidence that leads us to discount NTIAP's conclusions, nor do we think it likely such evidence will surface. Still (seen below), the GBC is always ready to hear new information, but we will only receive it through the proper channels--an individual communicating directly with the GBC Exec Comm. We are strong on this point because this is a volatile issue. Previous "investigations" have pointed fingers at Vaishnavas in our Society with no substantial evidence to back such dangerously serious accusation. While we want to remain open [...] irresponsible and unsubstantiated accusations are categorically unacceptable to us [...] despite claims of impartiality [...] this Commission could again bring about such accusations—directly or indirectly.

"These accusations have brought about even death threats--to several devotees, and the GBC fears... It is because of the seriousness of this issue that [...] the GBC has instructed ISKCON office bearers to not be involved in this Commission. All office bearers originally involved in the Commission have now resigned. They did so either after discussions with members of the GBC or after seeing disturbing elements in the procedure and mood of the Commission's members. Although all office bearers have now resigned, we have chosen to include this point in the resolution to emphasize our concern. Naturally office bearers and ISKCON devotees in general are free to look into issues and voice opinions as they see fit, but on this subject which [...] led to threats against devotee's lives, we stand firm that it be directly with our Exec Comm.

RESOLUTION: *Whereas the issue of Srila Prabhupada's alleged poisoning was considered with great concern at the GBC 2000 Mayapur meeting, Whereas the GBC accepted the conclusion of the book NTIAP [...], Whereas devotees who had ongoing concerns about the subject were invited to discuss the issue with the GBC Exec Comm, but they did not do so, Whereas Naveen Krishna and others have, without GBC consultation, set up a Commission to review the issue [...], It is hereby resolved that: The GBC does not recognize the N14C, nor is N14C considered an acceptable response to GBC resolution #10 (Mar. 2, 2000): "The GBC Body requests Naveen Krishna das and others to give careful and dispassionate consideration to the case presented in the book NTIAP and, after doing so, to enter into discussion with the EC for a resolution of this and any related issues. While not recognizing the Commission, if any individual has meaningful new evidence regarding this matter it should be presented to the GBC executive committee. No GBC member or office bearer of ISKCON should participate in this Commission. If they do so, disciplinary action will be taken against them."*

THE GBC CATCH 22: NO CIVIL OR ISKCON OPTIONS

"If they do so, disciplinary action will be taken against them." The only avenue left open to devotees with concerns about the poisoning of Srila Prabhupada was now private communication with the GBC EC, those who cut off Balavanta's funding, ignored his advice for further investigation, and commissioned a whitewash cover-up from the chief suspect's disciples. It was obvious what the GBC's answer to any call for investigation or presentation of evidence would be: *"the matter is already investigated, settled, and there was no poisoning."* The GBC had orchestrated a denial of the mountain of evidence linking that Srila Prabhupada was homicidally poisoned. They give sanctuary to the suspects so as not to disturb their "preaching and disciples." No wonder devotees call the GBC as "KGB-C." (KGB: feared Soviet secret police.)

We now refer to a bedrock portion of the ISKCON "lawbook" which further illustrates the siege mentality in ISKCON and the extent to which the GBC have felt it necessary to squelch any viewpoints not compatible with their institutional policies. It is: *"Iskcon Law No: 12.8 ...and however much he may be dissatisfied with the exercise of that jurisdiction, he shall refrain from invoking the supervisory power of the Civil Court, but shall seek redress of any grievance(s) through the ISKCON judicial process. Otherwise, he may be removed from office and /or his membership in ISKCON terminated.(88)"* The GBC respects no judicature or jurisprudence beyond itself, not even the intervention of the Civil Court, what to speak of its members' humble, sincere pleas and concerns. This is tyranny; to silence the opposition by force, intimidation, or economic, political, or deceitful means. The oligarchical GBC is beholden and obliged to no one but itself.

GBC AND ISKCON COVER-UP IS POLITICAL EVIDENCE

This GBC resolution is based upon a fraudulent so-called "investigation" (the book *NTIAP*) and forcefully silences voices of concern and the search for truth. *But this repression only increases the conviction and suspicions that Srila Prabhupada was indeed poisoned.* Their whitewash cover-up constitutes political evidence, and closely resembles the typical patterns of deceit and corruption in so many tainted institutions, from major religious institutions to prominent governments. The GBC excuse that devotee's lives have been threatened is ironic; what about Srila Prabhupada, who was not simply threatened, but slowly poisoned with heavy metals? The death threats (even if true) were an easy rationale for ending discussions of the issue. It is ridiculous to forbid investigation (someone might make a threat) so we can all live

281

peacefully in ignorance. The N14C agenda was gentlemanly and professional, as seen in the caliber of its participants. Although N14C did not achieve dramatic success, it solidified a growing consensus amongst those dedicated to uncovering the full truth about Srila Prabhupada's disappearance. Upon closer examination of the GBC denials of the poisoning evidence, and seeing the high levels of dishonesty, deceit, and fraud, this becomes further evidence to support the poisoning. One who tries to hide something, is usually guilty of that same thing.

SABOTAGE DOES NOT MEAN SOLUTION

N14C tried to coax the GBC to properly investigate Srila Prabhupada's poisoning. When the GBC forcibly sabotaged participation in N14C by prominent ISKCON members, it was not a solution but rather an end to hopes of GBC cooperation. All private investigative inquiries must now pursue the truth outside ISKCON, a bastion of lies. N14C lost momentum. Naveen became heavily involved with writing, editing, and publishing a third book on the poison issue, titled *Judge For Yourself*. Tamal, the primary suspect in Srila Prabhupada's poisoning, was killed in a car crash in March 2002. This subtly had an effect of lessening the urgency to pursue the issue, at least for some. With this successful repression of its own senior members, the fate of ISKCON and its GBC was sealed: at a future date when the truth becomes established, the entire ISKCON leadership will be replaced.

The present GBC is insincere and incapable of true leadership. Aiding, abetting, and benefitting from the repression of the truth in such a serious matter as Srila Prabhupada's poisoning irrevocably disqualifies them from any leadership role. Even after so much evidence was published and even after it was obvious that so many devotees were very concerned about the circumstances surrounding Srila Prabhupada's disappearance, why the brick wall of prohibition? The GBC have not actually studied the body of evidence, but have refused investigation, becoming complicit in the poisoning of Srila Prabhupada. In time, the "poison issue" will explode in their faces, to say the least.

CHAPTER 46:
JUDGE FOR YOURSELF IGNORED

Already there were four books on the poisoning issue. First Tamal came out with *The Final Pastimes of Srila Prabhupada* in 1988 (see

Volume 2). Then came *TKG's Diary* in 1998 which Tamal intended as his response to the poison controversy, doctoring accounts of 1977 events to show there was no poisoning. Restore The Mission published *SHPM* in May 1999. Then the ISKCON GBC endorsed in March 2000 the prime suspects' whitewash book *NTIAP*. Naveen's attempt to organize a professional commission in further investigation into Srila Prabhupada's departure was also squelched by GBC intimidation. ISKCON had declared the poison issue resolved and settled.

The Asian contingent of the private poison research team held meetings in Australia and the Philippines in 2002. Jitarati, Mandapa, and others liaised with Naveen Krishna, Gupta, and Nityananda, developing action strategies to continue with further investigation. They met with scientists dealing with the Bengal arsenic crisis and with many Vrindaban residents, who gave valuable information. They interviewed kavirajas and doctors who treated Srila Prabhupada in 1977, and hired a private detective agency in Australia to uncover fraud in *NTIAP*. They met with lawyers and judges in India. Nityananda had engaged with various scientific experts for further forensic studies, and he sent the Asian team these results and other materials and research. They decided to produce a book titled *Judge For Yourself*

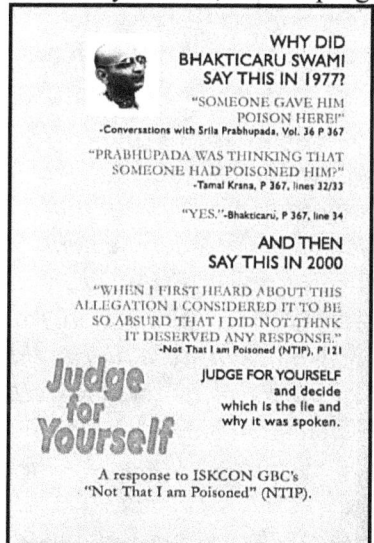

WHY DID BHAKTICARU SWAMI SAY THIS IN 1977?

"SOMEONE GAVE HIM POISON HERE!"
-Conversations with Srila Prabhupada, Vol. 36 P 367

"PRABHUPADA WAS THINKING THAT SOMEONE HAD POISONED HIM?"
-Tamal Krsna, P 367, lines 32/33

"YES."-Bhakticaru, P 367, line 34

AND THEN SAY THIS IN 2000

"WHEN I FIRST HEARD ABOUT THIS ALLEGATION I CONSIDERED IT TO BE SO ABSURD THAT I DID NOT THINK IT DESERVED ANY RESPONSE."
-Not That I am Poisoned (NTIP), P 121

Judge for Yourself

JUDGE FOR YOURSELF and decide which is the lie and why it was spoken.

A response to ISKCON GBC's "Not That I am Poisoned" (NTIP).

to specifically rebut the book of deceptions (*NTIAP*) and present the new evidence, including an audio CD, arranged by Naveen Krishna, of "enhanced" poison whispers, the "poison" conversations with Prabhupada, and Tamal's 1977 interview where he claims Srila Prabhupada asked for "medicine" to die.

Naveen also was a co-editor. Nityananda contributed advance chapters from his upcoming successor book to *SHPM* as well as new forensic evidence. *Judge For Yourself* was published (2000 copies, 250 pgs) and widely distributed in 2003-4, mostly for free. Nityananda then completely suspended his work to see what the results of *JFY* would be. Unfortunately, ISKCON **simply ignored this fifth book completely**, and never issued any statement nor took any action in response. For ISKCON, it was as if the book never existed. But outside the walls of ISKCON, it was read and appreciated by many who came to better understand the facts and evidence that Srila Prabhupada was poisoned.

The Asian team was called Bhaktivedanta Investigation Force, and a website shared the poison whispers and *JFY* chapters with thousands of visitors. It was another concrete step towards disseminating the truth about Srila Prabhupada's disappearance. *JFY* focused on contradictions in ISKCON denials and statements, especially the suspicious statements by the prime suspects. *JFY* expertly connected what the suspects, the doctors and kavirajas, and Srila Prabhupada himself had said in late 1977, highlighting the many questions that ISKCON and its whitewash book failed to answer. The hope that ISKCON could be induced towards the road of honesty, integrity, and cooperation had proved ill-founded, as ISKCON had become fully corrupted. Truth was no longer a guiding principle in ISKCON. *JFY* included a "Demand to Redress" summarizing the need for an honest and thorough investigation.

DEMAND FOR REDRESS (abbreviated): *We, the Bhaktivedanta Investigation Force (BIF), have taken note of your statement and endorsement of the book NTIAP [...] we find your statements to be unfounded, unsubstantiated and incorrect. We have also noted that after making the endorsement, you withdrew from further involvement in investigating Srila Prabhupada's alleged poisoning. You cited your "conclusion" as derived from "two independent reports" commissioned by you. Both were thoroughly examined and found to be contradictory to the facts. No "conclusive" investigation was undertaken. The first "attempted" investigation was by Balavanta. (1) It wasn't "independent," being commissioned by the GBC on an instalment basis and therefore subject to its will; (2) it was never completed and therefore not conclusive. From Balavanta's "final report" to the GBC, showing clearly that his investigation was terminated due to a lack of funding by the GBC, and because of sabotage, which was done under your instructions.*

"As for the second 'conclusive report,' this was enacted by the GBC inner circle only. Why the GBC decided to remove Balavanta and replace him with a new disciple (Hooper) of a suspect (Jayapataka), has left us to assume that Balavanta's public disclosure of Dr. Morris' arsenic findings brought about his swift replacement, and your own position as seeking self-preservation rather than the truth. Your second 'commission' resulted in a report entitled NTIAP, covertly financed by another suspect: Bhakticharu Swami, whose name is missing from the credits. BIF has engaged private investigators in double-checking "expert" witnesses and "testimonies" proffered in NTIAP. We have found the book to be wrongful in its purposeful, misquoting of professional submissions; inaccurate and deceptive in its interpretation of facts; unfounded in its assumptions; biased in favor of those who

commissioned its authorship; unprofessional in its ethic and its attempts to use the weight of authority to quell inquiry and subvert the truth.

"Our report is published in a CD/book titled Judge For Yourself. GBCs have already received copies. We request you to reconsider your position, the gravity of the situation, and we demand that the investigation into His Divine Grace's alleged poisoning be reopened. Set aside corporate concerns in the higher quest for truth. We ask all to avail themselves of the facts in Srila Prabhupada's disappearance, and raise voice with us, so righteousness and truth may prevail. [...] We will spare no expense or effort on the path of due process: investigation and revelation. [...] We have independent, accredited investigators waiting, accomplished personnel who are discreet, familiar with the case, and more than capable of producing a truly independent report." **(END)**

Hare Krishna movement participants could be categorized: **(1)** those who were already convinced of poisoning or who saw the need for a real, honest, and complete investigation, **(2)** those who denied Srila Prabhupada was poisoned, and **(3)** the fence sitters. Yes, no, and uncommitted. *JFY* did not include the 2002 breakthrough in forensic hair tests (Part 1). By 2005 the final hair tests were completed, and although Nityananda tried to finish his new book project by compiling all the evidence, it became too difficult and painful for him, and his book project dragged on for years. Somehow it was not the time for it to be made public. After 2004, the poison issue went very quiet until the book *Kill Guru, Become Guru* was published online in May 2017.

CHAPTER 47:
WAS IT THE WATER?

NTIAP claims the high arsenic was due to contaminated drinking water in India, and thus was not due to poisoning, devising a theory using the Bengal arsenic tainted water crisis. But facts show there is no truth to this idea. Srila Prabhupada's drinking water in Mayapur and Vrindaban was tested and normal. After *NTIAP* was published, cadmium was found to be the primary poison, and there is no cadmium crisis in drinking water anywhere. Still, we will expose the GBC's dishonesty and cover-up mentality in their "arsenic was in water" theory.

BENGAL TUBEWELL ARSENIC CRISIS

The Bengal arsenic water crisis only became known in 1989. The largest poisoning crisis in earth's modern history has been unfolding in the Bengal Ganges basin since the World Bank and Red Cross financed up to three million deep tube wells (20-80 meters), starting *after* the early 1980's. About half of these new deep tube wells became arsenic contaminated, some worse than others, while many others are safe. The tainted wells are randomly located near safe wells. Only testing can determine whether a well is safe. Typically it takes years before manifestation of slow chronic arsenic poisoning symptoms. *Previous to the early 1980's, namely when Srila Prabhupada used to reside in Mayapur on and off, all wells were only a few meters deep, and had normal arsenic levels.* Srila Prabhupada departed in 1977, before the origins of the Bengali arsenic crisis. *How could Srila Prabhupada imbibe arsenic from wells that were not drilled yet?*

DR. CHAKRABORTI'S MAYAPUR TEMPLE WATER TESTS

USA's EPA has set acceptable arsenic levels in drinking water at 50 parts per billion (0.05 pp million). But India and Europe's standard is 10 ppb (0.01 ppm). In 2002 our private investigation team interviewed Dr. Dipankar Chakraborti in India, learning he had tested three Mayapur West Bengal ISKCON wells at Satadhanya's request in the early 1990's. While other area wells were highly contaminated, ISKCON's were normal. *The water at the temple complex was safe to drink,* and thus cannot be blamed for Srila Prabhupada's high arsenic levels. Of course, these wells were also drilled after Srila Prabhupada departed. Dr. Chakraborti is Director of the School of Environmental Studies at Jadavpur University in Bengal, and heads up the crisis team dealing with the arsenic crisis in India. Asked about 2.6 ppm arsenic in hair, he said: *"Horrible !"* This was before we knew of the sky-high levels of Srila Prabhupada's cadmium, which would be termed "catastrophic."

Balavanta tested Srila Prabhupada's drinking water sources in both Vrindaban and Mayapur. There was no elevated arsenic level in the Vrindaban water source or the well supplying the Mayapur guest house in which Srila Prabhupada stayed. The Mayapur well near the front gate had a slightly higher level of arsenic just equal to the USA's maximum allowable amounts, but *Srila Prabhupada did not drink from this well.* The tests were performed by Advanced Technologies & Testing Laboratories in Gainesville, FL on May 25, 1999.

The exact results were: **(1)** Vrindaban "Old Well": 4.3 parts per billion arsenic **2)** Vrindaban "Present Well": 6.69 parts per billion **(3)** Mayapur "Old Deep Well" (Guesthouse): 6.16 pp billion **(4)** Mayapur

"New Well" (Front Gate): 50.1 pp billion. Srila Prabhupada stayed only 6 weeks in Mayapur, Feb. 7 to March 22, 1977. The manifestations of illnesses from well water contaminated with arsenic, however, involved *permanent* residents *over a period of years*, not constant travelers like Srila Prabhupada. *But the wells were normal anyway: Prabhupada's arsenic was not from the Vrindaban or Mayapur water.*

SRILA PRABHUPADA'S "LAST WATER" TESTED

Many years ago, Sadhusangananda das, former temple president of ISKCON Boston, acquired a small quantity of Srila Prabhupada's "last" water from Bhaktisiddhanta das, who had saved it since late 1977, mixing in a little water from Radha Kund. In 2004 Nityananda das acquired this collection of Srila Prabhupada memorabilia, with the last water, which

Drinking Water Specimen
Labeled: "Prabhupada's Last Water"
Assigned ID: Q1
Received: March 30, 2004
Report Date: September 7, 2004

Element Concentrations in Nanograms/Milliliter (ppb)			
Sample ID	Arsenic (As)[1]	Cadmium (Cd)[2]	Antimony (Sb)[3]
Sample Q1 rep 1	19.01	3.55	1.32
Sample Q1 rep 2	19.36	3.60	1.22
Sample Q1 rep 3	20.01	3.71	1.21
Sample Q1 rep 4	21.35	3.80	1.20
Sample Q1 rep 5	21.67	3.88	1.19
Mean conc.	20.28	3.71	1.23
Standard deviation	1.18	0.14	0.05
%RSDM	5.84	3.69	4.35

[1] The Maximum Contaminant Level (MCL) is a regulatory limit set by the U.S. EPA as the highest level of a contaminant allowed in drinking water. The MCL for arsenic has recently been lowered from 50 to 10 ppb effective January 23, 2006. Health risks, if any, associated with the consumption of drinking water containing arsenic at the level found in Q1 would be long-term and cannot be unequivocally, in whole or in part, attributed its consumption.
[2] The MCL for cadmium is 5 ppb. See Note 1 for a definition of MCL.
[3] The MCL for antimony is 6 ppb. See Note 1 for a definition of MCL.

he sent to Dr. Morris for ICP-MS testing. The results showed arsenic was below the old EPA limit but above the new EPA limit, Dr. Morris noted in his report: *"Health risks, if any, associated with the consumption of drinking water containing arsenic at the level found in (the sample) would be long-term and cannot be unequivocally, in whole or in part, attributed to its consumption."*

Srila Prabhupada's "last water" was found with *normal arsenic and cadmium*: **(1)** 20 parts per billion arsenic (MCL 50 ppb) **(2)** 3.71 parts per billion cadmium (MCL 5 ppb) **(3)** 1.23 parts per billion antimony (MCL 6 ppb). Heavy metals concentrations in water do not equate to the same levels in hair by one who drinks that water. Obviously drinking water was not the source of Srila Prabhupada's arsenic (or cadmium) poisoning, because of the simple fact that Mayapur and Vrindaban temple residents have been drinking this same water for the last 50 years.

Drinking water was not the cause of Srila Prabhupada's arsenic or cadmium. **CONCLUSION:** *the Vrindaban or Mayapur drinking water was normal… about 1/1000 of Srila Prabhupada's levels.*

CHAPTER 48:
SRILA PRABHUPADA'S ARSENIC

SP: *Let them talk all nonsense. We say in Bengali, pagale ki na bole, chagale ki na khaya. The goat can eat everything, and a madman can speak anything. (laughter)* (SPConv Jan. 3, 1974)

In light of finding far higher amounts of cadmium than arsenic in Srila Prabhupada's hair, the issue of whether 2.6 ppm arsenic (1998 test) is significant is now not so relevant to the forensic proof of poisoning. The review below of *NTIAP*'s statements on Srila Prabhupada's arsenic levels is more to show the GBC fraud, deceit, shifty tactics, and not to maintain a premise that arsenic was the primary poison. Srila Prabhupada's arsenic was unusually high, but it is now secondary to the sky-high cadmium levels. See Part 1 for the cadmium effects and toxicity; Srila Prabhupada's levels were lethal.

NTIAP tried to dismiss the 2.6 ppm arsenic in Srila Prabhupada's hair, even by rejecting hair analysis science altogether. *NTIAP* is full of bluff, error, fraud, deceit, smoke and mirrors. It is a crooked script of twisting details to cover-up truth. It is doubted that even a few GBCs have studied the poison evidence, or even glanced at their own book of shameful lies and deceit, which would upset any intelligent, honest man. *NTIAP*'s first chapter is *Hair Analysis Shows No Signs of Poisoning*, minimizing the significance of 2.6 ppm by dishonest use of the scientific literatures. It states trace amounts of arsenic are in everyone's hair. Yes, but Srila Prabhupada had 20 times normal. The GBC also claims 2.6 ppm is a normal trace amount of arsenic. But this is definitely false.

MAYAPUR DEVOTEES TESTED, BUT RESULTS NOT GIVEN

NTIAP cites a study done on a group of *"resident Mayapur devotees,"* with *"results of **up to** 1.4 ppm"* arsenic in their hair which had brought no known health problems. The implication was that 1.4 ppm arsenic is normal, not a health hazard, close enough to 2.6 ppm and therefore Srila Prabhupada's arsenic was ok. The highest value in that study was Didima's 1.4 ppm, but what was the average of all the persons in the study? *NTIAP* purposely omitted this data because this study will show Srila Prabhupada had many times the arsenic of the average Mayapur devotee. W*ouldn't that be embarrassing?* Scientific literature says 1 to 5 ppm over a lengthy time constitutes a chronic arsenic poisoning level and that skin tumors and lesions may appear with various diseases and very negative health effects. We wish Didima well.

NTIAP (p. 35): *"Because of the large range of "normal" values for hair arsenic levels, some authorities actually recommend that these values shouldn't be relied upon at all when applied to an individual, but should only be used where a group of individuals from the same area can be measured and compared to the average of that particular group."* OK, so why not compare Srila Prabhupada's 2.6 ppm to the Mayapur devotees, who have many similarities? The Mayapur study could serve as a control to compare to Srila Prabhupada. Yet *NTIAP* did not give their study's average but instead only used the highest value in that study. That is cheating "science." Srila Prabhupada had MANY times the average arsenic of Mayapur devotees. The GBC should also do a Mayapur test for average levels of hair cadmium, and compare that to Srila Prabhupada. They would undoubtedly find that he had 250 X more than the average Mayapur resident.

BENGAL ARSENSIC CRISIS

NTIAP accuses *SHPM* of "passing off" the Bengal tube well arsenic crisis and that Navadwipa and Mayapur are "…seriously affected areas," mentioning one family living north of Mayapur in Murshidabad with 4.78-9.78 ppm hair arsenic and *"two additional members of the family… happened to be there on the day of the testing, had hair arsenic levels of 2.35 and 3.36 ppm… (with no) adverse health effects."* Thus *NTIAP* plays scientist with making their own conclusions. But the scientific literatures clearly state if anyone maintain those very unhealthy levels for a year or more, they will definitely develop serious health problems. *NTIAP* also foolishly stated 10-12 ppm arsenic is normal. The Jadavpur University arsenic crisis team confirms these levels are dangerous.

NTIAP implies everyone in Mayapur has elevated arsenic, that this is not a problem, and Srila Prabhupada's 2.6 ppm was not a problem either. ***Then what is the Bengal arsenic crisis all about?*** After claiming his levels are normal, then *NTIAP* says it is no surprise Srila Prabhupada had higher arsenic since he was drinking Bengal well water (GBC argues it both ways). But *NTIAP* did not refer to Balavanta's tests done on the ISKCON Mayapur and Vrindaban temple wells, which they had in hand, and which had no abnormal levels of arsenic. Also, the Bengal arsenic crisis began with wells drilled after Srila Prabhupada departed. *NTIAP* cheats in so many ways one becomes dizzy…

NTIAP also refers to 3.36 ppm hair arsenic in a *"person who only occasionally visited the Ganges arsenic affected area."* But normal arsenic levels are 0.13 ppm in hair- ***that is scientific truth.*** *NTIAP* confuses by cherry picking high level "outliers". There are 250,000 souls dying in Bengal with 1-10 ppm hair arsenic but *NTIAP* makes a false interpretation that "up to 10 ppm is normal." Fact-check!

GBC "EXPLAINS" ARSENIC IS RELATIVELY COMMON

NTIAP cites arsenic as the 20th most abundant element and as commonly found in pesticides to medicines, thus minimizing its extreme toxicity, saying "it is everywhere," and so, a little (2.6 ppm) is normal. But the scientific fact is tiny amounts of arsenic negatively affect human health, and can quickly kill. There are many common elements that are very poisonous, yet locked up safely in nature. Arsenic's *relative* abundance means it is rarely found in any quantity except produced as *poisons* in herbicides and insecticides. When extracted from nature, arsenic often causes death or severe illness due to its highly poisonous nature. Arsenic is not innocent, as *NTIAP* would have us believe. Ask the arsenic victims. Once the amount of arsenic being ingested daily is tripled, chronic poisoning will follow with serious health ramifications.

The body is extremely sensitive to arsenic. Arsenic trioxide equal to the weight of a 2 inch square of paper can be lethal. A fatal human dose of arsenic trioxide is c. 300 mg (3/10 gram, or 1/100 ounce). Death by arsenic is one of the most horrible. Arsenic in human hair is measured in parts per million (ppm); a few atoms/ molecules out of millions is a health threat. The USA deems over 10 parts per *billion* unsafe. Arsenic is very insidious, poisonous. *"Daily consumption of water with greater than 50 ppm of arsenic, less than 1% of the fatal dose, can lead to problems with skin, circulatory and nervous systems. Greater problems can occur if arsenic poisoning is chronic, resulting in neural disorders, vital organ damage and eventually death." (WQA)* The truth on arsenic is that it is extremely negative to human health in even slightly higher amounts than normal. And what about cadmium at 250 X normal?

"COOKING THEIR BOOK" BY CHERRY-PICKING STUDIES

Regarding the 2.6 ppm arsenic in Srila Prabhupada's hair, *NTIAP* erroneously states: *"...cannot be taken as proof of poisoning. Rather this value falls within the range of average values reported in various studies around the world."* This is further from the truth than an octopus being the mother of an elephant because they both have legs. *NTIAP* **cherry-picked** ONLY two scientific studies that *"have shown levels of 4.6 ppm (Mexico City) and 3 ppm (Glasgow) average arsenic content of hair in normal populations." NTIAP:* (1) Sifted through *hundreds* of hair arsenic studies, taking the 2 highest values (2) Thus being inconsistent with the whole body of arsenic studies (3) Ignored the clear consensus of scientific studies that 2.6 ppm arsenic is a serious health threat (4)

"Cooked" their book to suit their needs **(5)** Ignored differences in ranges, averages, and "normal." This is cheating dishonest research. The average normal arsenic level in unexposed persons is 0.13 ppm (see below).

NTIAP quoted *"a study performed in the 1970's showing an average of 3 ppm hair arsenic in the population of Glasgow,"* claiming it justifies *"any value up to 10 ppm arsenic can be considered to be 'normal' levels."* This unusually high value study had 30 words with no details. Normal is **not** 3 to 10 ppm, as *NTIAP* claims. The vast majority of studies show 3 ppm as being highly elevated; normal is 0.1-0.2 ppm. The Glasgow study contradicts all other studies and is an anomalous "outlier;" *NTIAP* chose it because nothing else fit their ideas. Another Scotland study came with 0.46 ppm. *(Handbook on the Toxicology of Metals*, Vol. II, Friberg, 1986) A third Glasgow arsenic study found higher levels due to its heavy industrialization. Srila Prabhupada did not live in Glasgow. *The 30 word, 40 year old Glasgow "study" is an "outlier" three-liner cherry-picked to bypass scores of studies putting normal hair arsenic at 0.13 ppm.* Then *NTIAP* quotes a MIT Cambridge Toxicology Dept. study by Rogers: *"...gives a range of average values for normal people as being 0.13 to 3.71 ppm arsenic, based on 15 different studies."* But 3.71 ppm hair arsenic is not normal since out of hundreds in 15 groups, ONE person had 3.71 ppm, who was abnormal and an extreme outlier. The *average normal* is 0.13 ppm. The same Rogers is quoted by UN's WHO (1997): *"...in people with no known exposure to arsenic the concentration of arsenic in hair is generally 0.02–0.2 ppm."* So 2.6 ppm arsenic was a seriously elevated level.

CLOSER LOOK AT THE MEXICO CITY STUDY

NTIAP: *"Dr. Armienta tested hair samples from Zimapan residents in Mexico... residents complained of ailments caused from arsenic via well water. The tests showed hair arsenic to be 9.22 ppm. Even more interesting was results for a reference group of unaffected 'normal' people ...of Mexico City and showed the average was 4.6 ppm arsenic in hair. Remember that these are perfectly healthy individuals with no particular exposure to arsenic. The authors explained that the high value could be from **the air pollution prevalent in Mexico City.**"*

Well, they had no particular exposure to arsenic EXCEPT their high levels could be from the air pollution prevalent in Mexico City. So this study is NOT of normal people. Further, upon obtaining a full copy of Armienta's study for $70, it explained: *"...normal levels of arsenic in hair are between **0.3 and 1.75 ppm** (Galvao & Corey, 1987). The average concentration of arsenic for our reference group of 17 persons* *was* **4.6 ppm ± 1.96 ppm.** *This value, which is higher than the international "average" value, could be explained as a result of the air pollution prevailing in Mexico City."* It stated that the reference group's 4.6 ppm was about 3 X over the **limits** of the "international standard" due to severe Mexico City air pollution. Armienta **did not say** they were *"perfectly healthy individuals with no particular exposure to arsenic."* *NTIAP* **added these words to the study**, which is **FRAUD**.

Also, in Armienta's comparison group of 120 Zimapan victims of environmental poisoning (97 had arsenic poisoning symptoms) the range of hair values was 2.4-14.1 ppm (Mexico City's 4.6 ppm is in this range). The Mexico City group and Srila Prabhupada are in the same range as the environmentally poisoned Zimapan victims. Also, Armienta had a very poor accuracy variance of 30%, so 4.6 ppm might be 6.56 ppm. (Dr. Morris' 2.6 ppm accuracy was from 2.5-2.7 ppm).

Also Armienta's study was 3 lines in the 7 page Zimapan study: or *worthless Mexican quality and accuracy.* It tested 17 out of 35 million residents. *Mexico City, like Bengal, also has serious arsenic water contamination issues.* Mexico City's loosely restricted environmental pollution and smog is described as "out of control." A 1983 (40 years ago!) global study by L Friberg & M Vahter showed no place on earth with worse lead pollution than Mexico City (arsenic is a by-product of lead smelters). There was 4 X the lead (225 mg/liter) in Mexico City residents' blood than in the polluted industrial centers of Tokyo or Beijing. *NTIAP's* 4.6 ppm arsenic is NOT normal. H. Hironaka of Fukuoka City Institute inspected hair arsenic levels of 20+ persons in Torreon, Mexico, Oct. 2000 and they were confirmed as chronic arsenic poisoning victims due to tainted drinking water. Skin diseases, pigmentation, pneumonia were present. The three **highest** values in Hironaka's study: 1.1, 1.3, and 4.1 ppm. *The UN says levels over 1 ppm are associated with chronic arsenic poisoning.* 4.6 ppm is healthy? Such is the fraud and deceit by the GBC. They do not know what truth is.

THE LOW-DOWN ON LARRY KOVAR

NTIAP claims that "expert" scientists working with hair analysis and neutron activation agree that any amount up to 10 ppm arsenic can be considered normal. **This is absolutely untrue.** *NTIAP* said Dr. Morris is not an expert on arsenic and hair analysis (ridiculous: App. 1), presenting instead their own *"real"* expert, Larry Kovar, supposed NAA specialist. Why Kovar is better than Dr. Morris? He suited *NTIAP's* dishonesty. Kovar worked at General Activation Analysis (CA), a commercial testing facility. Kovar stated *his opinion* that average hair arsenic levels are 3-10 ppm. Nityananda contacted him in Sept. 2001 and he said something different: *"Arsenic in normal hair may vary from less than 0.1 ppm to about 10 ppm."* When told his opinion of normal did not concur with scientific findings in toxicological literature, he conceded: *"Some of the references indicate that "normal" is 1 ppm arsenic, depending on several factors including diet and occupation... The data can be found in the scientific literature... I have data on <u>acute poisoning</u>, not chronic."* So, he does not know what is normal; his 10 ppm refers to acute poisoning, not normal. So much for *NTIAP's* quack experts. Scientific literature shows 0.13 ppm arsenic as normal. Normal being 3-10 ppm is **rubbish**. The GBC sent hair samples to Kovar, who was unable to test such low mass samples. Kovar later went out of business.

SECOND GBC "EXPERT" AND 12 ppm?

The second *NTIAP* expert was Dr. Cashwell at the University of Wisconsin. Kovar sent the GBC's Srila Prabhupada hair samples to this testing facility, but it was **AGAIN** determined that their facilities could not test such small samples. A true expert would first determine if there was sufficient mass of material for his equipment, but Dr. Cashwell never asked. Dr. Cashwell *supposedly* once tested a student with 12 ppm hair arsenic, and *NTIAP* thus claims 2.6 ppm is normal. This 12 ppm story was likely concocted just like the other *NTIAP* frauds to discredit the whispers and the science of audio forensics. But even so, would one student set the international standard? *NTIAP* bypasses the consensus of scientific literatures, pulling up a few "outlier" data points, twisted into supposed proof of something. *NTIAP's* so-called experts gave personal opinions contradictory to the volumes of scientific studies and were also incapable of testing the GBC's hair samples.

GBC BOOK TRIES TO CREATE DOUBTS

Many texts state that skin afflictions such as eczema are not typical in chronic arsenic poisoning until after one or more years, explaining why Srila Prabhupada did not have skin symptoms of arsenic poisoning. Srila Prabhupada's arsenic poisoning was not long enough to cause arsenic skin symptoms. Mee's lines in the fingernails and keratosis of the soles of the feet thus would need more time to manifest. *NTIAP* says, *"There is no hard and fast rule for arsenic levels."* Nonsense. The GBC book tries to cast a cloud of all kinds of doubts to discredit the importance and significance of Srila Prabhupada's 2.6 ppm hair value, pretending to thus defeat the "poison theory."

WHY DOES THE GBC SO FEAR THE POISONING ISSUE?

The frantic efforts at total denial of the obvious evidence, saying there is *no valid evidence*, begs: what is the GBC afraid of? Why do they feel that, even in light of mountainous evidence, they must ridicule and dismiss *all of it*? Why the Inquisition and witch-hunt tactics, condemning those wanting an honest inquiry as enemies and envious blasphemers? The GBC also did this (1) when devotees objected to the "appointed eleven" zonal acharyas who were imitating Srila Prabhupada, (2) when devotees wanted to discuss the initiation issue, (3) when devotees objected to GBC approval of active child sex abusers as absolute gurus.

The GBC/guru hierarchy knows if Srila Prabhupada's poisoning is factually established, that the positions and benefits of everyone who has participated in or supported their guru regime will be finished. The poisoners wanted to take Srila Prabhupada's place, which they did via an appointment hoax and a deviant system where anyone could become a guru. *If Srila Prabhupada was poisoned, all the gurus will be exposed as complicit beneficiaries of the poisoning.* Everything they have is at stake, lest their guru system collapse. The "poison theory" threatens all they have established since 1977 since it is based on a homicidal takeover. And to perpetuate their fraud, truth was an early casualty.

HOW DOES ARSENIC FIT IN WITH THE CADMIUM?

So: *"If Srila Prabhupada was poisoned with cadmium, how the high arsenic level fit in to the updated evidential picture?" The arsenic was secondary and coincident to the primary poison cadmium.* The antimony was also elevated (8 X normal) in the three high-cadmium samples compared to three pre-poisoning samples. The dramatically higher levels of cadmium (avg. $\pm$ 16 ppm) found in *Samples D, A,* and *Q-2* is definite proof of deliberate homicidal poisoning, far more so than the 2.6 ppm arsenic in *Q-1*. *The debate whether 2.6 ppm arsenic was health detrimental is now less relevant because the cadmium levels are far more deadly and triple-confirmed as well. Srila Prabhupada was maliciously poisoned by lethal levels of cadmium.*

Cadmium being the principal poison, why the abnormal amounts of arsenic and antimony? Perhaps: **(1)** As *impurities* present in the cadmium compound used as poison. **(2)** As a secondary, earlier, or coincident poison *in addition* to cadmium. Recent political poisonings were mixtures of several ingredients. Maybe there is another explanation.

With the available evidence in 1999, arsenic was the best conclusion, and not an incorrect one. Arsenic and cadmium act similarly, both very destructive to health. **Cadmium is more lethal.** The main update to *SHPM (1999)* is: New hair tests show the primary poison was cadmium, at a vastly higher level of ± 16 ppm. Srila Prabhupada's poisoning was a ***heavy metals "cocktail."*** The evidence has evolved from chronic arsenic poisoning to sky-high lethal cadmium poisoning. 250 X normal cadmium over many months is lethal. (Ch. 7) Dr. Morris' 1998 report on 2.6 ppm arsenic: *This concentration is approximately 20 times higher than what I would consider a normal average for unexposed individuals living in the United States."* Dr. Morris initially told Nityananda that 2.6 ppm was at least 15 X normal; in *SHPM* it was conservatively stated as 5 to 10 X normal levels. Afterwards, thorough research showed the ***average normal*** level for arsenic in hair as ± 0.13 ppm. Thus Srila Prabhupada had 20 X the average normal.

CHRONIC ARSENIC POISONING IS 1-5 PPM

NTIAP's audacious position is Srila Prabhupada's 2.6 ppm is *"absolutely NO GROUNDS to claim a clear indicator of poisoning,"* calling it "arsenic idiocy" and "utter ridiculousness." But 2.6 ppm hair arsenic is a seriously elevated level and very detrimental to health, especially if maintained over a longer time. (App. 4) Although not near-term lethal, it is very significant, and legitimately causes great concern. Controversy arose in 2020 over "high" arsenic levels in Whole Foods' bottled Starkey Spring Water when arsenic was 9-12 pp <u>billion</u> (10 ppb max allowed by law). And this was 300 X less than Srila Prabhupada's level. The many references cited below which determine 0.13 ppm as the average normal for hair arsenic also confirm 2.6 ppm is a serious level of chronic poisoning. Srila Prabhupada sustained that level over many months. Wisconsin Laboratory Hygiene Ref. Manual: *"concentrations of arsenic in chronic poisoning are generally in the 1-5 ppm range,* but may range as high as 40 ppm." USA's EPA says: *"and levels in individuals with chronic (arsenic) poisoning range between 1-5 ppm."*

So 2.6 ppm is in the middle of the EPA's range for chronic poisoning. Many studies on arsenic contaminated water state that from 1-2 ppm and up hair arsenic resulted in lung, liver, blood and skin disease, including cancers, and *a lethal dose may be indicated by as little as 5 ppm of arsenic in the hair.* Srila Prabhupada's 2.6 ppm is thus "half-way lethal," yet *NTIAP* says, "no consequence." The Praxis Post and Nando Times (June 2001) reported 5 samples of Napoleon's hair were tested at Forensic Institute of Strasbourg. The director, Bertrand Ludes, said the tests showed from 7 to 38 ppm, confirming "chronic long-term poisoning by arsenic." He said also: *"one nanogram per milligram (1 ppm) is at the high end of an acceptable level of arsenic."* The GBC statements are to be seen as deceptive, erroneous, unscientific, inaccurate, shameful.

CHAKRABORTI AND MUZAMDAR WEIGH IN

We interviewed two prominent scientists in India in April 2002 and received their poignant opinions on the significance of 2.6 ppm hair arsenic. Google their names. They have worked on the Bengal arsenic crisis for decades, and know how to judge the effects of 2.6 ppm hair arsenic. **(1)** Dr. Dipankar Chakraborti, Dir. Environmental Studies, Jadavpur Univ., at the head of the Bengal arsenic crisis said: *"Oh, he will be finished!" "Red Alert?" "Yes."* **(2)** Dr. Muzamdar, Dir. Dept. Sanitary Engineering, All India Inst. of Hygiene Public Health, Calcutta: *"Oh, that is too high." "Red Alert?" "Yes."* The definitive text entitled *Arsenic* (Nat'l Acad. of Sci.) refers to a study by Lander, et al. of acute and chronic arsenic poisoning cases where patients had hair arsenic from 3.0 to 26 ppm, displaying serious physical reactions. Thus Srila Prabhupada, in an extremely debilitated condition, having 2.6 ppm of hair arsenic, had chronic arsenic poisoning. The scientific evidence establishes that 2.6 ppm is consistent with chronic arsenic poisoning.

COMPARING ARSENIC PRE AND POST POISON LEVELS

Two pre-1977 tests of Srila Prabhupada's hair (pre-poisoning) had normal levels of 0.112 ppm arsenic (averaged), and compared to his elevated levels, there is a jump of **23 X** from 0.112 to 2.6 ppm. Do we see the problem? The latent adverse effects of arsenic poisoning can result in hair levels returning to normal while the internal damage to health is irreversible and invisible until an advanced stage. Studies on retired German vineyard workers showed normal hair arsenic, but they had advanced diseases due to past poisoning. Because the blood mostly cleanses itself of arsenic in 3-5 days, thereafter there is minimal arsenic deposition in the hair. But the accumulated arsenic burden remains fixed in the internal organs. The seriousness of 2.6 ppm is reinforced by Friberg's reference to a study by Ishinishi on retired workers who had in the past been extensively exposed to arsenic, had normal hair arsenic levels, but with serious symptoms of chronic arsenic poisoning *(Handbook: Toxicology of Metals* Vol.2: Specific Metals, Friberg, 1986.) Current hair levels may not reflect the health damage already done by past poisoning. Was Srila Prabhupada's arsenic higher at other times, with health damage continuing due to those previous higher levels? E.g., a war veteran still suffers from his wounds even after the war is over.

EIGHTEEN ARSENIC DISHONESTIES FROM ISKCON

NTIAP postulates speculations that 2.6 ppm is meaningless. These dishonesties are summarized: **(1)** Srila Prabhupada drank from tainted wells in India which caused his elevated arsenic levels. *But* the wells he drank from were tested and normal. **(2)** That normal hair arsenic is 3-12 ppm. **But** the vast number of studies show normal is 0.13 ppm. **(3)** Ignoring the serious health effects of West Bengal residents with 1-10 ppm hair arsenic. **(4)** Ignoring that scientific studies put chronic arsenic poisoning in the 1-5 ppm range. **(5)** Deceitful omissions in Mexico City, Glasgow, Mayapur studies, cherry-picking "outlier" values. **(6)** Quoting scientific literatures out of context re: 2.6 ppm significance. **(7)** Falsely implying that high end outliers in ranges of "normal" people leads to good health. **(8)** Comparing seafood eaters' high arsenic levels as "normal" for Srila Prabhupada (below). **(9)** Falsely suggesting Ayurvedic medicines had enough arsenic to result in 2.6 ppm. **(10)** That 2.6 ppm is "normal" so there was no poisoning. False. **(11)** Hair analysis for arsenic is unreliable. False. **(12)** That 2.6 ppm could be from malnourishment and not poisoning. False. **(13)** Character assassination, name-calling, ridicule. **(14)** Rejecting Dr. Morris and promoting Larry Kovar as an expert. **(15)** That arsenic up to 12 ppm is normal. False. **(16)** Exaggerating limitations in scientific methods to falsely discredit them. **(17)** Misinterpreting why Srila Prabhupada had no skin lesions, Mee's lines. **(18)** Arsenic is everywhere, so why worry? False.

ARSENIC CASES WITH SIMILARITIES AND PARALLELS

We compare the arsenic levels and similarities in the following cases to Srila Prabhupada's case. **(1)** In 1955 in Japan over 12,000 infants were fed powdered milk tainted with arsenic; 130 died. The subacute poisoning symptoms were fever, abdominal swelling, enlarged liver, *coughing, runny nose (rhinitis), conjunctivitis,* vomiting, diarrhea. **(2)** In 1901, 500 persons drank arsenic tainted beer, with digestive symptoms, especially vomiting, diarrhea. In weeks *conjunctivitis, runny nose (rhinitis), laryngitis, heart irregularities, bronchitis* appeared. **(3)** In 1956 Mizuta reported on 220 patients poisoned by arsenic tainted soy sauce in Japan. Symptoms included anorexia, liver swelling, and symptoms of the *upper respiratory tract* were predominant. Hair arsenic 3.8-13.0 ppm. This was a more serious poisoning than with Srila Prabhupada's 2.6 ppm (but which lasted many months).

(4) Many chronic arsenic poisoning cases in Chile in 1960's came from 0.8 ppm arsenic tainted water. Symptoms were *chronic coryza (mucus) and chronic cough, broncho-pulmonary* disease, diarrhea, loss of taste, thickening of skin *(hyperkeratosis), abdominal pain.* **(5)** A diabetic female age 55 was hospitalized for diarrhea, nausea, vomiting, weakness. Five weeks earlier she ate noodle paste and developed great illness. The husband died. A urine test revealed 16.4 ppm arsenic. With chelation therapy she survived. *Many tests were required.*

Cadmium symptoms are quite the same as those of arsenic- Srila Prabhupada's health symptoms came from both cadmium and arsenic.

AVERAGE OF AVERAGES MAKES AN AVERAGE NORMAL

Below is a list of 23 scientific studies which are averaged to obtain a true figure as to the "average normal" level of arsenic in human hair. This *average of the averages is 0.13 ppm*. Thus Srila Prabhupada's 2.6 ppm arsenic was **20 X** the average normal. The GBC may cherry-pick studies with outlier values, but by averaging many studies we arrive at a value "immunized" from the outliers and "jury rigging" games found in the GBC's cover-up books.

(1-12) Twelve (12) separate studies from *WHO: Water And Sanitation* are quoted: **(a)** Valentine, et. al. 1979 **(b)** Olguin, et. al. 1983 **(c)** Narang, et. al. 1987 **(d)** Takagi, et.al. 1988 **(e)** Koons and Peters, 1994 **(f)** Wang, et. al. 1994 **(g)** Wolfsperger, et. al. 1994 **(h)** Vienna, et. al. 1995 **(i)** Raie, et. al. 1996 **(j)** Paulsen, et. al. 1996 **(k)** Rogers, et. al. 1997 **(l)** Kurttio, et. al. 1998. The average of these 12 studies cited above is 0.11 ppm hair arsenic.

(13) Arsenic Contamination In Bangladesh Groundwater: S. Tsushima at *www.kfunigraz.ac.at* did a study of hair arsenic levels in a control group with **0.08–0.25 ppm.** The median of this range is **0.165 ppm**.

(14) Handbook On The Toxicology Of Metals: In Japan, an industrialized country, the median arsenic content of human hair was **0.174 ppm**. (Vol. II: Specific Metals, by Friberg, et al, 1986).

(15) Bulgaria, washed hair/ range: 0.037–0.625 ppm & average **0.158 ppm**. **(16) USA Males**: Average **0.13 ppm**

(17) Pakistan: Range of 0.04-1.41 ppm; Average **0.26 ppm** **(18) Analytical Research Labs, Phoenix AZ:** Head chemist Russ Madarash estimated the average of ARL tests for arsenic hair levels at **0.10 ppm**.

(19) Pan, et.al. (1993): A study of 28 healthy Taiwanese: average **0.27 ppm**. **(20) Yamato** (1988): Japan, 100 samples, 0.04-0.33 ppm with average of **0.08 ppm**.

(21) A Hair Analysis in 2000 by ARL. Arsenic was **0.13 ppm**.

(22) Physics Dept, Univ. Of Tehran: Pazirandeh, et al published a NAA study (Appl Radiat Isot 1998) of arsenic in hair of 3 groups in an Iran village. The healthy group had an average of **0.2 ppm**.

(23) Srila Prabhupada's Pre-1977 Hair Arsenic Levels: Average of 4 tests, Srila Prabhupada's pre-1977 hair arsenic levels: **0.112 ppm**.

These 23 sources averaged gives a normal value of 0.13 ppm.

STUDIES WITH INTER-INDIVIDUAL VARIATION

Some studies give range and average, and we see how ranges can be misleading. *The Heavy Elements: Chemistry, Environmental Impact and Health Effects, p 488* cites human hair arsenic studies with wide ranges: Pakistan: range 0.04–1.41 ppm, average of 0.26 ppm. We see the average is 16% the range's upper end, so the higher values are "outliers." From a 2500 person study in Hungary (which has a water arsenic problem), a few had up to 3 ppm with the average "well below 1 ppm." Outliers distort the actual normal average. A few cases out of 2500 do not make a normal value. *This phenomenon is called "inter-individual variation."*

"When studies of arsenic… are scrutinized, a substantial inter-individual variation in the relative amounts… is obvious, although group averages seem to be fairly consistent between studies." (Arsenic in Drinking Water, 1999, p235) Ranges can prejudice towards outliers. Science adjusts to statistical problems of ranges, as those assumed normal will inevitably include some who are unexpectedly abnormal. Also in *Handbook on the Toxicology of Metals, Sec. Ed., Vol. II: Specific Metals, 1986,* p56: a study of hair arsenic in 1960's Scotland found a wide range of 0.02-8.17 ppm, with average 0.46 ppm. The vast majority of the 1250 subjects had under 1/2 ppm. Thus the outlier 8.17 ppm was not "normal."

MORE STUDIES: ARSENIC AVERAGES WELL UNDER 1 ppm

(1) USA's EPA: Safety Healthcare Handbook (arsenical pesticides): *"Hair has been used for evaluation of chronic exposure. Levels in unexposed people are less than 1 ppm."*

(2) Poisindex® Toxicological Managements:: A hospital guide (Sect. 4.1.4) quotes from Baselt & Cravey, 1989: *"Normal concentrations of arsenic in hair and nails is less than 1 ppm."* **(3) Wyoming Analytical Laboratories, Golden, Co:** *"...the normal Arsenic levels in human hair is less than 1 ppm."* NTIAP mentioned this lab, but these values were omitted, which is dishonesty.

(4) Wisconsin State Hygiene Laboratory: Their Reference Manual: normal arsenic in human hair is *less than* **0.5 ppm**.

(5) Associated Regional And University Pathologists: www.aruplab.com gives "reference interval" to testing laboratories, specifies normal hair arsenic levels of **0.00-0.90 ppm**. **(6) Analytical Research Labs (ARL):** Head chemist Russ Madarash July 5, 2001: Average arsenic is 0.1 ppm.

(7) UN Synthesis Report On Arsenic In Drinking Water, Ch. 4.1: diagnostic criteria of chronic arsenicosis is *"arsenic level in hair above 1* *mg/kg (1 ppm)" without history of seafood." and: "in people with no known exposure the Arsenic in hair is generally 0.02 –0.2 ppm."*

SOURCES CONFIRM OVER 1 PPM IS CHRONIC POISONING

(1) World Health Org: ascribes 3-10 ppm hair arsenic levels to victims of chronic arsenic poisoning. **(2)** Arsenic In Bangladesh Groundwater: Cites a hair arsenic study at *www.kfunigraz.ac.at* in an arsenic poisoned group with **1.1-19.84 ppm.** **(2)** Forensic Institute, Strasbourg, Switzerland: new tests of Napoleon's hair showed from 7-38 ppm, confirming "chronic long-term poisoning by arsenic" and "**[1 ppm]** is at the high end of an acceptable level of arsenic." **(3)** Three case studies 20 years ago involving ingestion of a traditional Chinese anti-asthmatic medicine called Sin Lak, by ST Wong, et al state arsenic poisoning is diagnosed when symptoms are combined with biochemical evidence of over **1 ppm** in hair or 0.01 ppm in urine. All 3 patients developed serious health problems, one dying, and 2 *" escaped detection for years..."* **(4) Ronpibool, Thailand:** arsenic contaminated water: Study by C. Choprapawon (2000) tested 500+ children to find relationships between elevated arsenic hair levels and intelligence: Levels above **1 ppm** showed dramatic decreases in intelligence. Elevated arsenic levels related to stunted height, weight.

(5) Hair Arsenic Levels and arsenicosis in 3 Cambodian provinces: Hashim JH· et al. (2013): *"Natural, inorganic arsenic contamination of groundwater in Cambodia tube wells was discovered in 2001 leading to the detection of the first cases of arsenicosis in 2006. [...] A cross-sectional epidemiological study of 616 respondents... The most prevalent sign of arsenicosis was hypomelanosis with a prevalence of [...] 32.4% among respondents with a hair arsenic level of over 1 µg/g. This was followed by hyperkeratosis, hyperpigmentation and Mee's lines. Results suggest a **1.0 ppm hair arsenic level** to be a cutoff point. This hair arsenic level, together with the presence of one or more of the classical signs of arsenicosis, seems to be a practical criteria for a confirmed diagnosis."* So, <u>32.4% of those over 1.0 ppm hair arsenic displayed symptoms of arsenicosis.</u> **(8)** Diagnosis, Treatment of Chronic Arsenic Poisoning: Diagnostic criteria of chronic arsenicosis to the UN's WHO for health was: Arsenic in hair above 1 ppm and nail above 1.08 ppm.

Chronic arsenicosis begins at 1 ppm. (NTIAP says 12 ppm is ok?) NTIAP also stated: if 2.6 ppm arsenic is abnormal, then why did Srila Prabhupada not show physical signs of arsenicosis? This probably was because it lasted months, not years. Dr. Morris confirmed that *2.6 ppm borders between "dangerous and very dangerous.*

CHAPTER 49:
HAIR ANALYSIS

SCIENCE OF HAIR ANALYSIS IS A RELIABLE INDICATOR

NTIAP, Ch. 1, #8, tried to discredit the science of hair analysis: *"Hair analysis for arsenic is a very unreliable indicator of serum arsenic levels when a specific individual is tested without a range of reference values from a group of the same time and place for comparison. This unreliability is even more marked when a small amount of hair sample is tested."* This may sound scientific, implying testing hair for metals and poisons is unreliable or inaccurate, but this is false and misleading. **(1)** The GBC had a reference group in their cited study of Mayapur devotees, but did not use it. **(2)** Also, we do not need to correlate Srila Prabhupada's hair levels to his blood. Hair levels in themselves reliably indicate levels of heavy metals *as related to health.* **(3)** Testing methods like NAA should be (and were) used to obtain accurate results on small samples. **(4)** To compare Srila Prabhupada to normal values found in various unexposed groups is a *valid, reliable, scientifically accepted method of determining abnormal exposure or poisoning.* **(5)** Hair analysis is reliable, widely used and accepted.

There are established normal/ abnormal levels. The EPA, WHO, UN, scientists, doctors, all accept hair analysis to be accurate for arsenic and cadmium. **(1)** *"Human head hair is a recording filament that can reflect metabolic changes of many elements over long periods of time and thus furnish a print-out of post nutritional events."* W.H. Strain, 1972. **(2)** *"The analysis of blood, excreted by-products, and human head hair represents a method for determining body element levels."* H.C. Hopps, 1977. **(3)** *"There is now a considerable body of literature on the use of hair in forensic science, in the diagnosis of disease states, and in the assessment of nutritional status."* B.J. Stevens, 1983. **(4)** *"Hair may provide a continuous record of nutritional status."* T.H. Maugh, 1978. **(5)** EPA (US Gov't) did a 1979 study reviewing 400 $+$ hair testing reports, concluding hair is a *"meaningful and representative tissue for biological monitoring of most of the toxic metals."* **(6)** Great Smokies Diagnostic Laboratories: *"There are numerous papers on the accuracy and efficacy of hair testing, particularly for toxic metals such as mercury. For more than 30 years, the significance of measuring element concentrations in scalp hair, blood, and urine has been studied."*

(7) A 1986 study by V Bencko, et al called *"Biological monitoring of environmental pollution and human exposure to some trace elements"* states: *"In addition to analyses of plant and animal specimens, the element content of human hair as an indicator of exposures to <u>arsenic</u>, mercury, <u>cadmium</u>, lead, antimony, manganese, nickel and cobalt has been <u>repeatedly confirmed as reliable</u>, if the analyses were carried out and evaluated on group diagnostic basis and were done in groups of individuals occupationally not exposed to these metals."* **(8)** From Nutri-Test Analytical, Edmonton: *"Blood, urine and hair are the most accessible tissues in which to measure elements in our body, and they are sometimes referred to as indicator tissues. Blood and urine concentrations usually reflect recent exposure and correlate best with acute effects. Hair is useful in assessing variations in exposure to metals over the long term. It is a useful tool for diagnosis of heavy metal exposure."* **(9)** A 1980 study by JS Lee and KL White called "A review of the health effects of cadmium" found that *"hair values correlate well with exposure"* to <u>cadmium</u>, whereas blood values did not. **(10)** A 1979 study published by the EPA/ DW Jenkins called "Toxic metals in mammalian hair and nails" found that *"hair analysis, when properly performed, is a reliable measure of tissue levels of <u>cadmium</u>."*

(11) A 1973 study by RW Thatcher et al called "Effects of low levels of cadmium and lead, etc" found that *"hair analysis is superior to blood in reflecting long term <u>cadmium</u> exposure."* **(12)** *"Determination of the trace element levels in hair and nails is the subject of interest in biomedical sciences. <u>Cadmium</u> levels in blood, urine, hair and nails samples are often determined in paraclinic lab tests."* www.ncbi.nlm.nih.gov/pmc/articles/PMC5596182: **(13)** Serdar MA, et al in 2012 on trace elements in hair: *"Hair analysis is a promising tool for routine clinical screening and diagnosis of heavy metal exposure and essential trace element status in the human body. Systemic intoxications have been identified by anomalously high values of toxins in hair samples."* **(14)** US Dept Health & Human Services (1999): *"Hair levels of <u>cadmium</u> have been used as a measure of cadmium exposure, and external contamination is found primarily in those exposed to occupational or environmental pollution, and even in those cases, not significantly in hair close to the scalp."* **(15)** Frery et al (1993) evaluated hair levels in those exposed to tobacco smoke, concluding that <u>cadmium hair analysis was a reliable indicator in those with higher exposures,</u> although not sensitive enough to resolve differences at lower levels.

(17) www.greatplainslaboratory.com: *"Heavy metals toxicity caused by increasing levels of pollution and industrial chemicals is a growing* *health threat. [...] Extensive research established that scalp hair element levels are related to human systemic levels. Many researchers consider hair as the tissue of choice for toxic and several nutrient elements. [...] As protein is synthesized in the hair follicle, elements are incorporated permanently into the hair with no further exchange with other tissues. Scalp hair is easy to sample, and because it grows 1-2 cm /month, it contains a 'temporal record' of element metabolism and exposure to toxic elements. [...] These elements levels in hair are correlated with levels in organs and tissues. Toxic elements may be 200-300 times more highly concentrated in hair than in blood or urine. Therefore, hair is the tissue of choice for detection of recent exposure to elements such as arsenic, aluminum, cadmium, lead, antimony, and mercury. With new vast improvements in technology, instrumentation, and application of scientific protocols, hair element analysis is now a valuable tool in providing dependable, useful data for physicians and patients. The EPA stated in a recent report: '...if hair samples are properly collected... analyzed by the best analytic methods, using standards and blanks as required, in a reliable laboratory, the data are reliable.' (US EPA 600/4-79-049) Hair element analysis is a valuable, inexpensive screen for physiological excess, deficiency, and maldistribution of elements."*

CONCLUSION: *Hair analysis gives excellent indicators of abnormal bodily elemental exposures compared to normal levels in human society, especially at higher levels, as with Srila Prabhupada.* It is an excellent indicator of metals poisoning. That hair analysis is so widely used in science, medicine, and law enforcement proves its usefulness. Hair analysis reliability, accuracy, and validity is widely accepted in the scientific community when properly performed with advanced equipment and technology, and a few common sense stipulations. There are endless references in the scientific literatures about the practical use of hair analysis for study of heavy metals toxicity/ poisoning, albeit with deference to variabilities and uncertainties.

So much for *NTIAP's* dishonest so-called scientific postulations!

WERE DR. MORRIS' HAIR TESTS ACCURATE?

Dr. Morris stated that the accuracy of his 2.6 ppm arsenic test on tiny amounts of hair was within 0.1 ppm of arsenic, which is "very adequate and plenty good." He said the accuracy of his methods and equipment are extremely good and that poorly executed and ill-equipped commercial scams are of questionable accuracy. MURR NAA tests are highly advanced, accurate, and reliable. The GBC referred to abuse by shady companies to disparage the science of hair analysis. The existence of quack doctors does not mean there are no good doctors. Also *NTIAP* contradicts itself: **(1)** On p. 123, BCS minimizes the evidence: *"...based on some whispers and <u>an incorrect and dubious analysis of some hairs</u>..."* **(2)** Yet on p. 318, the *NTIAP* author relates how he, on behalf of the GBC, approached Dr. Morris for testing Srila Prabhupada's hair *Samples A* and *D*. After abandoning those samples, he then concluded *NTIAP*: *"The ministry for the protection of ISKCON extends an open invitation to anyone who would like to fund <u>this analysis by Dr. Morris</u>"* The left and right hands say the opposite. *NTIAP* also stated the tiny hair amounts tested by Dr. Morris cannot be accurate and are unsuitable as evidence. ISKCON apologists and the prime suspects will say and do whatever they can to create doubts and distraction from the real, hard evidence. Attesting to the accuracy of Dr. Morris' hair tests are the close correlations amongst the 18 values in the six tests he performed. This consistency even applied to samples that greatly varied in mass.

Some think very small hair samples cannot be accurately tested. Hari Sauri said this about *Sample Q-1*: *"Balavanta dismantled the clippers and found some hair fragments under the blades but these were <u>not nearly big enough to do reliable tests on</u>. The hair samples I got later on from Daivi Shakti ...were much bigger and probably sufficient to get a fairly accurate reading."* Yet, *Samples Q-2* and *A* produced very similar readings of sky-high cadmium even though *Q-2* was 20% the mass of *A*. There are few places on this planet that can do NAA tests on hair samples of this size, and the GBC failed to find one. Hari Sauri speculated in ignorance of the accuracy of NAA testing.

Dr. Morris at MURR was fully capable of obtaining accurate results from samples of 0.00012 and 0.00310 grams in weight, and he wrote about accuracy in early 2000: *"As you have already discovered, these small samples are beyond the reach of most NAA laboratories. We can accurately analyze them at MURR for arsenic with a sensitivity of 1 E-11 grams. Assuming the mass of the sample to be 1 milligram (0.001), our sensitivity translates to a detection limit of approximately 0.01 to 0.1 ppm. This is well below the level of arsenic one would expect in a hair specimen from a person who had been subjected to arsenic poisoning. (However,) these analyses are costly, primarily because of the sample size."* His accuracy in *Sample Q-1* was ± 0.1 ppm, or 2.5-2.7 ppm. Dr. Morris did not have an accuracy problem.

The FBI tested two single hairs of Napoleon, achieving accurate findings with equipment and techniques appropriate for small samples. These hairs were lineally, segmentally tested for the various arsenic levels from one end of the hair to the other, giving a poisoning timeline history. NAA is an extremely sensitive method. Dr. Morris also compensated for background readings. Countless scientists use hair analysis for accurate and useful results, if performed properly. Dr. Morris does not run hundreds of commercial tests daily by an automated process. He prepared *each* test with its own fine-tuned parameters and settings of his precise testing equipment. NAA hair analysis is a valid and accurate scientific method. Or why are scientists/ researchers the world over testing hair? Or why fund Dr. Morris' MURR facility with tens of millions dollars for 40+ years to do useless hair tests?

NEW MICROANALYTICAL HAIR ANALYSIS METHODS

Years after Dr. Morris' tests, science developed new, even more accurate methods for tiny amounts of hair analysis, in measuring heavy metals or in DNA comparisons. *Hair analysis by qualified labs is extremely accurate and reliable.* Wikipedia (2015) Arsenic Poisoning: *"Thus for a temporal estimation of exposure, an assay of hair composition needs to be carried out with a single hair which is not possible with older techniques requiring homogenization and dissolution of several strands of hair. This type of biomonitoring has been achieved with newer microanalytical techniques like Synchrotron radiation based X ray fluorescence (SXRF) spectroscopy and Microparticle induced X ray emission (PIXE). The highly focused and intense beams study small spots on biological samples allowing analysis to micro level along with the chemical speciation."* Future tests of one piece of Srila Prabhupada hair only 3-5 mm long could show various cadmium levels over a month.

EXOGENOUS OR ENDOGENOUS?

One skeptical response to high heavy metals levels in a hair test is: ***"Maybe it is due to external contamination."*** Did the poison in the hair come from the internal blood deposition process, called endogenous, or from external sources called exogenous? Was the poison bound into the hair internally from the blood at the growing hair root, or was it adsorbed externally through the hair walls' surface area from air, dust, oils, shampoo, etc? Yes, a hair sample test should reliably and reasonably exclude external contamination as a possibility. The factors by which such exogenous origins occur are discussed below. Dr. Morris did not wash *Samples A* and *D* before testing, as this can have serious effects in compromising of results and was of limited value anyway. *By powerful microscopic examination he had not found any significant amount of external debris on the hair samples; they did not show evidence of external contamination, such as oils, dust, dirt, chemicals.* Also, he referred to scientific findings that hair very close to the scalp, as these samples were (the first half inch), was by far least likely to have *external contamination*. A study on hair test validity found that much of the variance in results was actually due to the washing steps themselves. Concern about misleading results due to external contamination, in no way invalidates the science of hair analysis. "Buyer beware" means finding a reputable lab who knows how to deal with the external contamination issue. And, we are NOT dealing with an exposed industrial worker with a few multiples over normal. Srila Prabhupada had 250 X normal levels. Srila Prabhupada's head was bathed 2 times a day, and being very short, his hair was not externally contaminated.

COSMETICS, SHAMPOOS, HAIR CREAMS, MASSAGE OILS

Selenium dandruff shampoos can result in high hair selenium values due to "external contamination." Hair dye, creams, sprays, straighteners, etc cause external contamination and produce false positives in hair tests. These external chemicals can be adsorbed into the hair. Therefore the personal history and habits of a person should be learned to reasonably rule out the possibility of external hair contamination. Srila Prabhupada did not use these compounds, and anyway, none of those items contain such high amounts of cadmium as found in his hair. Mustard seed oil was used to massage Srila Prabhupada daily, including his head, but it has no discernable cadmium. Even if the massage oil did have sky-high cadmium levels, those persons giving massages would also be poisoned through their hands; but none of the masseurs were poisoned. Massage oils are not an external cadmium/arsenic source. The hair clippers were tested for cadmium plating (negative). The clippers' lubricating oil had no arsenic, and we presume no cadmium either. How could 3 different hair samples have such similar levels of external contamination? The cadmium was NOT EXOGENOUS, but endogenous, or internally assimilated from the blood. Further, external contamination does not explain the "mystery" medical symptoms documented in Ch. 31.

TOTAL BODY BURDEN IS NOT OUR INTEREST

Some references *appear to say* that from hair values to body burden there is a poor correlation. Elemental levels in muscle, fat, organs, blood, and urine may not be directly indicated by hair tests. But so what? As the CDC's website says about cadmium in hair: *"Studies of exposed workers have not found a quantitative relationship between hair cadmium levels and body burden."* We are not interested in what specific levels of abnormal heavy metals would be in various organs. Hair tests do determine abnormal levels of poisons in the general body.

RANGE PROBLEMS AND META-ANALYSES

Scientific studies of hair mineral levels give results with means, ranges, averages, and medians. Averages and means are the same. Range is the lowest to highest values. Median is the middle value, different than the average. So: **(1)** Ranges with abnormal outliers are misleading. **(2)** There should be diet and occupational adjustments in understanding Srila Prabhupada's normal arsenic levels (see below). **(3)** The wealth of evidence in scientific literatures state "normal" to be far under 1 ppm arsenic in hair, an average 0.13 ppm. **(4)** The critical function of exposure duration in relation to dosage. **(5)** Srila Prabhupada's pre-poison normal levels (0.11 ppm) match societal norms (0.13 ppm).

Outlier values in studies of presumed normal people are aberrations, so averages better define what is normal. Better yet is to discount high-end outliers from a study. *Best is an average of many studies' averages,* which is a ***meta-analysis***, an average from many independent studies. We calculated this for both arsenic and cadmium, arriving at 0.13 ppm and 0.064 ppm respectively as overall ***average normal*** values. While we use the actual science, the GBC abuses it with their data doctoring.

ELEMENTS VARY IN EXTERNAL ADSORBABILITY

Scientific studies have ascertained the degree that each element is likely to adsorb externally into human hair. Copper in hair originates about 20% from external sources. However, cadmium, antimony, and arsenic are not easily adsorbed from external sources into hair. Great Smokies Diagnostic Labs: *"Experience has shown that hair is not very sensitive to exogenous contamination from environmental exposure to antimony."* The studies of those residing in cadmium polluted areas usually had only slightly higher levels of hair cadmium than normal. A study in 1990 by M Wilhelm et al called *"Cadmium, copper, lead, and zinc concentrations in human scalp and pubic hair"* stated: *"It is concluded that hair metal analysis in samples close to the scalp is not seriously invalidated by sources of external contamination."* So, external contamination is not a plausible explanation for Srila Prabhupada's arsenic/ cadmium levels. Endogenous origins is the correct conclusion. His hair had cadmium/ arsenic due to ingestion via malicious homicidal poisoning. *NTIAP* employed sensationalism, exaggeration to confuse us, preying on ignorance of hair test science. It may be boring, but this is for those interested in how the GBC twisted these details to suit their own agenda, even claiming hair analysis is not accurate or useful.

CONTAMINATION FROM AIR OR THE CONTAINERS?

Residents near industrial smelters will have the microscopic crevices of the hair surface contaminated by smelter dust and give misleading test results. However, Srila Prabhupada did not reside near smelters or industrially contaminated areas. *Samples D and A's containers were even tested by Dr. Morris and found to have "no evidence of significant contamination sources for arsenic, cadmium, antimony, or mercury."*

GBC BURNS CANDLE FROM BOTH ENDS

NTIAP p. 34: "...explains that the upper limit of NORMAL arsenic concentration with 99% confidence in people NOT exposed to arsenic is 5 ppm." But this is in reference to seafood eaters or one with an unexpected temporary exposure where elevated levels quickly return to normal. *NTIAP: "normal arsenic concentration of hair varies with nutritional, environmental and physiological factors." NTIAP* confuses normal and abnormal. Accommodation of the variable factors is vital, of which *arsenic-rich seafood consumption and occupational exposure* are primary. Elevated levels are often due to these 2 factors, otherwise hair arsenic levels would be much lower. Scientific studies are now adjusting for these variances. But *NTIAP* duplicitously compares seafood eaters and those occupationally exposed to Srila Prabhupada, and then they also say such variances make it impractical to ascertain normal values. Srila Prabhupada did not eat seafood or work in a high-exposure industry, so why compare him to those who do? *Science Magazine (May 2001)* had a report by G. Stohrer that arsenic levels can be either "standard" or "safe," making an important distinction between ranges and averages. The upper ends of ranges in arsenic studies, with over 1 ppm in hair, are almost always due to seafood or occupational exposure. The UN qualifies their "normal" acceptable hair arsenic levels by *eliminating* seafood eaters.

VARIANCES IN ARSENIC LEVELS DUE TO DIET

Toxicological literature points to normal arsenic level variances due to diet. Hair arsenic studies in a random cross-section of populace often include some who have multiples the average level due to eating meat, poultry, seafood, shrimp, seaweed, kelp, or mushrooms with high content of organo-arsenic compounds. These **organic** exposures have little known mammalian toxicity, unlike **inorganic** arsenic exposure, which is very toxic. 89-96 % of arsenic intake comes from seafood alone. Many higher values in arsenic studies are due to seafood with no poisoning symptoms due to the non-toxic nature of its organo-arsenic compounds. Since Srila Prabhupada did not eat these foods, it is unscientific to compare him to non-vegetarians. The seafood factor must be discounted in any analysis about normal hair arsenic values. Thus his 2.6 ppm arsenic cannot be compared to those who eat seafood.

VARIANCES IN ARSENIC LEVELS DUE TO OCCUPATION

The toxicological literature also cautions to account for variances in what is a normal arsenic level because of industrial exposure to toxic inorganic compounds. Electronics industries use gallium arsenate, agriculture uses arsenic herbicides and insecticides, arsenic is often an air pollutant in mining and smelting, "treated" lumber is pressurized with arsenic, arsenic sprays and dips are used in animal husbandry, etc. Chronic arsenic poisoning effects can lie hidden for decades. Those exposed to occupational hazards often appear "normal." In recent times occupational arsenic contamination has been largely reduced from acute levels to chronic levels and even to intermittent, low-dose levels.

Many scientific studies will unwittingly include apparently "normal" subjects who have hidden, unrecognized abnormal exposures. The Singapore Medical Journal states: *"With newly industrializing countries and expanding use of arsenic in industries like carpentry, electroplating and semi-conductor industries, the possibility of chronic poisoning remains."* **But Srila Prabhupada had no occupational exposure.** It is unscientific to compare his arsenic levels' significance to those that did.

OTHER VARIANCES IN ARSENIC LEVELS

Hazardous Materials Toxicology (74.822) specifies another variance in hair arsenic levels: *"...black women appear to have significantly increased arsenic content in the hair."* Also tobacco smoking results in higher arsenic, and science is now studying arsenic and lung cancer from smoking. But <u>Srila Prabhupada was not a black woman nor a cigarette smoker</u> and should not be compared to the high ends of studies.

ADJUSTMENTS FOR VARIABILITY AND UNCERTAINTIES

Also, major studies address **need for "adjustments" due to "variability and uncertainties"** in ascertaining what arsenic levels are detrimental. The factors of diet, occupation, etc must be considered when establishing acceptable levels of arsenic. EPA studies took into account these variables so that *"the implications of model uncertainty"* are minimized. *NTIAP* deviously exploited these "uncertainties." The UN has adjusted their standards on acceptable arsenic levels in drinking water and hair by <u>excluding seafood eaters</u> who distort "normal" values. *NTIAP* said diet and occupation are variables making arsenic testing unreliable, but actually, since we know Srila Prabhupada's lifestyle, diet, occupation– we must ***adjust downwards*** the arsenic to be expected as normal in his hair when compared to others where variables such as seafood, mushrooms, hazardous occupations, tainted drinking water, tobacco use, black genes, etc are factors. He had no reason to have more than 0.13 ppm hair arsenic, the average normal. These variables actually *magnify, not minimize,* the significance of Srila Prabhupada's 2.6 ppm.

VARIANCE DUE TO MALNOURISHMENT

Physiology is another variance. *NTIAP* refers to research that malnourished persons exhibit a 50% increase in the concentration of trace metals in their hair, due to slower hair growth while metals deposition into the hair remains constant. *NTIAP* implies that since Srila Prabhupada was malnourished, he was expected to have higher levels of hair arsenic than normal. *The sick irony here is that arsenic poisoning caused his malnourishment in the first place.* This is a cold, circular logic. The poisoning was first and caused malnourishment. With declining health, poisoning becomes more lethal. Arsenic poisoning becomes more deadly as the body weight declines. We note how Srila Prabhupada's health declined dramatically immediately *after, and only after,* his July 1976 and Feb. 1977 poisonings.

CONCLUSIONS: *NTIAP* searched scientific literatures for things to twist, to cause doubts rather than to seek truths, like a lawyer defends a guilty client. Unfortunately the GBC rejects more hair tests and suspect/witness interviewing. For them denying the truth is politically necessary. *NTIAP* failed to designificate Srila Prabhupada's 1977 hair arsenic levels, deceitfully defiling actual science. They said "normal" hair arsenic can be 12 ppm, but it is actually 90 X less, or 0.13 ppm. *NTIAP* failed to discredit the "poison theory" and to attribute the arsenic to drinking water. Their misapplication of variances in normal arsenic levels actually goes against their own arguments as Srila Prabhupada did not eat seafood, smoke, and was not environmentally exposed. The GBC revealed themselves as dishonest deniers and enemies of truth.

CHAPTER 50:
DEAF TO THE WHISPERS

FORENSIC ANALYSIS SUBJECTIVE? OR NTIAP DECEPTIVE?

GBC denial book *NTIAP,* Ch. 5: "The Will O' The Whispers" (9 pg) preposterously states: *"we must reject the so-called 'whispers' evidence as invalid. Firstly, the technical analysis is subjectively based on the hearer's ability to put certain sounds together to make coherent phrases. Secondly, the spectrographic method is questionable, especially when applied to whispers, and lastly, each time the 'incriminating' whispers were found, we also find corresponding conversations about the same topics in normal speech. These whispers show no hidden agenda…"*

What? Because caretakers were talking out loud about poisoning, the poison whispers mean nothing? Thus *NTIAP's* Mr. Hooper attacked CAE's audio forensic confirmation of several whispers on recordings from Srila Prabhupada's room in his last days as being about poisoning. *NTIAP* **had** to fault find the whispers because they are very damaging evidence. Hooper declared Mitchell's analyses as "highly subjective" and "slim evidence." Though there are parts of the whispers that are less audible, in the three primary whispers the word "poison" is very clear. The poison word was agreed upon by **ALL** the seven forensic studies that would be done in the next few years. Hooper also posed himself as an imminently qualified expert to appraise neutron activation analysts and dismiss Dr. Morris as "not an expert." He laughingly attempted the same with Jack Mitchell. Hooper also resorted to arguing about the secondary whispers, as though that would invalidate the poison words.

On Feb. 12, 2000, Naveen Krishna interviewed Jack Mitchell about his findings on the poison whispers (Ch. 21). On Oct. 15, 2001 Nityananda also discussed with Jack Mitchell about *NTIAP's* discrediting his forensic study. Yes, Mitchell's technical analysis was to a degree based on subjective ability to put certain sounds together into coherent phrases. But he pointed out that the difference between a layman and expert in audio forensics is *training, experience, reputation, and a developed skill.* Visual technical evidence and expert aural perception are combined in a process of "artistic science." Granted, the nature of sound and language is not the same as in the "pure sciences" of chemistry or calculus. Thus an audio forensics expert ***should*** be consulted, not a layman like the GBC spin doctor. Jack Mitchell had decades of training and education in music and sound, as did the other specialists we would engage in the years to come, seen in Part 3. Why do all the intelligence agencies use audio forensics? Recordings by terrorists are verified by audio forensics. Court cases accept audio forensic testimony. But *NTIAP* rejects the science: *"We do not hear anything."*

Several texts re: the bona fides of the audio forensic science: **(1)** Psychology of Hearing by Brian C J Moore **(2)** Pyscho Acoustics by Zweicker and Fastle **(3)** Sounds of Speech Communication by JM Pickett **(4)** Acoustic Analysis of Speech by RB Kent & Reed.

IT TAKES AN EXPERT TO CONTRADICT ANOTHER EXPERT

NTIAP's disparaging of Mitchell's work is ludicrous, arguing that poison whisper #1 should be heard as, ***"the boys is going down."*** A few weeks later Hooper called again to argue he was now certain it was **"the swelling's going down."** He did not have the skills (or honesty) to analyze the whispers, and refused to acknowledge real experts. Mitchell rendered an unflattering reply to Hooper's critique of his analysis: *"This guy is full of himself. He's an idiot spin doctor. [...] The fact that Tom Owens, Helen McCaffrey, Dr. French and I all agree on the basic poison words in the whispers will be practically indisputable in the courtroom. Who will he find to contradict the best experts in audio forensics? No other reputable expert would agree to dispute these findings."*

As for *NTIAP's* claim that the spectrographic method is questionable, Jack Mitchell replied that this was utter nonsense: *"...this attack on the scientific, investigative methods accepted in courts shows he has no idea what he is talking about."*

THE *NTIAP* REFINERY HOAX

Next is the embarrassing Refinery hoax, revealing how far Hooper went to disparage Mitchell's report. On *NTIAP's* p. 74: *"...we took the original archive copy of tape T-46 to 'The Refinery' digital mastering studios in Brisbane, Australia who have done extensive audio forensic work for many different organizations, including the Australian Federal Police."* NTIAP states that Dave, the sound engineer, agreed that the whisper was "the swelling's going down" and that no poison word was found, stating: *"We both agreed that the alleged 'poison's going down' whisper simply does not exist."* Also, Dave Was quoted that spectrum *"analysis is currently being questioned within the audio industry."*

Later we hired a private investigator, International Detective Agencies (IDS), to question David Neil, former owner of The Refinery, defunct since 2000. When Dave was informed of statements attributed to him in *NTIAP*, he became upset and provided a detailed affidavit. IDS reported: *"...to interview David Neil and confirm or negate various statements made in* Not That I Am Poisoned. *...suffice it to say that Neil has no accredited qualifications in audio forensics and has been* misquoted *in NTIAP."* Mr. Neil highlighted 6 major discrepancies in *NTIAP,* which actually amounted to a serious and prosecutable fraud:

(1) No Police Work: *"I have been quoted as saying that I had performed audio forensic work for the Australian Federal Police. This is a false statement."* NTIAP outright lied.

(2) A Sham Of A "Study:" *"...over the next 30-60 minutes an examination of the tape was conducted."* Actually Dave's business was unregistered and specialized in music production, mastering and editing services, and was not suited for audio forensics or computer audio engineering. This so-called "study" by Hooper cost less than $100, and the short visit was the entire "study." *NTIAP's* exaggeration.

(3) Unsure Of The Whisper: *"My assessment of what appeared to be said on the audio cassette… contained the words, "the swelling is going down," or words to that effect. The words, "it's going down," were quite clear, however the balance of that sentence was not (clear)…"* NTIAP misquoted Mr. Neal confirming "the swelling is going down." *NTIAP* lied.

(4) No Credentials: *"I have no training in forensic audio studies… I am in no way qualified to speak as a qualified expert witness, due to the lack of certified accreditation."* NTIAP claims The Refinery did *"extensive audio forensic work for many different organizations…"* *NTIAP* lied.

(5) No Preview As Promised: *"…it was agreed that I could be quoted on the provision I was to check the article before published. However I was not given the opportunity to peruse the draft."* NTIAP's promise broken.

(6) Spectrum Analysis Not Questioned, This Was A Set-Up: When David Neal heard he had been quoted as casting doubt on the method of spectrum analysis, he became more upset, denying he questioned the method of spectrographic analysis, and said the experience with the GBC author as a "set-up." *NTIAP's* fraud, they lied.

The Refinery episode was a shameful hoax and dishonest, disgusting fraud by the GBC, whose charge it is to lead Srila Prabhupada's followers through the dense forest of material illusions. Instead, the GBC is contributing to the darkness, being a phony spiritual leadership.

TAMAL SPEAKS WHISPER #1: "POISON'S GOING DOWN"

But *NTIAP* did admit one thing (p. 74): *"(we) will immediately recognize him (Tamal) as the speaker of the whisper."* Tamal also admits speaking the poison whisper, but he claimed it was "the swelling's going down." Tamal, p. 75: *"I would have been excited by this good indication and therefore repeated myself. If I was speaking to Prabhupada… I would not have spoken in a whisper."* Tamal was the speaker of whisper #1, verified by many audio forensic experts to be ***"the poison's going down."*** This is why Tamal is the chief "person of interest" in the poisoning of Srila Prabhupada. Tamal never gave a formal deposition or interview. *NTIAP* said Tamal has a "New York Jewish accent," implying spectrographic analysis will be confounded by *"the large variation in pronunciation between different speakers."* We do not use the car's brakes because it might skid and crash? Jack Mitchell easily coped with

Tamal's distinctive accent. *NTIAP* tries to hide truth to protect suspects. Again, 95% of devotees and many forensic experts have verified the poison word in the 3 main whispers.

WHAT ABOUT THE OTHER TWO POISON WHISPERS?

Although *NTIAP* disputes the "poison's going down" whisper, it ***totally ignores*** the other two, namely "is the poison in the milk?" and "poisoning for a (long) time." Why? Instead, *NTIAP* devotes much space to non-poison secondary whispers found by Mitchell. "He's gonna die" and "Yes, a heart attack time" were explained by *NTIAP* to be discussions how parikrama could be fatal for Srila Prabhupada. *NTIAP* thus honored Jack Mitchell's skill in deciphering obscure whispers. Then surely his accuracy should extend to the three poison whispers which are much more audible? *NTIAP* agrees with innocuous whispers but not the primary ones? *None so deaf as those who will not hear.*

GBC SAYS "IMAGINARY" WHISPERS ARE IRRELEVANT?

NTIAP, p. 79: *"The audible portion of the tape contains many references to poison in the ordinary course of the conversation. ...between the kaviraja and Prabhupada's disciples on the matter. It is therefore no surprise that his disciples were talking about the issue and that the word 'poisoning' would be present... there is really no mystery as to why the same word would also be found in whispers."*

After jumping hoops in denying the existence of the poison word in the three poison whispers, now ***NTIAP reverses and admits their existence after all***, but saying they don't have relevance because they reflect the discussions about poisoning at the time. *NTIAP* thus has it both ways. Are there whisperings about poison or not? *NTIAP* first dismisses the whispers as imaginary ("will of the wisp"), then proclaim their irrelevance due to the out-loud poison discussions on the same tape, which they also claim to be about "no poisoning." We are left dizzy with their circular logic and confusing flip-flops:

(1) The poison whispers are imaginary (or not about poison) **(2)** But they are irrelevant (no surprise they are about poison) **(3)** Because they reflect discussions about no poison *("Not that I am poisoned.")* **(4)** Even though Tamal asks Srila Prabhupada, *"Who is it that has poisoned you?"*

This is the GBC's best explanation? They think we are so dumb?

CONVERSATION MAKES POISON WHISPERS OK?

NTIAP, p. 79: *"Because the word 'poison' had been mentioned many times in that particular day's conversation, there really is no mystery as to why the same word would also be found in whispers... were totally innocent."* Poison in the milk and the poison's going down… this is innocent? The truth is that both the poison whispers *and the previous days' poison discussions* are very alarming (Part 2). Srila Prabhupada spoke of being poisoned several times, and all the caretakers acknowledged homicidal poisoning. Whispers convey a secretive intent, and poisoning is done secretly. How can whispers about "poison" be innocuous if they are related to discussions in the previous days about homicidal poisoning and demons, murder, criminal poisoning cases, ground glass in the food? *(Nothing to see here, folks. Move along, now.)*

POISON WHISPERS *THE DAY AFTER* POISON DISCUSSIONS

NTIAP was dead wrong that the Nov. 9-10 poison discussions are on tape T-46; they are on T-44 and T-45. T-46 has no discussion of poison *except* for the three poison whispers. So it is a great surprise to find poison whispers on T-46 where there is only discussion about parikrama, oxcarts, etc. Why is Tamal whispering "the poison's going down" during talks of where to sleep during parikrama? Why does he whisper "is poison in the milk?" just before Srila Prabhupada is clearly heard drinking, sipping, and swallowing milk? Why does Jayapataka tell Srila Prabhupada "poisoning for a long time" to which he weakly asks, "To me?" Do these whispers sound innocuous? Not hardly, any honest person would say. But ISKCON leaders are not honest.

Any audible or whispered poison discussion is concerning and cause for urgent investigation, not denials. We note the poison whispers take place the day *after* Srila Prabhupada disclosed that *"Someone has poisoned me."* The poisoners reacted to Srila Prabhupada's revelation of poisoning and are whispering about further poisoning. How can one NOT think this? This is the natural, logical understanding.

What is the mathematical probability of: **(1)** In 2000 tapes, **(2)** in 1 day there are 4 certified whispers about poisoning, **(3)** within 3 days of Srila Prabhupada's departure, **(4)** and one day after he states 3 times *"Someone has poisoned me."*

Innocuous coincidence? No, not unless you are spin doctoring and severely dishonest. It is more reasonable that as a result of Srila Prabhupada's poisoning revelations, there was a final dose, and whispers about poison while giving poison? That seems pretty clear, and in light of the irrefutable forensic cadmium tests proving that a poisoning occurred, it just makes sense that these whispers were about poisoning. It is certain and demands acceptance as the truth. The whispers alone are very strong evidence of poisoning. In the face of overwhelming audio forensic evidence, the GBC still maintains their absurd denials of the poison whispers. Their statements are even contradictory.

CHAPTER 51:
SMOKE AND MIRRORS

OLD BENGALI DYING VAISHNAVA COMPLAINERS?

NTIAP, saying the "poison theory" is baseless, had the crass audacity to dismiss Srila Prabhupada's statements about being poisoned as: *"(it is) common terminology for elderly (dying) Bengali Vaishnavas to say that they've been poisoned when some treatment doesn't work."*

NTIAP refers to Srila Prabhupada stating Oct. 27, 1977 the effects of the makharadhvaja were *"...reacting adversely."* According to *NTIAP*, these 2 words "confirmed" how elderly dying Bengali Vaishnavas are culturally conditioned to think and say things about being poisoned, as when Srila Prabhupada spoke on Nov. 9-10 about being poisoning. *NTIAP* says Srila Prabhupada's words are to be discounted as a *"very common expression... to complain... the medicine is poisoning them"* and *"Another very interesting point which has come to light recently."* Is this a decades-later, retroactive rationalization for why the GBC ignored Srila Prabhupada's clear statements about being poisoned? Why is this "interesting"? Pray tell us, what should an elderly Bengali Vaishnava say when he actually *is being poisoned*? Their brushing off of Srila Prabhupada's alarming statements of being poisoned and having the symptoms of poisoning, characterizing them as typical of dying Bengali men, is: **(1)** ignorance of the absolute value of Srila Prabhupada's words, **(2)** a great insult and minimization of the pure devotee's stature, to see the pure devotee as an ordinary man, **(3)** an inappropriate and offensive explanation. **(4)** Tamal also claimed Srila Prabhupada said many things that we should not take seriously due to his having been old and dying (Volume 2), being conditioned by Bengali cultural behavioral traits...

ISKCON leaders take Srila Prabhupada as being under the effects of material nature and cultural conditioning. They are not qualified to lead Srila Prabhupada's mission and should be removed from all positions until they have developed a little faith in Srila Prabhupada being in fact a *shaktyavesh avatar*. While *NTIAP* accuses "poison theorists" of trying to second guess Srila Prabhupada's intentions (by being revealing his poisoning to outsiders first), this is exactly what the GBC has done. Their own words apply much better to themselves: *"We should understand clearly that this is an attempt to silence Srila Prabhupada and not allow him to speak for himself."* Characterizing Srila Prabhupada's statements such as, *"Someone has poisoned me,"* to be the complaints of an old, dying and seemingly senile man is silencing Srila Prabhupada. The GBC has a double standard, one for us, another for them. Dishonesty always leads to self-defeating contradictions.

CONTRADICTIONS IN THEIR HYPOCRISY

Dementedly, *NTIAP* contradicts itself in a telling way. First *NTIAP* quotes Ameyatma das, *"I told him (a Calcutta doctor) what Prabhupada said, how he was being poisoned."* Then *NTIAP* states, *"Srila Prabhupada never specifically said, 'I am being poisoned.'"* Well, did he say he was being poisoned or not? Moreover, **IF** Srila Prabhupada was saying that he was **NOT** poisoned, as *NTIAP* claims (see Ch. 11), why bring up this sick example of typical dying Bengali men who say that they **ARE** being poisoned? Which is it? Their logic and consistency is seriously deficient. What kind of garbage is this, such offensive characterizations about our exalted divine master, the Yuga Acharya, being compared to senile dying Bengali men who ramble about being poisoned? Instead, we should have an honest, open and complete discussion of the mountain of evidence proving Srila Prabhupada's homicidal cadmium poisoning. Then we must find who did this, and what are the ramifications and necessary rectifications to his mission.

HE SPOKE OF POISONING ONLY TO THEN DENY IT?

NTIAP (p. 47): *"However, although Prabhupada made indirect references to poisoning, relating to what he had heard from friends or what he had felt about the makharadhvaja etc, what they seem to overlook is the fact that he made very clear and direct statements to the effect that he wasn't being poisoned."* This statement is preposterous. If Srila Prabhupada "made very clear and direct statements "that he wasn't being poisoned," then why did he raise the issue, just to deny it again? Srila Prabhupada's clear statements are blatantly distorted by the GBC.

NOT THAT I AM POISONED MEANS WHAT?

In Ch. 11 we saw how *NTIAP* misquoted Srila Prabhupada as saying he was not poisoned. The actual "poison discussions:" **Tamal:** *Srila Prabhupada? You said before that you… that it is said that you were poisoned?* **SP:** *No, these kind of symptoms are seen when a man is poisoned. He said like that, not that I am poisoned.* /Srila Prabhupada clarifies that an informant did not say he was poisoned, but only said he had poisoning symptoms. Srila Prabhupada himself was not denying poisoning. Otherwise, why state on Nov. 9 that he had been poisoned, then say he was not poisoned, and then on Nov. 10 say he was being poisoned? *NTIAP* picks one phrase out of context and named their book accordingly. And, finally Tamal asked: **"…So who is it that has** *poisoned?"* Why ask who poisoned if there was no poisoning? Tamal, BCS, Shastri, and others all acknowledged Srila Prabhupada spoke of being poisoned, that Srila Prabhupada knew who was poisoning him but would not say who it was, and that Srila Prabhupada should be asked directly as to who was poisoning him. The GBC is cherry-picking little conversational pieces to confuse the actual conversations.

TAMAL'S POISONING DENIAL STATEMENT

In *NTIAP*, Tamal writes: *" Many of you might have wondered why I have not denied this charge if there is no truth to it. The reason is quite simple: I felt the most appropriate and beneficial way to do so was to publish my diary, TKG's Diary."* But we find that his diary incriminates him further (Volume 2). *TKG'S Diary*, Tamal's *The Final Pastimes of Srila Prabhupada,* and *NTIAP* are three felonious books written to bamboozle us that Tamal is innocent in this poisoning. *NTIAP* (p. 145): *"I did not poison Prabhupada. In fact, nobody poisoned Prabhupada."* Tamal contradicts himself, *TKG's Diary* (p. 340): *"We asked Srila Prabhupada later what was the cause of his mental disturbance. Prabhupada disclosed his thoughts that someone has poisoned him."*

More caretaker confirmations: **BCS:** *Someone has given him poison here!* **Kaviraja:** *Listen, this is the understanding that some rakshasa (may) have given (poison)...* **BCS:** *Yes.* **Kaviraja:** *...some rakshasa has given (poison). ...This is what Srila Prabhupada is saying then there must be some truth in it. In this there is no doubt.* **Tamal:** *What did Kaviraja just say?* **BCS:** *He said that when Srila Prabhupada was saying that (he is poisoned) there must be something truth behind it.* **SP:** *"That same thing... that someone has poisoned me."*

Why does Tamal says *"Nobody poisoned Prabhupada?"* This audacious denial flies in the face of all that was discussed and acknowledged by him and all caretakers on Nov. 10, 1977. Tamal assumes most readers will not read the actual tape transcriptions (see Part 2), which show a different picture than his lying denials.

Someone Has Poisoned Me ONLY REFERS TO YESTERDAY?

Another example of *NTIAP's* twisted logic is on p. 51 where Srila Prabhupada's last statement on the poisoning issue, namely, **"That same thing –that someone has poisoned me,"** is brazenly minimized as only a "possibility" and is then totally rejected by the earlier extracted phrase, *"...not that I am poisoned." NTIAP says: "The fact of the matter is this. Prabhupada never said, "Someone has poisoned me," in response to the question, "Have you been poisoned?" The only time he says these words are in response to, "What was causing you the mental distress this* *morning?" He replies that it was the talk from the day before about the possibility that someone had poisoned him."* Well, another time Srila Prabhupada said it was when he raised the subject with Balaram Misra. And the GBC infers "someone has poisoned me" might mean something only IF a certain question had been asked as a preface? or IF it did not refer to the previous day's talks? Sad, such word jugglery to avoid even the possibility that Srila Prabhupada was poisoned. What about Tamal's last question, "…who is it that has poisoned?" Why does Tamal ask if Srila Prabhupada has already denied being poisoned?

"TAKE IT TO THE AUTHORITIES"

Appendix 9 in *NTIAP* is a very technical opinion on the poison discussions by Adridharan das which disregards the caretakers' acceptance of poisoning. He concludes Srila Prabhupada's statements are not an absolute statement of being poisoned. But now the cadmium test results have provided the certainty that Adridharan felt was missing. Nityananda das, 2016: *"This is like Bir Krishna Maharaja telling me in 2012: 'If you have some new evidence, take it to the authorities.' In other words, the GBC have dismissed all previous evidence and are hiding from the issue, conveniently deferring to legal authorities who require a very high level of proof in order to convict and punish those who break secular laws. This allows the GBC to maintain their dishonest position, 'Oh, there is no proof of a poisoning' as long there are no convictions."*

This is Catch-22 hypocrisy- the GBC passed ISKCON laws requiring that all legal complaints and civil disputes (including poisoning) MUST be first "raised in-house" with ISKCON authorities for resolution, mediation, and disposition. ISKCON has prohibited discussion of the poisoning evidence, and banned the topic. ISKCON leaders had their chance to deal with this matter and they cheated and deferred, and so it will end up with legal authorities, just as they wanted. The GBC deflects to secular laws so they can avoid their spiritual responsibility of responding to thousands of very concerned devotees who want a proper investigation into the allegations of Srila Prabhupada's being poisoned. This is *stonewalling* by corrupt misleaders, intent on suppression, denials, character assassination, and excommunication for those advocating further investigation. Why do they fear an investigation? Because some in the ISKCON institutional hierarchy are afraid of the fallout if Srila Prabhupada's poisoning is proven? Their cover-up and denials are their *badge of guilt*; it is very suspect, and speaks of something very amiss.

CHANDRA SWAMI POISONS FOR INDIRA GANDHI?

In *NTIAP,* Ch. 8, is another lie: *"...[SHPM] tries to insinuate all kinds of unsubstantiated facts regarding the 'connection' with Chandra Swami. [...] the idea that Chandra Swami was acting as an agent for Indira Gandhi, and that he tried to poison Srila Prabhupada on her behalf."* This is false. No one even hinted Indira Gandhi used Chandra Swami to poison Srila Prabhupada. Indira Gandhi was favorably disposed to Srila Prabhupada and his movement. These strawman tactics are most dishonest, deceptive- to accuse someone of something they did not do as a way to discredit what they stand for. The ISKCON misleaders' first big lie, in early 1978, was that Srila Prabhupada had appointed 11 successor acharyas. Then so many more lies, intrigues, and falsehoods came, just to defend the original lie of removing Srila Prabhupada and his instructions from their rightful place at the front of the society. This is the nature of deceit: once started, it simply becomes more complicated. The liar himself no longer knows what is truth or lie.

Srila Prabhupada (June 2, 1975): *"That is the way of falsehood. If once you speak something false, then to protect that falsehood you have to take to so many other falsehoods."* The falsehoods propagated by ISKCON misleaders since 1978 need to be exposed and undone, including re: the poisoning of Srila Prabhupada's body and mission. *"No man, for any considerable period, can wear one face to himself and another to the multitude, without finally getting bewildered as to which may be the true."* (Nathaniel Hawthorne) The nature of lying is such that once detected, it destroys faith and trust. The GBC has wonderfully accomplished the destruction of trust in themselves through their lies, fraud, and dishonesty, which is well understood by its former members.

TAMAL ORCHESTRATED ISKCON'S POISONING DENIALS

With the advent of the poison issue in 1997, an ISKCON policy evolved to: **(1)** Organize devious, untruthful, and misleading denials of Srila Prabhupada's poisoning, the whispers, and all other evidence by misrepresenting and twisting facts to discredit the poison "theory" **(2)** Deny any investigation and make Balavanta's a secret, under-funded, and then a sidelined investigation **(3)** Characterize those who wanted an honest investigation as "poisonous," envious mischief-mongers, or demons **(4)** ax Balavanta's investigation and endorse the suspects' sham, whitewash, fraudulent "investigation" in the book *NTIAP.*

Tamal was the architect and inspiration behind ISKCON's poisoning denials and obstruction of honest investigation into the massive evidence that Srila Prabhupada was maliciously poisoned. Seen as the prime suspect by most devotees, Tamal served his own interest by orchestrating, behind the scenes, ISKCON's cover-ups and denials of the poison evidence. Leaked emails had Tamal cajoling and coaxing his subordinates, planting ideas for denials, counter-arguments, and strategies for discrediting "conspiracy theorists." Tamal marshalled loyalists into a disinformation campaign. In late 1997 he devised plans for the "autonomous" *CHAKRA* website to deny the poison crisis and for an ISKCON propaganda operation to fight the allegations against himself. The poisoning suspects *including Tamal* gave statements that the "poison theory" was too absurd for a response or investigation.

Tamal was the back-room manipulator/puppet-master, pulling the strings via lackeys and agents. Tamal paid for the *CHAKRA* website with his own check. Tamal used the pronoun **"we"** and **"us"** to involve everyone in his defense. *He saw false propaganda as the only means of escape.* The GBC is as corruptly black as coal tar while maintaining a pseudo-respectable façade for those who sadly cannot see beyond their smoke and mirrors deceptions.

THE LEAKED EMAILS RE: CHAKRA WEBSITE

Tamal: 13/12/97: *"Thank you for your assurance that CHAKRA will start spinning by Tuesday."* **16/12/97:** *"The supposed witness is Nara Narayan das.* **Shyamasundar must be contacted to discredit this false allegation.***"* **16/12/97:** *"How is it possible for* **our** *main writer and editor, Umapati Maharaja,* **to do his work** *if he cannot access the VNN website?"* **20/12/97:** *"The main thing* **I have to find out** *is how these tapes (poison whispers) differ from the Archive versions, and why. Ravindra Prabhu, can you* **give me a report of the proceedings of the investigation so I can keep a running account** *on the web page?"* **18/12/97:** *"...there is* **urgent need** *to evaluate Bhagwat's statement and its bearing on seeing SP as a martyr.* **Who will do it? Someone must comment** *on Bhagwat's statement re: that he is not strictly following. What is proof of loving SP? Persons strictly following are accused of poisoning SP, and subverting his movement by those who don't strictly follow but who truly love him. Does it sound right? This would be* **appreciated by readers** *and* **draw the line between the opposing sides. Again, who will write it?** *...any* **senior ISKCON devotee** *could..."*

[Tamal musters allegiance, allies in a proxy defense, in his style of discrediting facts, creating a phantom enemy, provoking a group defense as a grand manipulator, and defending himself, not ISKCON.]

Tamal: 20/12/97: *"May I suggest you post your need for* **help**--web literates, writers, researchers, etc. **You may** *just get many volunteers. ...many would* **like to help,** *but have not been asked?"* **20/12/97:** *"Is*

Madhusudhani (CHAKRA editor) working on this? Why not post a letter to all ISKCON gurus requesting they send us names of senior literate disciples who can write for us? ...post an appeal to all Temple Presidents... Also GBC Delegates. Ask them to write and suggest others. Madhusudhani, I request you please do this. So far most articles are Umapati's. We need variety. Writers! Vipramukhya or Umapati can write to sannyasis and articulate senior devotees to propose topics."
*20/12/97: "...a distinct, loud alarm call. **We cannot simply stand by and watch this happen. ICNA should contact** the same sources and send them a short info on Puranjana and his madness, as well as answer or rather **deny the accusations...**"*

Vipramukhya, *CHAKRA co-editor: "I agree **we need to prioritize our work of attack** and increase **our** writers team. I would appreciate **help** from computer/web page literates to do **work behind the scenes** to **handle all this stuff**."*

[Secret committees behind public "statements," arrangements made for writers, editors, literate "senior men" to rally in a propaganda war. Tamal pushes sannyasis, gurus and disciples into defending him].

Tamal: 20/12/97: *"...I would be charging **my opponents** with a host of sins. I don't think this kind of counter-attack is ultimately going to get **us** very far. This may have to be done by some, to win the "war of words," but I doubt that I should be one of those who do it since **nearly the entire attack is aimed at me**, and it will appear that I am simply "getting back." ...what is needed most is textual and forensic evidence... is what has brought the pot to boil and only that will take it off the burner. **We** need to give extended textual materials in which sentences like the one **we** claim "proves" that Prabhupada was not poisoned – the "not that I am poisoned comment" ...**Let's** get on the evidence and off the podium. But what **we** really need is to convince the "middle," the vast number of uncommitted. **We** need researchers who can delve into all the materials and establish the truth..."*

*20/12/97: "I wish to thank Puru prabhu for his trust and love for me. Can his remarks be published? Although that would not vindicate myself or others now falsely suspected of the poisoning of our spiritual master, at least it would present an alternative view. [...] Could there be a prominent link button to have a visitor counter, to give a sense of our popularity... This will be my last posting... CHAKRA, the flagship of this conference, is off to a strong start and **it is time for me to fight on other battlefields**. I will continue to send messages to individuals. Please continue to **war against misinformation**. An enlightened readership is the best protection against all forms of ignorance."*

[Ironic, isn't it, how in 1997 Tamal pioneered the corrupt media's war against "misinformation," being himself the master of cover-ups?]

Tamal: 6/6/99: *"...we benefit by two websites... Chakra's **mood is feisty and confident and clearly partisan**. I recommend a second website which is more news oriented and **apparently neutral**... We will be much stronger if we come to the bargaining table with two arms. **One can be the "heavy," the other apparently "sweet"**- a chutney. I would propose Umapati Swami as the editor for CHAKRA, Krishna Dharma as the editor for the other, with Vipramukhya Swami facilitating both. Is this too ambitious...?"* **6/6/99:** *"Writing is the best cure... request Gunagrahi Maharaja to contribute. **If he wishes to be anonymous, he can always use a pseudonym.**"*

Tamal was the manipulator/puppet-master, making *"statements"* and *"responses"* via lackeys. Chakra's editor confirmed Tamal paid for the website with his own check. Tamal was the ghostwriter for the title, theme, script of the cover-up *"Not That I Am Poisoned."* This contrasts with his own diary: *"Prabhupada disclosed his thoughts that **someone had poisoned him**."* He uses **"we"** and **"us"** to rally others to his defense and *he saw propaganda as better than doing new hair tests.* The GBC endorsed *NTIAP*, produced by the poisoning suspects in their own defense, maintaining a pseudo-respectable façade for those fooled by their smoke and mirrors deceptions.

DHIRA GOVINDA TO CHAIRMAN PRAGHOSH DAS (2002)

"With regard to Srila Prabhupada's disappearance pastime, my sense is that the GBC body, yourself included, is engaged, perhaps in some cases unwittingly, in acts of deception and cover up. Maybe there is nothing to cover up. Still, the GBC, yourself included, seems to me an organization with a lot to hide on this issue. I'm curious if you sincerely believe, as the GBC resolution states, 'There is no evidence at this time to support the allegations of poisoning of Srila Prabhupada.' From my study of the evidence available to me, including the GBC book NTIAP, it appears that there is certainly credible evidence indicating that such an event may have occurred. ...But to state, as you are doing, that there is 'no evidence...' seems to be an attempt to prevent [us] from looking at the available evidence, including Srila Prabhupada's words on the subject. [...] the GBC ...is fearful of the truth [...] or even the hint that such truth may be a possibility, may substantially upset the status quo. In this regard you are apparently an instrument for the maintenance of that status quo. I ask you in all earnesty to take an honest look at your role in this. It is a very serious matter. ...Still, by handling the situation as the

GBC is doing, gives the strong impression [it] is committed to cover up and self-preservation, at the expense of truth [...] some won't apply their cognitive faculties to the matter, and they will be happy to be numb followers of the GBC. But then, what sort of people do we wish to primarily attract and keep in the organization? [...]

"First, Srila Prabhupada clearly expressed concern that he seriously considered the possibility that he was poisoned. As far as the argument 'But maybe he was referring to unintentional poisoning effects from medicine'- I don't see how someone conversant with the relevant conversations, and who is sincere about excavating the truth of the matter, can pose such an argument. ...Clearly they were discussing murder by poison. ...If you haven't studied these conversations by this time, then I'm doubtful whether you should be in any sort of leadership position in Srila Prabhupada's movement [...] Srila Prabhupada expressed serious concern that he was deliberately poisoned. [...] It is not helpful, except maybe in the most short-sighted sense concerned solely with immediate institutional protection, to cover this up. ...I believe if the currently available evidence for such an alleged crime [...] were to be delivered to the NYPD, an investigative team would deem that there is surely compelling evidence to warrant a homicide investigation. There are the whispers. [...] audio forensic experts have indicated, using their professional methodologies that are accepted in criminal courts, that the whispers constitute at least potential evidence, and perhaps strong evidence, that Srila Prabhupada was poisoned. [...]

"I understand that the whispers are likely not conclusive evidence. [...] the totality of the body of documentation constitutes compelling evidence that murder by poisoning may have happened. ...although the status quo in the GBC organization may in fact be disrupted. It is also clear from JFY Ch.4 that NTIAP contains deception in addressing the whispers. [...] a thinking person will naturally wonder 'What is it that needs to be hidden and covered up?' ...unexplained inconsistencies between what was said by some key players in 1977 and what they said in NTIAP, and the lack of straightforwardness in several sections of NTIAP, and to conclude that there 'is no evidence at this time' seems to me to be disingenuous. It is clear, as far as I can perceive, from the conversations in Nov. 1977 that those surrounding Srila Prabhupada thought it wholly feasible that Srila Prabhupada was poisoned. In NTIAP some of these same devotees expressed it is absurd that Srila Prabhupada was poisoned. How do you explain their incredulity towards an idea to which they gave complete credence in 1977? ...Please look at the possibility you are allowing some basic human needs within you,

324

such as those for approval, acceptance and recognition, to enable others to use you as an instrument for cheating, cover up and fraud." **(END)**

RASCALS CANNOT SEE THE TRUTH

NTIAP attacks and faults each piece of evidence cited in *SHPM.* What *NTIAP* fails to address is that when ALL the pieces of evidence are put together with the later cadmium findings and several later audio forensic studies, there is too much evidence to dismiss with, *"Well, that piece may not be absolutely valid, neither this one, nor that one..."* The GBC's creating doubts and faultfinding do not amount to an honest investigation. But hell will freeze over first. They did not even complete their own hair tests. We did that for them. A cover-up is often more criminal than the original crime. It was his role in the cover-up that took down Richard Nixon, not the actual Watergate chicanery. ISKCON has covered up Srila Prabhupada's poisoning (and much else). The truth is blocked by the GBC/guru club. This is obstruction of truth and justice.

(1) *"The smart way to keep people passive and obedient is to strictly limit the spectrum of acceptable opinion, but allow very lively debate within that spectrum." (Noam Chomsky)* **(2)** *"We must not compromise with our principles. Those who are actually sincere about spiritual life will gradually see the purity of our movement as you are conducting it and they will become attracted to the real thing. Those who want to be cheated do not take the solution even when it is at hand but prefer to be cheated."* (SPL Jan. 1, 1974) **(3) SP:** *"No, no, truth is there, but they cannot present the truth rightly. That is rascaldom. ...But they cannot present the truth in right way."*(SPConv, 17.11.75)

THERE IS NO EVIDENCE?

The official GBC resolution, *"There is no evidence at this time to support the allegations of poisoning of Srila Prabhupada,"* makes a mockery of ISKCON leadership. This gives insight into why the poison issue has been covered up and the suspects have not been interviewed or questioned by anyone. **(1)** *"The example may be given of a man who is sleeping. If he is actually sleeping, he may be wakened by various means, but there is no doubt that he must wake up. However, if a man is pretending to be asleep there is no way at all to rouse him up. (SPL July 9, 1970)* **(2)** *"Untruthfulness, illusion, inability to ascertain the correct thing to be done, etc are characteristics of the mode of passion. Another symptom of the asuric mentality is the tendency for deceit. In the Ramayana, the story of Ravana disguising himself as a sannyasi, as a deceitful ploy to capture and snatch Sita devi, is one of the prime examples in the Vedic literature of this dangerous and devious* *mentality.*" (Yasodanandana das, 2016) **(3)** *"It is difficult to get a man to understand something, when his salary depends upon his not understanding it."* (Upton Sinclair)

Their "no evidence" theory is a duplicitous cover-up: their finding of supposed faults in the mountain of evidence is meant to create doubts in the minds of the innocent and uninformed. By creating 5% doubt in the evidence, by ridiculous posturing, then the deniers will snakily make their claim of "no evidence. But it is simply smoke and mirrors.

CHAPTER 52:
BEARING FALSE WITNESS

"The further a society drifts from the truth, the more it will hate those that speak it." (George Orwell) "Thou shalt not bear false witness against thy neighbor." (#9, Bible's Ten Commandments)

False witness or testimony means lying and making false reports. A lying witness is deceitful, mocks justice, and intends to cover another's knowledge with falsity. Lying is a direct offense against truth and is a fundamental infidelity to the Supreme Lord, undermining one's relationship with Him. Slander defames by emphasizing supposed faults, and is false witnessing, employed to discredit a person's position or message. *NTIAP* overflows with false witnessing to hide truth and promotes false understandings. Of course, this is the GBC's history (Volume 5, 6) It is laborious to confront so much untruth and hypocrisy, but to set the record straight and to keep truth in the light of the sincere man's discerning intelligence, we will dissect their lies and expose them.

FALSELY ACCUSING OTHERS OF POISONING SP?

ISKCON apologists say "poison theorists" commit grievous wrongs and bearing false witness by accusing certain "advanced devotees" of poisoning Srila Prabhupada, like Tamal or Bhakticharu. *NTIAP* harps on this theme to no end. *NTIAP's* contributors in this regard:

(1) p. 17-8 (Devamrita Swami): *"...we should indeed feel disturbed when witnessing offenses to the Lord and his devotees... the potential for malicious envy and ill will toward other devotees... The farce, 'the poisoning of Prabhupada,' has dramatized the effects of rampant Vaishnava aparadha... to blaspheme any devotee who has dedicated his life to preaching the glories of the Lord is injurious..."* **(2)** p. 121 (Bhakticharu Swami): *"Recently one of our Godbrothers... wrote a* *book... and alleged that... the ones who were serving His Divine Grace at that time administered him that poison."* **(3)** p. 129 (Bhakti Tirtha Swami): *"The leaders who have been accused of being involved in the conspiracy (so called) to poison Srila Prabhupada..."* **(4)** p. 143 (Jayadwaita Swami): *"As much as I dislike feeling obliged to respond to garbage, I think that I too ought to comment on the scuttlebutt that Srila Prabhupada, by a conspiracy of disciples, was poisoned... It pains me when those I saw serving His Divine Grace with extraordinary devotion and love are made out to be devious killers."* **(5)** p. 145 (Tamal): *"For quite some time rumors have been circulating that Srila Prabhupada was poisoned, murdered by his own disciples."*

(6) p. 149 (Trivikram Swami): *"...it is unimaginable that any one of Srila Prabhupada's personal servants could have even once entertained the thought of poisoning Srila Prabhupada ...To suggest... there was... a conspiracy of a number of his servants, who not only thought about it but actually carried it out, is so far beyond the pale of believability..."* **(7)** p. 151 (Danavir Goswami): *"The poison theory is **hatimata**... Mad Elephant Vaishnava Aparadha at its heaviest. The poison theory sets forth ...Srila Prabhupada unknowingly surrounded himself with envious disciples who were conspiring to poison him and actually did so. I consider it to be a great insult to my spiritual master and to his sincere disciples* **(8)** p. 241 (Ravindra Svarupa): *"author names and relentlessly indicts the purported chief assassins: [...] Accusing them of the greatest possible crime, he remorsefully assaults their devotion, their honor, their reputation... accusing some devotees of a monstrous crime."*

The above was in response to *SHPM,* as though some were accused of poisoning Srila Prabhupada without any foundation. Behind its air of indignation and righteousness *NTIAP* has sidestepped the central question of **whether Srila Prabhupada was poisoned** (never mind by whom), diverting instead to how certain persons are being falsely accused. This is another dishonesty. The idea is: it is crazy that those who loved Srila Prabhupada so much could be accused in this way, and therefore there was no poisoning. This is standard methodology in politics. They avoid the question of poisoning by claiming that Tamal and others could not have done it, so it never happened. It seems more important to the GBC to defend their own than to determine if Srila Prabhupada was poisoned. Their priorities are revealing, and incriminate them further. Very illogical and devious. However, the evidence strongly implicates caretakers in Srila Prabhupada's proven poisoning. Some are "persons of interest" based on solid evidence. Since *SHPM* 23 years ago, substantial new evidence has accumulated. In Volume 2 Tamal goes on a virtual trial, and he comes out guilty of poisoning Srila Prabhupada *beyond a reasonable doubt*. This is a serious evaluation of the bulky evidence which clearly implicates him in this crime.

HARD EVIDENCE IS MET WITH FALSE ACCUSATIONS

NTIAP criticizes, p. 17: *"How could someone concoct this poison madness! How many of our dear fellow devotees temporarily fell victim to this smut campaign? And why so much time and energy wasted, out of necessity, debating this crazy idea?...forced to cope with the poison mongers' agenda... Can we stop despicable nonsense like this from breaking out in ISKCON again? Undeniably, the deadly toxin played a significant role in a worldwide decline of enthusiasm and trust. Most devotees did not swallow the scam entirely... the original perpetrators of this madness... who fermented this potion know their motives..."*

It is ISKCON who is bearing false witness and making false accusations. We are pointing out facts and evidence, not making wild and unfounded accusations. A very many Srila Prabhupada followers consider Tamal, Bhakticharu, Bhavananda, Jayapataka as suspects in Srila Prabhupada's now proven poisoning. ISKCON is making false accusations against those wanting further investigation into the circumstances surrounding Srila Prabhupada's departure, and insult intelligent devotees with their obvious deceitful cover-ups. The suspicions about the poisoning suspects are justified, based on solid evidence, but ISKCON deniers rely on lies, fearmongering, character assassination, misrepresentations, and false accusations. *What exactly frightens ISKCON about the poison issue so much?*

EXAMPLES OF ISKCON FALSE WITNESSING

NTIAP has substantial false witnessing or duplicitous accusations mixed with its disparaging of the evidence that Srila Prabhupada was indeed poisoned. **(1) "The Arsenic Ruse"** *–NTIAP's* deceptive and flagrantly erroneous assertion that normal arsenic in hair is up to 12 ppm, but in fact chronic arsenic poisoning begins at 1 ppm, with 0.13 ppm the average normal level. **(2) "The Whispers Time Waster"** *–NTIAP's* claims they are imaginary and they cannot hear any poison whispers the day after Srila Prabhupada repeatedly spoke about being poisoned. However, multiple expert audio forensic analyses prove that there are indeed several whispers about poisoning. (Part 3) **(3) Not That I Am Poisoned** *–NTIAP* plucks this phrase out of context, claiming Srila Prabhupada denied he was poisoned. But in the recorded conversations all the caretakers acknowledge that Srila Prabhupada thought he had been poisoned. (Part 2) **(4) Diabetes Diagnosis** –Their claims about health problems being due only to advanced diabetes is put to rest by the later triple discovery of sky-high cadmium levels. (Part 1) **(5) The Poison Was Just Bad Medicine** –The false idea that when Srila Prabhupada spoke of being poisoned he was referring to medicine with bad side effects: this is a cover-up meant to confuse the truth (Ch. 28). **(6) Chandra Swami** –Their claims that Srila Prabhupada's medicine coming from such a dangerous and notorious scoundrel is of no concern and simply scare-mongering on our part (Volume 2) **(7) Reverse Speech** –After mocking it, *NTIAP* then admits 7 instances of confirmed reverse speech which indicate foul play. (Ch. 59)

ISKCON FALSE WITNESSING

Spiritual leaders should defend actual facts and not be implicated in false testimony. *"...Regarding the position of a person who does not speak even when he knows the truth:* jani saksi nahi deya tara papa haya. *A person who knows things as they are and still does not bear witness becomes involved in sinful activities..."* (SPLecture, May 17, 1975)

ONE: ACCUSATIONS ABOUT BROKEN CONTRACTS

NTIAP included a "report" by Suddha Jiva das (SJ) with an incredible distortion of truth. SJ had started a devotee community in Efland, NC, USA. After a tricky land deal by selling 12 acres and later trying to donate the same land to Bhakticharu Swami, SJ filed false charges in court. SJ made false accusations against Nityananda das and the GBC included them in their book without verifying the facts. Many devotees were cheated by SJ's shady dealings. An institution such as ISKCON that harbors dishonest and ambitious leaders results in a corrupted membership by a trickle-down effect. This explains why many Srila Prabhupada followers stay outside the institution, to avoid such experiences. The GBC strategy was to give the messenger a bad name, hang him, and reject his message. Bhakticharu, not getting free land after all, went elsewhere, and there is now no devotee community in Efland.

TWO: ACCUSATIONS OF BLASPHEMING DEVOTEES

Danavir Goswami declared that *SHPM's* suspicions that Srila Prabhupada's loving disciples such as Tamal and Bhakticharu could have poisoned him was **blasphemy** of the highest order, a Maha Vaishnava Aparadha. *"...at its heaviest. By drinking this deadly brew, bubbling with blasphemy of Vaishnavas, naïve devotees are ruining their spiritual lives. Please avoid listening to the poison theory... one who blasphemes a Vaishnava should be defeated by expert preachers or punished by virtuous ksatriyas or avoided by neophyte sadhaka-bhaktas.*

Many expert devotees have tried their best to talk some sense into the poison proponent blasphemers to no avail... Therefore the best policy for ISKCON devotees is to act on the platform of madhyama adhikaris and completely avoid (them)... The poison proponents desire to see ISKCON demolished..." How ridiculous. Let the evidence speak for itself. We are presenting confirmed, irrefutable evidence, not theories. Listening to Srila Prabhupada speaking is not blasphemy. Srila Prabhupada's caretakers clearly acknowledged a homicidal poisoning. Why accuse of blasphemy for pointing this out? *"Formerly anti-cult groups and atheists vigorously opposed the Krishna consciousness movement. Now we find a new anti-cult class of so-called devotees dedicated to disrupting ISKCON, misrepresenting Srila Prabhupada's words and defaming respectable Vaishnavas. These new anti-ISKCON people are certainly behaving like demons.*" These intimidation tactics are a desperate defense of a dying generation of corrupt institutional leaders prior to a cleansing revolution by sincere followers who will soon end ***their*** abominations and deviations. Virtuous ksatriyas? Best to live in exile.

THREE: AN AGENT OF KALI AND A WACKO

Bhakti Tirtha Swami added his opinion to *NTIAP* (4 pg) that the poison controversy is the work of Kali and her agents, meant to destroy the Hare Krishna movement. *"So it really shows to the degree that Kali has entered our society, that the greatest attack- it's like in war, it's not the enemy which is antagonistic, but the greatest enemies in war are those who do the espionage. They are the most trained, the most powerful and the most dangerous because they enter into an environment with the idea of supporting it, while they have a hidden agenda. So beyond a doubt some of the major agents who are pushing this issue have been highly influenced by Kali.*" So those disturbed by the valid evidence that Srila Prabhupada was poisoned are monsters of Kali, actually Srila Prabhupada's enemies with hidden agendas? The always-grinning "Black Lotus" swami explains: *"...we also have to appreciate that when devotees get so wounded, so disappointed with the institution, and most importantly with themselves, the tendency is to over-react, to scapegoat, try to find some justification for their own failure or ways to deal with their void...*" He portrays those who "propagate" the poison controversy to be mentally or psychologically imbalanced people who are emotionally "wounded," compensating for their own "void" and personal failures by creating unjustified trouble for others. So if you use your intelligence, you are a psycho-wacko. Condescending and devious.

Then: *"...if we allow the parampara to do the driving. If we try to drive ourselves, try to do things based on our intelligence, then there will always be some shortcomings."* So we must surrender unconditionally to the infallible and self-realized souls such as him. GBC-guru BT Swami, before he passed in 2005, advised we turn off our intelligence and allow ISKCON leaders to "drive for us." Some of these leaders are suspected of poisoning Srila Prabhupada, and the rest are covering up for them. ISKCON only wants sycophants; independent thinkers are not welcome. BTS concluded: *"They have been empowered by Kali, and so their mentality, perceptions and actions, the kind of chaos it is bringing into the movement is beyond just normal deviation, it is actually like an empowerment for destruction."* For compiling hard facts and evidence about Srila Prabhupada being poisoned, we are the ultimate anti-spiritual force. Arrogant BTS saw us like mushrooms to be kept in the dark. He advised giving mercy and kindness to lost souls like us. His "mercy" on the fallen Kali agents was just a phony show to attract more followers.

THEIR EXPOSER EXPOSED

10% of *NTIAP* (30 pgs) was Geoffrey Giuliano's (Jagannath das Puripada) rambling "confession:" *"The Inside Story On The Poison CD: A Revealing Expose by Jagannath Das. The following statement was spoken to Bir Krishna Goswami in Sept. 1999."* Herein

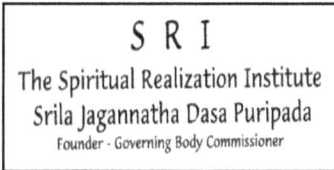

> **S R I**
> The Spiritual Realization Institute
> Srila Jagannatha Dasa Puripada
> Founder - Governing Body Commissioner

we examine the man ISKCON used to deny Srila Prabhupada's own recorded words about being poisoned. He is lifelong author and vendor of dubious celebrity sensationalism. He was never initiated. In 1999 he had a "Vedic center" in Lockport, New York, with the title Srila Puripada, intent on the "guru business." He distributed brochures: *"For Immediate Release: Self-Realized Spiritual Master, His Holiness Jagannatha Dasa Puripada On Tour Of America. The spiritual advisor and leader of thousands of people in India, His Holiness Jagannatha Dasa Puripada, has come to America to teach the 5000-year-old, non-sectarian, Vedic meditational technique of Bhakti, or Devotional Yoga, throughout North America."* (like Srila Prabhupada did?) He claimed he sponsored an orphanage in India (Bir Krishna Maharaja does as well) and a goshala. In his "expose" he makes many grossly false accusations.

TAPE TAMPERING ACCUSATIONS

Giuliano portrays himself as one who just wanted to help get out some information to devotees, but how he came to see the low character of those he was working with, namely Dhanesvara, Rochan, and Nityananda (Ch. 16). He accused us of attempted fraud: *"...did*

Nityananda request that in my studio, that you enhance, move around, juxtapose, some of the internal content of some of these whispers and sound bites, in order to present a stronger case or to put a finer point on it, or to make a more damning piece of taped evidence? My answer, 'Yes.'" Then Giuliano revealed he had experience in doctoring tapes to change the meaning or word content. He accused our team of manufacturing the poison issue's "false evidence" because of long-standing ill-will against ISKCON and its leaders. He stated our motivation was to pull down those in power and take their place in a "power-grab." This nonsense was copied into their book of denials.

He posted an article on the GBC website Aug. 26, 1999: *"Church of the Poisoned Mind, by Jagannath das: After undergoing the experience of working with devotee mobsters Rochan and Nityananda... drawn into their web of lies, innuendo and half-truth which is the hallmark of the professional agitator... the deliberate, pre-meditated fraud these men were out to sell to our worldwide family... I was asked point blank by Nityananda to falsify the taped 'evidence' by editing it in such a way it might seem both more damaging... a few words shuffled about... one dangling scrap of audio becomes a very different animal... you can make a person say ANYTHING, going so far as moving syllables and even breaths to make an edit go your way... that this entire campaign of terror was designed to bring about the fall of our sampradaya...should be seen as the Trojan Horse it is... and forever exposed."*

There was no attempt to alter or tamper with the tape recordings. How could anyone even hope to get away with that? The original tapes are at Bhaktivedanta Archives; any tampering would be quickly discovered. *Actually, it was Giuliano who suggested this on the phone, which was flatly rejected.* Forensic studies have validated the poison whispers. Fabrication of evidence is not the agenda for anyone on our team of private investigators. Obviously it would back-fire anyways.

GEOFFREY GIULIANO

After promising free use of his studio, Giuliano later demanded money. He also claimed that our just-finished CD was stolen from his premises and delivered to ISKCON by the Bengali devotees in his ashram that he accused of stealing various items and US$19,420 in cash. One of these Bengalis, Gaura Daya das, called us from Washington, DC, saying it was Giuliano who took the CD to Europe and sold it to Harikesh Swami. Bir Krishna Swami arranged to pay $10,000 for his *NTIAP* "expose," post a related article on VNN.org, and deliver our only and original Poison CD to Europe. Gaura Daya said they been abused and exploited for a year by Giuliano, who was a swindler, psychopath, and con-man. The very day the CD was completed, Giuliano instigated a terrible argument with Dhanesvara, who felt he was in danger and fled immediately. The Bengalis told of his shady practices and misuse of his tax exempt status. His career was selling dirt on celebrities to the smut media, and he is what ISKCON came up with to further their position? Desperate times, desperate measures?

GIULIANO'S HISTORY AND CHARACTER

The history and character of Geoffrey Giuliano is rather dodgy; he was involved in various libel lawsuits, and has attracted scrutiny for his controversial celebrity biographies. In 2021 Giuliano threatened to sue us if we published this chapter, saying it was libel and slander to his "good reputation." He refused to come clean on what had happened over 20 years earlier, saying he would not jeopardize his welcome on visits to ISKCON Vrindaban. Privately he admitted he had done wrong; he wanted to make amends in his life, and rejuvenate his spiritual life, but...

Before 1990 Giuliano invented/pioneered McDonald's mascot clown Ronald McDonald, even though he was vegetarian. He then sued McDonald's, decrying *"concerns who make their millions off the murder of countless animals and the exploitation of children."* He also was the actor for "the Marvelous Magical Burger King." With a supposed change of heart, he publicly courted himself as one redeemed by his conscience. He co-authored a John Lennon book with Julia Baird, Lennon's half-sister, and when Baird wrote another book *20 years later* for a movie, Giuliano sued her "for his share." A review on Beatles Collectors.com stated *"a tabloid style account covering only the negative publicity during the Beatles career."* He published many books about the Beatles, Hendrix, Townshend, Yoko Ono, Princess Diana with dirty gossip on their "secret" lives. A reviewer: *"If Giuliano's own double-talk isn't enough to diminish this work's credibility, his endless, voyeuristic descriptions of Lennon's sexual encounters are."* In addition to his audio CDs, books, radio shows, he became an actor in Thai movies; about a hunt for a dangerous tiger, Bangkok Adrenaline, Vikingdom, Scorpion King 3-- all grade-C, Asian glorified fantasy and violence.

We get hints of his character and quality as an author (or witness) from comments posted online: **Francie:** Giuliano is himself **a** fraud, culture vulture, liar and greed-driven. Hitler was a vegetarian too. **Roger Smith:** ...it's not good journalism. The sensational things, I don't know

where he got them from. I'm assuming he made it up."
Mom...@msn.com: This guy is a con-artist. I knew him in Jr. High and he was a whack-job then. I unfortunately got trapped into a business deal and that museum crap of his and was supporting him in Thailand via Walmart money orders for several months in 2006. He played the *"my son has a heart condition please send money, we are eating dirt over here."* I lost about $20,000 USD with the money I sent him and trying to secure his Lockport property & fix relations with the government.
Gordon: Giuliano tried to steal the multi-track tapes of TOMMY from Pete Townshend's attic. Pete caught him and, rightly so, threw him out...

Giuliano retorted: *"What is it that I don't have? People worship me. I'm famous. Why would I want to perpetrate fraud on anyone?"*

If his business was to make up and sell dirt about celebrities for profit, is it hard to imagine he approached Bir Krishna Goswami as a false witness for sale? Considering his international reputation, how could ISKCON allow him in their book? This puts ISKCON in the same league as Giuliano. Olivia, George Harrison's widow, wrote to the Guardian in 1992 re: Giuliano's misrepresentations about the Beatles: *"The sight of Geoffrey Giuliano's face is enough to make anyone a recluse. My husband once made the remark: 'That guy knows more about my life than I do'. Giuliano missed the joke and used it to endorse his book. To rate himself as the world's greatest rock 'n' roller biographer (a laughable title) is delusion. He has only ever been in the vicinity of my husband for about 10 minutes and considers himself an expert. He parades as a spiritual person while condemning the famous, yet without them his achievements in this life wouldn't rate one line. To judge Paul McCartney as vacuous and shallow comes from his arrogant mind, especially as Giuliano's own recognition is not because he is creative, but because, like a starving dog, he scavenges from his heroes, picking up bits of gristle and sinew along the way, repackaging them for consumption by a gullible public. His life is a 'curse;' his admitted 300 acid trips by age 19 has something to do with it. I'm sick of this guy."*

On July 20, 2006, Giuliano published in the Lockport newspaper an apology and a conceited rationale for his legal problems in New York: *"I lost my balance. I became arrogant, selfish and extremely self-centered. I showed off my new stature just like any poor boy might from the wrong side of the tracks. And then I found my faith. Now, as part of my spiritual growth, much of my wealth, career and even my once good name have been lost. I am now, at 52, a much kinder, quieter, more compassionate, caring person. Now I want to give something back to Lockport. I want to apologize for the times I was off base in my immature, aggressive approach. I have treated others wrongly. If, in the future I can use my time and talent ...I give my word I will do my very best to the people of Lockport, my home, wherever the wind may blow me."*

His above letter from Thailand sounds like a famous celebrity who expects forgiveness for their indulgences. But the truth is in the news:

Trouble With The Law: Friction With Authorities, J. Heaney, Buffalo News 5/28/00: *"So who is Giuliano? He changed his legal name to Jagannatha Dasa Puripada. In 1986, Giuliano wrote the first of his 23 books on popular music, 18 of them on the Beatles. <u>Giuliano has had his share of run-ins with the local authorities</u>. He received a one-year conditional discharge after authorities accused him of avoiding $21,672 in electric bills. One of his corporations pled guilty to a felony count of 4th degree grand larceny. ...by changing the name on the account every time NYSEG threatened to shut off service. ...refusing to pay the last one-third... He insists he was unfairly prosecuted- "they had nothing on me" ...the subject of several complaints filed ...that he threatened to "split their heads open"; and an obscenity-laced confrontation with police "They were simply allegations," ... "Charges were never filed."*

<u>World Beatles Forum Sept 2001: Repugnant Ruse On Grieving World</u>, B. Howard: *On Fri. Sept. 14, 2001, 7:54 PM, I received the following message from Geoffrey Giuliano's personal e-mail account: Indigo Editions today formally announces the death of author Geoffrey Giuliano in the tragic attack on the World Trade Center on his 48th birthday, 9.11, 2001. He is survived by his wife Vrinda and four children. No body has been recovered. An Indian funeral is planned near New Delhi. [This was a false announcement. He appears to have staged his own death for publicity]. Several people started investigating Giuliano's death. On Sept. 22, 2001, Steve Marinucci spoke with Geoffrey Giuliano, confirming he was alive and speculating someone in his ashram used his e-mail... It is incomprehensible someone would deliberately, falsely announce a death tagged to the WTC tragedy. How could anyone perpetrate this sick joke on a mourning world? Thousands of real people, innocent victims, died real deaths. Is nothing sacred?"*

Buffalo News Sept. 18, 2002: *"Geoffrey Giuliano was arrested two times in the past six days on charges ranging from grand theft to passing counterfeit checks... Giuliano, 49, was also arrested after he was accused of damaging property belonging to a woman who took care of his home since January while he was in Thailand. Giuliano also was arrested last week when he was in a car pulled over during a traffic safety blitz and identified himself as Eric Johnson... an outstanding warrant on counterfeit checks totaling $800."*

Geoffrey Giuliano: *"...I am physically unable to travel to the United States ...I require two surgeries, which ...I cannot afford as a full time monk without financial means of any kind."* (yeah right)

Summary: Bir Krishna Goswami, GBC Chairman, considered Giuliano worthy of providing an "expose" of the supposed truths on evidence that Srila Prabhupada was poisoned. However, this man is not at all worthy or reliable as telling truth. The GBC featured this false witness' lies in *NTIAP*, a man who faked his own death on 9/11; he worked in Thailand claiming to be a monk with no income; he wrote bad checks; he has a bad temper, threatens people, steals property, and yells obscenities; charged with financial fraud with utility companies; he is unduly proud of himself. He supposedly tried to steal master recordings from Pete Townshend's home. He admitted to us stealing the "Lost Kirtans" recording (Delhi, Jan. 1977) of Yamuna dasi and Srila Prabhupada, then selling it under his own label later. He was accused by his "ashram" members of stealing the "poison CD" in 1998 from Dhanesvara das and selling it to the GBC for $10k. He claimed we wanted to "edit" the poison whispers, but he is accused of concocting falsehoods and tampering with celebrities' photos in his own books.

Giuliano says he practices "devotional yoga," and that he is a student of Srila Prabhupada, claiming to have met and spoken with him in London in the 1970's. His brick manor house across from the Erie Canal supposedly served as a Vaishnava temple, guest house, animal sanctuary, and vegetarian food pantry. Through his Spiritual Realization Institute, Giuliano claimed he sponsored an orphanage, and distributing food and clothing in India. The GBC and Bir Krishna Swami have perpetrated a travesty of falsehoods by using Giuliano to discredit the validated evidence of Srila Prabhupada's poisoning and bearing false witness. *NTIAP* is a collection of lies, deceit, denials, fraud, and dishonesty as facts are twisted, butchered, altered, and ridiculed. It is a travesty how ISKCON has betrayed the truth.

CHAPTER 53:
DESERATE LIES OF *DECEPTION*

(1) *"Even the Devil can quote scripture."* (old Dixie saying) **(2)** *"The murder victim Sulochan and those who believed as he did had said the troubles (in ISKCON) were symptoms of a spreading cancer of denial."* (Betrayal of the Spirit, p.145) **(3)** *"He who establishes his* *argument by noise and command shows that his reason is weak."* (Michel de Montaigne) **(4)** *"Oh what a tangled web we weave when we first practice to deceive."* (Sir Walter Scott) **(5)** *"The ISKCON GBC stands strong in its assertion, 'There is no evidence at this time to support the allegations of poisoning of Srila Prabhupada.' I cite this statement as another category of evidence. That is, cover-up and concealment. If there is nothing to hide, why make such an absurd statement?"* (Dhira Govinda das, 2017)

In March 2000 Balavanta gave his investigative report at the GBC Mayapur annual meeting, recommending further investigation. Within minutes, a new 320 page book was presented, titled *Not That I Am Poisoned*. It had been secretly compiled in Australia by Deva Gaura Hari and Tirtharaj, disciples of Jayapataka and Tamal, and financed by Tamal and Bhakticharu, all primary suspects in Srila Prabhupada's poisoning. The book was endorsed by the GBC as the definitive conclusion to the poison controversy, stating there was no evidence and no poisoning, and therefore no need for further investigation. It grossly misrepresented and deviously manipulated the facts as a compilation of deceit and fabrication denying all the evidence, and even referring to Srila Prabhupada's words, *"Someone has poisoned me,"* as those of a senile, paranoid "Bengali gentleman."

The book's title is taken out of context and characterized as Srila Prabhupada's denial of being poisoned. The poison "theory" is ridiculed with fathomless dishonesty and character assassination, revealing the GBC as a corrupt entity more interested in their status quo than in reality, begging the question, *"What are they hiding and so afraid of?"* NTIAP is a shameless Kali Yuga masterpiece of hypocrisy and a sham whitewash cover-up. Bombarding us with bald-faced lies, exaggerations, perversions, falsities, and distortions, the GBC has bluffed and intimidated many into a silence of mental confusion. Apathy ensues as facts are clouded by doubts. Everyone already has too much they are trying to sort out. The GBC declares the poison "theory" as blasphemous to senior devotees, that the Hare Krishna movement can be destroyed by this "evil-minded" attack.

Researching medical toxicology textbooks, resolving apparent contradictions in scientific studies, and becoming knowledgeable in neutron activation analysis: this is not within the time constraints of most. How many can become well studied on heavy metal poisoning technicalities? The subject is challenging enough without the GBC deliberately trying to obscure the truth, create fearful paranoia, and then demonize legitimate concerns amongst Srila Prabhupada's followers.

This volume organizes and analyzes the evidence and issues in this matter and presents it clearly, to help others easily understand the truth.

GBC MEETING ON POISON ISSUE A "MACABRE CIRCUS"

The 2000 GBC Mayapur meetings had a scene where the GBC body apparently lost all sanity and sobriety: *"I was present during that presentation- at least, much of it. I found it difficult to be there, and didn't remain in the room for the entire presentation. I'd describe the mood as a sort of macabre circus. There was lots of laughter. They (most of those present) regarded Srila Prabhupada's alleged poisoning as a real knee-slapper. It was spooky. My sense was that very few there had malicious intent. If asked, I doubt that many of them could have explained what was so funny." (Dhira Govinda das, 2017)*

Sadly, ISKCON leaders cannot give Srila Prabhupada's poisoning evidence its due consideration. Those who voted in favor of adopting *NTIAP* as ISKCON's official position document have certainly shamed themselves and all those they represent. Part 6 shows how low the GBC went to discredit facts and evidence in a deceitful cover-up; they are thoroughly corrupted. Mandapa das (2017):

LOOKS LIKE YOU'VE HAD A BIT TOO MUCH TO THINK!

THOUGHT POLICE
Don't speak out or question.

"Tirtharaj is a Tamal disciple who joined in the 80's, eventually becoming Brisbane Temple President. He bought land to relocate the temple and had "fund raisers" with the Indian community. Some say he embezzled money. His most famous exploit was the money laundering scam. He had contacts in Columbia and he allegedly laundered over a million. He was caught when cartel agents went to the Sydney temple and wanted return of their funds. It was all done through ISKCON GBC bank accounts. Tamal called upon him to smash SHPM with a new book NTIAP, which was fraudulent in many ways. Tirtha engaged Deva Gaura Hari, (David Hooper) and together they came up with "Not that I am Poisoned." GBC member Tamal engaged Tirtharaj in his own vendetta."

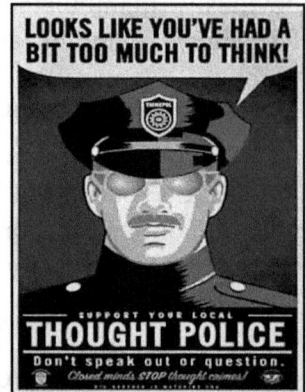

GBC RESOLUTION:THERE IS NO POISONING EVIDENCE

To understand how the ISKCON GBC has covered-up the poison evidence with their book of lies, fraud, and deceit, we review their position as recorded in the 2000 GBC resolutions:

*"**POISON CONTROVERSY: Where As,** the book NTIAP published by Ministry for Protection of ISKCON establishes that: Srila Prabhupada's medical history shows no evidence of poisoning, but*

rather confirms diabetes as the major factor in His Divine Grace's deteriorated physical health; Forensic (hair) analysis does not show any evidence of poisoning, in that the amount of arsenic is compatible with environmental levels and with normal physiological functioning. Recorded conversations indicate that Srila Prabhupada did not believe he was poisoned. Analysis of 'whisper evidence' is inconclusive or can be shown to correlate with spoken conversations of the time.

WHERE AS*, the report submitted by Balavanta das, commissioned by GBC Executive Committee, does not contradict the conclusions of the more detailed investigations by Ministry for Protection of ISKCON;*

*617. **(Statement) It Is Resolved That: (1)** <u>There is no evidence at this time to support the allegations of poisoning of Srila Prabhupada.</u> This conclusion is based on two independent reports commissioned by the GBC body, **(2)** The GBC body endorses NTIAP as the most detailed and comprehensive exposition of the allegations to date, and it recommends this book strongly to devotees who may have been affected by or who are interested in this issue. Approved by: (GBCs, including)* **Bhakticharu Swami***,* **Jayapataka Swami***,* **Tamal Krishna Goswami***.*

ISKCON's cover-up of Srila Prabhupada's poisoning hides the truth and real history of Srila Prabhupada's disappearance pastimes. It does not matter how definitively the poisoning is proven: the full spectrum dominance of the GBC in ISKCON is such that their lies are impossible to kill off, and they manage to implant their lies as the truth in the minds of a sufficient number of members to successfully conceal the truth. The ISKCON party narrative is that anyone challenging ISKCON's version of truth is dishonest or mad. The last leg of religiosity, truthfulness, is severely crippled and wavering, this being a dark time for what remains of a pure spiritual movement left to us only 45 years ago by Srila Prabhupada. ISKCON represses the poison evidence to preserve the status quo of ISKCON leadership.

This same leadership is suspected of poisoning Srila Prabhupada in 1977, and then hijacking, as aiders and abettors, the movement as phony gurus who have since established their franchises of temples, wealth, and followers. The future of Srila Prabhupada's mission, the Hare Krishna movement, is undermined by their refusal to properly investigate the poisoning issue. For this travesty, the complete ISKCON leadership must be sacked, as they have seriously breached their duty by placing material considerations above the cause of truth and faithfulness to Srila Prabhupada. ISKCON leaders care only about their livelihoods and positions. The poison issue threatens them. Naturally if ISKCON leaders' complicity in this poisoning is exposed, they stand to lose everything they have and possibly go to jail as well for either being party to the crime (or after the fact).

EVIDENCE TAMPERING?

In Oct. 2020 Dhananjaya das (Germany) visited Mayapur: *"Hari Sauri das has Srila Prabhupada's tooth and hair samples. In Mayapur Dhananjaya went to see Hari Sauri, who showed him all his Prabhupada items. He asked, 'Do you still have Srila Prabhupada's tooth and hair samples?' Hari Sauri said, 'No, someone came and took them.' Interestingly, instead of wasting money slamming the poison theory, all the GBC has to do is test the tooth and hair they took from Hari Sari and release the results! Instead they hide the facts and evidence, and fool us with a ridiculous video to appease Indian donors and zombie followers."*

COVER-UP CULTURE IN THE CORRUPTED INSTITUTION

ISKCON has resorted to all conceivable cover-up devices to forestall the recognition by its members and congregations of the overwhelming, convincing evidence that Srila Prabhupada was poisoned by his own men in 1977. They tried to explain the heavy metals with the drinking water in India, by alleging defects in the testing methodology of Dr. Morris, by disparaging the character and motives of the evidence messengers, by faulting the science of hair analysis, by cheating and cherry-picking scientific studies, by shopping around for contrary fraudulent scientific opinions, with smoke and mirrors tactics, using false witnesses and shady characters in their defense, and simply denying everything with an air of righteousness as they sit upon their institutional thrones, riddled and weakened by the termites of corruption (see Vol. 6).

The series of orchestrated Srila Prabhupada's poisoning cover-ups by those who took over ISKCON upon his departure (see Vol. 5) reveals how corrupted the institution, for which Srila Prabhupada had such high hopes, has become. First was Hari Sauri's Ministry cover-up in 1998, then a book of fraud and lies (*NTIAP)* in 2000, and finally the 400 page *Deception* book with an hour video in 2020. ISKCON leaders are very afraid of the truth about Srila Prabhupada's disappearance.

ISKCON denials are its recurring theme song. They cannot simply ignore the massive evidence in silence; they are compelled to react with further ***cover-ups*** each time the evidence hits the news wires. *Deception* exudes a palpable desperation of intense ridiculing, lampooning, and over-the-top, audacious denials and derogations of everything. They are circling their wagons and running out of ammo. The truth is closing in on them.

Betrayal of the Spirit (p. 118) describes the mid-80's dilemma for *ISKCON World Review* editors in ***covering up*** the endless bad news of guru fall-downs and debacles. Leadership credibility suffered in the eyes of the membership due to the guru scandals. New Vrindaban declared they had nothing to do with Sulochan's murder of in 1986, and community residents were instructed not to speak to the media or police. It was standard policy to hide all internal problems. ISKCON leadership covered up the massive child abuse scandal for decades by stonewalling and resistance to investigation. Dhira Govinda das, chairman of the Child Protection Office, stated 2015:

*"In places like Mayapur, where the most egregious abuse took place, the abuses were **covered up** again and again. **There is a culture of cover-up**. [...] In addressing cases of neglect of supervision by gurukula headmasters in schools where abuse was extensive, the CPO met with impassioned resistance from GBCs and other leaders... Considering the extent of child suffering and maltreatment in some ISKCON locations, a secular court would very possibly find criminal neglect on the part of [...] the administrators."*

Cover-ups are the norm in ISKCON. A lack of accountability culture prevails in ISKCON, resulting in the unreasonable and defiant denials of the poisoning evidence. Poisoning Srila Prabhupada is even more vile than child abuse: it is the (attempted) murder of the greatest saint and pure devotee, the very foundation of devotees' spiritual life and the Hare Krishna Movement.

Its response to the poison issue is *criminal obstruction of justice* and many heads will roll when their walls of denial crumble into dust, eroded by the relentless march of truth. That day is coming and it cannot come too soon. Truth will prevail. *"Secrets, lies, and hypocrisy are the hallmark of the GBC regime. A cover-up is very strong evidence of a crime, and the GBC has repeatedly engaged in covering up the poison issue." (Nityananda das, 2021)*

*"It is imperative to think for yourself, because **deception** is everywhere and the truth is often ridiculed. The problem is the privileged insiders will fight any reform tooth and nail, so the only real way to advance the interests of the common good is for the rigged, rotten, corrupt, unsustainable status quo to crumble to dust." (ZeroHedge)*

Mayeswara das, his trashy book *Deception,* and the GBC's cheating cover-ups are covered more in Vol. 7: *Kill Guru Become Guru- Crushing the Naysayer Cheaters.*

PART SEVEN:
THE QUEST FOR TRUTH

CHAPTER 54:
TRUTH AND COGNITIVE DISSONANCE

(1) *"It is certainly not good to write literature for money or reputation, but to write books and publish them for the enlightenment of the general populace is real service to the Lord."* CC Mad 19.132

(2) *"The highest courage is to dare to be yourself in the face of adversity, choosing right over wrong, ethics over convenience, truth over popularity. [...] Travel the path of integrity without looking back for there is never a wrong time to do the right thing."* (M Moore)

This volume is about ascertaining the truths of Srila Prabhupada's glorious disappearance pastimes. However, because it is Kali yuga, the age of hypocrisy and quarrel, to ascertain truth in any arena is fraught with many challenges. We all tend to be skeptical of being hoodwinked into some conviction based on faulty "evidence" or fake authority, and also we are apprehensive of "new" or controversial things. But if we can suspend our beliefs, prejudices, and preconceptions and try to keep an open mind, and allow the facts and evidence in the poison issue a fair hearing, we will be able to make a better determination of its validity. We must control our mind and trust our intuition and intelligence to distinguish fallacy from fact. At least, that is the theory…

Srila Prabhupada's triumphant departure pastimes deserve careful consideration. This volume is not an indoctrination program-- we honestly convey the full facts and unvarnished evidence. We do not use deceit, false analogies, or mind games. We do not present a conspiracy theory, although the facts and evidence may at first appear as such until given the fair and full hearing it deserves. Otherwise one gets only a superficial understanding of the facts. If we then pretend to be fully knowledgeable, our previous predispositions will again haunt us. Self-annihilating dishonesty and ulteriorly motivated denials should be scrupulously avoided. May we not be one of the general populace who is unaware of his cultural immersion in self-cheating and avoiding truths.

342

Many pride themselves on being "open-minded," but are so in name only. May discrimination, not conditioning, enable our enlightenment.

Galileo was jailed for saying the Earth was not the center of the universe and Columbus was deemed crazy to sail west across the Atlantic, lest he fall off the edge of the Earth. The mainstream media overhype of COVID-19's mortality rate and the claims of no evidence of fraud in elections are examples why we should be independent evaluators, and not blindly accept popular narratives or politically correct "truths" of the day. Most truths are at first ridiculed, feared, or labeled a "conspiracy theory." Thus we may lazily turn a blind eye to important issues, but a wise, courageous person withholds judgement until taking the due time to objectively examine an issue with their intelligence.

We all have faults and weaknesses which hamper us from recognizing those truths that threaten our closely held beliefs underpinning our social status, wealth, or identity. We are all inundated with societal values, norms, and propaganda that subtly shapes our worldview. It is the nature of the lost soul in the material world to be affected and molded by whatever he associates with. We are very pliable and "made" by our culture, friends, data sources, and authorities. It requires constant vigilance to be open to truth and not to become a programmed robot marching in lockstep to our external influences. Open discourse and free speech, amongst other things, are healthy and empowering to an enlightened person. Beware of the degrading influences of this age that lead us to ignore, minimize, blindly reject, or fear that which we "disagree" with or others insist is untrue.

Research has been done on *belief disconfirmation paradigm.* Dissonance is felt when people are confronted with information that is inconsistent with their beliefs. If the dissonance is not reduced by changing one's belief, it can result in restoring consonance through misperception, rejection or refutation of the information, seeking support from others who share these beliefs, and attempting to persuade others. Early on, cognitive dissonance theory appeared in Leon Festinger's 1956 book *When Prophecy Fails*, describing a deepening of cult members' faith following the failure of their prophecy that a UFO landing was imminent. They met at a set place and time, believing they alone would survive the Earth's destruction. The time came and passed. They faced acute cognitive dissonance: had they been the victim of a hoax? Most members chose to believe something less dissonant: Earth was given a second chance, and Earth-spoiling must stop. The group dramatically increased their proselytism *because of* the failed prophecy. Another case of belief disconfirmation paradigm was an orthodox Jewish group which believed their Rabbi was the Messiah. When he died of a stroke in 1994, some still concluded he was the Messiah and awaited his resurrection.

COGNITIVE DISSONANCE AND OPENING UP TO TRUTH

In psychology, cognitive dissonance is the mental stress or discomfort experienced by a person, when confronted with new information that contradicts existing beliefs, ideas, and values. This causes one to strive for internal consistency to avoid psychological discomfort. Many will experience shock when confronted with the evidence in this volume, and due to cognitive dissonance will try to reconcile the new information with their previously held convictions or hopes by insisting it is not true. By denial, avoidance, argumentation, or disbelief one may postpone acceptance of this reality. Similarly, it may take years for a sincere person to sufficiently overcome attachments and illusions to accept the process of bhakti yoga. The facts and evidence herein may require profound review of closely held values and beliefs. It may be a troubling, emotional journey to understand what happened to Srila Prabhupada in his last year. Not all his followers have the strength to deal with such an issue. The truth of Srila Prabhupada's disappearance pastimes are more than most tender hearts can accommodate, and they need a patient study to allow adequate time for assimilation.

It is not with any delight that this evidence is being conveyed. For many, coming to understand about Srila Prabhupada's passing away, based on his own statements and scientific confirmations, was the hardest time of their life. Even faced with irrefutable evidence, some will remain recalcitrant. Often disbelieving persons will shove aside the evidence and facts and cling to prior beliefs. Many devotees will vehemently resist accepting the evidence presented herein, as the truth disrupts their attachments, psyche, and major paradigms. Cognitive dissonance is a challenge to overcome, and it requires an open and honest mind (it helps if one is not subservient to the political pressures of the ISKCON institution). Difficult as it may be, we should not hide from the truth. It is a gradual process to dispel cognitive dissonance, step by step, and no one should be unkind, disrespectful, or impatient with those facing this struggle. In the end, truth is very healing.

"The biggest impediment in presenting your evidence is cognitive dissonance. When someone believes something and then is confronted with contradicting evidence, they may cope by finding an explanation to support their original belief." (Anuttama dasi, 2016)

Divine or Demoniac? (Dhanesvara das p. 378): *"The Aftermath of Realizing the Truth: [one] will likely be emotionally reeling ...This is normal, and expected, for anyone realizing that what they love is being destroyed by those they once trusted, and that their trust has been violated. It takes time to adjust to and accept these truths, to assimilate them, and to reconcile the many historical incidents and details. Those who have not previously or fully processed this history, will find themselves going through the stages of grief: denial, anger, bargaining, followed by depression, reconciliation, and finally acceptance [as] a natural response to a tragic event/great loss. Denial is generally the first reaction... The final stages are acceptance and reconciliation... one examines past events in light of the new information to reevaluate and make sense of history... [and] come to a new understanding."*

BRAINWASHED BY THE OFFICIAL NARRATIVE

Zero Hedge, May 6, 2020: *"There comes a point in the introduction of every new official narrative when people no longer remember how it started. Or [...] it doesn't make any difference anymore, because the official narrative has supplanted reality. [...] By [late] 2004, most had completely forgotten the propaganda that launched the Iraq invasion, and regarded the resistance as 'terrorists,' despite the fact the US had invaded and occupied Iraq for no legitimate reason. [...] there were no 'weapons of mass destruction,' and the US had invaded a nation that had not attacked it, and posed no threat to it, and so was perpetrating a textbook war of aggression. But these facts did not matter. We were totally immersed in the official War on Terror narrative, which had superseded objective reality. Herd mentality had taken over. [...] **it's a state of functional dissociation**. [...]*

*"They knew there never were any WMDs, and still they were certain there were WMDs, which would be found, although they clearly did not exist. In Nazi Germany most were not fanatical anti-Semites [...] or there was no need for Goebbels and his propaganda machine. They knew that their victims posed no threat, and also they believed the opposite, and did not protest as Jews were sent to death camps, which, in their dissociative state, simultaneously did and did not exist. This sounds like psychosis, but it is not an absolute break from reality. **People know what they believe is not real**. Still, they are forced to believe it, as the consequences of not believing it are more frightening than the cognitive dissonance of believing a false narrative. **Disbelieving the official narrative means excommunication** from 'normality,' the loss of friends, income, status, or punishments. Panicked herd animals instinctively run to the center of the herd or they will become easy prey for pursuing predators. Official narratives aim for this herd mentality, not to deceive, but to confuse and terrorize until they revert to their primal instincts,*

and are driven purely by existential fear, so that facts and truth no longer matter. Then an official narrative **is unassailable by facts and reason**. *It no longer needs facts, and reason cannot penetrate it. And arguing with its adherents is pointless."* **(END)**

This is often the case: we know or suspect there is truth to an idea that contradicts official narratives, but, being caught between **(1)** our own fear of making the practical, psychological, philosophical, and political adjustments in their life to realign with the truth **(2)** and the pressure from leaders and their peers (with potential losses in position, wealth, prestige, etc)… we choose to cling to our old closed-minded views, or even refuse to think about it. Such is the power of illusion…

BECOMING PROPERLY INFORMED WITH FACTS

Amongst the followers of Srila Prabhupada, so far, most are not well informed about the facts of Srila Prabhupada's departure. Strong emotions are invoked by this subject, and many have avoided becoming properly informed with the actual facts. Often it is assumed that "poison theorists" have an agenda based on material considerations, or the "poison theory" is not substantiated with real evidence. Some blindly believe what their family, friends, or ISKCON guru has told them. This is a shame because it is not a theory, nor a conspiracy, but based on an abundance of accumulated evidence amounting to rock-solid proof that Srila Prabhupada was indeed homicidally poisoned.

This evidence is suitably presented for even those who are not familiar with Krishna consciousness, so they have respect and appreciation for Srila Prabhupada's position and achievements. In light of so much false propaganda and obfuscation to block discovery of Srila Prabhupada's real departure pastimes, the record must be set straight. The aim is *historical revisionism,* to bring history into accord with verified facts. Usually official history and the facts are at odds because institutions falsify the past to keep their membership loyal and subservient to their corruptions (Orwell's *1984*). The material world is a dirty place, and it is difficult to expose the lies and misconceptions obscuring the hidden history and proper understanding of Srila Prabhupada's final pastimes.

The proper mood of inquiry in seeking truth is to face it and be blessed with its light. Let us find the truth, whatever it may be, even if unpalatable, bitter or distressing, or even if it turns our life upside down. Ultimately the truth is always good. There should be no fear of open discussion about Srila Prabhupada's departure because, if it is undertaken with honesty, it will be materially and spiritually beneficial.

Those falsely indoctrinated with "politically correct" partisan versions of reality require time to reach mature realizations and a clear view of the facts, to dispel the lies and fear that has been instilled in them. Truth is like the sunrise which causes darkness to dissipate. The truth always prevails over even in the darkest of all crimes.

ACCURACY, APATHY, HONESTY IN SEARCH FOR TRUTH

The evidence is laid out as it is, by *being truthful*. Facts may be loathed and condemned, but we should not deviate from the truth, even if cursed or at the risk of life and reputation. Years ago someone struggled to raise signatures on a petition endorsing further investigation into Srila Prabhupada's poisoning and was surprised at the indifference. This is lamentable, but expected in an institution constantly beset with scandals whereby everyone is now weary of the endless problems. It is difficult to rise above the weariness of cynicism, yet, spiritual strength will enable us to transcend the debilitating modes of nature. *As one would not be apathetic if their own parents had been murdered, so we must similarly respond to the poisoning of Srila Prabhupada, who is our eternal spiritual father, mentor, and primary beneficiary.*

This volume aims to set the facts straight and clear up confusion in the poison issue. It is an exhaustive attempt by disciples of Srila Prabhupada to illuminate for the benefit of sincere seekers the truth regarding historical and spiritual circumstances surrounding the mysterious last pastimes of Srila Prabhupada. It is not a lynch mob agenda, but is a crusade for discovery and recognition of facts. The sincere will be able to understand the truth whereas those under the spell of false preachers and narratives will miss out on the truth. The huge stock of evidence to date definitely proves Srila Prabhupada was indeed maliciously, homicidally poisoned with lethal amounts of heavy metals. This revelation came about by the arrangement of Lord Krishna.

ISKCON LEADERS SECRETLY DOUBT OWN NARRATIVE

Based on confidential information, we know that many senior ISKCON leaders accept that Srila Prabhupada was poisoned, or that it is likely. This was seen in 2002 when many ISKCON leaders supported further independent investigation into the issue with the N14C. However, because of ISKCON's heavy political pressure to tow the party line, all these leaders backtracked and now hold their views in private. Thus, out of misplaced calculations of loyalty, they remain silent and compliant with the GBC's repression. The GBC elite knows very well that if Srila Prabhupada's departure pastimes were to be properly investigated, major unpredictable disruptions and change in ISKCON would take place, jeopardizing their own positions. Better not to rock the boat. Their denials and repression is due to *vested personal interests* and *calcified institutional corruption*. Presentation of facts, evidence, actual ISKCON history, and philosophical siddhanta will rectify the institution. Truth be known. No more cover-ups. Take courage. Face the facts.

QUOTES FROM SRILA PRABHUPADA AND ELSEWHERE

(1) Hrdayananda: Sometimes, Prabhupada, when we expose them, their argument is, "Oh, you are a saintly person. Why are you criticizing me?" **SP:** No, it is not criticizing. It is opening your eyes. You are blind […] That is... ajnana-timirandhasya jnananjana-salakaya. You are blind with ignorance, so we are trying to open your eyes. See things as they are. It is favoring you. It is not criticizing you." (SPConv Feb. 6, 1976)

(2) SP: Ah. So this is sattvam jayate… What is this nonsense? Expose them. Bluffing. The bluffing should be exposed. (SPConv May 4, 1973)

(3) *"We are not proud of this; however, the truth must be explained."* (CC Adi 7.95 purport) **(4)** *"No one should resent the incisive words of a preacher; they should appreciate his straight-forwardness and beneficial instructions. As Chanakya Pandit says, 'He who speaks out plainly cannot be a deceiver.'"* (Niti Shastra 5:5, Srila Prabhupada)

(5) SBhag 1.17.25: You [Dharma] are now **standing on one leg only, which is your truthfulness**, and you are somehow or other hobbling along. But quarrel personified [Kali], **flourishing by deceit,** is also trying to destroy that leg. **Purport:** The principles of religion do not stand on some dogmas or manmade formulas, but they stand on four primary regulative observances, namely austerity, cleanliness, mercy and **truthfulness**. […] Gradually these attributes have diminished […] in this age of Kali to one fourth, which is also gradually diminishing on account of **prevailing untruthfulness**. […] and **by too much lying propaganda, truthfulness is spoiled**. The revival of bhagavata-dharma can save human civilization from falling prey to all types of evil.

(6) *"Facts are stubborn things; and whatever may be our wishes, our inclinations, or the dictates of our passion, they cannot alter the state of facts and evidence."* (John Adams) **(7)** *"Facts are peculiar things. They come together over time, and will prove what they will prove. And facts are, ultimately, immune to opinions and the people who hold them."* (Unknown) **(8)** *"A good journalist should present uncomfortable facts, question orthodoxies, highlight suppressed views."* (Unknown) **(9)** *"Everyone, without exception, has found some things to not believe in. Things that are demonstrably true that we just don't want to accept. A bit like a fingerprint, each person's pattern of disbelief is* *probably unique. You might believe that the moon is made of cheese. The question is: What has to happen for you to change your mind? What standard of proof, from what source, is sufficient for us to accept that something we're sure wasn't true, is true? That's a great place to begin."* (Seth Godin) **(10)** *"Facts are stubborn things, but statistics are pliable."* (Mark Twain) **(11)** *"Facts are facts and will not disappear on account of your likes."* (Jawaharlal Nehru)

(12) *"The internet's truth-telling has changed the Vaishnava world, and despite negative impact from facilitating false propaganda, it has allowed sincere persons to determine the truth in all transcendental topics by having easy access to search tools, databases, discussion groups, and faraway senior devotees. One may thus ascertain the real siddhanta of Srila Prabhupada's teachings, then take determined actions to secure their Krishna consciousness."* (Nityananda das)

CONCLUSION

The evidence proves Srila Prabhupada was deliberately poisoned with heavy metals to prematurely force him out of the scene. Srila Prabhupada's place was taken by "successor acharyas." This is ISKCON history. We must to go back to square one and re-evaluate the existing order in ISKCON, effecting a major housecleaning. If the acharya's seat was stolen illegitimately, with poisoning and deviant policies enabling the plunder of the society assets, then honest devotees must take determined steps to rectify the situation. The truth of Srila Prabhupada's final pastimes has yet to be assimilated into the Hare Krishna movement's collective psyche, but this is inevitable as the truth spreads, ending the cover ups. When the Sun of truth rises, all becomes self-evident. Dr. Sherri Tenpenny quoted research that when 10-11% recognize a truth, a societal paradigm shift occurs, and that truth quickly becomes accepted. We advocate truth-telling: 1%, 2%, 3%... TRUTH: Conformity to fact, reality; correspondence with what actually occurred.

CHAPTER 55:
PRIVATE INVESTIGATION

PRIVATE IMPARTIAL INVESTIGATION

After the evidence presentation in *Someone Has Poisoned Me* (1999), the GBC organized their cover-up book *NTIAP* in 2000, pretending it was all a nonsense conspiracy theory. The GBC has never completed an honest investigation, and that was true for the child abuse scandal, the guru appointment hoax, and Srila Prabhupada's poisoning. Only when they are compelled by circumstances and obvious facts, will they reluctantly respond by perpetuating another deviation.

Since 1997 some of Srila Prabhupada's disciples outside the ISKCON institution have privately investigated the suspicious circumstances surrounding Srila Prabhupada's departure, working independently and with their own resources. Early on, they knew that if the truth was to be discovered, it would have to be by their own endeavors, as ISKCON has always obstructed and opposed the discovery of the truths in key issues. The private investigation was opposed at every turn by an uncooperative, hostile ISKCON which has banned internal discussion of the issue and participation in any investigation. Those who do so are branded as envious, poisonous, agents of Kali, portrayed as offenders, fault-finders, troublemakers. When we tried to interview various devotees, most had no interest in helping, made no reply, did not remember anything, etc. The quest for the truth in this matter has been met with much resistance. Many feared retribution or loss of privileges should they be linked to the "poison conspiracy theory." Yet, the total evidence speaks convincingly for itself. Although Srila Prabhupada's poisoning has been investigated to the point of certainty, there are some open questions, such as: Who was involved, who knew about it, and who did what?

While ISKCON was denying, confusing, lying, deceiving, and whitewashing, a real investigation was underway, and irrefutable evidence accumulated to establish the certainty of Srila Prabhupada's chronic, malicious, homicidal cadmium poisoning. (Part 1) There was no choice but to organize a private investigation outside ISKCON.

A heuristic process is an educational method where learning occurs through discoveries resulting from investigations made by the student (disciple). The private investigation was heuristic, as each discovery built upon others, dispelling myths and revealing truths. From the discovery of the "poison whispers" in 1997, the evidence continued to accumulate, now compiled and organized to counteract the denials, fraud, and lies from the GBC. The phony, so-called ISKCON "investigation" in *NTIAP* was a denial whitewash and classic, sham cover-up by the prime suspects themselves. However, a private investigation has heuristically certified Srila Prabhupada's poisoning as a proven truth and fact. Former temple presidents and GBC members, and other senior devotees have supported the private investigation and production of this volume; those inside ISKCON have not contributed much save from a few sympathetic moles. Those in exile, either forced out or self-imposed, have worked together to find and distribute the truth in the face of cover-ups and stonewalling from ISKCON.

"WHERE'S THE PROOF?"

When Prahladananda Swami began to visit Australia years ago, a few devotees approached him. He seemed gentle, honest, not like the rest of the GBC and gurus they had seen. They explained the crisis in the Australian yatra, that local GBC and temple presidents were engaged in improprieties, illegalities, abuse, mismanagement, self-dealing, and corruption. Listening carefully, while they were hoping for a brighter future, he replied: *"Where's the proof?"* And that was the end of their hopes. The corruption had seeped into every nook of the institution, even Prahladananda Swami. Maybe he would follow up somehow, or bring it up at the next annual GBC meeting, or discuss their complaints with local leaders. But nothing happened and nothing changed.

LOYALTY TO THE INSTITUTION OR THE TRUTH?

An internal investigation into Srila Prabhupada's poisoning was "dead on arrival" because ISKCON is anti-truth and has only engaged in denials and deceitful cover-ups. (Part 6) By Krishna's arrangements, through a private investigation, a heavy metals poisoning has been proven, although there are areas requiring further investigation. The private investigation since 1997 was successful, and ideally government will now take up the matter. Suspects may confess or not, they may all die, yet Srila Prabhupada remains in his Vrindaban samadhi as the ultimate, preserved evidence, and he will be there for a long time. ISKCON employs tactics of repression, fear, institutional pressure, cover-ups, dishonesty, influencing, bribery, and dishonesty, all in true Kali Yuga fashion. ISKCON's non-cooperation and harboring of suspects and their followers reveals a spiritually compromised institution that will not agree to interviews and cross-examination until forced by state agencies. They have a lot to hide for as long as they can. ISKCON struggles to maintain the allegiance and loyalty of its members by insisting on its official narrative that there is no poisoning evidence. It bans critical thinking, open discourse, and any honest atmosphere based on facts and evidence whereby intelligent persons can freely discern truth. Its self-serving interpretations are imposed by claiming divine privileges, using coercive and unethical measures in repression. This is done by rewriting history, propaganda, sanctions, and sponsoring false witnesses. These mundane techniques, however, will fail in concealing truth. ISKCON's corruption is a disease which is gradually killing the host. Pity those whose sincerity and spiritual aspirations are eviscerated in a hopeless servitude to such a polluted institution.

The GBC's lies and deceit in its cover-up of Srila Prabhupada's poisoning is opposed by those who want a comprehensive, truly independent probe into the poison issue. The truths about Srila Prabhupada's life and pastimes will not be hidden. Enlightenment of one devotee at a time is how real and positive change will take place in the Hare Krishna movement, as the Golden Age continues to progress. To investigate and properly deal with this issue, we will not look to the corrupt GBC, but do it among honest devotees. No matter what the evidence is, ISKCON leaders say: *"Where's the proof?"* or *"Take it to the legal authorities."* Faced with final proof, they pretend it is faulty and inconclusive. This is duplicity. They will never willingly take the medicine of truth until forced by a revolution of consciousness and a grass roots rebellion. It is our duty to defend Srila Prabhupada and his movement from those who have *poisoned his body and mission.*

We did not know of the poisoning in 1977, but at least we can act now to protect his mission from the contaminating deviations of his poisoners and their successors. Some are certainly still within Srila Prabhupada's institution, and they, their heirs, and their influence must be removed. This crime against Krishna and His devotees, truth, and spirituality is perhaps the worst since Ravana and Hiranyakasipu. We do not intend to prescribe specific legal action and remedies, but to enlighten Srila Prabhupada's followers about the facts and evidence of Srila Prabhupada's poisoning, to counteract the cover-ups. Our forum to promote justice and historical truth is the public domain. Proof of the crime is now in hand, and further evidence will follow. We have a difficult task in restoring the divine mission that has been corrupted by the poisoners. With the mountain of evidence that Srila Prabhupada was intentionally poisoned, how can one remain silent? **Silence and complicity are close friends.** This is not entertainment reading. It is ISKCON history that the gurucrats hide truths from the rest of us. This is not a matter of airing our dirty laundry in public. It is a question of defending Srila Prabhupada, the truth, and his mission –which is the prime benediction for humanity. Devotees deserve the truth. This volume is a study of the internal and external features of Srila Prabhupada's transcendental, mystical disappearance pastimes.

PRIVATE RESEARCH IN INDIA

From 2002-06 an independent team conducted an extensive investigation into Srila Prabhupada's poisoning at their own expense. Consisting primarily of Mandapa, Jitarati, Sakshi Gopal, Nityananda, and Naveen Krishna, this team accomplished the following: **(1) Research, Interviews, Contacts In India.** The devotees interviewed prominent Indian scientists and experts on poisoning and the Bengali arsenic crisis, as described earlier. They interviewed many residents of Vrindaban and elsewhere in India. **(2)** *Judge For Yourself.* **(2003)** This third book (250 pg, 2000 copies) on Srila Prabhupada's poisoning, with much new evidence and analysis, was distributed throughout ISKCON. The GBC simply ignored the book and gave no sign of recognition or reply. Many leaders, however, privately acknowledged concern and sympathy, but had their hands and mouths tied by institutional policy. **(3) Star Tv Show (2005):** *www.youtube.com/watch?v=0h4YmilaL-c* */16 min.* Jitarati das (John Hanton) was interviewed on a major TV show special in India about the poisoning of Srila Prabhupada. The devotee team was disappointed at its quality, but it was a best effort. In the show, Braj Dulal Goswami testifies at length about his father Bonamali's 1977 urine test and medical assessment that Srila Prabhupada was poisoned. **(4) Legal Action In India:** The team was able to establish contacts in Delhi to initiate a government investigation into Srila Prabhupada's poisoning. The attorney who was chosen led the team on a dead end trail; she was actually working for ISKCON, being a life member. She misled and betrayed the team and the Indian government investigation into Srila Prabhupada's poisoning was sabotaged. This was a setback.

WHAT ARE THE REMAINING OPEN QUESTIONS?

Srila Prabhupada's poisoning has been proven by the accumulation of undeniable evidences. That Tamal was a party to this deed beyond a reasonable doubt is presented in Vol. 2. The primary suspects are examined in Vol. 3. The history of ISKCON deviations are examined in Vol. 5 and 6 to complete the picture of what happened to Srila Prabhupada's institution after 1977. *Prabhupada Truth Commission continues with its private investigations.* Some of the open ends:

(1) Interview Dr. Sri Pran Gopal Acharya (Gopinath Bazaar), Balarama Misra's son, who was present when Srila Prabhupada first stated someone told him he had been given poison. ISKCON may silence him as they have done with other witnesses. **(2)** Why was the death certificate filed so late, who filed it, and why was "heart attack" listed as the cause of death? **(3)** A legal deposition with Bhakta Vatsala,

Adhoksaja, Nandaprana, and other Mexican devotees be done. **(4)** Dr. K. Gopal of Mathura should be legally deposed. **(5)** Interview Panchadravida Swami who defected to the Gaudiya Math (1986) and has intimate knowledge of 1970's ISKCON internal affairs. He was often with Srila Prabhupada in 1977. **(6)** Investigate ISKCON Houston, Dallas to trace the existence or history of about 240 "missing" Srila Prabhupada tapes. **(7)** Tamal's original diary should be located, made available and studied. **(8)** The remaining makharadhvaja should be properly tested. **(9)** Former New York devotees should be interviewed to ascertain relationships between Chandra Swami, Adi Keshava, and Tamal. **(10)** Living witnesses should be officially interviewed: Bhavananda, Jayapataka, Braj Dulal Goswami, Bhaktisiddhanta das, Naveen Krishna das, many Vrindaban residents, Bhagatji's (Sri Vishvambar Dayal) family, and more. **(11)** The original May 28 tape at the Archives could be safely tested for editing, tampering.

WHAT WE DO **NOT** YET KNOW

The private investigation into Srila Prabhupada's poisoning has completed Phase One, answering the question: Was Srila Prabhupada poisoned? The substantial body of evidence is presented in this volume. Although much is not known about Srila Prabhupada's poisoning, this does not change the fact Srila Prabhupada *was homicidally poisoned.*

What we do not yet know: **(1)** Everyone involved in the poisoning and what were their roles? **(2)** Who knew of the poisoning in 1977, although not directly involved? **(3)** Who came to know of the poisoning after 1977? **(4)** Where was the cadmium chemical obtained for the poisoning? **(5)** How was the poison administered and who taught the poisoners how to use it? **(6)** When exactly did the poisoning start, and when was it given thereafter? **(7)** Who else in ISKCON knows that Srila Prabhupada was poisoned but has denied it until now? **(8)** What is the relationship between those who poisoned Srila Prabhupada and those involved in the ISKCON guru takeover conspiracy? **(9)** Who knew in 1977 of Tamal's claims that Srila Prabhupada wanted to commit suicide by being given a medicine/poison to die immediately?

The N14C (Ch. 45) originally had significant participation (2002) from active ISKCON leaders, who were then blackmailed and coerced by Tamal and the GBC into disengaging, withdrawing, and going silent. As a result, N14C's momentum was sabotaged by ISKCON, and the program became dormant, as it was based on cooperation with the GBC (who were not interested). However, Prabhupada Truth Commission is ready to accept sincere participation from any ISKCON member.

Whoever is willing to put their name on the line for the sake of truth and justice is welcomed to assist with the continuing investigation. ISKCON cannot be trusted to investigate this matter because of a fatal conflict of interest, in that the leadership is protecting those in their own ranks who are likely involved in or have knowledge of this crime.

AREAS OF PRABHUPADA TRUTH COMMISSION WORK

(1) Funding: Any contributions towards the ongoing private investigation into the poisoning of Srila Prabhupada are welcomed. To date total expenses are over US$400,000. Broader participation is sought. To assist with funding in any amount, contact: srigovinda@gmail.com or naveenusa01@gmail.com **(2) Professional Private Investigative Agency:** Through the professional contacts of one of the N14C supporters, an agency was located that had a very noteworthy history. Divulgence of details in this area would be counter-productive to the impact of possible upcoming legal actions. **(3) Criminal Investigation In India:** There is no statute of limitations on murder in India or USA. **(4) Interviews:** Conduct in-depth interviews and cross-examinations, including all suspects. **(5) Legal Actions:** (Ch. 63) **(6) Forensic Specialists, Criminologists, Toxicologists, Legal Experts**: As necessary, and underway. **(7) Forensics Tests:** Further tests on authenticated hair samples. Only a few pieces of Srila Prabhupada's hair (1976 to late 1977) are required for a high accuracy test. Many devotees and temples have such sacred relics.

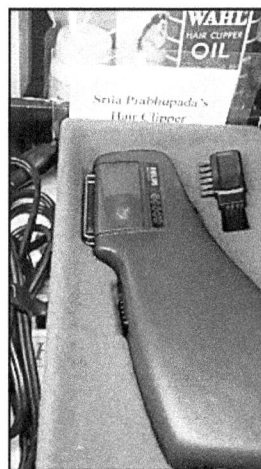

OTHER AREAS TO INVESTIGATE

(1) Aditya Dasi- The Bombay Almira And Desk: She was helping Tamal in Bombay as a secretary in 1977-78 and had the keys to SP's Bombay Almira and desk where Tamal kept many tapes and correspondence. This Almira (and all Bombay cabinets, safes) was searched by a Bhaktivedanta Archives' agent in 2016 for documents, recordings, letters, but nothing was found. Aditya dasi passed away in May 2017 and the whereabouts of her personal estate and effects is unknown. **(2) Prabhupada Museum**: ISKCON Vrindaban Mandir, has artifacts of Srila Prabhupada's hair, clothes, personal items, medical prescriptions, *face shaver (photo above),* medical logbook, SONY tape recorder, containers, etc. In 2004 a PTC member saw 3 medical prescriptions written by Damodara Shastri in the display showcase. **(4)**

355

Non-Public Minutes Of Meetings Of GBC (West Bengal Society Inc). Many "sensitive" resolutions of the GBC from 1976 onwards were never made public and should be obtained for evidence. **(5) Communications, Documents** in possession of GBC re: the poison issue. **(6) Estate Of Tamal, Prime Suspect:** office effects, notebooks, his 1977 diary, computers, hair samples, etc, in his Dallas temple quarters. There were 3 trustees for Tamal's estate, to execute his will, to manage, disperse the millions he accumulated as an ISKCON guru. Giriraj Swami and Carl Herzig (Tamal's brother) are believed to be trustees. Tamal's Dallas quarters are closed… *"years ago TKG's computer was stolen from some devotee's home in Dallas, so items are kept in TKG disciple's home."*

(7) Hair Samples: Abhiram, Satyanarayan, Dinatarine (Yamuna dasi), others have 1977 samples for testing. **(8) Personal Records And Effects** of Bhakticharu, Bhavananda, Satsvarupa, others. **(9)** More tests on Srila Prabhupada relics (hair samples and teeth). **(10)** Expert opinions from toxicologists, medical examiners, criminologists, and forensic experts. Ongoing. **(11)** New audio technologies be applied to further forensic study of poison whispers (Ch. 27). **(12)** Certified Voice Stress Analysis and new technologies applied to study 1977 audio recordings to determine stress, untruths by suspects (some tests were done, Volume 2).

COMMUNICATIONS WITH HARI SAURI DAS

After the May 4, 2017 release of the *Scientific Breakthrough* YouTube video, Nityananda wrote to Hari Sauri to explain that the hair samples he had arranged for testing in 1999 had been completed by PTC and that Yudhisthira das, who wrote him in 2002 for details on the GBC hair samples, had been actually Nityananda das (Ch. 2). Hari Sauri das was asked for his reactions to the findings of sky-high cadmium. He responded: *"So in other words you are saying that you were impersonating someone else in order to mislead me?"* Nityananda das replied: *"The only way I could have gotten the information on the hair samples was to approach you as someone else... to obtain the truth, sometimes unusual measures are required. I am sorry about that, but it was the only way... the hair samples you had arranged for Deva Gaurahari were tested after all. They were sent directly from Wisconsin to Dr Morris. NTIAP offered to allow others to complete the tests, which we did, and the results from Dr. Morris are proof Srila Prabhupada was poisoned with very high amounts of cadmium, a heavy metal similar to arsenic. Please read the two chapters I sent you to see how the hair tests took place. I would be interested in your thoughts."* There was no reply from a likely very shocked and consternated Hari Sauri das.

ISKCON'S PROPAGANDA, DISINFORMATION CAMPAIGN

With ISKCON's repeated cover-ups (Part 6), disinformation (Ch. 53), and stubborn adherence to lies, dishonesty, and denials of the facts and evidence in Srila Prabhupada's poisoning, this corrupted institution has become parallel to the "global elite" who are also engaged in other types of lies and tyranny. The planet is run by great powerful demons who exploit the innocent people in the most horrible ways possible, as they ruthlessly oppress the masses with medical fraud, endless wars, fiat currency, and corrupt politics, academia, science, and culture. Srila Prabhupada: *"By propaganda, you can do any false thing [...] propaganda is called in Bengali, dasha cakre bhagavan bhutha [...] By propaganda you can establish a false thing as real."* (Apr. 14, 1975)

INVESTIGATION STATUS

ISKCON claims they had already investigated whether Srila Prabhupada was poisoned or not, and they concluded with the deceitful pronouncement that there was no evidence to that effect. Actually, their first investigation, done by Balavanta, had found substantial cause for concern of poisoning and Balavanta recommended further investigation with proper funding. However, a secret, second "investigation" was organized by the primary suspects themselves through their disciples, which denied all the evidence by fraud, lies, irrelevancies, hyperbole. Frustrated and dissatisfied disciples of His Divine Grace banded together outside the precincts of the tyrannical institution and continued the investigation into the circumstances surrounding Srila Prabhupada's disappearance with their own funding. By chance, in 2002-05 three hair tests on GBC-authenticated samples of Srila Prabhupada's hair discovered sky-high, lethal levels of cadmium. This settled the question whether Srila Prabhupada was poisoned. The Prabhupada Truth Commission (PTC) continues their investigation and works to make the truth of Srila Prabhupada's departure pastimes known.

Srila Prabhupada knew he was being poisoned, strongly indicated by his asking for makharadhvaja which is a counteraction to poisoning. (https://www.kesarherbals.com/product/siddha-makardhwaj) It is a testament to the stark and brutal reality of the material world where such an exalted and pure Vaishnava would be so mercilessly poisoned. Thus we were denied more years of his divine physical presence. It was a long and horrible ordeal for Srila Prabhupada.

HOW MANY COINCIDENCES ARE NOT A COINCIDENCE?

(1) There are four poison whispers on the same day, Nov. 11, 1977. None have been found in any other out of thousands tape recordings. (2) The four poison whispers come the very next day (out of thousands of

days) after extensive discussions about homicidal poisoning and Srila Prabhupada revealing he thought he was being poisoned. **(3)** The poison whispers come just days before Srila Prabhupada's departure. **(4)** The poison whispers are from some of the most ambitious disciples. **(5)** In two days, out of over 4000 days, Srila Prabhupada stated three times he thought someone had poisoned him, something he never said before. **(6)** Srila Prabhupada had 12 unique physical symptoms attributable to cadmium poisoning BUT which are not found in diabetes/kidney disease, and there are 10 physical symptoms typical to diabetes/kidney disease which Srila Prabhupada did not have at all.

(7) Sky-high lethal cadmium poisoning 250 X above normal was found in similar levels in three separate hair tests. **(8)** Three of the tested hair samples also had elevated arsenic and antimony, whereas three hair samples from earlier years were normal in all 3 elements. **(9)** Out of over 2000 tape recordings made of Srila Prabhupada, about 10%, or 200, are missing, exactly from those times when Srila Prabhupada spoke about the future arrangements in ISKCON after his departure, namely May through Sept. 1977. **(10)** Never before were there such big gaps of missing tapes as there were under Tamal's 1977 management, even though he was a meticulous manager with great attention to detail, accuracy, efficiency. **(11)** Tamal was present with Srila Prabhupada on all his major downturns in health: July 20, 1976; Feb. 26, 1977; May 16, 1977; Sept. 8, 1977; as well as in the poison whispers and "Ravana will kill" episode. **(12)** Immediately after Srila Prabhupada departed, Tamal moved into Srila Prabhupada's Bombay quarters, and when he was ousted from Bombay, he then moved into Srila Prabhupada's Dallas quarters. **(13)** There are many similarities in the heavy metal poisonings of Srila Prabhupada with Napoleon and other victims, including the inflammation/blockage of the urinary tract, requiring circumcision. **(14)** The makharadhvaja in Delhi just happened to have been completed hours before Adi Keshava and Satadhanya picked it up; unusually it was given for free, and involved Chandra Swami, a notorious criminal involved in assassinations (Volume 3).

(15) Days after Srila Prabhupada departed, Tamal gives a highly incriminating interview claiming Srila Prabhupada wanted "medicine to die now," implying a mercy killing, obviously a defense against the poisoning he feared would be imminently exposed (Vol. 2). **(16)** ISKCON leaders have stubbornly denied ALL the evidence even beyond the pale of credibility and reasonableness, in a series of cover-ups orchestrated by the suspects themselves. **(17)** Srila Prabhupada's poisoning suspects happen to be those acknowledging Srila Prabhupada was speaking being homicidally poisoned, yet they did nothing, not contacting the police, nor any doctors, nor notifying other devotees, and decades later claimed Srila Prabhupada was not in his right mind, senile, and we should not take what he said seriously (Volume 2). **(18)** Srila Prabhupada chose to first disclose his poisoning to an outsider and not his own "trusted" close disciples. **(19)** Srila Prabhupada is attended by maybe 40 kavirajas and doctors in 1977, and none could correctly diagnose his declining health nor cure it with any medicine. **(20)** Why would Srila Prabhupada be in distress about being poisoned (Ch. 13) if he wanted a "mercy killing" (Vol. 2)?

All coincidences? How many does it take to not be coincidental?

PURPOSE OF THIS VOLUME

The purpose of this volume is simply to distribute the truth, facts, and evidence to all Srila Prabhupada followers about his glorious and triumphant disappearance pastimes. Then whatever happens, it is up to Krishna. Scientific discoveries have proven beyond doubt that Srila Prabhupada was maliciously, homicidally poisoned for minimum 10 months in 1977 at lethal levels with the heavy metal cadmium. This truth is highly relevant to all in the Hare Krishna movement and has deep ramifications for its future. The truth always serves us well, whereas ignorance and falsehood are always detrimental. *Srila Prabhupada's mission was hijacked by those who physically poisoned him, who have subsequently poisoned the mission as well with defective doctrines introduced to serve their corruption and exploitation of the mission's assets.* Thus Srila Prabhupada's mission to save and deliver humanity into transcendence was practically ruined. Knowing this true history, Srila Prabhupada's faithful followers will restore his mission, by removing poisoners, their accomplices, allies, heirs, and then their deviant doctrines.

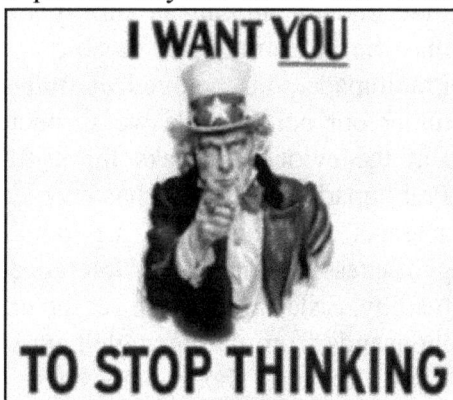

There are many sincere devotees both inside and outside the corrupt ISKCON institution. To varying degrees they have come to understand this sad situation, while others have been fully indoctrinated by the corrupt leaders, adversely influenced by "Tamalism," which is the institutionalized pursuit of personal ambitions (Volume 2) The truth is freedom, and thus it is gradually becoming accepted Srila Prabhupada was poisoned and his mission hijacked (gurujacked). No one is proud or happy about this truth that has been concealed and covered up for almost a half century. The truth about the facts, evidence, and history of Srila Prabhupada's disappearance and ISKCON's history since 1977 must be openly discussed and understood accurately. Those who cannot accept the evidence and scientific proof that Srila Prabhupada was maliciously, lethally poisoned with cadmium at levels 250 X above normal, often raise various objections (Ch. 58). Still, it is a proven fact. It is not so much that people disagree with the evidence, *but that they do not know what it is.* They most likely never even read the 1977 "poison discussions" with Srila Prabhupada and his caretakers. If they did, there would be 99% less doubts and questions.

Another reason why someone cannot appreciate the poisoning evidence is if they are dependent upon ISKCON misleaders or gurus, who all strenuously denied, repressed, and covered-up the issue. Independent thinking is almost impossible in ISKCON. A third reason may be if someone is unable to bear the emotional pain that Srila Prabhupada, our beloved eternal spiritual master, was poisoned right under our noses while we suspected nothing. There are other reasons. But the evidence speaks for itself. It is not a concocted theory. Srila Prabhupada's poisoning has been conclusively proven and established by science. In discussing the poisoning truth, we advocate patience, gentleness, compassion, tolerance, and open discourse; this will be healthy. Srila Prabhupada set the example by tirelessly working to rescue thousands from the entanglement of material existence, and so we must assist likewise those who have been adversely influenced by false information. Most devotees are sincere and when presented the facts and evidence, they connect the dots and in time understand everything quite well. Devotees are intelligent, so we should appeal to their intelligence. There is no use in quote-bashing, anger venting, or arrogance.

For example, many devotees seem compromised and lost, in league with the ISKCON corrupt leaders. They are subjected to intense institutional pressures. Many ISKCON devotees who have been resistant to the truths of Srila Prabhupada's poisoning are basically honest persons who can appreciate truth, facts, and evidence. The truth will convince one by one until the majority is "enlightened." Those who have been away from the influence of the ISKCON institution and leaders for at least some years generally find it much easier to see these truths.

Truth tellers have been banned, exiled, demonized by ISKCON. Only those who conform to the official ISKCON narratives and policies, as dictated by its misleading GBC, are allowed institutional facility or participation. Others are castigated, reviled, excluded, ridiculed, and demonized (sidelined at the minimum), and thus the most vital members have migrated outside the tyrannical boundaries of the corrupted institution operating for the benefit of its elites. Many have left to preserve their honor, spiritual principles, honesty, and virtue. Change and purity will return to the institution with a revolution of consciousness. Truth telling is essential to facilitate this awakening.

May violence, chaos, schisms, divisions, and strife not disturb the movement, but history shows this unlikely. Somehow change will come. The corrupt regime of tyranny will end and Srila Prabhupada's divine influence will prevail. Once the poisoners' regime and their heirs are identified and purged, along with their deviant doctrines (Volume 6), the devotee society can heal and thrive through Srila Prabhupada's living instructions. When it is understood how Srila Prabhupada was maliciously poisoned, devotees will understand exactly where ISKCON went astray since Srila Prabhupada's departure and they will set things back on track again by the divine will of Lord Chaitanya and Srila Prabhupada. We have faith in Krishna's guiding hand. Meanwhile, ISKCON continues their cover-ups. We can expect bribes, dishonest "experts," threats, pay-offs, forged documents, character assassinations, death threats, and worse. But these are their "end times." Srila Prabhupada's mission and mercy will be restored and revitalized.

PUT THEM IN JAIL? AND THEN ALL DONE?

Volume 2 determines that Tamal was involved in Srila Prabhupada's poisoning beyond a reasonable doubt. Volume 3 examines the evidence on Srila Prabhupada's other poisoners. Living suspects must be confronted: "Either submit to full cooperative interviews or go away" (and dead ones investigated further.) It is far more important to restore the mission than it in getting some legal convictions. What good will it be for a few men in jail, and leaving the movement as it is, corrupted and deviated by the poisoners' deviant doctrines? Volume 6 explores ISKCON corruptions; Volume 8, 9 looks at restoring the divine mission.

Anyone having any relevant information should send it to PTC. Constructive advice, clarifications, corrections, additions, deletions are welcomed. Thank you for being among Srila Prabhupada's followers who want to establish the truth about Srila Prabhupada's glorious disappearance pastimes and the restoration of his transcendental mission. Please send your feedback and comments to: srigovinda@gmail.com

CHAPTER 56:
ENORMOUS RAMIFICATIONS

THE MAIN ISSUE IN THE HARE KRISHNA MOVEMENT

The honest investigation into Srila Prabhupada's departure under suspicious circumstances is of great relevance and importance to the future success of the Hare Krishna Movement, even though many years have passed. The evidence is that Srila Prabhupada was indeed poisoned, as a fact. Srila Prabhupada's poisoners gurujacked ISKCON and then deeply influenced it with deviant policies and doctrines which were not given by Srila Prabhupada. Thus there was a poisoning of Srila Prabhupada's body *and then his mission and movement*. Everything in ISKCON since 1977 would be colored by this poisoning and the poisoners (Volume 2, 3, 5, 6). How can this be good? The ramifications of this pollution of Srila Prabhupada's mission are enormous and requires a complete reset. The slate must be cleaned and we must go back and begin over. Dishonest, corrupted, and compromised ISKCON misleaders in bed with the poisoner hijackers' regime will of course deny the facts and evidence. The evidence that Srila Prabhupada was poisoned should be **the primary issue** in the Hare Krishna Movement: all other issues are secondary to this "crime of the millennium." Book changes issue. Guru issue. Initiations issue. Deviations. Child abuse. *All this came after (and because of) Srila Prabhupada's poisoning.* This compilation of facts, evidence, documents, and forensic studies, with theological discussions, realizations, and conclusions is needed since ISKCON has only given us cover-ups and denials. History often requires corrections from verified evidence of the accurate picture of the past. Srila Prabhupada said: *"Among the public, those who are more honest will not dislike, but rather respect our straightforwardness. If we just go on giving our message as it is, it will gradually be accepted for what it is."* Truth is an end in itself, always worthy and necessary.

Anyone who has affection for Srila Prabhupada or has received a measure of his divine grace, upon understanding that Srila Prabhupada was poisoned with heavy metals, will quickly grasp how the Hare Krishna movement has been corrupted, and that the poisoners of the Founder-Acharya's physical body have also poisoned his mission and his mercy. How could those who defiled Srila Prabhupada's body not do the same to ISKCON? In fact, as seen in Volume 5, they engineered a "gurujacking" of the movement by illegally assuming the post of supposed acharyas and instituted a flawed guru regime based on fealty and patronage. Srila Prabhupada's being poisoned by insiders for personal gain explains the turbulent history and troubles of the Hare Krishna movement since His Divine Grace physically departed.

The profound ramifications of a homicidal attack on the Founder-Acharya, followed by a coup by senior men, is the crux and essence of all ISKCON anomalies. An overhaul of Srila Prabhupada's mission is required to restore its spiritual health. Srila Prabhupada's mission has been usurped by his poisoners, those who then proclaimed their divine right as his inheritors. It would be a great disservice to His Divine Grace if his followers did not rectify this dire situation. Deep discussion and sincere cooperation is needed to correct the endemic corruption that has consumed ISKCON and Srila Prabhupada's mission. This disease must be eliminated in a restoration of the Hare Krishna movement.

BIG WAKE UP CALL (Uttamasloka das, 2017)

"Srila Prabhupada stated clearly to Nanda Kumara (NK) that there were infiltrators in ISKCON trying to destroy it from within. That means they were in the leadership, not rank and file. NK said: 'SP told me something personally: "There are those among us wearing dhoti, sikha, tilaka and neck beads, but they are not devotees. They are agents of Kali who are here to try to stop our movement. You should find out who they are and weed them out." That's an exact quote.'"

"SP wrote Hansadutta in 1970, regarding problems within ISKCON: 'It is a fact however that the great sinister movement is within our Society.' Bhaktivinoda Thakura also confirms: 'After the time of Sri Chaitanya Mahaprabhu, those faithful to Him kept apart from non-devotees, to avoid contamination. Seeing this, the personality of Kali sent his representatives in disguise to pollute the Vaishnava sampradaya. Posing as Vaishnavas, they spread their wicked doctrines, and appeared so intelligent and devoted that <u>only pure devotees could detect their real identity</u>. Most devotees- not only the most neophyte- were enchanted by their tricks. In this way Kali's agents expertly introduced karma, jnana, and anyabhilasa in the Vaishnava sampradaya and caused suddha-bhakti to vanish from the world.'

*"So: IF there is clear and compelling evidence to indicate that there was an 'attempt' to poison SP, that must be brought to light and made public. [...] If there was, then it further validates SP's statements about infiltrators. We cannot ignore SP's statements in that regard. And, more importantly, it means **those infiltrators are still in the movement**. And it doesn't matter that all the GBC from the 70's are almost all gone.*

"*Infiltrators get new people to take over for them. They don't just fade away. Infiltrators are not 'lone wolves'. They are agents of a much larger conspiracy that does not go away. Many will not be able to process the idea of 'infiltrators' due to their cognitive dissonance and lack of understanding about how the world really works. There is valid evidence to suggest that there were infiltrators at the top in ISKCON. Just consider these facts: If you wanted to destroy a movement like ISKCON from within after SP left, what would you do? There's no way you could turn SP's disciples against him or get them to destroy the movement in any way. So you get rid of 90% of them, somehow, by making it so intolerable they leave in disgust or are kicked out, which is precisely what happened. Then you exalt 11 pretenders as 'pure devotees' on the level of SP, and tell SP's disciples that they now have to go through them to get to him. What arrogance, aparadha. Does that sound like loyal loving disciples of SP? After all his instructions, do you think SP would approve of this distorted philosophy?*

"*Then you fill up ISKCON with your own disciples who treat you just like SP and obey your every command like mindless zombies, not giving them much deep philosophy. Just enough to make them feel 'spiritual' and 'loyal to the cause'. That way, you control everything with no Godbrothers to interfere with your dirty work. Then you wait for the 11 to fall from grace in various modes of disgraceful behavior and the whole thing crumbles, top down, which is inevitable, since they were barely kanisthas. The new disciples lose faith in bhakti and it is a big mess. You also allow pedophilia to run rampant and cover it up and protect the perpetrators, just like the elite do in the world today. That was the plan, and it almost worked, but Krishna didn't allow ISKCON to fail completely. But it's a stinky mess underneath with a nice facade.*

"*I'm not doubting the sincerity of the rank and file and even some leaders, but that's how Kali does it. It only takes a few at that top to orchestrate these things. They are centralizing management, which is directly against Srila Prabhupada's instructions. The GBC is now an independent West Bengal corporation, which conveniently shelters them from any law suits against ISKCON, thus protecting their personal finances, etc. YES this needs to be made public IF it in fact did happen, i.e.: the 'attempt' to kill Srila Prabhupada. This idea to stifle things, "Would Lord Chaitanya or Srila Prabhupada want this to be made public?" is also bogus. If it's true, then everyone needs to know, and more importantly, it means the infiltrators are **still in ISKCON**. For that reason alone it should be exposed. It is a BIG wake up call.*" **(END)**

"GREAT SINISTER MOVEMENT IS WITHIN OUR SOCIETY"

This famous phrase from a Srila Prabhupada letter in 1970 to Hansadutta das was a mystery to devotees: what was Srila Prabhupada referring to? The Gaudiya Math's envious Godbrothers who wanted to take over ISKCON? Maybe... But we think it refers to the ambitious insiders wanting to take Srila Prabhupada's place, his seat. The 1970 incident was about senior disciples who tried to take over, relegating Srila Prabhupada to a figurehead role. *The great sinister movement is the personal ambition to be guru.* Later it evolved into a plot to poison Srila Prabhupada's body and then poison his mission with doctrines to facilitate disqualified men taking the post of Acharya. With the pure devotee's unparalleled success, ambitious men sought to steal that success for themselves, being attached to profit, adoration, and distinction. The purpose of poisoning Srila Prabhupada was to take his place, and the zonal acharya successors did this until they were forced by maya to include other ambitious men too (and they all keep biting the dust). Thus the disease of serving one's dirty heart became an accepted practice, all disguised as holy preaching (one cannot preach without sitting in Srila Prabhupada's seat?) For 45 years the great sinister movement of facilitating personal ambition by exploiting the assets of the real Acharya Srila Prabhupada has been staining, defiling, and seeping into the fabric of Srila Prabhupada's mission. ISKCON became a guru franchise operation, from ultra-large (Jayapataka, Radhanath, 50K disciples each) to small-timers (1-2 disciples). The purity of the mission was lost, more so in the institution itself than in the greater movement.

Untold thousands of ISKCON devotees have refused to cooperate with the jackals and hyenas who ravaged Srila Prabhupada's society assets for selfish desires, and they left the institution. The real history of ISKCON must be made known. Volume 5 and 6 will put together how the poisoners and their heirs ruined Srila Prabhupada's hard work, one deviation at a time until ISKCON is unrecognizable to Srila Prabhupada himself. Today's officially accepted policies and doctrines are those Srila Prabhupada clearly spoke against. Srila Prabhupada's instructions are de-emphasized, and new gurus are free to audaciously enunciate their own interpretations, no questions allowed. *"But when the guru departs, sadhu and shastra can take on a new import, as those who succeed him become the new interpreters of past precedents, scriptural law, and the new set of circumstances."* (Perils of Succession, Tamal 1996)

The great sinister movement of personal ambition (Tamalism) must be weeded out and purged from Srila Prabhupada's mission. Whether that means a restoration of the original ISKCON institution, which seems hopeless considering the corruption, or it means a new ISKCON, such as breakaway temples or starting again from scratch, only by the open discussion of issues and distribution of facts, evidence, and truths will positive results come about. The truth dispels all ignorance; just as when the Sun rises, darkness is dissipated. Lord Chaitanya and Srila Prabhupada's mercy, as preordained, will change the face of this planet for 10,000 years. The great sinister movement does not stand a chance. Of course, how soon personal ambition is purged from the Hare Krishna movement depends on sincere and proactive devotees who strive to please Srila Prabhupada with all they have. Without fear. What happened to ISKCON may be how Srila Prabhupada described Christianity:

"Now, after taking instruction from Christ, first of all they killed Christ. That means they could not understand the instruction. Therefore their first business was to kill the instructor. And after that, two thousand years passed, still they are killing. So when they have accepted the teachings of Lord Christ?" (SPConv, 1975, Perth) Can we see the parallel? Hopefully this is not ISKCON's long-term fate. ISKCON was hijacked by low-minded men who mercilessly poisoned Srila Prabhupada and conspired to sit on his seat, stealing the assets of the Movement with the demonic idea they were the ones to continue initiating spiritual seekers and to manage the sacred mission. They lied that they had been appointed as successor acharyas and goaded everyone into worshipping them as pure devotees.

WHY BRING THIS POISON ISSUE UP AGAIN?

This question implies two misconceptions: **(1)** the poisoning is unprovable and simply speculation, and **(2)** the issue has already been disproved and settled. But Srila Prabhupada's poisoning with heavy metals *is now proven as a fact*, clear to any reasonably honest person.

Some may say what is done is done and now we must focus on "positive" work going forward. Two quotes on this: **(1)** *"Suppose if I am here and somebody kills me, and if you do not protest, is it a very good business? People will be surprised that, 'So many disciples are there, and this man is being killed, and **nobody does anything?**'"* (SPLecture Oct. 27, 1974) **(2)** NOD Ch. 9: *"'The devotee should be more tolerant than the tree and more submissive than the grass. He should offer all honor to others, but may not accept any honor for himself.' In spite of Lord Chaitanya's being so humble and meek as a devotee, when He was informed about injuries inflicted on the body of Sri Nityananda, He immediately ran to the spot and wanted to kill the offenders, Jagai and Madhai. This behavior of Lord Chaitanya is very significant. It shows that a Vaishnava may be very tolerant and meek, forgoing everything for* *his personal honor, but when it is a question of the honor of Krishna or His devotee, he will not tolerate any insult..."* [or poisoning!]

Srila Prabhupada's followers cannot tolerate physical injury against Srila Prabhupada, much less a torturous chronic cadmium poisoning. Upon the pure devotee being offended, shastra advises one to defeat the offender, give up his life, or leave that place, lest *"he falls down from his position of devotion."* It is too late to prevent it, but not too late to investigate, find the truth, and to "defeat" the culprits and their defilement of the movement. With the irrefutable evidence validating the crime, who can neglect their duty to defend Srila Prabhupada and his work? We need to revisit this issue because hardly anyone understands the facts and evidence. Most don't even read anymore; it is the age of two minute video clips. Who has time, clarity of mind, or determination to properly understand any issue? Almost everything now is propaganda or entertainment. Still, we made a comprehensive reference manual to cover the whole subject with objectivity, accuracy, honesty, and clarity. The pen is mightier than the sword, and we hope this volume is useful.

THE RELEVANCE OF THE DISAPPEARANCE PASTIMES

Some think the circumstances of Srila Prabhupada's passing away are not as significant as his life and achievements, and that we should focus on his life instead. This, however, imposes an unnecessary either/or scenario and does not recognize the grave consequences for Srila Prabhupada's life work of preaching Krishna consciousness due to his mission being usurped by poisoners who have infiltrated and ruined ISKCON. We must preserve Srila Prabhupada's life accomplishments. Srila Prabhupada's poisoning raises immense concerns for the integrity and purity of Srila Prabhupada's mission. *Should a robbed bank just go on with its business as usual, even after the bank robbers killed the manager and diverted all future incoming bank deposits to their own accounts?* Our conscience should be clear when we meet Srila Prabhupada again, that we had acted in his defense, better late than never. *"All it takes for evil to triumph is for good men to do nothing."* Someone wrote: *"These written records will eventually expose the full truth. In time people will question without bias or hindrance. An expansive and in-depth account of events should be available for assessment. All this hard work will ultimately bear fruition."*

Those who poisoned Srila Prabhupada either still have a place or hand in Srila Prabhupada's institution, or their followers, heirs, and beneficiaries are managing ISKCON with the poisoner-hijackers' post-1977 policies. The hijacking is factual history (Volume 5). The poisoners directly or indirectly continue to defile Srila Prabhupada's mission. How can we neglect this? All of us should study the facts, evidence, post-1977 deviations (Volume 6) and set matters right again. Honest devotees must restore the movement *as it was when Srila Prabhupada left it* in our care. Will we: **(1)** support the present ISKCON leadership which has covered up and denied what is now proven to be true, or **(2)** act as guardians of his movement (Volume 8). The age of hypocrisy has deeply corrupted the Hare Krishna Movement as its misleaders defend their illicit regime by obscuring the truth that Srila Prabhupada was poisoned. When this truth is known, their ill-gotten corrupt regime (Volume 6) will be unsustainable. This is the reason for their denials.

It is said, "You can lead a horse to water, but you can't make it drink." Srila Prabhupada also said we cannot wake one up who is pretending to be asleep. Imagine getting a horse to drink while it is pretending to be asleep? The GBC is not interested in the truth. Continually revising their entry requirements by concocted revisions, they are a guru club, with supposed divine authority, receiving godly treatment, worship, wealth, prestige, perks and surrendered followers. The truth of Srila Prabhupada's poisoning seriously threatens this status quo, and thus it is belied as demonic and spiritually dangerous. But their hypocritical regime will crumble when enough devotees understand that *Srila Prabhupada's poisoning was the means by which their hijacking and deviant policies were established.*

It is best to examine the evidence that Srila Prabhupada was poisoned with an open and unbiased mind, make one's own judgement, and then consider what should be done. Should we be acquiescent, keep sitting on the fence, support the poisoners' administration, and continue to be "cooperative, gentle-hearted, and unoffensive"? *"So you all write very strongly, vehemently. Even it is a little offensive, still these rascals should be taught a lesson. Yes. They're misleading..."* (SPL Apr. 19, 1973) We should not avoid free discourse and discussion of controversial or sensitive issues, thereby tacitly endorsing the corruption of Srila Prabhupada's instructions and mission. It is spiritually healthy to cope with controversies that arise and which have everything to do with our progress in Krishna consciousness. Without careful thought and deliberation there cannot be a true spiritual society. *Siddhanta baliya cite na kara also/ Iha ha-ite Krishna lage sudrdha manasa... "A sincere student should not neglect to discuss the conclusions of the shastras, considering them controversial, for such discussions strengthen the mind. Thus one's mind becomes attached to Krishna."*

CHAPTER 57:
EVIDENCE AUTHENTICITY

AUTHENTICITY: A VALID CONCERN

As in any crime, the evidence is critical to the determination of truth and the appropriate remedies to pursue. There are always concerns about the authenticity of the evidence. Was the evidence gathered by Prabhupada Truth Commission fabricated, tampered with, or somehow fudged to make a bogus case that Srila Prabhupada was poisoned? No, the evidence is authentic, and no attempt was made to twist or misrepresent, deceive or mislead, and this can easily be verified. Forensics, histories, interviews, and testimonies have been faithfully scrutinized for veracity and they are factual, truthful, and relevant. This can be seen simply by examining them, and one's instinct can intuitively discern the truth. Contrary views and opinions are addressed without hyperbole, straw man arguments, selective omissions, or other mechanisms of dishonesty and deceit, methods which have been widely employed by ISKCON misleaders. More tests can be done for further confirmation, but they should be monitored by neutral observers.

MUCH OF THE AURAL EVIDENCE IS MISSING

There is no way to fabricate poison whispers or Srila Prabhupada's conversations and lectures. These original tape recordings are safe-guarded in a vault at the Bhaktivedanta Archives in North Carolina and high-quality copies can be obtained from them at a low cost. Anyone can verify their contents. The whispers, the poison discussions, and other relevant recordings are untamperable, authentic evidence. Still, incredibly, the ISKCON GBC paid for and endorsed false accusations Prabhupada Truth Commission tried to tamper with the poison whispers, just to sow doubts about the audio evidence. (Ch. 52) However, recordings may have been tampered with *before* they were given to the Archives in 1978. There are doubts in the May 28 "appointment" tape's integrity. There is much evidence of 200 missing 1977 tape recordings which had critical instructions from Srila Prabhupada about the future of the movement. The missing tapes are a brutal tampering with the aural record given by Srila Prabhupada. (Volume 2) The poison whispers are online for anyone to hear as they are.

FORENSIC AUDIO EVIDENCE IS CERTIFIED, AUTHENTIC

All the forensic specialists who analyzed the poison whispers have professional credentials and are recognized as performing honest and quality services, in stark contrast to the GBC's "experts" Larry Kovar and The Refinery who are now defunct ventures. The poison whispers were analyzed from direct copies of original tape recordings made by Bhaktivedanta Archives, sent directly to the forensic labs. These tapes' integrity is unchallengeable. Even Tamal verified the whispers, but he gave a different version, not confirmed by any audio analysis. The four poison whispers have been certified by various audio forensic analysts, all of whom confirmed the essential "poison" word. While ISKCON misleaders deny them, *the "poison whispers" are forensically certified secret discussions of caretakers talking about poisoning Srila Prabhupada.* This is an undeniable fact. Tom Owens described that they: *"justify consultation with a homicide investigator."* The audio forensic studies speak for themselves. (Part 3)

AUTHENTICITY ISSUES

One critical element of any forensic hair tests is the authenticity of the samples. Were they really Srila Prabhupada's hair? It is necessary to document and preserve the credibility and authenticity of the samples being tested. No one in the private investigation had contact with any hair samples that Dr. Morris tested, so they could not have been tampered with. Hair tests which revealed sky high cadmium and elevated arsenic levels were analyzed by a very qualified scientist at the uniquely equipped MURR nuclear research center. There are few places in the world able to do accurate NAA analyses. To disparage Dr. Morris' findings is like barking at the Moon. The three hair samples which confirmed cadmium (*A, D, Q-2*) were passed from the custody of ISKCON temples, GBC leaders, and their deputed agents **directly** to testing laboratories, and **never** were in anyone else's possession. The chain of custody is given below. There was no chance to tamper with these samples or the clippers from which they were removed. It would be impossible to taint these 3 samples with the same amounts of cadmium when they originated from different sources. How could such tainted hair then be inserted into the clipper blades? The cadmium hair samples were authenticated at length by Hari Sauri das, Srila Prabhupada's former personal servant (Ch. 2). PTC completed the GBC's hair tests for them with only phone calls, emails, and payment. More hair tests can be done as further confirmation (if conformed to chain of custody protocols).

There is no doubt in *Samples A, D,* and *Q-2*: they were arranged by Hari Sauri das, Srila Prabhupada's personal servant. He confirmed the chain of custody for all 3 samples. If someone wants to settle any doubts that these hair samples were actually from Srila Prabhupada's head, micro DNA testing and other methods are reliable and accurate. In early

2017, Hari Sauri *again verified* the authenticity of hair *Samples A & D*: *"SAMPLE A: In small plastic container, was brushed off outside of Srila Prabhupada's hairclippers in 1978 and kept in the Vrindaban museum on display until Hari Sauri took it and gave it to Deva Gaura Hari in 1999. SAMPLE D: Hari Sauri went to the Melbourne temple and retrieved a part of the Srila Prabhupada hair sample on display there, which he had donated to Melbourne ISKCON years earlier, and which he had cut from Srila Prabhupada's head as his servant in early March 1977."* There is no doubt in these hair samples' authenticity.

EVIDENCE CERTIFIED BY IMPARTIAL EXPERTS

It would be impossible to fabricate or falsify all of the various reports issued by the many unrelated experts that are evidence of the poisoning. Still, ISKCON has conjured doubt in a few pieces of evidence and then rejected ALL evidence as bogus. But the facts dictate *Srila Prabhupada was indeed maliciously poisoned.* George Blackwell, Jack Mitchell, Tom Owens, J.P. French, Dr. Steven Morris, Dr. Aggarwal, Dr. Page Hudson, Dr. Callery, James Reames, and recently, a major investigative forensic laboratory, do not make for a list of dodgy parties: they are all top notch authorities with high reputations in their fields. The GBC is cornered and now desperate. The credible witness testimony of Bhakta Vatsala, the Mexican gurukuli, is collaborated by other Mexican devotees, namely Durlab, Nandaprana, Adhoksaja, and Ramanya. He did not make up a story out of the blue – his story has been consistent with all those who have heard it throughout the last 25 years, and it existed long before the poison issue arose in 1997. The testimony of the Vrindaban residents and kavirajas concur with each other. Did they make up their matching stories? Bhaktitirtha Swami stated the poison theory was promoted by agents of Kali, but he did not substantiate this. The evidence is being delivered as it is. Rather, it is those who have covered up Srila Prabhupada's poisoning with lies, fraud, misrepresentations, and denials that must wear the moniker of *agent of Kali.*

CHAIN OF CUSTODY ON TESTED HAIR SAMPLES

SAMPLE Q-1: Arsenic 2.6 ppm (Hairclippers):

(1) This hair was cut by Srila Prabhupada's exclusive personal hairclippers, accumulated from many cuttings Nov. 1976 to Sept. 1977. Pieces stuck around the clipper blades from different cuttings. **(2)** The hairclippers were in locked display cases in Srila Prabhupada's Vrindaban rooms from 1977-1998. **(3)** In 1998 Daivi Shakti dasi, caretaker of Srila Prabhupada's Vrindaban rooms, gave the hair clippers to Hari Sauri das (Denis Harrison), who had GBC man Sesa das bring them to Balavanta das (William Ogle) in Alachua, Florida. **(4)** Balavanta sent the clippers to Dr. Morris who removed some hair stuck between the clipper blades, tested them by NAA and found 2.6 ppm arsenic. **(5)** This hair was hidden safely inside the hairclippers from 1977-1998.

SAMPLE D: Cadmium 19.9 ppm (Melbourne sample):

(1) This hair was cut by Srila Prabhupada's exclusively personal hairclippers by Hari Sauri just before Mar. 13, 1977, and was saved by him as a sacred relic, and he later gave it to Melbourne Australia ISKCON temple to be locked securely in Srila Prabhupada's rooms as a worshipable relic. **(2)** In 1999 Hari Sauri retrieved some of this hair sample and gave it to Deva Gaura Hari das (David Hooper) in Australia, who was the GBC agent. **(3)** Hooper sent this *Sample D* (with *Sample A*) to Larry Kovar at General Activation Analysis (CA.) who could not test such small amounts of hair, and who was instructed to send *Samples D & A* to Dr. Richard Cashwell at Univ. of Wisconsin, Madison, WI, USA. **(4)** Dr. Cashwell also could not test such a small amount of hair and the samples stayed there from late 1999 until Oct. 25, 2001, when Nityananda das requested Dr. Robert Agasie (Dr. Cashwell had retired) to directly Fedex *Samples D & A* to Dr. Morris in Columbia, MO, USA. **(5)** This hair was *always* in the hands of ISKCON and authorized agents. **(6)** Dr. Morris received *Samples D & A* on Nov. 1, 2001. **(7)** Dr. Morris tested *Sample D* on Mar. 5, 2002, finding 19.9 ppm cadmium.

SAMPLE A: Cadmium 12.4 ppm (Daivi Shakti dasi sample):

(1) This hair was cut by Srila Prabhupada's personal hairclippers in many cuttings, Nov. 1976 to Sept. 1977, as pieces stuck around the clipper blades. **(2)** Shortly after Srila Prabhupada's departure, Daivi Shakti dasi, caretaker of Srila Prabhupada's artifacts in his Vrindaban rooms, brushed off some hair that stuck on the clipper blades, put it in a small container, and locked it in a glass case in the Prabhupada temple museum. **(3)** This container was *Sample A*. **(4)** In 1999 Hari Sauri received *Sample A* from Daivi Shakti and gave it to Hooper in Australia, who sent it with *Sample D* (in separate containers) to Larry Kovar in CA, USA. **(5)** Kovar could not test it, and sent it to Dr. Cashwell, who could not test it either, and he soon retired. **(6)** Oct. 25, 2001 Nityananda das asked Dr. Robert Agasie to send *Sample A & D* directly to Dr. Morris by Fedex. **(9)** This hair was *always* in the hands of ISKCON managers and authorized agents. **(10)** Dr. Morris received *Sample A* on Nov. 1, 2001, and tested it on Apr. 18, 2002, finding 12.4 ppm cadmium.

SAMPLE Q-2: Cadmium 14.9 ppm (Hairclippers):

(1) July 22, 2005: Dr. Morris found more hair UNDER the blades of the same hairclippers referenced above by removing some parts.

(2) *Sample Q-2* would therefore be closely related to *Sample A*. Both *Samples A* and *Q-2* were collected from hair that stuck onto or in Srila Prabhupada's exclusively personal hairclippers. **(3)** This hair was hidden safely inside the hairclippers from 1977 until 2005. **(4)** Dr. Morris tested *Sample Q-2* July 25, 2005, finding 14.9 ppm cadmium.

All three samples never left GBC and their agents' custody. Further hair tests by the GBC may have credibility issues.

CHAPTER 58:
FLAWED OBJECTIONS ANSWERED

STATEMENT ATTESTING TRUTH

I, Nityananda das (Nico Kuyt), do hereby attest that all the information I have submitted in the private investigation, to the best of my knowledge, are true and accurate. I have not altered, tampered with, concealed, fudged, or in any way misrepresented this information. I swear by Lord Krishna that I have been totally honest and forthright in the research, investigation, presentation, and discussion of all information I have submitted in various books. I also confirm under oath that all other information, testimonies, and submissions included in this volume have been accurately represented and that they were properly vetted for veracity and are included only because of their value to the investigation and issues at hand. I have no motive other than the establishment of the truth in these matters and the restoration of Srila Prabhupada's mission to its pure condition as desired by Srila Prabhupada. In joining in the search for the truth of Srila Prabhupada's poisoning, I have lost friends, money, reputation, and become the whipping boy of my Godbrothers. Often I have feared for my life and I have lived as a recluse in remote places. I was formally excommunicated in 1990. But regardless of the costs or consequences, a disciple must remain true to his exalted guru, conscience, and the unvarnished facts and evidence, which I hope will be of use to others as presented herein. Signed: Nico Kuyt (Nityananda das), July. 4, 2022.

Those who deny Srila Prabhupada's poisoning even in the face of all the evidence and proof that he was in fact poisoned put forward various false theories and objections which are mostly dishonest maneuvers to avoid the truth. Some are emotional reactions which fear the truth, or they come from being misinformed, misled, or ignorant of the facts and evidence. A 41 min. film was made: ***Poisoning Objections Answered:***

https://www.youtube.com/watch?v=gOLeHjRhZMc

A complete examination and unwrapping, debunking of common objections offered by ISKCON deniers is given in Volume 7: *Kill Guru Become Guru: Crushing the Naysayer Rogues.*

CHAPTER 59:
HORSES, FOLLY, COMPLICITY

By Nityananda das
THE FIRST CHALLENGE HORSE

In the GBC's *NTIAP* Ravindra Svarupa reminded me of my "challenge horse" to the GBC in 1989 regarding demands for proper justification, based on Srila Prabhupada's teachings, for the ISKCON guru and initiation system, otherwise to accept the "officiating acharya" initiation system. The GBC has yet to provide convincing evidence, other than defectively interpretive policy papers, that Srila Prabhupada wanted self-appointed, ecclesiastically rubber-stamped, non-self-realized gurus. ***This first challenge horse*** released by the Vedic Village Review in 1989 has never been "captured" by the GBC and is still roaming at large, although they will dispute this. Under what authority have they approved "initiating gurus" in Srila Prabhupada's institution? The onus is on the GBC to prove that Srila Prabhupada actually gave the order to be initiating gurus. (see Vol. 9)

THE SECOND CHALLENGE HORSE

Now a new challenge to the GBC and Ravindra Svarupa das is to set up a scientific study where we feed the GBC enough heavy metals to maintain their hair cadmium and arsenic levels equal to those of Srila Prabhupada for a year, comparing all physiological changes in the GBC to those seen in Srila Prabhupada during 1977. After all, if these hair levels were normal and Srila Prabhupada was not poisoned, all this should be good for them too. Any takers? Put your poison where your mouth is… Or will they plead exclusion because they have diabetes? This is the second challenge to those who thought I had offended Srila Prabhupada and senior devotees by presenting factual evidence of the poisoning. *A second challenge horse* was given in 2017 to the GBC:

"If Srila Prabhupada was not poisoned, as the GBC claim in their book Not That I Am Poisoned, and he actually had normal levels of heavy metals in his hair, then they should: (1) Eat arsenic salts until they all maintain for a year 10 ppm arsenic in their hair, which they claimed is healthy and normal, or at least up to the 2.6 ppm that Srila Prabhupada had in his hair, and (2) Eat enough cadmium salts to maintain for one year the 15.73 ppm average cadmium level that was in Srila Prabhupada's hair, and show us all that this is normal and unproblematic, as they have claimed." The GBC resolution, *"There is no evidence at this time to support the allegations of poisoning of Srila Prabhupada,"* makes a mockery of ISKCON leadership. Mayeswara das, the outspoken GBC apologist, should join Ravindra Swarup and all GBC members to show their denials are sincere and not empty words. Will the GBC back up their fraudulent claims or not?

ISKCON GURUS IMPLICATED IN THE POISONING

Whether directly involved in Srila Prabhupada's poisoning or not, all ISKCON gurus after the original 11 "zonal acharyas" are implicated in Srila Prabhupada's poisoning. Their positions were falsely created by the poisoners who claimed they were appointed as acharyas and that they could add others later. Tainted by this assassination crime and hoax, all subsequent ISKCON gurus have aided and abetted the original crime by sharing in the "take" of illicit gains, and supporting a regime based on murder and theft, making them deeply complicit. This is like becoming the beneficiary of a murder. *It is also like accepting dirty money or stolen property- it is still theft, even if you did not directly steal it yourself.* Accepting stolen property knowingly is also criminal. The original 11 and then the 100+ ISKCON vote-approved gurus gained guruhood from Srila Prabhupada's poisoning and ISKCON's hijacking, first based on the lie that Srila Prabhupada had appointed successor gurus, and then that the GBC was authorized to approve more gurus. And, post-1977, deeply controversial GBC policies allowed anyone to "become" replacement diksha gurus, something even the GBC is deeply divided as to whether it is shastricly valid. (see Vol. 9)

Srila Prabhupada's poisoners and other senior disciples lied (in a collaborative conspiracy) about their appointment as initiating gurus. Overwhelming direct and circumstantial evidence implicates at least Tamal Krishna beyond reasonable doubt in this proven poisoning (see Vol. 2). _All ISKCON gurus have their guruship because some of the original 11 poisoned Srila Prabhupada._ Tamal and Bhakticharu are gone, but other poisoners remain in ISKCON's top leadership. It is not known yet exactly how the sordid affair was executed, but the whispers implicate at least 4 senior men in the poisoning, and surely others knew or were involved. The definition of abetting a crime includes assisting the criminals escape and by refusing to honestly investigate the voluminous poisoning evidence. ISKCON misleaders are sheltering the prime suspects and holding onto illicit gains that came to them only because Srila Prabhupada was poisoned. _They all share in the sin of the poisoning crime by aiding and abetting._ Since 1956 the law in India is that a murderer cannot inherit the property of their victim. Yet the murderous ISKCON GBC-guru regime has inherited their poisoned guru's assets. Let us not mince words here.

POISONING FOLLY IS THE ULTIMATE BLASPHEMY

Ramesvara (RV): [...] this movement will go on unimpeded for 10,000 years. **SP:** Yes, provided we keep it uncontaminated. You should take this opportunity. **RV:** So after ten years we have gotten so many devotees and so many houses, so I can't imagine how big this movement will be after 10,000 years. **SP:** Yes. You'll get the government. **RV:** The whole world will be delivered? **SP:** Yad yad acarati sresthah. America will be the best; people will follow. (SPConv June 11, 1976)

"But even, even one-fourth percent people come to this, then it will be successful. [...] Literatures are selling, they are appreciating, learned circle. Takes some time, but if we stick to our principles and do not make any compromise and push on in this way [...] it will never stop [...] At least for 10,000 years it will go on." (SPConv June 21, 1976)

So the Hare Krishna movement will go on as divinely ordained. It is futile to undermine or stop it, even by the attempted removal of Srila Prabhupada by poisoning his body and then his mission. The Supreme Lord's will is that this movement will flourish, prosper, and spread all over the world, to every cowpath village and town.

Sometimes, out of fear, the uneducated, weak, or cowardly tolerate blasphemy or deliberate offenses against the bona fide spiritual master.

Srila Prabhupada has oft pointed out such tolerance is condemned in scripture. **(1)** *"One should not at any time tolerate blasphemy and insults against Lord Vishnu or His devotees. A devotee is generally very humble and meek, and he is reluctant to pick a quarrel with anyone. Nor does he envy anyone. However, a pure devotee immediately becomes fiery with anger when he sees that Lord Vishnu or His devotee is insulted. This is the duty of a devotee. Although a devotee maintains an attitude of meekness and gentleness, it is a great fault on his part if he remains silent when the Lord or His devotee is blasphemed."* (SBhag 4.14.32) **(2)** SP: *"Suppose if somebody comes to kill me, and you will see and laugh? You'll do? Will you do that? Why? That is sinful."*

WHAT DIFFERENCE DOES HIS POISONING MAKE?"

Bhakti Vikas Swami: *"After seeing your video, it seemed to me that your position was almost incontrovertible... IMHO only a court case could settle this. But what would be the point? What difference would it make to ISKCON today?"* (May 26, 2017) Seriously, would the poisoners, after their poison business was completed, have faithfully carried out Srila Prabhupada's desires and the movement was in good hands with them? In any country and in international politics, an assassination and secret coup d'état would be met with great opposition and demands for popular elections, not a shrug of the shoulders to pretend it makes no difference. Those who poisoned Srila Prabhupada then took over the movement and his seat, diverting the Acharya's assets to their guru franchises (including Bhakti Vikas Swami). ISKCON gurus today just want the poisoners' guru regime to continue undisturbed.

A few differences are the resulting institutional corruptions: child abuse culture, endless book changes, siddhantic deviations, loss of 95% of SP's disciples, demigod worship, unaccountability, and prolific guru scandals that are just excused as "unfortunate." Another difference is that the hijacked movement was ruined by the poisoners and their successors with the disease of material ambition (Tamalism). Sincere followers of Srila Prabhupada want to confront and undo the pollution of the poisoners, their accomplices, supporters, and deviant doctrines. The poisoning speaks of a total corruption of ISKCON since 1977.

CHILDREN WANT JUSTICE IF THEIR FATHER IS KILLED

If your older brothers inherited the family estate when your father died under suspicious circumstances, and later you learned the father was poisoned, would you maybe look into it further? What difference does it make? Maybe the father's last instructions and will had been hidden or even changed? Maybe your inheritance was stolen by the older brothers who stole the estate for themselves and the father's intentions were subverted? Your rights were denied, and you were deprived of your rightful inheritance, and it makes no difference? Would you not even care if your dear father's will had been honored or not? After all, don't you owe your father so much, to at least see that his will was executed as he wanted? If not, isn't that cold-hearted? Truly, such an unconscious disposition is pathetic and criminally immoral.

Damaghosh das: *"Only a heartless, brain-dead person would have no feelings when they heard Srila Prabhupada was poisoned, at such advanced age, and who did so much for all humanity. The difference is- that the crime of murder must be punished first of all, the culprits be made known or jailed, and the ISKCON leadership begging forgiveness would be a good start. Every deviation in ISKCON today stems from this primary hati mata sin of killing guru and becoming guru. The world in general would not be the same today, if the Hare Krishna movement had not been hijacked. Nothing could have stopped us- and it wouldn't have, as Srila Prabhupada told us- we ourselves were the only ones who could stop 'us.' And that is exactly what happened."*

DELIBERATELY DESTROYING HIS MOVEMENT

Dhanesvara das: *"The difference to ISKCON today is that when it is added together with the other destructive elements in the society, a clear picture evolves of a leadership that is deliberately destroying Srila Prabhupada's mission -phalena paricyate. Consider the heinous abuse of gurukulis, the unnecessary changing of Srila Prabhupada's books, the centralized corporate-type bureaucracy despite Srila Prabhupada's multiple efforts to undo this and instructions that this would make ISKCON a mundane institution, the apasiddhanta in ISKCON's guru/initiation system, the hiding of the Direction of Management which accidentally became public knowledge in 1990s, the GBC's total neglect of what Srila Prabhupada said was 50% of his mission - Varnashrama Dharma, and the GBC making themselves as absolute authorities that can even contravene shastra. If all of this is taken as a whole the " difference" is obvious - the demons have control of the society."*

WE MUST OVERCOME OUR APATHY

The corrupted, deviant ISKCON (Vol. 6) suppresses the intelligent and free-thinking devotees, having alienated tens of thousands of dedicated devotees into exile, those who could not sell their hearts and souls to the tyranny of the deviated institution. Some left due to spiritual weakness, finding no support. Most could not reconcile their intelligence with the institution's corruptions. They found no place in a house of frauds, where discussion and thought is limited to the elite's narratives and facts are twisted accordingly. Truth is sacrificed to the deviant doctrines of the gurocracy. Brown-nosers, bootlickers, sycophants, and those ambitious for power and guruhood are what remain of its members (and the newcoming naïve). The honest have left ISKCON, built for all to live in, but hijacked by misleaders led by the poisoners.

Witnessing the insanity and fraud in this world, a sense of futility is difficult to overcome. Devotees need the wisdom, courage, and spiritual conscience to recognize truth, and that they have the *"shakti"* to deal with the truth that ISKCON was gurujacked by those who poisoned Srila Prabhupada. Estranged and banished devotees tend to think: *"What difference can I make?"* This sense of *futility* leads to apathy and a reluctance to validate and accept the truth of the poisoning even when it stares us in the face. *"Oh, it can't really be true."* When we are confronted with monstrous evil, we first reject it, not because we don't believe it exists, but because admitting its reality implies a responsibility to do something about it. And stopping evil requires personal sacrifice. People would just rather live in peace, so why fight hypocrisy?

But Srila Prabhupada struggled and sacrificed so much to give us Krishna consciousness and a perfect process of spiritual advancement, and if we take his mercy and improve ourselves with his gifts, we are indebted to him. We should consider how to repay Srila Prabhupada? He wants us to stick to the process of chanting Hare Krishna, and *he also wants us to preserve and propagate his pure teachings*. We must try to put aside feelings of futility and do our duty as best we can to defend Srila Prabhupada's transcendental mission and divine mercy. This starts with making our voices heard, and taking a stand for the truth.

"They are now taking action how to stop this Hare Krishna movement... They are trying. Of course, we are not afraid of this attempt. They will never be successful, rest assured... Krishna was attempted to be killed from the very beginning of His life. That is the nature of this material world, 'How to kill God,' [and guru] *'God is dead.' This is their attempt. So, from the life of Krishna we can understand that so many attempts were made by the demons and the rakshasas to kill Krishna, but actually Krishna killed them all. So, if you are sincere, if you follow the principles and push on this Krishna consciousness movement, nobody can kill you. You'll go forward, rest assured. We are not going to be killed."* (SPLecture Nov. 19, '76)

PART EIGHT:
TRIUMPHANT DEPARTURE

Translation (CC Mad 15.163): *My dear Lord, let me suffer perpetually in a hellish condition, accepting all the sinful reactions of all living entities. Please finish their diseased material life.* **Purport:** *Srila Bhaktisiddhanta Thakura gives the following commentary on this verse.*

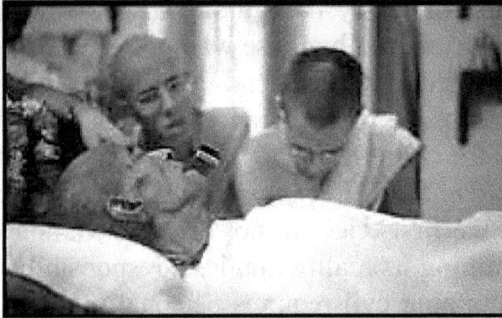

In the Western countries, Christians believe that Lord Jesus Christ, their spiritual master, appeared in order to eradicate all the sins of his disciples. To this end, Lord Jesus Christ appeared and disappeared. Here, however, we find Sri Vasudeva Datta Thakura and Srila Haridasa Thakura to be many millions of times more advanced even when compared to Lord Jesus Christ. Jesus Christ relieved only his followers from all sinful reactions, but Vasudeva Datta is here prepared to accept the sins of everyone in the universe. A Vaishnava is so liberal that he is prepared to risk everything to rescue conditioned souls from material existence. Srila Vasudeva Datta Thakura is universal love itself, for he was willing to sacrifice everything and fully engage in the service of the Supreme.

CHAPTER 60:
SRILA PRABHUPADA'S HOROSCOPE

Birth: Tuesday, Sept. 1, 1896, 4:00 pm. Calcutta, Rasi: Metthuna

Astrology is not being proposed herein as legally acceptable evidence, but solely for deeper insights. His Divine Grace accepted astrology as a bona fide science, although wary it could cause distraction from spiritual life, as it deals with the karma of the conditioned soul. Some Vaishnava astrologers have posited that Srila Prabhupada's horoscope supports his being poisoned by his own servants, others have said it does not. This is largely due to questions of his exact birth time leading to readings from different charts. We take no position on this debate, but will look at 1977 conversations and recent discussions on Srila Prabhupada's horoscope in the spirit of remembering his pastimes.

Those with the ability to interpret the stars to understand Srila Prabhupada's divine horoscope face a fundamental difficulty, namely, ascertaining which rising sign is the correct one. Srila Prabhupada gave his time of birth as [about] 4:00 pm, which is Capricorn rising, but many Vedic astrologers believe that a "chart rectification" indicates an actual time of birth a few minutes earlier with Sagittarius rising as a better fit for his life and activities. Both charts have been widely discussed. Vedic astrologers favoring Sagittarius (rectified at 3:30 pm) include Patita Pavana das, Nalinikanta das, Dharmapada das; and those favoring (or were instructed) Capricorn at 4:00 pm include Asutosh Oja, Shyamasundar das (astrologer), and Sudarshan das (Denver).

When Srila Prabhupada became very ill mid-1977 with a relentless deterioration of his health, he called for astrological consultations to get insights into his future. We cannot say that Srila Prabhupada did not know what his future was, nor that he needed to resort to astrology to decide his actions. Still, in some manner of transcendental pastime, Srila Prabhupada sent Yasodanandana Swami to obtain Asutosh Oja's reading in Delhi, and he sent other devotees for other astrologers' calculations.

"...for no matter how carefully a killer may try to cover his tracks, there is always one piece of evidence he can never destroy: namely, the position of the planets at the time of his crime." (W Henry)

LETTERS FROM TAMAL AND SURABHI SWAMI

Tamal to Ramesvara Aug. 5, 1977: *"One very capable astrologer has given horoscope and recommended the wearing of a blue sapphire stone of at least 7 carats weight. Hopefully by now money has been sent for the purchase of this stone. In addition there are various prayers which have been recommended to be chanted and Pradyumna will chant these regularly daily. Srila Prabhupada has recommended that all of the devotees may as a daily routine, pray, 'Dear Lord Krishna, if You desire, please cure Srila Prabhupada.' The horoscope describes Prabhupada's entire life very accurately (acknowledged by Srila Prabhupada), and the next six months will be very critical and difficult to pass over."*

Surabhi Swami wrote Aug. 10, 1977: *"Srila Prabhupada's health has become worse than ever before. He requested us to consult an astrologer to find out what will happen [...] Yasodanandana Swami went to Delhi to see one astrologer and myself went to Jaipur to see a numerologist. Both reports were quite similar. When I came back SP was eager to know what happened. He said, 'Will I live?' I explained that the* *pandit had said that <u>his disease was incurable by any medicine</u>... The next three months would be the most critical in his life. Of these three months these nine days would be even worse. Anyhow he predicted that he will most probably travel around the world again after three months. Although his health would not permit him. I know that it sounds strange that we have become dependent on this sort of people but Srila Prabhupada was extremely pleased with these reports. Tamal asked SP whether these types of science were bona fide and SP said 'Yes.'"*

ASUTOSH OJA'S FIRST ASTROLOGY REPORT AUG. 11, 1977

Asutosh Oja saw the chart as Capricorn rising, from the time he was given as 4:00 pm. Asutosh Oja's first reading was in June 1977, and the update below is from Aug. 11. On Oct. 8 another update was obtained.

Abhiram: I went to see the [Delhi] astrologer with Yasodanandana Swami, and he did more calculations on your chart. [...] So basically he explained when the difficult times will come, according to the planets. [...] it would be very difficult for calculations for a person in your position. For an ordinary man he can say very clearly. [...] but he cannot say for sure how much they [planets] will affect, because being a saintly person, there is naturally some resistance to these influences. [...] you should not think that these are final. [...] according to your birth, the longevity shows very clearly [...] Feb. 28, 1978, 6 months from now. This is according to birth and stars arrangement [...] Due to pious activities, due to the hand of Krishna, this can change. [...] during the next 6 months, the 1st week of Sept., Saturn will pass over Ketu, ... the resistance will go down, will become weaker. *Then he mentioned that there may be some trouble from, maybe financial or maybe from juniors, from subordinates.* Then this period, if you can pass through 1978, then there is 4 or 5 more years clear ahead [...] according to birth arrangement, the fatal date is Feb. 28, 1978 [...] there's what's called the completion of a Ketu maha-dasa, which began at your birth. [...] a man of spiritual advancement will have the ability to overcome his fate. [...] for a man of your position he could not even say for sure. [...] the blue sapphire would have some beneficial effect, at least to relieve you to some degree... [...] **Tamal:** That means divine intervention... **SP:** The chart is given. The calculation there is finished. That doesn't matter. Rather, if I am finished now, it will be glorious. (ConvBk 35, p.50)

ASUTOSH OJA ASTROLOGICAL UPDATE OCT. 8, 1977

Tamal: ...reading of your chart for free, Srila Prabhupada. The man is a devotee. [...] His name is Gopesh Kumar Ojah, and his son's name is Asutosh Ojah. All the calculations are given. He said Sukra as Muntesa, Varsa-lagnesh has no directional strength. Therefore the solar return is not good. The lord of the 6th is conjunct, mangala, not good. The following days are not auspicious: Sept. 27-8, Oct. 24-5, Nov. 20-2, Dec. 3-4. ...at present undergoing the fag end of Ketu Mahadasa, until Jan 13, 1978. Ketu is in the 8th. "...the house of death, with the Sun, which is the lord of the 8th, and Krusu, the lord of the 12th and 3rd houses. They are all in the 8th house. Mercury in Ketu started from Jan 16. Budha is the satesh also, disease. Shani has gone to the 8th house, which is the house of death, from the Sept. 7. That's the day you had your operation.

Shani as lagnesh in the 8th house and the transit over Jupiter and Ketu. The negative effect continues throughout Oct. '77, Nov. '77, and from the 1st of Dec. '77, Saturn becomes almost stationary and becomes more malefic. [...] In Jan. '78 until April '78 it again traverses the same degrees and becomes stagnant on Jupiter and Ketu in the last week of Feb. [...] you're supposed to have lived for 75 years, but everything beyond that was an extension by Krishna. [...] The Moon is in the 8th house, which is very bad. The patient may not recover. Then he gives various planets which are also not well aligned. He says the conjunction of another two planets is very bad. Hospitalization and ill health are intensified in the present year. The days which are not good is when the Moon passes in the 22nd to the 23rd of nakshatra, which are Sept. 27-8, that's already passed, then Oct. 24-5, then some days in Nov. and Dec. Surya will apply for Rahu on Oct. 8. That's today. This is very bad.

Surya will apply for Rahu. Brashna, Lagnesh, Mangal, in the 8th house. The medicine will not give any relief. The native will make a fight for life as Surya-Mangal are good friends, and Saturn, or Shani, and Sukra are enemies. There is no benefics in the 9, 6, 11 and 3. Mangal indicates the effects of Sakini. There is difficulty in recovery. The seventh dasa starts on Jan. 13, '78. [...] the periods are all negative until Mar.-April '78, and the main trouble was due to Shani. [...] blue sapphire [...] he should keep it on. Hospitalization and travels are indicated. Then he says the worst days of all for you are today and tomorrow. He says it is very negative, as well as the 11th, which is mixed. But these are all very inauspicious days. Oct. 4, 5, 8, 9, and 11. The only remedy is to do maha-mrtyum-jaya japa and havana. [...] Astrologically it is up to the 81 years, 4 months, approximately. Japa and havana. (SPConv 35, Oct. 8, 1977 p. 129)

SRILA PRABHUPADA'S TRUE HOROSCOPE IS SAGITTARIUS

Dharmapada das (dean@uninet.com.br), Jan. 13, 1998: *"I read an article that Srila Prabhupada's horoscope does not indicate death by poisoning, such that the case is solved (a tidy solution). [...] the chart itself was wrong [...] because a contention exists about **which** chart is actually SP's true horoscope. The chart with ascendant Capricorn has been championed by a respected astrologer in ISKCON [...] That the Sagittarius chart is actually SP's chart was brought to my attention by Nalinikanta das,* *another well-known ISKCON astrologer. First, it seems SP was given his calculated chart and told he was Capricorn ascendant [but] It's not as if SP affirmed this as his divine instruction. If SP's reported birth time was off by as little as 5 minutes or so, the ascendant would change from Capricorn to Sagittarius.* **They are entirely different.** *The ascendant would be either 29 degrees Sagittarius or in the first few degrees of Capricorn. [...] the round number of 4 pm may not be exact. The true ascendant is up for grabs until determined. With a rising sign on the cusp of a sign, first of all I ask what the source of the birth time is.*

"*Then I ask about indications which could only be true in one chart or the other. E.g., one chart may support having younger brothers, while the other does not. It is best to start with the chart, interrogate, go backwards and adjust the birth time rather than to take a borderline birth time for granted. The term for this is* **chart rectification.** *All practiced astrologers understand this problem [and use this method]. Which facts from SPs life correspond to one chart and not the other? I could argue for the existence of children and pharmaceutical business from both charts. But there are two blatant things about SP's life which can* **only be explained by the Sagittarius chart:** *His authorship and the 1970's success of his movement. First of all, there are two basic elements of a chart which we must consider. On one hand, we look at the house which stands for the thing in question, its occupants, any aspects which it might receive and the position of its lord. On the other hand, we examine the karaka or natural significator. So just as any issue has a house which represents it, there is a corresponding planetary indicator which naturally represents it, too.*

"*So, let's examine the authorship issue from the two charts. The karaka in the Capricorn chart is Mercury, the indicator of writing, authorship and books. In this chart, Mercury occupies its sign of exaltation, Virgo, in a benefic and pious house, the ninth. It forms raj yoga there with Venus, raj yoga being a tremendous combination for power and influence. First glance, the Capricorn chart supports the type of religious authorship that Srila Prabhupada enjoyed. But the lord (Jupiter) of the house of authorship (the third) occupies the 8th house. The 8th is the most evil house in any horoscope. The affairs represented by any planet or lord who falls there are said to disintegrate and the strength of such a planet is described as "feeble." In spite of the strength of the karaka Mercury, and the fact Mercury aspects or throws its influence on the house of authors, the absolute weakness of the lord of the house does not support the idea of a world-famous author who wrote and organized the distribution of many millions of books. The nature of any religious writings indicated by Jupiter in the evil 8th house afflicted by the Rahu - Ketu axis would not be of the nature of the pure Krishna bhakti of which Srila Prabhupada wrote. The Rahu-Ketu combination together with Jupiter goes by the name of Guru-*

Chandala yoga, indicative of dharmas of lesser understanding. When this combination is prominent in a horoscope, the traditional texts indicate that the person takes up Islam or Christianity, religions of the meat-eaters.

"I have seen this combination indicate comprehension troubles in the charts of many regular devotees, without carrying the added affliction of occurring in the evil 8th, as in the case of the Capricorn chart. In other words, the evil can be corrected if the combination receives other benefic influences, such as good association or aspects. But this combination doesn't cut the mustard because Jupiter is himself afflicted by being there and is the lord of bad houses. So this afflicted third-lord Jupiter with the Rahu-Ketu axis, in an evil house is not indicative of Srila Prabhupada's pure writings. The degenerate influence of Rahu and Ketu over Jupiter is fatal by being in the 8th house. The Sagittarius chart has 4 resounding indications suggesting great literary success with no blemishes. (1) Again, the natural indicator Mercury still occupies his sign of exaltation- Mercury occupies the house of occupation and career, which is certainly a natural place for it to be in Prabhupada's chart. (2) Rahu occupies the house of authorship. Rahu gives very good results from that house. (3) Jupiter and the Sun aspect the house of authors from the ninth house, a very pious and benefic house, wherefrom they form a great raj yoga. This greatly strengthens the house. (4) Finally, the lord of the house of authors occupies his sign of exaltation; (Saturn in the 11th). Not only is Libra the best sign for this planet, but the 11th is the best house!

"These are the indications which make an author a multimillion-dollar seller. These combinations are not seen often. Also the fact is that the heyday of the Hare Krishna movement took place during the major planetary period of Ketu. The idea is that during the period of a planet, the indications promised by it in the chart become activated. The Ketu period started in May, 1971. Previous to that, the major period corresponded to Mercury, the minor period belonging to Saturn from August of '68 until May of '71. In the Capricorn chart, does Ketu in the evil 8th house with the Rahu- Ketu axis indicate any great spirituality? The answer is no. Does Ketu in the 8th even suggest any type of strong success? Especially next to such a weak Jupiter, the answer again is also no. In the Sagittarius chart, however, any natural evil of the Rahu-Ketu axis would be overshadowed by dint of the fact that Ketu sits in the pious house of religion, by the fact Ketu is with a strong Jupiter, who is the karaka of religion and spiritual understanding (Jupiter is Brihaspati), and by being with the lord of the house of religion, the sattvic Sun.

"Ketu would not only reflect the piety of this 9th house situation of the Sagittarius chart, but also reflect and intensify the force and power of that combination, and give success in his period. It is the nature of both Rahu

385

and Ketu to reflect the results of the planet in whose sign they are placed. They are largely chameleons. They soak up and intensify the indications around them. In predictive astrology also, Rahu and Ketu act like their associated planets and reflect the qualities of the house they are in. It is only natural in the Sagittarius chart for Ketu to reflect and intensify the great success and piety of the raj yoga (Jupiter, Sun combination) of which he is a part. Ketu's inherent materialism is not reinforced as in the Capricorn chart, with Ketu in an evil house next to an afflicted and weak Jupiter. Ketu's intensifying nature accounts for the results which were not given in the major Jupiter period by itself, which took place in the 1920s, when Srila Prabhupada didn't have such success. So, Ketu was able to synthesize and intensify the combined effects of Jupiter and the Sun in a synergistic way. This is typical of the nature of Rahu and Ketu; we are used to seeing planets manifest their results through Rahu and Ketu. In the Capricorn chart, however, everything requires a bit of stretching. A much more tenable and natural interpretation results from the Sagittarius chart. I hope which chart is the real chart of Srila Prabhupada has become revealed. But, let's not hastily judge any astrologer who favors the Capricorn chart." (END)

COMMENTS: (by noted devotee Vedic astrologer): *"Interestingly, Dharmapada das in Brazil has written an essay published on the Sun some years ago that astrologically it is discernable that Srila Prabhupada was poisoned by his disciples. Here is the rationale of that: The lord of the 5th house of disciples (Mars) is in the 6th house of diseases and enemies. There Mars is conjoined the Moon, lord of herbs and medicines. And the Moon is the lord of the 8th house of death. So this conjunction of the violent Mars with the 8th lord Moon in the house of enemies points a finger at disciples, he stated."*

MORE CONVERSATIONS IN 1977 ABOUT ASTROLOGY

JPS: *[...] The tantric astrologer there, he gave some predictions.* **SP**: *What is that?* **JPS**: *[...] up 'til Nov. 28, the last date of sickness, and that after that... You would take a month or so to fully recuperate, and that from Jan. on you'd be quite healthy again, and that for at least 7 years you wouldn't have any trouble with health... He put the big day at Nov. 28.* **SP**: *Why Nov. 28?* **JPS**: *...He may or may not be accurate.* **BHAV**: *[...] That's the day Venus changes houses.* (SPConv Oct. 14, 1977)

SP: *So the final inauspicious day is not come yet. [...]* **Tamal**: *Fatal day. [...]* **Tamal**: *Well, it says, "You are presently undergoing the fag-end of Ketu Mahadasa, and it will last until 13 Jan. 1978. It mentions a lot of things. I don't understand these astrological terms. I could read them to you. [...]* **Pradyumna**: *Ketu is in the 8th house with Sun, Lord of 8th house, and guru, Brhaspati, Lord of 12th and 3rd houses. Mercury and Ketu* *started from 16/1/77, Budha... Budha Sasthesa also. 'Sasthesa means' Lord of house of disease. That is not good. Budha is Mercury. Mercury is Sasthesa also. That means disease, Budha. "Sani has gone to 8th house, house of death, from 7 Sept. 1977."* **Tamal**: *That's SP's Appearance Day.* **Pradyumna**: *"Sani is Lagnesa in the 8th house and in transit over Jupiter from 24 Sept. exact, and Ketu from 16 Sept. exact."* **Tamal**: *What does that mean? Unless you know astrology...* **Pradyumna**: *That is not good, with this Sani and Ketu. "A negative effect continues throughout Oct. 1977, to Nov. 1977, and from 1 Dec, 1977 Saturn becomes almost stationary." This is not a good time. "And becomes more malefic (evil)." That means it goes Vakrabhava. It goes retrograde and that is not good.* (SPConv. Nov. 8, '77)

PRABHUPADA'S ASTROLOGICAL CHART RE: POISONING

By Jai Hari das, Vedic astrologer, jyotish@vancouver.net:

[It is not clear which rising sign he has used.] Abbreviated:

"Srila Prabhupada had an interesting 8th house of death (which rules one's life force, the ability for the soul to stay in the body). He has Ketu, Sun and Jupiter in this house. Jupiter is malefic, the Sun is benefic. Because the Sun is the karmic controlling planet in this situation, we must give Lordship to his power of rulership in this house. Srila Prabhupada would experience some difficulties in life during Sun, Ketu major or minor periods. Worst case scenario, Sun and Ketu periods are life threatening periods. Jupiter periods would be much more auspicious.

"In this horoscope, Sun, Ketu and Jupiter are three killers sitting in the 8th house of death, waiting to be triggered by Saturn's entrance into his 8th house. Saturn was in the 8th house when Srila Prabhupada left this planet. Saturn is not a direct killer here and only pointed to the time. Sun, Ketu and Jupiter did the killing. The 8th house is a moksha house. Every planet in his 8th house is in a state of moksha. Jupiter owns his 12th house, a Moksha house. Although Jupiter is a killer, he is also a liberator. Ketu is in the 8th and is the planet of liberation and wisdom. The Sun is the spirit-soul. It's presence, ownership of the 8th produces three enlightened planets in the 8th. All three are under strong karmic forces due to Ketu's influence, which highly spiritualizes his natal Sun. He was a great teacher on how to die.

"At the time of his departure, Saturn was transiting the 8th house of death. At his birth Saturn was exalted in the 10th (status and worldly recognition). Saturn is a karmic controlling planet in his life, and is Lord of his Lagna, indicating rise to great recognition and the highest qualities of life. Saturn gains dispositorship of Rahu who sits in the 2nd house of speech, food, knowledge, wealth. He reaped the rewards of his

exalted, highly spiritualized Saturn, as Lord and master of his destiny. Saturn in the 8ᵗʰ is very auspicious, and due to this, all other planets were in samadhi at the time of death. The whole 8th house was in a state of liberation. The forces of Saturn and Rahu are unsurpassed in strength and influence in the life of Srila Prabhupada. Rahu is in the 2nd house. Rahu protects this house and malefic Sun, Ketu and Jupiter do not control Rahu in the 2nd. He attained great wealth and power. But he was totally renounced; a true quality of a highly evolved Saturn person.

"Rahu/Saturn protects Srila Prabhupada from death by poisoning.

*"Speaking from a material point of few, his Jupiter, Ketu and Sun are certainly malefic, very capable of death, sickness, adversity, **deceit, hidden factors, slander, mystery and intrigue,** [...] which all belong to his 8th house. He would face these types of issues in his life and after also. To say that persons may want to kill Prabhupada, to deceive, defame, poison him is indicated by Jupiter, Ketu and Sun. **There would be plots against him.** Threats known or unknown. The 8th house indicates this. Still, the plot could not succeed due to the protective forces of Saturn and Rahu which controlled his the destiny, both being exalted in Srila Prabhupada's chart."* [COMMENT: The stars strongly indicate a poisoning intrigue, although due to great spiritual power, Srila Prabhupada was not killed, but chose the time of his own death.]

CONCLUSION

Amar Puri das, taking Srila Prabhupada's birth particulars as Sept. 1, 1896, 3:24 pm, Calcutta: *"I will cite such an example from the horoscope of SP [...] At the date and time of SP's birth place, the configuration of the planetary arrangement was very auspicious. The Sun was in his own sign of Leo in 9th house of Dharma and in association with Jupiter and Ketu.. Mercury was exalted in her own sign of Virgo in 10th house of profession. Lord of the 3rd house Saturn was exalted in 11th house as well as Moon was exalted and so on. That is why SP is a Self-Realized Soul and is accepted worldwide as a true authority in the science of self-realization. In other words, he is a Nitya Siddha personality, empowered by the creator, Sri Krishna."*

To find a good Vedic astrologer in Kali Yuga is difficult and interpretations will differ. Srila Prabhupada was transcendental to all mundane influences, including those of the stars. The actual details of events are stored in the Akashic Record in the subtle dimension of the material energies.

CHAPTER 61:
HIS AMAZING TOLERANCE AND MERCY

(1) *"Suppose if I am here and somebody kills me, and if you do not protest, is it a very good business? People will be surprised that, 'So many disciples are there, and this man is being killed, and nobody do anything?'"* (SPLecture Oct. 27, 1974) **(2)** *"So as Krishna was attempted to be killed... And Lord Jesus Christ was killed. So they may kill me also."* (SPConv May 3, 1976) **(3)** *"Srila Prabhupada, Shastriji says that there must be some truth to it if you say that. So who is it that has poisoned?"* (Tamal Nov. 11, 1977) **(4)** *"An advanced devotee, therefore, does not live within the material body but within his spiritual body, just as a dry coconut lives detached from the coconut husk, even though within the husk. The pure devotee's body is therefore called cin-maya-sharira--spiritualized body. In other words, a devotee's body is not connected with material activities, and as such, a devotee is always liberated, brahma-bhuyaya kalpate."* (BGita 14.26)

(5) *"The difference between sakama and akama devotees is that when sakama devotees, like the demigods, fall into difficulty, they approach the Supreme Personality of Godhead for relief, whereas akama devotees, even in the greatest danger, never disturb the Lord for material benefits. Even if an akama devotee is suffering, he thinks this is due to his past impious activities and agrees to suffer the consequences. He never disturbs the Lord. [...] Even while suffering in the midst of difficulties, devotees simply offer their prayers and service more enthusiastically."* (SBhag 6.9.40 Pt) **(6)** *"Regarding your question about sufferings of master, you can simply ponder over Lord Christ's crucification."* (SPL Rebatinandan 12.31.72)

"HE WOULD HAVE PUT AN END TO THE POISONING..."

Some say that if Srila Prabhupada was poisoned, he would have known, since he is a pure devotee, and to protect his movement, he would have exposed or stopped his poisoning, and since he did not, there was no poisoning. There are problems with this line of thinking. Srila Prabhupada **_DID_** expose his own poisoning on Nov. 9-10, 1977. There were extensive discussions about being poisoned, and Tamal directly asked, *"So who is it that has poisoned?"* Also we must be cautious about interpreting Srila Prabhupada's activities as a liberated soul. Maybe he did not stop his own poisoning because: **(1)** He decided to tolerate it, just as Jesus Christ did not stop his crucifixion. **(2)** He accepted it as

Krishna's will. **(3)** He did not want to inconvenience his assailants, like Haridas did not want to inconvenience the soldiers flogging him to death. **(4)** Srila Prabhupada saw no need to protect his movement by stopping his own poisoning, because he felt himself too unimportant to make an issue out of it, or that it was part of Krishna's bigger plan. Speculating what Srila Prabhupada should have done is a mistake; he is a completely selfless pure devotee, uninterested in his own welfare. Whatever he did was perfect and under the authority and purview of the Supreme Lord.

Tamal also said Srila Prabhupada would have stopped his own poisoning. But we should not second guess the pure devotee. *TKG's Diary (p. 179)*: *"Prabhupada's mind works so transcendentally! No one can possibly understand how the acharya thinks."* (At least once, Tamal understood.) Did Christ object to his crucifixion? Was it the end of Christianity when he was crucified? No, but Christ's teachings were later adulterated by false followers. Srila Prabhupada's mission is corrupted by deviating from his instructions, and he lives forever for those who do follow them, who will struggle to protect Srila Prabhupada's movement from poisoners and their deviations. Srila Prabhupada had a perfectly logical, transcendental rationale to quietly tolerate his poisoning.

"The devotee does not do anything not sanctioned by the Supreme Personality of Godhead. As it is said, vaishnavera kriya mudra vijneha na bujhaya. Even the most learned or experienced person cannot understand the movements of a Vaishnava, a pure devotee. No one, therefore, should criticize a pure Vaishnava. A Vaishnava knows his own business; whatever he does is precisely right because he is always guided by the Supreme Personality of Godhead" (SBhag 9.4.68 Purport) In *Perfect Questions, Perfect Answers* (p. 51)

Srila Prabhupada said Bhaktisiddhanta had a disciple who had the *"personal motivation to do business with my guru Maharaja,"* but he took the high road and did not reject his disciple, just as Lord Krishna accepted Putana as His mother. Similarly, Srila Prabhupada knew how fallen and dangerous some of his disciples actually were, and he carried on trying to reform and train them, accepting the positive service they gave him, in spite of their poisoning him. We cannot demand Srila Prabhupada do as we (imperfectly) think is best.

"SP was obviously not in the mood of accusation in his final days. He may not have wanted a bloody riot at the last stage. When Tamal asked, 'Who is it that has poisoned?' he was silent. He did not deny, at this point, that someone gave him poison. He may not have answered because the poisoner was standing right in front of him. And apparently

he (they) had already subverted the movement and where were all those he had called to see him in his last days?" (Narasimha das, 2016)

THE PURE DEVOTEE'S TOLERANCE

Srila Prabhupada was not a conditioned soul fixed on self-defense. His poisoning can be seen as a "ghastly rasa" which teaches us tolerance.

(1) *"Even if he suffers some reversals in life, a devotee is never agitated."* (SBhag 4.24.20 purport) **(2)** *"Being situated in such a position, one is never shaken, even in the midst of greatest difficulty."* (BGita 6.23) **(3)** *"An unalloyed devotee is never disturbed by any kind of trying circumstance."* (SBhag 6.12.19 purport) **(4)** *"If one is situated in Krishna consciousness, then even in the greatest calamities he will not be disturbed."* (Life Comes From Life)

(5) *"While engaged in preaching work, he has to meet with so many opposing elements, and therefore the sadhu, or devotee of the Lord, has to be very tolerant. Someone may ill-treat him because the conditioned souls are not prepared to receive the transcendental knowledge of devotional service. They do not like it; that is their disease. The sadhu has the thankless task of impressing upon them the importance of devotional service. Sometimes devotees are personally attacked with violence. Lord Jesus Christ was crucified, Haridasa Thakura was caned in twenty-two marketplaces, and Lord Chaitanya's principal assistant, Nityananda, was violently attacked by Jagai and Madhai. But still they were tolerant because their mission was to deliver the fallen souls. One of the qualifications of a sadhu is that he is very tolerant and is merciful to all fallen souls. He is merciful because he is the well-wisher of all living entities."* (SBhag 3.25.21 purport)

(6) About the mood of the pure devotee who endures his suffering and does not become his enemy's enemy: *"A pure devotee is never disturbed in any circumstance... Thus it is better to suffer than to protest... Therefore he is calm, quiet and patient, despite many distressful conditions. A devotee is always kind to everyone, even to his enemy... He is tolerant, and he is satisfied with whatever comes by the grace of the Supreme Lord... He is a completely perfect mystic..."* (BGita 12.13-14) **(7)** *"SP asked Hamsaduta to join him soon in Hawaii. He would try to rectify his disciple and encourage him to be more careful and go on with his duties. This wasn't the first time one of his leaders stumbled. But Prabhupada never rejected them. He had always done everything to save the person. Prabhupada kept the doors open and welcomed whoever repented his mistakes and willingly resumed the fight against maya."* (Vedavyasa das)

(8) SBhag: *"The devotees of the Lord are so forbearing that even though they are defamed, cheated, cursed, disturbed, neglected or even killed, they are never inclined to avenge themselves. Purport: Rsi Samika also knew that the Lord does not forgive a person who has committed an offense at the feet of a devotee. The Lord can only give direction to take shelter of the devotee. He thought within himself that if Maharaja Pariksit would counter curse the boy, he might be saved. But he knew also that a pure devotee is callous about worldly advantages or reverses. As such, the devotees are never inclined to counteract personal defamation, curses, negligence, etc. As far as such things are concerned, in personal affairs the devotees do not care for them. But in the case of their being performed against the Lord and His devotees, then the devotees take very strong action."*

SRILA PRABHUPADA WAS EXTREMELY TOLERANT

Satsvarupa Oct. 14, 1977: *"Just yesterday she [SP's sister] arrived here. After so many doctors tried to prescribe cures for SP and mostly failed, she has come and given Srila Prabhupada prasadam cooked by herself, and it is the first solid food he has been able to eat in months."*

This indicates Srila Prabhupada deliberately fasted because he did not trust his food. When Pishima came, however, he again tried to eat, trusting her cooking. It seems Srila Prabhupada was well aware of the poisoning, but tolerated it while trying to avoid it as well. It may be said that Srila Prabhupada would have known, would have put a stop to it and rejected those who were, in essence, attacking him and his movement. But Srila Prabhupada would accept service from those who were poisoning him: *"Srila Prabhupada revealed in a matter-of-fact tone that he had no choice but to accept the service of anyone who Krishna sent to him. He had left Vrindaban because his Guru Maharaja asked him to preach in the West, so whoever Krishna sent <u>he had to accept that service to satisfy his Guru Maharaja</u>."* (Unalloyed Devotion, p. 208)

"A perfect yogi can have command over death and quit the body at the right moment, when he is competent to transfer himself to suitable planet. The bhakti-yogi, however, surpasses all yogis because, by dint of his devotional service, he is promoted to the region beyond the material sky and is placed in one of the planets in the spiritual sky by the supreme will of the Lord, the controller of everything." (SBhag 2.3.29 purport)

Arjuna das: *"This excellent Calcutta kaviraja came to Vrindaban to treat Prabhupada. He was sober, brahminical, from the Sri-sampradaya, wore big white and red tilak, very reverential to Prabhupada. One day he said, 'At first I doubted your Guru Maharaja was a paramahamsa. I have treated 1000s of dying people, and in this condition- when there's no more muscle and fat to cushion the nerves from being pressed against the bone- usually people are in such agony that I have to administer morphine. However, your Guru Maharaja never manifests the slightest expression of pain.' I also saw this in March-April in Bombay when Prabhupada's whole jaw was swollen. When we get a toothache, we can't tolerate it. But he tolerated it without any difference in his mannerisms, in his way of dealing with anyone, and he never complained. When the devotees tried to induce him to take care of his body, Prabhupada wasn't agreeable. He transcended his body. It was very evident that Srila Prabhupada was a successful astanga-yogi, that he had totally transcended his bodily conception and was a true living saint."*

"ALL RIGHT, LET ME DRINK (POISON)"

Scriptures explain why Srila Prabhupada was so tolerant.

"The Supreme Personality of Godhead sometimes <u>puts a devotee to severe tests that are almost unbearable</u>. One could hardly even live under the conditions forced upon Bali Maharaja. [He] endured all these severe tests and austerities is the mercy of the Supreme Lord. The Lord certainly appreciates the devotee's forbearance, and it is recorded for the future glorification of the devotee. This was not an ordinary test. [...] one of the mahajanas, the Supreme Personality of Godhead <u>not only tested him but also gave him the strength to tolerate such adversity</u>. The Lord is so kind to His devotee that when severely testing him the Lord gives him the necessary strength to be tolerant and continue to <u>remain a glorious devotee</u>." (SBhag 8.22.29-30 purport)

*"Sadhu is titiksava, tolerates all kinds of miserable conditions [...] A sadhu learns how to tolerate [...] never disturbed. [...] A sadhu, who has got the shelter of Krishna, if he is placed in the severest type of dangerous condition, he is never disturbed. Just like Prahlad Maharaja, his father was putting him in so many dangerous conditions [...] He knew that 'My father has **given me poison to drink. All right, let me drink**. If Krishna likes, He will save me. [...] He forced the mother, Prahlad's mother, 'Give your son this poison.' [...] he was a rascal demon. 'No, you must give.' So the mother knew, the son knew that the rascal father is giving this poison. What can he do, a small child? 'All right, let me drink." [...] He is not agitating. "All right, if Krishna likes, I will live.' This is the position of sadhu. He is not disturbed. [...] **In all circumstances, he is tolerant**. [...] Sadhu does not become disturbed. [...] He is himself disturbed, but he is merciful to others. Just like Jesus Christ. He is being crucified, and still he is merciful: 'God, these people*

do not know what they are doing. **Please excuse them***.' This is sadhu. He is personally being disturbed by the demons, but still, he is merciful to the general people. They are suffering for want of Krishna consciousness. So even up to the point of death, he is trying to preach Krishna consciousness. 'Let the people be benefited. Eh, what is this material body? Even if I am killed, I am not killed. This body is killed, that's all.' This is sadhu. [...] In one side he is tolerant, and other side, merciful."* (SPLecture July 18, 1973)

TOLERATED HIS POISONERS OUT OF COMPASSION

It is hard to understand on the basis of our experiences in this cruel, material world, but Srila Prabhupada tolerated his poisoners because of his great compassion for them. They were doing devotional service, mixed-bhakti perhaps, but he considered that more important than his own physical welfare. A pure devotee will not act in his own defense nor ask anything for himself, not even his own life. A remarkable feature of Srila Prabhupada's disappearance pastimes is how he did not move to save himself nor to name or accuse his poisoners. Similarly, Christ on the cross prayed, *"Forgive them, O Lord, for they know not what they do."* This is the nature of a bona fide saint like Srila Prabhupada, yet some expect Srila Prabhupada to behave like them- to defend and fight. Haridas Thakur, still alive after being beaten mercilessly, said to his executioners, *"If my being alive for even one minute inconveniences you, then I will die immediately."* And he became apparently dead, to be thrown into the Ganges. Jesus Christ also did not protest when crucified, even though he had the power to escape. Surely Srila Prabhupada knew who his poisoners were, but he did not care about himself, nor want to disturb the poisoners who were giving him at least some "shadow" service. Srila Prabhupada was reconciled to his departure and to being poisoned, only making the poisoning known in his last days so the truth be known to us. These are his glorious disappearance pastimes.

COMMENT: *"Srila Prabhupada's final pastime closely reminds me with that of Jesus Christ, as I was born Christian. Like Jesus on the cross SP's body was "nailed" to his bed and suffered numerous days of horrible torture. Jesus was described as extremely weak, dehydrated and suffocating. His true greatness is that even with all his suffering, he thought of others rather than himself. His words from the cross were, 'Father, forgive them; for they know not what they do."*

WHY DID HE NOT SAY MUCH ON BEING POISONED? *(Narasimha das)*

"If he had called out the poisoners, it would have caused turmoil and the movement's forward momentum could have been lost. The

momentum could have been lost and probably few would have joined after 1977. A likely scenario: one faction would have believed SP; they would have immediately reacted with violence. Others would have defended the caretakers, who would create more offenses claiming SP was mistaken or demented (as they now say openly). SP had asked for all devotees to come to Vrindaban, but they were not told and no one came. He was likely thinking the movement had already been hijacked. SP said going on parikrama would cure him. But they didn't want him to go. He saw those near him were controlling the situation, and the devotees were scattered around the world. There are many possible reasons why he didn't say or do more regarding both initiations and being poisoned:

"(1) He wanted to spend his last days in the mood of a paramahamsa, not chastising neophytes and rascals. (2) He wanted the momentum he had created in ISKCON to continue for some time more. (3) He wanted the cheaters to expose themselves. (4) He wanted more soul searching among his real disciples. (5) He wanted to delay things until later when it would be much easier to see that the GBC had gone rogue. (6) He wanted to leave sooner, seeing the situation of intrigue and deceit. (7) He was hearing and heeding the call of Krishna and another mission. (8) This lila is like Christ's crucification and ultimately meant for his glorification and his mission. Also, possibly some outside agency feared Srila Prabhupada and the Hare Krishna movement's rising power. The Hare Krishna movement's great success had likely riled the ruling powers. Srila Prabhupada did say that the planet was controlled by powerful rakshasas, so this is not just a silly idea." (END)

ALL-REDEEMING SERVICE WAS MOST IMPORTANT

Regarding Srila Prabhupada's vagueness, ambiguity, and refusal to name his informant or poisoner, and his unwillingness to disclose more, he was either: **(1)** wary that his poisoners would cause disruption to his mission if he named them, or **(2)** concerned they would cease their all-redeeming (shadow) service if he exposed them. /Srila Prabhupada put his poisoners' service, by which they were earning immeasurable, eternal spiritual benefit, even above his own physical well-being.

The pure devotee accepted poison from those who were rendering service to the movement. The poisoners were circumstantially locked in to the ongoing preaching, even if their secret desire was only to use it for material gains. Srila Prabhupada understood that if exposed as poisoners, they would just deny it, and that, if unexposed, they would continue to expand the movement even *because* of their personal ambitions to enjoy his assets, sit on his seat. Srila Prabhupada always encouraged everyone to keep chanting and serving Krishna, *in all situations and regardless of motives, as this would eventually lead to a completely purified heart.*

Partrikananda das reported, 1996: *"Srila Prabhupada told Bhagatji that his disciples were not very advanced and he would not be surprised if they tried to do him great physical harm."* Srila Prabhupada knew all that was going on: *"One who executes Sri Chaitanya Mahaprabhu's mission must be considered eternally liberated. He is a transcendental person and does not belong to this material world. Such a devotee, engaging in the deliverance of the total population, is as magnanimous as Sri Chaitanya Mahaprabhu Himself. [...] because his heart is always filled with compassion for all conditioned souls."* (CC Mad 15.163)

FURTHER ON SRILA PRABHUPADA'S TOLERANCE

"A devotee, however, is never disturbed by dangers, reverses, or calamities. Rather, he welcomes them. Because he is a surrendered soul, he knows that both dangers and festivals are but different demonstrations of Krishna, who is absolute. In the shastra [...] it is said that religion and irreligion, which are complete opposites, are merely the front portion and the back portion of God. But is there any difference [...]? God is absolute, and therefore a devotee, either in opulence or in danger, is undisturbed, knowing that both of these are Krishna. When a devotee is in danger, he thinks, 'Now Krishna has appeared before me as danger.' In His form of Nrsimhadeva, the Lord was dangerous to the demon Hiranyakasipu, but the same Nrsimhadeva was the supreme friend to the devoted Prahlad Maharaja. God is never dangerous to the devotee, and the devotee is never afraid of dangers, because he is confident that the danger is but another feature of God. 'Why should I be afraid?' the devotee thinks. 'I am surrendered to Him.'" (TQK Ch. 8)

"Many of us remain silent, not doing anything, continuing the enjoyment business. [...] Should I protest or keep my mouth closed for all the injustice taking place in this world? What if I was put in a similar situation to Srila Prabhupada? Would I still be silent or would I protest? After all everything is in God's control. Jesus Christ was crucified, Srila Prabhupada poisoned. But they did not protest. It was God's plan. They preached Krishna consciousness. It was their only concern. Jesus said, 'Father, forgive them, for they do not know what they are doing.' Prabhupada thought, 'Krishna, we should not take it seriously. They are demons. Our mission is to deliver them.' Jesus Christ and Srila Prabhupada were fighting with arrows of compassion thrown to each and every sinner equally. It is only Srila Prabhupada who delivers the whole universe. He is Guru, the spiritual master of everyone. Let us all

COMPLETE BOOK OF POISONING EVIDENCE

humbly bow down to Srila Prabhupada. Let's follow a true master. Never should we imitate such a great soul." (Gauranga das, Aug. 2017)

"...this is Srila Prabhupada's final and perfect departure pastime. How else could the world understand the true compassion and tolerance of our acharya? Srila Prabhupada did not protest very much because he could see his duty from Krishna's direct speaking, same as Jesus could ask forgiveness of his crucifiers. But we must try our best to act in such a way that the Hare Krishna movement will be purified... to our best ability... we should not remain silent." (Dharma das, Aug. 2017)

After Srila Prabhupada said 3 times he thought he was being poisoned, he simply dropped the matter, decided to tolerate it, and did not mention it again before his departure. There are many indications he expected to be poisoned or killed, and he knew exactly what was going on months before Nov. 9-10, 1977. He accepted it with great tolerance as the Lord's will. Srila Prabhupada accepted those who came to render him service and who were furthering his mission, even if they were doing so disruptively with their personal ambitions. He accepted the poisoners as his servants and prayed for their deliverance. *It is hard to appreciate this level of tolerance and mercy, but Srila Prabhupada was the personification of the highest levels of such divine qualities.* Lord Krishna also showed tolerance and mercy to Putana, who came to poison him in disguise. (see Vol. 11: *Shaktavesh Avatar of Truth and Mercy*)

SBhag 9.4.47 describes the tolerance of the pure devotee Ambarish Maharaja under deadly attack, and the same applies to Srila Prabhupada.

CHAPTER 62:
CAN THE PURE DEVOTEE BE KILLED?

"So real guru is never to be killed, but the so-called guru has to be killed. The so-called, pseudo guru, false guru, he should be killed." (SBhag 1.8.50 Lecture, May 12, 1973)

In light of the proof of Srila Prabhupada's lethal poisoning, the question whether Srila Prabhupada can even be killed is very interesting, as we know Srila Prabhupada is now not "dead" but has simply passed from our physical vision. Srila Prabhupada was not subject to the laws of material nature and his departure cannot be explained simply in material terms- he is in the custody of the Lord's internal potency, and thus his disappearance is a transcendental pastime. From the spiritual perspective,

Srila Prabhupada departed by the arrangement of Lord Krishna and he was not forced to leave this material realm due to poison. *"B.V. Puri Maharaja, who Srila Prabhupada said was his only Godbrother who was not envious of him, asked Srila Prabhupada, 'Please stay another 10 years with these boys.' Srila Prabhupada's answer was, 'They are all hard headed, I have done all I can do.' Prabhupada said, 'I can stay 100 years,' many times, but he left after 81 years."* (Gurukripa das, 2009)

Srila Prabhupada gave the example of the cat carrying in its mouth either the rat or its kitten. *"Prahlad Maharaja was tortured by his father in so many ways, but **he was not affected**. ... Superficially... Just like in the Christian Bible also, that Lord Jesus Christ was tortured, but he was not affected. This is the difference between ordinary man and the devotees or transcendentalists. Apparently it is seen that a devotee is being tortured, but he is not tortured. [...] it is seen that a cat is carrying its kitties in the mouth [...] But it is not in pain. [...] But when the cat... catches one mouse, his life is gone. ...she is carrying in the mouth both of them. Similarly, whenever you'll find that a great devotee is placed into torturing condition, he does not feel..."* (SPLecture 6.29.68)

Srila Prabhupada was given lethal amounts of heavy metals, and an ordinary man would surely have died much sooner, but he was not killed by poison- it was Krishna's divine arrangement how and when Srila Prabhupada would depart. But the poisoners were in maya.

GREAT DEVOTEES PERSECUTED THROUGH HISTORY

Throughout history, great religious preachers have been attacked, harassed, even apparently killed, by demoniac elements. Srila Prabhupada noted the most famous example of Lord Jesus Christ. John the Baptist was imprisoned, beheaded. Christ's Apostles were killed by leaders of secular or pseudo-religious society. Saint Thomas was beheaded by an envious, non-Vaishnava king in southern India who was goaded by false Brahmins into fearing the saint's powerful preaching. Prahlad Maharaja was the victim of many assassination attempts from his own father. In the early 1500's, Haridas Thakura was homicidally tortured in 22 market places. Envious clerics in the 1930's tried to hire assassins to kill Bhaktisiddhanta Sarasvati. Srila Prabhupada said that his *guru* left this world early due to disgust of his leading disciples.

Hardened materialists often try to repress the transcendental teachings of pure God consciousness as taught by Lord Chaitanya and His great devotees, but they are never successful in their intrigues. A pure teacher of God consciousness, the *sad-guru*, boldly propagates the message of the Absolute Truth, the Supreme Lord, by showing the path back to the Kingdom of Godhead. Not everyone can appreciate this divine mission. Atheists, impersonalists, false religious leaders, and other materialists who want to maintain the status quo in this world, will oppose the Lord's missionary work. Others spoil and exploit the mission of the eternal guru for their own prestige and profit. Powerful preachers are often crucified, imprisoned, attacked, or poisoned—even by their own people or followers, as was Jesus Christ, who was betrayed by Judas and priests. Srila Prabhupada: **(1)** *"Just as they tried to kill Lord Jesus Christ, they may try to kill me also."* (May 1976) **(2)** *"Don't torture me and put to death."* (Nov. 3, 1977) **(3)** *"Better to kill me here."* (1977) **(4)** *"This is also suicide."* (Nov. 1977) **(5)** *"Killed by Rama or killed by Ravana. Better to be killed by Rama."* (Nov. 1977)

THE SOUL CAN EXIST EVEN THROUGH THE BONES

The soul can remain in a body even if only bones remain, as with Hiranyakasipu. *"A yogi can keep himself alive in a transcendental state even if buried not only for many days but for many years [...] the soul can exist even through the bones. [...] It appears that even if a yogi does not drink a drop of water, he can live for many, many years by the yogic process, though his outer body be eaten..."* (SBhag 7.3.18)

Similarly Srila Prabhupada fasted or ate only tiny amounts for almost a year, and his body became emaciated, only bones and no muscle or fat, yet he stayed fully Krishna conscious and his body continued to function. His kaviraja was amazed when his heart and other organs appeared on the verge of collapse and then his condition returned to normal overnight. Srila Prabhupada maintained his body by spiritual strength; he was in the body but apart from it, in full control of life or death. Imagine the poisoners' frustrations how he continued to survive long after anyone else would have succumbed. Srila Prabhupada had the *shakti* to live in spite of any amount of poison, and he departed when it was either his decision (or Krishna's) to do so. The poisoners then foolishly thought that they had killed Srila Prabhupada. Lord Krishna also neutralized lethal doses of poison given to Mirabai and Prahlad.

RAMANUJACHARYA WAS ALSO POISONED

Many objections to the "poison conspiracy" are based on the misconception that it is not possible Srila Prabhupada could have been poisoned, due to Krishna's protection of the pure devotee. However, the material world is the place of birth and death, and even pure devotees will appear and disappear when coming here. Is a pure devotee's departure due to diabetes or old age Krishna's protection, and by poisoning not? An envious king conspired 1000 years ago to kill

Ramanujacharya, who was poisoned, although he departed later because his mission was not yet complete, whereas apparently Srila Prabhupada's mission was complete. *"One day in the evening Ramanuja went to the temple. The high priest gave him sacramental water laced with a virulent poison. Ramanuja went into a trance-like state and staggered out of the temple. The next morning the high priest saw Ramanuja in a state of spiritual ecstasy with tears flowing down his cheeks. Ramanuja had lost all body consciousness and was absorbed in the beatific vision of the Lord. The high priest was filled with remorse and threw himself at Ramanuja's feet, beating his head on the ground. Ramanuja regained body consciousness and tenderly raised the postulant sinner, forgave him and healed his wounds with his touch."*

Jesus Christ was crucified but not killed, and then went on to Kashmir. Srila Prabhupada was poisoned, but left only when he was ready to go. Srila Prabhupada took far longer to leave than ordinarily possible, in view of such a catastrophic cadmium poisoning.

FIRST UNDERSTAND THE POISONING IS A FACT, THEN...

There are two stages in uncovering the truth of this matter: **(1)** Was Srila Prabhupada poisoned? Yes, the evidence is conclusive. **(2)** Then, who did it? /So, we cannot go to #2 unless #1 is first understood. ***Don't worry about who did it if you are not sure it happened.*** Often people deny Srila Prabhupada's poisoning due to disbelief that caretakers did it. Once one understands the evidence of a homicidal poisoning, ***then*** one can ask who did it. Unfortunately there are deniers with ulterior motives that are not impressed by what Srila Prabhupada himself said about being poisoned, or who do not have the power of critical, independent thinking to assess the conclusive evidence. They will need a mundane court or agency to confirm for them that there was indeed a poisoning. And some will still deny it. Meanwhile we take the evidence to the court of public opinion, where each can decide for themselves with their intelligence, hopefully without institutional influence. The truth will be understood by those with more sincerity and honesty than the GBC, which functions only to preserve the status quo of the elite's privileges, a status quo that the poisoning evidence mortally threatens. The GBC has and will continue to cover-up the truth of Srila Prabhupada's disappearance pastimes. ***There is no use for more begging, polite petitions, cooperation, or expectations of any kind from them.***

The GBC cannot be trusted and they are an enemy of the truth. Ours is a war against a corrupt establishment intent on spoiling Srila Prabhupada's mission and mercy. ***First they poisoned him physically,*** *then they poisoned his mission and mercy.* The empowered pure devotee His Divine Grace Srila Prabhupada was poisoned maliciously by those who then took over his institution. The GBC just deny and cover it up. Why didn't they order the suspects to submit to interviews, truth tests, or arrange for a trusted third party to handle further investigation? Or test Srila Prabhupada's hair and teeth that are in their possession? Why? Something to hide? They won't even look at the results of tests that they left unfinished and invited others to complete. Instead, they had Mayeswara das say Dr. Morris does not know how to do NAA tests. They know they are now in trouble, that hair tests show Srila Prabhupada *was* poisoned with 250 X normal cadmium, an unprecedented level not even found in the scientific literatures. This truth is resonating with Krishna bhaktas all over the world and will end GBC tyranny. Who wants to be part of the poisoner's regime? Srila Prabhupada's mission will be restored by the power of the truth and the sincerity of honest devotees, in spite of the institutional obstructionists, who need to be removed for good and for the good of all in the Hare Krishna movement.

MAYA CANNOT TOUCH A PURE DEVOTEE

(1) *"...maya cannot touch a pure devotee: when you find a devotee is supposed in difficulty it is not the work of maya but it is the work of the Lord by his personal internal energy. The Pandava's tribulation in so many ways, Lord Ramachandra's departure to the forest, his wife the Goddess of Fortune's being kidnapped by Ravana, Lord Krishna's death being caused by the arrow of a hunter, Thakura Haridasa's being caned in 22 markets or Lord Jesus Christ being crucified- are all acts of the Lord personally. We cannot always understand the intricacies of such incidences. Sometimes they are enacted to bewilder persons who are demons. [...] We should only try to understand everything from the standard of devotional service. [...] anyone who is cent per cent engaged in the service of the Lord is transcendentally situated and the influence of maya has no more any action on such body. The Lord and his pure devotees are always beyond the range of maya's action. Even though they appear like action of maya, we should understand their action of yogamaya or the internal potency of the Lord."* (SPL Apr. 3, 1968) (2) *"...Regarding my leaving, I'll not leave the planet until you order."* (SPL, Bhaktajan das, Sept. 25, 1972) (Being poisoned could be considered an order to leave and no longer being welcome.)

MURDER OF A SPIRITUAL BODY?

Did anyone murder Srila Prabhupada? No, he departed when he wanted, being under the full protection of the Supreme Lord. To think that Srila Prabhupada was killed by poison or that his departure was effected by poisoners is an inaccurate understanding. From the material viewpoint, it may appear Srila Prabhupada was murdered, but the pure devotee, by dint of his full knowledge and surrender to Krishna, is never limited by the workings of the material energy. **(1) Devotee:** *Does Lord Jesus Christ appear in the spiritual sky with the body he manifested on the earth?* **SP:** *Yes. Otherwise how there can be resurrection? Ordinary body cannot be resurrected. He appeared in his spiritual body, certainly. Jesus Christ told, if I remember, that "Lord, excuse these persons," who were crucifying him. Is it not? He knew that "These rascals, they are killing me, but... They are offending certainly. So they do not know that I cannot be killed, but they are thinking that they are killing." You see? But that was offensive, therefore he begged Lord to be excused because God cannot excuse to the offenders of the devotee. He can excuse one who is offender to God, but if somebody is offender to the devotee, God never excuses. Therefore he prayed for them. That is devotee's qualification. He prays for everyone, even of his enemy. And he could not be killed. That he knew. But those rascals, they thought they were killing Jesus Christ.* (SPLecture Jan. 3, 1969)

(2) *"You try to trace out the history of the world, you'll find always persons who are for Krishna or God, they have been persecuted. Lord Jesus Christ was crucified, Haridasa Thakura was caned in 22 market places, Prahlad Maharaja was tortured by his father. So there may be such things. Of course, Krishna will protect us. So don't be afraid. Don't be afraid if somebody tortures us, somebody teases us. We must go on with Krishna consciousness without any hesitation, and Krishna will give us protect."* (SPLecture Oct. 21, 1968) **(3) SP**: *These, these rascals, they thought that "Jesus had a material body. Let us kill him." So Jesus Christ bewildered them more, to remain rascal, that they will continue to think that Jesus had a material body.* **Jyotirmayi**: *Bewildered them?* **Yogeswara**: *Yes, he bewildered them more by saying: "All right, go on thinking like that."* **SP**: *That is their punishment. They remain always in darkness that Jesus had a material body. (SPConv June 15, 1974)*

(4) *"A pure devotee of the Lord does not live on any planet of the material sky, nor does he feel any contact with material elements. His so called material body does not exist, being surcharged with the spiritual current of the Lord's identical interest, and thus he is permanently freed from all contaminations of the sum total of mahat-tattva..."* (SBhag 1.13.55) **(5)** *"It is therefore enjoined, gurusu nara-matih: one should stop thinking of the spiritual master as an ordinary human being with a material body. Arcye vishnau sila-dhih: everyone knows that the Deity in* *the temple is made of stone, but to think that the Deity is merely stone is an offense. Similarly, to think that the body of the spiritual master consists of material ingredients is offensive. Atheists think that devotees foolishly worship a stone statue as God and an ordinary man as the guru. The fact is, however, that by the grace of Krishna's omnipotence, the so-called stone statue of the Deity is directly the Supreme Personality of Godhead, and <u>the body of the spiritual master is directly spiritual</u>. A pure devotee who is engaged in unalloyed devotional service should be understood to be situated on the transcendental platform."* (BGita 14.26)

The conclusion is Srila Prabhupada came in his spiritual body. He gave the example of the iron rod which has been heated until red-hot by the fire; essentially both are fire. Similarly the physical body of the spiritual master or pure devotee is completely "spiritualized" by its full contact with Krishna. Failure to understand Srila Prabhupada's transcendental position explains why many consider him to be "dead," unavailable, or no longer present in his instructions, murti or photo (Vol. 8, *He Lives Forever*). Srila Prabhupada was always under the Lord's protection and Srila Prabhupada said Krishna had left his staying or leaving in his hands. Srila Prabhupada's departure was not due to poisoning. *His departure is not about Srila Prabhupada's "murder," but more about the horrible sin and offense of trying to kill him.*

SRILA PRABHUPADA COULD NOT BE KILLED

Those who thought they could speed up Srila Prabhupada's departure by poisoning him with cadmium were truly in illusion, thinking Srila Prabhupada to be an ordinary man who could be killed by a secret attack of deadly chemicals. These dullards were among the senior leaders of ISKCON, and things have not improved since then. Prahlad Maharaja and Srila Prabhupada were both protected by Krishna: *"Thus the weapons of the demons had no tangible effects upon Prahlad Maharaja because he was a devotee undisturbed by material conditions and fully engaged in meditating upon and serving the Supreme Personality of Godhead..."* And in the purport: *"...thus he was protected by Govinda... They may think that they can kill the Supreme Personality of Godhead and His devotee, but all their attempts will be futile. The Lord knows how to deal with them."* (SBhag 7.5.41)

When one studies Srila Prabhupada's last pastimes, when he was being poisoned, we see several remarkable episodes which reveal truth to the above quotes. ***The pure devotee cannot be killed***- he departs only by his own will or by the desire of Lord Krishna. There were instances when his health symptoms indicated an imminent end of life, but then miraculously those symptoms vanished. *"Sept. 27: Prabhupada was completely exhausted. Mucus was filling his whole system, and his legs and hands were very swollen. Even his eyes had much mucus. I felt nearly hopeless... At night, Prabhupada said his condition had gone from bad to worse... Sept. 28: Most amazingly, Srila Prabhupada improved considerably... Today, the mucus was practically gone. Prabhupada slept soundly the whole night; he now looked well rested."* (*TKG's Diary*, p. 204-5) Also p. 338-9, Nov. 10, just days before SP's departure: *"The kaviraja said that Srila Prabhupada's pulse was missing some beats. Privately, the kaviraja said to us that since last night, he has become hopeless about Prabhupada's condition... Later in the day He took Srila Prabhupada's pulse, which measured 90 beats a minute and was stronger than in the morning, when it measured 115. The blood pressure, at 140/75, was perfectly normal. Now the heart was in order. From the pathological point of view everything was all right... The kaviraja was amazed that Srila Prabhupada's body was suddenly able to become better, not at all ordinary."*

Shastri several times explained how one day he determined Srila Prabhupada's health condition as very bad, and the next day, it was very good and normal. Srila Prabhupada was not under the influence of the material energy and he was an accomplished, perfect yogi. *"I'll be back to say that you defy all medical laws. Sometimes you become very weak and sometimes you become immediately strong."* (SPConv Nov. 8, 1977) They were astonished by this recurring phenomenon. The poison only acted as Srila Prabhupada allowed, and as a pure devotee and mystic yogi, he was actually unaffected by the poison. He departed after many months of lethal poisoning not because of the poison, but because it was the time chosen by himself or Lord Krishna. Anantacharya das: *"Shastri, the doctor, comes in at 8:00 a.m. and declares Srila Prabhupada's pulse to be normal. Kaviraj says that he has seen many, many patients, but never one with a body like Prabhupada's. One day everything will seem in disorder, but the next day everything will be perfect again. Today there is no more high blood pressure either."*

Srila Prabhupada amazingly endured 10 months of 250 X normal cadmium levels. In Oct. '77 he stated it was up to him to stay or leave. Fools will think he was killed. Those with proper realization know he departed when he chose. *"The unalloyed devotees of the Supreme Lord, who are totally surrendered souls, do not care when they leave their bodies or by what method... If the yogi is perfect, he can select the time and place for leaving this material world, but if he is not so perfect, then he has to leave at nature's will."* (BGita 8.23 Purport)

A PURE DEVOTEE CANNOT BE POISONED?

Shastra does not say that a pure devotee cannot be poisoned. Pure devotees Prahlad, Mirabai, and Ramanujacharya were all poisoned. Haridas Thakur was flogged in 22 markets, Christ was crucified; both appeared to die but did not. But eventually they all "departed." Does Krishna not protect his pure devotees from death? Is it Krishna's protection when the pure devotee appears to expire with a natural disease, but not when it is poisoning? The answer is that pure devotees depart this material world by divine arrangement and the conditioned souls do so by karmic force. Srila Prabhupada's disappearance was a divine arrangement. Srila Prabhupada withstood poison by mystic power for 10-18 months and then departed like Bhishma did, at his own time and will. Bhishma remained for 2 months, pierced by dozens of arrows.

Srila Prabhupada said he once, in Germany, experimented travelling via the sunshine to the Sun by mystic power. In Dallas in 1973, he joked about flying on American Airlines to be "one with us," and it was clear that he could have traveled around like Narada Muni, but that would have distracted from his message of bhakti. Many devotees experienced him to have read their minds and hearts. He had the power to negate the effects of any poison and to check the poisoners. But he chose to live like a humble devotee fully dependent on the Lord's arrangements. It is difficult to understand exactly how Srila Prabhupada was always protected, even when given poison, but shastra confirms it.

Swami In A Strange Land by Yogeswara das, p. 220: *"Trailanga baba, a friend of Yogananda's grand-guru, Lahiri Mahasaya, had lived not far from Prabhupada's childhood home and passed away when Prabhupada was still a boy. Rumors held that Trailanga had been more than 300 years old at the time. Visitors reported seeing him levitate,* **drink poison without harm**, *and shrink himself down to the size of a pea. Prabhupada described that as a boy he had witnessed mystic powers on display when his father took him to the circus... one popular yogi proved his resistance to rusty nails and another made a syrupy gulab jamun sweet appear from thin air."* If an ordinary yogi could drink poison without harm, then what of the pure devotee of the Lord? Is it really so fantastic if Srila Prabhupada counteracted the cadmium he was ingesting and that he departed by his own will at the time he chose, in spite of lethal poisoning? No, this was totally within his capabilities.

When the poison issue first broke out, Prahladananda Swami wrote on Dec. 18, 1997 to the GBC email discussions group: *"I don't agree with Ravindra Svarupa's idea that it is shastric evidence that Srila*

Prabhupada could not have been poisoned because he was a greatly empowered servant of Lord Krishna... Srila Prabhupada in his books never said that extraordinary empowered devotees do not die of unnatural means. He says the opposite, that even shaktyavesh avatars are sometimes killed while preaching Krishna consciousness."

He quoted: **(1)** *"There are many examples in history of devotees of the Lord who risked their lives for the spreading of God consciousness. ...Lord Jesus Christ. He was crucified by the nondevotees, but he sacrificed his life for spreading God consciousness. Of course, it would be superficial to say he was killed."* (BGita 11.55) **(2)** *"When something is arranged by the Supreme Personality of Godhead, one should not be disturbed by it, even if it appears to be a reverse according to one's calculation. ...sometimes we see that a powerful preacher is killed, or sometimes he is put into difficulty, just as Haridasa Thakura was. [...] Lord Jesus Christ was crucified, Prahlad Maharaja was put through so many tribulations. The Pandavas, who were direct friends of Krishna, lost their kingdom, their wife was insulted, and they had to undergo many severe tribulations. Seeing all these reverses affect devotees, one should not be disturbed; one should simply understand that in these matters, there must be some plan of the Supreme Personality of Godhead."* (SBhag 3.16.37) **(3)** *"...Just like Jesus Christ. He is being crucified, and still he is merciful: "God, these people do not know what they are doing. Please excuse them." This is sadhu..."* (SPLecture July 18, 1973) **(4)** *"A preacher has to face many difficulties in his struggle to preach pure Krishna consciousness. Sometimes he has to suffer bodily injuries, and sometimes he has to meet death also. All this is taken as a great austerity on behalf of Krishna."* (KRISHNA Book Ch. 29)

Srila Prabhupada, Prahlad, and Mirabai's poison was rendered impotent. Srila Prabhupada knew that while some were trying to harm him, this would not impede the transcendental mission of the Lord. *"The spiritual master, or acharya, is always situated in the spiritual status of life. Birth, death, old age and disease do not affect him. According to the Hari-bhakti-vilas, therefore, after the disappearance of an acharya, his body is never burnt to ashes, for it is a spiritual body. The spiritual body is always unaffected by material conditions."* (SBhag 10.4.21 purport)

Watering The Seed, p. 187: *"When Lord Nrsimha asked Prahlad to accept some benediction, Prahlad refused. ...though Hiranyakashipu tried to kill him, Prahlad prayed for his deliverance (and of all living entities). [...] So the guru is always so merciful. The guru will always be merciful to his disciple, even if the disciple tries to kill him. The disciple is ignorant, but the guru knows that the soul is eternal. [...] Although*

Valmiki wanted to kill Narada, still Narada gave him so much mercy. <u>*The guru will never reject a disciple because the disciple is sinful. Even*</u> <u>*if the disciple is offensive, when the guru sees that the disciple has*</u> <u>*rendered so much service, he will not leave him. He is so kind.*</u> *[...] We see in Brhad-bhagavatamrta how the guru of Gopa Kumara came to him again and again over so many thousands and millions of years. [...] Similarly one may not see the reciprocation of the guru. But actually he loves his disciples more than anyone, and he is serving them and reciprocating with them as no one else can."*

The philosophy of Krishna consciousness is supportive of Srila Prabhupada knowing he was being poisoned and tolerating it. Srila Prabhupada knew his mission was protected. He could have zapped his poisoners into dust, but this is not the mood of a devotee. *"Being protected by the Supreme Personality of Godhead, a devotee is always powerful, but a devotee does not wish to show his power unnecessarily..."* (SBhag 6.17.37 Purport)

SBhag 7.7.10: *"...Indeed he is a great devotee, a powerful servant of the Supreme Personality of Godhead. Therefore you will not be able to kill him. Purport: There have been many instances in which demons or nondevotees have attempted to kill a devotee, but they have never been able to destroy a great devotee of the Supreme Personality of Godhead. [...] impossible for you to kill the child, even though you are demigods, and certainly it would be impossible for others.'"*

The conclusion is that Srila Prabhupada, although lethally poisoned over many months, perhaps even 18 months, as is scientifically and forensically established, did not depart because of the poisoning, which he miraculously withstood, but because it was his desire to do so, by the arrangement of Providence. This is the correct philosophical understanding, as there is no doubt he was "a great devotee" of the Supreme Personality of Godhead.

CHAPTER 63:
EXHUMATION OR LEGAL CASES?

EXHUMATION NOT NECESSARY NOR ADVOCATED

There is considerable fear-mongering about an exhumation of Srila Prabhupada from his Vrindaban tomb: *"That there has actually been a call by some to exhume the body of Srila Prabhupada to test for poison is so antithetical to respect for the sacred it reminds me more of the ghoulish activities of Duryodhana's adepts who presented him with the heads of the Pandava children thinking it would please him. Do these ghouls actually believe Prabhupada wants them to dig up his body? Could they actually bear to face his vapu again after almost of a quarter century being in the womb of the Earth Mother? Who amongst them would be the first to bring him out and look into his face? If these aliens want to begin testing for poison in this grotesque way, they should start by testing what kind of blood runs through their own hearts."*

There has been considerable speculation that the poison issue will not be settled until Srila Prabhupada's transcendental body is exhumed for forensic tests. In murder investigations, exhumations involve the removal of an interred body from a grave and then testing is performed. *But no one is proposing an exhumation.* No one recommends or favors exhumation. There is no need to exhume. There are *already sufficient hair and teeth samples,* which are part of Srila Prabhupada's body, that never went into the samadhi pit, in the possession of various devotees kept as sacred relics, *making exhumation redundant and unnecessary.*

In Appendix 13 are listed 5 known teeth that are in the hands of devotees. Some of them were extracted after mid-1976 and can be tested to determine poisoning or not, and the GBC has custody over more hair samples post mid-1976 as well. Sky-high levels of cadmium were found in three Srila Prabhupada's authentic hair samples. The thought of disturbing the pure devotee's samadhi is horrific and it is inconceivable that Srila Prabhupada's followers would allow such a drastic measure. Even Indian government authorities would be sensitive to public sentiments when dealing with a great Acharya such as Srila Prabhupada. It is not expected that government agencies would conduct an exhumation, as is normally done in USA homicide investigations. Dr. P. Kumar, C.M.O., Dept of Forensic Medicine, Safdarjung Hospital, Delhi: *"The Indian government will not proceed with exhumations unless they are 95% sure of bringing down a murder indictment."* That applies to ordinary murder cases: Srila Prabhupada is not an ordinary person. Of note, however, is that sometimes the grave of a saint will be moved if threatened by erosion from a river or some other emergency.

PROBABLE CAUSE FOR A GOVERNMENT INVESTIGATION

Eventually a government investigation will be launched into Srila Prabhupada's poisoning. This would follow from establishment of probable cause of murder based on scientific and expert assessment of the existing evidence as found to date. This has already been confirmed to be true. Once the verified and accredited scientific and forensic evidence is properly presented to secular agencies, more than sufficient "probable cause" will be recognized, and government will take the investigation forward. *That is the next phase in the investigation.* Governmental investigative and law enforcement agencies will become involved in Srila Prabhupada's poisoning case. There is no statute of limitation for murder in India. Gradually the demands and pressures from devotees, the public, and religious leaders, who want to settle the matter as to whether Srila Prabhupada was poisoned, will compel government to act. State agencies may order some type of testing to incontrovertibly determine the truth, which no one could stop. There are now novel methods to micro-tunnel with precision instruments and penetrate the ground remotely and mechanically, with miniscule, remote cameras, to obtain a very small sample for testing. Biopsy samples for testing may be obtained from Srila Prabhupada's Vrindaban samadhi by new technology of non-invasive methods. This is much less intrusive than an exhumation. This may occur beyond anyone's control. Law enforcement may require direct tests from the body rather than from hair that has been moving about or in storage for half a century. *Still, no one is suggesting or calling for any kind of exhumation.*

We note that ISKCON has opposed any kind of honest internal or external investigation and has repeatedly covered-up the evidence and suppressed even discussion of the issue. *If there will be any kind of exhumation* done by secular authorities, it will be the fault of ISKCON's leaders who could have easily tested samples from Srila Prabhupada's body (hair, teeth) but have refused to do so. It is now feared that these samples have been confiscated and disappeared by ISKCON's GBC. Better if more tests are done or someone comes forward with information or confession which would make exhumation unnecessary. *Conclusive proof of Srila Prabhupada's poisoning is already in hand and detailed in this book.* But to overcome the institutional denials and obstruction of this truth, government may decide to do some sort of exhumation to settle the matter. And that would be the GBC's fault.

WILL PRABHUPADA'S POISONING GO TO LEGAL ARENA?

Srila Prabhupada's poisoning will be addressed in the secular legal arena, but ISKCON will oppose this with fraud, bribery, and influence, even while they chide "poison theorists" for not taking the evidence to legal authorities. They stonewalled the child abuse investigation and forced the gurukulis to sue them in court. They adulterated Srila Prabhupada's books bit by bit until they were poisoned, forcing many scholars to convene and deem this to be even academically prohibited what to speak of spiritually offensive. They never shastricly justified their concocted guru system, though often resolving to do so. They suspended gurus for sexual improprieties and then reinstated them as deliverers of the fallen (not just Bhavananda). How much chicanery and farce does it take to see that the institutional misleaders are not dedicated to truth? We must not cooperate with a *criminal organization* controlled by: **(1)** those who poisoned Srila Prabhupada or **(2)** those benefitting from the deviated systems and doctrines that the poisoners introduced into ISKCON after 1977.

Legal action should be directed against the GBC, a West Bengal corporation, and not ISKCON, which holds Srila Prabhupada's assets and which must be, like Sita, rescued from the Ravanas. This illegal GBC has no legal standing in ISKCON temples outside India except where congregations resolved to accept individual GBC members as local directors (who can be voted out). Charges of financial and administrative malfeasance, infliction of emotional distress, abuse of office, employing deception, fraud, abuse of members... would be appropriate, as well as disobedience to scripture and the will of the Founder-Acharya, inflicting spiritual damage upon millions of followers. Hell knows no fury greater than that of devotees who have realized their GBC are criminals...

Tamal expired in 2002, and Bhakticharu in 2020, and as the two chief suspects, this has some bearing on the case. Nevertheless, other suspects remain alive. There is no statute of limitations for murder in both India or USA. Before legally pursuing the poisoners, the crime of Srila Prabhupada's malicious poisoning must be secularly established. It would seem the legal system of India would be the most appropriate and receptive venue to initiate police investigations and then legal court proceedings. It is simply a matter of organizing and presenting the evidence in a proper manner and beginning the process of criminal inquiry. This should be done by experts in India who can contend with the expected obstruction from ISKCON India. Srila Prabhupada is now a famous Indian national hero, with postage stamps and commemorative coins issued, and Indian national pride would not tolerate the unsolved crime of his poisoning, especially being surrounded by western disciples at the time of his death. If law enforcement and a criminal court ascertained that Srila Prabhupada was lethally poisoned, even without knowing by whom, this would precipitate seismic reformatory upheaval within the Hare Krishna movement. The cover-ups and denials will be the downfall of the present institutional leadership and force a total housecleaning. Devotees will reject all that has happened in ISKCON since Srila Prabhupada's departure-- doctrines, guru system, everything. The coming governmental confirmation of poisoning would energize the drive to find the poisoners and unravel ISKCON's other dark secrets.

PUT THEM IN JAIL AND THEN ALL DONE?

For many persons, perhaps most, when the poison matter is raised, they think in terms of obtaining justice in a mundane court of law, seeing the poisoning as simply a mundane crime that should be punished. They envision poisoners being convicted and going to jail. But poisoning crimes do not lend themselves to easy convictions as courts need a high level of proof in order to convict and punish those who break secular laws. This allows the GBC to maintain their dishonest position, *"Oh, there is no proof of a poisoning"* as long there are no convictions. Yet many crimes are proven without any convictions. Again, it is necessary to first prove the crime was committed before finding who did it.

It is very doubtful secular courts and judges can do much to correct the deviations introduced into Srila Prabhupada's spiritual mission of delivering the fallen souls. This kind of justice lies beyond the jurisdiction of mundane courts and law. E. g., in the court of Yamaraja (punishment after death), the poisoning of a pure devotee warrants a far heavier punishment than the poisoning of an ordinary man, whereas today's laws treat all men equally. Mundane laws do not consider animal killing a crime either. Pro-abortionists proclaim "My body, my choice" while not considering the unborn child's body and rights. True justice is dictated by the laws of Manu or God, not via defective, contradictory, speculative modern laws. Today there are no courts administered according to Vedic culture and the laws of Manu. So relying on the secular authorities to restore the movement after being plundered and abominated by poisoners is a pipedream. Rectification of the spiritual movement is beyond the understanding, capabilities, and jurisdiction of mundane courts or authorities. Courts can only determine if there was a crime and who did it, and punish by mundane standards.

The Hare Krishna Movement can only be advanced by sincere devotees following Srila Prabhupada's instructions, and only they are capable to restore purity to Srila Prabhupada's mission. Thus our focus is to establish the truth regarding Srila Prabhupada's physical poisoning and curing the poisoning of his divine mission and mercy. Srila Prabhupada's followers must rectify the anomalies that have developed since Srila Prabhupada's departure. **Secular courts cannot do this**. Still, if some degree of mundane justice is obtained, namely poisoners convicted, that would be good. *But there are much greater concerns at* *hand than just sending some poisoners to prison.* We should not be so obsessed with whether the evidence we have uncovered is court admissible or whether convictions for murder can be achieved. If these do come about, it will satisfy those wanting mundane justice, *but will do little to put Srila Prabhupada's mission back on the proper course that he had fought so hard to establish.* We are more interested in restoring the movement's original purity and removing the poisoners' corruptions and deviations. (Vol. 8, *Restoring Srila Prabhupada's Divine Mission*)

PREPARING TO EXPOSE THE TRUTH TO THE WORLD

In 2003-04 some Prabhupada Truth Commission members tried to bring the matter of Srila Prabhupada's poisoning into the legal arena in India. Legal and judicial contacts were developed to bring Srila Prabhupada's poisoning case into the Indian legal system as a criminal court murder case, by lodging a First Information Report (FIR), followed by a required police investigation, and then filing the case in criminal court. A trial would then follow. The FIR was lodged, forensic test results and evidence given to Indian authorities. Television shows and news reports attracted widespread attention, including a feature report on India's Star TV. Team members toured India for research, interviews, and meetings. Despite vigorous attempts, the legal filings failed as the case was misfiled and dismissed. Apparently the attorney was an ISKCON mole sabotaging the case. To initiate a successful legal investigation is hard and even if the Indian courts accepted the case, it could get bogged down for decades due to ISKCON's political influence. In India justice is often delayed and effectively denied. The goal of realizing an impartial and full legal investigation in India is problematic. A much broader and effective program to expose Srila Prabhupada's homicidal poisoning to the world would need to be organized.

The PTC has worked quietly for 20 years to build an expansive team of journalists, religious leaders, lawyers, judges, scientists, forensic experts, politicians, and ISKCON insiders. This media/ legal/ forensic/ devotee team will challenge the GBC with Srila Prabhupada's poisoning evidence, with new forensic studies and conclusive presentations, which will lead to a collapse of thisdenier regime. Forensic toxicologists, investigative anti-corruption journalists, sitting members of government, representatives of religious organizations, court judges, lawyers, honest ISKCON leaders, NAA experts, a foremost crime forensic laboratory, etc, coordinated in a mixed secular-spiritualist campaign to expose the truth of Srila Prabhupada's glorious departure pastimes. Coming soon... Also a civil legal action against the GBC individually and collectively is inevitable in light of their criminal and fraud operations.

CHAPTER 64:
IRREFUTABLE EVIDENCE SUMMARY

AURAL EVIDENCE: Multiple studies by a long list of prominent forensic audio labs have authenticated background voices and whispers of Nov. 11, 1977 room conversation recordings to be discussions about malicious poisoning by Srila Prabhupada's caretakers. Tamal, Jayapataka, and Bhavananda's voices were forensically discerned as the speakers. The GBC claims these whispers are indecipherable, but most devotees and experts hear them clearly with minimal enhancement and filtering. They have no innocuous explanation. The whispers are *"The poison's going down, the poison's going down," "Is the poison in the milk?" "It's poison,"* and *"Poisoning for a (long time)." Why are they whispering about poisoning Srila Prabhupada 3 days before his departure?* Being a pharmacist, chemist, and mystic clairvoyant, Srila Prabhupada knew he was being poisoned and he clearly stated three times on Nov. 9-10, 1977 *"Someone has poisoned me."* All his caretakers fully acknowledged he was speaking of homicidal poisoning, and not of "bad" medicine as claimed by ISKCON today. Nothing was done or came of these "poison discussions." CVVS tests have determined that there was considerable amounts of deceit in key sections of spoken conversation by leading disciples in late 1977. (Volume 2, 3)

HAIR TESTS: Arsenic And Cadmium: Dr. J. Steven Morris, Ph.D. conducted seven separate hair tests by neutron activation analysis at University of Missouri (MURR). A 1999 test by Balavanta of Srila Prabhupada's hair (Q-1) taken from his hairclippers contained 2.6 ppm of arsenic, 20 X more than average. This is not lethal but detrimental to health. Average "normal" amounts of hair arsenic (excluding seafood eaters) are 0.13 ppm. Chronic arsenic poisoning with serious health deterioration starts with 1-5 ppm arsenic in hair. Srila Prabhupada's arsenic level is synonymous with chronic arsenic poisoning levels and is expected to be a considerable contributing factor to his demise.

In reaction, some of the suspects secretly arranged to test two of their own samples of Srila Prabhupada's hair in late 1999 but abandoned them. The hair samples were located by PTC and forwarded to Dr. Morris who did NAA tests 2002-05, and he obtained a third sample from the same hairclippers. He found an average of 15.73 ppm cadmium in three samples, which is a sky-high level about 250 X more than the average normal, would be lethal in a short time, and could not come from any environmental or occupational contamination. The average normal level of hair cadmium is 0.064 ppm. Srila Prabhupada had cadmium levels 40 X more than those who were industrially poisoned. There is no plausible explanation for these cadmium levels found in multiple differently-sourced hair samples, other than homicidal malice fed by food or drink. These cadmium levels are unprecedented and not found in cases of major environmental or occupational exposure and accidents. The hair tests establish massive cadmium poisoning for 10 months from at least Feb. 1977. Cadmium was the primary poison with arsenic and antimony secondary. Antimony was 10 X Srila Prabhupada's normal levels, 8 X normal societal levels. Dr. Morris found normal levels of cadmium, arsenic, and antimony in pre-1977 hair samples.

WITNESSES & TESTIMONIES: There are a number of witnesses and testimonies (truth ascertainment tests in Volume 2, 3) which directly support the assessment of homicidal poisoning by way of a poison conspiracy to take over ISKCON. (Volume 5) Srila Prabhupada stated that he heard others speaking about his poisoning. Days after Srila Prabhupada departed, prime suspect Tamal discussed at length with Satsvarupa das in a taped *BTG* interview about supposedly being asked by Srila Prabhupada for *"medicine to die now."* (Volume 2) This is a virtual admission that he and others poisoned Srila Prabhupada, with an assisted suicide as their justification. No explanation by ISKCON's GBC or Tamal has ever been given for these statements. Tamal's statements on this tape are extremely incriminating and shocking. Bhakta Vatsala das, a gurukula student, testified he overheard senior devotees discussing the poisoning of Srila Prabhupada, confirmed by Ramanya, Durlab, and others. A series of respectable Vrindaban residents have privately testified as to knowledge of Srila Prabhupada's poisoning, including the witnessing of a urine test and four kavirajas agreeing on the diagnosis of Srila Prabhupada's poisoning in Nov. 1977. An antidote was prescribed but never given. There are other testimonies as well.

MEDICAL EVIDENCE: A long string of doctors and kavirajas examined Srila Prabhupada throughout 1977 but their diagnoses were contradictory and incorrect. Srila Prabhupada's cause of ill health was elusive and insidious. The health symptoms analysis indicates chronic cadmium and arsenic poisoning. Srila Prabhupada's health history has a list of physical symptoms which are unique to chronic cadmium and arsenic poisoning, such as conjunctivitis, photophobia, rhinitis, constant mucus and cough, and not attributable to diabetes or kidney disease. Chronic heavy metal poisoning causes and exacerbates diabetes and kidney failure. Prior to 1977 Srila Prabhupada's health was very good, and his diabetes was mild and non-insulin dependent. In 1977 Tamal aggressively discouraged the involvement of competent doctors to diagnose or treat Srila Prabhupada. Although Srila Prabhupada himself was not keen on doctors and medicines, he was determined to find a medical cure, but his caretakers declined non-invasive and simple medical tests even when they could be performed "at home." There was an endless changing and rejection of Ayurvedic and allopathic doctors. One of Srila Prabhupada's medicines was donated by the notorious Chandra Swami, later found to be involved in assassinations and poisons.

POLITICAL EVIDENCE: Institutional Denials, Stonewalling, Cover Ups: ISKCON ignored the advice that further investigation was warranted from their own investigator Balavanta das, whom they had underfunded and then sidelined. The GBC's irrational, hardline refusal to conduct an impartial, honest investigation itself supports the poisoning conclusion. ISKCON has vigorously and unreasonably denied ALL poisoning evidence. ISKCON's GBC and prime suspects conducted a series of fraudulent, sham cover-ups in 1998, 2000, and 2020. The disgraceful GBC books *NTIAP* (produced by suspects in their own defense) and *Deception*, are devious evidence manipulations with fraud, lies, deceit. The GBC failed miserably trying to deny the poison whispers and to designify the arsenic levels found in Srila Prabhupada's 1977 hair. They erroneously claimed average "normal" arsenic in hair can be anything up to 10-12 ppm, while actually it is 80 times less. The GBC twisted Srila Prabhupada's statements about being poisoned into claims he denied being poisoned. The incredible resistance, denials, blackmail, and institutional repression represents a massive cover-up of Srila Prabhupada's poisoning, showing that ISKCON is hiding poisoners in their midst. Such fraudulent cover-ups are damning evidence in itself.

SUSPECTS: The character and history of the primary suspects in Srila Prabhupada's poisoning are such that it is no surprise that they poisoned Srila Prabhupada. (Volume 2, 3) The idea that Srila Prabhupada was only surrounded by loving disciples is naive. The evidence finds beyond a reasonable doubt that Tamal was deeply involved in Srila Prabhupada's poisoning. Incriminating evidence shows Bhakticharu, Jayapataka, and Bhavananda to be highly suspected as well. ISKCON's takeover by Tamal and others was a very compelling motive to eliminate Srila Prabhupada, and they profited immensely with enormous power, prestige, wealth, and thousands of followers. *ISKCON was guru-jacked and infiltrated by Srila Prabhupada's poisoners.* Tamal has been found to be guilty in this poisoning beyond a reasonable doubt with 97% certainty. His "mercy-killing" tape recording made days after Srila Prabhupada's departure is especially incriminating. There are also three other primary suspects in Srila Prabhupada's poisoning: Bhakticharu Swami, Jayapataka Swami, and Bhavananda. All the primary suspects had more than ample motive, opportunity, and means, and they became zonal acharyas as soon as Srila Prabhupada had been removed by the cadmium poisoning. Bhakticharu has multiple contradicting statements which means he lied and was hiding the truth.

EXPERT OPINIONS: The GBC has presented one expert opinion in 23 years to support their position of no poisoning evidence, but they misinformed Dr. VV Pillay that PTC claimed pure metal cadmium was the poison used. Dr. Pillay did not read our book and was engaged "off the cuff," ad hoc replying only to what little he was told, rendering his opinion useless. Our volume however, lists 10 expert opinions, several of which are composites of many scientific studies and opinions. Dr. Page Hudson, who gave his opinions on Dr. Morris' hair test results, was a poisoning expert and chief medical examiner for North Carolina, having studied and solved many heavy metal poisoning cases. Dr. Anil Aggarwal, Dr. Dipankar Chakraborti, and Dr. A. Chatt gave expert opinions, as did ARL (Arizona), a commercial firm specializing in hair tests for hundreds of thousands of clients. From the body of scientific literatures, we compiled a consensus of many studies on the average normal levels for cadmium, arsenic, and antimony in human hair, as well as regarding the lethality, morbidity, pathology, and toxicity of cadmium poisoning. Dr. J. Steven Morris, an expert NAA technician and nuclear scientist, verified the authenticity of seven hair tests, three normal, one with elevated arsenic, three with astronomical cadmium levels.

Expert opinions from audio forensic analysts about audio recordings made in 1977 have determined beyond doubt there were several caretakers of Srila Prabhupada in his last days who engaged in conversation, whispers, and murmurs about poisoning. Jack Mitchell (CAE, NM), Tom Owens (Owl Investigations, NJ), J.P. French (UK), James Reames (JBR Technologies, VA), and another major forensic firm (2022) all confirmed secretive, conspiratorial talk of poisoning.

CONCLUSIONS: For devotees who have faith in Srila Prabhupada's words, his statements about being poisoned are solid proof that he was given poison with homicidal intent. For others, the levels of heavy metals, especially cadmium, in Srila Prabhupada's hair is scientific and final proof of his being poisoned with homicidal intent. ISKCON leadership still includes some of those who poisoned Srila Prabhupada or knew about it, and includes those who learned of it afterwards. The ISKCON GBC will not cooperate with any further investigation. It is useless to expect anything honest from them.

Add it all up: the cadmium and arsenic in the hair, the medical symptoms unique to cadmium/arsenic poisoning and not to diabetes/kidney disease, the witnesses and testimonials, the forensically certified poison whispers ("the poison's going down, etc), the poison discussions about malicious poisoning ("Someone has poisoned me…"), the motives of the suspects (very ambitious), the institutional non-cooperation and cover-ups (the suspects ban any further investigation after their own deceitful whitewash report), Tamal's bizarre mercy-killing interview ("He asked for medicine to die…"), the four kavirajas concluded poisoning , and other evidence – there is no room for further doubt: Srila Prabhupada was poisoned with intent to murder.

The Founder Acharya of ISKCON, His Divine Grace AC Bhaktivedanta Swami Srila Prabhupada, was homicidally poisoned by heavy metals in 1977, involving a clique of ambitious disciples who took his seat and assets by falsely assuming the posts of "enlightened" guru-acharyas. In the last 45 years these poisoners and heirs who have shared the spoils of the "crime of the millennium" have gained vast wealth, power, fawning disciples, and phony prestige. The matter demands government investigation and that justice be served. Many books have been published on this subject: **(1) 1999:** *Someone Has Poisoned Me* **(2) 2000:** *Not That I Have Been Poisoned* (ISKCON denial) **(3) 2003:** *Judge For Yourself* **(4) 2017:** *Kill Guru Become Guru: The Poisoning of Srila Prabhupada's Body (online e-book)* **(5) 2020:** *Deception: Poison Conspiracy Fraud (from GBC).* **(6). 2022:** *Srila Prabhupada's Hidden Glories: His Inconceivable Tolerance and Mercy (hardcover print edition).* **(7)** This *Personal Ambition* series of 12 volumes.

ISKCON GBC WILL NOT BE EXCUSED

A possible future outcome of the growing, widespread acceptance that Srila Prabhupada was maliciously poisoned in 1977 by his own caretakers is that ISKCON's GBC will eventually be compelled to concede that, yes, this may have happened. But they will say: **(1)** this crime did not involve present-day institutional leaders, since it was done 50 years ago, maybe by Tamal and Bhakticharu, who are now dead, **(2)** by denying the evidence, the GBC was only trying to protect the movement, and now that the poisoning evidence seems conclusive, it can be accepted, **(3)** however, everything should continue in ISKCON unchanged, **(4)** meanwhile, they will stall until Bhavananda, Jayapataka, others pass away, since remaining suspects are now very old and frail.

We must expect and be prepared for this ultimate deceit by the ISKCON GBC. Srila Prabhupada's poisoners hijacked the institution and introduced poisonous doctrines and deviant siddhanta, causing horrible spiritual pain and chaos for countless devotees. They poisoned Srila Prabhupada's books, his instructions, his movement, and the minds of innocent devotees. They perpetuated devotee and child abuse either themselves or by allowing such in a club of abusers. They have turned millions away from Srila Prabhupada and towards themselves as false gurus, until they are exposed as fallen, and then Srila Prabhupada is given as a consolation prize, but only as the "grandfather." The present GBC has inherited their positions as elite managers and absolute gurus with fawning disciples, wealth, and worship solely due to Srila Prabhupada's poisoning. Their positions were falsely created by the poisoners. They cannot keep their ill-gotten, illegal positions that came as a result of Srila Prabhupada's poisoning, any more than accomplices of a bank robber can keep the bank's stolen money. They are heirs to the Acharya's poisoning.

The ISKCON GBC has proven itself to be incapable of protecting Srila Prabhupada's legacy and mission, by harboring the poisoners and in many other scandals. Their legitimacy is zero. The dictates of illegitimate leaders are also illegitimate. All that they have done with and to ISKCON is also illegitimate and must be scrapped. We must return to the situation on Nov. 14, 1977, and, without interference from the personally ambitious, hopelessly corrupted GBC, carefully ascertain how to go forward according to the will and instructions of Srila Prabhupada. The poisoners' heirs, as aiders and abettors after, or even during, the fact must be removed permanently. The corrupt regime cannot pass the blame for ISKCON's poisoned condition to Tamal and company alone.

RESTORE THE MISSION

"Whenever an acharya comes, following the superior orders of the Supreme Personality of Godhead or His representative, he establishes the principles of religion, as enunciated in Bhagavad-gita. [...] It is the acharya's duty to spread a bona fide religious system [...] Unfortunately, when the acharya disappears, rogues and nondevotees take advantage and immediately begin to introduce unauthorized principles in the name of so-called swamis, yogis, philanthropists, welfare workers and so on. Actually, human life is meant for executing the orders of the Supreme Lord, and this is stated in Bhagavad-gita (9.34): [...] The acharya, the authorized representative of the Supreme Lord, establishes these principles, but when he disappears, things once again become disordered. The perfect disciples of the acharya try to relieve the situation by sincerely following the instructions of the spiritual master."
SBhag 4.28.48 Purport

Srila Prabhupada's divine mission was hijacked by ambitious disciples who deviated from the Founder-Acharya's instructions and proceeded to inject deviant doctrines into the ISKCON institution. It began with Srila Prabhupada's horrendous heavy metals poisoning in 1977. Srila Prabhupada entrusted the Hare Krishna Movement to the hands of his faithful followers, and humanity with its billions of lost souls depend on them to rectify this transcendental movement. It is up to us. Now is the time to show what we are made of. *Speak truth in any way you can.* Let the voice of truth roar. Expose the corruption. Be full of hope and courage, because the truth always prevails. Srila Prabhupada's faithful followers need to confront the *criminal enterprise* of the ISKCON guru regime. It is a racket, a plundering of the true Acharya's assets and mission. We must expose them to the devotee world. Undo the indoctrinations in the minds of the innocent, exploited Krishna bhaktas, in a campaign of spiritual awakening. Never allow despair or fear to overcome. The truth sets us free. May the darkness spread by the "sinister movement" be exposed by the light of truth, and Srila Prabhupada's divine mission be restored as he gave it to us.

APPENDIX 1:
CHIEF MEDICAL EXAMINER'S STATEMENT

DELAWARE HEALTH AND SOCIAL SERVICES

Office of Chief Medical Examiner	Forensic Sciences Center
Richard T. Callery, M.D., F.C.A.P.	Dir., Forensic Sciences Laboratory
February 5, 1999.	Re: Srila Prabhupada

Dear Mr. Ogle: I have reviewed your letters of Jan. 7, 1998 and Jan. 6, 1999, with the two-sheet chronology of events from late 1976 to Oct., 1997, and the toxicology report from the Univ. of Mo-Columbia, Jan. 6, 1999. In your cover letter you state that Srila Prabhupada turned 81 year of age the Aug. prior to his death. During 1977, he progressively grew thin, becoming emaciated weighing no more than 75-80 pounds. At the time of his death, he was completely bedridden and could not walk or move himself. You also state that he had a history of multiple myocardial infarcts and non-insulin dependent diabetes mellitus related to age that was controlled. I note that the report from the Univ. of Mo-Columbia indicates that the arsenic concentrations found in the hair was approx. 20 times higher than what would be considered normal for unexposed individuals living in the US. You have discussed with me his living status and he was not exposed to endemic arsenic concentrations noted in some areas of India significantly prior to his death and that the hair trimming recovered from the shaving device would have been those expected to be found there from use shortly before his death.

Chronic arsenic poisoning can give a variety of symptoms, many of which are non-specific and likely to also be those associated with debilitating illnesses of other causes. Chronic arsenic poisoning results from a rather continuous exposure to very low concentrations of arsenic or repeated ingestions of small doses over varied intervals of time. In continuous exposures, gastrointestinal disturbances may be slight or non-existent and non-specific complaints of anorexia, weight loss, weakness and malaise predominant although dermatitis, stomatitis, peripheral neuropathy and hematological disorders may indicate possible arsenic poisoning. If the exposure was intermittent rather than continuous, the periodic ingestion of small doses of arsenic would be expected to produce gastric disturbances in addition to the other signs of chronic arsenic poisoning. It is my opinion, to a reasonable degree of medical certainty, that this individual, with the history of multiple myocardial infarcts (heart palpitations) and non-insulin dependent diabetes mellitus, and considering his age, would be an individual in frail health in which a chronic administration or exposure of arsenic leading to toxic levels would be expected to be a significant contributing condition to his death. If I can be of any further assistance in this case, please contact me. Yours sincerely, Richard T. Callery, M.D., F.C.A.P.

Chief Medical Examiner, Director Forensic Sciences Laboratory

---

APPENDIX 2:
TRANSLATIONS OF THE LAST TAPES

Translations arranged by Naveen Krishna das, former GBC. Notes inserted. **KEY:** H/Hindi; B/Bengali. **ConvBk Vol. 36 p. 354,** Vrindaban. (The actual date is Nov. 9, 1977). Tape dates were often inaccurate.

Tape T-44 side A: DP Shastri Kaviraja (KAV): (H) Ye apki darshan ke liye Balaramji Misra. Aap jante hai inko? Chaitanya Mahabrabhu ke... (*Here is Balarama Misra come to see you. Do you know him? (He) is from Chaitanya...*) **Balaram Misra (BM):** (B) Aami edike aachi Maharaja. Aami Balarama Misra, chinte perechen to aamake? (*I am over here Maharaja. I am Balarama Misra, do you recognize me?*) **SP:** Han. (*Yes.*) **BM:** (B) Kaviraj'er shonge aamar onek purono aalap aache. Taa, kalke aamar shonge dakhai holo. Bole ...Maharaja aamaye dekecchen? Aamar to boro shoubhagya to..mane eyi shutre aamaro dakhaa hoye jabe. Keno bohudin purbe jokhon Thakura boseni takhun..... (*I am known to kaviraja for a long time. Well, yesterday I met him (kaviraja), he said, Maharaja (SP) has called for me. It is a great honor for me...that is.. this way I get a chance to meet you. Because many days ago, when the deity had not been installed...*) **SP:** oi ta ke? se aldah? (difficult to confirm what is said) (*Where are they (Deities)?..are they there?*) **BM:** Han. Aache. Aache Maharaja. Ami bhaablaam jadi ektu dakhaa kore aashi aamio... (*Yes. They are there.*

They are there Maharaja. I thought, if I could come and see you...)

SP: (B) Hotat (sarir kharap) hoe gelo. Bes kaj cholchilo, ki jani ki holo? Keu bole je poison kore dieche. Hote pare. *(Suddenly I fell sick. Everything was all right, I don't know what happened. Somebody said that poison has been given. May be true.)* **BM:** Hain. *(Yes.)* **SP:** Besh kaaj cholche? *(Is work going on well?)* **BM:** Hain. *(Yes.)* **BM:** Hmm? **KAV:** (H) Kya farma rahe hai? *(What are you saying?)* **SP:** (H) Koi bolta hai je, koi poison deya hai. *(Someone says that, somebody has given me poison.)* **KAV:** Kisko? *(to whom?)* **SP:** Mujhko. *(To me.)* **KAV:** Kaun bolta hai? *(Who is saying?)* **SP:** Ye saab friends. *(All these friends.)* **BCS:** (B) Ke boleche Srila Prabhupada? *(Who said, Srila Prabhupada?)* **SP:** Ke boleche. *(Someone said.)* **Tamal:** Krishna das? *(Whispers)* **KAV:** (H) Aapko kaun poison dega? kisleye dega? *(Who will give you poison? For what, why?)* **Tamal:** Who said that, Srila Prabhupada? **SP:** I do not know, but it is said. **Devotee:** (whispers) *... said, it's poison.*

SP: (B) Aapni to... jotish janen? *(You do know astrology?)* **KAV:** (H) Kya bolte hain? *(What's (he) saying?)* **SP:** Balarama Misra... **BCS:** (B) Aapni to jotish janen? *(You do know astrology?)* **BM:** Na.. Na... *(No.. No...)* **KAV:** (H) Yea to jotish nahi, pundit ye hain. *(He is not an astrologer, he is a scholar.)* **SP:** Hain? *(What?)* **KAV:** Yea to pundit hain. Jotish nahi jante hain. *(He is a scholar. Doesn't know astrology.)* **SP:** Hmm. **KAV** Karam kanda jante hain. *(He knows Karma Kanda.)* **BCS:** (H) Aap to thora kuchh jante hain na? Thora mutlub aap to jante hain? *(You must know a little bit? Little meaning; you know something?)* **KAV:** Thora bahout dekhlete hai. *(I do look through it a bit.)* **BCS:** (B) Shastriji janen, Srila Prabhupada. *(Shastriji (kaviraja) knows, SP.)* **KAV: (H)** Aap ko kisne bataye tha ke abhi o kushti ke andar aapko mar-case hai? Koye jotishne bataya tha? *(Who showed you that under your horoscope your death had come? Some astrologer showed you?)* **SP:** (H) Kya bataya tha? *(What was shown ?)* **BCS:** (B) Oi je aapnar aayu sesh hoye gecche aapni bolicchelen, shete ke kono jotish bolecchen? (no answer) Kushthiko bicar me waisa tha. *(You were saying that your life has come to an end, did some astrologer tell you that?* (no answer) (Hindi) *There was something* (like that) *in the horoscope.)* [...]

NOTES: Shastri says Srila Prabhupada will stay 10 more years. They talk about medicine from the market. Srila Prabhupada, Shastri, Balarama Misra (BM), BCS discuss the Chaitanya Mahaprabhu temple needing repairs, who will make the estimate for the Bhaktivedanta Charity Trust. Raw tumeric was being sought. Balarama Misra is offered ten rupees by Srila Prabhupada as charity to a brahmana.

BM: (B) No. samman hi to samman... apni keyethe to samman... boleye... apna je, aapni bolecchen ayi aamar jotheshto, bujhlen naa? Oyi taakaate je aamar... eyi... aapnaar aashirbad, ebong aami chaayi je aabar aapni bhogoban aapnaake aabar. *(No. Respect is respect. You say it, that's enough... You said that I was an astrologer, do you understand? That's money to me... this... your blessing (I need). What I want is that again, God will again make you.)* **SP:** Se taa aapni chaaiben... Aamaro kortobyo aache. *(That of course you will want. I also must do my duties.)*

KAV: (H) Yeh Maharaja, yeh kotha aap kaise bola aaj ki koi bola hi ki poison diya hai? Ye aapko kuuch abhaas hua hai, kya? *(This thing, Maharaja. You know how you said today that someone said somebody gave you poison? Did anyone tell you or you got some indication somewhere?)* **SP:** Nahin. Eyse koi bola jo denese ye hota hai. Shayed koi kithabme likkha hai. *(No. Someone said that, this kind of symptoms* *manifest if someone is poisoned. May be there is such a mention in some book.)* **KAV:** Woh koi khana se ho jata hai. Kaccha mercury se ho jata hai. Ye aur koi bhi cheez aisa hai jis se ho jata hai. Mane aapke liye kaun karega? Ham to yeh samajhta... ki aise devpurush ke liye koi manshik aisa bichar karega woh be rakshasa hai. *(Yes I know that such things happen if raw mercury is administered. Or there are some other things also which can cause such illness. But who will do such a thing for a Godly person like you. According to me if someone has such thoughts for you then he is a demon.)* **Tamal:** What did Prabhupada say? **NOTES:** Discussions continue, with SP, Tamal, Balarama Misra, Kaviraj, Svarupa Damodara, Giriraj Swami. Deity installations and praise for Srila Prabhupada's achievements are mentioned.

Svarupa Damodar: Prabhupada wants to do here. He's going to... **Tamal:** Is he going to do it here? (speak together) **Svarupa Damodar:** Prabhupada's requesting here. He said it's better if we do it here. So he said, "Make all the arrangements necessary." **Tamal:** He wants to bring the brahmins to inaugurate the Bombay temple, Srila Prabhupada? **SP:** That we shall consider later. **Tamal:** Cause we already told these South Indian brahmins to come. **SP:** Some of them may go also. **Tamal:** Do you know this man from a long time ago? **SP:** Yes. **Tamal:** He wants some money for some temple? **SP:** Yes. **Tamal:** Here in Vrindaban? (**NOTES:** SP asks if 10 Rs was given. Talks about a bank account.) **Giriraj:** [...] I spoke to Bombay to see how things were doing, and Gopala Krishna said that everything is going nice, and he's coming here on Friday, after two days. So I told him that your condition was very serious and that I wanted to stay here for a little longer. So he said that was okay. And I confirmed with Yasodanandana Swami's assistant that he sent the letter to the South Indian brahmins to confirm that they could come on the dates which we have fixed. So we are waiting to hear that reply. **SP:** You can take some Brahmin from here. Balarama Misra. **Giriraj:** Yes. **SP:** They'll chant Veda-mantra very nice. **Giriraj:** Uh-huh... We can have these brahmanas and the South Indian brahmanas. (Letter from China) **END T-44-A. //Tape T-44 Side B,** ConvBk Vol. 36, p. 359, Nov. 9.

Tamal: *Srila Prabhupada? You said before that you... that it is said that you were poisoned?* **SP:** *No. These kind of symptoms are seen when a man is poisoned. He said like that, not that I am poisoned.* **Tamal:** *Yeah. Did anyone tell you that, or you just know it from before?* **SP:** *I read something.* **Tamal:** *Ah, I see. That's why actually we cannot allow anyone to cook for you.* **SP:** *That's good.* **Tamal:** *Jayapataka Maharaja was telling that one acharya, Sankaracharya, of the Sankaracharya line, this is a while ago, he was poisoned to death. Since that time, none of the acharyas or the gurus of the Sankaracharya line will ever take any food cooked except by their own men.* **SP:** *My Guru Maharaja also.* **Tamal:** *Oh. You, of course, have been so merciful that sometimes you would take prasada cooked by so many different people.* **SP:** *That should be stopped.*

Tamal: Are you feeling any pain, Srila Prabhupada? **SP:** No. Urine bottle. **Tamal:** Urine? You want to try for it? Okay. Should we again continue some kirtan Srila Prabhupada? Okay. (kirtan) **SP:** Hm. Through. **Upendra:** Fifty, Srila Prabhupada. (**NOTES:** Tamal reviews a letter from SP's son M.M. De; they discuss banks. There is discussion about arranging for the brahmanas from South India who will conduct the upcoming opening of the new Bombay temple.)

Tamal: Would you like to hear kirtan, Srila Prabhupada? **BREAK** (Hindi talks)

KAV: Aaj darad to nahin hua...pisab hote hue? Shyam ko hua kuchh? (*Today did you have pain while passing urine? Did anything happen in the evening?*) **SP:** Thodasa. (*Little.*) **KAV:** Kuchh thoda hota hai, ab to chalenge Mayapur? Iccha hai? (*Some little is happening, now off to Mayapur. You have a desire (to go)?*) **SP:** Iss avastha me, kahin nahin jayega. (*In this state, going nowhere.*) **KAV:** Theek yeh avastha thodi hi barabar rahegi. Mujhe iccha to hain na mansik. (*Your state (of health) is not going to remain like this forever. I have a desire in my mind.*) **SP:** Han. (*Yes.*) [More talk about repairing that temple.] **Devotee:** Ghabrahati to kam hi na? (*The distress is less now?*) **KAV:** Kuchh bechani to kam hai na? (*The uneasiness is less isn't it?*) **BCS:** It's less now, this restlessness and the pain. **KAV:** Pisab nahin hota time me ? Thoda? ab pisab? (*Urine is not happening on time? A little? Urinate now?*) **Devotee:** Prabhupada? **BCS:** He didn't pass urine after that. Last one is 5 past 12. **BHAV:** That's all. He hasn't passed any. **SP:** Hm? **BCS:** He asking about urine, Srila Prabhupada, whether you passed urine afterwards. **NOTES:** SP talks of his son's stipend. Bhagatji offers to go to see the temple and make an estimate for repairs. Bhagatji went to Agra the day before to check on stone signs. (Whispering in the background)

BCS: Srila Prabhupada, ektu han korun, to oshudh dicchi. (SP, open your mouth a little, giving oshudh.) **SP:** Ki abbar? (*What again?*) **BCS:** Aarok. (*medicine*). **SP:** Hmm. **BCS:** Ektu han, ektuhani aache, alpo ektu aache. (*Open your mouth. A little is left. Only a little bit.*) **KAV:** Thoda pani dedo. (*Give a little water.*) **BREAK/ END OF T-45 SIDE A. //TAPE T-45, SIDE B:** Conv Bks Vol 36 p. 365. Late Nov. 10, 1977:

KAV (H): Aaj tatti hua tha kya? (*Did you pass stool today?*) **SP:** Hmm. **KAV:** Subha? (*In the morning?*) **SP:** Hmm. **KAV:** Bhanna? (*Loose?*) **BCS:** 150. **KAV:** Bhanna hua tha? (*Was it loose?*) **BCS:** Han. Thodasa. Dark green. (*Yes, a little.*) **KAV:** Woh purya to aaj laiege, purya to daydia. (*Bring that dose (medicine) today... given a dose (already).*) **BCS:** He gave a medicine yesterday to control the stool, so we have to get it today. **KAV:** Pulse over ninety. **Tamal:** 90. That's not bad. But is it strong or weak? **KAV:** Stronger. **Tamal:**Your pulse is stronger now, Srila Prabhupada. Shastriji says that your pulse is normal rate and stronger. I think the kirtan is having a good effect, SP. **SP:** Hm. **KAV:** Yebhi to maha aushadhi hi hai... Krishna Naam. (*This is also a great medicine, Krishna's Name.*) **SP:** Bhagavan Sri. [Shastri talks about herbs.]

SP: Suna Hai. Yaad hota hai. (*Heard about (it). Memory is there.*) **KAV:** Uske mul chahiye hamko. Woh hone se kya hoga ki; automatic thora sa pisaab jaada hokarke aapko barabar trouble nahin hoga, ek saath hi pisaab ho jayegaa. Pisaab jaada hokarke jaldi jaldi aapki jo bimari, woh mitegi. (*Its root is needed. If I had that what would happen; automatically (your) urine will increase a little and you won't be troubled constantly. The urine will happen in one go. When the urine increases quickly your disease, will cure.* **SP:** Hmm. Dekhi. (*Hmm. Let's see.*) [...] **BCS** He's explaining about the medicine that if he gets the medicine it will be all right. **BHAV:** Which medicine? **BCS:** The one that he went to look for in the forest. **BHAV:** Oh. **BCS:** He's telling that Prabhupada's condition is not bad right now. (indistinct) take care of him and Prabhupada shouldn't be left alone. [...] **KAV:** 140 by 75. **Tamal:** 75. **KAV:** Ekdam correct. **Tamal:** Just right. What was the pulse this morning? **BCS** (Hindi): Subhe pulse kitne tha? (*What was the pulse rate this morning?*) **KAV:** Subhe bur gaya tha. Subhe ka pulse ka sthiti thi inki 115. (*It increased this morning. This morning his pulse rate was 115.*) **BCS** (English): Morning his pulse rate was 115. **KAV:**

Abhi to 90 pulse rate hai. Manye abhi heart bahut badya kaam karta. Ekdam jitna good condition mein kaam karna chaahiye, utna kaam kar raha. (Now the pulse rate is 90. Now his heart is working very well. As much as a heart can be expected to work, it is working that well.) **BCS**: Now his heart is in perfect order.

BHAV: So what was the cause of that distress? **BCS**: Kaise woh kai hua tha subha? (What happened this morning?) **KAV** (H): Ye Maharaja ne kya to, samajh me nahin aata kya. (What Maharaja did, it cannot be understood.) **BCS**: He says Srila Prabhupada has done it himself. **KAV**: Minton mein theek ho jate. Minton mein kur jate. Aapko itna sardi lagti hai, subhe to bola to ekdam sab kapda hata diye. Subhe garmi nahin laga? (One minute it (pulse) is good, the next minute it's done again. You feel irritable. (I've heard) in the morning (you) removed all cloth. Were you feeling warm this morning?) **SP**: Hain. *(Yes.)* **KAV**: Ekdam sab kapde phenk di aapne subha. (Absolutely all cloth was thrown off by you this morning.) **KAV**: Tatti ki liyen hum inko eisa karenge ya do roz se ek tatti hoga, to bariya hai. Mal jo hai, ab mal thoda roknese, inmaa takat lane ki aavabhyakta hai. (To make him pass stool, (I will) do something, so that (he) will pass once every two days. This will be very good. Now if stop the mal (?) some possibility is there for (building) strength.) **BCS**: Accha. Woh jo hai, tatti ka rung hua tha hara. (Okay. The thing is, the colour of (his) stool was green.) **KAV**: Hara hua tha? *(Was it green?)* **BCS**: Man hamara khayal, woh jo dawai hai, jo Makoi ka ras dete hai. (My understanding is, that medicine, that Makoi ka ras that's being given...) **KAV**: Nai, nai.Hara ko matalab... liver kaam karta aacha. *(No, no. Green means... the liver is working fine.)* [Talk about SP's liver and tonic].

KAV: Abhi, iss time, pathological test se inko koi taklif nahin hai. Ab kya test maniye, kya nahin maniye. Pulse ekdam theek. Heart theek. (Now, at this time, pathological tests, he is having no problems. Now what test to accept, what not to accept. Pulse is all right. Heart is all right.) **BCS**: He says from pathological point of view, there is nothing wrong. **KAV**: General condition ekdam *(very)* good. **BCS**: His condition of the heartbeat is perfect. **Tamal:** So what is wrong? **BCS**: Blood pressure is perfect. **Tamal:** That means a spiritual... **BCS** (Hindi): To taklif kiun hota hai aisa? (Then why are there problems like this?) **SP** (Hindi): Nahin, us samaye hua tha. *(No, it happened back then.)* **BCS**: Hmm, us samaye hua tha. At that time it happened, but now it's all right. **NOTES**: They talk about the effects of Saturn on SP's health.

Tamal: (background) But what did Prabhupada just say? **KAV** (speaking over BCS): Jaise subhe position tha, subhe inka position tha na taklif hui na? ham das purya dene se jaise heart eise good position... ki ek purya se heart aisa... kya bolega bataiye ? kya mahatwa lagayenge? (How the position was this morning, the position was; there were problems, wasn't there? Had I given ten doses his heart would not have been in the position it is. Now with one dose his heart is... What can I say tell me? What definition can attach?) **BCS**: He said, How can you define it? How can you explain it? **Tamal:** But what did Prabhupada just say? **BCS**: Like the condition couldn't have improved by ten medicines also, but one medicine it becomes perfect. **Tamal:**What did Prabhupada just say? **BCS**: Prabhupada just said that I mean, this morning his condition was bad not now.

BHAV: Prabhupada was complaining of mental distress this morning also. **BCS**: SP? **SP**: Hmm? **BCS**: (Beng) Ota ki byapaar hoyechelo? mental distress? (What is that problem? mental distress?) **SP**: Hmm. Hmm. **KAV**: (Hindi) Boliye, boliye. *(Say, say.)*

SP: (H): Wohi bat jo koi hamko poison kya. (That same thing, that someone has poisoned me.) **BCS:** O aacha, uno soch na ki koi. (Oh, okay, he thinks that someone.) **BHAV:** Eemm? **KAV** (speaking over BCS): Dekhiye bat yehi hai ki kisi rakshas ne diya ho. **BCS:** Someone gave him poison here. **KAV:** Caru swami... **BCS:** Yes. **KAV:** ...kisi rakshas ne diya ho. Yeh to ho sakta hai. Impossible nehi hain. Woh Sankaracharya the; unhe kisi ne poison diya. Cheh mahina tak woh bari taklif paye. Kanch to hota hai na ? botal ke kanch, yeh pees ke khane mein khila diya. To usko kya nitaja hua; bara mahina baad mai, leprosy ho gaya sab sharir ki undar. To karam to apna bhugte hai. Kintu jo medicine ham dai raka hai; jadi koi uska effect hoga poison to rahe nahin sakta, guaranteed bolta hai. Ki woh be effected hoga to rahin nahi sakta. Ki abhi to ham pakar nahin saktai usko unko diya hua hai. Abhi bhi pakarta hai jab kidney kharab ho gaya, kisi kahena ya bimari se ho, chai grahan se ho, chai poison se. (*See, the thing is, it's possible a demon might have given, Charu Swami, (BCS says "yes") some demon might have given, it's not impossible, Sankaracharya was there, someone gave him poison, for 6 months Sankaracharya was in lot of difficulty, someone ground the glass of bottle and mixed in the food, then what was the result, 12 months later, the man who gave this got leprosy in his entire body, so for that karmic reactions he has to face but the medicine that I am giving, if that has any effect, then the poison won't remain, I can guarantee that, now I cannot catch if it is given to him, if it is found that his kidney is spoiled then it could be by sickness or astrological reason or by poison.*)

Tamal: Prabhupada was thinking that someone had poisoned him? **BCS** (*not Adri*): Yes. **Tamal:** That was the mental distress? **BCS:** Yes. **KAV:** Yeh bolte hai to isme kuch na kuch satya he. Isme koi sandeha nahin. (*This is what he says, then there must be some truth in it. In this there is no doubt.*) **Tamal:** What did KAV just say? **BCS:** He said that when Srila Prabhupada was saying that, there must be something truth behind it. **Tamal:** Sheessh... (*Everyone speaking*) **BCS:** ...ya that someone gave him poison... you know ... they powdered the glass... **KAV:** Koi rakshas hai... daina wallah. Pan me ek cheez de doon. Kya batun, doodh me de doon. Khana ek pan me dwai de doon, subhe me jindagi be bhool sakhoge. (It's some rakshasa... the poisoner, will put something in pan. What to say (or) something in milk. To eat, will put a medicine in pan, by the morning whole life can be forgotten.) **Tamal:** Srila Prabhupada, Shastriji says that there must be some truth to it if you say that. ***So who is it that has poisoned? (SRILA PRABHUPADA DOES NOT ANSWER; SILENCE.)***

KAV: Sabse bada poison to hota hai woh mercury ka hota hai. (The most powerful poison is mercury.) **BCS:** Woh to Gaya tha unka woh jo... (*That thing of his was gone...*) **KAV:** Nahin nahin, woh to Svarupa Guha tha. Aap para tha na swamiji? Kalkatte me? (*No, no, that was Svarupa Guha. You read about it didn't you, Swamiji? In Calcutta?*) **SP:** Hmm. **KAV** Svarupa Guha? **BCS:** Unko malum nahin. (*Svarupa Guha. He doesn't know (about it).*) **KAV:** Uska pati ne diya tha. (*Her husband had given it.*) **BCS:** Aacha. (*Okay.*) **KAV:** Uski koi medicine nahin aatha aap ki leya. Itni dose de diya. jisko hamlok Rashkapoor bolte hain. (*For it there is no medicine or antidote. Such a heavy dose was given. It's what we call Rashkapoor.*) **BCS:** Nahin. Woh jo mercury isme tha woh makharadhwaja. (No. That mercury was in the makharadhwaja.) **KAV:** Nahin, nahin. Woh mercury nahin hain. Uska doosra nam bolte hai. (No, no, not that mercury, there is different form of it.) **BCS:** Aacha.

BHAV: What did he say? **BCS:** He said that it's quite possible that mercury, it's a kind of poison...

Bhagatji: That makharadhwaja... **BCS:** No, he's saying not that. **KAV:** Rashkapoor **BCS:** Rashkapoor? **KAV:**.Aamer Rash. woh ekta (dota?) preparation aache. Eta very poison. (Aamer Rash. That's one preparation. It's very poisonous.) **BCS:** Woh to makharadhwaja jaise hai kya? *(Is that like makharadhwaja?)* **BHAV:** *Who is he thinking Prabhupada [indistinct]? Who is that?* **KAV:** Makharadhwaja to amrit hota hai, inke liye nahin suitable hota hai, yeh bat doosri. Baki woh to sab ki liye poison hota hai. (Makharadhwaja is like nectar although it's not suitable for him, that's for sure. But that (Raskapoor) is poison for everybody.) **BHAV:** What medicine was he taking before that? **BCS:** Konsa? Yogendra-ras *(What? Yogendra-ras)* **KAV:** Kuuch nahin. *(Nothing.)* **BCS:** No, he was referring to a case, a big murder case in Calcutta, the husband poisoned the wife. **BHAV:** Oh, Guha. Oh yes. **KAV:** Svarupa Guha, abhi uska case... *(the case is now...)* **BCS:** Shankara Dev Bannerjee was... **BHAV:** Our lawyer is the... *(sniggers).* **Tamal:** Bhagatji doesn't think the (indistinct) **KAV** (H): Manye (par?) inka sharir aisa hai, jeh bajra (ke?) hai chahe haazaar de do, kuch nahi hone wala. *(But his body is like that, it's like diamond, even if you give him thousands, nothing will affect him.)* **BCS:** Nain ghabrana ka jo... Bhagwan jise raksa karte hai, waise to Prahlad Maharaja ke bhi to *(No need for bewilderment. The way God protects his own, similarly Prahlad Maharaja was also.)*

KAV: Swamiji, ek sloka yaad aata hai (sloka) Aapto siddhanta Maharaja to, isliye koi shankhya karneka darkar nahin hain. *(Swamiji, one verse comes to my mind (verse) you are a divine soul, that is why there is no need to be anxious.)* **Tamal:** No poison is strong enough to stop the Hari Nam, Srila Prabhupada. **KAV:** (H) Bas. Hari Nam ke samne. Woh Mira ko jitna poison diya tha; ek boond parjanese aadmi ka death ho jate. Woh sub pegeya woh, batlayie? Jo Bhagavan ke prasad lag jate na, woh poison amrit ho jata, samajhte. *(Right. Before the Holy Name. How much poison was given to Mira, a single drop was enough to kill a man. Mira drank it all. Poison when offered to the Lord becomes nectar.)* **BCS:** Prahlad Maharaja. **KAV:** Prahlad se jada poison diya tha Halal isko Mira. Itna jabardast banaya woh. Jaise ek allopath me ek poison aata ka uska taste aaj tak koi bataa nahin sakaa. (Halal gave Mira a stronger dose of poison than Prahlad got. It was so strongly made. Like there is one poison in allopathy, even till today nobody can tell the taste.) **Tamal:** Would you like some more kirtan Srila Prabhupada? Lokanatha can lead. Lokanatha, you lead. **Tamal:** Lokanatha. **Lokanatha:** Not for chanting, Srila Prabhupada. **SP:** Hm.

Loka: We just had a big kirtan, but I could chant more. I have come a long way to see you and chant for you. So if you allow I will chant. **SP:** Yes. **Loka:** Yes. [...] **SP:** I wish that you GBC manage very nicely and consider I am dead and let me try to travel all the tirthasthana. Without any responsibility. If I become recovered from this malady I shall come back and then I shall die in, what is it when the dead body is there, let them bring to Mayapur and Vrindaban. I am thinking in this way. Bring little medicine and no medicine, little milk, and travel one place to another and if there is death, what is the lamentation? My age is ripe. In the open air and bullock cart or during daytime, eh? Or you can say semi-suicide, although living what consider me dead for the time being. You manage and nowadays there is in India ample sunshine. So during daytime I shall travel and nighttime you make a camp under the tree. In this way let me travel all the tirthas. I am thinking in this way. What is your opinion?

BHAV: Srila Prabhupada, we promise that we'll manage everything to the best of our ability. **SP:** No, no, you are managing, I know, but you are all important men and unnecessarily you are bound up. You cannot go. So Lokanatha party has got some experience and let me go. In India the climate is now good. If I recover, it is very good. You know. So what is the wrong? If I die, then the body will be brought either in Vrindaban or Mayapur, that's all. And if I live, it will be a great end of a life. You are all experienced. **Jayapataka (JPS):** As much as you have trained us, SP, that is only how much we are experienced. We don't want that you be burdened any more with material management problems but... serving... **SP:** No, not from that point of view. What is the use of lying down here? **JPS:** The kaviraja said...

SP: Kaviraja may say... **JPS:** That even that your body is going to, is got a life of six to ten years but he said even a healthy cow, if it's kept locked up in a room, then it will deteriorate. **SP:** Therefore I say, (laughs) don't keep me locked up. You do your duty as I have trained you and let me be free and if money required, he'll come and take and go back again as he is coming to take book. **JPS:** What? **SP:** They've got experience Indian, you can go village to village and, arrangement as you may, but it is trouble taken, and I am no longer, you manage. If I live, I can come again. I shall be very glad. **Devotee:** Previously it was mentioned that there was some risk in travelling. **SP:** What is the risk? Nowadays there is no risk. What is the risk? Mm? **Devotee:** Well from the medical point of view it's something with the organs or something, I don't know exactly but it's been considered. **SP:** This is my proposal and... **JPS:** That would be after you gain some strength, Srila Prabhupada? **SP:** Yes. If I've free air and free movement.. with some sunshine? and I can come back within a year. **JPS:** You will be translating while you're travelling, Srila Prabhupada? **SP:** No, Yes and no. **BHAV:** I think it's a good idea, Srila Prabhupada. **SP:** Ha. **BHAV:** Only factor at this point is not to take any unnecessary risk. **SP:** No. As I think free, so I remain. Mm. Then when I am sane man, I shall come back again either Mayapur or Vrindaban or Bombay, any other. **JPS:** You would travel by a minibus.

SP: Mm? **JPS:** You would travel by a bus. **SP:** That you think of. **BHAV:** We all sit down and discuss the different arrangements that have to be made, plans that have to be made. It's a very nice idea. Real sannyas life. **SP:** Yes. Mm. You've tried doctor, kaviraja, medicine, everything. Everything has failed. Now I suppose I am taking the risk of death, what is wrong? When the I am dead you go India, within India, you go and bring the body either in Mayapur or Vrindaban. Mayapur the land is already there. Vrindaban I think on the gate side, that's all. That's wherever you like you'll do. **JPS:** Srila Prabhupada, you commented that when Thakura Bhaktivinoda was put on the gate side that was no way to respect a Vaishnava. **SP:** Mm. **JPS:** So then doesn't seem proper to put you by the gate. **SP:** No, not by the gate. There is ample land. Or in Mayapur, that will be very nice. Mm. **JPS:** This kaviraja assures that by taking little milk frequently during the day... **SP:** I will take milk. Milk is available everywhere. (laughter) I shall take little milk and sleep, that's all. If I live, that's all right. If I don't live, that doesn't matter. **BHAV:** Very nice program. We can all accompany you at different times of the month. **SP:** Yes. Not very many, but you can come and go back.

JPS: Which holy places you would like to visit, Srila Prabhupada? **SP:** India is full of holy places. **JPS:** Krishna-lila, Mahaprabhu-lila. **SP:** Gradually go to Mayapur... Is someone here? **Tamal:** Yes, Srila Prabhupada. **SP:** I... **BHAV:** He has heard everything. **SP:** Mm. **JPS:** By you going to the holy places, you will purify the holy places. **SP:** There are two things, life or death. So if I die where's the wrong? And if there is death, that is natural. **JPS:** For you Srila Prabhupada, to be alive or to die is no different because you are in the transcendental position, but for us when you leave the body then we are bereft of your association. So for us it is very unfortunate. **SP:** Then live by my words, by my training. Mm. (pause)... So you like this idea? Mm? **Hamsaduta:** I liked it. **SP:** Who is it? **Adridharan:** It's Hamsaduta Maharaja. **SP:** Oh. Most places you beg from the local bread and subsist, otherwise purchase. **JPS:** You are very famous, Srila Prabhupada, wherever you go there will be crowds of people to have your darshan. **SP:** So they will see me, I have no objection. I want little milk from them, that's all... So far my presence is required (for) management, I think I have bequeathed, properly you can manage. Hm. It is to be admitted failure, the so called medical treatment, failure. **JPS:** All the doctors say that you defy all medical laws. Sometimes you become very weak and sometimes you become immediately strong. **Giriraj:** I think this is a good idea. **SP:** Who's this? **Devotee:** Giriraja. **SP:** Oh. **Giriraj:** Because, I mean, I don't have any faith in the doctors or their treatments because they're never working and ultimately it depends on Krishna and Krishna is everywhere. He can exercise His will in any condition and you know, as you say, that if you go out and if you recover then it's very good. And even otherwise, I mean, if that is the decision of Lord Krishna, then this is a very glorious way. **SP:** All seriously consider this submission and let me go. **END OF T-45-B. T-46, Side A, begins on p. 373 of the ConvBk Vol 36:**

BHAV: We should begin the parikrama in Vrindaban. **SP:** Yes. **BHAV:** Because quite honestly, Srila Prabhupada, I think most of us are very worried. If you go off down the road and send us all back to our different assignments, we would not be able to serve with our full attention, knowing that our beloved father and spiritual guide was in such weak condition. So if we begin in Vrindaban, we're all here now, we can see so that we know what arrangements to make for the future when you want to leave. **SP:** Hm. You make me flat. **BREAK Whispers: "The poison's going down. (giggle) The poison's going down."** (Next to the microphone are: Tamal, Jayapataka, Bhavananda.) **JPS:** We heard that Your Divine Grace had a dream that a kaviraja of the Ramanuja sampradaya would treat you and bring you back to strength, and this kaviraja says that in a very short time, following the treatment, you would regain your strength. Although he hasn't got all of the medicines yet, but within a day or two they'll all be prepared, and he says within fifteen days you should be quite improved in strength. So far, he seems to have been quite sincere. **SP:** No, no, he's sincere. I'll drink milk. Whatever strength is obtainable, there will be. **JPS:** Like to follow the same treatment, only while travelling.

Whispers: "Is the poison in the milk"... "Uh huh." (Tamal, Bhavananda voices)

Hamsaduta: So we should meet and make a program for going around Vrindaban. **SP:** Yes. **Hamsaduta:** You want to begin tomorrow morning? **SP:** Yes. **Devotee:** If Prabhupada travels in a van it would be very bumpy. He should have a big bus. **Hamsaduta:** Let's discuss it. **SP:** Bus? **Devotee:** A big bus. **SP:** No, no, bus will be not good. Bullock cart. **BHAV:** Bullock cart. **JPS:** That is very bumpy. **BHAV:** Your Guru Maharaja used to have bullock cart travel from Hulorghat (on the banks of the Ganges in Mayapur) up to the Chaitanya Matha. You told me you put a nice mattress down in the back and a cover, and you lay down there. You even told me once to go to Calcutta that way. You lay down at night ; you go little bit, little bit; and in the morning, when you wake up, you're in Calcutta. **SP:** Bullock, you get the cow dung. **Tamal:** Cook with it. **JPS:** In this part of India it's very cold for your Divine Grace. **SP:** Underneath the tree it is not cold. **Tamal:** You sound like you are very determined to go, Srila Prabhupada. **SP:** Daytime we expose in the sunshine, and camp underneath a tree at night. That has to be arranged.

BCS: (B) Srila Prabhupada, ektu doodh debo akhon? *(close to microphone) (Srila Prabhupada, would you like some milk now?)* **SP:** Hmm. Dao. Ektu garam diyo. *(Give. Give it a little warm.)* **BCS:** Ektu han korun. Garam theek ache? *(Open your mouth a little. Is it warm enough?) Sounds of drinking milk.* **SP:** Beshi mishti hoyeche. *(It is too sweet.)* **BCS:** Oh...Ektu han korun Srila Prabhupada. *(Oh, could you open your mouth Srila Prabhupada? A little more.)* **SP**: Bas. Aar na. *(Stop. No more.)* **BCS**: Ektu jal Srila Prabhupada? Jal o khaben na? *(Would you like some water Srila Prabhupada? You won't drink water?)* **SP:** Na *(No)* **BCS:** Aacha *(OK)* [Devotees ask to go for lunch prasadam.] [...] **BREAK**

Tamal: We were discussing how to make this parikrama possible, and we've concluded that the best thing was, as we said earlier, to parikrama around Vrindaban to begin with. And for that purpose we sent Lokanatha Maharaja and Panchadravida Maharaja and Trivikram Maharaja to get a bullock cart ready. **SP:** Hired or purchased? **Tamal:** No, for now just hired, not purchased. Later on we can make a more permanent arrangement, and it can be fixed up as nicely as possible. At the same time while we were meeting, the kaviraja, he also was present. So we inquired from him what he thought about this program, from a medical point of view of course. Spiritually he is in complete agreement. So from a medical point of view, he said that you would not at all be able to withstand this kind of a trip. He said that in a bullock cart, moving around, bumping on the road, you might not be able to live more than a couple of hours. He's here now. He wanted to speak to you. **BCS:** (H) Aap boliye kuchh. *(You (kaviraja) say something.)* **KAV:** Bolo Maharaja kya baat hai? kya bichar hai? *(Tell us Maharaja, what's the problem? what do you think?)*

SP: Bichar hai... jo idhar me to... sarte sarte bilkul sab energy nasht ho gaya. Usliye parikrama jayega. *(My thoughts are... that here... rotting and rotting and all my energy is being wasted. That is why I want to go on parikrama.)* **KAV:** Aacha, yeh bicar hai. To parikrama to apko ek nahin, do dila denge. Thoda sharir me takat ane dijye. Maine saath chalenge, kya baat hi? Abhi apke is haalat mein; oos roz dhekiye, parikrama mein gaya aapko chakkar aa gaya... kal apko thodi shikayat hogi. To abhi thoda strength aane dijye, thoda aur roz thairiye. Uske baad mein aap ke yahan ke parikrama shuru kar denge. Bahar ke parikrama aapka shuru kara denge. Thoda bal aana chahiye. Bal nahin hone se heart par sabse jada asar parta hai. Jo eek hi cheez; apka sabse majboot hai, jiske zariye hame yeh atmabal hai ki hamlog aapka yeh bimaar, mitadenge ki aapka tabyat bhi theek ho jaye. Ees halat mein aapka jana accha nahin hain. Yeh meri vyaktigat rai hai. *(Okay, so these are (your) thoughts. So*

429

parikramas I will deliver you not one but two. Let some strength get back into your body, we will go together, what's the problem? Now your situation is; the other day you went on parikrama and started getting dizzy. Yesterday you were a little uncomfortable. Let some strength return, wait a few days. After that I will start your parikrama here then begin the parikrama outside. A little strength needs to come. If there is no strength, the heart feels the stress most of all, and this is the one thing of yours that is strongest of all. Based on its well-being, we have confidence in your recovery. Your health will be fine. In this state though, you should not go. This is my personal conviction.) **SP:** Lokanatha? **Svarupa Dam:** Lokanatha has already gone, Srila Prabhupada. **Hamsaduta:** He has gone to Mathura for renting.

Tamal: He has gone out for renting the bullock cart. **SP:** Oh. (indistinct) **Tamal:** Lokanatha says that the bullock cart could probably go around Vrindaban in about five to six hours, parikramming Vrindaban town. **SP:** Make an experiment. Then we shall decide. **Tamal:** Prabhupada said, "Make an experiment. Then we shall decide." **JPS:** What is that experiment? **Tamal:** Jayapataka's asking what that experiment is, Srila Prabhupada. **SP:** Vrindaban parikrama. **Tamal:** Prabhupada said, "Vrindaban parikrama." **Hamsaduta:** Prabhupada, does it mean with Your Divine Grace, or we should go alone first and see? **SP:** Hm? **Hamsaduta:** Does it mean that Your Divine Grace will come on the experiment, or we should go without Your Divine Grace and experiment? **SP:** Why? **JPS:** See if the road is very rough, if the road is passable by bullock cart the whole way. **SP:** Bullock cart is not smooth. **Tamal:** Bullock cart is not smooth. How would you propose that we go, Srila Prabhupada? **SP:** Come, let us take the risk. **Tamal:** Go anyway. Let us take the risk. **Svarupa Damodar:** As your disciples, Srila Prabhupada, we're all neophytes. We don't know what is right and what is wrong. But at the same time we feel that we're very hopeful that you'll get strength slowly and slowly. And this morning you were telling us that you get a little strength, so we are hoping every day that "Prabhupada will gain even stronger and be with us for many more years." So we are taking advice from kavirajaji that you take milk more and more, day by day, so that Prabhupada will get stronger. Like kaviraja is suggesting that when Your Divine Grace gets stronger, he'll go with you in the parikrama he will accompany you. **SP:** So let us make experiment in Vrindaban. **Svarupa Damodar:** Shall we do that immediately? **SP:** Hm. Hm. **BCS: (H)** Unhe sthir kya woh bailgari me Vrindaban parikrama karenge pehle karke dekhta hai kaisa hota hai. *(He has decided to do Vrindaban parikrama in bullock cart. So he'll do it and see how it goes.)*

KAV: Yeh bilkul nahin karna chahiye. *(This should absolutely not be done.)* **BCS:** Shastriji's saying that he shouldn't do it under the circumstances. **BHAV:** Srila Prabhupada, if we follow the kaviraja's instructions and advice, then he feels that within 15 days, 20 days, you will have strength. To take an unnecessary risk at this time, we have to practically appraise what will be the loss. You have said, "If I live or die on this parikrama, it will be glorious," but the loss will be that Srimad Bhagavatam will not be finished, so many works will be unfinished. If it's just a matter of being a little patient and waiting fifteen more days- is only two weeks- then when you have strength, then we can all go on the parikrama, and you'll be able to hopefully gain more strength and finish up all of these works. But I think that the risk, in terms of the future of the whole world, is too great. **SP:** Vrindaban parikrama is not risk.

KAV: Vrindaban me dhakka lagenge Maharaja. Ham chahte vishwa parikrama karane. Abhi aap is bicharico ko mere hisab se sthagit kar dijye. Aap ka machine ko dekhte mein apko mane anumati nahin deta hun ki aap jayenge. Hamari atma nahin manti hai. Iss sthiti meh ki jaldi jaldi mai apko Mayapur le chulun phir aap vishwa mai jana life (?) ho jai. Ye kam na karti. Ye abhi jo Vrindaban ka parikrama ka bichar aap chhor dijye. Yeh meri rai hai. Phir aap sab ne dekhiye. *(In Vrindaban you will get jolted about Maharaja. I want to do a world parikrama. For now you should keep this decision on hold in my account. By looking at the state of your machine, I cannot give permission to go on this parikrama. My soul is not permitting. The situation is such that as soon as possible we shall take you to Mayapur. Then you will gain enough life (?) to go on a world tour. It will not work, give up the idea of this Vrindaban parikrama. This is my verdict. From now on the decision is up to all of you.)*

Tamal: Srila Prabhupada, when you went on this parikrama the other day around the temple, you became dizzy just going around the temple four times. That's when you were even able to sit up in bed a lot more. How is it going to be possible to go four, five or six hours, when you couldn't even... **SP:** Not four, five, six... **Tamal:** That's how long it takes to go around Vrindaban by bullock cart. It takes three hours walking at a good pace, and it takes at least five or six hours, Lokanatha says, by bullock cart. How? We couldn't even go half hour just around this temple. **SP:** No, I traveled. It takes two hours in the morning.

Tamal: Walking, by walking? **SP:** Yes. **Tamal:** But not by bullock cart. That's when a man walks very quickly you can do it in two hours, but by bullock cart it will take five hours. We have... You had difficulty even doing a half hour parikrama around the temple. You became very faint. Whether you think that you can go five hours in a row? **SP:** From Madhava Maharaja's Matha, bring Krishna dasa Babaji. **Tamal:** We should bring Krishna dasa Babaji here? OK **SP:** And Indu. **BCS:** Indu-mati Prabhu? **SP:** Indu-mati. **Tamal:** Indu-mati. **SP:** Then talk. **Tamal:** Okay. Krishna Balaram, you know Madhava Maharaja's Mandir? You know Krishna dasa Babaji, Prabhupada's Godbrother? You know? So Krishna-Balarama will go with you. Prabhupada wants to see Indu-mati and Krishna dasa Babaji. You bring them both. You go in one of the cars. Madhava Maharaja's Matha. Krishna Balarama-not the Krishna dasa Babaji from Radha-kunda. Madhava Maharaja. **Svarupa Damodara:** As your humble disciples, Srila Prabhupada, we are ready to take up any instructions that you've kindly given us, but at the same time, you have advised us many times that we shouldn't take unnecessary risk. Just like few days ago you were telling a Bengali saying, saying that when you are doubtful, don't do it. You instructed us. **SP:** That is material. (laughter) **Jagadish:** Srila Prabhupada, can you tell us why you want to go on the parikrama? **BCS:** (B) Srila Prabhupada, ekhon ektu doodh diya apnake? *(Srila Prabhupada, shall I give you some milk now?)* **SP:** Good... paddy (?)

Tamal: This seems like suicide, Srila Prabhupada, this program. It seems to some of us like it's suicidal. **SP:** And this is also suicidal. **Tamal:** Hm. Prabhupada said, "And this is also suicide." (speaks to side) Now you have to choose which suicide. **SP:** The Ravana will kill and Rama will kill. Better to be killed by Rama. Eh? That Marica- if he does not go to mislead Sita, he'll be killed by Ravana; and if he goes to be killed by Rama, then it is better. **Tamal:** Who is this Prabhupada's talking about? **Devotees:** Marica.

Tamal: Srila Prabhupada? I mean, just judging the symptoms, which is all that we can do, certain symptoms have certainly picked up. For instance, you're passing more urine, stool is coming naturally, and you're able to drink milk without getting any cough. These things were never there before. **SP:** Hm. That will continue. **Tamal:** So if the treatment is continuing, if the treatment is working, why not continue it under the guidance of this kaviraja for some time? His point is this. This is what I've seen, Srila Prabhupada, being your secretary all these months, that whenever you took milk you would get cough. For the first time I see there is no cough coming. Another problem, you couldn't pass urine. Now there's double the amount of urine. Another thing, you couldn't pass stool. Now it comes normally. At least it comes without any artificial means. So the one thing that has not yet come is strength, and kaviraja is suggesting what you yourself have always said, "If I can drink milk, I will get stronger." So if the kaviraja's treatment... to my feeling it has worked. At least the symptoms... the symptoms have been better under his treatment than any other doctor so far.

SP: That will work. **BHAV:** It will work. **Svarupa Damodara (SD):** Also Srila Prabhupada's resting is better than before. **Tamal:** But the idea is that... according to him... I mean, obviously we're all conditioned, and... I mean, he's not claiming not to be a conditioned soul either, but according to him, going on this bullock cart is a suicide. He said within an hour or two hours, the bouncing and jumbling of the bullock cart will cause a heart attack. Just like you were having heart, a little heart spasm the other day, just laying in bed two days ago. He says this going in a bullock cart, up and down, within one, two hours it can cause a heart attack. So as his treatment has been better at least than any other doctor, and certain symptoms have improved, why are we giving up his advice? If you say his advice is wrong, then there's no comment, but all along, his advice seems to have been more accurate than any other doctors that we've had. I mean we who are closely around you, Srila Prabhupada, your servants, secretary, our opinion of him is far superior than our opinion of any of these others. I see that he's able to take care of one symptom after another somewhat successfully. He's able to deal with these problems. He can deal with the problem of not enough urine... **SP:** That I know. **Tamal:** He feels quite confident that you can live for six, seven more years, Srila Prabhupada.

SD: We also feel very confident. **Tamal:** Better that you live for six or seven years productively than that you go on this parikrama and die within two hours gloriously. Why not live for six or seven years and then go on parikrama and die? If the parikrama can always be done, why not put it off for six or seven more years of preaching? **SD:** You've already been glorious, SP, all over the world. Whether you're here or outside doesn't really matter. You're already glorious. **JPS:** By your presence countless souls will attain devotional service. That's more glorious. **SP:** But I think I shall be cured. **Tamal:** Prabhupada says he thinks he will be cured by the parikrama. **BCS:** (Hindi to kaviraja) Srila Prabhupada je ne bolta hain ki unhe sochta hain ki parikrama se cure ho jayega. (*Srila Prabhupada is saying that he thinks that he will be cured by this parikrama.*) **KAV:** Hmm. **BCS:** Yeh parikrama karne se... (*If he does this parikrama...*) **KAV:** (Hindi Conversation) (*All the roads are broken.*)

(He) will feel the jerking. His heart will not be able to bear the jerking. Not at all. Later, after he is better, one way or another we will do parikrama, what's the problem with this? Sitting here, or even lying down you can do parikrama (mentally). You should renounce your decision. There are so many pot-holes that even our hearts get jolted, and we travel by car. In a bullock cart? It cannot be done, not even for 15 minutes.)

Hamsaduta: Under the circumstances we have to consider whether Prabhupada's opinion is more or less than the kaviraja's, is what it comes down to. **Tamal:** We can't continue, consider. Srila Prabhupada has to. **Hamsaduta:** If Prabhupada says that by going on parikrama he feels he'll be cured, then how can we continue to place arguments against him? **KAV:** (Sarira madhyam khalo dharma sadhan (sloka)) *Aur apko dharam ki apko koi aava shyakta hi nahin hai. Aap to oos jagah se pareh hain. Swayam prakasha hi manlo kya? Ess ye Bhagawan ke dharamsala hai. Panch loke sarira hai. Yeh abhi sahan karne layak nahin hai, isiliye hamlog mana karte hain. Nain aise kaam ke liye koi bhi mana nahin kar sakta hain, karna wale ko paap lagta hain. Sharirk sthiti dekhite hue hamara ji nahin manta kiaiki mein apko anumati de.* (sloka) (sloka) *And you do not need any additional purification. You are from there (in the pure state). You are yourself effulgent, understand this; this is God's rest-house, the body is made of the five elements of matter. This (parikrama) you will not be able to bear with. This is why we are forbidding it. Otherwise no one can object to this (holy) work. Those who do incur misfortune. Judging by your health, I do not feel you should be permitted to go. (sloka).* **Tamal:** Ultimately what Prabhupada decides, we will do. **Hamsaduta:** Well, it just... **Tamal:** Yeah, but it goes on. As Prabhupada goes on, his disciples also go on. [...] **Lokanatha:** So we're discussing bumping, so won't be much bumping on the cart. Also, we always could go slow. If Prabhupada wants to make an experiment, we could make one day... **Gopal Krishna:** A few hours. **SP:** I am thinking I am lying here. **End T-46-A.// T-46, Side B. ConvBk Vol 36 p. 383 line-36:**

Hamsaduta: Srila Prabhupada? The main concern of the devotees is that whether you will be able to survive such an experiment. But before, you said that you felt that such a parikrama would actually cure you. You said that. So your vision is transcendental, because you are the spiritual master. You're a pure devotee of Krishna. So if you say that it will cure you and that it will be beneficial for you, then we have to carry out that, whatever you desire. We do not know. We are just on the mundane platform. **SP:** One day experiment. It is for one day. **Lokanatha:** We have hired it for one day. **SP:** Rest assured. I will not die in one day. [...] **JPS:** Keu pathiye debo, seta manaar jonye naa aapni jaben? [Should someone be sent (to bring it), or will you go yourself?] **Krsna Das Babaji:** Jabo. [Trans (I will) Go.] **JPS:** Gari ekbar jabe. [The car will go once.] **KDB:** Na hoyle, riksha kore chole jaabo. [If it doesn't happen, I'll go by rickshaw.] **SP:** Aajke kombe. [Today reduced.] **KDB:** Han kombe. [Yes reduced.]

TIME 35.14: JPS: Should there be kirtan, Srila Prabhupada? You like kirtan? **SP:** Yes. (Bengali Speaker): Kayek din pare asha (In a few days' time.) **JPS: POISONING FOR A (long) TIME (OR "Poison ishvarya rasa")** **SP:** To me? (high, squeaky, weak voice) Unknown: (that's really) original. **JPS: Get ready to go.** Unknown: Anything might of happened today. Unknown: (Look) I'm not afraid to die. Soft elder voice:

Very good. **Unknown: You're taking it right now. Soft elder voice: How's this? Unknown: Let it go. (Break) [...]**

Tamal: Well Srila Prabhupada, I'll tell you, I'm getting so upset sitting in the room upstairs. I mean I just... I was walking around. Two of the devotees told me this road is so bad that if you go on this road, you're going to be jolted back and forth. The road is terrible. I just can't understand, Srila Prabhupada, why it has to be tomorrow that we have to go. If anybody wants you to travel, I do. My whole desire is to take you all over the world. I want to take you on parikrama, but why do we have to go when you're in this condition? I can't understand it. It just... I was standing outside. This kaviraja, he has worked so hard. He's so much disappointed. He can't understand why he... He says that now, today, you've taken half a kilo of milk. No mucus has been produced. No stool is being passed. He says that tomorrow he wants to give you a medicine that will begin to build the milk into muscles. He's going to get you to a point where you can take two kilos of milk a day. And he says very soon you'll be able to have the strength to actually do parikrama. So why are we throwing everything out the window, that we must go tomorrow? I cannot understand. **SP:** All right. **BCS:** Jaya Srila Prabhupada.

BHAV: Thank you, Srila Prabhupada. **SP:** I cannot refuse all your requests. **Tamal:** And we cannot refuse your request. We will take you all over tirtha-yatra, to all the places. Just that you get a little stronger. You'll be free of all management. You simply go to tirthas and take darshan of all the Deities in India. Everyone will stay in their respective places. They'll manage. But we just want you to be stronger. **SP:** All right... That will satisfy you? (laughter) **Tamal:** Babaji Maharaja also, you also thought that? We did not talk to him. **BHAV:** We were just on our way down the stairs to come and see your Divine Grace. **SP:** Bhavananda? **BHAV:** Yes, Srila Prabhupada? **SP:** You are satisfied?

BHAV: Now I am, Srila Prabhupada, yes. (laughter) I was in too much anxiety. **SP:** No, I cannot put you in anxiety. You have done so much. You have suffered for Mayapur so much. I cannot out you in anxiety. So I shall do what you like. [...] **Tamal:** I mean I'm amazed, Srila Prabhupada. A half a kilo of milk you've drank today--no mucus, no stool, and that is wonderful. You could not have done this two weeks ago. [...] **SP:** Yes, other devotees can go. I cannot go. **Tamal:** No, they'll go on your behalf, but you will go one day. That we promise you. **SP:** All right. **Tamal:** Our greatest pleasure will be to take you on tirtha-yatra, Srila Prabhupada. We wanted so much to go with you on that. **SP:** Thank you very much. **Tamal:** Actually, Srila Prabhupada, we're so much attached to you that you practically drive us to madness sometimes. Tonight we were becoming mad. **SP:** No, no, I shall not do that. [SP speaks with Krishna das Babaji] **SP:** So you will take bath in Radha-kunda on my behalf. **Tamal:** We'll get you better, Srila Prabhupada, and you will also be able to take bath personally there. We'll see you get better. **SP:** That's all right. **Tamal:** Krishna will make all our words come true, Srila Prabhupada. **BCS:** (B) Doodh niye aashbo Srila Prabhupada? *(Shall I bring milk Srila Prabhupada?)* **SP:** Han, niye esho. Kaviraja ato khatche. Aakhere gushkhora. *(Yes, bring. Kaviraja works hard. The result is?)* **Tamal:** Oh, this kaviraja, I mean we are fortunate to get this sincere man. **SP:** Where is kaviraja? **Tamal:** He's out working, at work. **BHAV:** Adri, see if he's here, kaviraja. **Tamal:** As soon as he comes, he can come and see Prabhupada. **END**

APPENDIX 3:
McCAFFREY REPORT

Summary Report
Acoustic Analysis of Speech
Helen A. McCaffrey, Ph.D., CCC/A
3913 W. 4th St
Fort Worth, TX 76107

Received 4.13.98

This document certifies that I am in agreement with the findings of acoustic analyses submitted by Jack Mitchell, Computer Audio Engineering that were completed with my consultation. Recorded signals were digitized and prepared for analysis by Jack Mitchell. Digitized signals were forwarded to this consultant via e-mail. The consultation was conducted over the telephone while Mr. Mitchell and this consultant simultaneously viewed the signals under consideration each using SoundScope speech analysis software, thus permitting each individual to view the same information throughout the consultation. Mr. Mitchell's report is a record of the findings and conclusions from that analysis session. I am in agreement with the content of that report.

This consultant first listened to the digitized signal and identified the possible phrase or word being said. Mr. Mitchell then supplied his interpretation. In the case of disagreement in perception, signals were replayed until a consensus could be reached. Following perceptual analysis, computerized acoustic analysis was conducted. The absolute frequencies and intensities of speech sounds (vowels and consonants) vary with speaker and with consonant/vowel context. Consequently, acoustic speech analysis does not yield absolute identification of speech sounds. Instead, an analysis reveals the most likely categories of sounds (e.g. made with the lips, produced with signal stopping as in /d/ or noisy signal frication as in /s/). Thus, acoustic analysis may confirm a message that has been perceived via listening to a signal and may also yield alternatives that can be further specified by attending to which word/sound choice is the most logical in the context of the probable message.

To that end, the acoustic analysis was conducted to confirm or disconfirm the perceptions of the listeners. Four analysis approaches were employed. The first and primary procedure was spectrographic analysis which is a three dimensional visual display of the digitized signal along the parameters of time, frequency, and amplitude and will be referred to as an F-T-A display for consistency with Mr. Mitchell's designation. FFT and LPC analyses provided spectral (amplitude by frequency) information and were used to identify frequency peaks in the signal at particular instances in time. An amplitude envelope of the utterance was obtained to identify amplitude peaks that are consistent with syllable production (for example, 2 peaks appear in the envelope for two-syllable words or for two one-syllable words).

Helen A. McCaffrey, Ph.D., CCC/A
Audiologist

APPENDIX 4:
ABOUT ARSENIC AND ANTIMONY

Arsenic General Information: Arsenic is found in nature in low levels, and has been a common environmental contaminant in the twentieth century. In its various chemical forms, it can be highly poisonous and has been used for thousands of years in political intrigue, revenge, murder, war, and the elimination of enemies. Medicinally, arsenic compounds have been useful in the West at least since the 5th century BC. In modern times, arsenic has been used to treat skin diseases, anemia, syphilis, and other ailments. Arsenic is a natural element having both metal and non-metal physical and chemical properties. In nature it exists as an element, and also in stable compounds. Inorganic pentavalent compounds are somewhat less toxic than arsenites, while the organic pentavalent compounds incur the least hazard of the arsenicals, with widespread use in pesticides. Inorganic arsenite as arsenic trioxide is the most prevalent natural form and is also the most toxic. Goldfrank's: *"Tasteless and odorless, arsenic is well-absorbed via the gastrointestinal, respiratory, and parenteral routes."* Ingestion has been the usual basis of poisoning. *Once absorbed, many arsenicals accumulate in and cause extensive toxic injury to cells of the kidney, liver, spleen, lungs, heart, nervous system, blood vessels, gastrointestinal tract, and other tissues.* Much smaller amounts accumulate in muscle and neural tissue, but cause great toxic injury there as well. If a victim survives arsenic poisoning after the first few days, the liver and kidneys show degenerative changes.

Arsenic causes toxicity by combining with sulfhydryl (-SH) enzymes and interfering with cellular metabolism. *Most arsenic compounds are tasteless and odorless.* Arsenic trioxide (As_2O_3) used to be a common cause of accidental poisoning because it is readily available, is practically tasteless, and has the *appearance of sugar as a white crystalline powder.* Also known as arsenious oxide, white arsenic or simply as arsenic, is extremely toxic as *one of the deadliest known poisons, with 60-200 mg fatal. This is about 1/300 oz.* Arsenic is used and stored for military purposes as a poison gas. A nickel's weight of arsenic is 25 lethal adult doses. Children, embryos, the chronically-ill, and *the elderly are more sensitive to arsenical intoxication.* The type of compound, dosage, health condition and duration of exposure are critical factors. Arsenic compounds are commonly found commercially in *treated lumber,* wood preservatives, pesticides, herbicides, fungicides, dyes, and paints, and is often present in tainted tobacco and old folk remedies. Tryparsamide, carbasone and arsphenamine are a few arsenic compounds used in medicine to treat ailments such as intestinal parasites, syphilis, psoriasis and dysentery. In cases of suspected arsenic toxicity in which the urinary arsenic measurements fall below accepted toxic levels, analysis of hair and nails may permit a diagnosis. Because of the high sulfhydryl content of keratin, high concentrations of arsenic are deposited in hair and nails. Deposition in the proximal portions of hair occurs within 30 hrs of ingestion, and stays fixed at this site. Hair grows 0.4 mm/ day (1/2 inch/ month) while nail grows 0.1 mm/ day. Full fingernail growth takes 3-4 months; toenails take 6-9 months. Because of its chemical similarity to phosphorus, arsenic is deposited in bone and teeth and stays there.

Arsenic can be eliminated by many routes although most is excreted in urine. The half-life for *urinary* excretion is 3-5 days, during which time *great damage is done to the internal tissues and organs.* Another half of the remaining amount is eliminated within another week, the next half-life in another month, etc. After 6 weeks there still remains about 10 to 15 % of the original amount in the urine. Thus repeated doses will begin to accumulate in the body quickly despite the process of elimination. As arsenic takes its toll, the body loses its ability to eliminate it, compounding the toxic accumulation and the rate of internal destruction of tissues and organs. In single or acute arsenic poisonings, the arsenic is deposited throughout the body. If there is chronic poisoning of repeated doses over a long period of time, the efficiency of elimination by the body dramatically decreases and arsenic accumulates much more permanently in the internal organs and tissues. The blood, liver, brain, heart and kidneys are top priority in the body's cleansing, while arsenic is pushed out the urine and into the hair, nails and skin as much as possible. Chronic poisoning gradually takes a serious irreversible toll of damage to the blood manufacturing capability, the kidneys and liver, the brain and heart, the central nervous system progressing from the periphery inwards, and the muscular system, among other areas of acute damage. *Chronic (low level) arsenic poisoning from repeated absorption of toxic amounts generally has an insidious (subtle or stealthy) onset of clinical effects and is **very difficult** for a doctor to recognize as many of the symptoms are seen with other illnesses. It is easily misdiagnosed as more commonly understood ailments and diseases, such as kidney disease.* Arsenic poisoning can be detected by studying the patient's symptoms, or by the testing of tissue samples, hair, fingernails, teeth, or urine. The onset of gastrointestinal symptoms may be so gradual that the possibility of arsenic poisoning would be easily overlooked.

THE NATURE OF ARSENIC POISONING

Chronic poisoning means exposure over a prolonged period of time in smaller amounts and acute is more all at once. Subacute poisoning is in between. Because Srila Prabhupada's health declined over 10 months, chronic poisoning is compatible with his health history. Signs and symptoms of arsenic toxicity vary depending on the amount and form ingested; the rate of absorption, metabolism and excretion; and the time course of ingestion (chronic, sub-acute or acute). The principal manifestations of arsenic poisoning are gastrointestinal disturbances and in four most common symptoms: thickening skin, discoloration of skin, swelling, and muscle weakness. In chronic cases, skin manifestations may not appear for years. When toxicity is more acute, symptoms typically begin with nausea, vomiting, abdominal pain, and diarrhea. Arsenic exploits certain pathways in our cells, binds to proteins, and creates molecular havoc. Arsenic poisoning results in the gradual onset of skin, blood and neuralogic manifestations, and less dramatic gastrointestinal symptoms. *Initially patients (or victims) report progressive weakness, anorexia and nausea.* With prolonged ingestion of small doses there may be increased salivation, inflammation in the mouth, running nose, vomiting, diarrhea, weight loss and many other symptoms. Small and repeated doses of arsenic poisoning may finally result in death or totally broken health after many months or years. Cardiovascular instability often accompanies or quickly follows these symptoms. Acute renal failure has often occurred. The etiology may be multifactorial, including renal ischemia secondary to hypotension, myoglobinuric- and hemoglobinuric-induced failure, renal cortical necrosis, and a direct toxin effect on renal tubules. Patients may complain of a metallic taste. Arsenic irritates mucous membranes which can appear to be pharyngitis or laryngitis, leading to a *misdiagnosis of upper respiratory tract infection*. Dry hacking cough and buildup of mucus is common, necessitating further coughing to spit out the mucus. The possibility for misdiagnosis of bronchitis, viral pneumonia, flu, cold, or persistent upper respiratory infection exists. Several hospital visits may occur before a correct diagnosis can be rendered in the case of chronic arsenic poisoning.

In addition, liver damage has been reported. Virtually all parts of the human body are effected by arsenic poisoning. Laboratory tests for diagnosis should include complete blood count, liver and renal function tests, and blood and urine arsenic levels. An abdominal radiograph (X-ray) may well show radiopaque contents after ingestion of arsenic. Mee's lines of the nails, horizontal 1 or 2 mm white lines which represent arsenic deposition, occur about 5 % of the time in acute or chronic cases. Facial and peripheral edema may develop as well as diaphoresis. Other potential toxic manifestations include fatigue, malaise, chronic cough, anorexia with weight loss, as well as persistence of acute gastrointestinal symptoms. The minimum lethal exposure of ingested arsenic is only about one milligram per kilogram of weight. A dose of 200-300 milligrams would usually be lethal in an adult.

NORMAL LEVELS IN HUMAN HAIR

The normal average arsenic in human hair is about 0.13 ppm. *Sample Q-1* had 2.6 ppm, which was the highest arsenic in any of our tests. Cadmium was the primary poison, with elevated amounts of arsenic and antimony. The average normal level of antimony in hair is 0.066 ppm. Srila Prabhupada's antimony was about 8.5 X more than his own pre-77 average. The antimony levels in Srila Prabhupada's hair were unusual and seem to be coincident with the cadmium. **Antimony Sources:** A silvery-white metal often mined as a by-product in lead mines, and is used in alloys for lead storage batteries, solder, sheet and pipe metal, bearings, castings and pewter. Antimony oxide is added to textiles as a fire retardant, and also in paints, ceramics, fireworks and enamels. Antimony is naturally present in tiny amounts in the environment, often undetectable, and in larger amounts where industry, incinerators, smelters or coal burning plants have unduly polluted the local area. Antimony is found in antiperspirants, ammunition, phosphorous fertilizer production, and smelting processes. **Antimony Poisoning Symptoms:** Gastrointestinal problems, heart disease, inflammation of respiratory tract, nausea, vomiting, diarrhea, metallic taste, mouth sores, abdominal pain, eye irritation, lung damage, weight loss, kidney disease, high blood pressure, fatigue, muscle aches and weakness, headache, liver failure, anemia. Antimony also can cause elevated uric acid in the blood, or uremia. **Metabolism:** Hair was found to be a good indicator of antimony ingestion and hair is not easily contaminated externally by antimony. Like AS, antimony has a high affinity for sulfhydryl groups on many enzymes.

APPENDIX 5:
DR. J. STEVEN MORRIS CREDENTIALS

The ISKCON leadership tried to discredit Dr. J. Steven Morris, who performed the NAA tests on hair samples for Balavanta and Prabhupada Truth Commission, but there is no justification for these kinds of devious maneuvers. There is no question that Dr. Morris is in the very top of his scientific field. A 2008 bulletin from MURR, p. 3: **Trace-Element Epidemiology:** The Role of Selenium in Human Health.

For 30 years, Dr. J. Steven Morris, a senior research scientist at MURR, has led a trace-element epidemiology (TEE) research program focused on better understanding the influences of both required and toxic trace-elements on human health. Epidemiology is broadly defined as the study of disease in defined populations and strives for an understanding of incidence and risk factors hopefully leading to prevention, or at least delaying onset, of chronic disease. The MURR TEE research program was launched in 1978 using neutron activation analysis to investigate the hypothesis that dietary selenium is protective against cancer. Thirty years later, hypotheses linking selenium to cancer and other chronic diseases, including heart disease, diabetes, AIDS and arthritis, are still of great interest. Over this period the program has participated in approximately 50 population, case control, and intervention trials of selenium and human health – and numerous animal studies, to elucidate selenium's biological roles and how it is distributed in critical organs. So, what has been learned? First, for large population-based epidemiological studies of selenium to be feasible, an accurate biomonitor of selenium intake and status was needed. It was demonstrated that toenail clippings, which are largely protein, satisfy the monitoring requirements for selenium. Second, selenium expresses its essentiality through a collection of selenoproteins growing in number through new discoveries. Third, selenium is classified as a micronutrient, meaning the daily requirement is less than 1/1000th of a gram.

Selenium becomes toxic at intakes not greatly in excess of the requirement. Hence, the optimal range of selenium intake is narrow. Fourth, a subset of the population has been identified in some epidemiological studies to benefit from a daily intake of selenium somewhat in excess of the requirement as established in clinical studies. This controversy regarding actual requirement has led to reports in the media that frequently overstate the benefits of selenium, resulting in a growing number of people who not only take a selenium supplement, but over-supplement with selenium. In response, a major goal of the TEE research program has been to establish a selenium-status diagnostic, using the toenail biomonitor. From research, it's suggested that the optimal range in selenium status is reflected by a toenail selenium concentration in the range of 0.75 to 1.50 PPM. Fifth, a comprehensive study of thousands of Missourians done in 2000-2002 indicates approximately 25 percent may have sub-optimal selenium status. In contrast, the increased use of dietary supplements, and particularly ones containing selenium, has resulted in mis-formulated products in this unregulated health field. MURR is currently leading a follow-up study of selenium intoxication caused by one grossly mis-formulated selenium supplement that has caused serious adverse health effects and contributed to at least one death in the Southeastern U.S. The take-away message is to be wary of dietary supplements and become informed regarding their selenium status.

Dr. Morris works on projects in these areas: **(1)** University educational classes, projects, etc **(2)** Outside contract work for profit to supplement university funding for the Nuclear Reactor Department **(3)** Research in nutritional and environmental effects of various elements such as selenium, arsenic, cadmium, aluminum, etc on human health **(4)** Two major areas of research have been how lack of selenium is related to prostate cancer and how excess of arsenic leads to hardening of arteries and heart disease. **(5)** Study of Aztec and Peruvian mummies including NAA on hair samples thereof. We can all accept Dr. Morris as a pre-eminent expert on the testing for amounts of elements such as arsenic and cadmium in human tissue and hair, and as an expert on what constitutes normal and abnormal levels of the same.

University of Missouri Research Reactor Center: MURR is home to a tank-type nuclear research reactor that serves the University of Missouri's Nuclear Science and Engineering Institute (NSEI) in Columbia. As of March 2012, the MURR is the highest power university research reactor in the U.S. at 10 megawatt thermal output. The fuel is highly enriched uranium. **History and overview:** In 1959, University President Elmer Ellis proposed a research reactor, as part of the University of Missouri. The MURR began operation Oct. 13, 1966 just southwest of the university's main campus and the city's main business district. *In 1970, MURR scientist Dr. George Leddicotte gave the first courtroom testimony on murder trial evidence using neutron activation analysis.* Four years later MURR began operating at 10 MW, making it the highest powered U.S. university reactor. Ir-192 was first produced at MURR for fighting breast cancer in 1976. The first small angle neutron scattering (SANS) spectrometer in the U.S. was installed in 1980. In 1986 the first experiments were performed that led to developing Quadramet and TheraSphere, which were later approved by the U.S. Food and Drug Administration (FDA) for helping fight against bone and liver cancer respectively. Since 2000, systematic upgrades, renovation, and renewal to MURR facilities and instrumentation in preparation for the next 20 years of licensed operation have taken place. In 2002, a 6,000 sq ft building addition opened the way for expansion into cGMP scale up of isotopes. Groundbreaking began in 2006 on a 25,000 sq ft addition to house laboratories, classrooms and offices to advance interdisciplinary research, education and treatment of patients. As of 2012, MURR supports research of 400 faculty and 150 graduate students representing more than 180 departments from more than 100 international universities and 40 federal and industrial labs every year. A cyclotron that will supply mid-Missouri with isotopes for PET imaging and support additional research, development, and clinical trials has been installed.

Research: The MURR contributes to research in boron neutron capture therapy, neutron scattering and neutron interferometry, neutron transmutation doping of semiconductor materials, use of radioisotopes for imaging and treatment of cancer, epidemiology, and archaeology, along with many others. Archaeometry Laboratory: The Archaeometry Laboratory at MURR has been funded by National Science Foundation (NSF) since 1988. *The neutron activation capabilities are used to characterize over 30 major, minor, and trace elements in archaeological and geological materials.* In addition to neutron activation, the laboratory maintains and operates several X-ray fluorescence spectrometers, multiple ICP-mass spectrometers, and a multi-collector ICP-MS for isotope-ratio mass spectrometry. *The laboratory is one of only a handful of facilities in the world to have access to all of these analytical methods.* Data generated by the laboratory are typically used by archaeologists to study issues relating to provenance (geological source) that facilitate understanding of trade and exchange in prehistory. The laboratory also handles analyses of geological materials in support of geology, soil science, and other environmental sciences. Neutron scattering: MURR's neutron scattering program has a long history. Many prominent scientists have graduated from this program and benefited from the in depth, hands on experience afforded by MURR's unique combination of high neutron flux and proximity to a flagship campus (UM). On the other hand, cutting edge research continues on the four active neutron scattering instruments of MURR's beamport floor: Triax (a triple-axis spectrometer), NR/GANS (a neutron reflectometer with spin-polarized capability), 2X-C (a multi-detector diffractometer), and PSD (a high-resolution diffractometer with position sensitive detectors). Landmark neutron interferometry experiments done here have played an important role in opening the field of experimental quantum mechanics.

APPENDIX 6:
CREDENTIALS: DR. PAGE HUDSON

Dr. Richard Page Hudson, Jr., Chief Medical Examiner of the state of North Carolina for 18years from 1968, NC died September 30, 2012. He was a member of ODK honorary society at Richmond College of the University of Richmond where he graduated with a bachelor's degree in chemistry in 1952. At the Medical College of Virginia he served on the Honor Council, was president of Theta Kappa Psi fraternity, receiving a Doctor of Medicine degree in 1956. He was an intern at Johns Hopkins Hospital. He was 2 years into pathology residency training there before going to Japan as a Captain/Officer-in-Charge of the Histopathology Lab at the USAF Hospital Tachikawa for two years. He followed that with a year's Research Fellowship in the Department of Legal Medicine, Harvard Medical School. Pathology residency was completed at the King's County Hospital, Brooklyn NY. After two years on the faculty of the State University of NY, Brooklyn, Dr. Hudson joined the faculty of his alma mater, MCV, in 1964. He became associate professor and specialized in surgical pathology, directed a division of a revised medical student curriculum, oversaw the general pathology curriculum of the School of Dentistry, and presented scientific work results in national meetings and medical journals.

In 1968 Page was recruited to forensic pathology, as N Carolina instituted a medical examiner system to provide expert input to investigate suspicious, unnatural, and unattended deaths in counties as well as at the Chief Medical Examiner (OCME). The headquarters and central facilities were located with the Pathology Department of the University of North Carolina in Chapel Hill. Dr. Hudson was appointed Associate Professor, later Professor and Chief of the Division of Forensic Pathology, as well as serving as the state's first Chief Medical Examiner. In his 18 year tenure he led the development of the OCME to become arguably the best state-wide medical examiner system in the country. Close integration with the UNC-CH School of Medicine was necessary in his opinion in providing NC with a top-flight death investigation system. The OCME developed a forensic pathology residency training program that produced more than a score of young forensic pathologists in his tenure. As Chief Medical Examiner Dr. Hudson was also a co-founder of the Sudden Infant Death Program in NC, and of the model NC Child Medical Evaluation program for living children suspected of being victims of child abuse or neglect. He expressed throughout his professional life his admiration for the law enforcement officers of NC, the state's Superior Court and hundreds of practicing physicians who were NC's county medical examiners and regional pathologists. Enjoying the challenge of 'new,' he aided the medical school at East Carolina University. He taught and practiced pathology and forensic pathology, helping ECU develop a major extension of the Medical Examiner System. He retired as Emeritus Professor and then worked with attorneys, law enforcement and private citizens requiring forensic pathology consultation, testifying frequently in Court and depositions. He was a medical missionary in Bosnia, re: identification of the unknown dead and evaluating prisoner abuse.

APPENDIX 7:
CADMIUM POISONING CHARTS

Cadmium levels chart comparing amounts of cadmium, 0 to 16 ppm

(1) Srila Prabhupada had an average ±16 ppm cadmium in his 1977 hair. **(2)** This is compared to the worst USA toxic waste dump with 4 ppm, **(3)** to the highest value at ARL Labs of 2 ppm cadmium in 500,000 hair tests, **(4)** to Dr. Hudson saying 1 ppm cadmium was a hefty load, **(5)** to the average environmentally/ industrially contaminated person at 0.387 ppm, **(6)** the average normal person of 0.064 ppm cadmium.

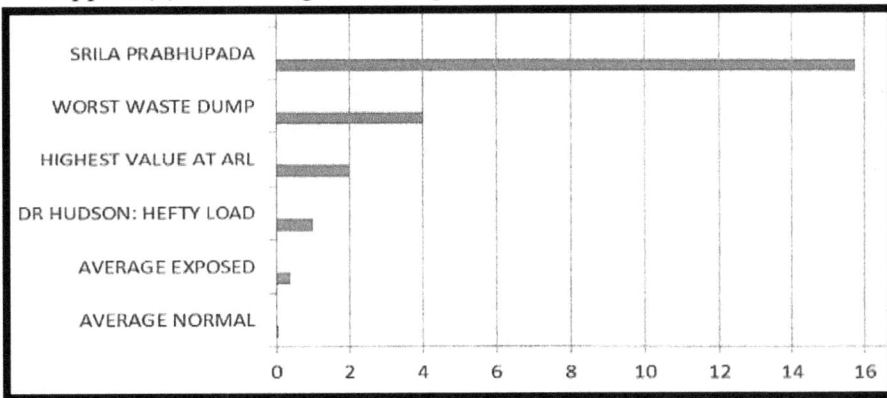

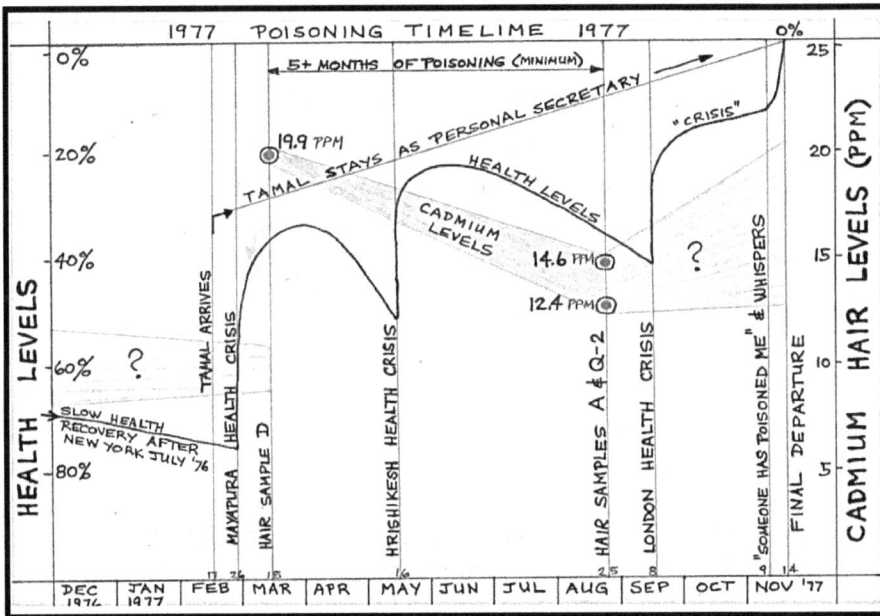

APPENDIX 8:
HEALTH HISTORY 1975-77

Srila Prabhupada's 1976-77 health history has been reconstructed by research and compiling from many biographical sources and devotee memories. No single source fully chronicles Srila Prabhupada's medications, health history, the various doctors, their diagnoses, and their treatments. Sources included *TKG's Diary* by Tamal K Goswami (**TkgD,**1998),

Bhaktivedanta Archives: Letters/Tamal **(Archives)**, Srila Prabhupada letters **(SPL)**, *Transcendental Diary* by Hari Sauri **(TransD**, 5 volumes), *Srila Prabhupada Lilamrita* **(SPLila**, Satsvarupa   ), *ISKCON in the 1970's* **(ISK70**: Satsvarupa, 1997), Abhiram das Memoirs **(ABHI**, Nov. 1978, Archives), Unpublished Hari Sauri diary **(HSUnpub**, Oct-Nov 77), Srutirupa dasi Memoir **(SRUTI**, Oct 1978 Archives), *Ocean of Mercy* **(OCEAN,** Bhakticharu 1977 memoirs**)**, *Srila Prabhupada's Conversation Books* **(ConvBk)** **Other abbreviations: SP:** Srila Prabhupada, **BHAV:** Bhavananda, **BCS:** Bhakticharu Swami

The following are only a few key excerpts from Srila Prabhupada's health history, and the full, unabridged version is found separately in *Srila Prabhupada: Mysterious Health Decline* (Volume 4).

Eight of Srila Prabhupada's ten "mystery" symptoms, unique to cadmium poisoning, are marked in the health history to highlight their prevalence and to assist in future research.

① **EXTREME PHOTOPHOBIA/ LIGHT SENSITIVE EYES**

② **EXCESSIVE MUCUS, CHRONIC BHRONCHITIS**

③ **COUGH, COLDS, CHRONIC RHINITIS & CONGESTION**

④ **SCRATCHY, HOARSE, HUSKY, WEAK VOICE**

⑤ **URINARY TRACT & KIDNEY INFECTIONS, PHIMOSIS**

⑥ **EXPRESSIONLESS, COLORLESS, PALE FACE**

⑦ **TEARFUL, SENSITIVE, MELANCHOLIC, EMOTIONAL**

⑧ **LIVER CHANGES, ANOMALIES, PROBLEMS**

A great deal of information came from the tape recordings as seen in the Conversations Books. This health history allows us to study Srila Prabhupada's medical conditions in his last year or so. Srila Prabhupada's poisoning likely started in May 1976 with consistent, unusual physical symptoms in Hawaii, New Vrindaban, and a severe health decline in New York, July 1976. Thereafter (London, France, Tehran, and India) followed a limited, slow recovery up to Feb. 26, 1977. Hair analyses prove a massive cadmium poisoning from Feb. through Nov. 1977, and the history of symptoms helps to see how far back the poisoning began.

One should be wary of the veracity and truthfulness in some of the biographical accounts, especially those by the poisoning suspects who whitewash historical incidents inaccurately. Also those who are compromised by institutional/ political influence and pressure or who are suspects will tend to explain things falsely. Tamal and BCS's accounts must be carefully screened for contradictory and unusual descriptions of events and statements unconfirmed by other sources. Both were trying to discredit the "poison theory." The tape transcripts are of course reliable. Satsvarupa's accounts were often distorted, such as his account of the May 28, 1977 talks. Tamal and BCS have clearly doctored and written their books with what they want us to believe. Still, by taking their versions with some "salt," in combination with other sources, we get a pretty accurate history of Srila Prabhupada's health in 1976-77. The "mystery symptoms" are indicated from mid-1976 since poisoning is believed to have started then.

DEC. 20, 1975: *"SP is not feeling well; swelling in his legs, feet, and hands trouble him. To see his body puffed with fluid is very disturbing. [...] SP said this is due to uremia, a toxic condition caused by waste products in the blood normally eliminated in the urine."*

DEC. 24, 1975: Dr. Patel: *You have taken that tablet for passing more urine?* **SP**: *I am passing (laughing).* **Dr. Patel**: *Yes, sir, but you have got the edema on the leg...* **COMMENT:** This shows that SP had some kidney problems well before the 1976-77 poisoning.

MAY 1976: At 1:00 AM, May 4, 1976, in Hawaii, SP rang his bell. *"Looking strained, SP informed us that he was ill and would not take his usual walk or give the morning Bhagwatam class. He is again having trouble with uremia, using the bathroom every hour. His feet are badly swollen and he is suffering dizzy spells."* Coincidentally Tamal had arrived from New York *"with a written report to give SP on their China preaching endeavors. Since the Mayapur festival, when SP ordered Tamal Krishna Maharaja to begin something in China..."* The report detailed the immense difficulties in trying to preach in China. SP said, *"Then give it up. If it is too difficult, don't waste time."* Thus the mission to China was cancelled. SP dictated a letter to all American GBCs, re-installing Tamal to his pre-Mayapur responsibilities as head of the Radha Damodar travelling parties and as a BBT trustee for North America. Tamal thereafter relieved Madhudvisa as GBC for the New York zone. On May 10, SP complained that he was not sleeping well, *"feeling ill with dizziness and passing too much urine."* On May 22 SP rested long in the afternoon and *"complained of weakness due to heart palpitations."* Then SP had no more striking health problems except for a cold.

JUNE-JULY 1976: *"...warning signs of His Divine Grace's deteriorating health grew stronger. He suffered attacks of toothache, high blood pressure, heart palpitations, kidney disease and flu with stoic indifference, and relentlessly pushed himself on despite his weakening bodily condition."* On June 23, in New Vrindaban: *"SP said very little on his walk and the class was short. He is experiencing disturbing heart palpitations and his uremia has caused his legs and feet to swell again... (but) his face is no longer swollen."* June 24: further heart palpitations and no walk. June 25, 26: no morning walks, and SP's heart was *"still giving him trouble."* June 28 SP felt *"heart strain"* riding in a pickup truck on a bumpy road. *"I am very weak nowadays. Still I am working... I think I shall not be* *able to go for walks. This morning my heart was beating too much."* June 30: *"SP was not well again today and had an ashen pallor...*⑥ *only a very short walk..."* Pradyumna gave class. *"When SP is unable to discourse on Krishna conscious philosophy, it is a serious matter indeed."* The next day SP skipped his walk and his class was only fifteen minutes. *"He is still weak and congested with mucus...*② *He doesn't eat much of anything..."* July 2: no morning walk. July 3: his health was *"still not good."* July 4: *"His respiratory system is quite blocked with mucus,*② *making his voice*④ *sometimes thick and husky."* These symptoms are the same as during 1977.

SP arrived in New York on July 9, hosted by Tamal as GBC, Adi Keshava Swami as temple president. July 12, 2:15 AM: *"...he looked very ill. He was gaunt and complained of severe chest pains and an inability to either rest or work. He had already changed his diet to simple kichari because of these symptoms, but the problem has persisted...."* At noon July 13 SP again complained of chest pains, which he attributed to *"too much anxiety."* Later SP had a pain in his foot, which was massaged for two hours. July 14: *"illness forced SP to cancel his afternoon darshan."* Early July 16, while visiting Gita Nagari farm, SP sat at his desk: *"He was ashen, and told me he was experiencing severe kidney pain and could not translate."* Back in New York, Dr. Bhagat, a life member, found very high blood pressure, a weak heart, and uremia likely due to a kidney stone. Diuretic, antibiotics, pain reliever, sleeping pills and psychotropic relaxant were prescribed. No sugar, salt were to be taken. SP took no medicines and did not change his diet.

July 20: SP *"now has a heavy cold which is worsening,"* SP took only a dry bath, skipped his massage. SP was encouraged to delay his scheduled departure that evening but he could not be convinced to stay. The overnight flight to London was very hard on SP. *"Racked by a heavy cold, SP spent practically the whole flight lying down, coughing*③ *up large amounts of mucus*② *every few minutes."* He hardly moved for over 6 hours. Deplaning, SP walked slowly, wobbly, and hesitatingly. He was very ill. *"SP has been very very sick since he has come. On the way back from the airport he vomited every five minutes, we had to stop the car. He did not eat for three days and is very weak."* Hari Sauri: *"It was alarming because it consisted more of thick, yellow bile and mucus*② *rather than food waste."* In London SP went straight to his rooms and rested until the next morning, SP *"had heart palpitations,"* was very weak, ate two spoonful's of fruit, refused massage, ate bit of kichari at lunch, asked for arrangements to return to Bombay at once. SP rested all afternoon again, still very ill.

July 26 SP rested all morning, *"although he has begun to eat more today."* When George Harrison visited, SP said, *"I have old man's disease, cough*[3] *and cold*[3], *so coughing."* July 27: SP was still coughing[3] and full of mucus[2]. The next day SP flew to Paris, and *"he is at least well enough to walk and resume his travels."* In France, he resumed some translation work. July 30: *"...still weak, and after a very short morning walk... He is still full of mucus*[2] *and alters his diet frequently to speed recovery."* July 31: *"Since we arrived SP has been resting until late in the morning, after 7 AM. He has not taken a full morning walk since leaving New York. This morning he ate very little for breakfast. He also told us to make all endeavor necessary to prevent him from catching cold*[3]. *He said that, 'With an old body, it means thin blood, and this turns to mucus*[2]."

AUG. 1-DEC. 1, 1976: Aug. 1, SP felt strong enough to make a short tour of the France farm grounds. Aug. 3: *"It was good to see him eating with relish even though it wasn't much."* The next day SP asked for some bada. Late on Aug. 4, SP *"...fell silent for a while, occasionally still coughing*[3], *but at least not dislodging the heavy mucus*[2] *of just a few days ago."* In Tehran on Aug. 11, during his morning walk, he spent most of the hour sitting on a park bench. Bombay, Aug. 14: *"...to go out onto Juhu beach... However, because of the persistent swelling in SP's legs caused by his malfunctioning kidneys he wasn't feeling up to it..."*

Aug. 27, New Delhi, SP's *"physical health is still weak, and so he took the opportunity for a little well-earned rest."* Aug. 28, morning walk, he was *"still feeling weak. He sat for most of the time on a bench... Since returning from Europe his health has definitely improved."* Vrindaban, Sept. 11: *"SP's health is not very good. He has been suffering from high blood pressure for several days... suffering a general decline in health and strength. At this time last year he was striding strongly down the road every morning for at least an hour and seemed quite full of vigor. Now he rarely takes such walks."* SP's muscle tone had declined. On Sept. 13, SP has *"great difficulty speaking very much at the moment due to his high blood pressure."*

Notably, Satsvarupa's biography includes *nothing* July 20, 1976 to Jan. 9, 1977. Hari Sauri's Transcendental Diary covers only up to Dec. 1, 1976. The tape recordings are in the Conversations Books. TransD: Vol. 5, Preface: *"...trying to cope with his failing health. High blood pressure was a major problem along with poor digestion."*

Oct. 13: After walking for 20 minutes, SP became tired and weak, and sat down to rest. Oct.17: Indicating a partial recovery from his severe July "illness:" *"He ate an unusually large amount, even calling for seconds."* *"...His strength is depleted and he complains sometimes of not having any appetite. Despite his blood pressure remaining high..."* Oct.31: *"SP is still suffering quite severely from high blood pressure and has hardly been seeing anyone. He is not taking his morning walks on a regular basis..."*

Nov. 3: *"SP is also coughing③ quite a lot and has had a lot of mucus②, so his voice is a little thick and nasal."* Nov. 4: *"SP is following his regular schedule, but his health is getting weaker and weaker."* Nov. 14: *"SP has been experiencing some weakness and poor digestion...* Nov. 20: *"I always follow close behind on the stairs out of fear that he may not have the strength to make it. His health seems to be on a continual decline, and he is commenting more and more on his bodily weakness.* Nov. 21: *"because of his poor health he is not keen to remain in Vrindaban in the winter season."*

SUMMARY 1976: SP had an illness in Hawaii for a few days in May, again in New Vrindaban in June, and a much more serious illness in New York in July, a severe health attack upon leaving New York, then recovering slowly for months travelling abroad. This illness was characterized by weakness, heart palpitations, swelling, poor appetite, and respiratory infection-like symptoms of cough③, cold③, and mucus②. It was an unusual combination of symptoms: digestive, cardiac, respiratory. It appears SP's poisoning began in 1976 but there is no forensic proof of this yet. SP was old and had a long-standing kidney weakness, yet the 1976 symptoms that began May 4, 1976 and became extreme in New York perfectly resemble the 1977 cadmium poisoning symptoms. Coincidence?

JANUARY 1977: SP's health partially recovered since a severe attack in July, and he even began to take beach walks in Bombay. Then another health downturn occurred at the Kumbha Mela on Jan. 12-13. Tamal was not there, but prime suspects Bhavananda, Jayapataka Swami were.

JAN. 13: All night SP was very cold, sitting fully clothed by his desk with a small kerosene heater. *"By morning, SP had a bad cold③ with runny nose and eyes... His hands and feet were swollen..."* **JAN. 14:** *"...not feeling well, very uncomfortable. His hands and feet were swelling, he was very ill with a mucus② problem ."* Rarely had SP been so sick. *JAN. 18:* *"SP had recuperated a couple of days in Calcutta. His head cold③ had gone away, but the swelling in his hands and feet persisted, as did other maladies(?)"* **JAN. 19:** *"SP said that he has no digestion and that he was not feeling strong. ...he could not eat foods cooked in ghee. SP referred to his kidneys."* **JAN. 23:** SP followed a careful diet, avoiding ghee and spices. *JAN. 26:* SP carried upstairs in a chair. *"...he (SP) began to stand, using his cane as a support, but suddenly, as he was about halfway up, he dropped down again onto the chair. Hari Sauri had to lift him to his feet..."*

FEBRUARY 1977: Feb. 7: Mayapur. *"As far as his health goes, SP is not really any better. The swelling is still there and digestion is still bad."* **FEB. 8:** *"But SP's ill health persisted – asked how he felt, he replied, "Very bad."* **FEB. 10:** *"while walking up the steep stone steps, SP's legs suddenly gave way, and he collapsed. Hari Sauri was close enough to catch him. It* *was the second time SP had collapsed in less than two weeks." **FEB. 12:*** Pishima cooked SP lunch and *"became sick. For the next two days he did not take anything except hot milk and medicine." **FEB. 16:*** SP: *"Actually it does not matter even if I die immediately. I have given the basis for everything, and now if they simply manage things nicely..."* **FEB. 17:** When Adi Keshava Prabhu came from New York, SP was energetic and showed few signs of illness or weakness. **FEB. 22:** Today Tamal became SP's permanent personal secretary and primary caretaker until SP's departure on Nov. 14.

FEB. 26: SP *"became very ill again."* Late in the day, *"SP's health deteriorated noticeably. Then a very serious illness began. His temperature rose to 104 or 105 degrees. For three days and two nights the high fever continued, and he was always moaning."* SP could not eat, His body was very swollen, there was great difficulty in urinating, and SP could not even talk. He remained in his quarters. SP said he thought he was going to leave his body. This was a major health attack. *"...Feb. 1977, when SP first started to get really sick... just lying in his bed... If he coughed③, you make sure he had his spittoon there ...or help him to go to the bathroom... SP was so sick that he was sometimes moaning, and he could not sleep, because he would be coughing③ so much."* SP was left extremely weak and semi-invalid. *" SP was extremely weak as he required to be carried on a palanquin."* SP: *"The last fortnight I was thinking I was dead..."*

MARCH 1977: SP was still very ill and weak from the sudden attack of ill health on Feb. 26. **MAR. 6, 7:** *"SP is getting sick and his appetite is failing him. He is feeling very bad, but he drank some barley water."* **MAR. 10:** *"SP is becoming very, very ill."* An expensive medicine with musk, gold and pearls produced no visible results. *"SP's health had been bad for months... He stopped going out for his usual morning walks, and he needed help just going to the toilet... Even using his cane, he needed support by reaching around his waist with one hand and holding his left shoulder with the other."* **MAR. 13:** Hari Sauri left SP's service. SP began to eat again, although not fully recovered. **MAR. 20: Tamal:** *...works for swelling. The swelling is due to urine, not...* **SP**: *(heavy coughing)* ③ **MAR. 22:** SP was lowered off the plane in Bombay by hydraulic lift. SP *"could not stand and walk without assistance..."* SP was carried on a palanquin. *"Ever since SP's extreme weakness of health had occurred in Mayapur, he would often sit for hours alone and silent. When he spoke his voice④ was often hoarse or faint."* **MAR. 25:** *"His health was not good and he was physically weak... Due to his poor health..."* **MA. 26: SP**: *Still I am 80% not good. But 20%.* **Tamal**: *It's very strange even now, because it doesn't seem to be anything apparently wrong, yet it's not good health.* **MAR. 27:** SP had a cough③. *"I am not keeping good health..."*

APRIL 1977: SP long ago stopped morning walks, remained almost constantly in his quarters, except for the morning greeting of the deities in the temple. SP arranged for quiet and solitude so that he could focus on his translation work. SP had no appetite and his health neither improved nor worsened. SP considered going to Kashmir. *"SP had little appetite. He could not eat anything heavy, and sometimes he had no appetite even for a cup of milk. One morning SP asked for orange juice..."* Bhavananda returned to Mayapur. *"His intelligence was ever sharp and alert, and yet his health did not improve..."* Glances, nods, hand motions and "Hmmm's" were common. *APR. 5:* SP: *I have no appetite. I cannot digest. APR. 10:* **Tamal**: *...you are taking so little prasadam that it is not to be expected that you can do very much physical activity... I think simply it is just weakness now... You've been maintaining a fast now for nearly two months* SP was averse to light, keeping his rooms dark①. *APR. 15:* SP was very weak and did not have the strength for vigorous preaching as before. *APR. 16:* *"Your suggestion that I come to Fiji for recovering my health is very good. We are now thinking of going to Kashmir... My health is very slowly improving."* *APR. 18:* Dr. Sharma found excess water in parts of the body, noting diarrhea and high blood pressure. Few were allowed to see SP. He instructed how to make neem paste compresses for his feet and legs, which reduced swelling. *APR. 23:* **Tamal**: *The milk has no taste...* **SP**: *I have no taste.* *APR. 29:* SP: *"...mentally to keep the brain, little fruit, milk, is sufficient. So I may live on fruit or milk. There is no difficulty. What is the use of taking chapattis and rice?"*

MAY 1977: SP discussed different locations favorable for his health. Bombay was hot in May, and it was decided to go to Rishikesh where the air, water and climate were pleasant. *MAY 1:* **SP**: *There is spasm in the heart. ...Lie down means spasm. Sit up, not so painful. MAY 3: "My health is not very good..." MAY 5:* SP: *"Actually, with this sickness I cannot sleep at night. ...I cannot eat also." MAY 7:* Arriving in Delhi, he walked down the plane's steps by himself. That night they all took the train to Hardwar. SP's limbs were greatly swollen again. *MAY 8:* SP liked Rishikesh and ate jalebis and kicharis heartily. *MAY 11: "Yes, my health is improving a very little. ...in Rishikesh. It is very nice and the climate is much better than Bombay's." MAY 14:* SP's voice④ was extremely faint. *MAY 15: "...a violent storm hit, and with the storm came a drastic turn in SP's health. He said the end was near, and he asked to go immediately to Vrindaban."* SP's hands and feet were swollen. *"From the material point of view, it is not good. Please consider how everything may be turned over to the G.B.C., so that in my absence everything will go on. You may make a will, and I will sign it."*

MAY 16: At 1:30 AM, suddenly SP called Tamal and BCS: *"...the symptoms are not good. I want to leave immediately for Vrindaban. If I am going to die, let it be in Vrindaban."* There was another drastic health downturn with heart spasms. *"SP rang his bell… 'The time has come for me to leave my body. …I want to leave my body in Vrindaban'… I ran downstairs and woke up Tamal"* **MAY 17:** Arriving in Vrindaban, he was carried by palanquin to his quarters. *"So I cannot speak. I am feeling very weak. I was to go to other places like Chandigarh program, but I cancelled the program because the condition of my health is very deteriorating. So I preferred to come to Vrindaban. If death takes place, let it take here..."* SP: *" Now take it that I am dead."* **MAY 18:** Due to heart palpitations last night, SP could hardly sleep. **MAY 20:** SP told what to do after his departure. *"The system of management will go on as it is now. There is no need of changing."* **Tamal:** *You've made such an effort to get better and it still hasn't improved. So how long one can keep trying like that?* **MAY 21:** Now SP would spend his mornings and evenings listening to kirtan or readings, usually lying in bed with eyes closed. Tamal would carefully restrict most visitors and letters, answering them himself. SP's morning rides and deity darshans all but ceased. Lying in bed, and sometimes sitting at his desk, he would be mostly silent, but would sometimes speak, albeit one would need to lean close to hear. *"Eating was almost nil."* SP requested the GBCs come to prepare for his departure. Tamal *was also happy that SP seemed relieved by giving up the struggle for life and giving up all worldly concerns.* Bhavananda also was happy that he would rejoin Krishna. *"…it was a great strain for him to remain within his body, which was now malfunctioning so badly. It would be much easier to give up his body and join Lord Krishna…"*

MAY 22: SP said: *"This disease is not ordinary. It is always fatal… Lost appetite means life is finished."* SP had grown very thin, appearing like an ascetic. *"…from the physical condition there is no hope."* SP's voice④ was hoarse and weak. **MAY 23:** SP signed his will. **MAY 24:** Jayapataka and Bhavananda arrived. SP decided to ask Dr. Ghosh to come to treat him. *"…SP sitting up behind his desk looking weak, pale and yellowish⑥, having a dim voice④, sagging eyes which were sensitive to light①. …SP had blue rings under his eyes."* **MAY 25:** SP would now spend more time lying down and less sitting up. SP has much trouble with heart palpitations, often caused simply by speaking. **BHAV:** *I noticed, SP, your complexion is yellowish⑥. Liver is…* **SP:** *There is no hope of life. Therefore we have called you. This condition is hopeless. We have given our will. …If I die in Vrindaban, there is no harm… We have become very, very weak. No appetite.* **MAY 26:** GBCs arrived. Tamal wanted to know where to repose SP's body after his departure. **MAY 28:** The famous conversation about initiations after SP's departure. **MAY 29:** SP: *I am not afraid of death. …Why shall I be afraid?"*

JUNE 1977: Early June brought hope of recovery; SP started his car rides and seeing the temple deities every morning with kirtan. SP often sat in his private garden next to his rooms; his voice *"soft and weak."* Sukhananda das to apply hot/ cold compresses and do massage. SP: *"Now it is not so bad. I am drinking fruit juices. ...by midnight it cools off. There is no need for me to eat cereals, ...gradually, I will increase my translating."* *JUNE 2:* SP: *"Soon I will get down and walk myself."* *JUNE 3:* "SP slept well and ate ...puris with fried portals."* The GBC all left. SP's health improved a little. The *Times of India* ran a front page story entitled, *"SP Seriously Ill,"* but a few days later the paper reported *"SP Now Better."* *JUNE 5:* SP was too weak for the morning car ride. Dr. Ghosh concluded SP had no chance of recovery. *"His organs were finished; his body was filling with urea"* and recommended dialysis in Delhi. *JUNE 7:* SP awoke in the night very weak. No appetite or taste. *"Unfortunately, His Divine Grace's health has taken a turn for the worst. Prabhupada's body is practically worn out and all of the internal organs are no longer functioning properly. This includes the kidneys, the liver, and the heart."* *JUNE 8:* Dr. Ghosh predicted SP would walk again in a week. SP said, *"I may stay or go, but in my books I will live forever."* Taking very little food, it appeared he was being sustained by kirtan and preaching reports. *JUNE 10:* Tamal has taken over SP's correspondence. *JUNE 20:* SP's heart gave pain. *JUNE 23:* Tamal: *"SP's health is a lot better than when you were here. He is eating regularly now, although not very much. And every night he is translating again."* *JUNE 30:* SP's eyesight had deteriorated so he could hardly do his translating. SP had conjunctivitis; his eyes runny, filled with mucus②.

JULY 1977: *JULY 5:* SP drank pineapple juice and had a cough③ and *"a cold"*③ the last two days. *JULY 7:* *"His health is maintaining, not getting any worse but not significantly better."* *JULY 8:* SP's cold③ has not improved; Vick's Vaporub used. *JULY 9:* SP is now too weak to sit up on his own. His health seemed stable, not improving but also not at the previous crisis level. *"SP is suffering from a cold③ just now, but amazingly his translation work has doubled."* *JULY 12:* BCS: "He asked me to go look for an Ayurvedic doctor named Vanamali Kaviraj... [who] sitting on a chair, felt his pulse for a long time... SP's kidneys were not functioning properly [which] was causing the swelling of his legs and pain in the body. ...I began cooking for SP regularly again. ...As SP's health improved, so did his appetite. Each morning he would tell me what he wanted for lunch."* *JULY 13:* The cough③ syrup prevented any translating. *JULY 17:* Tamal: *"It seems like your voice has become a little congested③ tonight."* *JULY 19:* Abhiram: *"[SP is] very ill, requiring a lot of physical assistance. It was taxing upon Upendra and Tamal."* *JULY 20:* SP said re: his hands and legs,

"It is reducing so much, soon I will be only bones... I want to eat, but I cannot..." **JULY 25:** Abhiram started to assist with SP's care.

JULY 26: In three weeks SP's pulse went down from 118 to 62. Bonamali: *"the internal fever had gone."* He thought appetite would return within two weeks. SP ate maybe a palmful a day; in three weeks he had taken only 2 or 3 sips of milk a day. BCS was cooking. **JULY 27:** *"SP's health seemed to be worsening again. And again he mentioned that the end might come at any moment."* **JULY 28:** SP's translating was decreasing; he was increasingly weaker from not eating. Tamal proposed a preaching tour to the West. SP became *"very enthusiastic about going abroad,"* and asked that three astrologers be consulted, *"whether I should go, whether I shall be cured, how long I shall live."* SP wore *"dark"* sunglasses① even in a dark room. He had trouble seeing properly and had sensitivity to light. **JULY 29:** A proposed travel itinerary was made. **JULY 30:** SP: *"This disease is in the kidney, so wherever I go, this kidney will go... According to medical science, the only cure is cutting or dialysis. But kaviraja medicine says there is cure."* **JULY 31:** Hardly eating in 6 weeks. Irregular in sleep, massage, translating. He approved a prayer: *"My dear Lord Krishna, if You desire, please cure SP."*

AUGUST 1977: Now SP was *"bedridden."* *"...sick all day with pain in the right side of his chest."* **AUG. 2:** *"SP is worse than he has ever been, taking some milk and fruit juices only. Today he has been vomiting, eating nothing, nausea and lack of digestion."* SP: *"I can no longer see properly."* *"SP has become very weak. Never in his life has he been this ill."* The *kaviraja* believed SP's appetite would gradually return. SP still went to see the deities every morning. SP drank apple juice but vomited, *"felt very ill all night."* SP: *"I am going through a difficult time and am now feeling restless."* *"(SP) has been very ill since Gaura Purnima. ...he is invalid and just to go to the latrine he requires the assistance of two persons. ...an acute case of dropsy..."* **AUG. 3:** SP remained nauseated. **AUG. 5:** SP ate some solid food. **AUG. 6:** Abhiram: *"...started to eat again, but his eyesight is gradually failing."* **AUG. 9:** *"He speaks less and with more difficulty. His sleep is not sound."* **AUG. 10:** SP: *"Not at all good. I am very, very weak."*

AUG. 11: SP used new Polaroid sunglasses① even inside and going for deity darshan. *"Now the kaviraja's medicine is doing nothing."* An astrological report: *"Then he mentioned that there may be some trouble from... maybe financial or maybe from juniors, from subordinates."* [danger from poisoners?] Three physicians from Ayurvedic Hospital in Delhi will come. **Satsvarupa:** *"New word is that he is 'even worse,' but I think I should go."* **AUG. 12:** SP: *"I have no taste. What is the use?"* Tamal: *"For the past few days, SP had been very quiet, almost transcendentally morose."* **AUG. 15:** *"Today was the day of doctors."* Naveen Krishna brought his father Dr. Khurana, who urged kidney dialysis. *AUG. 17:* *"Tamal said that SP's illness is psychological and subtle. A few days ago he was very bad. [...] SP is very thin. We watched through the doorway as he ate his lunch... eats here and there."* No tape recordings from Aug. 18 to Oct. 2.

AUG. 18: *"...he definitely wants to travel to the West" "I've tried to be cured here for the last six months. I have still a taste for milk, so it is not hopelessness."* *AUG. 19:* SP: *"'I'm disgusted... These kavirajas come, say they will get me well in four days, and then later they say it will take a long time... These are my last days."* *AUG. 20:* *"In this condition, anyone else would prepare for death, but I am going on a tour."* *AUG. 25:* *"(SP) was very sick. All night, he was awake and moaning. He said, 'Last night there was colic pain. It was a death-like pain. Just thinking of it, I am horrified. It is due to mucus②. Indigestion. It is a very critical situation.'"* Due to *"severe pain,"* Bonamali gave black salt for acid indigestion. SP tried to vomit all the previous night and through the day. *"For six months, all doctors and medicines have failed to produce an appetite." "He could not sit in any one position for more than a few minutes because of the pain."* SP was given enemas. *AUG. 27:* SP went to the Delhi airport lying in the Mercedes' back seat and moved by wheelchair to the plane. In London the devotees were shocked to see him so thin, weak, expressionless, and wearing dark sunglasses①. SP *"appeared like a powerful sage who had been undergoing long austerities for the benefit of humankind and who had become transcendental to his body, although living in it."* *AUG. 28:* SP came to the temple room by palanquin with dark sunglasses①. He sat expressionless⑥ during kirtan. *AUG. 29:* *"He hardly talked, constantly in trance as he sat absolutely still with his eyes closed."* *AUG. 30:* SP: *"I want to introduce varnashram at our Pennsylvania farm, the biggest problem of life is solved: food."* *AUG. 31:* SP was consuming mostly juices and had trouble passing urine⑤ but he rested well.

SEPTEMBER 1977: SEPT. 1: Abhiram: SP ate well, the swelling went down. *SEPT. 2:* Often SP would cry very easily⑦ as he *"was so sensitive."* His *"eyes①* would hurt in bright lights and he always wore sunglasses."* Srutirupa: *"He ate better today than for as long as I have been with him,"* and passing urine easier now. **COMMENT:** Noted are many unusual health ups and downs since February. *SEPT. 3:* SP's feet are swollen but he was in an *"upbeat mood,"* about touring the U.S. soon. *SEPT. 4:* SP did not eat and had pain in his left kidney; a hot salt compress was applied. *SEPT. 5:* SP had trouble again in passing urine today⑤. He had eaten practically nothing for days except some *"7-Up"* soda, but today took royal jelly with honey. His digestion and appetite were zero. *SEPT. 6:* Janmastami: SP took milk. SP. *"Now I have come to the West in a broken* *condition of health. ...no one would think of touring. An ordinary man would prepare for death. But I am not afraid of death, so why not let me see once again all of my beloved disciples and the Temples all over the world."*

SEPT. 7: Vyasa-puja day, SP shed many tears⑦. SP had swelling again, acute pain in the genital area. **SEPT. 8:** The swelling, genital pain had increased due to inability to pass urine⑤. This could lead to coma and death in hours. SP began to shake and he had a seizure. He fainted and his breathing stopped, his heart *"violently palpitating."* SP came to; his urinary tract⑤ was blocked. At Peace Memorial Hospital, Watford he was able to pass urine after a circumcision was done on the unusually thickened foreskin⑤ (phimosis). The doctor *"had never seen such a thing in his life."* (see a similar incident, Ch. 39). It is unknown if any tests were done. The doctor's analysis was: *"...difficulties in passing urine had produced a back pressure on the kidneys, causing gradual damage and a buildup of uric acid in the body, weakening the body, causing the nausea, non-digestion and a malnutritioned body of only 60 to 70 pounds."* **SEPT. 9:** *"...SP's health suddenly became much worse... he now requested that he be taken back to India... His health had been good... his health had suddenly taken a turn for the worse- he had developed a urinary-tract infection⑤ and had a minor operation. ...his condition had deteriorated. He had hardly been able to eat and had very little energy."* **SEPT. 10:** A record was kept on the amount of liquids in and out. SP had heart palpitations worse than when in Vrindaban. Tamal tried to encourage SP to go on to America. **SEPT. 11:** Despite the circumcision, *"SP says there is still difficulty in passing urine⑤."* **COMMENT:** Cadmium poisoning inflames the urethra.

SEPT. 12: SP decided to go to Bombay. Tamal refused to do the re-ticketing. Brahmananda had to do it. SP left London, boarding the plane by forklift. **SEPT. 14:** Bombay. *"I shall try to live on milk and fruit juice..."* Abhiram: *"SP appears to be getting stronger."* **SEPT. 15:** Mucus② buildup, much spitting and coughing③, and due to the mucus SP slept propped up on pillows. SP took a little fruit juice and mung bean water. SP was almost motionless and silent in bed all day, with no strength. SP said: *"Crisis."* **SEPT. 17:** SP was using a bedpan. Tamal: *"I presented a number of arguments against calling another doctor..."* SP could not see, recognizing visitors by their voices. *"His eyes were almost completely failing him."* **SEPT. 19:** *"SP's condition having grown worse, we now attend to him constantly."* **SEPT. 20:** SP became very congested③ with a bad cough③. SP could only sit in his wheelchair for a minute before returning to bed. **SEPT. 21:** SP could not go to see the deities in the temple. *"I feel that at any moment I could die."* No strength, started taking vegetable broth. Loose bowels. **SEPT. 23:** Took Horlicks supplement, cough[3] was the result. Wrapped by a large shawl, he was *"shaking slightly,"* though it was warm. His face was colorless[6], and his extremities were swollen more than usual. Massage was skipped due to the cough[3]. **SEPT. 24:** Kaviraja Ram Gopal came; SP had liver[8] and kidney problems. Tamal was criticized this doctor. **SEPT. 25:** Constipated and coughing[3] with too much mucus[2]. SP's limbs were swollen *"more than ever."* **SEPT.26:** No sleep due to mucus[2] and cough[3]; the cough syrup did not help. *"...again that SP's health is in crisis, 'the worst.' He is lying on his back and even to turn is a great effort. His secretary has called saying that all GBC men should come to Bombay at end Oct."* **SEPT. 27:** *"SP was completely exhausted. Mucus[2] was filling his whole system, and his legs and hands were very swollen. Even his eyes had much mucus[2]."*

SEPT. 28: *"Most amazingly,"* SP's condition suddenly became much better, with hardly any mucus, well rested. SP's signature *"was very unsteady,"* and he was very weak. **SEPT. 29:** SP decided to go to Vrindaban, invited discussion on the best course his treatment, and asked all his disciples be called to come be with him in Vrindaban. The message was changed: *"send only the leading disciples."* *"...his condition is very bad. ...he had not eaten anything solid for one and a half months. Now he takes a glass of mung water, one of grape juice, and a protein drink. A few days ago he took a few spoonful's of fruit and a piece of sandesh... The legs were so thin. ...He is 10 times worse than in June, he has no flesh on his body, just skin and bone. I saw his heart beating as the skin on his ribs moved up and down.* **SEPT. 30:** SP gave power of attorney to Tamal, Giriraja.

OCTOBER 1977: OCT. 1: Brahmananda carried SP to the car and train to Vrindaban. **OCT. 2:** Vrindaban. Much more deteriorated than when he had left a month ago. First, they *"closed the curtains and dimmed the lights[1]."* GBC men gradually came. SP instructed on a memorial and museum to honor him after departure. He instructed Kuladri not to allow anyone to cook for him without his permission. (Again? Did SP suspect foul play?) *"I could hardly hear him... whether SP's legs were paralyzed..."* SP eyes could not see who came and he could not hear the temple bells. *"In this condition, even I cannot move my body on the bed. Only chance you should give me- let me die peacefully, without anxiety. I have given in writing everything... Disaster will happen if you cannot manage it."* Satsvarupa: *"...he was going to leave his body at any moment. Everyone was called to be here at the end. The kaviraja came... and said his life is finished..."* **OCT. 3:** Bonamali ascertained weakness, no illness. Complan, milk, pomegranate and grape juices, honey, medicines. Milk produced mucus[2], causing cough③ at night, disturbing his rest. SP: *"The kaviraja said my life is finished, now by the grace of Krishna... whatever medicinal instructions he gives, strictly follow properly... Whatever he advises, that is good."* BCS came to help. SP went to see the deities in his chair, which exhausted him and he returned to bed. *"SP was coughing③ ...he is getting bed sores. SP is far less active... No longer speaking, no walking, no solid food ...We're doing all-night chanting vigils by his bed. ...no more Bhagwatam work nor answering mail. Hansadutta and Brahmananda cried, because if he doesn't eat or even drink, how can he continue to live? His body, as he said, is a bag of bones ...so how can he continue for long?"*

OCT. 4: SP slept poorly, coughing③, spitting mucus②. SP said in an inaudible voice④ the medicines were a *"complete failure."* *"The swelling has increased ...never so much as today. The mucus② was never so much as today."* He could not digest the medicine. The heart was good. Four raisins with honey. Today no medicines. Tamal complained Bonamali raised his fees; he was not recalled. Tamal wrote to Dr. G. Ghosh, Allahabad, asking him to come. *"During the night SP coughed③ a lot due to much mucus②. ...swelling in his arms, legs increased tremendously."*

OCT. 5: Tamal told SP, *"We should depend on Krishna, not on these kavirajas."* SP: *"Bhagwatam reading and kirtan. ...I'm not hungry. Let me hear kirtan."* Some Complan and one and a half teaspoon butter. *"...so weak that every little item has to be done for him."* *OCT. 6:* His cough③ was back. SP: *"Although drinking nothing, cough③ is coming."* **Tamal**: *...I don't know what to say, SP. It's certainly bewildering.* SP asked for rice water, honey and *"smashed"* cardamom. SP thought of Dr. Narottama Lal Gupta in Loi Bazaar. **Tamal**: *I don't advise it, SP. ...Because I don't see why we don't consult all 20,000 doctors...* **SP**: *No, they have good practice.* Balavanta confirmed in 1999 Dr. NL Gupta had examined SP in this time and determined poisoning. *OCT. 7:* Tamal: *"...so how will you live, SP? If you stop drinking everything, how will you get any strength? You're tired of trying anymore?"* SP had mucus② and was restless. SP declined to drink all day even though there was no coughing. SP: *"Survive?"* and laughed. Tamal: *"Yes. We're not ready to let you go yet."* SP rode in his palanquin around the temple, saw the deities, sat during kirtan. He spoke so weakly and hoarsely④. *OCT. 8:* Tamal read an astrological report. SP: *"Chant Hare Krishna. It is finished... We have the maha-mantra."* *"The general feeling for the last few days had been gradually more and more hopeless for SP staying with us. ...now he wants only caranamrita. Preparation for Samadhi and final ceremony are now openly discussed."* SP asked not to be taken to the hospital. *"SP rested... completely peaceful and quiet, hearing* *the kirtan."* Some of SP's Godbrothers came, discussed preparations for his departure. SP appeared resigned to his imminent departure. SP had not eaten or drunk for days; devotees anxious and agitated. SP refused to drink anything. Bags of salt were stocked behind the temple, meant for SP's samadhi. Satsvarupa: *"Some say there are still questions we haven't asked about who will initiate in the future, but actually, he has said it. Politics lurking among the devotees for sure... the patience of vultures. Waiting in the wings for the aftermath."*

OCT. 9: SP's pulse was weak. He was bathed in bed. He could not go out of his rooms. He only took a bit of caranamrita. He had more cough③. *" His body is like the picture of Rantideva- ribs sticking out, hip bones, no extra skin anywhere. To move a limb requires assistance."* **SP**: *Let me drink hari nama amiya vilasa... and charanamrita."* SP worried about mucus② if he drank more. **COMMENT:** Mucus is a reaction to cadmium/arsenic poisoning. SP could become dehydrated. SP: *"I feel no inconvenience. I am afraid of cough③."* *"You discuss amongst yourselves and decide what you want me to do."* Abhiram: *"About recovery?"* SP: *"I don't want."* SP, weakly said: *"If I want to survive, of course, I'll have to take something. It is not possible to survive without taking any food... Therefore I have decided to die peacefully..."* SP asked, *"Why do you want me to survive? ...Krishna wants me (to do) as I like. The choice is mine. Krishna has given me full freedom.* Kirtanananda pleaded emotionally, *"If Krishna gives you the choice, don't go. We need you."* [...] **Brahmananda**: *We have all met together, SP. We want you to remain and lead this movement and finish the Srimad Bhagwatam.* SP, yawning, casually said, *"All right."* *"It was the most completely casual decision on life or death ever made. At that moment, we understood SP's supremely independent position. He could stay or go as he chose."* **SP**: *So give me something to drink.* SP drank a glass of grape juice, took vegetable broth, speaking stronger and longer. The mood changed to hope and optimism, as the news spread that SP decided to stay. *"The entire atmosphere completely changed... Instead of withdrawing his energy as he has done steadily for the last few days, he came to life again."* SP decided to stay longer and began eating again.

OCT. 10: He increased his liquids. He took Complan, barley water, but coughed③ a lot as the drink turned to mucus②. SP complained of weakness. Raj Vaidya Pandit Lakshmi Narayan happened to come by and there was a lengthy examination. The *vaidya* recommended checking the blood pressure and testing a urine sample. Upendra: *"But SP hasn't got any taste."* The *vaidya* said SP should drink as much fluid as possible. SP said, *"I have no desire for water."* **OCT. 11:** *"SP seems to be slightly better today."* Took some sweet lemon juice. Total liquids today was more than in two weeks. **OCT. 12:** Sweet lemon juice, but the cough③ came again. Dr.

Ghosh, Kodaikanal, came. *"Kirtanananda offered to take charge of SP as far as ...medical care. SP said twice ...there must be no hospitalization. ...SP passed blood and pus⑤ in his urine. ...as soon as he lays down he fills up with cough③.* SP may have told Pishima he was being poisoned. SP translated with Pradyumna. Kirtanananda Swami took charge of feeding SP specified liquids. ***OCT. 13:*** *"Samples of SP's urine have been sent to the doctor due to the blood and pus⑤ passed last night. He asked his sister Pisima to cook for him... The last time he took anything solid was last month. ...SP took a dozen spoonful's of solid food... SP complained that he had no taste)."* Kirtanananda hoped Dr. G. Ghosh would be able to enforce some discipline of medical treatment. SP's urine⑤ was milky and bloody. Abhiram took a sample to a lab to test; results showed the presence of blood and pus⑤. The next day the urine cleared. Bhagatji took some urine for analysis, returning with pills, saying otherwise death could come in days. SP declined the pills sent by Dr. Gopal in Rama Krishna Hospital. *"He is the best doctor in Mathura district."* Kirtanananda, trying to nurse SP back to health, began to be more aggressive. **Kirtanananda**: *SP, you're not really going to try and eat that khicori are you?* **SP**: *Really? Why not?* Kirtanananda opposed SP taking the rich food Pishima was cooking for him, fearing a negative reaction. Upendra announced, *"Prasadam has come, SP."* SP: *"So you can for the time being, disperse. Let me... Whatever possible, I'll take."* *"SP ate quite heartily for the first time in many months."* He took lavan bhaskar and lay down. SP said, *"Medical science finished."* Hari Sauri: *"When all these doctors come, they can't understand how it is that you're still here."* SP seemed determined not to take any medicines. Kirtanananda: *"SP, even the astrologers all say that you are transcendental, that if you want, you can change your horoscope. ...that Krishna said the choice is up to you."* **Tamal**: *…what you ate today was more than I saw you eat in three months...* SP: *"Where is Kirtanananda? He is annoyed?"* Kirtanananda was upset about SP's refusing allopathic medicines. Later SP took Sandesh, wanting glucose and sweet lemon juice, but no medicines.

OCT. 14: SP asked Pishima to chant Nrsinghadeva mantras over him while massaging his chest. Amazingly, the urine was clear. *"But unlike yesterday, he had no taste and hardly ate anything."* SP asked for Bonamali to come again. As for soup, vegetable juices, SP: *"Cannot take. No taste."* **Tamal**: *...try to drink and eat whenever you have a little desire... You shouldn't try to fast until death.* **SP**: *No. That is useless. Do you recommend that?* **Tamal**: *No, definitely not... You shouldn't artificially fast or stop eating.* **SP**: *No, no. That is suicidal.* *"SP asked Pisima to make dal and roti for him. He showed no discomfort from the solid food yesterday, so he will take again today. He takes sips of Yamuna water every 15 minutes or so."* SP decided against milk due to risk of mucus②. Satsvarupa: *"...After so* *many doctors tried to prescribe cures for SP and mostly failed..."* **OCT. 15:** Hot mustard oil massage from Rupanuga. *"If this rubbing goes on, I think I can eat."* Bhagatji brought a masseur for this treatment. *"He applied a hot water bottle."* Bonamali checked the pulse, saying it was good and that there was only weakness, no complaint in the body. SP asked Pishima to make chana dal, a soup. SP could not even click the button for the dictaphone; he had almost no body left. SP's urine was *"very colored again."* Tamal told SP the cure was to drink sufficient liquids to clean the *"bodily poisons." "If you take no liquid, then it's very dangerous. You don't have to eat anything."* SP agreed to drink a half cup every four hours or so. SP coughed③ up mucus②. Tamal: *"I don't think this milk should be given again... it has caused maybe this mucus②."* SP: *"Hm? What is that phish-phish?"* Tamal and Giriraj whispering in the room. SP had pain in one hip. Hari Sauri thought the Persian citrus drinks were too strong for the kidneys, causing the blood and pus⑤ to make the urine cloudy.

OCT. 16: Cough③ returned, maybe from a little milk the day before. Took cough③ syrup, pomegranate juice, concerned about possible pneumonia. Nathiram gives massage twice daily. Bonamali said SP's discolored urine⑤ as due to a gonorrhea-type disorder which could block the ureter. Lunch of vegetable broth and fruit paste. Dr. G. Ghosh, Allahabad came. *"SP had a very bad morning, coughing③ up large amounts of very thick jelly-like mucus②. ...some milk yesterday evening.. ...a prolonged enema treatment and he felt better. He is actually very weak and talks with a very low voice④."* Dr. Ghosh wanted a new urinalysis and to reduce the swelling. The car took Dr. Ghosh to Agra for the urinalysis. Abhiram asked to leave SP's service.

OCT. 17: Dr. Ghosh found no problem with the liver or stomach, and asked SP to eat more solids and liquids. Pishima cooked; SP *"ate very heartily. Dr. G. Ghosh gave vitamin C, B-complex and Lassix tablets."* Dr. G. Ghosh brought Dr. Gopal. SP's pulse was 96; medications were prescribed for a serious chronic kidney infection⑤. Both doctors agreed on this diagnosis. *"The heart skipped a beat every 18. Blood pressure normal at 130. SP's urine was very dark, so he needs to drink more liquids. SP drank a full glass of Complan. The caretakers struggled to encourage SP to take his medicines and drink more."* **BHAV:** *...you have a chronic kidney infection⑤ ...it could develop into uremia, which could be fatal. ...everything is functioning well, but the kidneys are not ...they all insist that you have to take more liquid. ...you have to take rich protein foods. Milk, curd, chana, Proteinex, fruits, juices...* **Tamal:** *Bhagatji says that this Dr. Gopal is the best doctor in Mathura district...*

OCT. 18: SP did not rest all night. The pulse was improved, the swelling went down. SP blamed the allopathic medicines for inability to sleep, calling for Bonamali instead. Bhavananda noted the urine had cleared up due to the allopathic medicine, and asked SP to take it for at least one more day. **Hari Sauri:** *It definitely seems to be having a good effect.* **BHAV:** *They said that one of the symptoms of this infection - this poisoning - is that you become averse to taking any liquid or any food...* Later the urine was darker, cloudy⑤; SP drank very little. **BHAV:** *...your inability to eat and drink as a result of this poisoning from the kidney infection*⑤. **COMMENT:** Poisoning? Weird that a poisoning suspect uses this word about an infection. **SP**: *When I don't take anything, I feel more comfortable.* **Tamal**: *But you don't get better. That is the policy of death.* **SP**: *So let me die peacefully.* **Tamal**: *But we already explained to you that we don't want you to die.* **Hari Sauri**: *But the other day you said that to fast like this means suicide.* SP finally agreed to drink a whole glass of Complan and some fruit juice. This day SP drank 1000 cc liquids and passed more urine than any other day.

OCT. 19: SP still had no strength, lying silently, and unable to move without help. BCS cooks, Satadhanya and Upendra attend to SP's physical needs, and Bhavananda and Tamal struggle to maintain the taking of medicine and drink. Dr. Gopal said strength would come in a few days, and deemed the frequent bowel movements favorable, natural. SP ate mashed potatoes and custard and vomited *"after hardly a mouthful. So much mucus*② *and saliva immediately came out."* **COMMENT:** by now we can understand the mucus is coming from the poisoning. What else? SP was disturbed by frequent bowel movements, vomiting, and argued over the use of eating when there was no increased strength. *OCT. 20:* SP's *"skin has taken on a shiny appearance, as if he were perspiring."* **Dr. Gopal:** *Do you feel any difficulty during urination?* **SP:** *Not at all.* Only 290 cc urine yesterday. Dr. Gopal asked what else he could take besides some water. SP: *"Harinama."* The swelling had gone done. After eating cold custard, SP said, *"I... I'm feeling nicely... after eating."* *OCT. 21:* SP took no medicine, was more relaxed, alert. Dr. Ghosh left, saying SP was: *"in good hands with Dr. Gopal."* SP slept *"many, many, many hours..."* **Tamal:** *Now your urine is clear. ...to recover your strength, but that has not happened.* The room was dark①. SP asked why he was given no medicines in a day. **Tamal**: *Formerly, even if you didn't ask, we were encouraging you, 'Please take medicine...' So today we decided that whatever you ask, that we will do. ...so you direct what you want to be done... It's not good... to too much push something... If you want... then we can call the kaviraja. ...I think we can wait to see the results of NOT taking any medicine are.* **COMMENT:** Here we are a week into Dr. Ghosh/ Dr. Gopal's treatment. First

Bhavananda and Tamal are fighting to get SP to take the medicines otherwise he would die, then they whimsically change course and discontinue medicines. Strange! Is this to precipitate another rejection of doctors and medicines? This smells of manipulation. Now they will wait for SP to ask for medicine? Maybe in this way the doctors would be rejected? Were they worried about the new "expert" Dr. Gopal discovering the poisoning? **SP**: *So go on with the treatment.* Tamal then says the medicine would continue but Dr. Gopal would come *only when called*. The feast was brought but SP rejected all the preparations, *"being unable to taste any of them satisfactorily."*

OCT. 22: SP dreamt of a Ramanuja *kaviraja* preparing *makharadhvaja (MKD)*. Bonamali had delivered to BCS supposed *makharadhvaja*. Dr. Gopal thought it was *moti-dristi*. SP should be stronger before taking MKD and wait for cold weather. Dr. Gopal was perplexed because SP was not getting strength after taking his medicines for many days. He suggested a lung problem or asthma and prescribed a strong drug, wanted X-rays. Tamal said Dr. Gopal's treatment was a failure, that he was now simply speculating. **SP***: ...This doctor's treatment is failure.* **Tamal:** *Yes, he's starting to guess...* **SP:** *...Now take MKD, one dose, and leave everything to Krishna.* **BHAV:** *Yes. We felt that your dream, SP, was very significant.* **SP:** *Doctor treatment finished. Don't try any... They will simply guess and make huge complication.*

Tamal, Bhavananda suggested the urine clearing was from increased liquid intake, *not* Dr. Gopal's medicines. Dr. Gopal thought there might be a lung infection due to less air in the left lung. *"So he's prescribing that antituberculin drug called Isotoxin [Isonayazid]."* Tamal protested: *"But he doesn't even know... if it's tuberculosis."* SP: *"Then he'll say, 'Remove to the hospital'... Then who will take care of me? Hm?... Don't move me to the hospital. Better kill me here."* **COMMENT:** Better kill me here? Svarupa Damodar encouraged X-rays to test the tuberculosis theory, but Tamal disallowed it, even though the X-ray machine could have been brought to SP's room. **COMMENT:** Heavy metals are radiopaque and show up X-rays. Tamal: *"Actually the whole thing only began when Dr. Ghosh came... you didn't want Dr. Ghosh to come, but it was too late. ...we were obligated to try these allopathic medicines. ...Dr. Ghosh who brought Dr. Gopal... you always don't like the allopathic."* SP: *"I'll treat myself. Let the kavirajas come. And MKD... And stop all medicine."* **BHAV:** *"His desire was to remove you from here somehow or other. First to remove you for an X-ray, then..."* **Tamal:** *"Another trick they have is that you have one trouble, so they give you a medicine, but the medicine causes a worse trouble. And eventually such bad trouble is created that they get you depending on them, and then they say, 'Now the only thing left, you must come to the hospital for operation.' Then they kill you."* Many medical horror stories were recounted.

The mood was very anti-Dr. Gopal and his medicines.

COMMENT: It seems they were afraid Dr. Gopal might find the real cause of SP's illness. They discussed moving SP to Mayapur. SP sent BCS to search for the Ramanuja *kaviraja* in his dream. BCS found a *kaviraja* at the Janaki Vallabha temple and brought him to SP. He diagnosed malfunction of kidneys and digestion. Bhagatji wanted Dr. Gopal to test SP's urine and the X-ray machine be brought to SP's room, saying thus a proper diagnosis and proper treatment be made. But Tamal vigorously criticized allopathic doctors and medicine, telling more medical horror stories (e.g., scissors left inside the body after an operation). Bhagatji: *"Why sometimes pus⑤ and blood comes out of the urine?"* Tamal: *"Only for two or three days."* Bhagatji: *"Why is it? They have to test it. They have to find out. That is the reason of all this."* But Tamal had his way, and Dr. Gopal never returned nor X-rays or urine tests done. **Tamal**: *Prabhupada gave us an opportunity to try this allopathic medicine… And factually you saw he was vomiting, dizzy, and losing sleep. Then yesterday we didn't give any medicine, and he was much better off. You heard how he was speaking strongly… So Prabhupada said… "Then no more allopathic. It is finished." …it didn't work… But that whole science of Western medicine is very speculative… And as soon as we agree to X-ray, X-ray is only the first step… it means you are ready to take his treatment."*

COMMENT: Tamal uses scare tactics. A treatment can be stopped anytime if found unacceptable. Did they not reject Dr. Gopal after a week? Tamal's logic is so faulty; we see he feared the doctor's expertise. Dr. Gopal was getting too close to discovering the poisoning.

Tamal argued more and concluded allopathic doctors were useless and encouraged the use of Ayurvedic *kaviraja*s, if a qualified one could be found. Bhagatji offered to bring one that he knew from Mathura but Tamal wanted to see stick with the Ramanuji *kaviraja*. **COMMENT:** Tamal blocked Dr. Gopal. Would X-rays reveal the heavy metals? Dr. Gopal suspected something unusual which evaded his diagnosis. The problem was not only a kidney infection. If he continued, Dr. Gopal would soon find the poisoning. Tamal opposed to Dr. Gopal is suspect.

OCT. 23: SP's left leg felt: *"very heavy"* and he thought it paralyzed. SP did not want to be hospitalized under any circumstances. The Ramanuja *kaviraja* said the train jerking going to Mayapur would damage internal organs. He advised waiting. He could only make fresh MKD at his own dispensary, cost 3500 Rs ($300), and said it was the only medicine *"effective at this late stage."* They now doubted the authenticity of any MKD. SP directed the devotees find another bonafide Ramanuja *kaviraja*, giving ideas of how to find one. *OCT. 24:* SP now has no *kaviraja* although the masseur comes daily. To find quality MKD Smarahari was sent to South

India where Ramanujas are prevalent. Tamal created doubts in the Vrindaban Ramanuja *kaviraja* and Bonamali's MKD, calling them cheaters. Then Adi Keshava called from Delhi, regarding Chandra Swami whom he knew from NY and who donated a quantity of fresh MKD. Satadhanya would bring the medicine.

OCT. 25: The Delhi MKD was a mystery in that coincidentally it had just been prepared. *(Unlikely odds?)* Satadhanya: *"I have brought the MKD from the kaviraja in Delhi. ... he's not Ramanuja-sampradaya, but many people say in Delhi that he's the foremost kaviraja in India. He treats the Prime Minister, Morarji Desai, and all the ministers also... He was mixing it for some other person, but when he heard that you were ill, he gave it to us..."* SP asked the cost. *"Nothing. We got it for free because we got it through one influential man named Chandra Swami."* **Tamal**: *"Oh, Chandra Swami. That's that person Adi Keshava was always working with."* (Tamal already knew where the medicine came from; why does he say "Oh" as though it's news to him too?) **Tamal**: *"You met Chandra Swami?"* **Satadhanya**: *"No, he's in Madras..."* SP took his first dose of MKD. SP: *"...Die or live, it doesn't matter... Let me have parikrama. If I live, that's all right; if I die, that's all right."*

OCT. 26: SP felt that devotees were avoiding him, *"Now I have become poisonous."* Most had left Vrindaban a few weeks earlier. SP seemed stronger after two MKD doses, sitting for an hour, not tired after the temple tour. SP decided to take MKD only once a day. Then he stopped it altogether, as it was causing diarrhea. Tamal: *"How can we reject the medicine so quickly?"* SP: *"Because it is reacting so adversely... Don't give me any medicine. Simply chant and parikrama."* They talked about expanding the parikrama into the Vrindaban area by camping for several days. **SP:** *"Therefore I say stop it.* **BHAV:** *Still, we saw some positive signs. Of course, it might not have been from the medicine, but it is... You appear stronger. ...Baradraja Prabhu was just telling me that he's noticed- he's been massaging your legs- that your legs and feet are warmer today than they were yesterday."*

OCT. 27: SP again did temple parikrama. He took a third dose of MKD but there was a bowel movement again. SP could not tell the sun had already risen because the room was so dark①. BCS noted *"Even the swelling is down."* SP implied that whatever little blood he had left was being changed into stool by the medicine, robbing his little remaining strength. **Tamal:** *I agree... SP. I think it's a good idea to stop the medicine for a day and to consult the kaviraja ...What is the stool coming from if he's not eating?* **SP:** *Whatever little blood is there.* **BHAV:** *I think it's a mistake, SP, to take this strong medicine without having the kaviraja actually come and diagnose himself and...* **SP:** *Yes.*

First they convinced SP to start the MKD; now they remembered it shouldn't be taken without the *kaviraja*'s presence. These were the "qualified" caretakers. Bhavananda reminded SP, *"But you did say Krishna advised you through that dream to take that MKD medicine."* SP: *"But Krishna directed Ramanuja Vaishnava."* (The Delhi *kaviraja* was a Shaivite) **Tamal:** *"...they have arranged for one Ramanuji kaviraja there in Bengal side..."* SP asked if this Ramanuja *kaviraja* could come to Vrindaban to be the very last doctor. Adridharan was called about flying the Calcutta *kaviraja* to Delhi and then on to Vrindaban. Reflecting on the Delhi MKD SP said, *"It is acting adversely. If still I take, then, knowingly..."* Trivikram finished, *"Drinking poison."* **Tamal:** *" We had waited so long for this MKD, and now it had turned into poison."* (The actual poison was cadmium.)

OCT. 28: SP enjoyed temple parikrama. Adridharan was bringing the Calcutta *kaviraja* that morning. SP: *"Rice I cannot touch even."* Tamal: *"Vomiting tendency. [...] First we had that... Ramanuji came from Sri Rangaji temple, and he seemed to be a cheater. Then... We got this medicine from that sakta-kaviraja... turned out to be poison. And now this kaviraja who's supposed to be coming from Calcutta..."* Near midnight Adridharan arrived with the Calcutta *kaviraja,* named Damodar Prasad Shastri, with Ramanuja tilak. Shastri felt the pulse, used the stethoscope. BCS: *"He's saying that in this condition, SP can't take makharadhvaja. That any medicine that contains mercury and arsenic is poison to him."* Shastri said SP would recover due to his strong heart. His medicines would repair the liver[8] and kidneys, then *rasayana* would increase the bodily strength. In 10-15 days he thought SP might recover enough to travel to Mayapur. SP: *"Take his chart and strictly follow. I'll not object. I'll strictly follow. This is the last resort. Whatever it may be. No more trials."* *OCT. 29:* SP became emotional, cried[7], sorry he could not return his servants' service. Shastri prescribed medicines: the intestines have no digestion or secretions due to extreme shrinking. Kidney malfunctioning caused the skin to shine with salt due to uremic poisoning. SP slept until 5 PM, being very weak and tired, then took the medicine prepared by Shastri who collected herbs in the local forests. SP ate three spoons of loki. Tamal, BCS and Shastri deliberated how which Shastri sought to borrow a special apparatus from Dr. NL Gupta for distilling SP's medicines. (Ch. 36). Shastri advised SP drink a kilo of milk a day. Shastri needed to return to Calcutta but was convinced to stay. Shastri was very confident of his diagnosis and medicines. Shastri was devotional, first-class. Shastri was chanting mantras while preparing SP's medicines. SP's diarrhea had ceased.

OCT. 30: *"SP, your voice[4] is much stronger now."* SP *"had a cough[3] that gradually increased."* Shastri used a herbal medicine to reduce the increased swelling. An assistant *kaviraja* from the Rangaji temple would help in distillation of medicines. SP ate some solid foods, but not parathas and eggplant: *"No taste. It is desired, but no taste. The juice has taste. Now if I can just take some milk, I will become strong."* He was going daily on temple parikrama. **OCT. 31:** Bhavananda: *"You seem to be better."* SP: *"Yes."* SP took cough③ medicine with his milk and barley water, and had clear urine. Shastri saw good progress in SP's recovery. He distilled 22 ingredients to make *brikka-sanjivani-arak* to revitalize the kidneys. Renewal of strength would come from a return of appetite: this was the objective. SP asked to sit up. Tamal: *"...SP passed more urine than ever before, and very clear-colored. [...] He is saying it's impossible, that he had cough③ today, and tomorrow there is no sign of it. So these are all SP's pastimes."* SP said, *"This is last resort. Whatever it may be. Is that all right?"* **Tamal:** *"We might as well try. We've tried everyone else."* Bhavananda: *"He did agree with your own diagnosis, SP. He said MKD at this point would be poison and today you said that it was poison."* **COMMENT:** Why are they using the poison word so often? To confuse their poisoning with medicines and illness?

NOVEMBER 1977: **NOV. 1:** SP fainted during the temple parikrama. SP asked why there was no dramatic recovery yet. SP took milk and barley, and 12 spoonful's of solid food for lunch. BCS said: *"...and ever since you started taking the medicines there has been some good effect, like you started passing more urine, you started getting a little appetite, little taste, your swelling has gone down, to some extent."* Shastri: *"You are weak, but the heart is strong. There is little blood in the system, and this causes weakness and fainting."* **NOV. 2:** The trip to Mayapur did not take place because the cars from Delhi were too late. Tamal: *"This resting is very good. ...constant resting means that the body is getting a chance to renew itself and take strength."* Shastri left for Calcutta, to return in about 7-10 days. The *kaviraja* assistant came to check SP. SP skipped the parikrama due to weakness. **NOV. 3:** *"...SP asked BCS to soak chickpeas and almonds."* SP found a little taste in some avocado for lunch. **NOV. 4:** Tamal: *"This time, until the kaviraja comes, from now until then, you should rest as much as possible, take these medicines. I think it's having a positive effect. You mentioned this morning that when you sit up you feel a little stronger now."* **SP:** *So far I am thinking, I'm not improving in strength. And how can I improve by drinking little barley and milk and little fruit juice? I have no appetite for anything else... I am losing my willpower, because practically I see that I am becoming more and more weak.* SP said that in case the treatment failed, *"Yes, that starving and chanting and a little ganga-jala or... In this way let me pass away peacefully.* Krishna das Babaji was astonished to see SP's extremely depreciated physical condition while still maintaining such perfectly clear consciousness. SP again emphasized never to be hospitalized. Tamal agreed: *"We see one example after another that these hospitals, they are simply meant to kill, not to save life."* SP: *"This is the decision, that in case it does not improve, let me die here."* When the *kaviraja* assistant came to check on SP, he was not allowed in, but given a report by BCS. Tamal noted that after a few days, SP finally had a good bowel movement and felt relieved. Tamal: *"I think that this is the last kaviraja that we should take the help of. If his medicine works, that's very welcome. And if it doesn't, then I don't think that we should try any more kavirajas or any doctor. We've tried enough… At least we've seen that with other kavirajas there were so many negative effects. Remember? Now, with this kaviraja, nothing has even happened badly with the medicine he's prescribed…"* After fifteen days of curing the liver⑧ and kidneys, then Shastriji would begin to administer strength-increasing medicines such as *makharadhvaja*.

NOV. 5: *"…after passing stool five times, SP said that all medicine should be stopped."* The assistant *kaviraja* prescribed ginger and honey to add to the other medicines. **Tamal**: *This is a common ailment that people have, diarrhea or passing stool too often, loose bowels. That's not a very major problem.* **SP**: *No, you have to stop.* **Tamal**: *No, that's not necessarily the only solution, to stop… The medicine you're getting is supposed to be doing good to your kidney and liver⑧. That it causes you to pass stool, that is not good, but at the same time, it may be doing good for the kidney and liver…* Tamal wrote: *"SP's health has not shown any marked improvement. He is still quite critical."*

NOV. 6: *"…in the middle of bathing, he had to lie down, he was so weak. When it was time for him to eat, he said he could no longer sit up; however, he would take very little prasadam while lying down. We could understand SP's condition was becoming very serious, that unless we did something immediately, SP would soon stop eating altogether."* Adridharan was called for bringing Shastri back immediately. SP was convinced to continue the medicine and drinking liquids until Shastri arrived. Meanwhile, Tamal observed, SP's liquid intake and urine have recently doubled. SP did not want to be sat up for drinking any more. He would drink what he could while lying down. **SP**: *I cannot take anything. I feel comfort only lying down.* SP said his willpower to remain, *"That strong desire has now disappeared."* The assistant *kaviraja* came and the heartbeat had increased a little. **SP**: *No appetite.*

NOV. 7: Shastri arrived at 4 AM with Jayapataka. *"When we asked SP to drink, he retorted, "How can I drink? There is no thirst, no hunger. I cannot sit up."* *"SP was becoming increasingly weaker, despite the medicine. The kaviraja said all organs, except for the kidneys, were all* *right. There was no blood, marrow, flesh or muscles."* SP ate a little, asked about malpoora. Tamal: *"Everything in SP's body was drying up. Although the kaviraja had high hopes, improvement would be slow..."* SP's swelling was much less than before, there was no heart weakness. SP expressed interest in *shrikand* (thick sweet milk). Shastri wanted 3 more days before starting his strength-giving medicines. Points discussed with Shastri: **(1)** The main problem was the kidneys, which were still working, otherwise there would be no urine. **(2)** The medicine over the last week has improved the kidneys, thus the increase of urine. **(3)** There is very little blood due to no eating for so long, resulting in great weakness, practically no muscles left. **(4)** Due to weakness, strong medicines must be avoided or given in small amounts. **(5)** A new medicine was started today to make new blood, even if increased strength was delayed. **(6)** Better to eat lying down and not strain the heart. **(7)** Solid food was not necessary. **(8)** SP's chances of full recovery were quite good if the treatment was followed for 3-4 months. **(9)** Shastri had worse cases who survived, encouraging SP to keep up good spirits.

NOV. 8: SP had a strong pulse; in four or five days, SP should be fit for Vrindaban parikrama. Shastri searched long hours in the forests for specific herbs. Swelling increased today. SP: *"I think I am feeling a little strength."* A urinalysis report came from Dr. Gopal. There were too many pus⑤ cells due to poor kidney functioning. This was very serious; there was pain in the left kidney, but no kidney stones were detected. The passing of urine⑤ was somewhat painful, coming *"in installments."* The *arak* medicine for the kidneys would need to be increased. *NOV. 9:* SP's old acquaintance, Balaram Mishra, came and SP casually told him he thought he was being poisoned. See Part 2, the "poison discussions." *"[Shastri] found the pulse to be very weak. SP has felt cold all day, asking to be covered by a quilt. ...was due to so little blood. SP's urine was very cloudy⑤ and brown.."*

NOV. 10: "SP was very restless." Shastri gave some medicine. SP's *"pulse was missing some beats. Privately, the kaviraja said to us that since last night, he has become hopeless about SP's condition."* At noon Shastri came to see SP again. The pulse was 90 per minute, stronger than that morning. Blood pressure was normal at 140/75. *"Now the heart was in order."* Shastri was amazed how SP was *"suddenly able to become better."* The color of stool indicated the liver was working, and Shastri thought pathologically the general condition was good. There were long discussions about mental distress, homicidal poisoning after SP repeated again: *"Someone has poisoned me."* All the caretakers acknowledged SP thought he was being maliciously poisoned. Yet nothing was done and the matter was ignored. (see Part 2) *NOV. 11:* SP said: *"I am not getting strength. Even to lift my leg, I need help. Practically my left leg is not working. What*

468

should be done now, you consider." Shastri advised milk, not yogurt. Shastri had consulted Sri Ramduttji in Delhi, the best *kaviraja* in India and a specialist in kidney and heart problems, saying SP's *"disease could definitely be cured and that the most immediate necessity was to increase his strength. For that purpose, milk was very important."* Shastri said he would *"give medicine to control the cough③ and the passing of stool. The kaviraja said that he was not afraid of the disease, rather of SP's weakness."* (But what was the disease?) Shastri said he would cure him in a week, he should eat a little bit often.

SP wanted to go on pilgrimage to various holy places, camping and cooking outdoors. SP did not want to expire in his room: *"I wish that you GBC manage very nicely and consider I am dead and let me travel all the tirthasthana, without any responsibility... You have tried doctor, kaviraja, medicine, everything. Everything has failed. Now suppose I am taking the risk of death (by going on parikrama), what is wrong?... I have bequeathed, properly you can manage. Hm. It is to be admitted failure, the so-called medical treatment, failure... All seriously consider this submission and let me go."* SP rejected attempts to restore his health by going on a final parikrama. The devotees left his room to discuss this. Some tried to dissuade SP from going on parikrama in a cart, saying it would jeopardize his frail life. On tapes a series of extraordinary and incriminating whispers were discovered and forensically analyzed to be about poison and poisoning. **(Whisper: The poison's going down. (Giggle) Poison's going down.)** JPS: *"Like to follow the same treatment, only while traveling."*

Then another whisper: **"Is the poison in the milk? Uhh huh."** Minutes later, BCS gives SP milk to drink. Was there poison in this milk?

Tamal: *"Spiritually he (Shastri) is in complete agreement. So from a medical point of view, he said that you would not at all be able to withstand this kind of trip. He said that in a bullock cart, moving around, bumping on the road, you might not be able to live more than a couple of hours."* Shastri discouraged the parikrama, as did others. Later: **Tamal**:

This seems like suicide, SP, this program. It seems to some of us like it's suicidal." **SP**: *And this is also suicidal.* (Why is it suicide to stay?) **Tamal**: *Hm. SP said, "And this is also suicide." Now you have to choose which suicide.* **SP**: *The Ravana will kill and Rama will kill. Better to be killed by Rama. Eh? That Marica, if he does not go to mislead Sita, he'll be killed by Ravana; and if he goes to be killed by Rama, then it is better.* **COMMENT:** SP compared staying in his room as suicide, being killed by Ravana, which is chilling. Ravana was in his room? SP knew he was being poisoned, so better to die on parikrama, killed by Rama rather than the Ravanas.

Shastri thought SP would get a heart attack within 1-2 hours from the rough roads. SP said the parikrama would cure him. Hansadutta: *"...we have to consider whether SP's opinion is more or less than the kaviraja's..."* Then Tamal speaks softly, ***"We know he's trying to trap us."*** And, ***"He's as sly as they come."*** Then Tamal said: *"We're voicing different opinions..."* which many thought to be *"Put poison in different containers."* The bullock cart would be ready at 5 AM in the morning. SP discussed with devotees how his Vrindaban bullock cart parikrama program would be organized. Krishna das Babaji came later and spoke with SP convincingly about not going on a parikrama. Another whisper, after **JPS** asks, *"Should there be kirtana, SP? You like kirtan?"* Then a Bengali phrase, and **JPS** says, ***"Poisoning for a long time..."*** SP, asked, ***"To me?"*** Then another voice: *"That's really original."* Next, **JPS**: ***"Get ready to go."*** Then kirtan begins.

SP relented. *"All right... I cannot refuse your request... No, no, I cannot put you in anxiety... So I shall do what you like... I cannot refuse."* Tamal said, in relief: *"Actually, SP, we're so much attached to you that you practically drive us to madness sometimes. Tonight we were becoming mad." "Tomorrow, he (kaviraja) will give medicine for building muscles. The next day, he wants to go to Jaipur for medicine. For now the kaviraja was giving medicine made from crushed pearls and will be giving crushed emeralds later, which are even more powerful than crushed diamonds."* SP felt stronger. *"[Shastri's] saying that SP's pulse is ninety, which is normal, and he gave three other medicines for SP's heart. That missing beat that SP was having- that's no more there... he hasn't seen a body like SP's. In one moment it is very critical, and the next moment it's in perfect order. And he is now absolutely confident that SP is going to get well... And he's just requesting SP that he keeps on taking the milk and the fruit juice and the medicine." "SP is incredibly thin but his hands and feet are noticeably swollen. He is so weak that he can only move the lower parts of his arms."*

NOV. 12: *"At 8 AM Shastri felt SP's pulse and stated that it was perfectly normal again; he had never seen, of his many patients, one who had a body like SP's. One day it would be in disorder then the following day everything would be perfect. Also the blood pressure is not abnormally high. The Kaviraj again assured the devotees that if SP takes the medicine prescribed then all would be well."* SP wanted to go on parikrama, even after he had agreed not to. SP said, *"...since a long time I have got a desire." "...SP taking rest most of the time, and devotees always performing kirtan. ...he complained of pain in his left thigh, the same leg which he has had us keep elevated on a pillow for so many weeks now."* ***NOV. 13:*** SP had severe pain in his left leg. Hot salt compresses and Sloan's liniment were applied to his thigh. *"...but this did not bring sufficient relief... The devotees had stopped kirtan and were surrounding his bed. ...rubbing witch-hazel had produced too much coldness."* With a heating lamp, SP was now able to rest again. SP felt very cold, wanting many blankets, but then also threw off the blankets. **BHAV:** *SP was saying he is heavy all over his body. Just before* *all this pain, he was feeling heavy. [...] The swelling's gone down every day.* The pain returned every three hours. SP drank 1150 cc, half of it milk, and he passed urine sufficiently. In the evening Krishna das Babaji and Bon Maharaja came. Satsvarupa: *"Don't wish for SP's departure. Pray he recovers." "He has caught a cold③ and is very weak."*

NOV. 14: *"Today, the attacks continued in regular three hour intervals. SP was in deep consciousness, not external. The kaviraja came frequently, but SP took medicine only with great efforts on behalf of BCS. When the attacks came again, SP moved his right arm back and forth gracefully in the air, but we could not properly understand him. Although we all wanted to help him, we felt we could not. The kaviraja confirmed SP's condition was very serious. ...the end was approaching. Thus the room was packed with devotees, and chanting was continuous."* The *kaviraja's* request to catherize SP for emptying of the bladder was not approved. SP had before disliked how Tirtha Maharaja expired with tubes in his body. *"At 11:30 AM SP was completely uncovered and awake and the devotees were surrounding, all gently massaging various parts of his body. He occasionally moved his hand in the air. The Kaviraj said that since SP had not passed any urine that his liver would be very affected and predicted he would only live for 6 to 10 hours."* The Kaviraj knew that SP was experiencing great pain and that he would depart when we wanted, that he had complete control. Asked to pass urine, SP spoke his last words: "Iccha nahin hai" meaning **"I have no desire."** BCS gave some drops of water into his mouth and sometimes SP would wave his hand around or make some noise or groan. His breathing was very slight, and at the end it became very heavy, heaving. The Kaviraj read SP's lips: "Hare Krishna."

The devotees crowded around SP very tightly. Pishima, SP's sister, came in and repeatedly asked SP if he had eaten something, but there was no answer. She put Ganges water in his mouth. Bon Maharaja, Krishna das Babaji, Ananda das and Narayan Maharaja came and sat on benches at the side of the bed. *"They... watched intently, observing SP's consciousness. Narayan Maharaja spoke in SP's ear, but there was no response; but when BCS spoke into SP's ear, telling him that Narayan Maharaja and others were present, SP slowly raised his left hand to his head in salutation and started crying⑦."* SP's Godbrothers thought the attacks were not painful, being only movements of body airs, noting his perfect consciousness. They left, promising to return upon being called.

Devotees chanted, waited. The last attack was at 3 PM; SP rubbed his hand quickly back and forth across his heart. Upendra massaged the heart area. For hours, *"SP was very peaceful. At 7:25 PM, Prabhupada opened his eyes, which were very clear, more so than in many months. His mouth opened, his tongue moved, and then he became still."* The *kaviraja* detected no movement of air by placing a cotton swab under the nostrils. Srila Prabhupada had departed at the most auspicious time of the day. Srila Prabhupada was brought before the temple deities and kirtan was held all night. At 6:30 AM, Nov. 15, Srila Prabhupada was taken on Vrindaban parikrama, visiting the seven major temples. He rode tied sitting up on his palanquin and gave his last darshan to all the Vrijibasis. At 9:30 AM the funeral ceremonies were held and Srila Prabhupada's transcendental body was interred in his samadhi. Arati was done to Srila Prabhupada's picture, placed on a small mound over his transcendental repose.

Later, a glorious memorial shrine was built on that spot which has since been visited by many millions of his followers and admirers.

APPENDIX 9:
ABHIRAM AND WIFE TESTIMONIES

ABHIRAM DAS STATEMENT: Nov. 5, 1997

Abhiram das posted a letter before any investigations began which described his knowledge of Srila Prabhupada's health in 1977, presenting evidence including an opinion of advanced diabetes.

"I have recently become aware of incredible theories of the poisoning of Srila Prabhupada, circulated by some poorly informed devotees. I acted as Srila Prabhupada's nurse and assistant secretary from July 25 to October 16, 1977, and was therefore in the best position to evaluate the factors influencing his health during this time. I kept a diary which often documented his physical condition, food intakes, and discomforts. I also was [there] when he was taken to hospital in Watford England during his last stay at the Manor. I convinced His Divine Grace to go to a hospital, accompanied him there, negotiated with the surgeon not to give general anesthetics and intravenous feeding, provided most of the post-operative care to SP. [...] Dr. McIrvine, made a very clear and definitive diagnosis of SP's condition, namely that he,

(1) had, due to diabetes (and dropsy) suffered swelling which affected the flow in his urinary tract over many years (2) That he had since birth a slightly constricted urethra which further reduced the urinary flow. (This was the reason for surgery and gave a great deal of relief) (3) The combination of these two major factors had put a constant and harmful back pressure on his kidneys, which along with a general deterioration due to age, had inflicted serious renal damage. SP complained he had difficulty urinating and finally was completely blocked leading to this surgery (4) The kidney failure would cause an increase in his system's uric acid which

would probably affect digestion and appetite. Both being prominent symptoms in SP's condition. (5) The loss of digestion and appetite led to malnutrition which caused an already aged and intensely taxed system to go into a total collapse.

This is an accurate account of the diagnosis of the doctors who examined Prabhupada at Peace Memorial Hospital on Sept. 8, 1977, and all of my/our observations prior and subsequent to this generally confirmed this diagnosis. When SP first arrived at the hospital, they had refused to treat his urethra constriction unless he was totally hooked up to intravenous feeding and any other life support systems they may need to employ. SP ...did not want to die in a hospital and I had convinced him to visit on a promise that he would receive only minor surgery to open the urethra ("some minor plumbing work"). I had to use considerably persuasive arguments to convince the surgeon to risk an operation on someone he said was nearly dead, without all the support systems required by hospital policy. ...I pleaded that SP wanted only enough relief to be able to travel back to his home (Vrindaban) to die as he wished. I challenged the doctors that "if he submits to all of your treatments, how much time can you extend his life?" They answered he was so far deteriorated they could hardly understand how he was living at all; and they could not even propose adding three more months to his life with all of their medical interventions employed. As his nurse I had been instructed by him to "never leave my side day or night" and had spent most days in 24 hour contact with him. I slept holding his hand, I bathed, dressed, fed and carried him. In short, I am a credible witness...

My assessment of the accusations of SP being poisoned are: (1) SP's exoteric conditions were carefully observed by a variety of care givers and medical professionals. (2) All diagnoses generally confirmed that his body was in an overall crisis, precipitated by his diabetes, dropsy, kidney damage, and overstressed due to age, travel, etc. (3) Prognosis was not optimistic; death seemed imminent, at least from Sep '77. (4) There was no indication of any other cause of his ill health (i.e. poisoning) noticed by me or any medical professional up to 16 Oct. and SP did not say anything to indicate that he suspected such a thing during my time with him. (5) His eventual physical departure within one month of my departure as his nurse, was a logical and expected conclusion to the above mentioned indications. I was not at all surprised, although I will remain broken hearted over his departure throughout my life. I have written these details for those who wish to know them. I have no ulterior motive and pray that my effort will help to maintain a truthful historical perspective on SP's departure. **(END)**

COMMENT: Contrary to Abhiram's sincere assessment, a careful review of all historical records for Srila Prabhupada in 1977 shows that he and his caretakers in 1977 had no idea as to the cause of Srila Prabhupada's illness. They engaged many doctors and undertook many different treatment programs, none of which was for diabetes. Diabetes was never discussed in any existing known conversations except in early Feb. 1977 when Srila Prabhupada said he had "a little diabetes." Dr. Khurana, Naveen Krishna's father from Delhi, prescribed kidney dialysis, something that was rejected by Tamal. Abhiram's understanding is more from hindsight. Did he ever discuss with Srila Prabhupada a diagnosis of diabetes, its proper treatment, and then, what was the use of all the other treatments for indigestion, liver problems, malnutrition, conjunctivitis, cough, etc? If Abhiram was there on November 9-10 to hear Srila Prabhupada say three times, *"Someone has poisoned me,"* he might have a different overview. He left Srila Prabhupada on Oct. 16. Of course, even if there was serious diabetes, that does not rule out poisoning, which causes, exacerbates diabetes. Three tests of Srila Prabhupada's 1977 hair averaged 16± ppm cadmium renders the theory that Srila Prabhupada's demise was due to serious diabetes irrelevant. *The clear and proven over-riding factor in Srila Prabhupada's health was his heavy metals poisoning.*

ABHIRAM ON THE CADMIUM YOUTUBE FILM May 17, 2017

"I watched the 'new' video from the PTC, which seemed to be trying to add some zest to the sad proposal that SP was poisoned and yet I saw nothing substantive or 'new' to me, it was just the same twisting of minuscule details, completely taken out of the context of how SP spoke and the myriad of circumstances that were going on at that time. **COMMENT:** Did Abhiram miss the part about the cadmium in three authenticated GBC hair samples done by the laboratory chosen by the GBC? *"I will make here only a few of many points that I, as the natural witness to the final days observed; which should smash any further doubts among sincere devotees who genuinely want to understand the truth of what really happened. The rest will always see and hear what they want to. [...] but for now, I give only these skeletal points to help you all heal from the pain of doubt about your Godbrothers. If they ever were actually serious to investigate, why did they not contact me?* **COMMENT:** *"What really happened..."* Abhiram's experiences do not negate the hair tests on three GBC-certified hair samples tested at a laboratory chosen by the GBC, confirming homicidal poisoning.

"I was SP's nurse from May/June 77 till Oct. and traveled with Him substantially preceding that all the way back to early 76. Everything that happened was entered into my diary at the time, so I am the only living witness from the full-time party of servants and probably a fairly credible one, since I obviously got no benefits from SP's departure. Neither I became a guru, GBC... [I never] noticed something untoward, considering that I

was following the order that SP's had given to me; "never leave my side, day or night" for most of that time as His 'nurse'.

COMMENT: There is no reason to suspect Abhiram in the poisoning. He was a caretaker July 25-Oct. 16, 1977, for 84 days. He was also previously with Srila Prabhupada for another 2 ½ months. But were he and his wife watching Srila Prabhupada constantly 24 hours a day? No, of course not. Poisoning is a very secretive undertaking. They could have missed many things, and according to Dr. Morris' report, they did miss the poisoning. "I was there and saw nothing untoward" only means they did not see it. How would they know if tasteless, colorless, odorless cadmium was in something, say, once a month? They wouldn't know. **FROM GUPTA DAS, ATTORNEY:** *"Abhiram's testimony is certainly relevant, but you may want to ask him to confirm that, when he was nurse to Srila Prabhupada, whether there was a 24 hour shift of only him and his wife (Srutirupa), and, if not, who else was around Srila Prabhupada during the periods that those two were not awake and right around SP."*

"Nearly everything that went into His mouth was prepared by my wife or me (all supplements, medicines, etc) and if not, it was usually eaten by me as mahaprasad (and her), as he hardly took much of what was prepared. I was then extremely healthy and remain healthy…

COMMENT: Poison would have been introduced in such a way that only Srila Prabhupada was poisoned, and not others. Did Abhiram drink ALL the leftover water, milk, and fruit juices that were given to Srila Prabhupada? Did he take his medicines? Were he and his wife the only ones giving medicines, food, and drink? The answer is no to all those questions. Abhiram did not even suspect poisoning in 1977 and would not have thought at that time to watch specifically for that in mind. Further, he was not a caretaker on July 20, 1976 or on February 26, May 15, June 2, 1977, when Srila Prabhupada had serious health declines. If Srila Prabhupada himself did not witness his own poisoning, how could Abhiram, being present only part-time? **(Narasimha das:** This argument that "I was closest to Prabhupada and would have known about it" is sentimental, a bit naive and misleading. The poisoners would let him see what they were doing?)

"It was only I who spoke to SP about going to hospital in Watford and it was only I who spoke directly to the surgeon on His behalf. Not TKG, nor anyone else. Gurukripa was there at the hospital as well […] The surgeon gave me a very simple explanation for SP's condition; namely that his dropsy, caused by diabetes, created swelling. This compounded with a congenitally small urethra to cause blockage of the urinary tract. This created back pressure during urination, over time causing renal (kidney) damage. The renal damage caused an excess of uric acid in His system, which made him nauseated and unable to eat or digest properly. This in

turn, caused 'malnutrition' which was all exactly in line with everything I observed as His primary care giver, during those months. **COMMENT:** This diagnosis sounds good, but cadmium poisoning CAUSES and ACCELERATES both diabetes and kidney disease. And the fact is he was poisoned with sky-high cadmium.

"That surgeon conducted normal blood tests, affiliated with the circumcision he performed, to successfully help relieve the blockage. **COMMENT:** We also interviewed the "surgeon" Dr. McIrvine in 2001, and he could not confirm if (or which) blood tests might have been done- he **assumed** this because it is normal procedure. But any tests would have been for blood counts, hemoglobin, diabetes, infection, and McIrvine said there were no tests for poisoning since it was not suspected. Tests for poison must be ordered by the doctor, patient, or police for each specific poison, requiring MANY tests. The hospital records were destroyed in the early nineties. Even if there were tests, they would not have detected cadmium.

"There was also a significant discussion I had with HDG, subsequent to the surgeon's analysis, about the 'toxins inside of your system, essentially poisoning you' (my words to Him) that HDG took very seriously and we spoke a good bit about Him going on a juice fast, 'to eliminate the toxins/poisons.' I read him a few passages from Ann Wigmore's book, which was all the rage at the time and HDG said to me, 'Yes, we will do like this. Yogis adopt such simple diets for their health.' If anyone has actually spent private time serving SP, they would know it was perfectly normal for him to say 2 months later 'I am being poisoned' which I heard Him say and at the time seemed obvious to me that He was referring back to our several discussions about this. Once, when His sister Pishima was helping Srutirupa to cook for HDG, He told her; 'I am swelling from all the mustard oil she uses (in the shukta). She is trying to kill me. Do not let her back in the kitchen.' Should we now open an investigation into His sister? He spoke like that sometimes and anyone who was around Him, or anyone who actually researches His casual comments would know this. I suggest that there are still many senior devotees who would testify to this way of His speaking, who were either His servants or spent extensive time around Him. **COMMENT:** *"...it was perfectly normal for him to say 2 months later "I am being poisoned" which I heard Him say..."* Srila Prabhupada said "Someone has poisoned me," three times, and this was when **Abhiram was NOT THERE** on Nov. 9-10, 1977. Has Abhiram read the actual transcripts from Nov. 9-10, as the caretakers and Srila Prabhupada clearly discuss HOMICIDAL poisoning with reference to lawyers, courts, murders, rakshasas, dead by the morning, ground glass in the food, restricting the cooks and sources of Srila Prabhupada's food, etc? Abhiram's suggestions about eliminating toxins in the body is not in the audio record. SP's caretakers ARE NOT discussing bad medicine, mustard oil, toxic build up

in the body from food or medicines over the years, juice fasts, etc. *"I am being poisoned"* is not found. Abhiram cannot grasp the possibility of the poisoning that is now proven by forensic science as a fact. See Ch. 10-14.

"There is so much in my memory and diary that I probably could write another hundred points refuting this poison theory, but I never felt motivated to do so, since it is obvious to me that none of the proponents of this theory could be even half sincere, since they never even asked me to explain my observations and experiences, before publishing their mad theories and I am one person that should be considered an important and credible witness. Remember, I got nothing but sorrow and darkness by the loss of His Divine Grace ... I am sure you all are sincere to know the real truth, versus what some would want you to believe, for some reasons unknown to me. Abhiram Das (ACBSP)" **COMMENT:** Many are reluctant to accept the truth of irrefutable evidence of Srila Prabhupada's poisoning, as the very idea of Srila Prabhupada being homicidally poisoned is more than they can bear.

FURTHER SUBMISSION FROM ABHIRAM DAS, May 18, 2017

"[...] SP had been discussing the shortage of servant help with TKG over a few weeks, when I came to visit HDG in Vrindaban and it was SP who suggested that I stay on and not TKG. [...]" **COMMENT:** Abhiram had no part in Srila Prabhupada's poisoning nor was he aware of it. *"On his other point about cadmium. I did not see their lab work [...] I cannot answer something that is firstly unproven to me and secondly am unqualified to interpret, as, I suspect, is he. He claims "it was off the charts" as if he is qualified to interpret [...] there seems to be no published history of cadmium being used to poison someone [...] the symptoms of cadmium poisoning is almost always from environmental contamination and also do not correspond to the health problems manifest in HDG's external body, according to my direct experience.* **COMMENT:** We sent the chapters on hair tests and cadmium levels to Abhiram (June 2017) with a number of points on the evidence that Srila Prabhupada was poisoned with very high levels of cadmium. We agree that only experts in toxicology, forensics, and pathology should give opinions as to the impact of these high cadmium levels; these expert opinions are found in Ch. 6. Examples of homicidal cadmium poisoning are in Ch. 9. SP's levels of cadmium were far beyond anything seen in cases of environmental contamination, and this betrays homicidal intent. Srila Prabhupada's health symptoms lead to cadmium poisoning (Ch. 31). Cadmium causes diabetes, kidney failure (Part 4).

"I also have some of the hairs that I cut from SP's head, during His illness and will have it tested someday, but everyone born in and around West Bengal will have super high levels of mercury, since the waters all around WB are the most contaminated with mercury of practically

anywhere on earth. **COMMENT:** It is an arsenic crisis, not mercury, and it was cadmium poisoning. Abhiram is not clear on what the issues are about. Six samples of SP hair all had normal mercury. We ask Abhiram to test 3 little pieces of his 1977 hair sample by NAA for arsenic and cadmium.

"Also, we should ask if the cadmium or mercury levels (depending on which theory is promoted) are present throughout the hair sample, or only in one small area. [...] To infer that HDG was not in complete control of His surroundings and that His mental state was anything but crystal clear is totally incorrect [...] He was lucid and powerful to the last breath [...] Knowing a little about SP's manifest personality directly, I cannot imagine He would have tolerated being poisoned, bullied, manipulated or controlled. [...] **COMMENT:** There are 3 NAA hair tests finding sky-high cadmium. There are no cadmium or mercury theories. Philosophical discussion on whether or not Srila Prabhupada would tolerate his own poisoning does not change the fact that his hair contained lethal levels of cadmium that could only come from a deliberate homicidal attack. We cannot impose on SP how he must react to being poisoned. He would tolerate being poisoned, just as Christ and Haridas Thakur tolerated their deadly abuses. SP chose to depart by his own time and will. But the lethal cadmium levels are facts. Someone TRIED TO KILL Srila Prabhupada.

"...how do they explain away the statement made by Sruti Rupa, that TKG was not even on the scene for a few months after HDG began to fade? Did TKG have the mystic power to be in two places at once? [...] **COMMENT:** Before discussing Tamal and assuming this and that, what about the fact that Srila Prabhupada was deliberately, homicidally poisoned with cadmium at levels about 250 X above normal? *[...] SP would have never tolerated [...] Abhiram Das (ACBSP)"* **COMMENT:** Yes, devotees on the internet who issue wild statements, not knowing what they are talking about. That is the reason for this volume with all the real evidence.

SUBMISSION FROM SRUTIRUPA DASI IN 2017 (abbreviated)

"I was personally with SP in 1975, 1976 and 1977 when he was in India. I was cooking with Palika and then on my own in 1977. I was Srila Prabhupada's last 'official' cook and flew with him to London. [...] SP began getting sick in Dec. 1976 in Bombay. [...] Tamal Krishna was not even on the scene yet. **COMMENT:** Actually Srila Prabhupada became extremely ill in New York in July 1976 with Tamal when she was not present. In Dec. 1976 Srila Prabhupada was still ill from July. *[...] he was told by a Ayurvedic doctor to stop ghee and salt, so he would come into the kitchen in Bombay and cook for himself [...] Then we went on to Kumbha Mela, Bhubaneswar, Calcutta and Mayapur and I was the cook along with Palika and she then left and it was only Pishima and myself cooking for him from Feb. 1977. During his stay in Mayapur he told me 'not to let Pishima*

back into the kitchen because of the mustard seeds and that 'she was killing him with the mustard seeds'! This was not a literal statement! We stopped the mustard seeds and nothing more was ever said! BUT if you heard this on a tape, you would think differently, it seems, not understanding [...] how Srila Prabhupada spoke in these circumstances." **COMMENT:** The mustard seed story does not negate Dr. Morris' tests finding lethal cadmium poisoning, which show poisoning from at least Feb. 1977, during the time Srutirupa was with Srila Prabhupada. Srutirupa's testimony does not negate the hard proof of lethal cadmium poisoning. Regardless how Srila Prabhupada spoke about his sister, the hair tests are scientific proof.

"Tamal did not join Srila Prabhupada till Feb. in Mayapur. SP's health continually deteriorated from Dec. and he was bed ridden in Mayapur by now and only continued to get worse and TKG had just arrived on the scene after SP had been ill for several months now and deteriorating.
COMMENT: Srila Prabhupada became very ill on July 20, 1976, and spent the next 7 months recovering slowly, being weak but doing fairly well, going on walks and traveling. But on Feb. 26, 1977 he suddenly became more ill than ever, bedridden and in great pain. Two major health collapses on July 20, 1976 and Feb. 26, 1977, both in Tamal's presence. Srutirupa thinks if Tamal was not there, then there was no poisoning? Then what of the forensic, triple-confirmed scientific proof of poisoning?

"[...] This whole idea that he was poisoned is madness and ever who says this, never spent time around SP. [June] in Vrindaban and SP went 2 weeks without anything solid to eat and was skin and bones! He then called for me and said that he 'wanted to test me' and then what I made was the first thing he had eaten in 2 weeks [...] for the next several months what he ate in a day on the palm of my hand... it was simply tiny, tiny amounts for he had lost all appetite. [...] There was NO poisoning going on. I was there and in and out of his rooms and saw him daily, spoke to SP and gave him his medicines, barley milk, Ayurvedic teas etc. [...] no matter how one feels or felt about TKG, he loved SP so intensely and did everything he could to care for SP during this time and wanted him to remain. He was what he was, but he loved Srila Prabhupada [...] I am sorry, but this idea of poisoning is simply madness and words taken out of context or not understanding. Never at any time did SP think that he was being poisoned. AND yes, with all the blood work in London, it would of been obvious if he was. [...] your servant, Srutirupa devi dasi"

COMMENT: Srutirupa ignores the actual forensic poisoning evidence and is relies on her experiences of the time to judge if there was a poisoning or not. Even expert doctors are fooled by poisoning and cannot ascertain the real cause of health decline. The hair tests confirm a homicidal poisoning, confirmed also by many forensic certifications poisoning whispers and "poison discussions" with caretakers about a homicidal poisoning. The body of evidence is irrefutable, which Srutirupa obviously has not understood. Talk of mustard seeds, Pishima "killing him," bad medicine, a toxic buildup, etc... none of this changes the scientific proof of a lethal poisoning.

CONCLUSION: Whether or how much Srila Prabhupada had diabetes, still, cadmium was the primary cause of Srila Prabhupada's ill health. In these testimonies we see how devotees, out of emotion, will overlook the evidence that proves poisoning, and cling to their limited experiences in disbelief. This is cognitive dissonance, fear of the truth, takes time to overcome. In mid-2022 when Abhiram das attended the opening of the Krishna Hill temple in Bangalore, he discussed and was open to the poison evidence when presented with the book: Srila Prabhupada's Hidden Glories: His Inconceivable Tolerance and Mercy.

APPENDIX 10:
NONE SO BLIND AS THOSE WHO WILL NOT SEE

"Facts are stubborn things; and whatever may be our wishes, our inclinations, or the dictates of our passion, they cannot alter the state of facts and evidence." (John Adams)

PTC has disseminated the 1977 statements and discussions by and with Srila Prabhupada about his being poisoned, along with scientific forensic tests on hair samples and audio recordings. It brings forward other evidences such as witnesses; medical symptom analysis; analysis of motive; institutional cover-ups, fraud and deceit; the worsening history of deviations and corruption in ISKCON; why certain persons are suspected; and shastric quotes to counter objections that a pure devotee could be poisoned. The evidence is conclusive that Srila Prabhupada was maliciously poisoned in 1977, which he himself confirmed. But there are those who insist the evidence messengers are mind-poisoners with a false message. They speak of a "poison antidote" to counteract what they characterize as an envious and demonic mentality. They nitpick the poisoning evidence with clever misrepresentations, and ignore the bald facts. They allude to imaginary faults, then proclaim the entire "poison theory" as null and void, and that there is no evidence at all (as in, 0%).

In Oct. 2017 Mayeswara das of Ojai, CA compiled his reply to the "poison theory." His 80 page e-book was the precursor to his 2020 *Deception* book (400 pg.) that ridiculously fault-finded with all the evidence of Srila Prabhupada's poisoning. E.g., he boisterously exclaimed that Dr. Morris at MURR did not know how to test hair samples, etc. A full analysis of Mayeswara's bluster, as well as the GBC flawed arguments against the poisoning evidence, is presented in Vol. 7: *Kill Guru Become Guru: Crushing the Naysayers Cheaters*.

APPENDIX 11:
SP'S TRAVEL ITINERARY 1976-77

1976: Jan 01   -Jan 02   Madras   Jan 03 -Jan 09   Nellore
Jan 10 -Jan 12   Bombay, Calcutta
Jan 15 -Mar 22 Mayapur/Haridaspur: Mayapur Fest. Tamal exiled to China
Mar 22 -Mar 24 Calcutta   Mar 24 -Mar 28 Delhi
Mar 29 -Mar 29 Modi Nagar   Mar 30 -Mar 30 Aligahr
Mar 31 -Apr 10 Vrindaban   Apr 11 -Apr 11 Delhi
Apr 11 -Apr 17 Bombay
Apr 18 -Apr 26 Melbourne: Health is strong, brisk walks in cold mornings
Apr 27 -Apr 28 Auckland   Apr 28 -May 02 Fiji
May 03 -May 31 Hawaii: Tamal visits, pleads not to go to China, SP gets ill
Jun 01 -Jun 10 Los Angeles
Jun 11 -Jun 15 Detroit: No apparent health problems
Jun 16 -Jun 20 Toronto: his cold, mucus, cough returns
Jun 21 -Jul 01 New Vrind: Weeks of weakness, heavy cold, cough, very ill
Jul 02 -Jul 06 Washington, DC   Jul 07   -Jul 09   Balt., Wash.
Jul 09 -Jul 14 NY (Rathayatra): As Tamal's guest, SP's swelling reappears
Jul 15 -Jul 15 Gita Nagari Farm, PA. Not well.
Jul 16 -Jul 20 New York: Leaving SP becomes ill, on plane extremely ill
Jul 21 -Jul 27 London UK: Vomiting, in bed for days, no eating or walks
Jul 28 -Jul 28 Paris   Jul 29   -Aug 05 France farm
Aug 06 -Aug 07 Paris: Next 6 months, slowly recovers his strength a bit
Aug 07 -Aug 13 Tehran: Travels, Asia, India
Aug 13 -Aug 15 Bombay   Aug 16 -Aug 16 Hyderabad
Aug 17 -Aug 24 Hyderabad   Aug 25 -Sep 02 Delhi
Sep 03 -Oct 08 Vrindaban   Oct 09 -Oct 10 Aligarh
Oct 11 -Oct 12 Delhi   Oct 13 -Oct 18 Chandigarh
Oct 19 -Oct 19 Delhi   Oct 20 -Nov 30 Vrindaban
Dec 01 -Dec 01 Delhi   Dec 02 -Dec 05 Hyderabad
Dec 06 -Dec 17 Hyder Farm   Dec 17 -Dec 17 Train
Dec 18 -Dec 20 Venkatesvara   Dec 20 -Dec 21 Bombay
Dec 22 -Dec 22 Poona   Dec 23 -Dec 31 Bombay
1977: Jan. 1   -Jan 10   Bombay   Jan 11 -Train Hardvar
Jan 12 -Jan 15 Allahabad/ Kumbha Mela   Jan 16 -Jan 18   Calcutta
Jan 18 -Jan 18 Train to Bhubaneshv   Jan 19 -Jan 24   Bhubaneshv.
Jan 25 -Jan 25 Jagannath Puri   Jan 25 -Feb 02   Bhubaneshv.

Feb 03 -Feb 03   Train to Calcutta   Feb 04 -Feb 06   Calcutta
Feb 07 -Mar 01   Mayapur Festival, Tamal comes 16th, SP deathly ill Feb 26
Mar 02 -Mar 30   Bombay Pandal, cannot take walks, no appetite
Mar 31 -May 06   Bombay Juhu New Quarters   May 07 -May 07   Delhi
May 08 -May 15   Rishikesh for heath, but becomes extremely ill late May 15
May 16 -May 16   Train to Delhi: back to Vrindaban, thinking death is near
May 17 -Aug 27   Vrindaban GBCs come/Final Will/May 28 talks/July 9 Order
Aug 28 -Sep 13   London: Minor operation Sept 8, health declines further
Sep 14 -Oct 02   Bombay: SP cancelled his US tour, bed-ridden, very weak
Oct 03 -Nov 14   Vrindaban: GBCs come, poison whispers and discussions
Nov 14 -SP departs/intrigue/ambitions/full takeover by March 26, 1978

APPENDIX 12:
SHARP SWORD TRUTH FILMS

Video One: "Kill Guru, Become Guru: The Forensic Breakthrough"

https://youtu.be/PIBqNBMbPvY   May 4, 2017 a 54 min. film on the history of the private investigation into Srila Prabhupada's poisoning and how the scientific forensic breakthrough into proving Srila Prabhupada's poisoning was accomplished by discovery of sky-high levels of cadmium in 3 authentic Srila Prabhupada hair samples. The "poison issue" was resurrected and again brought to the attention of the Hare Krishna movement after about 15 years. By 2022 there were 36,000 views and hundreds of very appreciative comments. The message was that SP's poisoning had now been definitely proven with hard scientific proof.

Video Two: "Poisoning Objections Answered"

https://www.youtube.com/watch?v=gOLeHjRhZMc On June 27, 2017 PTC released a second film of 41 minutes, and by 2022 there were over 13,000 views. A review and more in depth look of the evidence was undertaken and 20 common objections to Srila Prabhupada's poisoning were answered or refuted. It was necessary to deal with emotional and illogical objections such as: Srila Prabhupada could not have been poisoned because no one saw it happen. Emphasis was placed on the scientific proof of cadmium poisoning. Some responses: *"I live close to Dallas temple... devotees here are stating openly that if this truth about Srila Prabhupada becomes known widely it will destroy Hare Krishna movement. I have the opposite opinion." (Anonymous)   "ISKCON has already been destroyed. The truth will help devotees see just how strong the material illusion really is and should revitalize the mission." (Anuttama dasi, 2017)*

Video Three: "Crime Of The Millennium: Poisoning Prabhupada"

https://www.youtube.com/watch?v=IMuUqqZDqTQ A third film was released by PTC of 31 minutes on Aug. 28, 2017 and by 2022 there were 21,000 views. This film reviewed further evidence in Srila Prabhupada's poisoning, and demanded that the ISKCON leadership publicly accept the scientific proof of the crime of the millennium, apologize for their cover-up of the facts and evidence, and resign from their posts sooner the better. It called upon devotees to remove the ISKCON leaders and elect new ones who could respond to the ramifications of the truth about Srila Prabhupada's poisoning. It also called upon devotees to take a public stand on the issue and to restore Srila Prabhupada's mission and mercy by going back to "Square One," as though it were the day after Srila Prabhupada's departure. By open discussion, debate, research, and study the proper understanding of Srila Prabhupada's teachings could be ascertained. On various public Facebook pages and websites, discussion and comments were 95% in agreement and favorable of the evidence and films. Of course, there was absolutely no response from any ISKCON leader nor the GBC on the issue, just dead silence. One comment: *"There are still followers of Srila Prabhupada who are sincere, active, not silent, spreading his mission. Nothing is fully lost and there is still hope. By the association with Srila Prabhupada and his sincere followers will the whole world be purified."*

Video Four: In Pursuit Of Prabhupada's Poisoners

https://www.youtube.com/watch?v=6unXi7jzSiI This film (25 min) came out Oct. 5, 2017, by 2022 had 58,000 views. This film focused on the suspects and the evidence implicating them, and has been the most watched of all the films, showing intense interest in the evidence implicating the prime suspects in Srila Prabhupada's heavy metals poisoning.

Video Five: "Reward On Prabhupada's Poisoners"

https://www.youtube.com/watch?v=GZg_rNP6HiY A short film was released Oct. 13, 2017 and by 2022 there were 2,000 views. It offered on a cash reward of US$50,000 for information that would lead to the felony conviction of anyone for poisoning Srila Prabhupada. No information has been forthcoming, but it is a tall order to obtain a criminal conviction.

Video Six: "We Could Have Done That (Poison Prabhupada)"

https://www.youtube.com/watch?v=XoRz1ENORFg This 24 min. film came out July 25, 2018 and by 2022 had 5,000 views. This film focused on Tamal's mercy killing *BTG* interview where he claims Srila Prabhupada wanted an assisted suicide, undoubtedly his defense for poisoning Srila Prabhupada if the matter became public. Tamal spoke of it again.

OVERWHELMINGLY POSITIVE COMMENTS

There are also foreign language subtitled versions of these films, such as in Russian. By 2022 the total views on all six films was over 150,000 (compared to 3,000 for the 2020 Mayeswara/GBC Deception film). Some comments: **(1)** *"When someone believes something to be true and then is confronted with evidence/data that contradicts that belief, one of the ways that they cope with the dissonance is to find evidence or an explanation that supports their original belief."* **(2)** *"This video is a home run in Prabhupada's service. It may take time for the effect to show. Krishna has a timeline. The forensic parts, Prabhupada's words, the different laboratories all combine for a perfect presentation. Even Christians do not deny the crucifixion of Christ."* **(3)** *"So now we have proof Srila Prabhupada was poisoned. What do we do next?"* **(4)** *"Let us pray that Lord Chaitanya will bless this endeavor, and expose these rascals in Iskcon leadership positions and thereby purify the Movement that was meant to purify us all."*

(5) *"Very well done, and there's no doubt in my mind that our guru was poisoned. I hope that your book gets printed and is widely distributed. Although I know it is an unpleasant topic. You've spent many years and lots of money on this project."* **(6)** *"Very impressive presentation. I also like the title you chose for the book. This covering of the truth by ISKCON leaders is consistent and prevalent in all of their activities. What is amazing is that everything they say or submit or allege is a lie. We need to isolate, expose, and remove the demons who have taken over this great movement and the BBT. It is war and we cannot back down from the fight."* **(7)** *"Most of the negative responders did not watch the video and had no reasonable arguments. Those who watch the video have less questions."* **(8)** *"The video is loud, clear, non-offensive. Thank you for your sacrifice."* **(9)** *"This was very well done, calm and factual. It's always wise to keep it cool and let the facts speak for themselves."* **(10)** *"Overall great response to the video so far. I have had emails, phone calls and personal visits. Many have expressed tremendous gratitude for this video."* **(11)** *"It is now very evident that they poisoned. I hope whole world will realize and kick out these so called authorities."* **(12)** *"Tamal is the master manipulator - but his words and actions spill out the truth- Tamal asks Srila Prabhupada several times about his poisoning. Tamal's interview with Satsvarupa. The suspects behind 'Not that I am poisoned' book. Not honest investigation. Passing resolution against devotees participating in investigation. Threatening punishment to devotees if they participate in investigation."* **(13)** *"Your talk in this video is very convincing."* **(14)** *"A powerful documentary on the poisoning of Srila Prabhupada. Well done."* **(15)** *"We must be most grateful for this great methodological and scientific research that shows, due to convincing forensic evidence, that Srila Prabhupada was poisoned with arsenic and cadmium. This also identifies the prime suspects Tamal, etc."*

(16) *"I watched your expose twice now and it is quite convincing. So you seem to have hit a chord with the devotees and pray that it is just the start of an avalanche of interest in regards to Prabhupada's attempted slaying. As with everything, the 250 times normal, lethal dosage has to put* *to rest that Srila Prabhupada was a mere human."* **(17)** *"This is a hard hitting piece of video journalism that cannot help but put the "poisoning of Srila Prabhupada" back on a very public platform and possibly into a few court rooms. This is a very compelling presentation with a narrative citing solid, verified evidence. The video does a very professional job presenting the evidence- It will be difficult to disarm the arguments and conclusions. Reasonable people will view this evidence with interest and find that a strong case is presented that deserves a full, open, impartial hearing and a court of law would appear to be the next proper venue."* **(18)** *"Does anyone think that the scientists who conducted the studies are Ritviks? Moron alert! No one can doubt the overwhelmingly compelling case made here in this video. The data is stacked up pretty high."*

(19) *"If Prabhupada said so, why do they not believe him? They use Prabhupada's words like gospel, yet here they choose to ignore him. It's an utter disgrace. They are deceiving so many people. Breaks my heart. How can we say we love Prabhupada while worshipping people who were involved in his poisoning? Time to pull the head out of the sand and use the brain that Krishna gave us. Heart breaking."* **(20)** *"Irrefutable evidence."* **(21)** *"...the evidence is clear and irrefutable. You have done amazing research work. The video I shared with other Godbrothers- changed their perspective."* **(22)** *"You have provided overwhelming and conclusive proof of poisoning that can't be denied, and the evidence will remain for future devotees to assimilate. Only Srila Prabhupada could survive that long."*

The six videos presented the various pieces of evidence with a deep analysis. PTC has as its goal to widely distribute the facts and evidence about Srila Prabhupada's poisoning. The truth does make a huge difference. **http://killgurubecomeguru.org**

DISCUSSION BANNED FROM SP DISCIPLES FB GROUP

There is a closed Facebook group with 850 original Srila Prabhupada disciples who share and participate in discussions of interest. Nityananda das was invited to join about 2014, but was not familiar with Facebook and did not reply. When the first PTC video came out, a fiery discussion ensued about the "poison issue" and whether it had any new value, new evidence, etc. One of the members suggested Nityananda das join the group and answer questions to clear up misunderstandings about the facts and evidence. The proposal was put to the group, and the idea invoked such a firestorm from a number of members, who were then rebutted by those in favor... that a vote was taken and the idea was axed. The group administrators deleted all posts on the "poison issue," banned further discussion on the subject, and decided not to post the video link for those who might be interested. Nityananda was advised that the FB group had successfully navigated discussions on the child abuse, book changes, guru fall-downs, Gaudiya Math, and many other subjects, but that the "poison issue" was too volatile, resulting in offensive and super-emotional posts which were inflammatory and unacceptable. Some members were so viscously disturbed over the "false theory that Srila Prabhupada was poisoned" that the administrators felt there was no option but to avoid the topic altogether, lest the group self-destruct.

WEBSITE AND BOOKS ON THE POISON EVIDENCE

(1) WEBSITE: http://killgurubecomeguru.org

Books On Amazon: (8) Srila Prabhupada: Triumphant Departure- Complete Book of Poisoning Evidence:

https://www.amazon.com/dp/B0BBPPFMFV

(2) Private distribution only: *Srila Prabhupada's Hidden Glories* (hardcover 2 book set, 880 pg each, ask for PDF, available free) Book One: *His Inconceivable mercy and Tolerance,* Book Two: *Inevitable Restoration of His Divine Mission* (contact: srigovinda@gmail.com)

(3) *Judge For Yourself* (out of print) book) 300 pgs Book with CD of the poison whispers and more

(4) *Kill Guru, Become Guru* (see website above) 800 pgs, EBook

(5) *Someone Has Poisoned Me* (1999, out of print) 400 pgs Book

(6) *Not That I Am Poisoned* (2000, GBC book of denials, cover-up)

(7) *TKG's Diary* (1998, by Tamal, his doctored version of events as his own efforts at a cover-up of the poison evidence) 350 pgs Book

---

APPENDIX 13:
SRILA PRABHUPADA'S TEETH AS EVIDENCE

(Nityananda das, 2020): The flow of blood in the human body nourishes all parts of the body, including tissue, bones, hair, fingernails, and teeth. Whatever is in the blood will be deposited in the hair and teeth. Any degree of heavy metals in the blood will be proportionately deposited in hair and teeth. As hair grows, the contents of the blood are deposited in the growth of the hair shaft at each point of time, showing a history. Tests on Napoleon's hair showed rising and falling arsenic levels from month to month over a year's time. Each inch of hair represents a month or two growth and history of blood contents. Deposits of minerals and toxins from the blood in teeth, however, will accumulate over time because grown adult teeth are sustained. Thus a poisoning over time would show in teeth an accumulation of poison, not simply a signature amount (as in hair or fingernails). Testing teeth for poisoning evidence thus gives another type of picture from that from hair tests. Further confirmation of Srila Prabhupada's poisoning could come from testing Srila Prabhupada's teeth extracted in 1976-77. His fingernail clippings, if any could be located, would also accurately validate if any poisoning that took place. Such tests could confirm the levels of poisons as was done in the hair tests. Discussions with Sadhusangananda das, former president of Boston ISKCON, about the location of Srila Prabhupada's teeth which had come from his mouth while still living, believed there were four teeth in the possession of various devotees. "Sadhu" formerly had an incomparable collection of Prabhupada memorabilia. We have identified 5 of Srila Prabhupada's teeth.

ONE: REAR MOLAR, MID-1975

One of Srila Prabhupada's teeth is owned by Radha Govinda Vedic Charitable Foundation, purchased in 1996 from Rakshanam's brother Lalitanath for $10,000. Srila Prabhupada nonchalantly took it from his mouth in mid-1975 on a cross-country US plane flight, and it was given by Srila Prabhupada's servant Hari Sauri das to Rakshanam, who was then serving as Srila Prabhupada's bodyguard. Being that it was separated from Srila Prabhupada's body before poisoning is believed to have begun in mid-1976, testing should show normal pre-poisoning levels of cadmium as comparison to values during poisoning. Sophia Kuyt stole this tooth in Fiji from a heavily locked museum room in Dec. 2017 and it is with her brother in Wash, DC. It is encased in acrylic in a 1.25 inch silver container with lid. It has four roots.

TWO: LOWER CANINE: AUG. 15, 1976

Another tooth is owned by Hari Sauri das, Srila Prabhupada's personal servant from 1975-77. This one came from Srila Prabhupada's mouth in Bombay during the early hours of Aug.15, 1976, noted in *A Transcendental Diary*, Vol. 4, p. 124: *"I entered his room, offered my obeisances, looked up- and got a shock. Srila Prabhupada was smiling- revealing a gap where his tooth should have been. With mixed dismay and surprise I asked, 'Srila Prabhupada, what happened to your tooth?' Without saying anything, Srila Prabhupada reached down and pulled open the drawer of his desk. The tooth was lying inside. During the night it has either fallen out, or Srila Prabhupada had pulled it out.... The tooth, a lower canine, is astonishing: a huge cavity has eaten away more than half the side at the point where the tooth entered the gum. Bits of prasadam (spices and the like) are lodged inside..."* Hari Sauri, as stated in his writings, has this tooth on his personal altar as a worshipable item. It is very important to test this tooth if possible. Only an unnoticeable and extremely tiny portion would be required for a forensic test, and best would be neutron activation analysis (NAA). It could establish whether poisoning had started by Aug. 1976 and could also further confirm the forensic tests on hair samples that had discovered sky-high levels of cadmium in 1977. A correlative confirmation between hair and tooth tests would be very powerful further evidence of homicidal poisoning. Hari Sauri, as GBC for Australia after he left Srila Prabhupada's service in March 1977, wrote a letter to the Australian devotees about this tooth when he visited Vrindaban: *"I also brought out Srila Prabhupada's tooth for a special*

Hari Sauri dasa ACBSP

In front of Srila Prabhupada there is a golden drinking lota and next to that a gold casket with his tooth in it.

darshan for the devotees, placing it before the temple's deity of Srila Prabhupada, Who was appropriately sitting just in front of Lord Balarama." Hari Sauri is still today an Australian resident, usually in Melbourne or Mayapur. In early 2020, David Paulig (Dhananjaya das, Germany) noted how he had just visited Hari Sauri in Mayapur and was told that his hair samples and tooth had "been taken," presumably by an GBC directive, as an obstruction of justice.

THREE: TYPE UNKNOWN: EXTRACTED APRIL 1977

A third tooth has great relevance to the investigation at hand as crucial evidence. In April 1977 Srila Prabhupada, while speaking in his Bombay quarters to devotees, paused and casually took a loose tooth from his mouth and placed it in his desk drawer. Tamal asked Srila Prabhupada for this special item and was granted it. This incident is from memory and now the source cannot be located. This tooth was referred to by Hari Sauri, who wrote in a 1978 letter: *"According to Satsvarupa, Srila Prabhupada's secretary* [Tamal?] *wears a tooth in a reticule (small handbag) around his neck."* Hair *Sample D*, also dated from early 1977, had sky-high levels of cadmium, and this tooth would very likely further confirm Srila Prabhupada's cadmium poisoning. Tamal passed away in 2002, and this tooth is actually now entombed along with Tamal's body in his Mayapur samadhi, according to Sruta Kirti das and Hari Sauri das (two former personal servants to Srila Prabhupada) in separate December 2019 emails. Garuda das advised that there were three trustees for Tamal's estate, to execute Tamal's will, to manage and disperse the millions he had accumulated while an ISKCON guru, and to care for his personal properties. Giriraj Swami and Tamal's brother Carl Herzig are believed to be two of the trustees and Tamal's other possessions are likely in his closed-down locked apartment at Dallas ISKCON, such as his original diaries. In any investigation by law enforcement into Srila Prabhupada's poisoning, this tooth must be secured as a priority.

FOUR: RIGHT FRONT UPPER INCISOR: Late 1975 To Mid-1976

There are many photos of Srila Prabhupada in his last years where one of his upper front teeth is clearly shown missing. In 2019 this tooth was located in the hands of Kumara das (USA):

"My devotee name is Kumara Dasa [Craig Thompson]. I was in New Vrindaban for 19 years from 1979-1998. I was one of the artists at the community responsible for a lot of what you see there (worked in the mold shop also). *Presently, I live in Pittsburgh, PA and am a full time commercial, architectural and fine art photographer. I'm sure you may be wondering how I came into its possession. Here is its history. Back in 1980 or thereabouts, could have been a bit later, His Holiness Tamal Krishna Goswami visited New Vrindaban, possibly for the Palace of Gold opening. As you probably know, Tamal was Srila Prabhupada's personal secretary. (I assume) TAMAL acquired the tooth from Srila Prabhupada during his time as his assistant/secretary. I don't know the exact specifics of how he got the tooth but imagine Srila Prabhupada had to have it pulled. Tamal*

presented the tooth to Kirtanananda Swami during the above mentioned visit. I was Kirtanananda Swami's part time personal assistant at New Vrindaban at the time (and up until he left New Vrindaban in 1994). The tooth was kept in a safe that I only had access to for the remaining years I was in New Vrindaban. Before Kirtanananda Swami left the community, the tooth and a few other Srila Prabhupada belongings were given to me. I have had the tooth in my possession ever since TKG brought it to Kirtanananda Swami in New Vrindaban in early 80's."

New Vrindaban's Palace of Gold grand opening was in mid-1980. However, since photos show this upper front tooth missing well before 1977, this tooth would ***not*** be the one that was extracted in April 1977 and given to Tamal. Kumara's dentist examined the tooth and declared it is the upper right central

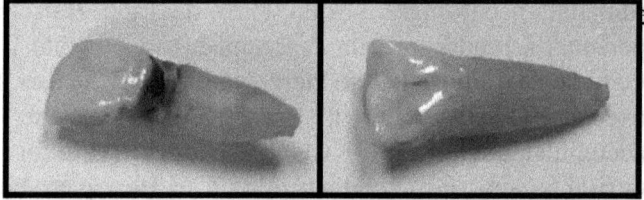

photos we note that the left central incisor is different than the right one, which has a flat edge and very square shape. Kumara's assumption that it is from Tamal's time as Srila Prabhupada's secretary is mistaken; Tamal would have acquired this tooth before 1977 and given to Kirtanananda in 1980. It is also not the "lower canine" that is held by Hari Sauri. The date of its extraction is unsure, between late 1975 and mid-1976. Since Srila Prabhupada's medical symptom history indicates that poisoning very likely began at least by July 20, 1976, this tooth might be relevant to the investigation but maybe was extracted before poisoning began.

FIVE: VISHVADEVI DASI IN UK

Email Dec. 9, 2019 from Hari Sauri to Chaitanya guru: *"I am not sure when Prabhupada lost the front tooth [#4 above]. I need to go through my photos and see. Apart from that here's what I know about his other teeth: I was given one by Prabhupada in August 15 1976 [#2 above]. Tamal Krishna Maharaja had one which was put in his samadhi in Mayapur on his request in his will [#3 above]. Padmagarbha das has one. He lives in NC as far as I know [this would be #1 above, as Padmagarbha was close neighbor and friend to Lalitanath and Rakshanam in Los Angeles]. Vishvadevi dasi has one in the UK. I was told that Kirtanananda had one which was put under Prabhupada's murti in New Vrindaban [this is #4]. I can't think of any others at the moment but if I do I will let you know."*

Vishvadevi is an original Prabhupada disciple who was one of the early London devotees in the mid-seventies.

All Glories to His Divine Grace Srila Prabhupada!

www.ingramcontent.com/pod-product-compliance
Lightning Source LLC
Chambersburg PA
CBHW071234290326
41931CB00038B/2951